P9-DTV-784

DEVELOPMENTAL DOMAINS IN EARLY CHILDHOOD STAGE

DEVELOPMENTAL DOMAINS IN EARLY CHILDHOOD STAGE

NEW APPROACHES TO STUDY CHILD GROWTH AND DEVELOPMENT

PRELIMINARY EDITION

Edited by Elmira Jannati, EDD

California State Polytechnic University—Pomona

cognella®

SAN DIEGO

Bassim Hamadeh, CEO and Publisher
Mieka Portier, Field Acquisitions Editor
Tony Paese, Project Editor
Christian Berk, Production Editor
Emely Villavicencio, Senior Graphic Designer
Stephanie Kohl, Licensing Coordinator
Natalie Piccotti, Director of Marketing
Kassie Graves, Vice President of Editorial
Jamie Giganti, Director of Academic Publishing

Copyright © 2021 by Cognella, Inc. All rights reserved. No part of this publication may be reprinted, reproduced, transmitted, or utilized in any form or by any electronic, mechanical, or other means, now known or hereafter invented, including photocopying, microfilming, and recording, or in any information retrieval system without the written permission of Cognella, Inc. For inquiries regarding permissions, translations, foreign rights, audio rights, and any other forms of reproduction, please contact the Cognella Licensing Department at rights@cognella.com.

Trademark Notice: Product or corporate names may be trademarks or registered trademarks and are used only for identification and explanation without intent to infringe.

Cover image: Copyright © 2019 iStockphoto LP/FatCamera.

Printed in the United States of America.

cognella® | ACADEMIC PUBLISHING
3970 Sorrento Valley Blvd., Ste. 500, San Diego, CA 92121

CONTENTS

Unit V   Language and Speech   339

INTRODUCTION

M ore than a decade of teaching child development courses has brought me in contact with so many students with different educational needs, interests, and goals for the future. My goal in preparing the *Developmental Domains in Early Childhood Stage* is to provide a textbook that meets the course objective as well as students' diverse needs and goals. *Developmental Domains in Early Childhood Stage* will help readers gain a better understating of each area of development through comprehensive and significant research on human development.

The first section of *Developmental Domains in Early Childhood Stage* offers an essential perspective on most developmental theories that have become the science of human development and beginning of a human's life. This chapter describes the interaction of genes and surrounding chemicals that influence human growth, defines terms, introduces research design, and presents a general overview of the first significant domains of child development such as the cognitive, physical, social, emotional, language-related, and speech-related domains. All articles in part one demonstrate a developmental perspective and focus on particular stage of the lifespan and human development.

The second section of *Developmental Domains in Early Childhood Stage* reviews multiple perspectives on early cognitive development: Piaget's cognitive development theory, Vygotsky's sociocultural theory, and information processing theory. This chapter focuses on how children develop perspective taking and comprehend the concept of the world around them based on their age and ability to process incoming information along with their capabilities to represent objects and experiences. Furthermore, this chapter describes the influence of children's social interaction and language development on their intellectual progress, cognitive achievement, and the flexibility of their thinking.

The third section of *Developmental Domains in Early Childhood Stage* explains the importance of physical development throughout a child's life. This chapter comprises theories and perspectives on children's physical development such as fine and gross motor skills, the strengthening of bones and muscles, and the ability to move and touch from birth to early childhood age. During the first year of life, children will learn to control their movements. From birth to one year, children will make a drastic change in physical mobility and dexterity; as a result, in this section of the book readers will learn about the sequence of motor skill development starting from the inner body, including the head, neck, arms, and legs, then moving to the outer body, including the hands, feet, fingers, and toes. In addition to discussing a sequence of physical growth and mobility, selected research articles in this section explain and validate the significant influence of an appropriate physical environment on children's developmental need of trust, flexibility, and sensory exploration aspects.

The fourth section of *Developmental Domains in Early Childhood Stage* highlights the significance of children's social and emotional development. This part of the book defines various social–emotional theories through which children obtain the capacity to recognize, express, experience, and manage their emotions. Human babies depend on caregivers to survive. They require adult attention and care to provide them with necessities for development; as a result, this chapter will help readers acquire knowledge on how newborn babies interact, attract adult attention, and develop meaningful relationships with caregivers or people around them.

Finally, the fifth and last section of *Developmental Domains in Early Childhood Stage,* discusses language development in early childhood. By considering the innate ability of the human to learn language, babies and children must build multiple networks in their brains and develop social understanding in order to relate verbal language and gestures as they communicate with others. Section five describes children's simultaneous use of many language skills, such as vocabulary retention, putting words together into sentences, understanding the social context of what is begin said, and using proper grammar as they communicate with others.

In summary, understanding primary developmental domains and the concept of early childhood is the foundation for childhood educators. Early childhood development is best understood when its multiple domains and dimensions are examined both independently and interdependently as the whole process. Understanding the dynamics of these developmental domains and how they intersect is not only a critical component for educating children but is also essential for children's educational success. Once educators perceive children's development as a "whole," they will recognize the vital fact that educating children is more complicated than teaching letters and numbers. My intention in designing this book was to bring some of the readings in the field of child development together in a single volume based on each significant developmental domain (cognitive, physical, social and emotional, and language and speech). Unlike the existing readers in the field, a reader that is divided by these significant domains helps students realize how each domain is interrelated to the other domains and how the entire development is a holistic process. The *Developmental Domains in Early Childhood Stage* is designed for advanced undergraduates and introductory graduate-level students. This book has clear and direct relevance to development concerns, and each of the chapters in this textbook clarifies a particular domain of human development through the review of theories and research of the discipline and subdisciplines.

UNIT I

INTRODUCTION

Selection from Human Development

Lester M. Sdorow, Cheryl A. Rickabaugh, and Adrienne J. Betz

In 1987 Hulda Crooks climbed Mount Whitney in the Sierra Nevada Mountains of California for the 23rd time. This would be a noteworthy feat for any person, given that at 14,495 feet, Mount Whitney is the tallest mountain in the contiguous 48 states. What made it more impressive was that Hulda was 91 years old at the time, making her the oldest person ever to reach the summit. That year she also became the oldest woman to climb Mount Fuji, the tallest mountain in Japan. The Japanese sponsors of her ascent honored her with a banner reading "Grandma Fuji."

The following year Hulda decided to add the U.S. Capitol to her long list of conquests. She barely worked up a sweat as she ascended the 350-step staircase in the building's dome in just 30 minutes. Hulda, a physical fitness proponent who also held eight Senior Olympics world records in track and field at the time, made the climb to celebrate National Women in Sports Day (Connors, 1988).

Source: Lightspring/Shutterstock.com.

CHAPTER OUTLINE

Research Methods in Developmental Psychology

Prenatal Development

Infant and Child Development

Adolescent Development

Adult Development

Lester M. Sdorow, Cheryl A. Rickabaugh, and Adrienne J. Betz, Selection from "Human Development," *Psychology*, pp. 107-148, R1-R74. Copyright © 2019 by Academic Media Solutions. Reprinted with permission.

In 1991 a peak near Mount Whitney was named Crooks Peak in Hulda's honor. "You have not only highlighted the importance of physical fitness for all Americans, but also served as a role model for senior citizens everywhere," wrote President George H. W. Bush in a letter recognizing her accomplishments. At the ceremony naming the peak, Hulda observed, "It's never too late to change your lifestyle if you realize it's not appropriate. I want to impress to young people that they're building their old age now" (Kuebelbeck, 1991).

Hulda, who died in 1997 at the age of 101, was a vegetarian who took up hiking in her 40s following a bout with pneumonia. She did not scale her first peak until she was 66, when many people are content to lead a more sedentary life. Hulda advocated a sparse diet, vigorous exercise, and avoiding caffeine and alcohol. She also credited her healthy life to her spirituality as a devout member of the Seventh Day Adventist Church. Hulda published her memoirs, *Conquering Life's Mountains*, as a testament to the importance of mental, physical, and spiritual well-being. At a book signing, she was treated as a celebrity. Mountaineers lined up to have her sign their copies. One of them laughed when he realized that he had retired from mountain climbing at 55, when he was more than 10 years younger than Hulda was when she began her climbing career (Fieckenstein, 1996).

Hulda Crooks' accomplishments in old age contradict the stereotype of the elderly as frail and lacking in vitality. Psychologists who study the aging process find that severe mental and physical decline is not necessarily a characteristic of old age. As Hulda noted, by keeping mentally and physically active in adulthood we can have rich, rewarding lives throughout our later years. **Developmental psychology** is the study of the physical, perceptual, cognitive, and psychosocial changes that take place across the life span. Though opinions about the nature of human development can be found in the writings of ancient Greek philosophers, the scientific study of human development did not begin until the 1870s.

> **developmental psychology** The field that studies physical, perceptual, cognitive, and psychosocial changes across the life span.
>
> **maturation** The sequential unfolding of inherited predispositions in physical and motor development.

That decade saw the appearance of the "baby biography," usually written by a parent, which described the development of an infant. Though much of infant development depends on learning, it also is guided by physical **maturation**—the sequential unfolding of inherited predispositions (as in the progression from crawling to standing to walking). Developmental psychologists recognize that most aspects of human development depend on the interaction of genetic and environmental factors (Belsky & Pluess, 2009). The 1890s saw the beginning of research on child development after infancy (White, 1990), most notably at Clark University by G. Stanley Hall (1844–1924). Hall based his views on Darwin's theory of evolution, earning him the title of "the Darwin of the mind." He applied research findings to the improvement of education and child rearing, and today he is recognized as the founder of *child psychology*. Until the 1950s the study of human development was virtually synonymous with child psychology. During that decade, psychologists began to study human development across the life span. More recently, psychologists have come to realize the importance of considering social-cultural factors in human development.

Research Methods in Developmental Psychology

Though developmental psychologists often use the same research methods as other psychologists, they also rely on methods that are unique to developmental psychology. These include *longitudinal research*, *cross-sectional research*, and *cohort-sequential research*, which enable researchers to study age-related differences and changes in their participants.

Longitudinal Research

Longitudinal research follows the same participants over a period of time, typically ranging from months to years. The researcher looks for changes in particular characteristics, such as lan-

> **longitudinal research** A research design in which the same group of participants is tested or observed repeatedly over a period of time.

guage, personality, intelligence, or perceptual ability. Suppose you wanted to study changes in the social maturity of college students. If you chose to use a longitudinal design, you might assess the social maturity of an incoming class of first-year students and then note changes in their social maturity across their 4 years in college. Longitudinal research has been used to study numerous topics, such as factors associated with the development of creativity in children and adolescents (Weller, 2012), the relationship between identity, intimacy, and well-being in midlife (Sneed, Whitbourne, Schwartz, & Huang, 2012), and older adults' evaluations of their physical health as they age (Sargent-Cox, Anstey, & Luszcz, 2010).

Though longitudinal research has the advantage of permitting us to study individuals as they change across their life spans, it has major weaknesses. First, the typical longitudinal study takes months, years, or even decades to complete. This often requires ongoing financial support and continued commitment by researchers—neither of which can be guaranteed. Second, the longer the study lasts, the more likely it is that participants will drop out. They might refuse to continue or move away or even die. If those who drop out differ in important ways from those who remain, the results of the research might be less generalizable to the population of interest (Feng, Silverstein, Giarrusso, McArdle, & Bengtson, 2006). For example, a 14-year longitudinal study of changes in adult intelligence found that those who dropped out had scored lower on intelligence tests than did those who remained. This made it unwise to generalize the study's findings to all adults. Including only those who remained in the study would have led to the erroneous conclusion that as adults age they show a marked increase in intelligence (Schaie, Labouvie, & Barrett, 1973).

Cross-Sectional Research

The weaknesses of longitudinal research are overcome by **cross-sectional research**, which compares groups of participants of different ages at the same time. Each of the age groups

> **cross-sectional research** A research design in which groups of participants of different ages are compared at the same point in time.
>
> **cohort** A group of people of the same age group.

is called a **cohort**. If you chose to use a cross-sectional design to study age-related differences in social maturity of college students, you might compare the current social maturity of four cohorts: first-year students, sophomores, juniors, and seniors. A cross-sectional research design was used in a study of differences in male sexuality across adulthood. The researchers compared samples of men in their 30s through 90s. The stereotypical view of old age as a time of asexuality was countered by the finding that all of the participants in the oldest groups reported feelings of sexual desire (Mulligan & Moss, 1991). Cross-sectional research designs have been used to study topics as varied as differences in attitudes about love, sex, and "hooking up" among students during their first year of college (Katz & Schneider, 2013) and the relationship between medical education and differences in moral reasoning across four years of medical school (Self & Baldwin, 1998).

Like longitudinal research, cross-sectional research has its own weaknesses. The main one is that cross-sectional research can produce misleading findings if a cohort in the study is affected by circumstances unique to that cohort (Fullerton & Dixon, 2010). Thus, cross-sectional studies can identify differences between cohorts of different ages, but those differences might not hold true if cohorts of those ages were observed during another era. Suppose that you conduct a cross-sectional study and find that older adults are more prejudiced against minorities than are younger adults. Does this mean that we become more prejudiced with age? Not necessarily. Perhaps, instead, the cohort of older adults was reared at a time when prejudice was more acceptable than it is today. Members of the cohort might simply have retained attitudes that they developed in their youth.

Cohort-Sequential Research

One way to deal with the shortcomings of longitudinal and cross-sectional research is to use **cohort-sequential research**, which begins as a cross-sectional study by comparing different cohorts and then follows the cohorts longitudinally. As an example, consider how a cohort-sequential research design was employed in a study of alcohol use in old age. Healthy cohorts ranging in age from 60 to 86 years were first compared cross-sectionally. The results showed a decline in the percentage of drinkers with age. The

cohort-sequential research A research design that begins as a cross-sectional study by comparing different cohorts and then follows the cohorts longitudinally.

cohorts then were followed longitudinally for 7 years. The results remained the same: as the drinkers aged, they drank less. This made it more likely that the decline in drinking with age was related to age rather than to life experiences peculiar to particular cohorts (Adams, Garry, Rhyne, & Hunt, 1990). Another cohort-sequential study found that participation in sports, athletics, or exercising was related to lower levels of substance abuse by teenagers and young adults rather than merely being associated with different patterns of substance abuse for different age cohorts (Terry-McElrath & O'Malley, 2011).

Cohort-sequential research designs also may reveal age differences that are cohort effects rather than being age-related effects. This was the case in the Seattle Longitudinal Study. Cognitive abilities of participants in the longitudinal aspect of the study were measured in 1956, 1963, 1970, and 1977. At each of those times, the cognitive abilities of participants of different ages were compared cross-sectionally. The findings showed that there was a larger cognitive decline in the cross-sectional comparisons than in the longitudinal comparisons. This indicates that observed differences in cognitive ability at different ages is more related to factors affecting particular cohorts than to changes that naturally accompany aging (Williams & Klug, 1996).

Longitudinal research, cross-sectional research, and cohort-sequential research have long been staples of research on development from birth to death. Today, technology permits developmental psychologists to study ongoing developmental processes even before birth, during the prenatal period.

SECTION REVIEW: Research Methods in Developmental Psychology

1. What is maturation?
2. What are the strengths and weaknesses of cross-sectional and longitudinal research designs?

Prenatal Development

All of us began life as a single cell. The formation of that cell begins the prenatal period, which lasts about 9 months and is divided into the germinal stage, the embryonic stage, and the fetal stage.

The Germinal Stage

The **germinal stage** begins with conception, which occurs when a *sperm* from the man unites with an egg (or *ovum*) from the woman, usually in one of her two *fallopian tubes*, forming a one-celled *zygote*. The zygote contains 23 pairs of chromosomes, one member of each pair coming from the ovum and the other coming from the sperm. The chromosomes, in turn, contain genes that govern the development of the individual. The zygote begins a trip down the fallopian tube, during which it is transformed into a larger, multicelled ball, called a *blastocyst*, by repeated cell divisions. By the end of the second week, the blastocyst attaches to the wall of the uterus. This marks the beginning of the embryonic stage.

The Germinal Stage

The germinal stage begins with conception, when one sperm penetrates the outer layer of the egg in a fallopian tube. Once this occurs, cells divide until a multi-cell clump, called a blastocyst, which continues on its journey to the uterus.

Source: Ralwel/Shutterstock.com.

> **germinal stage** The prenatal period that lasts from conception through the second week.

The Embryonic Stage

The **embryonic stage** lasts from approximately the end of the second week through approximately the tenth week of prenatal development. The embryo, nourished by nutrients

> **embryonic stage** The prenatal period that lasts from the end of the second week through the tenth week.

that cross the placenta, increases in size and begins to develop specialized organs, including the eyes, heart, and brain. What accounts for this rapid, complex process? The development and location of bodily organs is regulated by genes, which determine the kinds of cells that will develop and also control the actions of *cell-adhesion molecules*. These molecules direct the movement of cells and determine which cells will adhere to one another, thereby determining the size, shape, and location of organs in the embryo (Rungger-Brändle, Ripperger, Steiger, Soltanieh, & Rungger, 2010). By the end of the embryonic stage, development has progressed to the point at which the heart is beating and the approximately one-inch-long embryo has facial features, limbs, fingers, and toes.

But what determines whether an embryo becomes a female or a male? The answer lies in the 23rd pair of chromosomes, the sex chromosomes, which are designated *X* or *Y*. Embryos that inherit two X chromosomes are genetic females, and embryos that inherit one X and one Y chromosome are genetic males. The presence of a Y chromosome directs the development of the testes; in the *absence* of a Y chromosome, the ovaries differentiate. Near the end of the embryonic period, the primitive gonads of male embryos secrete the hormone *testosterone*, which stimulates the development of male sexual organs. And the primitive gonads of female embryos secrete the hormones *estrogen* and *progesterone*, which stimulate the development of female sexual organs. Thus, the hormonal environments of female and male fetuses differ at the embryonic stage of development.

Human Embryonic and Fetal Development

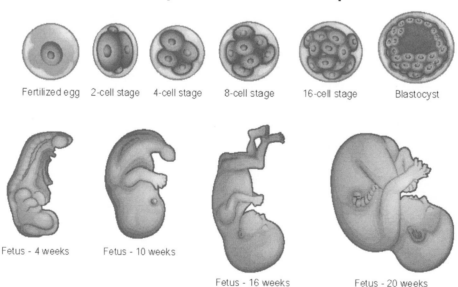

Prenatal Development

Human prenatal development is the process in which a fertilized egg becomes an embryo and develops as a fetus until birth. In the fetal stage, many organs are formed.

Source: BlueRingMedia/Shutterstock.com.

Prenatal hormones direct the differentiation of sexual organs and the brain, especially the hypothalamus. The secretion of testosterone by the male fetus directs the differentiation of the male sexual organs. In cases where testosterone is absent, female sexual organs differentiate. There is evidence, though, that estrogen plays a greater role in sexual differentiation of the female fetus than has been estimated in the past (Collaer, Geffner, Kaufman, Buckingham, & Hines, 2002).

The Fetal Stage

The presence of a distinctly human appearance marks the beginning of the **fetal stage**, which lasts from the beginning of the third prenatal month until birth. By the fourth month, pregnant women report movement by the fetus. And by the seventh month, all of the major organs are functional, which means that an infant born even 2 or 3 months prematurely has a chance of surviving. The final 3 months of prenatal development are associated with most of the increase in the size of the fetus.

> **fetal stage** The prenatal period that lasts from the end of the eighth week through birth.

The fetus also develops rudimentary sensory and cognitive abilities, including the ability to hear sounds and form long-term memories. In one study, 143 fetuses were exposed to a series of conditions. First, there was 2 minutes of silence. Second, there was a tape recording of their mother reading a story. The recording was played for 2 minutes through a speaker held about 4 inches from the mother's abdomen. Then, they were exposed to another 2 minutes of silence. Fetal heart rate increased in response to the mother's voice and decreased when they were exposed to silence. This indicates that the fetus can perceive and form a memory of its mother's voice (Kisilevsky & Haines, 2011).

Premature infants tend to be smaller and less physically and cognitively mature than full-term infants. For example, when an object approaches the eyes of a premature infant, the infant might not exhibit normal defensive blinking (Pettersen, Yonas, & Fisch, 1980). Moreover, though prenatal development usually produces a healthy infant, in some cases genetic defects produce distinctive physical and psychological syndromes. The chromosomal disorder called Down syndrome, for example, is associated with intellectual disabilities and abnormal physical development. Other sources of prenatal defects are **teratogens**, which are noxious substances or other factors that can disrupt prenatal development and prevent the individual from reaching her or his inherited potential. (The word *teratogen* was coined from Greek terms meaning "that which produces a monster.")

> **teratogen** A noxious substance, such as a virus or drug, that can cause prenatal defects.

Most teratogens affect prenatal development by first crossing the placenta. A potent teratogen is the German measles (rubella) virus, which can cause defects of the eyes, ears, and heart—particularly during the first 3 months of prenatal development. Many drugs, both legal and illegal, can cross the placenta and cause abnormal physical and psychological development. These drugs include nicotine (Piper, Gray, & Birkett, 2012) and marijuana (Keegan, Parva, Finnegan, Gersen, & Belden, 2010). And alcohol consumption during pregnancy is

fetal alcohol syndrome A disorder, marked by physical defects and intellectual disability, that can afflict the offspring of women who drink alcohol during pregnancy.

associated with **fetal alcohol syndrome**. Fetal alcohol syndrome is associated with facial deformities, intellectual disabilities, attentional deficits, and poor impulse control. Researchers have demonstrated the striking teratogenic effect of alcohol in animal studies. When pregnant rats were given alcohol during the embryo stage, their offspring had physical deformities and behavioral deficits similar to those seen in humans (Sulik, Johnston, & Webb, 1981).

Factors that are correlated with parental substance abuse also may have harmful long-term effects. Recreational drug use has adverse effects on the father's health, including damaged DNA that results in abnormal sperm (Pollard, 2000). Parents with a history of substance abuse also are more likely to have turbulent relationships. One study found that women who were heavy cocaine users were more likely to report that the father of the child abused alcohol or other drugs. And fathers with a history of a drug or alcohol problems were more likely to subject their partner to physical or mental abuse during her pregnancy (Frank, Brown, Johnson, & Cabral, 2002). Sadly, children with a history of prenatal drug exposure also are at risk of receiving poor-quality parental care after birth (Eiden, Schuetze, & Coles, 2011). Thus, teratogens not only have a direct effect upon prenatal development, they also may harm the child indirectly by contributing to an environment that fails to ensure the child's well-being.

SECTION REVIEW: Prenatal Development

1. What are cell-adhesion molecules?
2. What are the symptoms of fetal alcohol syndrome?

Infant and Child Development

Childhood extends from birth until puberty and begins with **infancy**, a period of rapid physical, cognitive, and psychosocial development, extending from birth to age 2 years. Many developmental psychologists devote themselves to studying the changes in physical, perceptual, cognitive, and psychosocial development that occur during childhood.

childhood The period that extends from birth until the onset of puberty.

infancy The period that extends from birth through 2 years of age.

Physical Development

Newborn infants exhibit reflexes that promote their survival, such as blinking to protect their eyes from an approaching object and rooting (searching) for a nipple when their cheeks are touched. Through maturation and learning, the infant quickly develops motor skills that go beyond mere reflexes. The typical infant is crawling by 6 months and walking by 13 months.

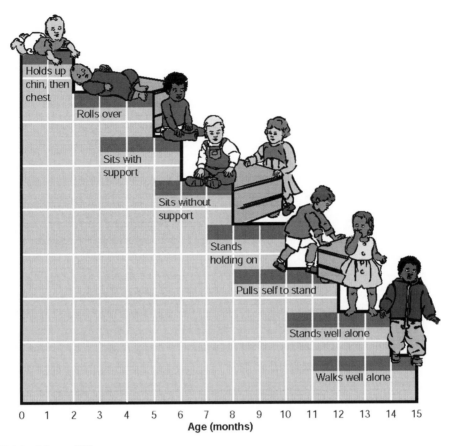

FIGURE 1.1 **Motor Milestones**

Infancy is a period of rapid motor development. The infant begins with a set of motor reflexes and, over the course of little more than a year, develops the ability to manipulate objects and move independently through the environment. The ages at which healthy children reach motor milestones vary somewhat from child to child, but the sequence of motor milestones does not.

Though infant motor development follows a consistent sequence, the timing of motor milestones varies somewhat from one infant to another. Figure 1.1 depicts the major motor milestones.

Infancy also is a period of rapid brain development, when many connections between brain cells are formed and many others are eliminated. Though some of these changes are governed by maturation, research studies by Marian Diamond and her colleagues over the past few decades have demonstrated that life experiences can affect brain development (Diamond, 1988). One of these studies determined the effect of enriched and impoverished environments on the brain development of rats (Camel, Withers, & Greenough, 1986). A group of infant rats spent 30 days in an enriched environment and another group spent 30 days in an impoverished environment. In the enriched environment, the rats were housed together in two large, toy-filled cages, one containing water and one containing food, which were attached to the opposite ends of a maze. The pattern of pathways and dead ends through the maze was changed daily. In the impoverished environment, the rats were housed individually in small, empty cages.

Microscopic examination of the brains of the rats found that those exposed to enriched environments had longer and more numerous dendrites on their brain neurons than did those exposed to the impoverished environment. The increased size and number of dendrites would provide the rats exposed to the enriched environment with more synaptic connections among their brain neurons. The benefits of enriched environments on neural development also have been replicated in studies of children (Bryck & Fisher, 2012).

After infancy, the child's growth rate slows, and most children grow two or three inches a year until puberty. The child's motor coordination also improves. Children gradually learn to perform more sophisticated motor tasks, such as using scissors, tying their shoes, and riding bicycles. The development of motor skills even affects the development of cognitive skills. For example, children's ability to express themselves through language depends on the development of motor abilities that permit them to speak and to write.

Perceptual Development

Over a century ago, in describing what he believed was the chaotic mental world of the newborn infant, William James (1890/1981, Vol. 1, p. 462) claimed, "The baby, assailed by eyes, ears, nose, skin, and entrails at once, feels it all as one great blooming, buzzing confusion." But subsequent research has shown that newborn infants have more highly developed sensory, perceptual, and cognitive abilities than James believed. For example, though newborns cannot focus on distant objects, they can focus on objects less than a foot away—as though nature has programmed them to focus at the distance of the face of a person who might be holding them (Aslin & Smith, 1988). Newborn infants can use their sense of touch to discriminate between objects with different surface textures (Molina & Jouen, 1998). Newborns also have a more sophisticated sense of smell than James would have presumed. In one study, infants were exposed to either the odor of amniotic fluid (which they experienced while in the womb) or another odor they had not been exposed to before. The results showed that the infants were more likely to turn their heads toward the odor of amniotic fluid than toward the other odor (Schaal, Marlier, & Soussignan, 1998).

Ingenious studies have permitted researchers to infer what infants perceive by recording changes in their eye movements, head movements, body movements, sucking behavior, or physiological responses (such as changes in heart rate or brain-wave patterns). For example, a study of newborn American infants found that they could discriminate between Japanese words with different pitch patterns as indicated by their sucking harder on a rubber nipple in response to particular patterns (Nazzi, Floccia, & Bertoncini, 1998). Infant preferences can be determined by recording which targets they look at longer or by presenting them with a stimulus, waiting for them to *habituate* to it (that is, stop noticing it—as indicated by, for example, a stable heart rate), and then changing the stimulus. If they notice the change, they will show alterations in physiological activity, such as a *decrease* in heart rate.

Studies using these techniques have found that infants have remarkably well-developed sensory-perceptual abilities. Tiffany Field has demonstrated that infants less than 2 days old can imitate sad, happy, and surprised facial expressions (Field, Woodson, Greenberg, & Cohen,

1982). Nonetheless, other studies have been inconsistent in their findings regarding neonatal imitation of facial expressions. The most consistent finding has been that neonates will respond to models who stick out their tongues by sticking out their own (Anisfeld, 1996).

The Research Process box illustrates one of the ways in which psychologists study infant perceptual development. The study made use of a "visual cliff" to test infant depth perception.

Infants also have good auditory abilities, including the ability to localize sounds. Between the ages of 8 and 28 weeks, infants can localize sounds that shift in location by only a few degrees, as indicated by head turns or eye movements in response to the shifts (Morrongiello, Fenwick, & Chance, 1990). Infants can even match the emotional tone of sounds to the emotional tone of facial expressions. In one study, 7-month-old infants were shown a sad face and a happy face. At the same time, they were presented with tones that either increased or decreased in pitch. When presented with a descending tone, they looked longer at a sad face than a happy face, as if they were equating the lower tones with a sad mood and the higher tones with a happy mood (Phillips, Wagner, Fells, & Lynch, 1990). As the preceding studies attest, infants are perceptually more sophisticated than William James presumed.

Cognitive Development

Infancy also is a time of rapid cognitive development, during which infants show the unfolding of inborn abilities and their talent for learning. In regard to inborn abilities, for example, newborn infants can distinguish groups of objects that differ in number (Wynn, 1995). In regard to learning, by 4 or 5 months of age, an infant's response to the sound of its own name differs from its response to hearing other names (Mandel, Jusczyk, & Pisoni, 1995).

Jean Piaget (1896–1980), a Swiss biologist and psychologist, put forth the most influential theory of cognitive development. Piaget (1952) proposed that children pass through four increasingly sophisticated cognitive stages of development (see Table 1.1). According to Piaget,

TABLE 1.1 Piaget's States of Cognitive Development

Stage	Age	Description	Developmental Outcome
Sensorimotor	Birth–2 Years	Infants learn to integrate sensory input and motor output and begin to use symbolic thought.	Object permanence
Preoperational	2–7 Years	Children become more sophisticated in their use of language and symbolic thought, but they have difficulty in reasoning logically.	Loss of egocentrism
Concrete operational	7–11 Years	Children become proficient in reasoning logically about concrete situations, such as the ability to make transitive inferences.	Conservation
Formal operational	11–15 Years	Many adolescents learn to use abstract reasoning and to form hypotheses about future events based on relevant current knowledge.	Abstract reasoning and hypothesis testing

a child is more than an ignorant adult; the child's way of thinking is qualitatively different from the adult's. Moreover, infants are not passive in developing their cognitive views of the physical world. Instead, their views depend on their active interpretation of objects and events in the physical world.

Though Piaget assumed that complete passage through one stage is a prerequisite for success in the next one, research suggests that children can achieve characteristics of later stages without completely passing through earlier ones (Berninger, 1988). The issue of whether human cognitive development is continuous (gradual and quantitative) or discontinuous (in stages and qualitative) remains unresolved (Fischer & Silvern, 1985). The stages put forth by Piaget are the *sensorimotor stage*, *preoperational stage*, *concrete operational stage*, and *formal operational stage*. Some psychologists have criticized Piaget's theory for its assumption that cognitive development follows a universal pattern (Elkind, 1996). Cross-cultural research indicates that children throughout the world do tend to pass through these stages in the same order, though the timing varies (Segall, Dasen, Berry, & Poortings, 1990).

Sensorimotor Stage

Piaget called infancy the **sensorimotor stage**, during which the child learns to coordinate sensory experiences and motor behaviors. Infants learn to interact with the world by sucking, grasping, crawling, and walking. In little more than a year, they change from being reflexive and physically immature to being purposeful, locomoting, and language-using. By the age of 9 months, for example, sensorimotor coordination becomes sophisticated enough for the infant to grasp a moving object by aiming her or his reach somewhat ahead of the object—using its speed and direction—instead of where the object appears to be at that moment (Keen, Carrico, Sylvia, & Berthier, 2003).

sensorimotor stage The Piagetian stage, from birth through the second year, during which the infant learns to coordinate sensory experiences and motor behaviors.

Piaget claimed that experiences with the environment help the infant form **schemas**, which are cognitive structures incorporating the characteristics of persons, objects, events, procedures, or situations. This means that infants do more than simply gather information about the world. Their experiences actively change the way in which they think about the world. Schemas permit infants to adapt their behaviors to changes in the environment. But what makes schemas persist or change? They do so as the result of the interplay between **assimilation** and **accommodation**. We *assimilate* when we fit information into our existing schemas and *accommodate* when we revise our schemas to fit new information.

schema A cognitive structure that guides people's perception and information processing that incorporates the characteristics of particular persons, objects, events, procedures, or situations.

assimilation The cognitive process that interprets new information in light of existing schemas.

accommodation 1. The cognitive process that revises existing schemas to incorporate new information.
2. The process by which the lens of the eye increases its curvature to focus light from close objects or decreases its curvature to focus light from more distant objects.

Young infants, prior to 6 months old, share an important schema in which they assume that the removal of an object from sight means that the object no longer exists. If an object is hidden by a piece of cloth, for example, the young infant will not look for it, even after watching the object being hidden. To the young infant, out of sight truly means out of mind. As infants gain experience with the coming and going of objects in the environment, they accommodate and develop the schema of **object permanence**—the realization that objects not in view may still exist. Infants generally fail to search for objects that are suddenly hidden from view until they are about 8 months old (Munakata, McClelland, Johnson, & Siegler, 1997). But researchers have questioned Piaget's explanation that young infants fail to search for hidden objects because they lack a schema for object permanence. Perhaps, instead, they simply forget the location of an object that has been hidden from view (Bjork & Cummings, 1984).

> **object permanence** The realization that objects exist even when they are no longer visible.

THE RESEARCH PROCESS

When Do Infants Develop Depth Perception?

Rationale

One of the most important perceptual abilities is depth perception. It lets us tell how far away objects are from us, preventing us from bumping into them and providing us with time to escape from potentially dangerous ones. But how early can infants perceive depth? This was the subject of a classic study by Eleanor Gibson (1910–2002) and Richard Walk (Gibson & Walk, 1960).

Method

Gibson and Walk used a "visual cliff" made from a piece of thick, transparent glass set about four feet off the ground (see Figure 1.2). Just under the "shallow" side was a red and white checkerboard pattern. The same pattern was placed at floor level under the "deep" side. The sides were separated by a one-foot-wide wooden board. The participants were 36 infants, aged 6 to 14 months. The infants were placed, one at a time, on the wooden board. The infants' mothers called to them, first from one side and then from the other.

Results and Discussion

When placed on the board, 9 of the infants refused to budge. The other 27 crawled onto the shallow side toward their mothers. But only 3 of the 27 crawled onto the deep side. The remaining ones instead cried or crawled away from it. This indicated that the infants could perceive the depth of the two sides—and feared the deep side. It also demonstrated that depth perception is present by 6 months of age. Replications of the study using a variety of animals found that depth perception develops by the time the animal begins moving about on its own—as early as the first day after birth for chicks and goats. This is adaptive, because it reduces their likelihood of being injured. More recent research on human infants, using decreases in heart rate as a sign that they notice changes in depth, indicates that rudimentary depth perception is present in infants as young as 4 months (Aslin & Smith, 1988). But research findings indicate that human infants will not fear heights until they have had several weeks of crawling experience. Infants will not avoid the deep side of the visual cliff until they have been crawling for at least 12 weeks (Kretch & Adolph, 2013).

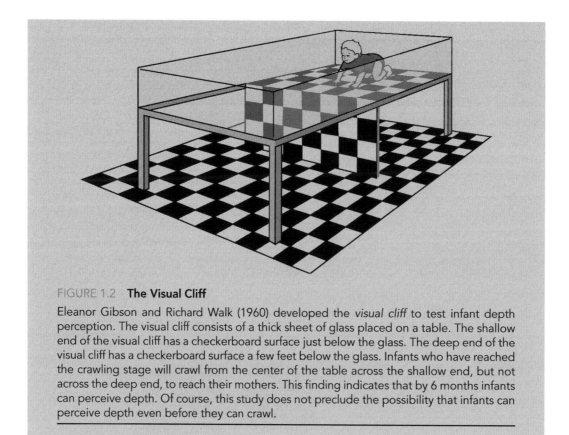

FIGURE 1.2 **The Visual Cliff**

Eleanor Gibson and Richard Walk (1960) developed the *visual cliff* to test infant depth perception. The visual cliff consists of a thick sheet of glass placed on a table. The shallow end of the visual cliff has a checkerboard surface just below the glass. The deep end of the visual cliff has a checkerboard surface a few feet below the glass. Infants who have reached the crawling stage will crawl from the center of the table across the shallow end, but not across the deep end, to reach their mothers. This finding indicates that by 6 months infants can perceive depth. Of course, this study does not preclude the possibility that infants can perceive depth even before they can crawl.

After the age of 8 months, most infants demonstrate their appreciation of object permanence by searching at other places for an object they have seen being hidden from view. At this point in their development, they can retain a mental image of a physical object even after it has been removed from their sight, and they realize that the object might be elsewhere. This also signifies the beginning of representational thought—the use of symbols to stand for physical objects. But Piaget might have placed the development of object permanence too late, because infants as young as 6 months have been found to show an appreciation of it (Shinskey, 2012).

Preoperational Stage

According to Piaget, when the child reaches the age of 2 years and leaves infancy, the sensorimotor stage gives way to the **preoperational stage**, which lasts until about age 7. The stage is called preoperational because the child cannot perform what Piaget called *operations*—mental manipulations of reality. For example, before about the age of 5 the early preoperational child cannot perform mental addition or subtraction of objects. During the preoperational stage, however, the child improves in the use of language, including a rapid growth in

preoperational stage The Piagetian stage, extending from 2 to 7 years of age, during which the child's use of language becomes more sophisticated but the child has difficulty with the logical mental manipulation of information.

vocabulary and a more sophisticated use of grammar. Thus mental development sets the stage for language development. Unlike the sensorimotorstage child, the preoperational-stage child is not limited to thinking about objects that are physically present.

During the preoperational stage, the child also exhibits what Piaget called **egocentrism**, the inability to perceive reality from the perspective of another person. Egocentrism declines between 4 and 6 years of age (Ruffman & Olson, 1989). Children display ego-centrism when they draw a picture of their family but fail to include themselves in the drawing. In

> **egocentrism** The inability to perceive reality from the perspective of another person.

some capital criminal cases, lawyers might gain a reduced sentence for a child defendant if they can convince the jury that the child had not progressed beyond egocentrism and therefore was unaware of the effect of the criminal act on the victim (Ellison, 1987).

Concrete Operational Stage

At about the age of 7, the child enters what Piaget calls the **concrete operational stage**, which lasts until about the age of 11. The child learns to reason logically but is at first limited to reasoning about physical things. For example, when you first learned to do arithmetic problems, you were unable to perform mental calculations. Instead, until perhaps the age of 8, you counted by using your fingers or other objects. An important kind of reasoning ability that develops during this stage is the ability to make **transitive inferences**—the application of previously learned relationships to infer new

> **concrete operational stage** The Piagetian stage, extending from 7 to 11 years of age, during which the child learns to reason logically about objects that are physically present.
>
> **transitive inference** The application of previously learned relationships to infer new relationships.

ones. For example, suppose that a child is told that Pat is taller than Lee, and that Lee is taller than Terry. A child who can make transitive inferences will correctly conclude that Pat is taller than Terry. Though Piaget claimed that the ability to make transitive inferences develops by age 8, research has shown that children as young as 4 can make them—provided they are given age-appropriate tasks (Andrews & Halford, 1998).

By the age of 8, the child in the concrete operational stage also develops what Piaget called **conservation**—the realization that changing the form of a substance or the arrangement of a set of objects does not change the amount. Suppose that a child is shown two balls of clay of equal size. One ball is then rolled out into a snake, and the child is asked if either piece

> **conservation** The realization that changing the form of a substance does not change its amount.

of clay has more clay. The child who has not achieved conservation will probably reply that the snake has more clay because it is longer. Figure 1.3 shows a classic means of testing whether a child has developed the schema of conservation. Conservation has implications for children as eyewitnesses. Children who have achieved conservation are less susceptible to leading questions than are children who have not achieved it (Muir-Broddus, King, Downey, & Petersen, 1998).

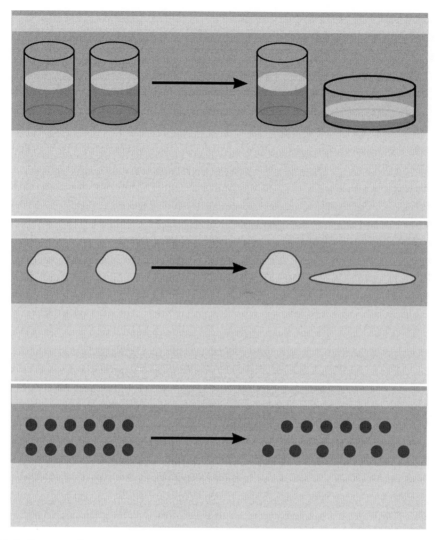

FIGURE 1.3 **Conservation**

During the concrete operational stage, children develop an appreciation of conservation. They come to realize that changing the form of something does not change its amount. For example, they realize that pouring water from a tall, narrow container into a short, wide container does not change the amount of water.

The effect of sociocultural experiences on the timing of conservation was demonstrated in a study of children in a Mexican village whose parents were pottery makers. The children who normally helped their parents in making pottery acquired conservation (at least of mass) earlier than other children did (Price-Williams, Gordon, & Ramirez, 1969). Moreover, certain nonverbal variations of the conservation of liquid volume problem show that children might develop conservation earlier than indicated by studies that have used the traditional verbal demonstration procedure (Wheldall & Benner, 1993).

In early adolescence, the concrete operational stage might give way to the formal operational stage, which is discussed in the section of this chapter devoted to adolescent development.

Psychosocial Development

Just as Piaget believed that the child passes through stages of cognitive development, psycho-analyst Erik Erikson (1902–1994) believed that the child passes through stages of psychosocial development. Erikson observed that we go through eight distinct stages across the life span. Each stage is marked by a conflict that must be overcome, as described in Table 1.2. Research has supported Erikson's belief that we pass through the stages sequentially—though people differ in the ages at which they pass through them (Vaillant & Milofsky, 1980). Erikson also was one of the first researchers to consider sociocultural differences in psychosocial development, noting that the society, not just the family, affects the child's development (Eagle, 1997). This view was influenced by Erikson's studies of children in Sioux, Yurok, and other Native American cultures.

TABLE 1.2 Erikson's Stages of Psychosocial Development

Age	Social Conflict	Successful Resolution of Conflict
Birth–1 year	Trust vs. mistrust	A sense of security and attachment with caregivers.
2 years	Autonomy vs. shame and doubt	A sense of independence from caregivers.
3–5 years	Initiative vs. guilt	The ability to control impulses while still being spontaneous.
6 years–puberty	Industry vs. inferiority	A sense of competence in regard to a variety of everyday activities.
Adolescence	Identity vs. role confusion	A mature sense of self characterized by living according to one's own values, interests, and goals.
Young adulthood	Intimacy vs. isolation	The establishment of mature relationships characterized by personal commitment and emotional attachment.
Middle adulthood	Generativity vs. stagnation	An investment in others and concern about their well-being.
Late adulthood	Integrity vs. despair	A sense of acceptance from reflecting on a meaningful life.

You also should be aware that there might be sociocultural differences among peoples we normally might consider to be members of a homogenous cultural group. In Central Africa, for example, infants have markedly different experiences among Ngandu farmers and neighboring Aka hunter-gatherers. Aka infants are more likely to be held, and Nkandu infants are more likely to be left alone, possibly contributing to early behavioral differences that are observed between them (Hewlett, Lamb, Shannon, Leyendecker, & Schoelmerich, 1998).

Social Attachment and Interpersonal Relationships

Erikson found that the major social conflict of the first year of infancy is **trust versus mistrust**. One of the most important factors in helping the infant develop trust is **social attachment**, a strong emotional relationship between an infant and a caregiver that develops during the first year. Beginning in the 1930s, British psychiatrist John Bowlby (1907–1990) became interested in the effects of early maternal loss or deprivation on later personality development. Much of his theorizing was based on his study of orphans whose parents were killed in World War II. Bowlby favored an evolutionary viewpoint, suggesting that infants have evolved an inborn need for attachment because their survival depends on adult caregivers (Bowlby, 1988). Thus, infants seek to maintain physical proximity and evoke responses from adults through crying, cooing, smiling, and clinging. Similarly, Sigmund Freud assumed that an infant becomes attached to his or her mother for a functional reason—she provides nourishment through nursing.

> **trust versus mistrust** Erikson's developmental stage in which success is achieved by having a secure social attachment with a caregiver.
>
> **social attachment** A strong emotional relationship between an infant and a caregiver.

Freud's assumption was contradicted by research conducted by Harry Harlow and his colleagues on social attachment in rhesus monkeys. Harlow separated infant monkeys from their parents and peers and raised them for 6 months with two "surrogate mothers." The surrogates were wire monkeys with wooden heads. One surrogate was covered with terry cloth and the other was left bare. Harlow found that the monkeys preferred to cling to the cloth-covered surrogate, even though milk was available only from a bottle attached to the bare-wire surrogate. Harlow concluded that physical contact is a more important factor than nourishment in promoting infant attachment (Harlow & Zimmerman, 1959).

Harlow's research findings inspired interest in the possible role of attachment in human psychosocial development. Of course, today's ethical standards would prevent the replication of Harlow's experiment with human infants (and perhaps even with infant monkeys). Much of what we know about attachment in human infants comes from research by Mary Ainsworth (1913–1999) on the mother-infant relationship. She was inspired by her long-time collaboration with Bowlby. Ainsworth conducted her first studies of infant-mother attachment patterns after visiting Uganda. Though cross-cultural studies have found differences in infant behaviors and maternal behaviors and beliefs, the importance of infant-mother attachment patterns has been found to generalize across many cultures (Pierrehumbert et al., 2009).

In assessing attachment, Ainsworth made a distinction between *securely attached* and *insecurely attached* infants. This becomes an especially important issue at about 8 months of age, when infants show a strong preference for their mothers over strangers and show separation anxiety. To test this, Ainsworth developed the Strange Situation: The mother and infant are in a room together; the mother leaves the room, a stranger enters the room, the stranger then leaves, and the infant's response to the mother is assessed when she then returns to the room. The securely attached infant seeks physical contact with the mother, yet, despite mildly protesting, freely leaves her to play and explore, using the mother as a secure base. In contrast, the insecurely attached infant clings to the mother, acts either apathetic or highly anxious when separated from her, and is either unresponsive or angry when reunited with her.

A meta-analysis of 21 studies using the Strange Situation with more than 1,000 infants found a moderately strong relationship between the mother's sensitivity and the infant's attachment security (De Wolff & van IJzendoorn, 1997). An infant whose mother is more sensitive, accepting, and affectionate will become more securely attached. Infants who are securely attached, in turn, have better relationships with their peers in childhood and adolescence than infants who are insecurely attached (Gorrese & Ruggieri, 2012). And research indicates that the relationship between maternal responsiveness and the quality of infant attachment generalizes across cultures. Cultural differences have been observed, though, in the maternal and infant behaviors observed in the Strange Situation, especially in measures of visual referencing—infants' willingness to play at a distance while keeping mothers within eyesight—and physical proximity seeking, such as clinging and cuddling (Leyendecker, Lamb, Fracasso, Schölmerich, & Larson, 1997; Zach & Keller, 1999).

Until recently, research on attachment has been limited to use of the Strange Situation in assessing the quality of attachment with the infant's primary caregiver—typically the mother (Field, 1996). Researchers investigating the role of the father in social development have found that paternal interaction also promotes secure attachment in infants. Moreover, families may be described as reflecting a system of attachments between infants, young children, and family members who provide care and engage them in social interaction (van IJzendoorn & DeWolff, 1997).

One study assessed the quality of attachment between mothers, fathers, and two of their children. The Strange Situation was used to measure attachment in the younger children (aged 18 to 24 months), and a questionnaire was used to measure attachment in older children (4 to 5 years of age). Parental caregiving was assessed through naturalistic observation and questionnaires. Results indicated that the majority of the children had developed secure attachments with both parents. Moreover, the quality of parental care-giving predicted secure attachment in only one case: between mothers and their younger children. Maternal caregiving was unrelated to the quality of attachment in older children. And paternal caregiving was unrelated to the quality of attachment of younger and older children (Schneider-Rosen & Burke, 1999). These findings suggest that care-giving is only one avenue by which parents, usually mothers, contribute to the development of a secure attachment in infancy. Moreover, the quality of attachment in older children appears to be related to other aspects of family interaction, such as the quality of parent-child play (Grossmann, Grossmann, Kremmer-Bombik, Scheuerer-Englisch, & Zimmerman, 2002). And, though neglected by early research in attachment, fathers do contribute to the development of attachment in infancy and early childhood.

Researchers also have investigated the stability of attachment security across the life span. Two longitudinal studies found that attachment security is remarkably stable from infancy through adolescence (Beijersbergen, Juffer, Bakermans-Kranenburg, & van IJzendoorn, 2012) and early adulthood (Fraley, Roisman, Booth-LaForce, Owen, & Holland, 2013). In these studies, attachment category had been assessed in infancy. Later, participants completed questionnaires assessing the quality of their attachment or were interviewed by raters blind to their original classification. In both studies, the majority of the securely attached participants' classification was unchanged. But what predicts changes in attachment security? Attachment security can be adversely affected by negative life events that disrupt a family's functioning and the psychological well-being of adults in the household—and in turn their responsiveness and sensitivity to their offspring (Waters, Weinfield, & Hamilton, 2000).

According to Erikson, during the second year the child experiences a conflict involving **autonomy versus shame and doubt**. The child explores the physical environment, begins to learn self-care skills, such as feeding, and tries out budding motor and language abilities. In doing so, the child develops a greater sense of independence from her or his parents. This might account for the popular notion of the "terrible twos," when the child enjoys behaving in a contrary manner and saying no to any request. Parents who stifle efforts at reasonable independence or criticize the child's awkward efforts will promote feelings of shame and doubt. Elementary and high school teachers who support autonomy in their students have a more positively motivating style of teaching (Reeve, Bolt, & Cai, 1999).

> **autonomy versus shame and doubt** Erikson's developmental stage in which success is achieved by gaining a degree of independence from one's parents.

At 3 years of age, the child enters the stage that involves the conflict Erikson calls **initiative versus guilt**. The child shows initiative in play, social relations, and exploration of the environment. The child also learns to control his or her impulses, feeling guilt for actions that go beyond limits set by parents. So, at this stage, parents might permit their child to rummage through drawers but not to throw clothing around the bedroom. Thus, the stage of initiative versus guilt deals with the development of a sense of right and wrong.

> **initiative versus guilt** Erikson's developmental stage in which success is achieved by behaving in a spontaneous but socially appropriate way.

At about the age of 6, and continuing until about the age of 12, Erikson observed, the child faces the conflict of **industry versus inferiority**. The industrious child who achieves successes during this stage is more likely to feel competent. This is important, because children who feel academically and socially competent are happier than other children and have more positive relationships with their peers (Mouratidis & Michou, 2011). A child who develops a sense of inferiority may lose interest in academics, avoid social interactions, or fail to participate in sports. Successful resolution of the conflict over industry versus inferiority also leads to more positive feelings of vocational competence in high-school students (Gribble, 2000). The importance of this stage in psychosocial development has been demonstrated in both Western and non-Western countries, including the People's Republic of China (Zhang & Nurmi, 2012).

> **industry versus inferiority** Erikson's developmental stage in which success is achieved by developing a sense of competency.

Parent-Child Relationships

One of the most important factors in psychosocial development is the approach that parents take to child rearing. This is especially important, given the increasingly diverse family configurations within the United States. Stepparents, for example, who try to develop a friendship with their stepchildren before marrying and who continue their friendship after marrying have relationships with their stepchildren that are more likely to be marked by liking and affection. Stepparents who, instead, try to control their stepchildren are less likely to develop a positive relationship (Ganong, Coleman, Fine, & Martin, 1999). And a frequently expressed concern is whether the children of gay or lesbian parents will suffer from personal or social adjustment problems. An extensive review of research studies found no differences between the children of gay and lesbian parents and those of heterosexual parents on a number of measures of psychosocial adjustment (Wainright, Russell, & Patterson, 2004).

Parenting Style Psychologist Diana Baumrind (1966) distinguished three parenting styles: *permissive*, *authoritarian*, and *authoritative*. Permissive parents set few rules and rarely punish misbehavior. Permissiveness is undesirable because children will be less likely to adopt positive standards of behavior. At the other extreme, authoritarian parents set strict rules and rely on punishment. They respond to questioning of their rules by saying, "Because I say so!"

Authoritarian parenting, likewise, is undesirable. Authoritarian parents exert coercive power over their children, which is arbitrary and domineering (Baumrind, 2010), and which may lead to emotional abuse (Hamarman, Pope, & Czaja, 2002). Authoritarian parents also are more likely to resort to physical discipline—perhaps escalating to physical abuse. Aside from the potential for injury to the child, physical child abuse is associated with lasting emotional effects on the target of the abuse. Abused children have lower self-esteem and are more depressed (Leeson & Nixon, 2011), they tend to be more aggressive (Barry, Lochman, Fite, Wells, & Colder, 2012), and they are more likely to develop behavior problems in adolescence (Thompson, Hollis, & Richards, 2003).

Another form of physical and emotional child abuse is sexual abuse—in many cases by a parent or close family member. A review of research studies published between 1989 and 1999 found that about 10 percent of child abuse cases involve sexual abuse and about 17 percent of women and 8 percent of men had histories of sexual abuse as children (Putnam, 2003). The scourge of child sexual abuse makes it imperative that children be taught to avoid situations that might make them potential targets of sex abusers. Of great concern is the vicious cycle in which abused children become abusive parents. However, though most child abusers were abused as children, only one-third of abused children become abusers—a far cry from claims that being an abused child automatically makes one a future child abuser (Putnam, 2003). So, if you were unfortunate enough to have a history of child abuse, you may very well be able to break the vicious cycle when rearing your own children.

Baumrind has found that the best approach to child rearing is **authoritative parenting** (Baumrind, 1983). Authoritative parents tend to be warm and loving, yet insist that their children behave appropriately. They encourage

> **authoritative parenting** An effective style of parenting in which the parent is warm and loving yet sets well-defined limits that he or she enforces in an appropriate manner.

independence within well-defined limits, show a willingness to explain the reasons for their rules, and permit their children to express verbal disagreement with them. By maintaining a delicate balance between freedom and control, authoritative parents help their children internalize standards of behavior.

Children of authoritative parents report better physical and psychological well-being than children of authoritarian or permissive parents Children who have authoritative parents are more likely to be socially competent, independent, and responsible. They are less likely to drink alcohol or smoke (Piko & Balázs, 2012), more likely to perform well in school (Mattanah, Pratt, Cowan, & Cowan, 2005), and more likely to be autonomous and display a mastery orientation, which is essential for motivation (Kudo, Longhofer, & Floersch, 2012). But, as cautioned in Chapter 2, be wary of concluding that parenting style causes these effects. Remember that only experimental, not correlational, research permits statements about causality. Perhaps the direction of causality is the opposite of what one would assume. For example, children who behave properly might evoke authoritative parenting.

Research tends to support a positive relationship between authoritative parenting and children's competence. But we still do not know how or why it does so (Darling & Steinberg, 1993). Though the relationship between authoritative parenting and healthy child development appears to be a universal phenomenon (Zhou et al., 2008), we must be aware of cultural differences in child rearing—both between and within societies. Cultural differences in beliefs about parental and child roles and the nature of child rearing influence parents' interactions with their children (Rudy & Grusec, 2001). For example, Chinese parenting may be seen as authoritarian and controlling. Chinese cultural beliefs about parenting stress the concept of *chiao shun*, or training the child to meet social expectations. Thus, parental control may have different meanings in cross-cultural contexts (Chao, 1994; 2001).

Day Care Another important, and sometimes controversial, factor in child rearing is day care. The number of American children placed in day care increased during the 1990s, with more than half of infants and toddlers spending at least 20 hours per week in the care of adults other than their parents (Singer, Fuller, Keiley, & Wolf, 1998). Though day care, overall, seems to have neither strong benefits nor strong detrimental effects (Lamb, 1996), research findings are contradictory in regard to the effects of day care on infants. On the negative side are studies finding that infant day care of more than 20 hours a week in the first year of life is associated with insecure attachment during infancy and greater noncompliance and aggressiveness in early childhood (Hill, Wadlfogel, Brooks-Gunn, & Han, 2005) and that children who enter day care before age 2 later perform more poorly in high school than do children who enter day care after age 2 (Ispa, Thornburg, & Gray, 1990). Of course, we can never be sure about the cause and effect from studies such as these. On the positive side are studies finding that infants in day care do not become insecurely attached (Burchinal, Bryant, Lee, & Ramey, 1992) and that they later do well in school and act less aggressively than other children do (Field, 1991). And a longitudinal study that examined preschoolers' behavior before and after their mothers returned to work showed no negative outcomes (Chase-Lansdale et al., 2003). These contradictory findings reflect the complex nature of the issue, which involves numerous variables, including the characteristics of the infants, their parents, their caretakers, and the day-care settings.

Because many working parents have no choice but to place their infants in day care, it is reassuring to know that research indicates that high-quality infant day care is probably not harmful (Maccoby & Lewis, 2003). According to findings of the National Institute of Child Health and Human Development Study of Early Child Care, "high-quality" means that the number of children and the adult-child ratio are small, the adults practice nonauthoritarian caregiving, and the environment is safe, clean, and stimulating (NICHD Early Child Care Research Network, 1997). Some researchers have found that high-quality daycare can have long-term benefits on children's cognitive and social emotional development (Peisner-Feinberg et al., 2001). High-quality day care has been found to be especially influential in the prevention of behavior problems in low-income boys and African American children (Votruba-Drzal et al., 2010). Though, overall, day care has neither positive nor negative effects on infants or children, poor day care and lack of a stable care provider tend to have a negative effect (Lamb, 1996). But the cost of high-quality day care—if it is, in fact, available—makes it unaffordable to many families. Nonetheless, even day care that is not optimal tends not to have damaging effects on most children. Heredity and home environment tend to outweigh the effects of day care, even when it is not of high quality (Scarr, 1998).

Parental Conflict Children are affected not only by parenting styles and day-care practices but also by the quality of their parents' relationship. A meta-analysis of relevant studies found that parental discord spills over into negative parent-child relationships (Erel & Burman, 1995). Moreover, marital discord can undermine the child's feeling of emotional security and lead to adjustment problems in childhood and adolescence (Klahr, Rueter, McGue, Iacono, & Alexander, 2011) and marital discord in adulthood (Davies & Cummings, 1994).

In some cases marital discord leads to divorce. Because about half of all marriages in the United States end in divorce, many children spend at least part of their childhood primarily with one parent. Though it is easier for two adults to meet the stressful demands of providing the consistent, responsive caregiving that promotes children's well-being, research on single parents indicates that one responsible, emotionally available adult can provide the social and emotional bond that is essential to optimal childhood development (Silverstein & Auerbach, 1999). More than one-third of American children born in the past three decades will experience parental divorce. And they will be more likely to suffer emotional problems, particularly depression (Aseltine, 1996). The long-term effects of divorce on children include greater personal distress and more problems in intimate relationships in adulthood (Christensen & Brooks, 2001).

Because divorce involves so many variables, including the age and economic status of the parents, the age of the children, and the custody arrangements, different combinations of these variables can have different effects on the children (Lamb, 2012). The effects of each combination remain to be determined. It should be noted, however, that children from divorced families have a greater sense of well-being than children from intact families with intense parental conflict (Amato & Keith, 1991). Moreover, divorce itself might induce less distress in children than parental conflict prior to the divorce. A meta-analysis of research studies published during the 1990s on the well-being of children of divorce versus children from intact families found that children of divorce were worse off on variables such as self-esteem, personal conduct, psychological adjustment, interpersonal relationships, and academic performance. These differences were slightly greater in later studies than those reported in studies conducted during the 1980s (Reifman, Villa, Amans, Rethinam, & Telesca, 2001).

Interaction with Peers

Children are affected by their relationships with friends and siblings as well as those with their parents. Friendships provide the context for social and emotional growth (Newcomb & Bagwell, 1995). Secure attachment to both mothers and fathers provides a solid basis for friendships (Verissimo et al., 2011). And childhood friendships may have a bearing on adult emotional well-being. Consider a study that compared young adults who had a best friend in fifth grade and young adults who had no friends in fifth grade. Those who had a best friend had higher self-esteem than those who had no friends. And those who had no best friend were more likely to have symptoms of psychological disorders (Bag-well, Newcomb, & Bukowski, 1998). Of course, you must be careful not to assume that there is a causal relationship in which friendships promote healthy personalities. Perhaps, instead, children with certain personalities are simply more likely to make friends and to have higher self-esteem.

Few children develop friendships before the age of 3, and 95 percent of childhood friendships are between children of the same sex (Hartup, 1989). Girls tend to have fewer, but more intimate, friendships than do boys (Berndt & Hoyle, 1985). A meta-analysis of children's peer relations found that socially and academically competent children are popular with their peers. In contrast, children who are withdrawn, aggressive, or academically deficient tend to be rejected by their peers (Newcomb, Bukowski, & Pattee, 1993).

Peer relationships in childhood involve play. A classic study (Parten, 1932) found that the interactive play of children gradually increased between 2 and 4 years of age, but that throughout this period, children engaged mainly in parallel play, as when two children in a sandbox play separately from each other with pails and shovels. Parallel play provides a transition into social play, in which children play interactively, with children as old as 4 years alternating between the two (Anderson, 2001). There also are cultural differences in play. For example, whereas gender-segregated play appears to be a universal phenomenon, there are cultural differences in the extent to which children engage in cross-sex play (Aydt & Corsaro, 2003).

Gender-Role Development

One of the most frequently studied aspects of psychosocial development in childhood is the development of **gender roles**, which are behavior patterns that are considered appropriate for men or women in a given culture. The first formal theory of gender-role development was put forth by Sigmund Freud. He assumed that the resolution of what he called the Oedipus (in the case of boys) and Electra (in the case of girls) complexes at age 5 or 6 led the child to internalize the gender role of the same-sex parent. The Oedipus and Electra complexes begin with the child's sexual attraction to the

gender roles Behaviors that are considered appropriate for women or men in a given culture.

other-sex parent. According to Freud, because the child fears punishment for desiring the other-sex parent, the child comes to identify with the same-sex parent. But studies of children show that children develop gender roles even when they live in single-parent households. Because of the lack of research support for Freud's theory, most researchers favor more recent theories of gender-role development.

Social learning theory stresses the importance of observational learning, rewards, and punishment. Thus, social learning theorists assume that the child learns gender-relevant behaviors by observing gender-role models

> **social learning theory** A theory of learning that assumes that people learn behaviors mainly through observation and mental processing of information.

and by being rewarded for appropriate, and corrected or punished for inappropriate, gender-role behavior. This process of gender typing begins on the very day of birth and continues through the life span. In one study, new parents were interviewed within 24 hours of the birth of their first child. Though there are no observable differences in the physical appearance of male and female newborns whose genitals are covered, newborn daughters were more likely to be described by their parents as cute, weak, and uncoordinated than newborn sons were (Rubin, Provenzano, & Luria, 1974). But an influential review of research by Eleanor Maccoby found that parents reported that they did not treat their sons and daughters differently (Maccoby & Jacklin, 1974). Of course, parents might believe that they treat their daughters and sons the same, while actually treating them differently. A meta-analysis, however, supported Maccoby by finding that gender-role development seems, at best, weakly related to differences in how parents rear their sons and daughters (Lytton & Romney, 1991).

Parents are not the only social influences contributing to gender-role development. As noted earlier in this chapter, children tend to socialize with same-sex peers and engage in sex-segregated play. Children reward each other for engaging in gender-appropriate activities and punish or exclude children who engage in cross-gender behavior. Moreover, this peer pressure is stronger for boys than for girls. Considering the inconsistent evidence for the role of differential parental reinforcement of children's behaviors, it is very likely that peers may wield a stronger influence on gender-role development than do parents (Bussey & Bandura, 1999). One such factor is the sex of one's siblings. A large-scale study of 3-year-olds found that both boys and girls with an older brother were more masculine and less feminine. Boys with an older sister were more feminine but not less masculine. And girls with an older sister were less masculine but not more feminine (Rust, Golombok, Hines, Johnston, & Golding, 2000).

An alternative to the social learning theory of gender-role development is Sandra Bem's (1981) **gender schema theory**, which combines elements of social learning theory and the

> **gender schema theory** A theory of gender-role development that combines aspects of social learning theory and the cognitive perspective.

cognitive perspective. Bem's theory holds that people differ in the schemas they use to organize their social world. People may have schemas relevant to age, ethnicity, gender, occupations, or any number of social categories. *Gender schemas* are specialized cognitive structures that

Gender Roles

According to social learning theory, children learn gender-role behaviors by being rewarded for performing those behaviors and by observing adults, particularly parents, engaging in them.

Source: XiXinXing/Shutterstock.com.

assimilate and organize information about women and men. Children are *gender schematic* if they categorize people, behavior, activities, and interests as masculine or feminine. In contrast, *gender aschematic* children do not categorize these types of information into masculine and feminine categories. Gender schematic individuals are likely to notice, attend to, and remember people's behavior and attributes that are relevant to gender. For example, one study found that gender schematic adults recalled more gender- stereotypic information than did gender aschematic adults (Renn & Calvert, 1993).

Gender schemas develop early. One study found that toddlers were able to label same-sex toys—operationally defined as touching a masculine or feminine toy—as early as 2 years of age (Levy, 1999). Social experiences can modify the development of gender schema, though, as shown in studies of traditional and egalitarian families. A meta-analysis of 48 studies found that parents' gender schemas were correlated with their children's gender schemas. Though the effect size was small, traditional parents were more likely than nontraditional parents to have children who thought about themselves and others in gender-typed ways (Tenenbaum & Leaper, 2002). Gender schema theory provides a glimpse into the development of gender stereotypes and how gender stereotypes influence social behavior (Deaux & Major, 1987).

Moral Development

American psychologists have researched and tested the development of morality in children and adults for more than a century (Wendorf, 2001). Today, the most influential theory of moral development is Lawrence Kohlberg's (1981) cognitive-developmental theory.

Kohlberg's Theory of Moral Development Kohlberg's theory, formulated in the 1960s, is based on Piaget's (1932) proposal that a person's level of moral development depends on his or her level of cognitive development. Piaget found that children, in making moral judgments, are at first more concerned with the consequences of actions. Thus, a young child might insist that accidentally breaking ten dishes is morally worse than purposely breaking one dish. As children become more cognitively sophisticated, they base their moral judgments more on a person's intentions than on the consequences of the person's behavior. Kohlberg assumed that as individuals become more cognitively sophisticated, they reach more complex levels of moral reasoning. Research findings indicate that adequate cognitive development is, indeed, a prerequisite for each level of moral reasoning (Walker, 1986).

Kohlberg, agreeing with Piaget, developed a stage theory of moral development based on the individual's level of moral reasoning. Kohlberg determined the individual's level of moral reasoning by presenting a series of stories, each of which includes a moral dilemma. The person must suggest a resolution of the dilemma and give reasons for choosing that resolution. The person's stage of moral development depends not on the resolution, but instead on the reasons given for that resolution. What is your response to the following dilemma proposed by Kohlberg? Your reasoning in resolving it would reveal your level of moral development:

> In Europe, a woman was near death from a very bad disease, a rare kind of cancer. There was one drug that the doctors thought might save her. It was a special form of radium that a druggist in the same town had recently discovered. The drug was expensive to make, but the druggist was charging 10 times what the drug cost him to make. He paid 200 dollars for the radium and charged two thousand dollars for a small dose of the drug. The sick woman's husband, Heinz, went to everyone he knew to borrow the money, but he could get together only about one thousand dollars, which was half of what it cost. He told the druggist that his wife was dying and asked him to sell it cheaper or let him pay later. But the druggist said, "No, I discovered the drug, and I am going to make money from it." So Heinz got desperate and broke into the man's store to steal the drug for his wife. (Kohlberg, 1981, p. 12)

The levels of moral development represented by particular responses to this dilemma are presented in Table 1.3. Kohlberg has identified three levels: the *preconventional*, the *conventional*, and the *postconventional*. Each level contains two stages, making a total of six stages of moral development. As Piaget noted, as we progress to higher levels of moral reasoning, we become more concerned with the actor's motives than with the consequences of the actor's actions. This was supported by a study of moral judgments about aggressive behavior, which found that high school and college students at higher stages of moral reasoning were more concerned with the

TABLE 1.3   Kohlberg's Theory of Moral Development

Level of Moral Development	Stage of Moral Development
Preconventional level: Concern with consequences of behavior for oneself	*Stage 1:* Moral choices made to avoid punishment
	Stage 2: Moral choices made to gain rewards
Conventional level: Concern with social laws and values	*Stage 3:* Moral choices made to gain social approval
	Stage 4: Moral choices made to fulfill duty, respect authority, and maintain social order
Postconventional level: Concern with moral principles, agreed-upon laws, and human dignity	*Stage 5:* Moral choices made to follow mutually agreed-upon principles and ensure mutual respect of others
	Stage 6: Moral choices made to uphold human dignity and one's own ethical principles

aggressor's motivation than were students at lower stages (Berkowitz, Mueller, Schnell, & Padberg, 1986).

People at the **preconventional level** of moral reasoning, which typically characterizes children up to 9 years old, are mainly concerned with the consequences of moral behavior to themselves.

> **preconventional level** In Kohlberg's theory, the level of moral reasoning characterized by concern with the consequences that behavior has for oneself.

In stage 1, the child has a punishment and obedience orientation, in which moral behavior serves to avoid punishment. In stage 2, the child has an instrumental-relativist orientation, in which moral behavior serves to get rewards or favors in return, as in "you scratch my back and I'll scratch yours."

> **conventional level** In Kohlberg's theory, the level of moral reasoning characterized by concern with upholding laws and conventional values and by favoring obedience to authority.

People at the **conventional level** of moral reasoning, usually reached in late childhood or early adolescence, uphold conventional laws and values by favoring obedience to parents and authority figures. Kohlberg calls stage 3 the good boy/nice girl orientation because the child assumes that moral behavior is desirable because it gains social approval, especially from parents. Kohlberg calls stage 4 the society-maintaining orientation, in which the adolescent views moral behavior as a way to do one's duty, show respect for authority, and maintain the social order. These four stages have even been used to show differences in moral reasoning among members of the U.S. Congress about political issues (Shapiro, 1995).

At the end of adolescence, some of those who reach Piaget's formal operational stage of cognitive development also reach the **postconventional level** of morality. At this level of moral reasoning, people make moral judgments based on ethical principles that might conflict with their self-interest or with the maintenance of social order. In stage 5, the social-contract orientation, the person assumes that adherence

> **postconventional level** In Kohlberg's theory, the level of moral reasoning characterized by concern with obeying mutually agreed-upon laws and by the need to uphold human dignity.

to laws is in the long-term best interest of society but that unjust laws might have to be violated. The U.S. Constitution is based on this view. Stage 6, the highest stage of moral reasoning, is called the universal ethical principle orientation. The few people at this stage assume that moral reasoning must uphold human dignity and their conscience—even if that brings them into conflict with their society's laws or values. Thus, an abolitionist who helped runaway American slaves flee to Canada in the 19th century would be acting at this highest level of moral reasoning.

Criticisms of Kohlberg's Theory Kohlberg's theory has received mixed support from research studies. Children do appear to proceed through the stages he described in the order he described (Walker, 1989). And a study of adolescents on an Israeli kibbutz found that, as predicted by Kohlberg's theory, their stages of moral development were related to their stages of cognitive development (Snarey, Reimer, & Kohlberg, 1985). But Kohlberg's theory has been criticized on several grounds. First, the theory explains moral reasoning, not moral action. A person's moral actions might not reflect her or his moral reasoning. Yet some research supports a positive relationship between moral reasoning and moral actions. For example, one study found that college students who believed that the use of illegal drugs was morally wrong based on principle were, in fact, less likely to use drugs than peers who believed that illegal drug use was a matter of simple personal choice (Abide, Richards, & Ramsay, 2001).

A second criticism is that the situation, not just the person's level of moral reasoning, plays a role in moral decision making and moral actions. This was demonstrated in a study of male college students who performed a task in which their goal was to keep a stylus above a light moving in a triangular pattern—a tedious, difficult task. When provided with a strong enough temptation, even those at higher stages of moral reasoning succumbed to cheating (Malinowski & Smith, 1985).

Other critics insist that Kohlberg's theory might not be generalizable beyond Western cultures, with their greater emphasis on individualism (Sachdeva, Singh, & Medin, 2011). This criticism has been countered by Kohlberg and his colleagues. They found that when people in other cultures are interviewed in their own languages, using moral dilemmas based on situations that are familiar to them, Kohlberg's theory holds up well. Moreover, in other cultures, the stages of moral reasoning unfold in the order claimed by Kohlberg. For example, a study of Taiwanese children and young adults found that they progressed through the moral stages in the order and at the rate found in Americans (Lei, 1994). Nonetheless, postconventional moral reasoning is not found in all cultures (Snarey, Reimer, & Kohlberg, 1985).

Still another criticism of Kohlberg's theory is that it is biased in favor of a male view of morality. The main proponent of this criticism has been Carol Gilligan (1982). She points out that Kohlberg's theory was based on research on male participants, and she claims that Kohlberg's theory favors the view that morality is concerned with detached, legalistic justice (an allegedly masculine orientation) rather than with involved, interpersonal caring (an allegedly feminine orientation).

Thus, Gilligan believes that women's moral reasoning is colored by their desire to relieve distress, whereas men's moral reasoning is based on their desire to uphold rules and laws. Because Kohlberg's theory favors a male view, women are unfairly considered lower in moral development. Despite some research support for Gilligan's position (Garmon, Basinger, Gregg, &

Gibbs, 1996), there does not appear to be a moral chasm between men and women—there are no significant differences between men and women in their use of justice and care orientations. For example, a recent study lent only mixed support to Gilligan's position. More than 200 men and women rated hypothetical mixed (containing elements of both care and justice orientations) and real-life (conflicts they had personally experienced) moral dilemmas. As Gilligan would predict, women scored higher on care reasoning and men scored higher on justice reasoning on the hypothetical mixed dilemmas. However, there were no gender differences in the ratings of the real-life moral dilemmas. Regardless of participant sex, real-life moral dilemmas involving ongoing personal relationships elicited care reasoning. And real-life moral dilemmas concerning the self or casual acquaintances elicited justice reasoning (Skoe, Cumberland, Eisenberg, Hansen, & Perry, 2002). Moreover, a meta-analysis found that females exhibit a care orientation only slightly more than males, and males exhibit a justice orientation only slightly more than females (Jaffee & Hyde, 2000).

Other critics claim that both Kohlberg's and Gilligan's theories are simplistic and do not consider enough of the factors that influence moral development. These critics believe that an adequate theory of moral development must consider the interaction of cultural, religious, and biological factors (Woods, 1996).

SECTION REVIEW: Infant and Child Development

1. What has research discovered about infant depth perception?
2. What are Piaget's basic ideas about cognitive development?
3. What has research found about the importance of infant attachment to a caregiver?
4. What are the differences between permissive, authoritarian, and authoritative parenting?

Adolescent Development

Change marks the entire life span, though it is more dramatic at certain stages than at others. Biological factors have a more obvious influence during adolescence and late adulthood than during early and middle adulthood. Social factors exert their greatest influence through the **social clock**, which includes major events that occur at certain times in the typical life cycle in a given culture. In Western cultures,

social clock The typical or expected timing of major life events in a given culture.

for example, major milestones of the social clock include graduation from high school, leaving home, finding a job, getting married, having a child, and retiring from work. Being late in reaching these milestones can cause emotional distress (Rook, Catalano, & Dooley, 1989).

There also is some evidence for cross-cultural and cohort differences in young adults' beliefs about the timing of life events. For example, one study of Australian undergraduates found that the "best" ages associated with adult milestones differed from American age norms of the 1960s. Moreover, participants suggested later ages for marriage and grandparenthood and a wider age range for retirement (Peterson, 1996).

Cultural and historical factors can have different effects on different cohorts. Depending on your cohort, your adolescent and adult experiences might differ from those of other cohorts. A Swiss study compared young adult participants born between World Wars I and II (the "Between the Wars" cohort) participants born in the years immediately after World War II (the "Early Baby Boomers" cohort) and participants born in the early 1970s (the "Generation X" cohort) regarding their views concerning the main tasks of young adulthood. The largest difference was between the "Between the Wars" cohort and the "Generation X" cohort. Whereas the "Between the Wars" cohort placed relatively more value on work and family, the "Generation X" cohort placed relatively more value on higher education and leisure-time activities (Bangerter, Grob, & Krings, 2001). Thus, as you read, keep in mind that although common biological factors and social clocks might make generations somewhat similar in their development, cultural and historical factors that are unique to particular cohorts can make them somewhat different from cohorts that precede or succeed them.

Adolescence is unknown in many developing countries. Instead, adulthood begins with the onset of puberty and is commonly celebrated with traditional rites of passage. With the advent of universal free education and child labor laws in Western countries, children, who otherwise would have entered the adult work world by the time they reached puberty, entered a period of life during which they developed an adult body yet maintained a childlike dependence on parents. Formal study of **adolescence**, the transitional period between childhood and adulthood, began with the work of G. Stanley Hall (1904).

> **adolescence** The transitional period lasting from the onset of puberty to the beginning of adulthood.

Physical Development

Recall your own adolescence. What you might recall most vividly are the rapid physical changes associated with **puberty** (from the Latin word for "adulthood"). As illustrated in Figure 1.4, puberty is marked by a rapid increase in height; girls show a growth spurt between the ages of 10 and 12, and boys show a growth spurt between the ages of 12 and 14. The physical changes

> **puberty** The period of rapid physical change that occurs during adolescence, including the development of the ability to reproduce sexually.

of puberty also include the maturation of primary and secondary sex characteristics. Primary sex characteristics are hormone-induced physical changes that enable us to engage in sexual reproduction. These changes include growth of the penis and testes in males and the vagina, uterus, and ovaries in females. Secondary sex characteristics are stimulated by sex hormones but are unrelated to sexual reproduction. Pubertal males develop facial hair, deeper voices, and larger muscles. Pubertal females develop wider hips, larger breasts, and more rounded physiques, caused in part by increased deposits of fat.

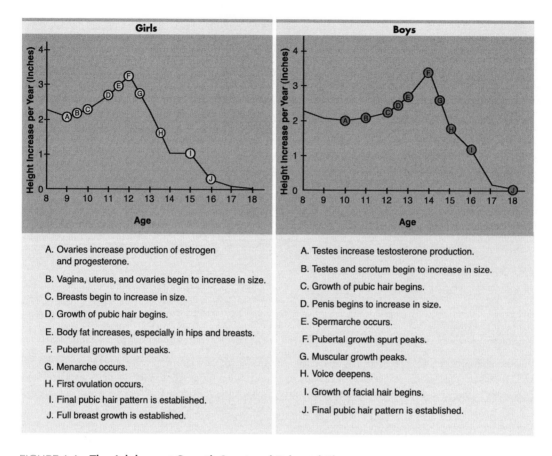

FIGURE 1.4   **The Adolescent Growth Spurt and Pubertal Change**
The onset of puberty is associated with a rapid increase in height. The growth spurt of girls occurs earlier than that of boys. Note that the ages given for the timing of particular physical changes during puberty are based on averages. Individual pubertal changes may vary from these averages without falling outside the range of normal development.

These physical changes are triggered in girls by a spurt in the secretion of the sex hormone estrogen between ages 10 and 11 and in boys by increased levels of the sex hormone testosterone between ages 12 and 13. Boys generally experience **spermarche**, their first ejaculation, between the ages of 13 and 15, typically while asleep (so-called nocturnal emissions). Girls exhibit earlier physical maturation than boys and generally experience **menarche**, their first menstrual period, between the ages of 11 and 13 (Paikoff & Brooks-Gunn, 1991). The average age at menarche is lower than in the past; this decline in the age of menarche has been attributed to improved health and nutrition. For example, the average age of menarche declined from 16.5 to 13.7 years over a span of 40 years in two rural counties of China. During this period of modernization, the health and living conditions of the rural Chinese population improved dramatically (Graham, Larsen,

spermarche The first ejaculation, usually occurring between the ages of 13 and 15.

menarche The beginning of menstruation, usually occurring between the ages of 11 and 13.

Puberty

Because adolescents enter puberty at different ages, groups of young adolescents include individuals who vary greatly in height and physical maturity. As a consequence, a typical middle-school class might appear to include a wider age range than it actually does.

Source: Tracy Whiteside/Shutterstock.com.

& Xu, 1999). And increasing rates of obesity across the globe are associated with a decline in the average age of menarche. The Health Behavior in School-Aged Children study assessed the relationship between obesity and the average age of menarche among girls in 34 countries. The researchers concluded that most cross-cultural differences in the average age of menarche were attributable to childhood obesity (Currie et al., 2012).

Though the dramatic physical changes of puberty are caused by hormonal changes, adolescent mood swings are not necessarily the by-products of hormones run wild. Hormone fluctuations affect the adolescent's moods, but life events have a greater effect (Brooks-Gunn & Warren, 1989). Of course, the physical changes of puberty, including acne, rapid growth, and physical maturation, can themselves produce emotional distress. This is especially true if the adolescent is unprepared for them or is made to feel self-conscious by peers or parents. Boys find it difficult enough to deal with scruffy facial hair, unwanted penile erections, and voices that crack, without being made more anxious about those changes. Girls, likewise, find it difficult enough to discover suddenly that they have enlarged breasts, a monthly menstrual cycle, and possibly tower several inches above many of their male peers.

The timing of puberty may influence how adolescents respond to these physical changes. Research findings on the relative effects of early versus late puberty have been inconsistent, in part because of the different methodologies that have been used. Cross-sectional research findings indicate that late maturation is, overall, more negative for both males and females in regard to behavior and personal adjustment, but longitudinal research findings indicate that the timing of puberty, overall, has neither positive nor negative effects on adolescents (Dorn, Susman, & Ponirakis, 2003). Nonetheless, at times early maturation may bring with it certain problems. For example, boys and girls who enter puberty early drink more alcohol and become intoxicated more often than their peers who do not mature early. This correlation is stronger for boys than for girls (Kaltiala-Heino, Koivisto, Marttunen, & Fröjd, 2011).

Cognitive Development

Adolescent cognitive development is less dramatic, with no obvious surge in mental abilities to match the surge in physical development. According to Piaget's theory, at about 11 years of age, some adolescents pass from the concrete operational stage to the **formal operational stage**. A person who reaches this stage is able to reason about abstract, not just concrete, situations. The adolescent who has reached the formal operational stage can apply abstract principles and make predictions about hypothetical sit-uations. In contrast, an adolescent still in the concrete operational stage would rely more on blind trial and error than on a formal approach to problem solving.

> **formal operational stage** The Piagetian stage, beginning at about age 11, marked by the ability to use abstract reasoning and to solve problems by testing hypotheses.

To appreciate this, imagine that you are given four chemicals and are asked to produce a purple liquid by mixing them—but it is left up to you to discover the proper mixture. People at the concrete operational level would approach this task in an unsystematic manner, hoping that through trial and error they would hit upon the correct combination of chem-icals. In contrast, people at the formal operational level would approach it systematically, perhaps by mixing each possible combination of two of the chemicals, then each possible combination of three, and finally all four. Thus, people who reach the formal operational stage perform better on more complex intellectual pursuits. A study of seventh and eighth graders found that those in transition between the concrete operational stage and the formal operational stage showed better understanding of abstract concepts presented in a physics textbook than did those still in the concrete operational stage (Renner, Abraham, Grzybowski, & Marek, 1990).

Piaget found that so few people reach the formal operational stage that he gave up his earlier belief that it was universal. Those who reach that stage are more likely to have been exposed to scientific thinking in their academic courses (Rogoff & Chavajay, 1995). Though educational interventions have been effective in fostering the development of formal opera-tional thought in developing countries such as Pakistan (Iqbal & Shayer, 2000), people from cultures that do not stress science in their school curricula are less likely to achieve the formal operational stage.

Psychosocial Development

Erik Erikson noted that psychosocial development continues through adolescence into adulthood and old age. Perhaps the most important psychosocial tasks of adolescence are the formation of a personal identity and the development of healthy relationships with peers and parents.

Identity Achievement

According to Erikson (1963), the most important feat of adolescence is the resolution of the conflict of **identity versus role confusion**. The adolescent develops a sense of identity by adopting her or his own set of values and social behaviors. Erikson believed this is a normal part of finding answers to questions related to one's identity, such as these: What do I believe is important? What are my goals in life?

> **identity versus role confusion** Erikson's developmental stage in which success is achieved by establishing a sense of personal identity.

Erikson's emphasis on the importance of the identity crisis might reflect, in large part, his own life history. He was born in Germany, the child of a Danish Christian mother and father. Erik's father abandoned his mother while she was pregnant with him. She then married a Jewish physician, Theodore Homburger. Erik was given his new father's surname, making him Erik Homburger. But it was not until Erik reached adolescence that he was told that Homburger was not his biological father (Hopkins, 1995).

Erikson, uncomfortable among Jews and Christians alike, sought to find himself by traveling in European artistic and intellectual circles, as many young adults did in the 1920s. Eventually he met Anna Freud, Sigmund's daughter and an eminent psychoanalyst herself. Erikson underwent psychoanalysis with her almost daily for 3 years. In 1933 Erikson changed his name to Erik Homburger Erikson and left to pursue a career in the United States. His long, rich life was a testament to his success in finding his identity as a husband, writer, teacher, and psychoanalyst.

To appreciate the task that confronts the adolescent in developing an identity, consider the challenge of having to adjust simultaneously to a new body, a new mind, and a new social world. The adolescent body is larger and sexually mature. The adolescent mind can question the nature of reality and consider abstract concepts regarding ethical, political, and religious beliefs. The social world of the adolescent requires achieving a balance between childlike dependence and adultlike independence. This also manifests itself in the conflict between parental and peer influences. Children's values mirror their parents', but adolescents' values oscillate between those of their parents and those of their peers. Adolescents move from a world guided by parental wishes to a world in which they are confronted by a host of choices regarding sex, drugs, friends, schoolwork, and other things. Erikson's theory of adolescence has received support from longitudinal studies showing that, in fact, adolescents typically move from a state of role confusion to a state of identity achievement (Streitmatter, 1993). Among the factors that are related to successful identity achievement are positive parental involvement with the adolescent and active interest in the adolescent's school performance and social relationships (Brittain & Lerner, 2013).

There also is some evidence that Erikson's theory may generalize to adolescents' experiences across cultures. One study found that Hong Kong adolescents who achieved a sense of identity were more prosocial and exhibited fewer antisocial behaviors than adolescents who had not (Ma, Shek, Cheung, & Oi, 2000). And African adolescents who achieved a sense of identity reported more extensive exploration of career options and held broader vocational interests than adolescents who had not (Schmitt-Rodermund & Vondracek, 1999). Successful identity achievement is positively related to personal adjustment (Hunsberger, Pratt, & Pancer, 2001).

Failure to achieve a sense of identity is associated with emotional distress, including feelings of emptiness and depression (Taylor & Goritsas, 1994).

But Carol Gilligan (1982) believes that Erikson's theory applies more to male than to female adolescents. She points out that Erikson based his theory on studies of men, who tend to place a greater premium on the development of self-sufficiency than do women, who tend to place a greater premium on intimate relationships in which there is mutual caring. Thus, female adolescents who fail to develop an independent identity at the same time as their male age peers might unfairly be considered abnormal. One recent study compared self-descriptions and personality attributes of male and female undergraduates. Self-descriptions of men and women who had achieved identity were more similar than the self-descriptions of men and women who had not. However, gender differences were found in the relationship of personality variables that have been thought to contribute to identity development (Cramer, 2000). Though intimate relationships are important to both men's and women's well-being, psychologists studying gender differences in identity development believe that women's identity development emphasizes the self in relation to others.

Psychologists also have investigated the nature of ethnic identity, particularly among immigrants and members of ethnic minority groups (Phinney, 1990). Studies of ethnic and American identity in multi-ethnic samples have found that ethnic identity is positively correlated with self-esteem—regardless of participants' ethnicities. Thus, positive attitudes toward one's ethnic group contribute to high self-esteem. Ethnic and American identity, however, tend to be strongly

Identity Formation

During adolescence our peers play a large role in the development of our sense of identity. Generation after generation, this has distressed North American parents—though, as adolescents, their stylistic choices may have upset their own parents.

Sources: Left: Gina Smith/Shutterstock.com. *Right:* marcogarrincha/Shutterstock.com.

correlated only for European American participants (Phinney, Cantu, & Kurtz, 1997). Ethnic identity was found to be positively correlated with many measures of psychological adjustment, including optimism, mastery, and coping, in a multi-ethnic sample of over 5,400 American adolescents (Roberts et al., 1999).

This research has important implications for members of ethnic minority groups, many of whom consider themselves to be bicultural. One study assessed ethnic identity and measures of acculturation among 1,367 American undergraduates, most of whom were of Mexican origin. Ethnic identity was strongest for first-generation and less acculturated participants. And higher levels of acculturation were associated with a diminished sense of ethnic identity and belongingness. More positive outcomes were associated with participants who were high in biculturalism—that is, feeling a part of both majority American and traditional Mexican cultures. Participants who scored high on a measure of biculturalism had higher ethnic identity scores and were more socially oriented than participants who scored low on biculturalism (Cuellar, Roberts, Nyberg, & Maldonado, 1997).

Once again, this demonstrates the importance of considering the cultural context of theoretical positions. For example, the Inuit people of Canada see personal identity as inseparable from the physical, animal, and human environments. The Inuits would find it maladaptive if members of their culture formed more individualistic identities (Stairs, 1992).

Social Relationships

Because the adolescent is dependent on parents while seeking an independent identity, adolescence has traditionally been considered a period of conflict between parents and children, or what G. Stanley Hall called a period of "storm and stress." Parents might be shocked by their adolescent's preferences in dress, music, and slang. In trying out various styles and values, adolescents are influenced by the cohort to which they belong. Thus, male adolescents shocked their parents by wearing pompadours in the 1950s, shoulder-length hair in the 1970s, spiked haircuts in the 1990s, and piercings and tattoos at the turn of the 21st century. Though parental conflict, moodiness, and a tendency for engaging in risky behavior are more common in adolescence, there are considerable cross-cultural differences. Adolescents in traditional cultures tend to maintain traditional values and practices—even those experiencing the rapid pace of modernization and globalization. Moreover, there are considerable individual differences in behavioral and mood disruptions among adolescents (Arnett, 1999).

Despite the normal conflicts between parental values and adolescent behaviors, most adolescents have positive relations with their parents. In general, adolescence is a time of only slightly increased parent-child conflict. Though the emotional intensity of parent-child conflicts is somewhat higher at puberty, the rate of parent-child conflict declines over the adolescent years (Laursen, Coy, & Collins, 1998) as both adolescents and their parents adopt more positive conflict resolution styles (Van Doom, Branje, & Meeus, 2011).

Adolescents' increasing autonomy and involvement with their peers often leads to disagreements with their parents about family obligations. For example, Jean Phinney and Anthony Ong assessed beliefs about family obligations in a large sample of Vietnamese-American and European-American adolescents and their parents. Regardless of socioeconomic status or cultural background, disagreement over family obligations was negatively correlated with the adolescent participants' life satisfaction (Phinney & Ong, 2003). Conflicts also may be more frequent among first-generation immigrants and their children due to differential rates of acculturation within the family. Compared to non-immigrant families, immigrant Armenian, Vietnamese, and Mexican parents were more likely to stress family obligations than their children. Moreover, among immigrant families, inter-generational discrepancies in familial values increased as a function of time spent living in the United States (Phinney, Ong, & Madden, 2000).

In regard to their friendships, adolescents have more intimate friendships than do younger children, possibly because they are more capable of sharing their thoughts and feelings and understanding those of others. Adolescents who fail to develop intimate friendships are especially prone to loneliness. In fact, adolescent friendships are more important than relationships with family members in preventing loneliness (Ciftci Uruk & Demir, 2003). Though the level of intimate feelings expressed by boys and girls when interacting with their same-sex friends does not differ, there are gender differences in the ways adolescents establish and experience intimate friendships. Adolescent girls tend to establish intimacy through self-disclosure and discussion, whereas adolescent boys tend to establish intimacy through shared activities (McNelles & Connolly, 1999).

Adolescence is associated with an important biologically based psychosocial conflict between the powerful urge to engage in sexual relations and societal values against premarital sex. The proportion of sexually active American adolescents increased steadily from the 1930s, when less than 10 percent had premarital sex, to today, when most older adolescents engage in it. But the sexes differ in their sexual attitudes. Male adolescents are more willing to engage in casual sex, whereas female adolescents are more likely to prefer sex as part of a committed relationship, though this gender difference is not large and gender similarities in sexual attitudes have increased over time (Petersen & Hyde, 2010).

Psychologists recently have begun correcting the one-dimensional view of adolescent erotic relationships as consisting solely of sexual behavior. More researchers are focusing on the nature of adolescent romance, not just sexual behavior, including parental influences and changes in the nature of adolescent romance (Furman, 2002). A study of over 200 college students found that the quality of their romantic relationships was related to the nature of their relationships with their parents. Students who felt a low degree of trust, communication, and closeness in their relationships with their parents tended to feel devalued, disrespected, and emotionally controlled by their current romantic partner. Moreover, students who were unhappy in their current romantic relationship reported that their past relationships with their parents were marked by frequent, intense, and poorly resolved conflicts. A key factor moderating the relationship between their past negative relationships with their parents and their current romantic relationships was the expectation that their romantic partner would ultimately reject them. Such a pessimistic expectation may lead individuals to engage in behaviors that harm their romantic relationships (Gray, 2001).

Adolescence also is a period often involving experimentation with, or chronic use of, psychoactive drugs, including alcohol, nicotine, cocaine, and marijuana. Adolescent drug use, such as smoking, is influenced more by peers than by parents (Bauman, Carver, & Gleiter, 2001). But parental involvement, including monitoring their children's behavior, can help counter the possibility of the adolescent's being initiated into smoking by peers (Simons-Morton, 2002). The importance of avoiding unwise use of psychoactive drugs is highlighted by the association of adolescent smoking and drug use with risky sexual behavior, particularly engaging in sexual intercourse without using a condom (Wu, Witkiewitz, McMahon, & Dodge, 2010).

Drug use also has a negative effect on academic performance. A survey of more than 18,000 American adolescents assessed the relationship between using cigarettes, marijuana, alcohol, and cocaine and academic achievement. The main factors related to poor academic achievement were smoking cigarettes, getting drunk, and being under the influence of alcohol while at school. Cocaine use had a negligible relationship to academic achievement, perhaps because few adolescents reported being under the influence of cocaine while at school (Jeynes, 2002). Today, alcohol is the main drug of choice among adolescents in many countries. A survey of more than 2,600 Canadian adolescents found that alcohol use was associated with more problem behaviors than was the use of other drugs (Gfellner & Hundleby, 1994). Fortunately, despite the risks associated with sexual irresponsibility and drug and alcohol abuse, almost all adolescents enter adulthood relatively unscathed.

SECTION REVIEW: Adolescent Development

1. Why should adolescence researchers be concerned with cohort effects?
2. What is the formal operational stage?
3. According to Erikson, how does identity formation manifest itself in adolescents?

Adult Development

In Western cultures, **adulthood** begins when adolescents become independent of their parents and assume responsibility for themselves. Interest in adult development accelerated in the 1950s after being inspired by Erikson's theory of life-span development (Levinson, 1986) and brought an increased realization that physical, cognitive, and psychosocial changes take place across the entire life span.

adulthood The period beginning when the individual assumes responsibility for her or his own life.

Physical Development
Adults reach their physical peak in their late twenties and then begin a slow physical decline that does not accelerate appreciably until old age. Most athletes peak in their twenties, as is

shown by the ages at which world-class athletes achieve their best performances (Schulz & Curnow, 1988). Beginning in our twenties, our basal metabolic rate (the rate at which the body burns calories when at rest) also decreases, accounting in part for the tendency to gain weight in adulthood. This makes it especially important for adults to pay attention to diet and exercise, which are associated with healthier cardiovascular functioning in middle age and old age (Sawatzky & Naimark, 2002). Physical exercise also is associated with better cognitive functioning in old age (Colcombe & Kramer, 2003). Of course, one must be careful not to presume that exercise *causes* improved cardiovascular or cognitive functioning. Perhaps, for example, having a healthier cardiovascular system or good cognitive functioning makes individuals more likely to exercise.

The aging process is marked by hormonal changes in women and men. Typically, women experience **menopause**—the cessation of their menstrual cycle between the ages of 40 and 55. This is associated with a reduction in estrogen secretion, cessation of ovulation, and consequently the inability to become pregnant. The reduction in estrogen can cause sweating, hot flashes, and brittle bones, as well as atrophy of the vaginal tissue, uterus, and mammary glands (Freedman, 2002). Typically, men experience **andropause**—a gradual decline of testosterone after the age of 40. As testosterone levels decline, men produce fewer and fewer sperm and experience changes in their sexual response, such as slower erections and delayed or less frequent orgasms. However, they still can father children into old age (Morley, 2001).

> **menopause** The cessation of menstruation, usually occurring between the ages of 40 and 55.
>
> **andropause** The gradual decline of testosterone experienced by men after the age of 40.

Midlife hormonal changes do not signal an end to sexuality. Postmenopausal women still have fulfilling sex lives and social lives. A survey of 16,000 American women from five ethnic groups (European American, African American, Japanese American, Chinese American, and Latino) found that women's attitudes toward menopause were neutral to positive and that health status, not menopausal status, predicted the happiness of women in midlife (Sommer et al., 1999). Attitudes toward menopause, however, can vary by culture and social class. For example, one cross-cultural study found that French women generally reported positive attitudes toward menopause. However, Tunisian women, especially poor Tunisian women, reported more negative attitudes and physical symptoms than the French (Delanoë et al., 2012). Moreover, though the prevalence of erectile dysfunction does increase with age, many older men have satisfying sex lives. One large survey of more than 1,000 men aged 58 to 94 years found that positive sexual attitudes, good health, and a responsive sexual partner were associated with continued sexual activity (Bortz, Wallace, & Wiley, 1999).

Middle-aged adults tend to become farsighted and require reading glasses, as evidenced by an increasing tendency to hold books and newspapers at arm's length. But marked changes in physical abilities usually do not occur until late adulthood. The older adult exhibits deterioration in heart output, lung capacity, reaction time, muscular strength, and motor coordination (Maranto, 1984). Old age also brings a decline in hearing, particularly of high-pitched sounds.

Eventually, no matter how well we take care of our bodies, all of us reach the ultimate physical change—death. Though the upper limit of the human life span seems to be about 120 years, few people live to even 100 years of age. But why is death inevitable? Death seems to be genetically programmed into our cells by limiting their ability to repair or reproduce themselves (Hayflick, 1980). Animal research indicates that aging can be slowed by the reduction of daily caloric intake, which prevents the buildup of certain metabolic by-products that promote aging. For example, a study of rats found that those who ate a low-calorie diet lived longer (Masoro, Shimokawa, Higami, & McMahan, 1995). The effects of low-calorie diets on human aging and longevity remain unclear, but ongoing research with human participants suggests that there are positive benefits in reducing caloric intake (Roth & Polotsky, 2012). Longevity also is influenced by physical activity. One longitudinal study of 70-year-old residents of western Jerusalem found that mortality rates were significantly lower for participants who reported engaging in regular exercise. Moreover, walking as little as four hours per week was linked to increased survival in this sample (Stessman, Maaravi, Hammerman-Rozenberg, & Cohen, 2000).

Aging and Physical Health
These adults show that diet and exercise can contribute to a healthy old age.

Source: Lisa F. Young/Shutterstock.com.

We do know, however, that the mere act of continuing to work is associated with slower aging. In a study supporting this, elderly people who continued to work or who retired but participated in regular physical activities showed a constant level of cerebral blood flow over a 4-year period. In contrast, elderly retirees who did not participate in regular physical activities showed a significant decline in cerebral blood flow. Those who continued to work also scored better on cognitive tests than did the inactive retirees (Rogers, Meyer, & Mortel, 1990). One 30-year longitudinal study found that adults who were employed in occupations that required complex work—requiring thought and independent decision making—demonstrated higher levels of intellectual functioning compared to adults who were employed in less demanding occupations. Moreover, the beneficial effect of complex work was more pronounced in late adulthood compared to young adulthood (Schooler, Mulatu, & Oates, 1999). There is even evidence that individuals who engage in complex activities can generate new synapses in the brain, partly countering some of the negative effects of aging (Black, Isaacs, & Greenough, 1991). Thus, whereas physical aging is inevitable, people who maintain an active lifestyle might age at a slower rate. Note that these results do not conclusively demonstrate that activity causes a slowing of the effects of aging. Perhaps, instead, people who age more slowly are more likely to stay active.

Cognitive Development

One of the most controversial issues in developmental psychology is the pattern of adult cognitive development, particularly intellectual development. Early studies showed that we experience a steady decline in intelligence across adulthood. But this apparent decline is found more often in cross-sectional studies than in longitudinal studies. Longitudinal studies have found that a marked decline in intelligence does not begin until about age 60. This indicates that the decline in intelligence across adulthood found in cross-sectional studies might be a cohort effect (perhaps due to differences in early educational experiences) rather than an aging effect (Schaie & Hertzog, 1983). Moreover, the intellectual decline in old age does not encompass all facets of intelligence. Instead, it holds for fluid intelligence but not for crystallized intelligence (Ryan, Sattler, & Lopez, 2000). **Fluid intelligence** reflects the ability to reason and to process information; **crystallized intelligence** reflects the ability to gain and retain knowledge.

fluid intelligence The form of intelligence that reflects reasoning ability, memory capacity, and speed of information processing.

crystallized intelligence The form of intelligence that reflects knowledge acquired through schooling and in everyday life.

But what accounts for the decline in fluid intelligence in old age? The Seattle Longitudinal Study of 1,620 adults between 22 and 91 years of age conducted by K. Warner Schaie (1989) found that the speed of information processing slows in old age. This has been replicated in other research studies (Zimprich & Martin, 2002). This slowing is especially detrimental to short-term memory (Salthouse, 1991), which is the stage of memory that involves the conscious, purposeful mental manipulation of information. But the decline in fluid intelligence can be slowed. The Seattle Longitudinal Study found that a group of older adults who were given cognitive training did not show the same decline in fluid intelligence shown by older adults who were not given such training (Saczynski, 2002).

Older adults tend to do more poorly than adolescents and young adults on cognitive tasks. One factor that explains why is that they have been out of school for many years. This was the finding of a study that compared the recall ability of college students of traditional age, their peers not attending college, and older people not attending college. The average age of the younger groups was 22, and the average age of the older group was 69. The three groups were equal in their level of intelligence.

CRITICAL THINKING ABOUT PSYCHOLOGY

Are There Significant Psychological Gender Differences?

In the 19th century, scientific interest in gender differences was stimulated by Darwin's theory of evolution and promoted by Francis Galton, whose views were influenced by sexist attitudes of the Victorian era (Buss, 1976). Galton assumed that women and men had evolved physical and psychological differences that help them function in particular roles, and he insisted that they should remain in those roles (Shields, 1975). ... views like his were countered by some psychologists, such as Leta Stetter Hollingworth (1886–1939), who insisted that gender differences were due to social factors and did not denote the inferiority of women.

The first major review of gender differences was published by Eleanor Maccoby and Carol Jacklin (1974). They reported that women were superior in verbal abilities and men were superior in spatial and mathematical abilities. They also found that men were more aggressive than women. Nonetheless, they found fewer differences, and generally smaller differences, than were commonly believed to exist. Today, researchers who study gender differences are particularly concerned with cognitive abilities and psychosocial variables. Many of these researchers have used the statistical technique meta-analysis, which enables them to assess the size of gender differences and situational or sociocultural factors that influence these effect sizes.

Cognitive Abilities

In studying cognitive differences between women and men, researchers have studied differences primarily in three kinds of abilities. They ask, Are there gender differences in verbal abilities? spatial abilities? mathematical abilities?

Verbal Abilities

Research on children supports the popular belief in the verbal superiority of girls and women. Girls tend to be superior to boys in speaking, spelling, vocabulary, and reading comprehension. Yet the size of these differences decreases by adolescence. Overall, gender differences in verbal abilities have declined in size in recent decades until they are virtually negligible (Hyde & Plant, 1995). But what about talkativeness, which the popular stereotype holds to be the province of women? Research indicates that, contrary to the stereotype, men are consistently more talkative than women (Hyde & Linn, 1988).

Spatial Abilities

Research has tended to consistently find a large gender difference in one test of spatial abilities. Men are superior in the rotation of mental images (Hyde, Fennema, & Lamon, 1990). Gender differences in other spatial abilities, though, tend to be smaller and inconsistent. Moreover, a meta-analysis of research studies of gender differences in spatial abilities found that the sizes of the differences have decreased in recent years (Voyer, Voyer, & Bryden, 1995). However, gender differences in spatial abilities are observed in early childhood (Levine, Huttenlocher, Taylor, & Langrock, 1999) and in many nonlaboratory settings. For example, when providing directions, women are more likely to rely upon landmarks, whereas men are more likely to refer to north-south-east-west strategies (Halpern & LeMay, 2000). A recent study revealed, though, that gender differences also may be influenced by regional differences. In the Midwest and Western United States and in regions characterized by a grid-like pattern of roads, *both* men and women were more likely to refer to compass or left-right directions (Lawton, 2001). Thus, social experiences can influence spatial abilities.

Mathematical Abilities

Perhaps the most strongly established cognitive gender difference is that adolescent and adult men have higher average scores than adolescent and adult women on standardized mathematics tests. A national talent search by Camilla Benbow and Julian Stanley (1983) found that among seventh- and eighth-graders who took the mathematics subtest of the Scholastic Aptitude Test (SAT), the average score for boys was higher than the average score for girls. In fact, among those scoring higher than 700 (out of 800), boys outnumbered girls by a ratio of 13 to 1. Could this be attributable to boys having more experience in mathematics? Benbow and Stanley say no, having found little difference in the number of mathematics courses taken by females and males. And because they found no other life experiences that could explain their findings, Benbow and Stanley concluded that heredity probably accounts for the difference. This explanation has received some support from other researchers (Thomas, 1993).

But it has also provoked controversy. Critics argue that the gender differences in mathematical abilities reported by Benbow and Stanley might be attributable to as yet unidentified differences in girls' and boys' experiences with mathematics. Also, boys do not have a higher average score than girls on all measures of mathematical ability. Though boys have higher average scores on mathematics achievement tests, which stress problem solving, girls receive higher grades in mathematics courses (Halpern, 2000). A recent meta-analysis of 242 studies published between 1997 and 2007 based upon more than 1,200,000 participants found, overall, no gender differences in mathematical performance (Lindberg, Hyde, Peterson, & Linn, 2010).

It also is important to consider that gender differences in mathematics achievement are smaller than cross-cultural or ethnic differences in achievement (Kimball, 1995). In fact, the greatest gender difference in mathematics ability is found among European American samples (Hyde, Fennema, & Lamon, 1990). In cultures with comparatively smaller gender differences, parents are more likely to encourage academic achievement and advanced study in mathematics—for both sons and daughters (Hanna, Kundiger, & Larouche, 1990). Moreover, gender differences in mathematics are larger in countries where women do not share economic, social, and political power with men (Else-Quest, Hyde, & Linn, 2010).

As discussed, people's beliefs about group differences may lead to a self-fulfilling prophecy, which ultimately influences their behavior. And research has shown that women's and men's beliefs about gender and ethnic differences can affect their performance on mathematics tests (Smith & White, 2002). Thus, stereotypes about women's and men's cognitive abilities may contribute to gender differences in mathematics achievement.

Psychosocial Variables

Researchers also study gender differences in psychosocial behavior. They have been especially concerned with differences in personality and aggression.

Personality

Meta-analyses of research studies on personality differences have found that men are more assertive where-as women are slightly more extraverted ($d = -.14$) and more anxious, trusting, and, especially, tender-minded (that is, more caring and nurturing). These differences tended to be consistent across all ages and educational levels of participants, as well as across a variety of different cultures (Feingold, 1994). A recent meta-analysis found that male participants score slightly higher on standardized measures of self-esteem than do female participants. The size of this small gender difference does increase—at least temporarily—in adolescence (Kling, Hyde, Showers, & Buswell, 1999). And a recent meta-analysis (Else-Quest, Hyde, Goldsmith, & Van Hulle, 2006) found that girls score much higher on measures of self-control than do boys ($d = -1.01$), whereas there is a moderate gender difference favoring boys on factors related to rough-andtumble play, such as activity level ($d = .30$) and the intensity of their emotional experiences ($d = .33$).

Gender Differences and Similarities

Physiological and sociocultural factors play an important role in girls' and boys' cognitive abilities.

Source: Zurijeta/Shutterstock.com.

Researchers also have studied a variety of other personality variables with the use of meta-analysis. For example, do women reveal more of their private thoughts, feelings, and experiences than men do? Contrary to popular belief, women are only marginally more likely to self-disclose than men are (Dindia & Allen, 1992). But consistent with popular views, males are slightly more likely than females to take risks across a variety of situations (Byrnes, Miller, & Shafer, 1999) and women and girls are slightly more able than men and boys to delay gratification (Silverman, 2003). But what of the popular belief that women are more empathetic than men? This apparent gender difference depends on how empathy is measured. When asked to report on their level of empathy, women score higher than men. But when empathy is measured by physiological arousal or overt behavior, gender differences disappear. Evidently, social expectations that women will be more emotionally sensitive than men create differences in their subjective views of themselves but not necessarily in their actual behavior or physiological responses (Eisenberg & Lennon, 1983). This hypothesis was tested in a recent meta-analysis that found women's empathy scores were higher than men's only when participants were aware that their empathy was being assessed. This gender difference disappeared in experimental situations that lacked this demand characteristic (Ickes, Gesn, & Graham, 2000).

One recent study provided more evidence of gender similarities in basic values. Over 11,000 participants were surveyed in eight cultures (Chinese East Asia, Eastern Europe, Finland, France, Israel, Japan, Latin America, and the United States). Whereas some cross-cultural differences were found, results indicated that there were no consistent gender differences in the meaning of personal values across cultures (Struch, Schwartz, & van der Kloot, 2002).

Aggression

Just as women are reputed to be more empathetic than men, men are reputed to be more aggressive than women. Research has found that men are somewhat more physically aggressive than are women (Eagly & Steffen, 1986). Moreover, gender differences in aggression might be the product of gender roles. This was the conclusion of a study in which male and female participants were tested in the laboratory. When they were singled out as individuals, men were more aggressive than women. When they were deindividuated (that is, made to feel anonymous), men and women did not differ in aggression. The researchers attributed this difference to the power of gender roles: When we feel that we are being noticed, we behave according to gender expectations (Lightdale & Prentice, 1994). Moreover, when operational definitions of aggression are broadened to include behaviors that are more stereotypically female—such as indirect aggression—gender differences in aggression are minimized.

Explanations for Possible Gender Differences

If psychological gender differences exist, what might account for them? Researchers point to physiological factors and sociocultural factors.

Physiological Factors

Because of the obvious physical differences between men and women, researchers have looked to physiological factors to explain psychological gender differences. David Buss believes that men and women inherit certain behavioral tendencies as a product of their long evolutionary history. According to Buss, "Men and women differ ... in domains in which they have faced different adaptive problems over human evolutionary history. In all other domains, the sexes are predicted to be psychologically similar" (Buss, 1995, p. 164). Thus, men are more aggressive and women more nurturing because prehistoric males were more likely to be hunters and prehistoric females were more likely to be caregivers. They do not differ in traits unrelated to their prehistoric roles as males and females.

But how might heredity affect psychological gender differences? Evidence supporting the biological basis of gender differences in social behavior implicates hormonal factors. Girls whose adrenal glands secrete high prenatal levels of testosterone are more likely to become "tomboys" who prefer rough play and masculine activities (though most tomboys do not have this adrenal disorder). These girls' genitals look more similar to those of boys at birth (though they are usually modified by surgery), and this might make parents treat them as though they were boys, yet parents usually report that they treat these girls the same as parents treat girls without the disorder (Berenbaum & Hines, 1992). There is some evidence, though, for a hormonal basis for cognitive gender differences (Kimura & Hampson, 1994). There also is evidence of a hormonal basis for gender differences in play behavior in childhood and fairly strong evidence for its influence on gender differences in physical aggression (Collaer & Hines, 1995).

A second way that heredity might affect gender differences is through brain development. But efforts to associate specific cognitive differences with differences in brain structures have produced mixed results. Some studies have found that men's brains may be more lateralized than women's brains. Studies of people with brain damage have found that damage to men's left cerebral hemisphere is associated with impaired verbal skills, and damage to men's right cerebral hemisphere is associated with impaired nonverbal skills. In contrast, women's verbal and nonverbal skills do not seem to be influenced by the side of the brain damaged (Springer & Deutsch, 1998). Other studies, though, have failed to find gender differences in hemispheric lateralization (e.g., Snow & Sheese, 1985). And there are large individual differences in brain organization; biological sex is only one of many variables influencing brain organization (Kimura, 1987).

Sociocultural Factors

The possibility that gender differences in cognitive abilities are influenced more by sociocultural factors than by physiological factors is supported by studies that have found a narrowing of gender differences in cognitive abilities between North American male and female participants during the past 40 years (Hyde & Plant, 1995; Lindberg, Hyde, Peterson, & Linn, 2010). This might be explained in part by the cultural trend to provide girls and boys with somewhat more similar treatment and opportunities (Jacklin, 1989). Even Camilla Benbow (1988) agrees that environmental, as well as hereditary, factors play an important role in cognitive abilities such as mathematics. For example, minimal gender differences have been found among participants from the study of Mathematically Precocious Youth who had gone on to graduate study in math and sciences. The profiles of female and male participants included attributes that are critical to achieving excellence in these fields—exceptional quantitative abilities, scientific interests and values, and persistence in seeking out educational opportunities (Lubinski, Benbow, Shea, Eftekhari-Sanjani, & Halvorson, 2001).

After decades of extensive research, no gender differences have emerged that are large enough to predict with confidence how individual men and women will behave (Deaux, 1985). This has provoked a controversy about whether we should continue to study gender differences. Some psychologists, such as Roy Baumeister (1988), argue that we should no longer study them. Why study differences that are too few or too small to have practical significance? And why study gender differences when reports of even small differences might support sex discrimination? But Baumeister's view was countered by gender difference researchers Alice Eagly (1995) and Diane Halpern (1994), who believe that objective scientific research on gender differences should continue, even if it might find differences that some people would prefer did not exist.

A compromise position has been put forth by Janet Shibley Hyde, who favors studying gender differences but warns against relying on the results of studies that have not been replicated, interpreting gender differences as signs of female deficiencies, and automatically attributing such differences to inherited biological factors. She favors acknowledging the fact that gender similarities are the rule and that the few gender differences that have been found can be attributed primarily to sociocultural factors (Hyde, 2007).

The results showed that the recall ability of the college group was better than that of the other two groups. But there was no difference in the performance of the groups of older persons and younger persons who were not attending college. This indicates that it might be the failure to use one's memory, rather than simply brain deterioration accompanying aging, that accounts for the inferior performance of the elderly on tests of recall. When it comes to the maintenance of cognitive abilities, such as memory, the adage "Use it or lose it" might have some validity

(Hultsch, Hertzog, Small, & Dixon, 1999). One of the more intriguing longitudinal studies of cognitive aging and Alzheimer's disease is the Nun Study, which has involved following a large sample of Catholic religious sisters for more than 60 years—through the deaths of many of them (Santa Cruz et al., 2011).

Psychosocial Development

Social development continues through early, middle, and late adulthood. Keeping in mind that these divisions are somewhat arbitrary, assume that early adulthood extends from age 20 to age 40, middle adulthood from age 40 to age 65, and late adulthood from age 65 on. The similarities exhibited by people within these periods are related to the common social experiences of the "social clock." In recent decades, the typical ages at which some of these experiences occur have varied more than in the past. A graduate student might live at home with his parents until his late twenties, a woman working toward her medical degree might postpone marriage until her early thirties, and a two-career couple might not have their first child until they are in their late thirties. Of course, events that are unique to each person's life can also play a role in psychosocial development. Chance encounters in our lives, for example, contribute to our unique development (Bandura, 1982). You might reflect on chance encounters that influenced your choice of an academic major or that helped you meet your current boyfriend, girlfriend, husband, or wife.

Back to School

The myth that intellectual decline is a normal aspect of aging is countered by the increasing number of older adults who enroll in undergraduate degree programs. In the case of memory and other cognitive abilities, the adage "use it or lose it" seems to have validity.

Source: bikeriderlondon/Shutterstock.com.

Early Adulthood

Though Sigmund Freud paid little attention to adult development, he did note that normal adulthood is marked by the ability to love and to work. Erik Erikson agreed that the capacity for love is an important aspect of early adulthood, and he claimed that the first major task of adulthood is facing the conflict of **intimacy versus isolation**. Intimate relationships involve a strong sense of emotional attachment and personal commitment. The Rochester Adult Longitudinal study of a community sample supported Erikson's belief that the development of the capacity for intimacy depends on the successful formation of a psychosocial identity in adolescence. The achievement of identity during adolescence contributed to the development of intimacy in young adulthood. Participants who were capable of developing both identity in adolescence and a high degree of intimacy in young adulthood reported more successful romantic relationships and greater life satisfaction in midlife (Sneed, Whitbourne, Schwartz, & Huang, 2012).

> **intimacy versus isolation** Erikson's developmental stage in which success is achieved by establishing a relationship with a strong sense of emotional attachment and personal commitment.

Establishing Intimate Relationships. About 95 percent of young adults eventually experience the intimate relationship of marriage. Of course there is a variety of family arrangements. And at any given time many adults are unmarried—they are either widowed, divorced, not ready, or committed to remaining single. However, the results of a longitudinal study of six countries (Austria, Germany, the Netherlands, Great Britain, Ireland, and the United States) found that men's and women's attitudes are shifting away from the norms of traditional marriage. Participants reported a remarkable diversity of lifestyles and individual differences in the timing of marriage and parenthood (Gubernskay, 2010).

A strong and consistent positive correlation has been found between marriage and psychological well-being. The World Values Survey, a survey of 159,169 adults in 42 countries, found that married women and men reported higher levels of life satisfaction than cohabiting couples, single adults, and divorced or separated adults. Though there were significant cross-cultural differences, these differences were negligible. And men and women derive similar benefits from marriage (Diener, Gohm, Suh, & Oishi, 2000). These results recently have been replicated in nationally representative samples from Australia, Germany, and Great Britain (Luhmann, Lucas, Eid, & Diener, 2013). Unmarried status is correlated with greater physical and psychological risks, especially for men. A survey of more than 18,000 men conducted in England found that unmarried middle-aged men of all kinds—single, widowed, divorced, or separated—had higher mortality rates than did married men (Ben-Shlomo, Smith, Shipley, & Marmot, 1993). One reason for this is a lower risk of illness in the married, especially if their partner is responsive to their needs (Selcuk & Ong, 2013).

What characteristics do adults look for in potential mates? As you might expect, both women and men tend to seek partners who are kind, loyal, honest, considerate, intelligent, interesting, and affectionate. But men tend to be more concerned than women with the potential spouse's physical attractiveness, and women tend to be more concerned than men with the potential spouse's earning capacity (Buss et al., 1990). As discussed in Chapter 17, psychologists argue whether these preferences reflect the influence of evolution or of cultural norms that differentially affect men's and women's marital expectations.

What determines whether a relationship will succeed? An important factor is similarity—in age, religion, attitudes, ethnicity, personality, intelligence, and educational level (O'Leary & Smith, 1991). Willingness to talk about problems is another important factor, as found in a 2-year longitudinal study of newlyweds. Those couples who believed that conflicts should be discussed openly reported greater marital happiness than those who believed they should be ignored (Crohan, 1992). A 4-year longitudinal study found that high-quality, positive communication between couples was associated with higher levels of marital satisfaction. Moreover, marital dissolution was associated with marital conflict and aggression—especially if present early in the marriage (Rogge & Bradbury, 1999).

Communication is essential to marital satisfaction. One study examined videotapes of 78 married or cohabiting couples discussing a conflict they were having. Positive interruptions (agreement with what the partner was saying) were positively correlated with the couples' feelings about the conversation and their relationship satisfaction. Negative interruptions (disagreement with what the partner was saying) were negatively correlated with the couples' feelings about the conversation and their relationship satisfaction (Daigen & Holmes, 2000). Research indicates that marital satisfaction is greater when partners take a collaborative approach to resolving conflicts than when one or both take a competitive approach (Greeff & de Bruyne, 2000).

Dissolving Intimate Relationships. Unfortunately, for many couples, happiness is elusive, and they may eventually seek to end their relationship. In the United States, about half of first marriages are so unhappy that they end in divorce. In fact, the United States has the highest divorce rate of any industrialized country (O'Leary & Smith, 1991). A study that interviewed over 1,300 persons found that divorce has increased not because marriages were happier in the "good old days," but instead because barriers to divorce (such as conservative values or shared social networks) have fallen and alternatives to divorce (such as a wife's independent income or remarriage prospects) have increased. Thus, the threshold of marital happiness that will trigger divorce is lower than it was several decades ago.

The barriers to relationship dissolution associated with marriage are important in understanding the higher rate of relationship dissolution among gay and lesbian couples. One study compared relationship satisfaction and dissolution rates among heterosexual, gay, and lesbian couples. Heterosexual married couples' satisfaction with their relationship was similar to that reported by cohabiting gay and lesbian couples. Whereas relationship satisfaction declined among all three groups, gay and lesbian couples were more likely to have ended their relationships over the 5 years of the study. These results are attributed to the fact that gay and lesbian couples perceived fewer barriers to ending their relationship—for example, the cost of divorce or the loss of insurance or health benefits (Kurdek, 1998).

There are a variety of specific factors that contribute to divorce. One of the hallmarks of an unhappy marriage is the tendency of spouses to consistently offer negative explanations for their spouse's behavior (Karney & Bradbury, 2000). In dual-wage-earner marriages, perceived inequality in doing housework—particularly by wives—appears to contribute to divorces (Frisco & Williams, 2003). And even the nature of commitment may predict relationship dissolution. Couples who display avoidant commitment (that is, those who want to avoid the negative consequences of breaking up) are more likely than committed couples who display approach commitment (that is, those who want to retain the positive consequences of staying together) to break up (Frank & Brandstaetter, 2002).

Yet there is evidence that people might remain committed to spouses or partners who treat them poorly. You probably have known someone who sticks with a romantic partner who treats that person in a manner that you would not tolerate. Consider a study of 86 pairs of married couples from central Texas, with an average age of 32 years and an average length of marriage of 6 years (Swann, Hixon, & De La Ronde, 1992). The spouses took personality tests measuring their self-concepts. They also measured how the spouses appraised each other and how committed they were to each other. The results revealed that the degree of commitment to one's spouse depended on the degree of congruence between one's self-concept and how one was viewed by one's spouse. That is, those with positive self-concepts felt more committed when their spouses viewed them positively. Likewise, those with negative self-concepts felt more committed when their spouses viewed them negatively.

What could account for this finding, which runs counter to the commonsense notion that we all wish to be admired and treated well? The researchers found that though we might insist on being treated well in casual relationships, we insist on being treated in accordance with our self-concept within the intimacy of marriage. That is, we want our spouses to verify our self-concept so we are not confused about ourselves or about how other people will treat us. In addition, we will trust spouses more who do not try to "snow" us by telling us we're attractive when we feel ugly, intelligent when we feel stupid, and personally appealing when we feel socially inept. Moreover, whereas people with positive self-concepts might welcome high expectations of them, people with negative self-concepts might fear unrealistically high expectations that they could not meet.

Parenthood. For most couples, parenthood is a major component of marriage. Raising children can be one of the greatest rewards in life, but it can also be one of life's greatest stresses. Because women still tend to be the primary caregiver, their parental responsibilities tend to be especially stressful. But couples who share childcare responsibilities are more likely to successfully weather the stress of becoming new parents (Belsky & Hsieh, 1998). Overall, parents who live with their biological children show greater declines in marital happiness over time than do married, childless couples or married couples living with stepchildren (Kurdek, 1999). Of course, some couples remain childless. They are not necessarily unhappy. In fact, especially if they are voluntarily childless, they might be as happy as couples with children. This is attributable, in part, to the fact that they do not have the stress that parents experience from money woes, children's illnesses, loss of sleep, and lack of recreational outlets. Women who are childless by choice show higher levels of psychological well-being than women who are involuntarily childless (Jeffries & Konnert, 2002).

But what of single parents? In the 1960s and 1970s, divorce was the chief cause of single parenting. This has been joined by planned or unplanned childbearing outside of marriage. Though single parents are usually women, one in five is male. Many single parents, given social and financial support, are successful in rearing children. For example, one study of single parents serving in the U.S. military found that mothers and fathers readily used social, financial, and organizational resources to balance their family and work obligations (Heath & Orthner, 1999). But according to the U.S. Bureau of the Census, single-parent families, on the average, suffer disadvantages in regard to income, health, and housing conditions. The most disadvantaged are families consisting of children and a never-married mother (Bianchi, 1995).

Middle Adulthood

In 1850 few Americans lived beyond what we now call early adulthood; the average life span was only 40 years (Shneidman, 1987). But improved nutrition, sanitation, and health care have almost doubled that life span. What was the end of the life span more than a century ago is today simply the beginning of middle adulthood. Daniel Levinson (1978) found that during the transition to middle adulthood, men commonly experience a midlife crisis, in which they realize that the "dream" they had pursued in regard to their life goals will not be achieved or, even if achieved, will seem transient in the face of the inevitability of death. Other studies indicate, however, that the midlife crisis is less intense than Levinson found in his research (Fagan & Ayers, 1982). Moreover, the life dreams of women tend to be more complex than the life dreams of men. Whereas men typically focus on their careers, women focus on marriage and children, as well as their careers (Kittrell, 1998).

According to Erik Erikson, the main task of middle adulthood is the resolution of the conflict of **generativity versus stagnation**. Those who achieve generativity become less self-absorbed and more concerned about being a productive worker, spouse, and parent (Slater, 2003). They are more competent, continue to strive for achievement, and are more altruistic and trusting (Cox, Wilt, Olson, & McAdams, 2010). They also are more satisfied with their lives (McAdams, de St. Aubin, & Logan, 1993). One way of achieving generativity is to serve as a mentor for a younger person. This lets mentors realize their life dreams vicariously and know that their dreams will continue even after their own deaths (Westermeyer, 2004).

Generativity

According to Erik Erikson, people who successfully resolve the midlife conflict of generativity versus stagnation become less self-absorbed and more concerned with the well-being of the next generation.

Source: Pressmaster/Shutterstock.com.

generativity versus stagnation
Erikson's developmental stage in which success is achieved by becoming less self-absorbed and more concerned with the well-being of others.

Middle adulthood also brings transitions affected by one's parental status. You might be surprised to learn that parents become more distressed and experience more marital unhappiness after their first child leaves home than after their last child leaves home. In fact, after the last child has left home, parents tend to be relieved and experience improved marital relations (Harris, Ellicott, & Holmes, 1986). Perhaps the notion of an "empty nest syndrome" (after the last child has left home) should be replaced by the notion of a "partly empty nest syndrome" (after the first child has left home). Moreover, a growing trend in North America is the "revolving-door nest," caused by the return home of young adults who find it personally or financially difficult to live on their own (Dennerstein, Dudley, & Guthrie, 2002).

Late Adulthood

Now that more people in developed countries are living into their 70s and beyond, developmental psychologists have become more interested in studying late adulthood. In 1900 only one person in thirty was over 65. By 2020 one person in five will be over 65 (Eisdorfer, 1983). Though this increase in the elderly population, including many more retired people, will create more concern about physical well-being in old age, it also will create more concern about psychosocial development in old age. Research has provided inconsistent findings regarding whether retirement generally has positive, negative, or no effects on psychological well-being (Kim & Moen, 2001).

Erikson claimed that the main psychosocial task of late adulthood is to resolve the crisis of **integrity versus despair**. A sense of integrity results from reflecting back on a meaningful life through a "life review." In fact, Erikson claimed that pleasurable reminiscing is essential to satisfactory adjustment in old age. This was supported by a study of nursing home residents aged 70 to 88 years. Participants in the experimental group received a visitor who encouraged them to reminisce and engage in a life review. Participants in the control group received a friendly visit. Participants who engaged in a life review scored higher on a questionnaire that measured their level of ego integrity, as long as 3 years after the intervention (Haight, Michel, & Hendrix, 2000). Older adults who are able to review and accept their past are more likely to develop a sense of coherence and experience more positive psychological development (Wiesmann & Hannich, 2011).

> **integrity versus despair** Erikson's developmental stage in which success is achieved by reflecting back on one's life and finding that it has been meaningful.

And old age is not necessarily a time of physical decay, cognitive deterioration, and social isolation. For many, it is a time of physical activity, continued education, and rewarding social relations (Whitbourne & Hulicka, 1990). Many elderly adults optimize their cognitive and physical functioning by capitalizing on their strengths and compensating for their weaknesses. For example, they may allot more time to perform tasks, practice old skills, or learn new skills. The use of these strategies by elderly adults has been found to be associated with successful aging, characterized by more positive emotions, enhanced feelings of well-being, and less loneliness (Freund & Baltes, 1998).

Eventually, many adults must confront one of the greatest psychosocial challenges of old age—the death of a mate. During the period immediately following the death of their spouse, bereaved spouses are more likely to suffer depression, illness, or death than are their peers with living spouses. An increase in morbidity, mortality, and psychological well-being tends to be found among surviving spouses. This might stem from the loss of the emotional and practical support previously provided by the now-deceased spouse. One study tested this hypothesis with a sample of recently bereaved spouses. Widowers were more likely to experience greater deterioration in physical and mental health and receive less social support than were widows. However, there was no evidence that the loss of social support reported by widowers mediated this gender difference (Stroebe, Stroebe, & Abakoumkin, 1999). Thus, it is likely that other factors contribute to the poorer health and negative psychological outcomes experienced by bereaved widowers. For example, a study of older German adults found that widowers tend to be lonelier than widows (Pinquart, 2003). A variety of techniques have been used to aid the bereavement process, with varying success (Durland, 2000). In one study, 44 college students who had lost a loved one were randomly assigned to write about either their bereavement experience or about a trivial, unrelated topic. The results indicated that writing about one's bereavement experience helped reduce feelings of distress (Range, Kovac, & Marion, 2000). Similar findings were reported in a study in which college students wrote about their bereavement experience regarding a loved one who had committed suicide in the prior two years (Kovac & Range, 2000).

Though, as Benjamin Franklin observed in 1789, "in this world nothing's certain but death and taxes," we can at least improve the way in which we confront our own mortality. In old age, successful resolution of the crisis of ego integrity versus despair is associated with less fear of death (Goebel & Boeck, 1987). And a survey of 200 adults found that those with strong religious convictions and a greater belief in an afterlife have lower death anxiety (Alvarado, Templer, Bresler, & Thomas-Dobson, 1995).

Prior to the 20th century, death was accepted as a public part of life. People died at home, surrounded and comforted by loved ones. Today, people commonly die alone, in pain, in hospital rooms, attached to life-support systems. One of the most important developments to counter this approach to death and dying is the **hospice movement**, founded in 1958 by the British physician Cicely Saunders. She was motivated to do so by her colleagues' failure to respond sensitively to dying patients and their families. Hospices provide humane, comprehensive care for the dying patient in a hospital, residential,

hospice movement The providing of care for the dying patient with attention to alleviating the patient's physical, emotional, and spiritual suffering.

or home setting, with attention to alleviating the patient's physical, emotional, and spiritual suffering (Saunders, 1996). A study comparing hospices to traditional nursing homes found that elderly dying cancer patients received more effective pain relief and better quality of life during their time spent in hospice (Black et al., 2011).

SECTION REVIEW: Adult Development

1. What is the apparent relationship between caloric intake and aging?
2. What does research indicate about changes in intelligence in old age?
3. How do adults successfully resolve Erikson's conflict involving generativity versus stagnation?

EXPERIENCING PSYCHOLOGY

An Analysis of Children's Toys

Rationale

As discussed in this chapter, children as young as toddlers learn to classify toys as masculine or feminine. In fact, toys are examples of how social and cultural factors influence gender-role development. In this exercise you will examine a selection of toys, observe any gender-specific messages or gender typing, and discuss your work in the context of what you learned from reading this chapter.

Procedure

Find a local toy store that has a well-stocked selection of toys for boys and girls of different ages. Before you make your trip, consider the ways that gender typing may be reflected in a toy's attributes. For example, you might consider colors of the toys or pictures of children playing with the toys on packaging materials. Other factors to consider might be indicators that toys are for girls or boys. Some packages might indicate that the toy is appropriate for boys of a certain age range. Or, the store might group toys that girls would be interested in together.

Spend about an hour in the store, examining the toys, their packaging, and their placement in the store and make notes of any evidence of gender typing. Summarize your findings by answering the following questions:

1. Could you find toys that were easily identifiable as boys' toys? What types of toys? What type of play or activities do they encourage?
2. Could you find toys that were easily identifiable as girls' toys? What types of toys? What type of play or activities do they encourage?
3. Could you find any gender-neutral toys—that is toys, that were neither boys' nor girls' toys? What types of toys? What type of play or activities do they encourage?

Results and Discussion

Describe your findings. Did you find evidence of gender typing during your observation? As discussed in the chapter, cultural trends have indicated more similar treatment of boys and girls. Do your results support what you read in the chapter? Were there any other conclusions you reached after summarizing your observations?

Chapter Summary

Research Methods in Developmental Psychology

- Developmental psychology is the field that studies the physical, perceptual, cognitive, and psychosocial changes that take place across the life span.
- Research designs typical of developmental psychology include longitudinal research, cross-sectional research, and cohort-sequential research.

Prenatal Development

- The prenatal period is divided into the germinal, embryonic, and fetal stages.
- Cell-adhesion molecules direct the size, shape, and location of organs in the embryo.
- Teratogens can impair prenatal development.
- Women who drink alcohol, a teratogen, during pregnancy might have offspring who suffer from fetal alcohol syndrome.

Infant and Child Development

- Childhood extends from birth until puberty.
- The first 2 years of childhood are called infancy.
- Motor development follows a consistent sequence, though the timing of motor milestones varies somewhat among infants.
- Jean Piaget found that children pass through distinct cognitive stages of development.
- During the sensorimotor stage, the infant learns to coordinate sensory experiences and motor behavior, and forms schemas that represent aspects of the world.
- The preoperational stage is marked by egocentrism. In the concrete operational stage, the child learns to make transitive inferences and to appreciate conservation.
- Erik Erikson put forth an influential theory of psychosocial development. He believed that the life span consists of eight distinct stages, each associated with a crisis that must be overcome.
- An important factor in infant development is social attachment, a strong emotional relationship between an infant and a caregiver.
- Permissive and authoritarian child-rearing practices are less effective than authoritative ones.
- Children who receive high-quality day care do not appear to suffer ill effects from being separated from their parents, though this might not be true of infants.
- Research on the effects of divorce on children has produced inconsistent results, with some studies finding no effects, others finding negative effects, and still others finding positive effects.
- Though the causes of gender-role development are still unclear, social learning theory and gender-schema theory try to explain it.

- The most influential theory of moral development has been Lawrence Kohlberg's cognitive-developmental theory, which is based on Piaget's belief that a person's level of moral development depends on his or her level of cognitive development.
- Kohlberg proposes that we pass through preconventional, conventional, and postconventional levels of moral development.
- Carol Gilligan argues that Kohlberg's theory is biased toward a masculine view of morality. Research has provided mixed support for Kohlberg's theory.

Adolescent Development

- Adolescence is a transitional period between childhood and adulthood that begins with puberty.
- In regard to physical development, the adolescent experiences the maturation of primary and secondary sex characteristics.
- In regard to cognitive development, some adolescents enter Piaget's formal operational stage, meaning that they can engage in abstract, hypothetical reasoning.
- And, in regard to psychosocial development, adolescence is a time of identity formation, an important stage in Erik Erikson's theory of development.
- The adolescent also is increasingly influenced by peer values, especially in regard to fashion, sexuality, and drug use.
- Research on sex differences has found no consistent differences in male and female brains.
- Girls and boys differ little in their gross motor abilities until puberty, when boys begin to outperform girls.
- Women tend to have better verbal abilities, while men tend to have better spatial and mathematical problem-solving abilities.
- Men also tend to be more physically aggressive than women.
- Research on gender differences is controversial because of fears that its findings might be used to promote and legitimate discrimination.
- Gender differences are based on group averages, and most are so small that they should not be used to make decisions about individuals.

Adult Development

- Adulthood begins when adolescents become independent from their parents.
- In regard to physical development, adults reach their physical peak in their late twenties, at which point they begin a gradual decline that does not accelerate appreciably until old age.
- Middle-aged women experience menopause, which, contrary to popular belief, is rarely a traumatic event, and middle-aged men experience andropause.
- In regard to cognitive development, though aging brings some slowing of cognitive processes, people who continue to be mentally active show less cognitive decline than do their peers who do not stay active.

- In regard to social development, Erik Erikson saw the main task of early adulthood as the establishment of intimacy, typically between a husband and wife. About 95 percent of adults marry, but half of North American marriages will end in divorce.
- The most successful marriages are those in which the spouses discuss, rather than avoid, marital issues.
- Erikson saw the main task of middle adulthood as the establishment of a sense of generativity, which is promoted by parenting.
- After the last child leaves home, parents typically improve their emotional and marital well-being.
- Erikson saw the final stage of life as ideally promoting a sense of integrity in reflecting on a life well lived.
- Eventually, all people must face their own mortality.
- The hospice movement, founded by Cicely Saunders, has promoted more humane, personal, and homelike care for the dying patient.

References

Abide, M. M., Richards, H. C., & Ramsay, S. G. (2001). Moral reasoning and consistency of belief and behavior: Decisions about substance abuse. *Journal of Drug Education, 31,* 367–384.

Adams, W. L., Garry, P. J., Rhyne, R., & Hunt, W. C. (1990). Alcohol intake in the healthy elderly: Changes with age in a cross-sectional and longitudinal study. *Journal of the American Geriatrics Society, 38,* 211–216.

Alvarado, K. A., Templer, D. I., Bresler, C., & Thomas-Dobson, S. (1995). The relationship of religious variables to death depression and death anxiety. *Journal of Clinical Psychology, 51,* 202–204.

Amato, P. R., & Keith, B. (1991). Parental divorce and the well-being of children: A meta-analysis. *Psychological Bulletin, 110,* 26–46.

Andrews, G., & Halford, G. S. (1998). Children's ability to make transitive inferences: The importance of premise integration and structural complexity. *Cognitive Development, 13,* 479–513.

Anisfeld, M. (1996). Only tongue protrusion modeling is matched by neonates. *Developmental Review, 16,* 149–161.

Arnett, J. J. (1999). Adolescent storm and stress, reconsidered. *American Psychologist, 54,* 317–326.

Aseltine, R. H., Jr. (1996). Pathways linking parental divorce with adolescent depression. *Journal of Health and Social Behavior, 37,* 133–148.

Aslin, R. N., & Smith, L. B. (1988). Perceptual development. *Annual Review of Psychology, 39,* 435–474.

Aydt, H., & Corsaro, W. A. (2003). Differences in children's construction of gender across culture: An interpretative approach. *American Behavioral Scientist, 46,* 1306–1325.

Bagwell, C. L., Newcomb, A. F., & Bukowski, W. M. (1998). Preadolescent friendship and peer rejection as predictors of adult adjustment. *Child Development, 69,* 140–153.

Bandura, A. (1982). The psychology of chance encounters and life paths. *American Psychologist, 37,* 747–755.

Bangerter, A., Grob, A., & Krings, F. (2001). Personal goals at age 25 in three generation of the twentieth century: Young adulthood in historical context. *Swiss Journal of Psychology–Schweizerische Zeitschrift fuer Psychologie–Revue Suisse de Psychologie, 60,* 59–64.

Barry, T. D., Lochman, J. E., Fite, P. J., Wells, K. C., & Colder, C. R. (2012). The influence of neighborhood characteristics and parenting practices on academic problems and aggression outcomes among moderately to highly aggressive children. *Journal of Community Psychology, 40,* 372–379.

Bauman, K. E., Carver, K., & Gleiter, K. (2001). Trends in parent and friend influence during adolescence. The case of adolescent cigarette smoking. *Addictive Behaviors, 26,* 349–361.

Baumeister, R. F. (1988). Should we stop studying sex differences altogether? *American Psychologist, 43,* 1092–1095.

Baumrind, D. (1966). Effects of authoritative control on child behavior. *Child Development, 37,* 887–907.

Baumrind, D. (1983). Rejoinder to Lewis's reinterpretation of parental firm control effects: Are authoritative families really harmonious? *Psychological Bulletin, 94,* 132–142.

Baumrind, D. (2010). Differentiating being confrontive and coercive kinds of parental power-assertive disciplinary practices. *Human Development, 55,* 35–51.

Beijersbergen, M. D., Juffer, F., Bakermans-Kranengurb, M. J., & van IJzendoorn, M. H. (2012). Remaining or becoming secure: Parental sensitive support predicts attachment continuity from infancy to adolescence in a longitudinal adoption study. *Developmental Psychology, 48,* 1277–1282.

Belsky, J., & Hsieh, K. H. (1998). Patterns of marital change during the early childhood years: Parent personality, coparenting, and division-of-labor correlates. *Journal of Family Psychology, 12,* 511–528.

Belsky, J., & Pluess, M. (2009). The nature (and nurture?) of plasticity in early human development. *Perspectives on Psychological Science, 4,* 345–35l.

Bem, S. L. (1981). Gender schema theory: A cognitive account of sex typing. *Psychological Review, 88,* 354–364.

Benbow, C. P. (1988). Sex differences in mathematical reasoning ability in intellectually talented preadolescents: Their nature, effect, and possible causes. *Behavioral and Brain Sciences, 11,* 169–232.

Benbow, C. P., & Stanley, J. C. (1983). Sex differences in mathematical reasoning ability: More facts. *Science, 222,* 1029–1031.

Ben-Shlomo, Y., Smith, G. D., Shipley, M., & Marmot, M. G. (1993). Magnitude and causes of mortality differences between married and unmarried men. *Journal of Epidemiology and Community Health, 47,* 200–205.

Berenbaum, S. A., & Hines, M. (1992). Early androgens are related to childhood sex-typed toy preferences. *Psychological Science, 3,* 203–206.

Berkowitz, M. W., Mueller, C. W., Schnell, S. V., & Padberg, U. (1986). Moral reasoning and judgments of aggression. *Journal of Personality and Social Psychology, 51,* 885–891.

Berndt, T. J., & Hoyles, S. G. (1985). Stability and change in childhood and adolescent friendships. *Developmental Psychology, 21,* 1007–1015.

Berninger, V. W. (1988). Development of operational thought without a normal sensorimotor stage. *Intelligence, 12,* 219–230.

Bianchi, S. M. (1995). The changing demographic and socioeconomic characteristics of single parent families. *Marriage and Family Review, 20,* 71–97.

Bjork, E. L., & Cummings, E. M. (1984). Infant search errors: Stage of concept development or stage of memory development. *Memory and Cognition, 12,* 1–19.

Black, B., Herr, K., Fine, P., Sanders, S., Tang, X., Bergen–Jackson, K., Titler, M., & Forcucci, C. (2011). The relationships among pain, nonpain symptoms, and quality of life measures in older adults with cancer receiving hospice care. *Pain Medicine, 12,* 880–889.

Black, J. E., Isaacs, K. R., & Greenough, W. T. (1991). Usual vs. successful aging: Some notes on experiential factors. *Neurobiology of Aging, 12,* 325–328.

Bortz, W. M. II, Wallace, D. H., & Wiley, D. (1999). Sexual function in 1,202 aging males: Differentiating aspects. *Journals of Gerontology: Series A: Biological Sciences and Medical Sciences, 54A,* M237–M241.

Bowlby, J. (1988). *A secure base: Parent-child attachment and healthy human development.* New York: Basic Books.

Brittain, A. E., & Lerner, R. M. (2013). Early influences and later outcomes associated with developmental trajectories of Eriksonian fidelity. *Developmental Psychology, 49,* 722–735.

Brooks-Gunn, J., & Warren, M. P. (1989). Biological and social contributions to negative affect in young adolescent girls. *Child Development, 60,* 40–55.

Bryck, R. L., & Fisher, P. A. (2012). Training the brain: Practical applications of neural plasticity from the intersection of cognitive neuroscience, developmental psychology and prevention science. *American Psychologist, 67,* 87–100.

Burchinal, M. R., Bryant, D. M., Lee, M. W., & Ramey, C. T. (1992). Early day care, infant-mother attachment, and maternal responsiveness in the infant's first year. *Early Childhood Research Quarterly, 3,* 383–396.

Buss, A. R. (1976). Galton and the birth of differential psychology and eugenics: Social, political, and economic forces. *Journal of the History of the Behavioral Sciences, 12,* 47–58.

Buss, D. M. (1995). Psychological sex differences: Origins through sexual selection. *American Psychologist, 50,* 164–168.

Buss, D. M. Abbott, M., Angleitner, A., Asherian, A., Biaggio, A., Blanco-Villasenor, A. ... Yang, K.-S. (1990). International preferences in selecting mates: A study of 37 cultures. *Journal of Cross-Cultural Psychology, 21,* 5–47.

Bussey, K., & Bandura, A. (1999). Social cognitive theory of gender development and differentiation. *Psychological Review, 106,* 676–713.

Byrnes, J. P., Miller, D. C., & Schafer, W. D. (1999). Gender differences in risk taking: A metaanalysis. *Psychological Bulletin, 125,* 367–383.

Camel, J. E., Withers, G. S., & Greenough, W. T. (1986). Persistence of visual cortex dendritic alterations induced by postweaning exposure to a "superenriched" environment in rats. *Behavioral Neuroscience, 100,* 810–813.

Chao, R. K. (1994). Beyond parental control and authoritarian parenting style: Understanding Chinese parenting through the cultural notion of training. *Child Development, 65,* 1111–1119.

Chao, R. K. (2001). Extending research on the consequences of parenting style for Chinese Americans and European Americans. *Child Development, 72,* 1832–1843.

Christensen, T. M., & Brooks, M. C. (2001). Adult children of divorce and intimate relationships: A review of the literature. *Family Journal-Counseling and Therapy for Couples and Families. 9,* 289–294.

Ciftci Uruk, A., & Demir, A. (2003). The role of peers and families in predicting the loneliness level of adolescents. *Journal of Psychology, 137,* 179–193.

Collaer, M. L., & Hines, M. (1995). Human behavioral sex differences: A role for gonadal hormones during early development? *Psychological Bulletin, 118,* 55–107.

Colcombe, S., & Kramer, A. F. (2003). Fitness effects on the cognitive function of older adults: A meta-analytic study. *Psychological Science, 14,* 125–130.

Collaer, M. L., Geffner, M. E., Kaufman, F. R., Buckingham, B., & Hines, M. (2002). Cognitive and behavioral characteristics of Turner syndrome: Exploring a role for ovarian hormones in female sexual differentiation. *Hormones and Behavior, 41,* 139–155.

Connors, A. (1988, February 5). At 91, she's stepping up in class. *Los Angeles Times,* p. 2.

Cox, K. S., Wilt, J, Olson, B., & McAdams, D. P. (2010). Generativity, the Big Five, and psychosocial adaptation in midlife adults. *Journal of Personality, 78,* 1185–1208.

Cramer, P. (2000). Development of identity: Gender makes a difference. *Journal of Research in Personality, 34,* 42–72.

Crohan, S. E. (1992). Marital happiness and spousal consensus on beliefs about marital conflict: A longitudinal investigation. *Journal of Social and Personal Relationships, 9,* 89–102.

Cuellar, I., Roberts, R. E., Nyberg, B., & Maldonado, R. E. (1997). Ethnic identity and acculturation in a young adult Mexican-origin population. *Journal of Community Psychology, 25,* 535–549.

Currie, C., Ahluwalia, N., Godeau, E., Gabhainn, S. N., Due, P., & Currie, D. B. (2012). Is obesity at individual and national level associated with lower age at menarche? Evidence from 34 countries in the Health Behaviour in School-aged Children Study. *Journal of Adolescent Health, 50,* 621–626.

Daigen, V., & Holmes, J. G. (2000). Don't interrupt! A good rule for marriage? *Personal Relationships, 7,* 185–201.

Darling, N., & Steinberg, L. (1993). Parenting style as context: An integrative model. *Psychological Bulletin, 113,* 487–496.

Davies, P. T., & Cummings, E. M. (1994). Marital conflict and child adjustment: An emotional security hypothesis. *Psychological Bulletin, 116,* 387–411.

De Wolff, M., & van Ijzendoorn, M. H. (1997). Sensitivity and attachment: A meta-analysis on parental antecedents of infant attachment. *Child Development, 68,* 571–591.

Deaux, K. (1985). Sex and gender. *Annual Review of Psychology, 36,* 49–81.

Deaux, K., & Major, B. (1987). Putting gender into context: An interactive model of gender-related behavior. *Psychological Review, 94,* 369–389.

Delanoë, D., Hajri, S., Bachelot, A., Mahfoudg, D., Hassoun, D., Marsicano, E., & Ringa, V. (2012). Class, gender and culture in the experience of menopause: A comparative survey in Tunisia and France. *Social Science & Medicine, 75,* 401–409.

Dennerstein, L., Dudley, E., & Guthrie, J. (2002). Empty nest or revolving door? A prospective study of women's quality of life in midlife during the phase of children leaving and re-entering the home. *Psychological Medicine, 32,* 545–550.

Diamond, M. C. (1988). *Enriching heredity: The impact of the environment on the anatomy of the brain.* New York: Free Press.

Diener, E., Gohm, C. L., Suh, E., & Oishi, S. (2000). Similarity of the relations between marital status and subjective well-being across cultures. *Journal of Cross-Cultural Psychology, 31,* 419–436.

Dindia, K., & Allen, M. (1992). Sex differences in self-disclosure: A meta-analysis. *Psychological Bulletin, 112,* 106–124.

Dorn, L. D., Susman, E. J., & Ponirakis, A. (2003). Pubertal timing and adolescent adjustment and behavior: Conclusions vary by rater. *Journal of Youth and Adolescence, 32,* 157–167.

Eagle, M. (1997). Contributions of Erik Erikson. *Psychoanalytic Review, 84,* 337–347.

Eagly, A. H. (1995). The science and politics of comparing women and men. *American Psychologist, 50,* 145–158.

Eiden, R. D., Schuetze, P., & Coles, C. D. (2011). Maternal cocaine use and mother-infant interactions: Direct and moderated associations. *Neurotoxicology & Teratology, 33,* 120–128.

Eisdorfer, C. (1983). Conceptual models of aging: The challenge of a new frontier. *American Psychologist, 38,* 197–202.

Eisenberg, N., & Lennon, R. (1983). Sex differences in empathy and related capacities. *Psychological Bulletin, 94,* 100–131.

Elkind, D. (1996). Inhelder and Piaget on adolescence and adulthood: A postmodern appraisal. *Psychological Science, 7,* 216–220.

Ellison, W. J. (1987). State execution of juveniles: Defining "youth" as a mitigating factor for imposing a sentence of less than death. *Law and Psychology Review, 11,* 1–38.

Else-Quest, N. M., Hyde, J. S., & Linn, M. C. (2010). Cross-national patterns of gender differences in mathematics: A meta-analysis. *Psychological Bulletin, 136,* 103–127.

Else-Quest, N. M., Hyde, J. S., Goldsmith, H. H., Van Hulle, C. A. (2006). Gender differences in temperament: A meta-analysis. *Psychological Bulletin, 132,* 33–72.

Erel, O., & Burman, B. (1995). Interrelatedness of marital relations and parent-child relations: A meta-analytic review. *Psychological Bulletin, 118,* 108–132.

Erikson, E. (1963). *Childhood and society.* New York: W. W. Norton.

Fagan, M. M., & Ayers, K. (1983). Levinson's model as a predictor of the adult development of policemen. *International Journal of Aging and Human Development, 16,* 221–230.

Feingold, A. (1994). Gender differences in personality: A meta-analysis. *Psychological Bulletin, 116,* 429–456.

Feng, D., Silverstein, M., Giarrusso, R., McArdle, J. J., & Bengtson, V. L. (2006). Attrition of older adults in longitudinal surveys: Detection and correction of sample selection bias using multigenerational data. *The Journals of Gerontology: Series B: Psychological Sciences and Social Sciences, 61,* S323–S328.

Fieckenstein, L. (1996, May 20). Trailblazing Hulda Crooks, 100: Loma Linda resident publishes memoirs. *Press-Enterprise,* p. B03.

Field, T. M. (1991). Quality infant day-care and grade school behavior and performance. *Child Development, 62,* 863–870.

Field, T. M. (1996). Attachment and separation in young children. *Annual Review of Psychology, 47,* 541–561.

Field, T. M., Woodson, R., Greenberg, R., & Cohen, D. (1982). Discrimination and imitation of facial expressions by neonates. *Science, 218,* 179–181.

Fischer, K. W., & Silvern, L. (1985). Stages and individual differences in cognitive development. *Annual Review of Psychology, 36,* 613–648.

Fraley, C. R., Roisman, G. I., Booth-LaForce, C., Owen, M. T., & Holland, A. S. (2013). Interpersonal and genetic origins of adult attachment styles: A longitudinal study from infancy to early adulthood. *Journal of Personality and Social Psychology, 104,* 817–838.

Frank, D. A., Brown, J., Johnson, S., & Cabral, H. (2002). Forgotten fathers: An exploratory study of mothers' report of drug and alcohol problems among fathers of urban newborns. *Neurotoxicology & Teratology, 24,* 339–347.

Frank, E., & Brandstaetter, V. (2002). Approach versus avoidance: Different types of commitment in intimate relationships. *Journal of Personality and Social Psychology, 82,* 208–221.

Freedman, M. A. (2002). Quality of life and menopause: The role of estrogen. *Journal of Women's Health, 11,* 703–718.

Freund, A. M., & Baltes, P. B. (1998). Selection, optimization, and compensation as strategies of life management: Correlations with subjective indicators of successful aging. *Psychology of Aging, 13,* 531–543.

Frisco, M. L., & Williams, K. (2003). Perceived housework equity, marital happiness, and divorce in dual-earner households. *Journal of Family Issues, 24,* 51–73.

Fullerton, A. S., & Dixon, J. C. (2010). Generational conflict or methodological artifact? Reconsidering the relationship between age and policy attitudes in the U.S., 1984–2008. *Public Opinion Quarterly, 74,* 643–673.

Furman, W. (2002). The emerging field of adolescent romantic relationships. *Current Directions in Psychological Science, 11,* 177–180.

Ganong, L., Coleman, M., Fine, M., & Martin, P. (1999). Stepparents' affinity-seeking and affinity-maintaining strategies with stepchildren. *Journal of Family Issues, 20,* 299–327.

Garmon, L. C., Basinger, K. S., Gregg, V. R., & Gibbs, J. C. (1996). Gender differences in stage and expression of moral judgment. *Merrill-Palmer Quarterly, 42,* 418–437.

Gfellner, B. M., & Hundleby, J. D. (1994). Developmental and gender differences in drug use and problem behaviour during adolescence. *Journal of Child and Adolescent Substance Abuse, 3,* 59–74.

Gibson, E. J., & Walk, R. D. (1960, April). The visual cliff. *Scientific American,* pp. 67–71.

Gilligan, C. (1982). *In a different voice: Psychological theory and women's development.* Cambridge, MA: Harvard University Press.

Goebel, B. L., & Boeck, B. E. (1987). Ego integrity and fear of death: A comparison of institutionalized and independently living older adults. *Death Studies, 11,* 193–204.

Gorrese, A., & Ruggieri, R. (2012). Peer attachment: A meta-analytic review of gender and age differences and associations with parent attachment. *Journal of Youth & Adolescence, 41,* 650–672.

Graham, M. J., Larsen, U., & Xu, X. (1999). Secular trend in age at menarche in China: A case study of two rural counties in Anhui province. *Journal of Biosocial Science, 31,* 257–267.

Gray, D. E., (2002). Everybody just freezes. Everybody is just embarrassed: Felt and enacted stigma among parents of children with high functioning autism. *Sociology of Health and Illness, 24,* 734–749.

Greeff, A. P., & de Bruyne, Tanya (2000). Conflict management style and marital satisfaction. *Journal of Sex and Marital Therapy, 26,* 321–334.

Gribble, J. R. (2000). The psychosocial crisis of industry versus inferiority and self-estimates of vocational competence in high school students. *Dissertation Abstracts International: Section B. The Sciences and Engineering, 60,* 3618.

Grossmann, K., Grossmann, K. E., Fremmer-Bombik, E., Kindler, H., Scheuerer-Englisch, H., & Zimmerman, P. (2002). The uniqueness of the child-father attachment relationship: Fathers' sensitive and challenging play as a pivotal variable in a 16-year longitudinal study. *Social Development, 11,* 307–331.

Gubernskaya, Z. (2010). Changing attitudes toward marriage and children in six countries. *Sociological Perspectives, 53,* 179–200.

Haight, B. K., Michel, Y., & Hendrix, S. (2000). The extended effects of the life review in nursing home residents. *International Journal of Aging and Human Development, 50,* 151–168.

Hall, G. S. (1904). *Adolescence.* New York: Appleton.

Halpern, D. F. (1994). Stereotypes, science, censorship, and the study of sex differences. *Feminism & Psychology, 4,* 523–530.

Halpern, D. F. (2000). *Sex differences in cognitive abilities* (3rd ed.). Mahwah, NJ: Erlbaum.

Halpern, D. F., & LeMay, M. L. (2000). The smarter sex: A critical review of sex differences in intelligence. *Educational Psychology Review, 12,* 229–246.

Hamarman, S., Pope, K. H., & Czaja, S. J. (2002). Emotional abuse in children: Variations in legal definitions and rates across the United States. *Child Maltreatment: Journal of the American Professional Society on the Abuse of Children, 7,* 303–311.

Hanna, G., Kundiger, E., & Larouche, C. (1990). Mathematical achievement of grade 12 girls in fifteen countries. In L. Burton (Ed.), *Gender and mathematics: An international perspective* (pp. 87–98). New York: Cassell.

Harlow, H. F., & Zimmerman, R. R. (1959). Affectional responses in the infant monkey. *Science, 130,* 421–432.

Harris, R. L., Ellicott, A. M., & Holmes, D. S. (1986). The timing of psychosocial transitions and changes in women's lives: An examination of women aged 45 to 60. *Journal of Personality and Social Psychology, 51,* 409–416.

Hartup, W. W. (1989). Social relationships and their developmental significance. *American Psychologist, 44,* 120–126.

Hayflick, L. (1980, January). The cell biology of human aging. *Scientific American,* pp. 58–65.

Heath, D. T., & Orthner, D. K. (1999). Stress and adaptation among male and female single parents. *Journal of Family Issues, 20,* 557–587.

Hewlett, B. S., Lamb, M. E., Shannon, D., Leyendecker, B., & Schoelmerich, A. (1998). Culture and early infancy among central African foragers and farm ers. *Developmental Psychology, 34,* 653–661.

Hill, J. L., Waldfogel, J., Brooks-Gunn, J., & Han, W. J. (2005). Maternal employment and child development: A fresh look using newer methods. *Developmental Psychology, 41,* 833–850.

Hopkins, J. R. (1995). Erik Homburger Erikson (1902–1994). *American Psychologist, 50,* 796–797.

Hultsch, D. F., Hertzog, C., Small, B. J., & Dixon, R. A. (1999). Use it or lose it: Engaged lifestyle as a buffer of cognitive decline in aging? *Psychology and Aging, 14,* 245–263.

Hunsberger, B., Pratt, M., & Pancer, S. M. (2001). Adolescent identity formation: Religious exploration and commitment. *Identity, 1,* 365–386.

Hyde, J. S. (2007). New directions in the study of gender similarities and differences. *Current Directions in Psychological Science, 16,* 259–263.

Hyde, J. S., Fennema, E., & Lamon, S. J. (1990). Gender differences in mathematics performance: A meta-analysis. *Psychological Bulletin, 107,* 139–155.

Hyde, J. S., & Linn, M. C. (1988). Gender differences in verbal ability: A meta-analysis. *Psychological Bulletin, 104,* 53–69.

Hyde, J. S., & Plant, E. A. (1995). Magnitude of psychological gender differences: Another side of the story. *American Psychologist, 50,* 159–161.

Ickes, W., Gesn, P. R., & Graham, T. (2000). Gender differences in empathic accuracy: Differential ability or differential motivation? *Personal Relationships, 7,* 95–109.

Iqbal, H. M., & Shayer, M. (2000). Accelerating the development of formal thinking in Pakistan secondary school students: Achievement effects and professional development issues. *Journal of Research in Science Teaching, 37,* 259–274.

Ispa, J. M., Thornburg, K. R., & Gray, M. M. (1990). Relations between early childhood care arrangements and college students' psychosocial development and academic performance. *Adolescence, 25,* 529–542.

Jacklin, C. N. (1989). Female and male: Issues of gender. *American Psychologist, 44,* 127–133.

Jaffee, S., & Hyde, J. S. (2000). Gender differences in moral orientation: A meta-analysis. *Psychological Bulletin, 126,* 703–726.

Jeffries, S., & Konnert, C. (2002). Regret and psychological well-being among voluntarily and involuntarily childless women and mothers. *International Journal of Aging and Human Development, 54,* 89–106.

Jeynes, W. H. (2002). The relationship between the consumption of various drugs by adolescents and their academic achievement. *American Journal of Drug and Alcohol Abuse, 28,* 15–35.

Kaltiala-Heino, R., Koivisto, A.-M., Marttunen, M., & Fröjd, S. (2011). Pubertal timing and substance use in middle adolescence: A 2-year follow-up study. *Journal of Youth and Adolescence, 40,* 1288–1301.

Karney, B. R., & Bradbury, T. N. (2000). Attributions in marriage: State or trait? A growth curve analysis. *Journal of Personality and Social Psychology, 78,* 295–309.

Katz, J., & Schneider, M. E. (2013). Casual hook-up sex during the first year of college: Prospective associations with attitudes about sex and love relationships. *Archives of Sexual Behavior, 42,* 1451–1462.

Keegan, J., Parva, M., Finnegan, M., Gerson, A., & Beldon, M. (2010). Addiction in pregnancy. *Journal of Addictive Diseases, 29,* 175–191.

Keen, R., Carrico, R. L., Sylvia, M. R., & Berthier, & N. E. (2003). How infants use perceptual information to guide action. *Developmental Science, 6,* 221–231.

Kim, J. E., & Moen, P. (2001). Is retirement good or bad for subjective well-being? *Current Directions in Psychological Science, 10,* 83–86.

Kimball, M. M. (1995). *Gender and math: What makes a difference? Feminist visions of gender similarities and differences.* New York: Harrington Park Press.

Kimura, D. (1987). Are men's and women's brains really different? *Canadian Psychology, 28,* 133–147.

Kimura, D., & Hampson, E. (1994). Cognitive pattern in men and women is influenced by fluctuations in sex hormones. *Current Directions in Psychological Science, 3,* 57–61.

Kisilevsky, B. S., & Hains, S. M. J. (2011). Onset and maturation of fetal heart rate response to the mother's voice over late gestations. *Developmental Science, 14,* 214–223.

Kittrell, D. (1998). A comparison of the evolution of men's and women's dreams in Daniel Levinson's theory of adult development. *Journal of Adult Development, 5,* 105–115.

Klahr, A. M., Rueter, M. A., McGue, M., Iacono, W. G., & Alexandra, B. S. (2011). The relationship between parent-child conflict and adolescent antisocial behavior: Confirming shared environmental mediation. *Journal of Abnormal Child Psychology, 39,* 683–694.

Kling, K. C., Hyde, J. S., Showers, C. J., & Buswell, B. N. (1999). Gender differences in self-esteem: A meta-analysis. *Psychological Bulletin, 125,* 470–500.

Kohlberg, L. (1981). *Essays on moral development.* New York: Harper & Row.

Kovac, S. H., & Range, L. M. (2000). Writing projects: Lessening undergraduates' unique suicidal bereavement. *Suicide and Life-Threatening Behavior, 30,* 50–60.

Kretch, K. S., & Adolph, K. E. (2013). Cliff or step? Posture-specific learning at the edge of a drop-off. *Child Development, 84,* 226–240.

Kudo, F. T., Longhofer, J. L., & Floersch, J. E. (2012). On the origins of early leadership: The role of authoritative parenting practices and mastery orientation. *Leadership, 8,* 345–375.

Kuelbelbeck, A. (1991, August 23). A real high point. *Los Angeles Times,* p. E1.

Kurdek, L. A. (1998). Relationship outcomes and their predictors: Longitudinal evidence from heterosexual married, gay cohabiting, and lesbian cohabiting couples. *Journal of Marriage and the Family, 60,* 553–568.

Kurdek, L. A. (1999). The nature and predictors of the trajectory of change in marital quality for husbands and wives over the first 10 years of marriage. *Developmental Psychology, 35,* 1283–1296.

Lamb, M. E. (1996). Effects of nonparental child care on child development: An update. *Canadian Journal of Psychiatry, 41,* 330–342.

Lamb, M. E. (2012). Mothers, fathers, families and circumstances: Factors affecting children's adjustment. *Applied Developmental Science, 16,* 98–111.

Laursen, B., Coy, K. C., & Collins, W. A. (1998). Reconsidering changes in parent-child conflict across adolescence: A meta-analysis. *Child Development, 69,* 817–832.

Lawton, C. A. (2001). Gender and regional differences in spatial referents used in direction giving. *Sex Roles, 44,* 321–337.

Leeson, F. J., & Nixon, R. D. V. (2011). The role of children's appraisals on adjustment following psychological maltreatment: A pilot study. *Journal of Abnormal Child Psychology, 39,* 759–771.

Lei, T. (1994). Being and becoming moral in a Chinese culture: Unique or universal? *Cross-Cultural Research: The Journal of Comparative Social Science, 28,* 58–91.

Levine, S. C., Huttenlocher, J., Taylor, A., & Langrock, A. (1999). Early sex differences in spatial skill. *Developmental Psychology, 35,* 940–949.

Levinson, D. J. (1978). *The seasons of a man's life.* New York: Knopf.

Levinson, D. J. (1986). A conception of adult development. *American Psychologist, 41,* 3–13.

Leyendecker, B., Lamb, M. E., Fracasso, M. P., Schölmerich, A., & Larson, C. (1997). Playful interaction and the antecedents of attachment. A longitudinal study of Central American and Euro-American mothers and infants. *Merrill-Palmer Quarterly, 43,* 24–47.

Lightdale, J. R., & Prentice, D. A. (1994). Rethinking sex differences in aggression: Aggressive behavior in the absence of social roles. *Personality and Social Psychology Bulletin, 20,* 34–44.

Lindberg, S. M., Hyde, J. S., Petersen, J. L., & Linn, M. C. (2010). New trends in gender and mathematics performance: A meta-analysis. *Psychological Bulletin, 136,* 1123–1135.

Lubinski, D., Benbow, C. P., Shea, D. L., Eftekhari- Sanjani, H., & Halvorson, B. J. (2001). Men and women at promise for scientific excellence: Similarity not dissimilarity. *Psychological Science, 12,* 309–317.

Luhmann, M., Lucas, R. E., Eid, M., & Diener, E. (2013). The prospective effect of life satisfaction on life events. *Social Psychological & Personality Science, 4,* 39–45.

Lytton, H., & Romney, D. M. (1991). Parents' differential socialization of boys and girls: A meta-analysis. *Psychological Bulletin, 109,* 267–296.

Ma, H. K., Shek, D. T. L., Cheung, P. C., Oi Bun Lam, C. (2000). Parental, peer, and teacher influences on the social behavior of Hong Kong Chinese adolescents. *Journal of Genetic Psychology, 161,* 65–78.

Maccoby, E. E., & Jacklin, C. N. (1974). *The psychology of sex differences* (2 vols.). Stanford, CA: Stanford University Press.

Maccoby, E. E., & Lewis, C. C. (2003). Less day care or different day care? *Child Development, 74,* 1069–1075.

Malinowski, C. I., & Smith, C. P. (1985). Moral reasoning and moral conduct: An investigation prompted by Kohlberg's theory. *Journal of Personality and Social Psychology, 49,* 1016–1027.

Mandel, D. R., Jusczyk, P. W., & Pisoni, D. B. (1995). Infants' recognition of the sound patterns of their own names. *Psychological Science, 6,* 314–317.

Maranto, G. (1984, December). Aging: Can we slow the inevitable? *Discover,* pp. 17–21.

Masoro, E. J., Shimokawa, I., Higami, Y., & McMahan, C. A. (1995). Temporal pattern of food intake not a factor in the retardation of aging processes by dietary restriction. *Journals of Gerontology: Series A: Biological Sciences and Medical Sciences, 50A,* B48–B53.

Mattanah, J. F., Pratt, M. W., Cowan, P. A., & Cowan, C. P. (2005). Authoritative parenting, parental scaffolding of long-division mathematics, and children's academic competence in fourth grade. *Journal of Applied Developmental Psychology, 26,* 85–106.

McAdams, D. P., de St. Aubin, E., & Logan, R. L. (1993). Generativity among youth, midlife, and older adults. *Psychology and Aging, 8,* 221–230.

McNelles, L. R., & Connolly, J. A. (1999). Intimacy between adolescent friends: Age and gender differences in intimate affect and intimate behaviors. *Journal of Research on Adolescence, 9,* 143–159.

Molina, M., & Jouen, F. (1998). Modulation of the palmar grasp behavior in neonates according to texture property. *Infant Behavior and Development, 21,* 659–666.

Morley, J. E. (2001). Androgens and aging. *Maturitas, 38,* 61–73.

Morrongiello, B. A., Fenwick, K. D., & Chance, G. (1990). Sound localization acuity in very young infants: An observer-based testing procedure: Correction. *Developmental Psychology, 26,* 1003.

Mouratidis, A., & Michou, A. (2011). Self-determined motiviation and social achievement goals in children's emotions. *Educational Psychology, 31,* 67–86.

Muir-Broaddus, J., King, T., Downey, D., & Petersen, M. (1998). Conservation as a predictor of individual differences in children's susceptibility to leading questions. *Psychonomic Bulletin and Review, 5,* 454–458.

Mulligan, T., & Moss, C. R. (1991). Sexuality and aging in male veterans: A cross-sectional study of interest, ability, and activity. *Archives of Sexual Behavior, 20,* 17–25.

Munakata, Y., McClelland, J. L., Johnson, M. H., & Siegler, R. S. (1997). Rethinking infant knowledge: Toward an adaptive process account of successes and failures in object permanence tasks. *Psychological Review, 104,* 686–713.

Nazzi, T., Floccia, C., & Bertoncini, J. (1998). Discrimination of pitch contours by neonates. *Infant Behavior and Development, 21,* 779–784.

Newcomb, A. F., & Bagwell, C. L. (1995). Children's friendship relations: A meta-analytic review. *Psychological Bulletin, 117,* 306–347.

Newcomb, A. F., Bukowski, W. M., & Pattee, L. (1993). Children's peer relations: A meta-analytic review of popular, rejected, neglected, controversial, and average sociometric status. *Psychological Bulletin, 113,* 99–128.

NICHD Early Child Care Research Network (1997). The effects of infant child care on infant-mother attachment security: Results of the NICHD study of early child care. *Child Development, 68,* 860–879.

O'Leary, K. D., & Smith, D. A. (1991). Marital interactions. *Annual Review of Psychology, 42,* 191–212.

Paikoff, R. L., & Brooks-Gunn, J. (1991). Do parent-child relationships change during puberty? *Psychological Bulletin, 110,* 47–66.

Parten, M. B. (1932). Social participation among preschool children. *Journal of Abnormal and Social Psychology, 27,* 243–269.

Peisner-Feinberg, E. S., Burchinal, M. R., Clifford, R. M., Culkin, M. L., Howes, C., Kagan, S. L., & Yazejian, N. (2001). The relation of preschool child-care quality to children's cognitive and social developmental trajectories through second grade. *Child Development, 72,* 1534–1553.

Petersen, J. L., & Hyde, J. S. (2010). A meta-analytic review of research on gender differences in sexuality: 1993–2007. *Psychological Bulletin, 136,* 21–38.

Peterson, C. C. (1996). The ticking of the social clock: Adults' beliefs about the timing of transition events. *International Journal of Aging and Human Development, 42,* 189–203.

Pettersen, L., Yonas, A., & Fisch, R. O. (1980). The development of blinking in response to impending collision in preterm, full-term, and postterm infants. *Infant Behavior and Development, 3,* 155–165.

Phillips, R. D., Wagner, S. H., Fells, C. A., & Lynch, M. (1990). Do infants recognize emotion in facial expressions? Categorical and "metaphorical" evidence. *Infant Behavior and Development, 13,* 71–84.

Phinney, J. S. (1990). Ethnic identity in adolescents and adults: Review of research. *Psychological Bulletin, 108,* 499–514.

Phinney, J. S., Cantu, C. L., & Kurtz, D. A. (1997). Ethnic and American identity as predictors of self-esteem among African American, Latino, and White adolescents. *Journal of Youth and Adolescence, 26,* 165–185.

Phinney, J. S., Ong, A., & Madden, T. (2000). Cultural values and intergenerational value discrepancies in immigrant and nonimmigrant families. *Child Development, 71,* 528–539.

Phinney, J. S., & Ong, A. D. (2002). Adolescent-parent disagreements and life satisfaction in families from Vietnamese- and European-American backgrounds. *International Journal of Behavioral Development, 26,* 556–561.

Piaget, J. (1952). *The origins of intelligence in children.* New York: International Universities Press.

Pierrehumbert, B., Santelices, M. P., Ibáñez, M., Alberdi, M., Ongari, B., Roskam, I., ... Borghini, A., (2009). Gender and attachment representations in the preschool years: Comparisons between five countries. *Journal of Cross-Cultural Psychology, 40,* 543–566.

Piko, B. F., & Balázs, M. Á. (2012). Authoritative parenting style and adolescent smoking and drinking. *Addictive behaviors, 37,* 353–356.

Pinquart, M. (2003). Loneliness in married, widowed, divorced, and never-married older adults. *Journal of Social and Personal Relationships, 20,* 31–53.

Piper, B. J., Gray, H. M., & Birkett, M. A. (2012). Maternal smoking cessation and reduced academic and behavioral problems in offspring. *Drug and Alcohol Dependence, 121,* 62–67.

Pollard, I. (2000). Substance abuse and parenthood: Biological mechanisms—Bioethical challenges. *Women and Health, 30,* 1–24.

Price-Williams, E., Gordon, W., & Ramirez, M. (1969). Skill and conservation: A study of pottery-making children. *Developmental Psychology, 1,* 769.

Putnam, F. W. (2003). Ten-year research update review: Child sexual abuse. *Journal of the American Academy of Child and Adolescent Psychiatry, 42,* 269–278.

Range, L. M., Kovac, S. H., & Marion, M. S. (2000). Does writing about the bereavement lessen grief following sudden, unintentional death? *Death Studies, 24,* 115–134.

Reeve, J. M., Bolt, E., & Cai, Y. (1999). Autonomy-supportive teachers: How they teach and motivate students. *Journal of Educational Psychology, 91,* 537–548.

Reifman, A., Villa, L. C., Amans, J. A., Rethinam, V., & Telesca, T. Y. (2001). Children of divorce in the 1990s: A meta-analysis. *Journal of Divorce and Remarriage, 36,* 27–36.

Renn, J. A., & Calvert, S. L. (1993). The relation between gender schemas and adults' recall of stereotyped and countersterotyped televised information. *Sex Roles, 28,* 449–459.

Renner, J. W., Abraham, M. R., Grzybowski, E. B., & Marek, E. A. (1990). Understandings and misunderstandings of eighth graders of four physics concepts found in textbooks. *Journal of Research in Science Teaching, 27,* 35–54.

Roberts, R. E., Phinney, J. S., Masse, L. C., Chen, Y. R., Roberts, C. R., & Romero, A. (1999). The structure of ethnic identity of young adolescents from diverse ethnocultural groups. *Journal of Early Adolescence, 19,* 301–322.

Rogers, R. L., Meyer, J. S., & Mortel, K. F. (1990). After reaching retirement age physical activity sustains cerebral perfusion and cognition. *Journal of the American Geriatrics Society, 38,* 123–128.

Rogge, R. D., & Bradbury, T. N. (1999). Till violence does us part: The differing roles of communication and aggression in predicting adverse marital outcomes. *Journal of Consulting and Clinical Psychology, 67,* 340–351.

Rogoff, B., & Chavajay, P. (1995). What's become of research on the cultural basis of cognitive development? *American Psychologist, 50,* 459–477.

Rook, K. S., Catalano, R., & Dooley, D. (1989). The timing of major life events: Effects of departing from the social clock. *American Journal of Community Psychology, 17,* 233–258.

Roth, L. W., & Polotsky, A. J. (2012). Can we live longer by eating less? A review of caloric restriction and longevity. *Maturitas, 71,* 315–319.

Rubin, J. R., Provenzano, F. J., & Luria, Z. (1974). The eye of the beholder: Parents' views on sex of newborns. *American Journal of Orthopsychiatry, 44,* 512–519.

Rudy, D., & Grusec, J. E. (2001). Correlates of authoritarian in individualistic and collectivist cultures and implications for understanding the transmission of values. *Journal of Cross-Cultural Psychology, 32,* 202–212.

Ruffman, T. K., & Olson, D. R. (1989). Children's ascriptions of knowledge to others. *Developmental Psychology, 25,* 601–606.

Rungger-Brändle, E., Ripperger, J. A., Steiner, K., Conti, A., Stieger, A., Soltanieh, S., & Rungger, D. (2010). Retinal patterning by Pax6-dependent cell adhesion molecules. *Developmental Neurobiology, 70,* 764–780.

Rust, J., Golombok, S., Hines, M., Johnston, K., & Golding, J. (2000). The role of brothers and sisters in the gender development of preschool children. *Journal of Experimental Child Psychology, 77,* 292–303.

Ryan, J. J., Sattler, J. M., & Lopez, S. J. (2000). Age effects in Wechsler Adult Intelligence Scale-III subtests. *Archives of Clinical Neuropsychology, 15,* 311–317.

Sachdeva, S., Singh,P., & Medin, D. (2011). Culture and the quest for universal principles in moral reasoning. *International Journal of Psychology, 46,* 161–176.

Saczynski, J. S. (2002). Cognitive training gains in the Seattle longitudinal study: Individual predictors and mediators of training effects. *Dissertation Abstracts International: Section B. The Sciences and Engineering, 62,* 6001.

Salthouse, T. A. (1991). Mediation of adult age differences in cognition by reductions in working memory and speed of processing. *Psychological Science, 2,* 179–183.

SantaCruz, K. S., Sonnen, J. A., Pezhough, M. K., Desrosiers, M. F., Nelson, P., & Tyas, S. L. (2011). Alzheimer disease pathology in subjects without dementia in 2 studies of aging: The Nun Study and the Adult Changes in Thought Study. *Journal of Neuropathology & Experimental Neurology, 70,* 832–840.

Sargent-Cox, K. A., Anstey, K. J., & Luszcz, M. A. (2010). Patterns of longitudinal change in older adults' self-rated health, the effect of the point of reference. *Health Psychology, 29,* 143–152.

Saunders, C. (1996). Hospice. *Mortality, 1,* 317–322.

Sawatzky, J. V., & Naimark, B. J. (2002). Physical activity and cardiovascular health in aging women: A health-promotion perspective. *Journal of Aging and Physical Activity, 10,* 396–412.

Scarr, S. (1998). American child care today. *American Psychologist, 53,* 95–108.

Schaal, B., Marlier, L., & Soussignan, R. (1998). Olfactory function in the human fetus: Evidence from selective neonatal responsiveness to the odor of amniotic fluid. *Behavioral Neuroscience, 112,* 1438–1449.

Schaie, K. W. (1989). Perceptual speed in adulthood: Cross-sectional and longitudinal studies. *Psychology and Aging, 4,* 443–453.

Schaie, K. W., & Hertzog, C. (1983). Fourteen-year cohort- sequential analyses of adult intellectual development. *Developmental Psychology, 19,* 531–543.

Schaie, K. W., Labouvie, G. V., & Barrett, T. J. (1973). Selective attrition effects in a 14-year study of adult intelligence. *Journal of Gerontology, 28,* 328–334.

Schmitt-Rodermund, E., & Vondracek, F. W. (1999). Breadth of interests, exploration, and identity development in adolescence. *Journal of Vocational Behavior, 55,* 298–317.

Schneider-Rosen, K., & Burke, P. B. (1999). Multiple attachment relationships within families: Mothers and fathers with two young children. *Developmental Psychology, 35,* 436–444.

Schooler, C., Mulatu, M. S., & Oates, G. (1999). The continuing effects of substantively complex work on the intellectual functioning of older workers. *Psychology and Aging, 14,* 483–506.

Schulz, R., & Curnow, C. (1988). Peak performance and age among superathletes: Track and field, swimming, baseball, tennis, and golf. *Journal of Gerontology, 43,* 113–120.

Segall, M. H., Dasen, P. R., Berry, J. W., & Poortinga, Y. H. (1990). *Human behavior in global perspective: An introduction to cross-cultural psychology.* New York: Pergamon.

Selcuk, E., & Ong, A. D. (2013). Perceived partner responsiveness moderates the association between received emotional support and all-cause mortality. *Health Psychology, 32,* 231–235.

Self, D. J., & Baldwin, D. C., Jr. (1998). Does medical education inhibit the development of moral reasoning in medical students? A cross-sectional study. *Academic Medicine, 73,* S91–S93.

Shapiro, D. (1995). Finding out how psychotherapies help people change. *Psychotherapy Research, 5,* 1–21.

Shinskey, J. L. (2012). Disappearing décalage: Object search in light and dark at 6 months. *Infancy, 17,* 272–294.

Silverman, I. W. (2003). Gender differences in delay of gratification: A meta-analysis. *Sex Roles, 49,* 451–463.

Silverstein, L. B., & Auerbach, C. F. (1999). Deconstructing the essential father. *American Psychologist, 54,* 397–407.

Simons-Morton, B. G. (2002). Prospective analysis of peer and parent influences on smoking initiation among early adolescents. *Prevention Science, 3,* 275–283.

Singer, J. D., Fuller, B., Keiley, M. K., & Wolf, A. (1998). Early child-care selection: Variation by geographic location, maternal characteristics, and family structure. *Developmental Psychology, 34,* 1129–1144.

Skoe, E. E. A., Cumberland, A., Eisenberg, N., Hansen, K., & Perry, J. (2002). The influence of sex and gender-role identity on moral cognition and prosocial personality traits. *Sex Roles, 46,* 295–309.

Slater, C. L. (2003). Generativity versus stagnation: An elaboration of Erikson's adult stage of human development. *Journal of Adult Development, 10,* 53–65.

Smith, J. L., & White, P. H. (2002). An examination of implicitly activated, explicitly activated, and nullified stereotypes on mathematical performance: It's not just a woman's issue. *Sex Roles, 47,* 179–191.

Snarey, J. R., Reimer, J., & Kohlberg, L. (1985). Development of social-moral reasoning among kibbutz adolescents: A longitudinal cross-cultural study. *Developmental Psychology, 21,* 3–17.

Sneed, J. R., Whitbourne, S. K., Schwartz, S. J., & Huang, S. (2012). The relationship between identity, intimacy, and midlife well-being: Findings from the Rochester Adult Longitudinal Study. *Psychology and Aging, 27,* 318–323.

Snow, W. G., & Sheese, S. (1985). Lateralized brain damage, intelligence, and memory: A failure to find sex differences. *Journal of Consulting and Clinical Psychology, 33,* 940–941.

Sommer, B., Avis, N., Meyer, P., Ory, M., Madden, T, Kagawa-Singer, M., ... Adler, S. (1999). Attitudes toward menopause and aging across ethnic/racial groups. *Psychosomatic Medicine, 61,* 868–875.

Springer, S. P., & Deutsch, G. (1998). *Left brain, right brain* (5th ed.). New York: Freeman.

Stairs, A. (1992). Self-image, world-image: Speculations on identity from experiences with Inuit. *Ethos, 20,* 116–126.

Stessman, J., Maaravi, Y., Hammerman-Rozenberg, R, & Cohen, A. (2000). The effects of physical activity on mortality in the Jerusalem 70-year-olds longitudinal study. *Journal of the American Geriatrics Society, 48,* 499–504.

Streitmatter, J. (1993). Gender differences in identity development: An examination of longitudinal data. *Adolescence, 28,* 55–66.

Stroebe, W., Stroebe, M. S., & Abakoumkin, G. (1999). Does differential social support cause sex differences in bereavement outcome? *Journal of Community and Applied Social Psychology, 9,* 1–12.

Struch, N., Schwartz, S. H., & van der Kloot, W. A. (2002). Meanings of basic values for women and men: A cross-cultural analysis. *Personality and Social Psychology Bulletin, 28,* 16–28.

Sulik, K., Johnston, M., & Webb, M. (1981). Fetal alcohol syndrome?: Embryogenesis in a mouse model. *Science, 214,* 936–938.

Swann, W. B., Jr., Hixon, J. G., & De La Ronde, C. (1992). Embracing the bitter "truth": Negative self-concepts and marital commitment. *Psychological Science, 3,* 118–121.

Taylor, S., & Goritsas, E. (1994). Dimensions of identity diffusion. *Journal of Personality Disorders, 8,* 229–239.

Tenenbaum, H. R., & Leaper, C. (2002). Are parents' gender schemas related to their children's gender-related cognitions? A meta-analysis. *Developmental Psychology, 38,* 615–630.

Terry-McElrath, Y. M., & O'Malley, P. M. (2011). Substance use and exercise participation among young adults: Parallel trajectories in a national cohort-sequential study. *Addiction, 106,* 1855–1865.

Thomas, H. (1993). A theory explaining sex differences in high mathematical ability has been around for some time. *Behavioral and Brain Sciences, 16,* 187–189.

Thompson, A., Hollis, C., & Richards, D. (2003). Authoritarian parenting attitudes as a risk for conduct problems: Results from a British national cohort study. *European Child and Adolescent Psychiatry, 12,* 84–91.

Vaillant, G. E., & Milofsky, E. (1980). Natural history of male psychological health: IX. Empirical evidence for Erikson's model of the life cycle. *American Journal of Psychiatry, 137,* 1348–1359.

Van Doom, M. D., Branje, S. J. T., & Meeus, W. H. J. (2011). Developmental changes in conflict resolution styles in parent-adolescent relationships: A four-wave longitudinal study. *Journal of Youth & Adolescence, 40,* 97–107.

Verissimo, M., Santos, A. J., Vaughn, B. E., Torres, N., Monteiro, L., & Santos, O. (2011). Quality of attachment to father and mother and number of reciprocal friends. *Early Child Development and Care, 181,* 27–38.

Votruba-Drzal, E., Coey, R. L., Maldonado-Carreño, Li-Grining, C. P., & Chase-Lansdale, P. L. (2010). Child care and the development of behavior problems among economically disadvantaged children in middle childhood. *Child Development, 81,* 1460–1474.

Voyer, D., Voyer, S., & Bryden, M. P. (1995). Magnitude of sex differences in spatial abilities: A meta-analysis and consideration of critical variables. *Psychological Bulletin, 117,* 250–270.

Wainright, J. L., Russell, S. T., & Patterson, C. J. (2004). Psychosocial adjustment, school outcomes, and romantic relationships of adolexcents with same-sex parents. *Child Development, 75,* 1886–1898.

Walker, L. J. (1986). Experiential and cognitive sources of moral development in adulthood. *Human Development, 29,* 113–124.

Walker, L. J. (1989). A longitudinal study of moral reasoning. *Child Development, 60,* 157–166.

Waters, E., Weinfield, N. S., & Hamilton, C. E. (2000). The stability of attachment security from infancy to adolescence and early adulthood: General discussion. *Child Development, 71,* 703–706.

Weller, S. (2012). Evolving creativity in qualitative longitudinal research with children and teenagers, *International Journal of Social Research Methodology: Theory & Practice, 15,* 119–133.

Wendorf, C. A. (2001). History of American morality research, 1894–1932. *History of Psychology, 4,* 272–288.

Westermeyer, J. F. (2004). Predictors and characteristics of Erikson's life cycle model among men: A 32-year longitudinal study. *The International Journal of Aging & Human Development, 58,* 29–48.

Wheldall, K., & Benner, H. (1993). Conservation without conversation revisited: A replication and elaboration of the Wheldall-Poborca findings on the nonverbal assessment of conservation of liquid quantity. *Educational Psychology, 13,* 49–58.

Whitbourne, S. K., & Hulicka, I. M. (1990). Ageism in undergraduate psychology texts. *American Psychologist, 45,* 1127–1136.

White, S. H. (1990). Child study at Clark University. *Journal of the History of the Behavioral Sciences, 26,* 131–150.

Wiesmann, U., & Hannich, H.-J. (2011). A salutogenic analysis of developmental tasks and ego integrity vs. despair. *The International Journal of Aging & Human Development, 73,* 351–369.

Williams, J. D., & Klug, M. G. (1996). Aging and cognition: Methodological differences in outcome. *Experimental Aging Research, 22,* 219–244.

Woods, C. J. P. (1996). Gender differences in moral development and acquisition: A review of Kohlberg's and Gilligan's models of justice and care. *Social Behavior and Personality, 24,* 375–384.

Wu, J., Witkiewitz, K., McMahon, R. J., & Dodge, K. A. (2010). A parallel process growth mixture model of conduct problems and substance use with risky sexual behavior. *Drug and Alcohol Dependence, 111,* 207–214.

Wynn, K. (1995). Infants possess a system of numerical knowlege. *Current Directions in Psychological Science, 4,* 172–177.

Zach, U., & Keller, H. (1999). Patterns of the attachment-exploration balance of 1-year-old infants from the United States and northern Germany. *Journal of Cross-Cultural Psychology, 30,* 381–388.

Zhang, X., & Nurmi, J.-E. (2012). Teacher-child relationships and social competence: A two-year longitudinal study of Chinese preschoolers. *Journal of Applied Developmental Psychology, 33,* 125–135.

Zhou, Q., Wang, Y., Deng, X., Eisenberg, N., Wolchik, S. A., & Tein, J.-Y. (2008). Relations of temperament and temperament to Chinese children's experience of negative life events, coping efficacy, and externalizing problems. *Child Development, 79,* 493–513.

Zimprich, D., & Martin, M. (2002). Can longitudinal changes in processing speed explain longitudinal age changes in fluid intelligence? *Psychology and Aging, 17,* 690–695.

Theories of Human Development

J. Michael Spector

"All that is valuable in human society depends upon the opportunity for the development accorded to the individual" (Albert Einstein upon his departure from Germany in 1933)

Just as technologies change, so do humans. However, the changes within a human are quite different from changes in technology. Technologies evolve and new technologies are introduced on account of humans. Humans create and change technologies. Changes within a human are more complex. An individual human naturally changes over time. The physiological changes are perhaps most obvious as the infant becomes a child and matures into an adult. Those physiological changes tend to occur regardless of what other humans do or fail to do. Of course, the result of human growth can be nurtured or impeded by a number of factors, such as diet, exercise, exposure to others, and so on.

Humans also develop psychologically, in the sense that some things are simply not able to be easily understood at certain stages of development. As Piaget (1929, 1970) noticed, a very young child does not understand that a quantity (e.g., water in a container) does not change when its spatial arrangement has changed (e.g., the water is poured into a differently shaped container). Language and experience clearly play important roles in psychological development (Newman & Newman, 2007).

Moreover, humans develop socially, although there is perhaps more variation in social development than in physiological or psychological development.

Before taking a short tour of different theories of human development, two additional comments are in order. First, the physiological and psychological changes alluded to above might be regarded as macro-changes in the sense that they apply generally to all humans and refer to major aspects of being at a certain stage in life.

J. Michael Spector, "Theories of Human Development," *Foundations of Educational Technology: Integrative Approaches and Interdisciplinary Perspectives*, pp. 59-65. Copyright © 2012 by Taylor & Francis Group. Reprinted with permission.

In addition, these different stages of development are relatively easy to identify. However, humans also undergo many micro-changes that are particular to individuals and not so easily identified. For example, a person may experience a loss of hearing or lose a certain prejudice that had influenced many prior choices. Both macro- and micro-changes in human development have implications for learning and instruction. However, for the sake of brevity, physiological development is omitted from this discussion of human development. It is clear that hormones and other physiological factors affect learning and development, but such a discussion would take us far from the core concept of the foundations of educational technology.

Second, humans have the ability to bring about some changes in themselves. Not all of human development is pre-coded or determined by external circumstances. Humans make choices and decisions, and those choices and decisions can affect human development. For example, Marie Curie noticed unusual electromagnetic activity associated with pitchblende. She suspected it was related to something similar to uranium rays and decided to try to find out the cause. She devoted several years of concentrated investigation and discovered two new radioactive elements (polonium and radium) with the help of fellow physicist and husband, Pierre Curie. The point here is that because of her decision to investigate she developed a much deeper understanding of the substance called pitchblende, a mineral ore found in many parts of the world, now used in processing uranium. Within any field of inquiry or endeavor, one can cite levels of human development that might include absolute beginner, advanced beginner, competent performer, proficient performer, and intuitive expert (Dreyfus & Dreyfus, 1986).

Based on the notions of physiological, psychological, social, and self-directed development, a few prominent theories of human development are briefly reviewed. The point of understanding these perspectives on human development is to make more effective use of technology to improve learning and instruction in various circumstances with different learners. These theories point to differences in learners that are pertinent to proper support for learning. There are additional individual differences (e.g., prior knowledge and experience, learning styles, gender, culture, etc.) that ought to be considered when planning and implementing support for learning.

Cognitive Developmental Theory (Piaget)

Cognitive developmental theory is the notion that as a person matures, he or she naturally progresses through different stages of cognitive development. The theorist most closely associated with this theory is Jean Piaget, a Swiss genetic epistemologist who studied the cognitive structures of children. Piaget (1929, 1970) proposed four primary stages of cognitive development: (a) a *sensorimotor stage* in which motor control is developed and identifies the self as separate from other objects (roughly birth to age 2); (b) a *preoperational stage* in which objects are identified and associated with symbols through the use of language (roughly ages 3 to 7); (c) a *concrete operational stage*, in which the ability to think logically about objects and events and the notion of conservation is understood (roughly ages 7 to 11); and (d) a *formal operational stage*, which involves the ability to think logically about abstract objects and hypothetical propositions (roughly ages 11 and up).

Piaget's basic outlook is that as a person matures, he or she adapts to the world in different ways. The two basic processes of adaptation are assimilation and accommodation. Assimilation involves taking in that which is perceived, creating internal representations and associating them with pre-existing representations; the assimilation process implies that what is experienced is internally represented so as to fit with existing internal structures. Accommodation occurs when internal structures must change or be created in order to account for new experiences.

While assimilation and accommodation are complementary processes and often occur together, the process of accommodation is related to the notion of cognitive dissonance introduced by Festinger (1957). Festinger argues that people in general seek to avoid conflicting beliefs and opinions. When an occasion arises that creates such a conflict, the individual typically rejects or modifies one or both beliefs to eliminate the dissonance.

A related perspective can be found in Quine and Ullian's (1978) *The Web of Belief*, which is a landmark work in the area of naturalistic epistemology—the same field with which Piaget identified. Quine and Ullian (1978) argue that a person naturally strives for coherence among a set or sets of beliefs. When a new experience is encountered that appears to introduce an inconsistency, minor adjustments are made so as to make the internal representation of the new experience compatible with representations of existing experience. When such adjustments become excessive, the existing internal structure must be reconstructed, similar to Kuhn's (1962) notion of a paradigm shift. The related concepts of accommodation, cognitive dissonance, and paradigm shift within the context of naturalistic epistemology are captured in Wittgenstein's (1922) remark in the *Tractatus Logico-Philosophicus* that the world waxes and wanes as a whole (see *Tractatus* §6.43). While Wittgenstein noted in the *Tractatus* that a person creates internal representations in response to experiences (e.g., "we picture facts to ourselves" at *Tractatus* §2.1), he acknowledged that these internal representations are not separate entities unconnected to or uninfluenced by other internal representations.

A person does not process perceptions and beliefs in a discrete, one-at-a-time manner. On the contrary, a person gradually develops sets of internal mental structures, with the implication that multiple beliefs are nearly always involved in a learning experience. Figuring out how best to leverage existing beliefs and mental structures to make learning effective is an ongoing challenge for teachers and designers, as these beliefs and structures can vary dramatically from one individual to the next.

A final point associated with the cognitive developmental theory is the notion of internal mental structures, which are dealt with in different ways by different cognitive scientists. Johnson-Laird (1983) argues that mental models are fundamental to human reasoning and cognitive development. It is possible to distinguish internal representations created just when needed to explain an unusual phenomenon or puzzling situation from internal structures that are well established and invoked automatically (and often without conscious thought) in order to deal with a problem or situation. Some call the former transient structures *mental models* and the latter established structures *schema*. Mental models can be transformed into schema when created often in similar circumstances. The process of transforming mental models into schema is associated with the notion of developing automaticity in performing recurrent tasks, which is often a targeted outcome in training programs. The process of transforming or decomposing a schema into easily alterable sets of mental models is akin to the process of unlearning, which presents particular challenges to teachers and trainers. It is often more difficult to help a learner unlearn a procedure or complex set of beliefs that have been automated than it was to help that learner acquire the knowledge in the first place (for example, see https://lila.pz.harvard.edu/pdfs/Unlearning_Insightv2010.pdf).

Cognitive Social Mediated Theory (Vygotsky)

The emphasis in cognitive development theory is primarily on the individual. While cognitive development researchers acknowledge the influence of things outside the individual, the focus is on determining markers of individual progress and identifying different stages of cognitive development. However, it is obvious that children are influenced by their peers, teachers, and parents. Moreover, much learning is mediated by language. This realization has led researchers to enlarge the focus to include the social and cultural context in which individual cognitive development occurs. The general premise of cognitive social mediated theory is that individual development is in large part determined by the social and cultural context in which a person is situated (see www.funderstanding.com/content/vygotsky-and-social-cognition).

With regard to child development, it is clear that parents, teachers, and other children provide the context of many or most experiences associated with learning. A child growing up in a rural community on a farm will have experiences quite different from a child growing up in a large urban environment. I recall my parents taking me on a shopping trip to a large nearby city when I was six or seven. The department store had an escalator. I had no idea that such things existed. I had to ask how it worked and why there would be such a thing. The word "escalator" was not part of the vocabulary of a small-town child in the US in the 1950s. Likewise, one can imagine that whatever the context in which a child is raised, there will be some things with which that child will be familiar and many with which the child will not be familiar.

Introducing language about things completely alien to someone's prior experience is not likely to be very meaningful unless that language is accompanied with some kind of realistic experience with which the person can relate. This discussion then comes back to the fundamental role that language plays in learning. Language serves to mediate experience.

An early psychologist who realized this was Lev Vygotsky (1896–1934), whose work did not become widely known outside Russia until decades after his death (Vygotsky, 1962, 1978). In addition to emphasizing the important role of social and cultural interaction, Vygotsky contributed two other significant ideas to cognitive development. First, a more knowledgeable other (MKO), such as a parent, teacher, or another child with more experience, plays a critical role in individual development. Before a child internalizes an idea, it is presented in a social context by a more knowledgeable other. Second, the distance between a child's ability to understand a concept or perform a task independently (indicating internalization of the relevant concepts and individual cognitive development) and that child's ability to understand and perform with the assistance of an MKO is called the zone of proximal development (ZPD). The implication for educational technologists and teachers is that they should focus on the ZPD, as that is where learning progress will most often occur. These extensions to individual cognitive development theory are widely accepted, although there are many variants.

Psychosocial Development Theory (Erikson)

Erik Erikson (1902–1994) was a Danish–German–American psychoanalyst who was especially interested in the development of identity. Erikson (1959, 1968) postulated eight stages of development that span the entire life of an individual (see Table 2.1). The basic idea is that within each stage there are representative crises that form an individual's identity.

Erikson was influenced by Freudian psychology, partly through Sigmund Freud's daughter Anna. The Freudian influence can be seen in the central notion that a person's identity and personality develop in stages. Ego and personal identity play a central role in Erikson's theory of development; the way an individual responds to the inherent conflicts that arise at each stage of development largely determine a person's identity. A lasting aspect of Erikson's contribution is the extension of cognitive development theory beyond adolescence into adulthood, maturity, and old age. Those involved with designing and implementing learning environments, including those for adults, are well advised to consider Erikson's theory. As with all of the development theorists, one conclusion is that not all learners are the same. Many differences are due to different stages of development, whichever development theory guides one's work. In addition to individual differences due to stages of development, there are other individual differences that educational technologists and instructional designers will attend; these will be discussed in Part III of this volume.

TABLE 2.1   Erikson's Eight Psychosocial Stages of Development

Development Stage	Prototypical Psychosocial Crisis	Age Range/Description
Infancy	Hope: trust vs. mistrust	0–1.5 years, birth to walking
Early childhood	Will: autonomy vs. shame/doubt	1–3 years, toilet training, talking
Play age	Purpose: initiative vs. guilt	3–6 years, pre-school, reading
School age	Competence: industry vs. inferiority	5–12 years, early school
Adolescence	Fidelity: identity vs. role confusion	9–18 years, puberty, teens
Young adult	Love: intimacy vs. isolation	18–40 years, dating, parenthood
Adulthood	Care: generativity vs. stagnation	30–65 years, parenting, middle age
Maturity	Wisdom: integrity vs. despair	50+ years, old age

Test Your Understanding

Which of the following are generally regarded as true statements?

1. Some individual differences are a result of being at a particular state of development.
2. Language and thought develop independently.
3. Certain learning tasks are virtually impossible for individuals at an early stage of cognitive development.
4. Mental models are directly observable markers of development.
5. The concepts of a more knowledgeable other and the zone of proximal development are closely related.
6. Development theorists are engaged in descriptive research—describing how individuals develop rather than how individuals should develop.

A Representative Educational Technology Challenge

A government agency that wants to support foreign workers in the country has asked your organization to develop a second-language course for the families of workers being hired by business and industry. These families include spouses, children, and in some cases elderly parents. They come from a variety of different countries and speak different languages. The government agency would like the language course(s) to be offered online at no charge to these families. You have been asked to conduct a needs assessment and training requirements analysis, and report the critical factors that will then inform the design of the course(s).

Learning Activities

1. Identify and describe the key factors involved in a needs assessment and training requirements analysis for the representative problem above.
2. Identify and describe the key factors that are likely to become part of an implementation plan for this problem situation.
3. Indicate and describe the relationships among the key factors that have been identified.
4. Indicate what things are likely to change in the period involved in implementing the plan.
5. Create an annotated concept map that reflects the things indicated in response to the previous four tasks.
6. Reflect on your responses and your concept map, and then describe the assumptions you have made and what resources would be required to implement the solution you have in mind.

References

Dreyfus, H., & Dreyfus, S. (1986). *Mind over machine: The power of human intuition and expertise in the era of the computer*. New York: Free Press.

Erikson, E. H. (1959). *Identity and the life cycle*. New York: International Universities Press.

Erikson, E. H. (1968). *Identity, youth and crisis*. New York: Norton.

Festinger, L. (1957). *A theory of cognitive dissonance*. New York: Wiley.

Johnson-Laird, P. N. (1983). *Mental models: Towards cognitive science of language, inference and consciousness*. Cambridge, UK: Cambridge University Press.

Kuhn, T. S. (1962). *The structure of scientific revolutions*. Chicago, IL: University of Chicago Press.

Newman, B. M., & Newman, P. B. (2007). *Theories of human development*. Mahwah, NJ: Erlbaum.

Piaget, J. (1929). *The child's conception of the world*. New York: Harcourt, Brace Jovanovich.

Piaget, J. (1970). *The science of education and the psychology of the child*. New York: Grossman.

Quine, W. V. O., & Ullian, J. S. (1978). *The web of belief* (2nd ed.). New York: Random House.

Vygotsky, L. S. (1962). *Thought and language*. Cambridge, MA: MIT Press.

Vygotsky, L. S. (1978). *Mind in society*. Cambridge, MA: Harvard University Press.

Wittgenstein, L. (1922). *Tractatus logico-philosophicus* [Tr. C. K. Ogden]. London: Routledge & Kegan Paul.

Links

Explorations in Learning and Instruction: The Theory into Practice Database (TIP), created by Greg Kearsley: see http://tip.psychology.org/.

David Perkins on Unlearning: https://lila.pz.harvard.edu/pdfs/Unlearning_Insightv2010.pdf.

Funderstanding.com website on Lev Vygotsky and Social Cognition: see www.funderstanding.com/content/vygotsky-and-social-cognition.

Learning Theories site on Vygotsky: www.learning-theories.com/vygotskys-social-learning-theory.html.

Other Resources

George Mason University website with online resources for developmental psychology: http://classweb.gmu.edu/awinsler/ordp/index.html.

Lone Star College site with links to anatomy and physiology tutorials: http://nhscience.lonestar.edu/biol/tutoria.html.

NCREL (North Central Regional Educational Laboratory) on Theories of Child Development and Learning: www.ncrel.org/sdrs/areas/issues/students/earlycld/ea7lk18.htm.

Resources for Human Development: www.rhd.org/Home.aspx.

Early Childhood Education and Human Factor

Connecting Theories and Perspectives

Yomi A. Ogunnaike

Yomi A. Ogunnaike

College of Professional Studies

University of Wisconsin-Stevens Point

2100 Main

Stevens Point, WI 54481

oogunnai@uwsp.edu

> Children develop an understanding of the social world through a long slow process of construction. They use what they see in their lives as a basis for constructing an understanding of how people treat each other.
>
> —Carlsson-Paige and Lantieri

Abstract

Early Childhood Education theories provide a framework for understanding the nature, abilities, and how to create learning environments that enhance children's overall development. This article presents an overview of two theoretical perspectives of Lev Vygotsky and Howard Gardner. Through this overview, four essentials underlying Vgotsky and Gardner's ideas were identified and connected to the major tenets of the Human Factor (HF) perspective defined by Senyo Adjibolosoo. The essentials include the child, multiple abilities, learning environment, and teachers. Connecting Constructivists and Human Factor perspectives accentuates the importance of creating space to educate both the "head and the heart" of young children.

Yomi A. Ogunnaike, "Early Childhood Education and Human Factor: Connecting Theories and Perspectives," *Review of Human Factor Studies*, vol. 21, no. 1, pp. 9-26. Copyright © 2015 by International Institute for Human Factor Development. Reprinted with permission. Provided by ProQuest LLC. All rights reserved.

Introduction

This special edition of the HF is focused on Early Childhood Education—where it all begins. This article provides an overview of Constructivist theories, and relevant Developmentally-Appropriate Practices (DAP) that have guided early childhood programs. Further, the chapter examines the connections between the Constructivists and Human Factor proposed by Dr. Senyo Adjibolosoo. Adjibolosoo defined Human Factor (HF) as "the spectrum of personality characteristics and other dimensions of human performance that enable social, economic and political institutions to function and remain functional, over time" (2005, p.45).

For the purpose of this introduction, I focus on the work of two theorists—Lev Vygostky and Howard Gardner. Vygotsky has emphasized that knowledge is socially mediated; a framework that considers the significance of apprenticeship thinking or/and shared learning. Vygotsky's ideas provide a different view from the largely Westernized perspective that has emphasized the "individual exploration and discovery" as posited by Piaget. For Vygotsky, the adage of "it takes a village to raise a child" is central to growth and development. He implies the cultivation of a learning environment that fosters growth through joint participation, conversations, dialogues, interactions and apprenticeship—working with others who are more knowledgeable be it adult or peer.

Howard Gardner has also provided further insight related to child development through his emphasis on the different modes of learning that each child brings into the classroom. Contrary to the single quantitative measure of intelligence, Gardner has emphasized that intelligence is too broad and dynamic to be narrowly defined and restricted to the results of a single aptitude test referred to as the Intelligent Quotient. Intelligence is dynamic, cultural, and defined as the ability to engage successfully in problem solving a problem and creating products in an environment that is natural and rich in context (Armstrong, 2009 p. 6). Gardner has since posited nine different modalities or categories of intelligence.

The overarching question guiding this particular overview is "How do we build a bridge that connects Human Factor and the Constructivist perspective in Early Childhood Education?" In order to establish such a connection, I explore theorists who emphasize the active, sociocultural and dynamic nature of young children's development, and also insist on educating young children within an environment that speaks to more than skill or knowledge acquisition. These theorists emphasize and recognize the salience of caring adults, a safe learning environment, and the give-and-take dance between children's construction of knowledge through connection with others in their immediate and larger environment.

Several constructivists in the field of ECE include Piaget, Vygotsky, Gardner, Dewey, Montessori, Emilia, and Elkind. Here we focus our attention on the works of Lev Vygotsky and Howard Gardner. Vygotsky, a Russian Psychologist gave voice to the importance of the child's sociocultural milieu to provide a more holistic understanding of the child's growth and development. The theory developed by Howard Gardner, Multiple Intelligences, sheds light on the multiple ways that children not only learn, but that they excel in problem solving and understanding their worlds.

In the following sections, I begin with a general overview of the constructivists' perspective. This general overview is followed by a specific discussion of the ideas posited by Vygotsky and Gardner. Relevant Developmentally-Appropriate Practices (DAP) that integrate the ideas of these constructivists are briefly discussed to provide credence to the influence of the socio-cultural context of development and multiple intelligences on early childhood programs. The essentials of the Human Factor perspective and how these connect to the ideas of the constructivists conclude this chapter.

Constructivist Perspective

The Constructivist perspective is central to this theoretical discussion. This particular framework establishes five understandings:

1. **The child is the "protagonist"** on the world's stage of learning. The child creates, constructs, discovers, and decides the "what" and "how" of his or her learning journey.
2. As the protagonist, **the child actively constructs knowledge** through meaningful interactions with the learning environment. These interactions occur largely through play.
3. **Learning is holistic,** and hierarchical as it moves from concrete, simple, particular-to-particular frame of reasoning to a more abstract, flexible, and less egocentric frame. Such frames of learning also takes place within a social context that allows more knowledgeable adults and/or peers to mediate development, especially, cognitive.
4. **The learning environment is one that is deliberately prepared** and provides concrete resources that promote hands-on exploration, problem solving, pro-social behaviors, socio-emotional relationships, and experiences that challenge young children to think beyond their immediate "selves" or/and environment.
5. **The presence of caring adults that model pro-social and ethical behaviors** and also give voice to each child's idea, suggestions, and perspectives is important.

Lev Vygotsky. Vygotsky has emphasized that knowledge is socially-mediated—that is the socio-cultural context of learning reflected in the presence and interactions with more knowledgeable peers and/or adults has a profound impact on learning. Vygotsky has explained that learning occurs when more knowledgeable peers or/and adults "adjusts the amount of guidance needed to support a child's potential level of performance" (Beloglovsky and Daly, 2015, p.18). Further, Vygotsky would have us know that learning has the capacity to enhance development, especially in what Vygotsky called the "Zone of Proximal Development" (ZPD). In such a zone, the child is able to do more through collaboration than as an independent learner. According to Vygotsky, collaborating with another peer or adult facilitates the accessibility of the child's emergent skills, and such skills translate to a much better task performance at a later time. Vygotsky's claim is captured in his summary of the ZPD as "what the child is able to do in collaboration today he will be able to do independently tomorrow." How does a classroom promote ZPD? The answer is through play. Play is central to early childhood education because it allows young children to learn social, cognitive, emotional, language and physical skills that are essential to their overall development (Axelrod, 2015, pp. 57–58). Like many constructivists, Vygotsky makes a strong claim that play creates the Zone of Proximal Development in which children behave and act roles that are out of their reach in reality. Through make-believe play, children accesses emerging skills that enable them to create rules that must be followed, practice self -regulation, engage in problem solving, and deliberately activate prior memory. As such, play is serious work to a child because it facilitates higher cognitive functioning. For Vygotsky, the child in play seems "to stand a level above his head."

Also central to Vygotsky's theory is the significant role of the socio-cultural milieu on the overall development of children. He has stressed the fact that culture determines what a child learns, and that that the construction of knowledge is socially mediated. The socio-cultural context where learning occurs nurtures, expands, and builds a child's repertoire of knowledge and skills. Vygotsky also identified language, symbols, signs, numbers and pictures are cultural "tools" that are used to achieve specific cultural goals similarly to how physical tools are used to accomplish a task.

Summarizing the Vygotstkian framework, Bodrova and Leong (2007, p. 9) and Beloglovsky and Daly (2015, p. 17) highlight that: development is inseparable from its social and cultural context; children construct knowledge and such construction is enhanced through social interactions; language is central to mental development and learning can lead to development. Vygotsky explains that children use cultural tools provided by the adults in their social environments in constructing knowledge. Specifically, the child's manipulations of a toy can lead to incredible discovery of physical qualities such as size, how to hold it or place it (space) of that toy. However, such knowledge is further enriched by the information shared by the adult. For example, the adult can specify colors, specific spatial traits or other attributes outside the range of the child's construct. Thus, social interactions (between the child and other adults) mediate specific knowledge that broadens the child's repertoire.

Like his other constructivist colleagues, Vygotsky, has emphasized the child's ability to build his/her knowledge. However, Vygotsky differed from Piaget, also constructivist in perspective, based on his claim that the acquisition of higher cognitive functioning is a shared process. This claim is reflected in the main principles described as the "more knowledgeable other" and the "Zone of Proximal Development". Beloglovsky and Daly (2015) explain that according to Vygotsky, this "more knowledgeable other" is someone (an adult or another child) who has more experience in mastering a particular task, compared to the child. As such, during a learning episode, this more knowledgeable other is able to "adjust the amount of guidance needed to support a child's potential level of performance". During such an adjustment, the expert provides just enough support to facilitate child's task performance. However, as soon as child progresses, the expert then pulls back to allow child to build his or her mastery of the task. This process of gauged assistance or guidance is what has been popularly described as "scaffolding". Knowing the significant role played by "experts" be they peers or adults has given credence to group projects or peer learning in many Early Childhood classrooms.

The thrust of the Zone of Proximal Development (ZPD), has been summarized by Vygotsky as "what the child is able to do in collaboration today he will be able to do independently tomorrow" (Bodrova and Leong 2007, p. 40). Vygotsky defined the ZPD as "the distance between the actual developmental level as determined by independent problem solving and the level of potential development as determined through problem solving under adult guidance or in collaboration with more capable peers" (Vygotsky, 1978, p. 86). Inherent in this definition is that difference between what a child can do on her own and what she can accomplish through interactions or guidance provided by another. Such interactions may include but not limited to rephrasing questions, finding out what child knows/understands, and providing specific guidance through hints or using familiar words or symbols with child. Thus, as educators, we should aim for not just what the child is able to "learn" in the classroom, but to provide a developmentally-appropriate "challenge" that guides the child into becoming "more" or learning more with assistance. Providing such a challenge should not be a static experience or activity, but one that should be available and sensitive to children's needs or skills on the verge of emergence.

ZPD has the ability to reveal those skills that are about to emerge in a child, and also the limitations of a child's development at a given time. Beloglovsky and Daly comment on the implications of ZPD for learning in the ECE classroom (2015). First of all, educators need to assist children's performance of a task. A major avenue for assisting children's performance is through the provision of ample time for play, especially, make-believe. Vygotsky emphasized that play not only creates the zone of proximal development ZPD but it allows children to "stand taller above herself" as she practices those socio-cognitive skills that are on the edge of emergence. Through play, children create imaginary situations, create and follow specific rules, and act out those roles appropriately. For example, in pretending to be a firefighter, there are specific costumes, equipments and language used in such a context. Such rules cannot be used in practicing to be a teacher or police officer. Play enables children to practice self-regulation, separate thoughts from actions, and deliberately attend to specific stimuli. Similarly, ZPD also teaches educators how they can assess what children can do on their own, and what level of assistance or support is beneficial. ZPD helps to describe what is developmentally appropriate for young children. Vygotsky has explained that educators must teach to the higher level of a child's ZPD in order to enrich learning. If all learning were geared towards only what the child can achieve independently, then there is a limitation to what can be enriched through collaboration. Bodrova and Leong suggested that "teaching must identify both the independent level of performance that marks the lowest level of the ZPD as well as goals that are beyond what the child can do independently, reaching into the ZPD" (2007, p. 45).

For the purpose of this journal, Vygotsky would have us understand that all mental processes exist primarily in a shared space, before it transfers to an independent plane. Compared to the westernized concept of learning through individual construct, Vygotsky emphasized the "shared process of cognition" that propels and enriches the child's ability and knowledge. Such shared cognition acquired through the social context of learning is a prerequisite for the development of higher cognitive growth. Vygotsky also emphasized the fact that learning enhances development, although "there is a complex nonlinear relationship between learning and development"

(Bodrova and Leong, 2007, p. 13). Bodrova and Leong explained that while some children require great deal of learning for development to occur, other children may need only a minimal amount of learning with a resulting maximum development.

Regardless of the learning environment, Vygotsky emphasized that educators must be sensitive to a child's developmental level and abilities, but they must not be limited by such knowledge. Educators need to be able provide that balance between the knowledge of development(al) levels and the provision of learning opportunities that can propel child's development. To provide already mastered skills or learning is to bore those "experts" while an introduction of new skills in the absence of readiness is to frustrate the learning experience and its potentials for all. Parents, teachers, and peers all contribute to how the child's mind works in his or her attempt to learn and wield those important cultural tools in becoming a successful member of that particular society. Vygotsky mentioned that our cultural experiences influence our problem solving strategies because we are largely shaped by our social world. A child's social context or cultural background influences how he or she thinks, listens, communicates, and memorizes.

Howard Gardner. The essence of Gardner's multiple intelligences is in the recognition of differences in abilities, learning styles, and approach to problem solving. Beloglovsky and Daly (2015) explain Gardner's argument that intelligence is pluralistic and children are able to use these multiple intelligences to resolve real life/concrete problems or /and generate new problems for others to solve. Thus, in early childhood classrooms, children are able to use their intelligences to invent and be creative in problem solving. Others offer similar ideas about the significance of multiple intelligences. For example, Carlsson-Paige and Lantieri (2005) explain that Gardner's theory provides us with a broader understanding of how children learn. Children can read, write, are able to move their bodies, use music, numbers, inner explorations and social exchange in demonstrating their abilities to learn through different modalities. Such modalities or capabilities have been grouped into at least nine comprehensive categories. They are as follows:

1. **Bodily-kinesthetic intelligence:** Expertise in using one's body to express feelings, ideas, and engage in problem solving. It is also embodied in the ability to coordinate body movements in prescribed and differentiated ways, and use one's hands to transform or produce things. People who demonstrate this type of intelligence include athletes, sculptors, surgeons, dancers, and actors/actresses.

2. **Linguistic intelligence:** Ability to communicate effectively and sensitively through the written or spoken language. For example, orators that use rhetoric language to convince others, poets or playwright that manipulate the syntax, semantics, and phonology to write and/or tell stories, or report news in a compelling manner.

3. **Logical-mathematical intelligence:** The ability to effectively use numbers and logic to explain problems or situations. The strengths and interests reflective of this intelligence include math, logical reasoning, abstract thinking, pattern recognition, and scientific experiments.

4.   **Musical intelligence:** Ability to compose, produce and show appreciation for rhythm, pitch, and timbre. The strengths and interests reflective of this intelligence include dancing, singing, remembering songs and melodies, playing a musical instrument, and listening to music.

5.   **Spatial intelligence:** Ability to accurately perceive the visual-spatial world and manipulate and portray images. The strengths and interests reflective of this intelligence include completing jigsaw puzzles, sculpture, reading maps and charts, architectural designs/ drawings, doing art and 3-D models of various objects.

6.   **Interpersonal intelligence:** Ability to know and respond appropriately to others' moods, motivations, temperaments, and desires. The strengths and interests reflective of this intelligence include an ability to make friends, be a good listener, socializing, and collaboration with others. Strong leadership conflict resolution skills are also reflected in this intelligence.

7.   **Intra-personal intelligence:** Ability to access and accept one's strengths, limitations, needs, and dreams. The strengths and interests reflective of this intelligence include understanding self, reflecting, pursuing one's interests, and working alone.

8.   **Naturalistic intelligence:** Ability to understand the natural world, one species and habitat at a time. The strengths and interests reflective of this intelligence include an interest in animals, plants, minerals, water, weather, stars, and seasons. Those who enjoy hiking, outdoor adventures, caring for and about animals, preservation advocates demonstrate this intelligence.

9.   **Existential intelligence:** Ability to process information within the context of a larger picture, in relation to the big picture of human existence. The strengths and interests reflective of this intelligence include philosophical thoughts and sayings, global awareness, and advocates for worldwide peace, justice, and equity.

Constructivists like Vygotsky and Gardner emphasize very specific ideas that continue to guide practices in early childhood classrooms. For example, the significance of culture and the social context of learning influence classroom practices, namely the group projects that allow for learning through interactions and joint participation. Gardner's multiple intelligences help us to understand the different modalities or strengths that each child brings to the early childhood classrooms. The notion of culture and different modalities are a few of the Constructivists' ideas that guide major practices in early childhood classrooms referred to as Developmentally-Appropriate Practices (DAP). These practices are not static but they are dynamic as they are formulated in response to the changing framework of the American society and its effect on the young child.

Developmentally—Appropriate Practices (DAP)

Principles of Development and Learning in ECE: According to the National Association for the Education of Young Children (NAEYC), a national organization that provides a framework for practices in early childhood classrooms, there are specific principles of child development that guide the field of Early Childhood Education (see Gestwicki 2007, pp 12–15). Of these basic principles, six are particularly relevant to this discussion.

Development and learning occur in and are influenced by multiple social and cultural contexts: Gestwicki (2007) explains that educators must view development of the child within a communal context-first, within the family, followed by the school, and then within the larger society. Children are capable of learning in several contexts in which they find themselves, and to educate the child is to acknowledge where the child is coming from and provide additional resources that extend and enrich such communal learning. For example, research in ECE attests to the significance of respecting the home language and culture of children (see Ordonez-Jasis, and Ortiz 2006). Thus, educators must acknowledge the role of the child's culture, especially, the home language in the classroom.

Children are active learners, drawing on direct physical and social experience as well as culturally transmitted knowledge to construct their own understanding of the world around them: This principle underlies the major idea of the Constructivists who claim that children act upon their learning environment to figure out how things work.

Play is an important vehicle for children's social, emotional, and cognitive development, as well as a reflection of their development: Described as the optimum context for active construction of knowledge, play is that medium that allows children to interact with others, practice self-control, share personal knowledge and learn to express their emotions.

Development advances when children have opportunities to practice newly acquired skills, as well as when they experience a challenge just beyond the level of their present mastery: Inherent in this principle is the concept of scaffolding, a joint interaction in which the more knowledgeable learner adjusts guidance to build the learner's potential level of performance (see Beloglovsky and Daly 2015, p. 18).

Children demonstrate different modes of knowing and learning and different ways of representing what they know: Gardner posits the notion that there is no single way of showing or demonstrating knowledge. Instead, each person has different modes of learning or what he referred to as "intelligences" that enable him or her to solve a problem or creatively come up with a problem that others can solve.

Children learn best in the context of a community in which they are safe and valued, their physical needs are met, and they feel psychologically secure: Research in early brain development indicates that children learn best in environments that are physically, emotionally, and psychologically safe. In addition to the psychological and physical safety is the presence of caring and nurturing adults that model positive behaviors.

From the discussions of the works of Vygotsky, Gardner, and consideration of the Developmentally-Appropriate Practices, we emphasize the following factors are particularly salient to educating young children in the early childhood classroom: Children are capable of learning and constructing knowledge of their world in a learning environment that promotes diverse styles of learning, diverse resources, and integrates children's cultural background; adults must be respectful, create a safe, nurturing, hands-on, and problem solving learning environment that engages children in learning beyond their present capacity/ability adults must be mindful in observing, documenting, and modeling appropriate social behaviors that are worthy of emulation.

In the next few paragraphs, I will briefly discuss the Human Factor, its components, and connect its essential claims to the Constructivist perspectives.

Human Factor Perspective

Adjibolosoo defined Human Factor (HF) as "the spectrum of personality characteristics and other dimensions of human performance that enable social, economic and political institutions to function and remain functional, over time" (2005, p. 45). Adjibolosoo posits the following about the HF dimensions:

They have the ability to preserve and sustain how society operates,

They can be positive or negative depending on the "network of committed persons who stand firmly by them",

-There are six components to these dimensions, and they include *Spiritual Capital, Moral Capital, Aesthetic Capital, Human Capital, Human Abilities* and the *Human Potential* (see Adjibolosoo, 2005). The six components are defined as follows:

Spiritual Capital: This refers to a person's ability to connect with and to the Divine- highest power and authority that govern the universe—GOD.

Moral Capital: This refers to a person's ability to differentiate between wrong and right. This ability is reflected in honesty, trustworthiness, integrity and faithfulness.

Aesthetic Capital: This refers to the ability or quality of a person to appreciate beauty, and differentiate such from what is ugly. This ability is reflected in appreciation for the arts—music, dance, and drama.

Human Capital: This refers to a person's acquired skills and know-how, relevant knowledge and skills that promote an effective and successful participation in any societal institution. Human Capital is reflected in human experiences, analytical, technical, and communication skills, emotional health, and physical well—being. Human Capital is acquired through formal and informal schooling beginning during early childhood education.

Human Abilities: This refers to a person's ability to perform tasks in an effective and efficient manner. Human Abilities comprise of intelligence, diligence, motivation, wisdom, and competence. Adjibolosoo (2005, p. 47) did note "Human Abilities allows one to make effective and efficient applications of one's Human Capital".

Human Potential: This refers to a person's undeveloped abilities, talents, and skills. These skills need to be identified and "grown" in order for them to be successfully utilized by the individual.

Adjibolosoo (2005) claims that the quality of one's Human Factor is central to how the individual relates to others. The interactions among the six components of the Human Factor help to establish the individual's actions, attitude, and effectiveness, particularly, in leadership roles or position. To maximize one's potentials in relating to others, each of us must hone the quality of each of these six dimensions of the Human Factor. Following from these claims, several questions arise that include: *How are these qualities identified? Who does the identifying? How and Where are these honed?* The answers to these questions are reflected in the learning environment where the journey of education begins at the Human Factor Leadership Academy established by Adjibolosoo.

The Human Factor perspective, as with many Constructivist perspectives, believes and engages transformational education rather than programs that are solely aimed at knowledge and skill acquisition. It is about educating the individual in terms of recognizing, developing and honing those traits, abilities, and behaviors that promote fairness, justice, integrity, and the well-being of the community. Citing the ideas proposed by Berman, Carlsson-Paige and Lantineri (2005) explain that educating young children is a process that entails the recognition and encouragement of emerging behaviors and values. Where does such recognition and encouragement take place? They do in a learning environment where children know they are cared for and cared about. Secondly, where children are exposed to adults who model pro-social and ethical behaviors; and are provided opportunities to engage in problem solving, and practice the act of decision—making. Such an environment reflects Adjibolosoo's model of education described as Transformational Developmental Education [TDE] established at the Human Factor Leadership Academy, Akatsi, Ghana.

At the core of early childhood education at the Human Factor Leadership Academy (HFLA), is the provision of a propelling environment that recognizes, encourages, and nurtures the cultivation of desired behaviors, values, and skills underlying the components of the HF in every child. Adjibolosoo (2005) likens such an environment to a garden in which each child is likened to a fragile bud that is grown and tendered till it blooms. Thus, the adult is responsible for nurturing and nursing the traits that propel the child toward the achievement of her or his full potential. There is no hurried curriculum or emphasis on acquiring one particular skill over others. On the contrary, Adjioblosoo emphasizes two terms to describe the process of education at the HFLA.

These are "transformation" and "wholeness". Transformation takes place as the adult nurtures each child in developing desired traits of the HF, and wholeness "reflects the idea of assisting the individual to be transformed—in all aspects of being, body, soul, and spirit" (2005, p. 198).

Connecting Human Factor to Early Childhood Education

To establish any connections between Human Factor (HF) and the Constructivists' perspectives, it is imperative to identify and discuss four essentials of HF that resonate with the ideas of the Constructivists. The following represent the common essentials underlying the HF and Constructivists' perspectives:

Child/Individual: At the core of Adjibolosoo's definition of Human Factor is the individual—a child, an adult. Such an individual is dynamic, capable of learning from her environment, and possesses specific skills that are recognized and nurtured by others. These skills can be positive or negative depending on the "network of committed persons who stand firmly by them". The vision for a positive conglomeration of HF components is a major impetus for the establishment of Adjibolosoo's Human Factor Leadership Academy (HFLA) in his native country, Ghana, West Africa. Adjibolosoo strongly believes that the early childhood years matter because this is where the components can be observed and "tinkered" with in a nurturing environment (Adjibolosoo 2005). Knowing that others play a significant role in growing and transforming the child's skills and abilities, it is better that the child starts and continues the journey of life within positive social contexts, such as school, families, and the immediate community. Examining the ideas of the constructivists, beginning with Piaget, Vygotsky and Gardner, the child is active, capable of learning and constructing knowledge within multiple contexts. While the child is the "all in all" as she interacts with toys and the environment, Vygotsky emphasizes the socio-cultural context of learning in which others play a significant role in the child's learning adventures. Both the HF and constructivists acknowledge that the starting point is the child who is capable of learning and interacting with others. Further, the underlying premise of Developmentally-Appropriate Practices upheld by many early childhood programs is the belief in the child's capability (see Gestwicki (2007, pp. 12–15).

Skills/Abilities: Central to the definition of Human Factor is the notion of plurality. Adjibolosoo defined Human Factor (HF) as "the spectrum of personality characteristics and other dimensions of human performance that enable social, economic and political institutions to function and remain functional, over time" (2005, p. 45). HF has six components that include *Spiritual Capital, Moral Capital, Aesthetic Capital, Human Capital, Human Abilities* and the *Human Potential.* Such plurality is similarly reflected in Gardner's Multiple Intelligences. Nine intelligences have been identified so far and the include *Spatial, Logical Mathematical, Bodily-Kinesthetic, Musical, Interpersonal, Intra personal, Naturalist,* and *Existential.* Both Human Factor perspectives and the Multiple Intelligences provide specific explanations about the dynamics of the plurality that underlies their ideas. Adjibolosoo (2005, p. 48) emphasizes that all six dimensions must be honed because the quality of the Human Factor underlines human behavior and performance. Regarding Multiple Intelligences, Armstrong (2009, pp. 15–16) helps us to understand the following: that all intelligences interact in complex ways; each person has all the intelligences and is able to "grow" each to a certain level of mastery; people differ in their demonstration of talents within and across the intelligences. For example, a person may not be a good reader, yet is able to excel in telling stories.

Environment: As stated earlier, the development and honing of the HF components takes place in a propelling environment where there are caring adults that identify, nurture, and gently guide the development and transformation of the quality of the child's *Spiritual Capital, Moral Capital, Aesthetic Capital, Human Capital, Human Abilities* and the *Human Potential*. Likewise, the presence of others e.g. teachers, parents, and/or more competent peers is central to Vygotsky's socio-cultural theory. Vygotsky emphasizes that the social context mediates the acquisition of higher cognitive functioning, social context being everything in the child's environment with a direct or indirect influence by culture- family, school, community, and society (Bodrova and Leong 2007). Vygotsky notes that the key to a child's cognitive development is his/ her appropriation of cultural knowledge. Different cultures emphasize different styles of learning and problem solving. In cultures that emphasize the importance of non-verbal communication, apprentice-ship training requires the utilization of a different set of skills compared to another culture that emphasizes verbal skills. Rogoff andassociates have studied apprenticeship training in different cultures and their findings attest to the role of social context and cultural values in cognitive functioning (see Bodrova and Leong 2007). Gestwicki (2007) writes that children deserve to be cared for in healthy and safe environments where they can develop warm relationships with adults over time. Creating a healthy environment implies the provision of time, activities, and resources that enhance the child's developing skills and abilities. Inherent in such an environment is the opportunity for play, and stated earlier, play is central to the development of the child (Axelrod, 2015; Bodrova and Leong 2007; Gestwicki, 2007).

Teachers or Network of Committed Persons: Caring adults that model behaviors that teach kindness, fairness, and challenge young children beginning at age three to practice what is "right", "proper" and "respectful" are the educators at Adjibolosso's HFLA. These caring adults are the ones who prepare the enabling or propelling environment, observe, nurture, and gently support the transformation of the child's HF components into the fullness of their potential. They also continue to guide and build the child's potentials through "art of teaching and tools of socialization" that utilize life stories, proverbs, mythology, ancient wisdom, role modeling, riddles, personal studies, reflections and more (Adjibolosoo, 2005). According to Constructivists, e.g. Vygotsky, teachers, parents, adults, even peers, are major participants in the child's cognitive functioning. Bodrova and Leong write "children learn or acquire a mental process by sharing or using it when interacting with others. Only after this period of shared experience can the child internalize and use the mental process independently" (2007, p. 11). Central to the role of others in the acquisition of higher cognitive functioning is the Zone of Proximal Development (ZPD). This zone is defined as "the distance between the actual developmental level as determined by independent problem solving and the level of potential development as determined through problem solving under adult guidance or in collaboration with more capable peers" (Vygotsky, 1978, p. 86). In his words, Vygotsky has this to say about the ZPD "what the child is able to do in collaboration today, he will be able to do independently tomorrow" (Bodrova and Leong, 2007, p. 40).

Conclusion

Human Factor has a lot to teach us about the development of children and how adults contribute to the process of growing and cultivating those dimensions that enrich not only the child's life but those that create a just, honest, and compassionate society for all. These are also reflected in the ideas of the constructivists in their emphases on the active role of the child, nurturing adults, and presence of a deeply caring environment that challenges the child beyond his or her level of current mastery. Based on their beliefs that there is more to a child than the acquisition of skills and knowledge, both HF and Constructivists enjoin us to be mindful of how we view children, work and walk with them, engage their minds, and prepare them for a world beyond their immediate environment. Carlsson-Page and Lantieri (2005) explain that because children's ability to gradually move from concrete to more abstract ways of thinking occurs within family and societal contexts, and affect their social, cognitive, moral, and emotional development, educators must value what the child brings to the learning environment. Specifically, they suggest making space for what they refer to as "head and the heart" curriculum that values, equally, children's social, emotional and cognitive abilities.

References

Adjibolosoo, S. 2005. *The Human Factor in Leadership Effectiveness*. Mustang, OK: Tate Publishing.

Armstrong, T. 2009.*Multiple Intelligences in the Classroom*. Alexandria, VA: ASCD.

Axelrod, Y. 2015."Todos Vamos a Jugar, Even the teachers"-Everyone playing together". In Bohart, Charner, and Koralek. (Eds). *Spotlight on Young Children: Exploring Play*. Washington DC: NAEYC. (pp. 56–64).

Beloglovsky, M. and Daly, L. 2015. *Early Learning Theories Made Visible*. St. Paul, MN: Redleaf.

Bodrova, E. and Leong, D. J. 2007. *Tools of the Mind: The Vygotskian Approach to Early Childhood Education*. Upper Saddle River, NJ: Pearson Prentice Hall.

Carlsson-Paige, N. and Lantieri, L. 2005. A Changing Vision of Education in Noddings (Ed). *Educating Citizens for Global Awareness*. New York, NY: Teachers College Press (pp. 107–121)

Gestwicki, C. 2007. *Developmentally Appropriate Practices: Curriculum and Development in Early Education*. Canada: Thomas Delmar Learning.

Morrison, G. S. 2012. *Early Childhood Education Today.* Upper Saddle River, NJ: Pearson Prentice Hall.

Ordonez-Jasis, R and Ortiz, R. 2006. "Reading their worlds: Working with Diverse Families to Enhance Children's Early Literacy Development." *Young Children*; 61 1 42–48.

Vygotsky, L.S. 1978. *Mind and Society: The Development of Higher Psychological Processes.* Cambridge, MA: Harvard University Press.

Discussion Questions

1. Explain different stages of human development. In your opinion, what are some concerns at different stages of development?
2. Explain the distinguishing characteristics of Erik Erikson's psychosocial theory, Jean Piaget's cognitive development theory, Lev Vygotsky's sociocultural theory, and Howard Gardner's multiple intelligences theory?

UNIT II

COGNITIVE DEVELOPMENT

Selections from Cognitive Development During Early Childhood

Megan Clegg-Kraynok, Kelvin L. Seifert, and Robert J. Hoffnung

Source: Monkey Business Images/Shutterstock.com.

FOCUSING QUESTIONS

- What are the special features and strengths of preschoolers' thinking?
- How does the language of preschool children differ from that of older children?
- What social and cultural factors account for variations in preschoolers' language and speech?
- What constitutes good early childhood education?

Megan Clegg-Kraynok, Kelvin L. Seifert, and Robert J. Hoffnung, Selections from "Cognitive Development During Early Childhood," *Child and Adolescent Development: A Chronological Approach*, pp. 199-206, 216-219, R1-R36. Copyright © 2019 by Academic Media Solutions. Reprinted with permission.

COGNITIVE DEVELOPMENT

In addition to their physical changes, preschool children develop new abilities to represent objects and experiences. They begin to notice, for example, that their particular way of viewing the objects across a room differs from the perspective of a family member already sitting on the other side. They begin to distinguish between appearances and reality; that is, when you cover a doll with a costume, it still is "really" the same doll. And they become able to communicate new understandings such as these to others. The changes are in thinking, or *cognition,* and are called *cognitive development.*

Thinking among Preschoolers

Much of the research on cognitive development owes its intellectual roots to the observations and theorizing of Jean Piaget. During the 1960s and 1970s, considerable effort went toward testing his ideas about cognitive development. Overall, the research led first to modifications of, and in some cases, challenges to, Piaget's major proposals, such as the existence of comprehensive cognitive stages that unfold in a predictable order or the idea that thinking is really an individual activity rather than a social one. To put these later findings in proper context, however, we must first keep in mind Piaget's key ideas about the changes young children experience during the preschool years.

Piaget's Preoperational Stage

At about age two, according to Piaget, children enter a new stage in their cognitive development (Piaget, 1963; Wadsworth, 1996). Infancy has left them with several important accomplishments, such as the belief that objects have a permanent existence and the capacity to set and follow simple goals, such as emptying all the clothes from every drawer in the house. Infancy has also left them with the knowledge that all of their senses register the same world; now a child knows that hearing his mother in the next room means that he will probably see her soon and that seeing her probably also means he will hear from her.

The **preoperational stage**, roughly ages two through seven, extends and transforms these skills. During this stage, children become increasingly proficient at using *symbols*—words or actions that stand for other things. During this period, they also extend their belief in object permanence to include *identities,* or constancies, of many types: a candle remains the same even as it grows shorter from burning, and a plant growing on the windowsill remains the same plant, even though its growth changes its appearance from day to day.

preoperational stage In Piaget's theory, the stage of cognition characterized by increasing use of symbolic thinking but not yet by logical groupings of concepts.

Preoperational children also sense many *functional relationships,* or variations in their environments that normally occur together. Preschool children usually know that the hungrier they are, the more they will want to eat; the bigger they are, the stronger they tend to be; and the faster they walk, the sooner they will arrive somewhere. Of course, they still do not know the

The play of preschoolers often relies on their growing abilities to represent objects and events symbolically. A cardboard box becomes a car, and the porch becomes a racetrack.

Source: Orange-studio/ Shutterstock.com.

precise functions or relationships in these examples—exactly how *much* faster they will arrive if they walk a particular distance more quickly—but they do know that a relationship exists.

These are all cognitive strengths of preschool children, and they mark cognitive advances over infancy. But as the *pre-* in the term *preoperational* implies, Piaget's original theorizing actually focused on the limitations of young children's thinking relative to that of school-age children. The term *operations* referred to mental actions that allow a child to reason about events he or she experiences. Piaget's observations suggested that from age two to seven, children often confuse their own points of view with those of other people, cannot classify objects and events logically, and often are misled by single features of their experiences. As later sections of this chapter point out, however, more recent research has substantially qualified this perspective; in essence, it has found that children often are more cognitively astute than Piaget realized. Their specific cognitive skills are all based on a key ability that Piaget *did* recognize: the ability to represent experiences symbolically.

Symbolic Thought

As we just noted, *symbols* are words, objects, or behaviors that stand for something else. They take this role not because of their intrinsic properties but because of the intentions of the people who use them. A drinking straw is just a hollow tube and does not become a symbol until a preschooler places it in the middle of a mound of sand and declares it to be a birthday candle. Likewise, the sound /bahks/ lacks symbolic meaning unless we all agree that it refers to a hollow object with corners: *box*.

Probably the most significant cognitive achievement of the preoperational period is the emergence and elaboration of **symbolic thought**, the ability to think by making one object or action stand for another. Throughout their day, two-year-olds use language symbolically, such as when they say "Milk!" to procure a white, drinkable substance from the refrigerator. They also use symbolic thought in make-believe play by pretending to be people or creatures other than themselves. By about age four, children's symbolic play often combines complex actions (getting down on all fours), objects (using a table napkin for a saddle), language (shouting "Neigh!"), and coordination with others (getting a friend to be a rider).

> **symbolic thought** Mentally using one thing to represent something else.

Symbolic thinking helps preschool children organize and process what they know (Carlson & Beck, 2009; Goldman, 1998; Nelson, 1996). Objects and experiences can be recalled more easily if they have names and compared more easily if the child has concepts that can describe their features. Symbols also help children communicate what they know to others, even in situations quite different from the experience itself. Having gone to the store, they can convey this experience to others either in words ("I went shopping") or through pretend play ("Let's play school, and I'll be the teacher."). By its nature, communication fosters social relationships among children, but it also fosters cognitive development by allowing individual children to learn from the experiences of others. More precisely, communication allows individuals to learn from the symbolic representations of others' experiences.

Egocentrism in Preschool Children

Egocentrism refers to the tendency of a person to confuse his or her own point of view and that of another person. The term does not necessarily imply selfishness at the expense of others, but a centering on the self in thinking. Young children often show egocentrism in this sense, but not always. Piaget illustrated their egocentrism by showing children a table on which models of three mountains had been constructed and asking them how a doll would see the three mountains if it sat at various positions around the table. Three-year-olds (the ones in Piaget's preoperational stage) commonly believed the doll saw the layout no differently than they did (Piaget & Inhelder, 1967).

> **egocentrism** Inability to distinguish between one's own point of view and that of another person.

On the other hand, when the task concerns more familiar materials and settings, even preschool children adopt others' spatial perspectives (Steiner, 1987). For example, instead of using Piaget's three-mountain model, suppose we use a "police officer" doll that is searching for a "child" doll and place them among miniature barriers that sometimes obscure the dolls' "view" of each other and sometimes do not. When these procedures are followed, four-year-olds have relatively little difficulty knowing when the two dolls can "see" each other and when the barriers truly are "in the way."

In oral communication, preschoolers also show distinct but incomplete egocentrism. A variety of studies have documented that preschoolers often explain tasks rather poorly to others, even though their language and understanding are otherwise skillful enough to explain them better

(Nelson, 1996). Copying a simple diagram according to instructions from a preschooler can prove next to impossible, no matter how sensitive the listener is. On the other hand, preschool children do show awareness of the needs of a listener. They explain a drawing more clearly, for example, to a listener who is blindfolded, apparently because the blindfold emphasizes the listener's need for more complete information.

In these studies, young children show both similarity to and difference from the adults they will become. All of us, young or old, show egocentrism at times; indeed, our own thinking is often the only framework on which we can base our actions and conversations with others, at least initially. As we mature, though, we learn more about others' thoughts, views, and feelings, as well as more about how to express ourselves more precisely. In these ways, we (hopefully!) differ from four-year-olds.

Other Aspects of Children's Conceptual Development

Along with their symbolic skills, preschool children develop specific cognitive skills. They become able to classify objects, and by the end of the early childhood period, some can even attend to changes in objects involving more than one feature at a time. They move beyond rote counting to a meaningful understanding of the concept of *number*. They also acquire an intuitive sense of the differences among fundamentally different types of concepts, such as the difference between a living dog and a toy robot made to act like a dog.

Classification Skills

Classification refers to the placement of objects in groups or categories according to some specific standards or criteria. Young preschool children, even those just three years old, can reliably classify objects that differ in just one dimension, or feature, especially if that dimension presents fairly obvious contrasts. Given a collection of pennies and nickels, a preschooler usually can sort them by color, which is their most obvious dimension of difference. Given a boxful of silverware, a young child might sort the items by type: knives, forks, and spoons. Or she might group dishes by how they are used in real life, putting each cup with one saucer rather than separating all the cups from all the saucers. These simple groupings represent cognitive advances over infancy.

> **classification** Grouping of objects according to standards or criteria.
>
> **reversibility** Ability to return mentally to earlier steps in a problem.
>
> **conservation** A belief that certain properties (such as quantity) remain constant, despite changes in perceived features, such as dimensions, position, and shape.

Reversibility and Conservation

Some classification problems require **reversibility** in thinking, or the ability to undo a problem mentally and go back to its beginning. If you accidentally drop a pile of papers on the floor, you may be annoyed, but you know that in principle the papers are all there: you believe (correctly) that the papers that have scattered can be "unscattered" if you pick them up and sort them into their correct order again. Reversibility, it turns out, contributes to a major cognitive achievement of middle childhood: **conservation**, or the ability to perceive that certain properties of an object remain the same or constant despite changes in the object's appearance. On average, children do not achieve conservation until about age six.

To understand reversibility and conservation, consider the task shown in Figure 4.1. First, you show a preschool child two tall glasses with exactly the same amount of water in each. Then the child watches you pour the water from one of the glasses into a third, wide glass. Naturally, the water line in the wide glass will be lower than it was in the tall one. Finally, you ask the child, "Is there more water in the wide glass than in the [remaining] tall glass, or less, or just as much?"

Children less than five years old typically say that the tall glass has either less or more water than the wide glass, but not that the two glasses are the same. According to Piaget, this happens because the child forgets the identity of the water levels seen only a moment earlier; in this sense, the child is a nonreversible thinker and cannot imagine pouring the water back again to prove the glasses' equality. Instead, the child is limited to current appearances. More often than not, a big difference in appearance leads a child to say that the amount of water changes as a result of its being poured. In Piagetian terms, the child fails to conserve, or to believe in the constancy of the amount of liquid, despite its visible changes (Inhelder & Piaget, 1958). Not until the early school years do conservation and reversibility become firmly established.

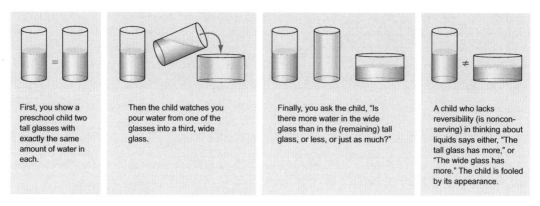

FIGURE 4.1 Conservation of Liquid Quantity

Does a child believe that liquid quantity remains constant (is "conserved"), despite changes in its shape? The method illustrated here, or some variation of it, is often used to answer this question.

In the meantime, tasks that require conservation are affected significantly by how they are presented or described to the child. When given a series of conservation tasks, for example, a child tends to alternate conserving with nonconserving responses (Elbers et al., 1991). Why? Perhaps repeating the question makes some children believe that the experimenter wants them to change their response; after all, why else would she repeat herself? Because most children begin the conservation task by agreeing that the glasses hold equal amounts of water, obliging children may feel compelled to give nonconserving responses against their own better judgment. It seems, therefore, that children may take Piagetian tasks as social events, as well as cognitive ones.

The Concept of Number

Like many parents, Piaget correctly noted that children do not fully grasp how the conventional number system works during the first few years of life (Piaget, 1952). Preschoolers may, of course, count, such as when a three-year-old says, "One, two, three, blast off!" before tossing a ball high into the air. But such counting, Piaget argued, lacks understanding; it essentially is a rote activity, though children as young as two or three understand the *magnitude* of numbers, which is demonstrated when a child asks for "more" or "a lot more" when a parent is doling out a treat (Ginsburg, Cannon, Eisenband, & Pappas, 2008). To fully understand the concept of number, a child must comprehend three ideas. The first is that a one-to-one correspondence exists between items in a set and number names. The second is *cardinality,* the idea that the total number of a set corresponds to the last number named when the items are counted. And the third is *ordinality,* the concept that numbers always occur in a particular order (the second item to be counted is always called the "second," for example).

Research stimulated by these ideas about number generally has concluded that Piaget underestimated preschoolers' knowledge of number. Many four-year-olds, and even some three-year-olds, can reliably say the numbers in sequence, at least up to some modest limit such as *five* or *six*. They also know that different sets of items should be counted with the same sequence of numbers, that each item should be counted only once, and that any set can be counted in more than one order. For this and other reasons, some psychologists have argued that children may have an innate conception of number, or at least that they can learn underlying notions of number from appropriate experiences during infancy (Case, 1998; Ginsburg et al., 2008; Kirschner, 1997).

Cognition as Social Activity

Variations in cognitive performance occur partly because young children depend on the social context or circumstances to develop new thinking skills. In spite of our stereotypes of thinking as a solitary, independent activity, children learn not only from interacting with objects and the physical environment but also from interacting with adults or others with more experience. Psychologists who study this sort of thinking often call it **situated cognition** and call their perspective **social constructivism** (Kirschner & Whitson, 1997; Rogoff et al., 1993). A parent who is cooking dinner, for example, may invite a four-year-old to help with preparations, during which the child observes and works on a number of cognitive tasks: measuring amounts for ingredients, sequencing the steps

> **situated cognition** Thinking that occurs jointly with others and is embedded in a particular context or activity setting.
>
> **social constructivism** A theory that views learning as resulting from active dialogue and interaction between an individual and his or her community.
>
> **activity settings** Group situations in which a shared focus of attention and shared goals facilitates an individual's learning from others in the group.

in the preparations, attending to the time needed for each task. Interactions about the tasks being pursued in common form a context, or **activity setting**, for learning (Lave, 1997). In an activity setting, the older or less experienced individuals provide problems and activities, as well as tasks that allow a younger, less experienced person to become a legitimate—though perhaps marginal or peripheral—participant in the situation. When cooking, for example, the parent determines the menu and in other ways sets the agenda for the activity: "We will make X instead of Y tonight." The parent also provides tasks for the apprentice-cook (in this case, the child) to do. The tasks ensure that the child belongs or participates successfully, although they also provide only a marginal role for the child at first, in keeping with his or her immaturity and lack of experience with the challenges of cooking.

Viewed this way, thinking seems far less solitary than Piaget pictured it, and far more social. Children figure things out not by manipulating objects and observing the results of the manipulations but by interacting (in activity settings) with a community of people, including parents, teachers, and peers. In doing so, the young, inexperienced preschooler is able to work on problems or tasks that might prove too difficult to attempt alone; yet the support and guidance of others allow considerable success! The interactions that allow the child to succeed are sometimes called the **zone of proximal development** (or **ZPD**). The concept of the ZPD originated with the Russian psychologist Lev Vygotsky (Newman & Holzman, 1993; Vygotsky, 1978) and has created a lot of interest among developmental psychologists because it suggests ways in which knowledge and thinking skills may originate and evolve. Consider this conversation between a six-year-old girl and her grandfather, while the two sort some scrap lumber piled behind the grandfather's hardware business:

> **zone of proximal development** According to Vygotsky, the level of difficulty at which problems are too hard for children to solve alone but not too hard when given support from adults or more competent peers.

Grandfather: We have to put the spruce here and the pine over there.

Girl: Spruce here? (Tosses one piece, but to the wrong pile)

Grandfather: No, there. (Moves her piece to the correct pile)

Girl: What's this? (Notices letter S scribbled in pencil on a piece)

Grandfather: That's for *spruce*. Put it with the spruce.

Girl: (Pondering the letter S). Spruce. OK. (Tosses piece correctly) So this is pine? (Looks at a piece with a *P* written on it)

Grandfather: Yep. Put it over there. (The two continue sorting for a while. Girl examines each piece for letters. Eventually she finds one with no letter written on it.)

Girl: Someone should write the name on this one. (Notices a knothole in the piece) I think it's pine.

Grandfather: You're right about that. Here's a pencil. (Tosses her a pencil)

Girl: (Writes *P* on the piece of scrap pine.) Know what? I can write *pine*! (Smiles) I bet I can write *spruce*, too.

Grandfather: (Looks at the letter *P* she has written.) Yeah, says *pine* all right. You might say it says *pine*.

In this example, the grandfather (and his pile of scrap wood) provided an activity setting in which the girl learned about differences between two woods, spruce and pine, as well as a way to represent the differences with letters. Without his presence and comments, considered *scaffolding* by Vygotsky, she might not have succeeded as well in this task. On the other hand, the grandfather did not simply "teach" the girl how to sort wood or to read the letters *S* and *P*, as a teacher might conventionally do in a classroom. Instead, he provided a task needed in his world (sorting the scrap wood is part of his business) and a way to involve the girl in the task. The interactions create a zone of proximal development for the girl. When she makes a mistake, the grandfather either simply corrects it matter-of-factly (such as when she tosses a piece in the wrong pile) or revises his own goals temporarily to fit hers (such as when

Much cognitive change occurs because of the mutual development of meaning that happens in the "zone of proximal development," where two people focus on a common activity. In this case, the mother stimulates her daughter to learn about cooking, and the daughter stimulates the mother to learn about the daughter's growing knowledge and abilities.

Source: Dragon Images/ Shutterstock.com.

she claims, mistakenly, that she has spelled the whole word *pine* using only its first letter). At the beginning of the task, the girl needs more assistance, or scaffolding. However, as the girl comes to understand and, eventually, become an expert at the task, she needs less scaffolding, or assistance.

As you might suppose, the nature of the ZPD depends on the experiences and circumstances of the child. Parents with "bookish" interests, for example, and the resources and time to provide book-related activity settings will more often provide ZPDs that encourage bookish and school-oriented skills in their children. Those with an outgoing, social disposition will provide ZPDs that encourage interpersonal interest and sensitivity in their children. Yet, reproduction of parents' priorities is not inevitable. Much also depends on how a child interprets an activity setting. An opportunity to learn to play the piano, for example, can be experienced as either attractive or boring, or as either an invitation or burdensome drudgery. What is provided is not necessarily what the child takes up or appropriates (Cobb et al., 1997; Guralnick, 2008).

Neostructuralist Theories of Cognitive Development

As the studies described so far suggest, preschoolers show considerable new strengths in using symbolic thought. They can take others' perspectives to some extent, develop a usable theory of how the human mind works, and distinguish between appearances and reality at least some of the time. Many of Piaget's classic observations on Swiss children have proven true: preschool children do have trouble focusing on two dimensions of an object at once and therefore have difficulty with conservation tasks throughout most of the preschool period. Other Piagetian observations have underestimated children's ability and stimulated research that has led to new ways of thinking about children's capacities. For example, unlike Piaget's claims, preschool children have a partial understanding of number.

Research has complicated our picture of children's cognitive development. Many psychologists have sought to keep Piaget's commitment to stagelike progressions in development and at the same time revise the content or details of those progressions (Case, 1998). Instead of proposing comprehensive, "grand" stages of thinking, as Piaget did, they argue that stages may be much more focused in content. Research based on this premise has, in fact, identified stages of spatial representation, of shapes, of mathematical ability, of patterns, and of interpersonal awareness, among others (Case, 1992; Ginsburg et al., 2008). Each of these skills seems to develop through predictable stages, but do so independently of the other domains. As individuals, children therefore show unique patterns and timing of development across many areas of thinking and skills (Wozniak & Fischer, 1993).

This newer view of cognitive stages is sometimes called **neostructuralist theory**, or *neo-Piagetian theory* because of its roots in the ideas of Piaget. As a result of focusing attention on more specific cognitive achievements, it has also paid more attention to *how,* or by what processes, children acquire new cognitive skills. One neostructuralist line of research explored the process of learning to draw by noting how it consists of the successive coordination of simpler skills

> **neostructuralist theory** Relates to recent theories of cognition that emphasize the structure or organization of thinking.

(Dennis, 1992). Natalia begins her second year of life able to visually track objects as well as reach for objects. With practice, by the time she reaches age three, Natalia has learned to coordinate these two schemes into a single cognitive skill that enables scribbling. As she continues to practice with this newly consolidated scheme, she begins coordinating it with other, more advanced schemes, such as *comparing* scribbles with the orientation and edges of the paper. When tracking edges of a paper and tracking scribbles eventually become coordinated, Natalia can finally begin controlling lines and curves. Now the stage is set for her first representational drawings, such as stick-figure people.

From the neostructuralist perspective, then, cognitive development during early childhood is not all of one piece when it unfolds but has many components—many forms of thinking, as well as perceptual and language developments. As a result, it is important to understand each piece separately from the others and to combine them to get a well-rounded picture of young children. Therefore, in the next section we look at another major piece of the puzzle of children's thinking: language acquisition.

WHAT DO YOU THINK?

What do you think parents of young children *believe* about preschoolers' cognitive abilities? What if you asked parents (1) how much their *children* know when *parents* are happy or upset and (2) would their children think that a clay ball was the same "amount" if it were squashed into a pancake shape? Would parents' expectations about these questions coincide with the research described in this section? If possible, interview a real-life parent or two to test your prediction.

WHAT DO YOU THINK?

How do you think early childhood teachers should respond to language variety in preschoolers? Should they encourage it, discourage it, or simply accept it? This is an important issue in education and would make for a lively debate in class!

Early Childhood Education

Developing cognitive skills influence an important experience for many preschool children: early childhood education. Programs for three- and four-year-olds take many forms. Look at these experiences:

- Juan goes to *family day care* for three full days each week. His care occurs in his caregiver's home, with only four other children.
- Denzel goes to a *childcare center* full time, five days a week. The center consists of two rooms modified from a church basement. About twenty children attend the center and are cared for by four adults.
- Cary goes to a part-time *nursery school* four mornings per week. There are twelve children and two adults.

Early Education and Cognitive Theories of Development

As with the diversity of these childcare arrangements, there is diversity in the developmental perspectives guiding the arrangements. Some programs draw heavily on Piaget's ideas about cognitive development, especially the notion that children construct knowledge by interacting with the environment actively (Marlowe, 1998). They provide sensorimotor activities, such as sand and water play, as a basis for fostering preoperational activities such as make-believe play. Other programs organize cognitive activities around structured materials, which teachers guide children to use in particular ways. Nurseries and centers inspired by Maria Montessori (Cuffaro, 1991; Montessori, 1964; Lillard, 2012) may give children sets of cylinders graded by size and designed to fit snugly into a set of size-graded holes in a board. A child experiments with the cylinders and holes to discover the best way to fit them.

Still other early education programs borrow from Vygotsky's views of cognition as originating in social and cultural activities. These programs emphasize cooperative problem-solving activities and *emergent literacy,* a way of introducing reading and writing by situating it in everyday, valued experiences (Morrow, 1996). For example, instead of teaching children to recognize letters or familiar words at a special time each day, the early childhood teacher might simply provide a classroom rich in print materials and encourage children to come to him with words or letters that they themselves want to learn.

Effectiveness of Early Childhood Education

Evaluations of early childhood programs suggest that a wide range of approaches, including those just mentioned, are about equally effective in promoting overall cognitive growth, although the choice of curriculum does seem to influence *the pattern* of skills children acquire (Lillard, 2012; Schweinhart et al., 1993).

Three factors seem to underlie successful early childhood programs, whatever their format and curriculum. First, the staff members of successful programs regard themselves as competent observers of children's educational needs and as being capable of making important decisions in tailoring a curriculum to particular children. Second, the vast majority of successful programs and teachers view an early childhood curriculum as an integrated whole, rather than as consisting of independent subject areas or skills. Singing a song, for example, is not just "music"; it also fosters language development, motor skills (if the children dance along), arithmetic (through counting and rhythm), and social studies (if the words are about people and life in the community).

Third, successful early childhood programs involve parents, either directly as volunteers in the classroom or indirectly as advisers on governing boards, in certain school activities, or in additional services that support families. The federally sponsored program of early education called *Head Start,* for example, owes much of its effectiveness to parent involvement (Ames, 1997; Love, Banks Tarullo, Raikes, & Chazan-Cohen, 2008). To get federal funding, local centers are required to create parent advisory boards to guide policy and practice at the centers. They are also encouraged to provide other family support services, such as parent support groups and dental screening for children.

Cultural Diversity and Best Practice in Early Education

A careful look at successful programs for young children raises an important question: are there "best" ways to support children's learning despite the cultural and individual diversity among children? A major professional association for early childhood education, the National Association for the Education of Young Children (NAEYC), argues that there are and has described its recommendations in detail in an influential book called *Developmentally Appropriate Practice: Birth to Age Eight* (Bredekamp & Copple, 1997; Copple & Bredekamp, 2009; Gestwicki, 1995). **Developmentally appropriate practices** are ways of assisting children's learning that are consistent with children's developmental needs and abilities. Table 4.2 lists a few of the practices recommended by the NAEYC as they relate to the preschool years.

> **developmentally appropriate practice** Methods and goals of teaching considered optimal for young children, given current knowledge of child development.

The NAEYC recommendations seem reasonable in many ways. Who can object, for example, to providing children with choices for their preschool play or to supporting their dialogues and initiatives with comments from the teacher or caregiver? Yet cross-cultural comparisons of early childhood programs complicate the picture somewhat by revealing that some practices in early education in North America are really culture bound rather than universally beneficial to children.

In Japan, for example, early childhood programs are more likely to value large-group activities (such as singing or putting on a skit) in the belief that such activities develop commitment to the

TABLE 4.2   Developmentally Appropriate Practices with Preschoolers

Principle	Examples
Caregivers provide ample space for active play.	Program has access to outdoor space or gymnasium with climbing apparatus, tricycles, etc.
Caregivers allow children choices in activities.	Classroom has several learning centers: dramatic play (dress-up), block building, books and reading area, art area, etc.
Caregivers provide long periods of uninterrupted time.	Group transitions (e.g., from indoor to outdoor activities) are kept to a minimum. Activities tend to begin and end individually.
Activities and materials are relevant to children's experiences.	Books are gender fair and culture fair. Relevant cultural holidays are noted and celebrated through appropriate activities in class.
Caregivers ensure that the environment is safe and free of hazards.	Climbing apparatus has soft mats underneath (if indoors) or soft sand (if outdoors). Furniture is sturdy. Sharp objects (knives, scissors) are supervised carefully when used.

Source: Adapted from Bredekamp & Copple (1997).

child's community—in this case, the community of the classroom (Kotloff, 1993). The time given to large-group activities, however, probably would seem excessive to some preschool educators in North America, where the development of individual initiative is more highly valued.

A MULTICULTURAL VIEW

Parents' Beliefs about Intelligence: A Cross-Cultural Perspective

In our society, parents mean particular things when they refer to children's *intelligence:* they are usually talking about a child's verbal skills and reasoning abilities, especially as they occur in school or school-like tasks. This view of intelligence is so deeply grounded in our culture that an entire psychological field has developed to measure it, complete with standardized "intelligence" tests and experts to help teachers and parents interpret the tests.

But not all societies think of intelligence in this way. The Kipsigis in East Africa frame the idea of intelligence rather differently, placing it more explicitly in its social context (Harkrtess & Super, 1992). They speak of a child being *ng'om,* meaning not only verbally skilled and sociable but also responsible to others. A child who is *ng'om* is quick to learn household tasks, for example, but also reliable about doing them without being reminded. The Kipsigis recognize, in principle, that a child can have verbal skill in the abstract. In practice, however, they regard such an isolated or abstract skill as a unique ability that requires a special term to describe it: *ng'om en sukul,* or "smart in school." Furthermore, *ng'om* is a quality shown only by preschoolers; neither an infant nor an adult can be *ng'om* because she or he is not expected to be responsible to others in the same way preschoolers are.

Such a socially embedded notion of intelligence differs radically from the usual North American idea. In our society, parents are likely to distinguish clearly between a child's sense of responsibility to others and his or her intelligence (Goodnow, 1996). They may consider the former desirable but not an intrinsic part of intelligence as such. When interviewed about the qualities shown by preschoolers, parents of preschoolers tend to name relatively "cognitive" features: an intelligent child is inquisitive, curious, imaginative, self-reliant, and able to play independently (Harkness & Super, 1992). These features of intelligence take individual autonomy for granted rather than social harmony: being intelligent is something you do by or on behalf of yourself, not with or on behalf of others.

These cultural differences begin to make sense if we consider the settings in which Kipsigis and North American parents and preschoolers live. A Kipsigis preschooler typically is part of an extended family. There are likely to be children of all ages close at hand, related to one another in largely complex ways; older children typically care for younger children from an early age; and children's chores are likely to take on "real" economic importance as children get older. Such a setting seems sure to reward children for showing responsibility to others.

In our own society, a preschooler is likely to live with a small family; relatively few or even no immediate relatives may be close at hand; parents expect that school will figure prominently in the preschooler's future; and parents themselves are likely to be working for a living. This sort of setting favors children who can "teach themselves" to a certain extent, that is, play with and learn from materials on their own. It also favors children who orient themselves toward school-like activities—toward number and memory games, for example, and books and letters. An "intelligent" child is one who can do these things, which have much less to do with responsibility to others than is the case for a Kipsigis child. Cultural differences such as these can pose problems for many preschoolers in our own society when they finally enter school. Historically, modern schooling has encouraged the culturally conventional definitions of intelligence as individual activity and those of cognitive activity as separate from the daily needs of the community. Students generally "do their own work" and focus on tasks (such as a set of math problems) that are created specifically for school settings.

When these assumptions do not fit the cultural expectations of particular children or their families, however, teachers are challenged to modify them. Teachers must then find other ways for children to "be intelligent"—ways that involve greater responsibility to others, for example, and greater concern for the real needs of the child's community (Gopaul-McNicol & Thomas-Presswood, 1998). Though it takes effort, there are ways to accomplish these changes in teaching philosophy; some of these changes are discussed in Chapter 8 in connection with bilingualism and the influence of school in the middle years.

In Italy, early childhood programs emphasize involvement of parents much more heavily than do most North American programs (Edwards & Kutaka, 2015). They also place children in permanent groups from their entrance at age three until they leave the program for public school at age six. Over recent decades, societal changes, such as higher divorce rates, increasing numbers of women working outside the home, and economic difficulties, have challenged the early childhood care systems, but Italian culture persists in supporting these programs (Edwards & Kutaka, 2015).

WHAT DO YOU THINK?

Is early childhood education a "social" or a "cognitive" activity? Decide what you think about this question. Then, if you can, talk about it with one or two experienced teachers of young children. How does your opinion compare to theirs?

These comparisons suggest that the best practices in early education may need to take account of cultural differences and values regarding children's development (Mallory & New, 1994). For programs in ethnically diverse societies such as the United States, this means more than including songs and brief mentions of the holidays of various cultural groups. The central values and attitudes of cultural groups served by a particular center or nursery school must find their way into the daily activities of the program. Particular centers, therefore, will experience cultural diversity in different ways.

As the "A Multicultural View" feature shows, in these culturally diverse programs, cognition, or thinking, itself can take on diverse meanings. Educators who work with young children therefore need to do more than understand preschool cognition: they also need to explore how it might be understood and used by particular children and communities with specific social relationships and values. The next chapter turns to these important topics.

From Preschooler to Child

The physical and cognitive changes we have talked about in this chapter create new relationships with parents and other caregivers, who in turn stimulate further changes. Preschoolers' new motor skills may stimulate adults to encourage various talents actively and with more focus than before. Once catching and throwing make their appearance, playing ball becomes a possibility; once scribbling stabilizes, skillful and interesting drawing seems just around the corner. And so parents and other interested adults encourage children toward these new skills, among others. Sometimes, the teaching and learning seem easier now, too, because adults no longer have to monitor a child's every move and can concentrate increasingly on the goals of movements. Just a few years before, "one false step" might have meant a child would literally fall. But now, this term has become only a metaphor for mistakes in general, not for physical mishaps specifically.

The cognitive developments of early childhood are equally influential on relationships. New cognitive abilities create new individuality in children. In spite of differences in temperament among infants, it is not they but preschoolers who have more identifiable personalities. By age four or five, conversations become possible; moods can be expressed not only through gestures and body language but also through words; and a child's lasting interests become more obvious to those who know the child. All of these changes create new meanings for the idea of parenting. Attending to physical needs begins to recede in importance (though not completely), and attending to psychological needs comes more to the fore. As parents shift their relationship to accommodate these changes, they are more likely to remember their own childhoods once again, and with renewed vividness. The memories can be good, bad, traumatic, or mixed; but whatever they are like, they force reassessment of parents' *own* personal histories and identities, and their relationships with their *own* parents, the preschooler's grandparents. We saw aspects of these changes in Chapter 5's discussion of attachment formation, and we will explore them further. We come to them first in Chapter 8, which describes where preschoolers' new physical growth and cognitive skills lead them during middle childhood. We come to them again in Chapter 13, which discusses the impact of parenting on parents in more detail. First, though, we must complete the portrait of young children by discussing the development of their social relationships and their emotional growth in the next chapter.

References

Ames, L. (1997). *Women reformed, women empowered: Poor mothers and the endangered promise of Head Start*. Philadelphia: Temple University Press.

Bredekamp, S., & Copple, C. (Eds.) (1997). *Developmentally appropriate practice in early childhood programs* (rev. ed.), Washington, DC; National Association for the Education of Young Children.

Carlson, S. M., & Beck, D. M. (2009). Symbols as tools in the development of executive function. In A. Winsler, C. Fernyhough, & I. Montero (Eds.), *Private speech, executive functioning, and the development of verbal self-regulation* (pp. 163–175). Cambridge University Press.

Case, R. (1992). Neo-Piagetian theories of intellectual development. In H. Beilin, & P. Pufall (Eds.), *Piaget's theory: Prospects and possibilities*. Hillsdale, NJ: Erlbaum.

Case, R. (1998, April). *Fostering the development of number sense in the elementary and middle grades*. Paper presented at the annual meeting of the American Educational Research Association, San Diego.

Cobb, P., Gravemeijer, K., Yackel, E., McClain, K., & Whitenack, J. (1997). Mathematizing and symbolizing: The emergence of chains of signification in one first-grade classroom. In D. Kirschner, & J. Witson (Eds.), *Situated cognition: Social, semiotic, and psychological perspectives* (pp. 151–234). Mahwah, NJ: Erlbaum.

Cuffaro, H. (1991). A view of materials as the texts of the early childhood curriculum. In B. Spodek, & O. Saracho (Eds.), *Issues in early childhood curriculum* (pp. 64–85). New York, NY: Teachers College Press.

Copple, C., & Bredekamp, S. (Eds.) (1997). *Developmentally appropriate practice in early childhood programs serving children from birth through age 8* (3rd ed.), Washington, DC: National Association for the Education of Young Children.

Dennis, S. (1992). Stage and structure in the development of children's spatial reasoning. In R. Case (Ed.), *The mind's staircase* (pp. 229–245). Hillsdale, NJ: Erlbaum.

Elbers, E., Wiegersma, S., Brand, N., & Vroon, P. (1991), Response alternation as an artifact in conservation research. *Journal of Genetic Psychology, 152,* 47–56.

Edwards, C. P., & Kutaka, T. S. (2015). Diverse perspectives of parents, diverse concepts of parent involvement and participation: Contrasts between Italy and the United States. Chapter prepared for S. M. Sheridan, & E. M. Kim (Eds.), *Foundational Aspects of Family-School Partnerships* (pp. 35–54).

Gestwicki, C. (1995). *Developmentally appropriate practice: Curriculum and development in the early years*. Albany, NY: Delmar.

Ginsburg, H. P., Cannon, J., Eisenband, J., & Pappas, S. (2008). Mathematical thinking and learning. In K. McCartney, & D. Phillips (Eds.), *Blackwell handbook of early childhood development* (pp. 208–230). Malden, MA: Blackwell Publishing.

Goldman, L. (1998). *Children's play: Mime, mimesis, and make-believe*. New York, NY: Oxford.

Goodnow, J. (1996). Collaborative rules: How are people supposed to work with one another? In P. Baltes, & U. Staudinger (Eds.), *Interactive minds: Lifespan perspectives on social foundations of cognition* (pp. 163–197). New York, NY: Cambridge University Press.

Gopaul-McNicol, S., & Thomas-Presswood, T. (1998). *Working with linguistically and culturally different children.* Boston: Allyn and Bacon.

Guralnick, M. J. (2008). Family influences on early development: Integrating the science of normative development, risk and disability, and intervention. In K. McCartney, & D. Phillips (Eds.), *Blackwell handbook of early childhood development* (pp. 44–61). Malden, MA: Blackwell Publishing.

Harkness, S., & Super, C. (1992). Parental ethnotheories in action. In I. Sigel, A. McGillicuddy-DeLisi, & J. Goodnow (Eds.), *Parent belief systems: The psychological consequences for children* (2nd ed., pp. 373–392). Hillsdale, NJ: Erlbaum.

Inhelder, B., & Piaget, J. (1958). *The growth of logical thinking from birth to adolescence.* New York, NY: Basic Books.

Kirschner, D. (1997). The situated development of logic in infancy: A case study. In D. Kirschner, & J. Whitson (Eds.). *Situated cognition: Social, semiotic, and psychological perspectives* (pp. 83–96). Mahwah, NJ: Erlbaum.

Kirschner, D., & Whitson, J. (Eds.) (1997). *Situated cognition: Social, semiotic, and psychological perspectives.* Mahwah, NJ: Erlbaum.

Kotloff, L. (1993). Fostering cooperative group spirit and individuality: Examples from a Japanese preschool. *Young Children, 48*(3), 17–24.

Lave, J. (1997). The culture of acquisition and the practice of understanding. In D. Kirschner & J. Whitson (Eds.), *Situated cognition: Social, semiotic, and psychological perspectives* (pp. 17–36). Mahwah, NJ: Erlbaum.

Lillard, A. S. (2012). Preschool children's development in classic Montessori, supplemented Montessori, and conventional programs. *Journal of School Psychology, 50*(3), 379–401.

Love, J. M., Banks Tarullo, L., Raikes, H., & Chazan-Cohen, R. (2008). Head Start: What do we know about its effectiveness? What do we need to know? In K. McCartney, & D. Phillips (Eds.), *Blackwell handbook of early childhood development* (pp. 549–575). Malden, MA: Blackwell Publishing.

Marlowe, B. (1998). *Creating and sustaining the constructivist classroom* Thousand Oaks, CA: Corwin Press.

Mallory, G., & New, R. (Eds.). (1994). *Diversity and develop-mentally appropriate practice. Challenges for early childhood education.* New York, NY: Teachers' College Press.

Montessori, M. (1964). *The Montessori method.* New York, NY: Schocken Books.

Morrow, L. (1996). *Motivating reading and writing in diverse classrooms: Social and physical contexts in a literature-based program.* Urbana, IL: National Council of Teachers of English.

Nelson, K. (1996). *Language in cognitive development: Emergence of the mediated mind.* New York, NY: Cambridge University Press.

Newman, F., & Holzman, L. (1993). *Lev Vygotsky: Revolutionary scientist.* New York, NY: Routledge.

Piaget, J. (1952). *The child's conception of number.* New York, NY: Norton.

Piaget, J. (1963). *The origins of intelligence in children.* New York, NY: Norton.

Piaget, J., & Inhelder, B. (1967). *The child's conception of space.* New York, NY: Norton.

Rogoff, B., Mistry, J., Goncu, A., & Mosler, C. (1993). Guided participation in cultural activity by toddlers and caregivers. *Monographs of the Society for Research in Child Development, 58*(8, Serial No. 236).

Schweinhart, L., Barnes, H., & Weikart, D. (1993). Significant benefits: The High/Scope Perry Preschool Study through age 27. (*Monographs of the High/Scope Educational Research Foundation,* No. 10). Ypsilanti, MI: High/Scope Press.

Steiner, G. (1987). Spatial reasoning in small-size and large-size environments; In search of early prefigurations of spatial cognition in small-size environments. In B. Inhelder, D. de Caprona, & A. Wells (Eds.). *Piaget today.* Hillsdale, NJ: Erlbaum.

Vygotsky, L. S. (1978). *Mind in society: The development of higher psychological processes.* Cambridge, MA: Harvard University Press.

Wadsworth, B. (1996). *Piaget's theory of cognitive and affective development: Foundations of constructivism.* 5th ed. White Plains, NY: Longman.

Wozniak, R., & Fischer, K. (1993). *Development in context: Acting and thinking in specific environments.* Hillsdale, NJ: Erlbaum.

Selection from The Developing Toddler and Early Childhood

Susan Whitbourne and Cynthia R. Davis

Cognitive Development

The development of cognitive skills is still in its early stages, but young children begin to show their emerging cognitive capacities and memory capabilities and can demonstrate them as they become increasingly verbal.

The Preoperational Stage

Swiss psychologist Jean Piaget believed that during early childhood children were in the **preoperational stage** of cognitive development. This stage focuses on the limitations of a child's thinking because, according to Piaget, children have yet to develop mental operations—the ability to mentally manipulate information from the environment using organized, formal, and logical processes. The images below demonstrate this theory. In the first image, the child can identify that both rows contain the same number of coins. In the second image, she reports that the top row has more coins. The child concludes that the row with the coins spread apart has more coins because it appears longer than the other row. Piaget would argue that this child is lacking the mental operations necessary to manipulate the information in front of her to understand that the two rows have the same *amount* of coins even though the rows look different in *size*. The realization that objects or sets of objects remain the same even when they are moved, manipulated, or made to look different, is known as **conservation**. Children in the preoperational stage lack this cognitive ability. During this stage, children experience **egocentric thought**, meaning that they focus on their own thoughts alone and have a hard time understanding the thoughts and feelings of others. During free play, children with egocentric thought may talk

Susan Whitbourne and Cynthia R. Davis, Selection from "The Developing Toddler and Early Childhood," *Lifespan Development: Biopsychosocial Perspectives*, pp. 114-116, 328-368. Copyright © 2018 by Cognella, Inc. Reprinted with permission.

FIGURE 5.1   A child in the preoperational stage could tell you that both rows have the same number of coins in the image on the left, but may think the top row has more coins in the image on the right.

Source: https://www.youtube.com/watch?v=whT6w2jrWbA.

in ways that simply reflect the verbalizing of their inner thoughts. Two children may be playing side-by-side, both talking, but the conversation may be confusing to an outside observer, because one child is verbalizing her thoughts, while the other is verbalizing his thoughts, which may have no relation to one another. On the other hand, while quietly playing with her toys, a child at this age may stop and ask a parent, "but Daddy, why did Elephant say that to Barbie?" It is likely that Elephant and Barbie were having a discussion in the child's mind, and the child assumed that the parent was also part of this inner conversation. According to Piaget, the child believes that everyone has the same inner thoughts and observations about the world as she does.

Memory

Around age 2, children begin to develop the ability to communicate their explicit memories. In other words, they can consciously recall and verbalize memories of events from the past. As we discussed in the previous chapter, this capacity is linked to their developing ability to understand and use language. Children can begin to talk about things they have done in the past or will do in the future. For example, a child may describe a special family event and say, "Remember when we went to California and we saw the fishies at the aquarium," or if his birthday is tomorrow he might say "After this sleep then it will be my birthday." Some of these memories stay with us as most adults can remember at least one event that occurred when they were 3 or 4 years old, whereas other adults can remember many events during this age period or one or two events from an even younger age (Strange & Hayne, 2013). Memories that are linked to particularly emotional events, like a trip to the hospital, are more likely to be remembered across the lifespan (Peterson & Whalen, 2001). Also, whether a parent continues to discuss these events with the child can make a difference on memory retention (Sales, Fivush, & Peterson, 2003). When asked about important events, such as the birth of another sibling, we can typically provide greater detail about the event when we are adults, though. This is not because adults have better memories. It is likely because the details of the event are not necessarily memories from that actual time, but are pieces of information that have been provided by others over time (maybe a parent) who were also there (Gross, Jack, Davis, & Hayne, 2013).

Executive Functioning

Executive functioning, a major component of cognition, involves mental processes that help "control, direct, or coordinate" cognitive functions such as memory, visual-spatial abilities, language, and motor skills. Executive functioning involves the ability to switch between various functions, to limit the influence of nonpriority functions and information, and to hold important information in working memory (Lee, Bull, & Ho, 2013). Some suggest executive functioning emerges when infants can regulate their eye movement, and it becomes increasingly sophisticated during infancy as young children demonstrate joint attention (De Luca & Leventer, 2008; Johnson, 1995). During early childhood significant development occurs in areas of the prefrontal cortex, which is thought to promote executive functioning during toddlerhood and the preschool years. In young children, specifically, it appears to allow for the behavioral regulation of both thoughts and emotions (Espy, Sheffield, Wiebe, Clark, & Moehr, 2011).

The development of executive functioning is dependent on the characteristics of the child, the larger environment and social experiences. Difficulties with executive functioning have been linked to genetic factors, increased activity in the frontal lobe during infancy (Kraybill & Bell, 2012) and a child's temperament characteristics such as negative emotionality (Leve et al., 2012). Caregiving behaviors can contribute to the development of executive functioning. For example, when a caregiver responds to a young child's cues it signifies to the infant that he has an impact on the environment. Parent–child interaction behaviors that promote a child's problem-solving abilities are also important, as are behaviors that interpret and verbalize the child's thoughts and feelings. These interactions provide the verbal skills needed to convey emotions and, in turn, help him understand and manage his feelings, or self-regulate (Carlson, 2003). The ability to interact with the environment, to problem solve, and to self-regulate are all important factors in executive functioning. It makes sense, then, that children who are raised in nonoptimal caregiving environments show deficits in executive functioning. For example, children who are adopted and experienced institutionalized care preadoption show reduced executive functioning. Researchers speculate that this is likely due to a lack of early caregiver attention and interaction, as well as poor physical care (Hostinar, Stellern, Schaefer, Carlson, & Gunnar, 2012).

Executive functioning is measured by assessing several child behaviors, including delay of gratification and the ability to maintain rules in a variety of tasks when given conflicting information (Conway & Stifter, 2012). During toddlerhood and early childhood it can be linked with learning skills and behavioral difficulties across the lifespan (Fitzpatrick & Pagani, 2012; Leve et al., 2012).

References

Carlson, S. M. (2003). Executive function in context: Development, measurement, theory, and experience. *Monographs of the Society for Research in Child Development, 68*, 138–151.

Conway, A., & Stifter, C. A. (2012). Longitudinal antecedents of executive function in preschoolers. *Child Development, 83*, 1022–1036. doi:10.1111/j.1467-8624.2012.01756.x

De Luca, C. R., & Leventer, R. J. (2008). Developmental trajectories of executive functions across the lifespan. *Executive functions and the frontal lobes: A lifespan perspective*, 23–56.

Espy, K. A., Sheffield, T. D., Wiebe, S. A., Clark, C. A. C., & Moehr, M. J. (2011). Executive control and dimensions of problem behaviors in preschool children. *Journal of Child Psychology and Psychiatry, 52*, 33–46. doi:10.1111/j.1469-7610.2010.02265.x

Fitzpatrick, C., & Pagani, L. S. (2012). Toddler working memory skills predict kindergarten school readiness. *Intelligence, 40*, 205–212. doi:10.1016/j.intell.2011.11.007

Gross, J., Jack, F., Davis, N., & Hayne, H. (2013). Do children recall the birth of a younger sibling? Implications for the study of childhood amnesia. *Memory, 21*, 336–346.

Hostinar, C. E., Stellern, S. A., Schaefer, C., Carlson, S. M., & Gunnar, M. R. (2012). Associations between early life adversity and executive function in children adopted internationally from orphanages. *Proceedings of the National Academy of Sciences, 109*, 17208–17212. doi:10.1073/pnas.1121246109

Johnson, M. H. (1995). The inhibition of automatic saccades in early infancy. *Developmental Psychobiology, 28*, 281–291. doi:10.1002/dev.420280504

Kraybill, J. H., & Bell, M. A. (2012). Infancy predictors of preschool and post-kindergarten executive function. *Developmental Psychobiology*. doi:10.1002/dev.21057

Lee, K., Bull, R., & Ho, R. M. H. (2013). Developmental changes in executive functioning. *Child Development*. doi:10.1111/cdev.12096

Leve, L. D., DeGarmo, D. S., Bridgett, D. J., Neiderhiser, J. M., Shaw, D. S., Harold, G. T., et al. (2013). Using an adoption design to separate genetic, prenatal, and temperament influences on toddler executive function. *Developmental Psychology, 49*(6), 1045.

Peterson, C., & Whalen, N. (2001). Five years later: Children's memory for medical emergencies. *Applied Cognitive Psychology, 15*, S7–S24. doi:10.1002/acp.832

Sales, J. M., Fivush, R., & Peterson, C. (2003). Parental reminiscing about positive and negative events. *Journal of Cognition and Development, 4*, 185–209.

Strange, D., & Hayne, H. (2013). The devil is in the detail: Children's recollection of details about their prior experiences. *Memory, 21*, 431–443.

Stage Theory of Cognitive Development

Janet Tareilo
Stephen F. Austin State University

Children develop their concept of the world around them based on their own understandings, their age, and their ability to process incoming information. Knowledge and learning result from this interchange. Each level of understanding then results in a continued complexity of thought (Brooks & Brooks, 2001). Slavin (2000) contends that "development refers to how people grow, adapt, and change through physical, personality, socioemotional, cognitive, and language development" (p. 28) and that by understanding that this occurs in and through various stages helps to define how learning takes place. The person who understood this phenomenon the most was Jean Piaget (1896–1980) who became a leading voice in the area of cognitive development of children by using skills of observation, having simple conversations, and listening attentively to children's responses (Atherton, 2011). Biehler (1978) suggests that Piaget "exerted more influence on theoretical discussions of development and on educational practices than any other [living] psychologist" (p. 150).

Though not an educator at heart, Piaget's work with Alfred Binet, who was studying the commonality of children's responses on a testing instrument, led him to question not only how the children responded but how they derived at their answers (Sadker & Sadker, 2005). His observations began by watching his own children grow and learn and broadened into an epistemological stance of understanding the acquisition of knowledge. His exploration into discovering the concept of cognitive development occurred because he proposed as a child aged, there were four distinct stages that allowed a child to receive new information and then process that information into learning (Slavin, 2000). Piaget's theory of cognitive development actually presented learning in such a way that parents and educators could understand a child's readiness to learn new skills as well as the type of experiences that would impact learning at each of the four stages (Seifert, 2011).

Janet Tareilo, "Stage Theory of Cognitive Development," *Handbook of Educational Theories*, ed. Beverly Irby, Genevieve H. Brown, and Rafael Lara-Aiecio, pp. 149-153. Copyright © 2013 by Information Age Publishing. Reprinted with permission.

While learning is the result of an individual child's interactions with his world and certain stimuli, Piaget believed that development and learning were dissimilar in fact due to the creation of distinct structures that enabled a child to process specific information (Siegler, 2005). Siegler (2005) further asserts that developmental sequences occur that enable a child to accept or adapt to new learning. The idea that the process of learning could be different but the path taken to learn was the same supported Piaget's conceptualization of cognitive development.

Stages of Cognitive Development

Piaget's four stages of cognitive development stood as collective reflections of his observations of what children had the capacity to learn and when certain skills and knowledge could be learned. He perceived that the stages never changed and every child passed through these stages in a sequential order. At each stage, children demonstrated new intellectual abilities and these abilities increased their levels of understanding (Wood, Smith, & Grossniklaus, 2001). The stages of cognitive development included (1) sensorimotor, (2) preoperational, (3) concrete operational, and (4) formal operational and stipulated that at each stage a child required specific experiences to ensure learning (Wood, et al., 2001). The progressive nature of each stage examined how age and cognitive abilities influenced learning and the acquisition of skills (see Table 6.1).

TABLE 6.1   Piaget's Stages of Cognitive Development

Sensorimotor	Preoperational	Concrete Operational	Formal Operational
Birth–2 years of age	2–7 years of age	7–11 years of age	Adolescence to adulthood

Every stage involves a child's encounter with stimuli, his or her ability to process information, and then a follow through with the organization of those thoughts to understand the world (Biehler, 1978). Brooks and Brooks (2001) view Piaget's stages as different places of thought processes that every child passes through according to the experiences provided at that particular time of growth as well as the actions taken by the child.

Sensorimotor Stage

During the first identified stage of cognitive development (birth to 2), a child primarily deals with his or her world through the use of their senses. Children experience trial and error thinking that leads to problem solving abilities appropriate for their age. Included in this stage is the concept of object permanence that allows a child to understand that an object, though out of sight, still exists. This ability leads a child to his or her learning of symbolic representation (Slavin, 2000).

Preoperational Stage

At approximately 2 years of age and until the age of 7, a child uses their concepts of symbols to make sense of objects. During this phase of development, the child acquires a great deal of language which in turn helps to stimulate his cognitive development. A major concept at this time is the principle of conservation that signifies an object stays the same regardless of other variables associated with the object. This stage also entails egocentric thinking in that everyone in the child's world thinks the way he or she does (Slavin, 2000).

Concrete Operational Stage

Many children enter school during this stage of cognitive development. This stage occurs between the ages of 7 and 11 and provides the child with experiences that develop his sense of reversibility and problem solving. Children during this stage are able to think logically but not abstractly. The child moves away from the importance of self (decentering) to being in the development of an imagination. Because of the age of the child, his world revolves around school, social interaction, and forming individual patters of thinking (Slavin, 2000).

Formal Operational Stage

The cognitive development at this stage includes a child's ability to move beyond the need for concrete objects to have an understanding of the world around them. Abstract and symbolic thinking are constantly in use as problem-solving and decision-making skills increase. This learning time brings children acceptances of things around them that help make acquire, process, and master new knowledge (Slavin, 2000).

Awareness of these stages of development provides a picture into the cognitive abilities of a child. Piaget realized there was a clear distinction in the differences that existed between the stages when objects were introduced, actions were required, and the thought process moved from a concrete to an abstract frame (Gardner, 1980). Seagal and Horne (1997) relate that recognition and understanding differences in the way children learn and acquire knowledge allow parents and educators to examine life and school experiences as well as instructional practices at the appropriate time when a child can accept what he or she is expected to learn.

Additional Piagetian Concepts Related to Cognitive Development

Cognitive development, as explained by Jean Piaget's four stages, includes additional concepts of learning that Piaget found equally important: (a) schemata; (b) assimilation; (c) accommodation; and (d) equilibration. These principles are ingrained into the learning experience based on Piaget's interest in biology and epistemology (Biehler, 1978).

Schema

In regards to Piagetian theory as defined by Wadsworth (2004), schemata are "the cognitive mental structures by which individuals intellectually adapt to and organize the environment" (p. 14). It is through the development of these schemes that children organize and process cognitive structures that determines their behaviors (Slavin, 2000). As a child moves through the cognitive stages of development, schema mature and change to allow children to develop necessary concepts related to their age and experiences. These changes occur through the ability a child has to assimilate and accommodate information.

Assimilation

Because each stage involves experiences that are varied and understood differently, a child must find a way to process incoming information. Assimilation allows children to comprehend the experiences by using existing schemata (Slavin, 2000).

Accommodation

When a child does not have a schema to make sense of the incoming information, he must modify or adjust an existing schema. This process is referred to as accommodation. By using this skill, children are able to understand new experiences (Slavin, 2000).

Equilibration

A key point in the discussion of developmental stages concerns the fact that children are constantly trying to remain balanced in their thinking and understanding. With equilibration, a child possesses the ability to remain in a state of stability and coherence to comprehend any inconsistency that arises in their experiences (Biehler, 1978).

Validation of the Theory Through an Educational Lens

Key to Piaget's foundation of cognitive development was the fact that the acquisition of knowledge was more important than being able to define knowledge (Campbell, 2006) and understanding this point was an essential element in the planning and implementation of instruction. Learning was a process that developed on a continuum with children taking an active role in the acquisition of skills and abilities because of a delineated readiness based on their ages (Duffy, 1996).

The goal of education then was not to consider results-based outcomes but to incorporate this belief with a child's eagerness to learn (Duffy, 1996). By addressing learning in developmental terms, Piaget contended that teaching and instructional strategies need to be addresses in relation to the child's level of cognitive ability (Wood et al., 2001). The concept of developmental and appropriate education could directly influence a teacher's use of resources, instructional materials, and the learning atmosphere (Slavin, 2000).

Seagal and Horne (1997) support these views when they discuss the importance of recognizing that learning does indeed occur in stages and children would acquire lasting knowledge by incorporating this thinking. Sadker and Sadker (2005) contend that using Piaget's theories could provide teachers with in depth ways to analyze a child's abilities and limitations to accept information based on their experiences.

Using Piagetian thinking, teachers should provide opportunities for the child to take an active role in their learning by presenting a variety of experiences, using open-ended questioning techniques, and individualizing instruction as much as possible (Biehler, 1978). The curriculum and materials used during the learning process would also be reflective of a child's abilities to absorb incoming information. Instruction and content should reflect a child's developmental level if mastery of subject matter and the acquisition of basic skills is expected (Wood et al., 2001). As a child progresses through school, Piaget's stages of cognitive development bring awareness to the most beneficial time to teach certain concepts, when to introduce abstract thinking, and give a child's ability to assess and process new information. With this in mind, a child will be given several opportunities to "discover and transform" knowledge on their own and by doing that a child discovers meaning, experiences a continual revision of existing knowledge, and plays as an active participant in their own learning (Slavin, 2000, p. 256).

The realization of this translates into specific practices for teachers (Berk, 1997):

1. provide appropriate learning opportunities;
2. ask students to explain their reasoning techniques;
3. provide discovery learning opportunities such as centers;
4. teach for mastery learning according to the specific stage of development; and
5. be prepared to accept children's individual differences.

Wood et al. (2001), using Piaget's stage theory advocate further suggestions for instruction:

1. use of hands-on learning;
2. provide learning situations that require a child to explore and experiment to develop new knowledge;
3. introduce complex terms at the appropriate time; and
4. encourage students to work together in problem-solving exercises.

In addition, Duffy (1996) recommends that teachers accept a Piaget frame of thinking by:

1. allowing students to discover answers on their own;
2. create learning situations that prompt the exploration of new concepts;
3. consider the individual intellectual abilities of each child; and
4. use teaching strategies that are appropriate and meaningful.

These beliefs about how children learn were instrumental in influencing the idea of constructivist learning (Brooks & Brooks, 2001) and led many to place the child at the center of cognition regardless of a prescribed curriculum or a predetermined grade level.

Constructivist thinking borrowed from the works of Piaget his idea that cognitive change occurs through a process and that process is determined by a child's age and his or her ability to use existing information to think in a more complex way (Slavin, 2000). Simply put, a child will learn what they need to know through self-discovery and student-centered instruction. A teacher acts as a facilitator during this process. Piaget's influence continues to be reflected in the use of Howard Gardner's Seven Intelligences and Marie Montessori's Method of Discovery

Learning (Duffy, 1996). Munari (1994) suggests that Piaget's experimental data serves as a building block for Gardner, Montessori, and others who insisted a relationship existed between learning, knowledge, and readiness.

Criticisms of Piaget and His Stage Development Theory

The works of Jean Piaget regarding the stages of cognitive development created as many questions as it did inquiry into how children learned and formulated understanding about themselves and their world. Because of his background in biology, he viewed the process of cognitive development as a systemic reaction to receiving and translating incoming stimuli. However, not all of his contemporaries agreed with his methods or his findings.

As a researcher, Piaget's methods of collecting data came under much scrutiny. He lacked a control group, his sample size was small, and his disregard for statistical analysis of his findings led to the belief that his research was limited and created additional concerns about the generality of his findings (*Criticisms of Piaget's Theories*, n.d.). By using different groups of children for different studies, Piaget failed to consider a child's individual differences such as gender, socioeconomic status, or family patterns. Continued criticism arose because it appeared that there was far too much theorizing about the stages and not enough evidence to support the theories as well as the concern that Piaget excluded any alternative explanations for his findings (*Criticisms of Piaget's Theories*, n.d.). The merging of his findings from various studies also led to many questions about the reliability and validity of those studies.

The idea that children could not acquire advanced skills because they had not reached a certain stage of cognitive development falls as one of Piaget's shortcomings. Critics argue that the tasks children were asked to complete were too difficult, it was inconceivable to accept that thinking would be the same through each of the stages regardless of the task, and trying to teach advanced thought processes to children early would prove unsuccessful (Wood et al., 2002). Wood et al. (2002) maintain that continued research in this area has produced a deeper understanding of children's abilities to accept and process advanced skills when the instructional level is appropriate, the learner is considered as an individual, and a wide scope of learning opportunities are provided.

Additional controversy developed over Piaget's beliefs that the stages of development were fixed and that development actually preceded learning (Slavin, 2000). In contrast to Piagetian theory, Slavin (2000) cited several studies that addressed these concerns:

1. Some of the skills presented by Piaget that developed at certain stages could be introduced at an earlier time (Black, 1991; Donaldson, 1978; & Kusaka, 1989).
2. If similar language was used in addressing certain skills, children could perform those skills at earlier stages (Gelman, 1979).
3. Cognitive abilities of children develop differently based on the task at hand and a child's previous experiences (Byrnes, 1988; Gelman & Baillargeon, 1983; & Overton, 1984).

If anything, Piaget caused fellow researchers to question the factors that influenced the way children learned and how that learning took place.

Probably Piaget's greatest criticism came from Jerome Bruner. Instead of four succinct stages in cognitive development, Bruner suggested that there were actually only three systems of representation and that language played a key role in the development of thought (Biehler, 1978). Bruner believed that Piaget's thoughts centered on maturation while his theories of cognitive development concentrated on the concept of internalization (Biehler, 1978). In terms of readiness, Bruner and Piaget also differed. Bruner did not agree that children should learn through their own experiences; instead, he thought that a child's experiences should be specific in their design to allow for later learning (1978).

Regardless of the criticisms placed on Piaget and his stages, he is still regarded as a scientist and psychologist whose innate interests regarding cognition opened doors of exploration and discovery on how children learn and acquire knowledge.

Piaget's Influence

The Russian psychologist, Lev Vygotsky (1896–1934), adopted several of Piaget's concepts regarding the process of learning. While Piaget and Vygostsky were interested in intellectual development, Vygotsky was concerned with how social and cultural factors influenced the cognitive development of children (Wadsworth, 2004). Piaget saw learning as a result in the development of a child's abilities while Vygotsky purported that learning was the driving force for cognitive development (Wadsworth, 2004). He did veer from some aspects of Piaget's thoughts regarding cognition because he maintained that "cognitive processes [were] determined by the subject's interactions with his/her social environment rather than emanating from his/her internal functioning" (Santiago-Delefosse & Delefosse, 2002, p. 728).

As children grown and begin to make sense of their world and their surroundings, explanation about their patterns of thought became essential. Piaget introduced a sense of reasoning as to what the child was experiencing. Gardner (1980) contends that Piaget's observations regarding children remains "without peer" (para. 5). Gardner (1980) continues with his praise for Piaget's efforts by crediting him with "more thought about what he had to say about cognition than what Skinner posited on overt behaviors or Freud's focus on motivation, personality, or the unconscious" (para. 4).

When faced with trying to explain certain phenomenon, scientists utilize various methods of inquiry and research techniques. The research process allows individuals to question, seek out additional information, and formulate new thinking from an original idea or hypothesis. From Piaget's simple observation of his children at play, he set in motion years of study and research that influenced how parents interacted with their children and even the educational system.

Through approximately 13 years of formal education, a child experiences a variety of teaching styles, a multitude of social interactions, and an assortment of learning opportunities. These occur in different settings with many variables that also influence how a child learns. Piaget's research recognized the importance of each stage of development and made a lasting impression on the area of early childhood education as well as influences a child needed during formative years (Sadker & Sadker, 2005).

Piaget looked at cognitive development as a result of the formation of knowledge that was a result of certain stages and times that a child experienced (Valsiner, 2005). The belief that the child was an active participant in his or her learning and that a child does possess cognitive abilities still remain valuable Piaget contributions to understanding how a child acquires lasting knowledge (Gardner, 1980). Piaget said (as cited in Feldman, 2008), "the only knowledge that is truly worthwhile is knowledge that each of us creates for our own purposes, that helps achieve goals that are important to us, that seeks answers to verify important questions, and that ultimately enriches the collective experiences of humankind" (p. 200).

References

Atherton, J. S. (2011, February). *Learning and teaching: Piaget's developmental theory.* Retrieved from http://www.learningandteaching.info/learning/piaget.htm

Berk, L. E. (1997). *Child development* (4th ed.). Boston, MA: Allyn & Bacon.

Biehler, R. F. (1978). *Psychology applied to teaching* (3rd ed.). Boston, MA: Houghton Mifflin.

Brooks, J. G., & Brooks, M. G. (2001). *In search of understanding: A case for constructivist classrooms.* Upper Saddle, NJ: Prentice-Hall.

Campbell, R. L. (2006). *Jean Piaget's genetic epistemology: Appreciation and critique.* Retrieved from http://hubcap.clemson.edu/~campber/piaget.html

Criticisms of Piaget's theory. (n.d.). Retrieved from http://ehlt.flinders.edu.au/education/DLit/2000/Piaget/critics.htm

Duffy, K. (1996). *Jean Piaget: The man behind the lab coat.* Retrieved from http://www.users.muohio.edu/shermalw/honors_2001_Fall/honors_papers_2000/duffy.html

Feldman, D. H. (2008). Darwin? Lamarck? Piaget? All of the above. *Human Development, 51,* 196–201.

Gardner, H. (1980, September 21). Jean Piaget: The psychologist as renaissance man. *The New York Times,* p. E20.

Munari, A. (1994). Jean Piaget. *International Bureau of Education, 24*(1/2), 311–327.

Sadker, M. P., & Sadker, D. M. (2005). *Teachers, schools, and society* (7th ed.). New York, NY: McGraw Hill.

Santiago-Delefosse, M. J., & Delefosse, J. M. O. (2002). *Spielrein, Piaget and Vygotsky: Three positions on child thought and language.* Retrieved from http:tap.sagepub.com/content/12/6/723

Seagal, S., & Horne, D. (1997). *Human dynamics: A new framework for understanding people and realizing the potential in our organizations.* Waltham, MA: Pegasus Communications.

Seifert, K. (2011). *The learning process: Major theories and models of learning.* Retrieved from http://cnx.org/content/m38002/1.2

Siegler, R. S. (2005, November). Children learning. *American Psychologist, 60*(8), 769–778.

Slavin, R. E. (2000). *Educational psychology: Theory and practice.* Needham Heights, MA: Allyn & Bacon.

Valsiner, J. (2005, January/February). Participating in Piaget. *Society, 42*(2), 57–61.

Wadsworth, B. J. (2004). *Piaget's theory of cognitive and affective development* (5th ed.). New York, NY: Pearson Education.

Wood, K. C., Smith, H., & Grossniklaus, D. (2001). Piaget's stages of cognitive development. In M. Orey (Ed.), *Emerging perspectives on learning, teaching, and technology.* Retrieved from http://projects.coe.uga.edu/epltt/index/php?title=Piaget%27s_Stages

The Development of Action Cognition

Antonia F. de C. Hamilton, Victoria Southgate, and Elisabeth Hill

Abstract

Humans learn motor skills over an extended period of time, in parallel with many other cognitive changes. The ways in which action cognition develops and links to social and executive cognition are under investigation. Recent literature is reviewed which finds evidence that infants advance from chaotic movement to adult-like patterns in the first two or three years of life, and that their motor performance continues to improve and develop into the teenage years. Studies of links between motor and cognitive systems suggest that motor skill is weakly linked to executive function and more robustly predicts social skill. Few, if any, models account directly for these patterns of results, so the different categories of models available are described.

Introduction

Humans are born with very limited motor skills and yet, over an extended period, develop into independent individuals capable of the precise control of skilled actions. Throughout this process, an increasing ability to control actions may also contribute to the development of other cognitive faculties such as language, executive control, and social interaction. Thus, action cognition concerns two topics: how the motor control system actually works, and how motor control relates to other cognitive processes. We begin by reviewing adult models of the motor system because it is useful to understand the end point of a developmental process. Thereafter we discuss the

Antonia F. de C. Hamilton, Victoria Southgate, and Elisabeth Hill, "The Development of Action Cognition," *The Pragmatic Turn: Toward Action-Oriented Views in Cognitive Science*, ed. Andreas K. Engel, Karl J. Friston, and Danica Kragic, pp. 35-47, 357-409. Copyright © 2016 by MIT Press. Reprinted with permission.

developmental changes that occur on the way to that end point, both within the motor system and in links between motor and other cognitive systems. We conclude with a consideration of some of the different theoretical frameworks that have been put forward to account for the *development* of action cognition.

Control of Human Movement

The task of reaching out to pick up a toothbrush, applying toothpaste, and brushing one's teeth may seem trivial to the adult who does this daily without much thought. However, learning this skill is not simple. Children develop some motor skills rapidly after birth, but many take years before expertise is fully achieved. To control a highly nonlinear and redundant system of muscles and bones in an efficient fashion, their motor systems must contend with signaling delays and sensorimotor noise (Franklin and Wolpert 2011). Despite this complexity, a preschool child can easily surpass the visuomotor skill of the best robots available today. The study of action cognition is the study of the information-processing systems that underpin motor abilities. While it draws heavily on basic computational motor control, action cognition[1] includes more abstract processes, such as motor planning and motor sequencing, which are sometimes studied in relation to executive control. It is important to explore the relationship between action cognition and other cognitive systems, in particular executive function and social cognition.

A large number of different models have been proposed to understand sensorimotor control in typical adults, and from these, two major categories of model emerge. Computational models describe human movement in terms of optimal feedback control (Todorov and Jordan 2002) and forward/inverse models (Kawato and Wolpert 1998), considering in detail the type of engineering required to control the human motor system. An alternative approach simplifies control to the idea of an equilibrium point and suggests that the spring-like properties of the musculature can be adjusted to move the equilibrium of the arm (Feldman et al. 1998). A similar principle is found in the more recent active inference model (Friston et al. 2011). However, a key difference between these two classes of models concerns whether prediction is separate to or fully integrated with control (Pickering and Clark 2014). We will draw primarily from the former class of models, because they have been tested in more detail in developmental populations.

To summarize current knowledge about the development of motor systems and action cognition, we will refer to recent studies in this area. The vast majority of published papers on motor development focus on clinically relevant behaviors (e.g., walking, writing) without regard to the underlying cognition. Here our discussion focuses on performance of specific motor tasks that link closely to particular computational components of motor control. We distinguish between

---

1   The term "cognition" is used as a synonym for "information processing." It does not imply a particular symbolic form of representation or a contrast to "affective" information but rather refers simply to any neural patterns of information between sensory input and muscle activation.

multisensory integration, visuomotor mapping, forward models, motor planning, and action comprehension, asking how each develops from infancy to adulthood.

Multisensory Integration

The human brain has many sources of sensory information which allow it to determine the current state of the world (e.g., visual, tactile, proprioceptive, and auditory input channels). A single physical event often impacts on many channels at once, and thus detecting congruency between different input channels and integrating inputs is helpful in building an accurate model of the state of the world. In adults, these different sensory information sources are integrated in a Bayes-optimal fashion (Ernst and Banks 2002). However, it is not yet clear how infants and children learn to integrate different senses. At a very young age, infants are sensitive to contingencies between different sensory modalities. An early study demonstrated that five-month-old children prefer to view a video of their own leg movements than a video of time-delayed leg movements (Bahrick and Watson 1985). However, this study did not distinguish which modalities (visual, tactile, proprioceptive, motor) are focused on by the infants.

Studies of visual and tactile integration suggest that this pairing is important from a very early age. Newborns (12–103 hrs old) prefer to view a face that is touched in sync with a touch to the infant's own face, than a face which is touched out of sync (Filippetti et al. 2013). This suggests they are able to detect synchrony between a face touch and a visual event. Similarly, seven-month-old infants prefer viewing a leg touched in sync with touches to their own leg (Zmyj et al. 2011), and the strength of this effect increases from seven to ten months. The integration of postural, visual, and tactile information also improves over the six- to ten-month age range, as shown by changes to somatosensory-evoked potentials in infants (Rigato et al. 2014). In older children (six-year-olds), visual-tactile integration can be similar to adults but is not mandatory, whereas adults cannot avoid integrating cues (Jovanovic and Drewing 2014). Visual-haptic cues for size discrimination are also not integrated in children before eight years of age (Gori et al. 2008). Similar results have been found for integration of different visual cues to depth (Nardini et al. 2010).

Visual-tactile-proprioceptive integration has also been examined using the rubber hand illusion (Botvinick and Cohen 1998). In older children (four- to seven-year-olds), the illusion is present and its magnitude remains constant over this age range (Cowie et al. 2013). However, the same children showed larger errors than adults in pointing to the true location of their hand, suggesting that visual-proprioceptive integration has not yet matured in this group. Further evidence of late maturation of visual-proprioceptive integration was found in a study of 7- to 13-year-old children in a hand localization task (King et al. 2010). Younger children in the sample were more reliant on visual information, which resulted in larger proprioceptive errors. A further study showed that noisy proprioceptive information could account for worse motor performance in six-year-olds compared to 12-year-olds (King et al. 2012). Together, these studies suggest very early sensitivity to sensorimotor congruency, together with very protracted development of the ability to integrate the senses.

Visuomotor Mapping

To obtain accurate control of hand actions, an infant needs more than multisensory integration; it must link motor commands and sensory input. This process is central to action cognition and has been studied from a variety of perspectives. A substantial number of studies that recorded from single neurons in monkeys found an occipito-parietal premotor pathway with a core role in transforming visual signals to motor actions (Cisek and Kalaska 2010). Within this pathway, mirror neurons are active when participants perform and observe actions (Rizzolatti and Sini-gaglia 2010). These neurons might provide a basic social mechanism for understanding other people (Gallese et al. 2004), but alternative interpretations are also available (Hamilton 2013a; Hickok and Hauser 2010). In cognitive terms, the link between visual and motor systems has been explored in the associative sequence learning model (Heyes 2001). Central to all these models is the idea that visual information (about objects in the world and the hand) must be mapped to motor information about the actions that the hand is performing. Specifically, the infant must learn to link the retinal image of a skin-colored moving shape to the motor outputs it sends to its own hand and arm muscles. This must involve transforming the retinal information into other, intermediate representations (e.g., visual primitives, kinematics, action goals, motor primitives). Such coordinate transforms have been studied in detail for spatial tasks (Andersen et al. 1997) but have been less often considered in studies of action cognition. In particular, it is not yet known what types of intermediate representation are required for action cognition or how these can best be studied. Nevertheless, it is clear that infants can learn and use visuomotor mappings. For example, the more opportunity infants have to acquire a visuomotor mapping for leg actions (via live video feed of their own legs), the more active their motor system becomes when they observe leg actions (de Klerk et al. 2014). Thus, forming early links between visual images and motor systems is critical to the developing motor system and may also contribute to social cognition.

There is evidence that building robust visual motor mappings is important for infants, even from the earliest days of life. Neonates (10–24 days old) will move their arm to keep it within a beam of light where they can see it (van der Meer 1997). Around four months of age, infants begin to make reaching movements toward objects, but their hand trajectories do not follow a smooth, adult-like path until at least three years of age, after which it continues to improve (Konczak and Dichgans 1997). The development of grasping is also prolonged. For example, an adult will typically use a large grip aperture when reaching for an orange but a small grip aperture when reaching for a grape. Infants reaching for objects of different sizes always use the same grip aperture at six months, but begin to scale their grip to the object by 13 months (von Hofsten and Ronnqvist 1988). One recent study suggests that four- to eight-month-old infants grasp as if their eyes were shut, relying on haptic cues; they only develop visual control of grasp by 24 months (Karl and Whishaw 2014). A study of four- to 12-year-olds reaching and grasping for objects showed clear improvements in trajectory and smoothness over this age range, with only the oldest children showing adult-like patterns of grip aperture scaling when reaching in the dark (Kuhtz-Buschbeck et al. 1998).

Another way to examine visuomotor mappings is to change these mappings, by asking a participant to make movements but giving false feedback about the location of the hand. Adults can adapt when a rotation of 45° is applied to the visual feedback given as the participant makes center-out movements, and then show aftereffects in the opposite direction when the false feedback is removed (Krakauer et al. 1999). The same method has been used to examine visuomotor transformation in four- to ten-year-old children. Results show that these children adapt to the new feedback like adults; however, the younger children showed smaller aftereffects when the false feedback was removed (Contreras-Vidal et al. 2005). This implies that younger children may have a broader tuning function in their visuomotor mapping than older children and adults. Overall, these studies show similarities to the studies of multisensory integration: early disorganized movements take on a recognizable pattern over the first year of life, and refinement of these movements continues for over a decade as the child gradually acquires adult levels of performance.

Prediction and Planning

A major challenge in motor control is the inherent delays in the visuomotor system. Sending a signal from motor cortex to the muscle takes around 20–30 msec (Matthews 1991), with another 25 msec required to translate that signal into a change in muscle force (Ito et al. 2004). If a visual input is required, delay in retinal and early visual systems must also be considered, giving rise to a delay in involuntary visual responses of around 110–150 msec (Day and Lyon 2000). Forward models or predictors can be used to circumvent these delays; that is, a copy of the outgoing motor command (efference copy) is used to predict what the sensory consequences of an action should be, and the predicted consequences are compared with the actual consequences (Davidson and Wolpert 2003; Miall and Wolpert 1996). One of the clearest examples of the use of forward models in the motor system can be seen in the programming of grip force. If you need to pick a raspberry from a bush without crushing it, it is important to grip inward and pull the fruit away from the bush with just the right force and timing. Studies in adults have revealed that grip force (the force inward between the finger and thumb) is closely correlated to load force (the upward force against gravity) when an object is lifted (Johansson and Cole 1992). This can best be explained by the use of a forward model in which the motor command to increase load force is also used to generate a prediction of the required grip force, so that grip and load can be controlled in parallel (Davidson and Wolpert 2003).

Studies of the development of grip force and load force over childhood demonstrate a very protracted developmental trajectory. The correlation between grip force and load force increases gradually over two to eight years of age (Forssberg et al. 1992) and continues to improve up to 14 years of age (Bleyenheuft and Thonnard 2010). Grip force dexterity in the more complex task of compressing a spring also improves over the four- to 16-year age range (Dayanidhi et al. 2013). A different way to measure predictive processes is to examine stability to unloading. In these tasks, a participant holds a heavy object in his/her left hand, thus requiring activation of muscles in the left arm to hold the object stable. In different trials, either an experimenter lifts the object from the participant's left hand (other-lift) or the participant lifts the object with their right hand (self-lift). In a self-lift, a participant is normally able to relax the left arm at just the same time as the object lifts, thus holding the left hand stable. In contrast, the timing of the other-lift cannot be predicted and so muscle activation in the left hand remains high for longer, with the left hand moving upward as the object is lifted. Performance on this task improves substantially from 4–16 years of age, but even 16-year-olds do not demonstrate the same level of performance as adults (Barlaam et al. 2012; Schmitz et al. 2002).

While predictive processes in motor control are helpful on a very short timescale (hundreds of milliseconds), planning processes can help performance on a longer timescale. One aspect of longer-term planning is seen in chaining tasks, where the kinematics of an action differs according to the next action performed. For example, a grasp followed by a throw has different kinematics during grasping compared to a grasp followed by a placing action (Becchio et al. 2012; Johnson-Frey et al. 2004). This is true for school-age children (Cattaneo et al. 2007; Fabbri-Destro et al. 2009) as well as ten-month-old infants (Claxton et al. 2003); however, detailed developmental studies have not been performed. More is known about planning based on end-state comfort. For example, when lifting a bar to place it in a particular location, adults will often begin the action with an awkward posture so as to end their action in a comfortable posture (Rosenbaum et al. 1990). The effect of end-state comfort provides a measure of action planning, and performance improves from three to ten years of age (Jongbloed-Pereboom et al. 2013; Stöckel et al. 2012; Weigelt and Schack 2010). Overall, these studies illustrate the very gradual development of predictive and planning abilities in the motor system, with changes in performance continuing up to 16 years of age.

Comprehension of Other People's Actions

An important component of action cognition is social (i.e., the ability to understand what another person is doing now and intends to do next when viewing their actions). Many studies have examined how this process develops in infancy and how it relates to other skills. From a young age, infants are able to interpret others' actions as movements directed toward goals and they use a variety of cues to identify a goal-directed action (Hernik and Southgate 2012). The dominant theory in this area suggests that if mirror neurons are central to action understanding (Gallese et al. 2004), then an infant's ability to understand an observed action should be dependent on their ability to perform that action. Data in support of this show links between performance and comprehension of actions. For example, three-month-old infants are not yet able to reach and grasp objects themselves and do not appear to understand actions as goal directed (Sommerville et al. 2005). However, if three-month-olds are provided with experience of grasping for objects by wearing Velcro gloves, which help them to pick up objects in their vicinity, they subsequently evidence an understanding that an observed reach and grasp action is goal directed (Skerry et al. 2013; Sommerville et al. 2005). Numerous other studies also demonstrate a relationship between developing action skill and various measures of action understanding (Cannon and Woodward 2012; Kanakogi and Itakura 2011).

One difficulty with these studies is that it is not always clear what it means for an infant (or an adult) to understand an action. Is it enough to predict what is next, or is a more elaborate representation of intention required? There is evidence that motor and mirror systems have a role in the former (Southgate et al. 2009, 2010, 2014). However, it seems that infants may also recruit their motor system during the prediction of others' actions that are outside of their own motor repertoire (Southgate and Begus 2013; Southgate et al. 2008). Thus, while infants' own motor skill does appear to influence their action understanding, the mechanisms mediating this relationship are unclear. There are also several reasons to believe that, at least in adults, intention understanding requires more than just motor prediction (Csibra 2007; Spunt et al. 2010). The relationship between motor and social cognition will be discussed in more detail in the next section.

Summary

Action cognition encompasses a variety of skills and computational components which must work together to allow coordinated and efficient action. Developmental studies suggest that infants rapidly learn motor skills in the first year of life, moving from helplessness to a state with some basic control systems in place. However, the acquisition of full motor skill remains very protracted. Even everyday skills, such as grasping objects, draw on a complex system for visuomotor transformation and predictive control, and performance continues to develop and improve into adolescence. Developmental trajectories for motor skills are likely to be nonlinear—with progress in an area followed by stagnation, followed by more progress—and different motor skills do not develop in synchrony, even in children.

How Does Action Cognition Relate to Other Types of Development?

Learning a new motor skill can change how a child engages with the world as well as how the world engages with a child. For example, an infant who can grasp an object might now perceive the potential of a cup for grasping in a way that a younger child might not. The grasping infant may also receive different social inputs from adults, who might place objects within reach (or remove them) and talk about the objects differently. Thus, learning a new motor skill has the potential to impact both a child's cognitive development and social development. Here we review work in this area to trace how different cognitive skills might be linked.

Intellectual and Executive Development

There are many reasons to believe that motor and intellectual skills are connected. In longitudinal studies, motor skill has been linked to later motor, social, physical, and mental health outcomes as well as to academic achievement (Bart et al. 2007; Ekornås et al. 2010; Emck et al. 2011). Several studies have focused particularly on executive function—a broad term used to describe skills, including working memory, inhibition, and cognitive flexibility (Diamond 2013), related to measures of intelligence. Some aspects of executive control can be seen even in infancy (Johnson 2012) but the development of these skills continues into adulthood (Best and Miller 2010). There is mixed evidence for a relationship between executive function skills and motor skills. Five-year-olds with motor difficulties show differences in executive function measured one year later (Michel et al. 2011). In a study of 100 typical seven-year-olds, only some correlations between executive function and motor performance were reliable (Roebers and Kauer 2009). Reliable but small correlations were also reported in a study of motor skill and intelligence in 250 children (Jenni et al. 2013). However, other studies report positive associations. For example, throwing and catching skills correlated in particular with IQ (Rigoli et al. 2012a), an effect that might be mediated by working memory (Rigoli et al. 2012b). Other work suggests that links between motor and cognitive skills might be mediated by visual performance (Davis et al. 2011).

Some theories claim strong links between motor skill, cognitive skill, and the development of the cerebellum (Diamond 2000; Wang et al. 2014). For example, in children with cerebellar tumors, there is a correlation between motor and cognitive skills (Davis et al. 2010), and cerebellar function has been linked to autism (Wang et al. 2014); direct evidence in typical children, however, is limited. Developmental coordination disorder (DCD) can also be examined as a test case. A study by van Swieten et al. (2010) demonstrated developmentally inappropriate *motor* planning in six- to 13-year-old children with DCD, but appropriate *executive* planning (using a Tower of London task) in seven- to 11-year-olds in this group. Pratt et al. (2014) identified, however, significant difficulties with both types of planning in a different group of children with DCD, compared by age and IQ to typically developing children. Leonard and Hill (2014) show that children with DCD performed worse than typically developing controls on *nonverbal* measures of working memory, inhibition, planning, and fluency, but not on tests of switching or verbal equivalents of the same tasks. Overall, these studies give mixed support to the claim that motor cognition and executive function are linked. There may be weak correlations between these cognitive systems, but the association is not a tight one.

Social Development

Much better evidence is available to suggest that motor skill contributes to social development. During infancy, motor development can affect how infants interact with individuals around them. For example, as infants improve in manipulating objects, they also show altered patterns of attention to others in the environment (Libertus and Needham 2010). The onset of crawling and walking is linked to greater joint attention and social referencing, perhaps because of the altered type and number of interactions the young child is then able to have with its caregivers (Campos et al. 2000; Karasik et al. 2011; Leonard and Hill 2014). Specifically, the ability to move around and explore the environment as well as manipulating objects and sharing them with others provides more opportunities to engage in joint attention and changes the types of vocalizations and expressions the infant receives from the caregiver. Evidence for relationships between motor development, language, and social communication skills can be seen from the outset in typical development through the tight coupling of motor and language milestones throughout infancy (Iverson 2010). There is also a feedback loop between produced and heard speech: children with autism produce less speech and, in return, receive less speech input from their caregivers (Warlaumont et al. 2014). Thus, motor skills can directly influence the child's social environment and opportunities to develop social skills.

Many studies of links between action cognition and other types of cognition have examined children with developmental disorders, in particular autism spectrum conditions diagnosed on the basis of poor social cognition. As many as 80% of children with autism have substantial motor difficulties (Green et al. 2009), and interest in the links between autism and motor cognition is increasing (Fournier et al. 2010; Gowen and Hamilton 2012). In particular, there is evidence for dyspraxia (poor performance of skilled hand actions) in autism beyond other possible motor impairments (MacNeil and Mostofsky 2012; Mostofsky et al. 2006). Infant siblings at risk of developing autism demonstrated differences in standardized motor tasks and face-processing tasks (Leonard et al. 2013). In children at high risk of developing autism, greater autism symptoms were also seen in those with poorer motor skills (Bhat et al. 2012; Leonard and Hill 2014).

Despite clear links between overall levels of motor and social skills, it is harder to identify specific differences in cognitive systems, and here results are more variable. Children with autism show poor performance in specific tasks involving motor planning in some studies (Hughes 1996) but not in others (Hamilton et al. 2007; van Swieten et al. 2010). Some studies report difficulties in chaining actions together in sequences (Cattaneo et al. 2007), but others do not (Pascolo and Cattarinussi 2012). Detailed testing of visuomotor adaptation in children with autism did not find group differences (Gidley Larson et al. 2008). Similar variability is found in studies of how children with autism understand other people's actions—a social component of motor cognition. Some studies report difficulties in answering questions about why a person performed an action (Boria et al. 2009) or in predicting what will come next in a movie (Zalla et al. 2010). Other studies, however, find no differences in the ability to make sense of hand gestures (Hamilton et al. 2007). Studies of imitation show intact performance on emulation tasks (copying the goal of an action) but poor performance on mimicry tasks (copying precise kinematic features) (Edwards 2014; Hamilton 2008). Some of these differences may be explicable in terms of links to executive function or top-down control (Wang and Hamilton 2012). Overall, there is no single aspect of motor cognition that can be directly linked to poor social cognition. More research is needed to understand how motor and social developmental processes interact.

Summary

Overall, data show reliable but small links between motor cognition and executive function, and larger more robust links between motor cognition and social cognition. In particular, changes in motor skill seem to drive changes in the child's social environment and predict later performance in situations involving communication and interaction. However, it is less clear what specific cognitive processes drive these effects. To assign motor-social links to a single brain system (such as the mirror neuron system) is probably premature (Hamilton 2013b). Instead, it will be important to consider how different systems *interact* in development, and how the acquisition of one skill gives the child more opportunities to learn other skills, in a complex interplay between the child and the social environment.

Theories for Understanding the Development of Action Cognition

There are many different theoretical frameworks under which we could try to make sense of the development of action cognition and its relationship to social cognition. Here we provide a brief overview of the different options, before ending with suggestions for future directions.

Cognitive Theories

The traditional way to understand information processing in the human brain is to develop cognitive or computational models that can reproduce that processing (Marr 1982). To understand action cognition, computational models provide a powerful way to test and explore the problems which the human brain must solve to move in the world (Franklin and Wolpert 2011). Similar computational mechanisms could be applied to social cognition: the motor control mechanisms that allow a person to predict and control a tennis racket might also allow a person to predict and control the actions of another person (Wolpert et al. 2003). Such models can incorporate gradual motor learning but do not say anything specific about development.

A related approach to action and cognition can be found in the mirror neuron framework (Rizzolatti and Sinigaglia 2010), which postulates how motor performance and action understanding could be linked to the same neural systems. The mirror neuron model has been set within a developmental context (Gallese et al. 2009), with strong claims that the failure to develop mirror systems in autism might account for difficulties in social cognition (for a critique, see Hamilton 2013b). This account also places a strong emphasis on prenatal and innate mechanisms of action and cognition, and does not leave much space for development after birth. Thus, neither of these models has much to say about the rapid improvements in action cognition during the first year of life.

One way to expand the cognitive approach, so as to consider developmental change, is to study developmental disorders. Developmental causal modeling (Morton 2004) and the ACORN framework (Moore and George 2011) provide tools for specifying and testing cognitive models of child development and developmental disorders. Using these tools, a developmental process can be formally specified in terms of the biological, neural, and cognitive changes that take place at different developmental time points, as well as the ways in which these influence each other. Such a formal model is more amenable to testing and clinical use than more weakly specified theories. For example, a developmental causal model of autism suggests that a primary difficulty in theory of mind can account for many of the observed difficulties in social cognition (Frith et al. 1991), and this has been tested in detail (U. Frith 2012). A key question for cognitive approaches to development is to identify the different modular systems and to determine if and how they might interact. For example, is the development of motor systems essential to theory of mind (Gallese et al. 2009), or not (U. Frith 2012)? It would be possible to place these questions and the relevant data on action cognition into a more formal modeling framework of causation to test out theories of developmental change, but this has yet to be attempted.

Interactionist Theories

An alternative approach that is gaining ground is to focus the study of child development on the process of development itself (Karmiloff-Smith 2012). Rather than starting from the adult end state and considering the child as an adult with some bits missing, this approach considers fully how new capacities can emerge out of the interaction between the infant and the social-motor environment. In the motor domain, dynamical systems models have been used to describe how motor skills emerge in infants from the interaction of the child and the environment (Thelen and Smith 1996). In social cognition, embedded and embodied accounts (Reddy 2008) view social skills as emerging from the interaction between infant and caregiver, rather than being internalized by the infant. A key prediction in these models is that developmental changes emerge out of the relationship between the child and the environment. For example, if a child who can walk obtains different physical and social inputs to a child who cannot walk, this will initiate the development of particular social and motor skills. The emphasis here is on a longitudinal, two-way relationship between the child and the social-physical world.

Interactionist theories are part of the push toward thinking of cognition not in isolation, but grounded in reality, embodied in the world, and created by the interaction between child and world. This push is similar to the new emphasis on "second person neuroscience" (Schilbach et al. 2013), where the emphasis is strongly on the interrelation between the developing child and that child's social-motor environment. This is a promising approach which is coherent with reports of close links between the child's social-motor experience and their further development (Leonard and Hill 2014)). However, the major limitation of this approach is its complexity. If the decomposition of behavior according to cognitive processes is abandoned, it is not clear how development should be decomposed. Yet without any decomposition, the problem of understanding a process and formulating testable models is difficult. Overall, interactionist models are intriguing but it remains very hard to find tractable experimental approaches to test their validity.

Future Directions

In this review of the development of action cognition, data suggest that motor development is a very protracted process—one that is linked to other areas of cognition, in particular to the development of social skills. Two categories of key unanswered questions include:

1. What is the best framework for understanding the development of motor control? Can we break down motor control into specific cognitive processes and track the development of each? Or is this only feasible through a holistic, interactionist account?

First column (top to bottom): Gottfried Vosgerau, Cecilia Heyes, Pierre-Yves Oudeyer, Peter König, Antonia Hamilton, Antonia Hamilton and Pierre-Yves Oudeyer, Robert Rupert

Second column: Giovanni Pezzulo, Atsushi Iriki, Peter König, Antonella Tramacere, Gottfried Vosgerau, Antonella Tramacere, Uta Frith

Third column: Uta Frith, Robert Rupert, Henrik Jörntell, Saskia Nagel, Cecilia Heyes, Giovanni Pezzulo, Atsushi Iriki

2. What processes link motor and social cognition? Are there specific cognitive mechanisms which might be shared between motor and social cognition and, if so, what are they? Alternatively, are the associations we observe in data between motor and social skills driven instead by changes in the child's opportunities to learn, or other facets of the environment?

To address these questions, more data is needed on how motor cognition actually develops. In young children, it would be particularly helpful to consider the substantial individual differences that are apparent at certain ages (e.g., walking at nine vs. 18 months) but resolved at later ages (almost all four-year-olds can walk in a similar way). It is also critical to consider the interplay between the child and the environment. Longitudinal studies which track the child's skill and social surroundings over time would be particularly valuable in this regard. Finally, the study of children with a range of developmental disorders (not just autism) are needed to understand why motor cognition sometimes goes wrong and what the implications of this are for both typical and atypical development.

Bibliography

Andersen, R. A., L. H. Snyder, D. C. Bradley, and J. Xing. 1997. Multimodal Representation of Space in the Posterior Parietal Cortex and Its Use in Planning Movements. *Annu. Rev. Neurosci.* **20**:303–330. [3]

Bahrick, L. E., and J. S. Watson. 1985. Detection of Intermodal Contingency as a Potential Basis Proprioceptive-Visual of Self-Perception in Infancy. *Dev. Psychol.* **21**:963–973. [3]

Barlaam, F., C. Fortin, M. Vaugoyeau, C. Schmitz, and C. Assaiante. 2012. Development of Action Representation During Adolescence as Assessed from Anticipatory Control in a Bimanual Load-Lifting Task. *Neuroscience* **221**:56–68. [3]

Bart, O., D. Hajami, and Y. Bar-Haim. 2007. Predicting School Adjustment from Motor Abilities in Kindergarten. *Infant Child Dev.* **16**:597–615. [3]

Becchio, C., V. Manera, L. Sartori, A. Cavallo, and U. Castiello. 2012. Grasping Intentions: From Thought Experiments to Empirical Evidence. *Front. Hum. Neurosci.* **6**:117–117. [3]

Best, J. R., and P. H. Miller. 2010. A Developmental Perspective on Executive Function. *Child Dev.* **81**:1641–1660. [3]

Bhat, A. N., J. C. Galloway, and R. J. Landa. 2012. Relation between Early Motor Delay and Later Communication Delay in Infants at Risk for Autism. *Infant. Behav. Dev.* **35**:838–846. [3]

Bleyenheuft, Y., and J.-L. Thonnard. 2010. Grip Control in Children before, During, and after Impulsive Loading. *J. Mot. Behav.* **42**:169–177. [3]

Boria, S., M. Fabbri-Destro, L. Cattaneo, et al. 2009. Intention Understanding in Autism. *PLoS One* **4**:e5596–e5596. [3]

Botvinick, M., and J. Cohen. 1998. Rubber Hands "Feel" Touch That Eyes See. *Nature* **391**:756–756. [3, 7]

Campos, J. J., D. I. Anderson, M. A. Barbu-Roth, et al. 2000. Travel Broadens the Mind. *Infancy* **1**:149–219. [3]

Cannon, E. N., and A. L. Woodward. 2012. Infants Generate Goal-Based Action Predictions. *Dev. Sci.* **15**:292–298. [3]

Cattaneo, L., M. Fabbri-Destro, S. Boria, et al. 2007. Impairment of Actions Chains in Autism and Its Possible Role in Intention Understanding. *PNAS* **104**:17825–17830. [3, 20]

Cisek, P., and J. F. Kalaska. 2010. Neural Mechanisms for Interacting with a World Full of Action Choices. *Annu. Rev. Neurosci.* **33**:269–298. [2–4]

Claxton, L. J., R. Keen, and M. E. McCarty. 2003. Evidence of Motor Planning in Infant Reaching Behavior. *Psychol. Sci.* **14**:354–356. [3]

Contreras-Vidal, J. L., J. Bo, J. P. Boudreau, and J. E. Clark. 2005. Development of Visuomotor Representations for Hand Movement in Young Children. *Exp. Brain Res.* **162**:155–164. [3]

Cowie, D., T. R. Makin, and A. J. Bremner. 2013. Children's Responses to the Rubber-Hand Illusion Reveal Dissociable Pathways in Body Representation. *Psychol. Sci.* **24**:762–769. [3]

Csibra, G. 2007. Action Mirroring and Action Understanding: An Alternative Account. In: Sensorimotor Foundations of Higher Cognition: Attention and Performance, ed. P. Haggard et al., vol. 12, pp. 453–459. Oxford: Oxford Univ. Press. [3, 9]

Davidson, P. R., and D. M. Wolpert. 2003. Motor Learning and Prediction in a Variable Environment. *Curr. Opin. Neurobiol.* **13**:232–237. [3]

Davis, E. E., N. J. Pitchford, T. Jaspan, D. McArthur, and D. Walker. 2010. Development of Cognitive and Motor Function Following Cerebellar Tumour Injury Sustained in Early Childhood. *Cortex* **46**:919–932. [3]

Davis, E. E., N. J. Pitchford, and E. Limback. 2011. The Interrelation between Cognitive and Motor Development in Typically Developing Children Aged 4–11 Years Is Underpinned by Visual Processing and Fine Manual Control. *Br. J. Psychol.* **102**:569–584. [3]

Day, B. L., and I. N. Lyon. 2000. Voluntary Modification of Automatic Arm Movements Evoked by Motion of a Visual Target. *Exp. Brain Res.* **130**:159–168. [3]

Dayanidhi, S., A. Hedberg, F. J. Valero-Cuevas, and H. Forssberg. 2013. Developmental Improvements in Dynamic Control of Fingertip Forces Last Throughout Childhood and into Adolescence. *J. Neurophysiol.* **110**:1583–1592. [3]

de Klerk, C. C. J. M., M. H. Johnson, C. M. Heyes, and V. Southgate. 2014. Baby Steps: Investigating the Development of Perceptual-Motor Couplings in Infancy. *Dev. Sci.* **18**:1–11. [3]

Diamond, A. 2000. Close Interrelation of Motor Development and Cognitive Development and of the Cerebellum and Prefrontal Cortex. *Child Dev.* **71**:44–56. [3]

————. 2013. Executive Functions. *Annu. Rev. Psychol.* **64**:135–168. [3]

Edwards, L. A. 2014. A Meta-Analysis of Imitation Abilities in Individuals with Autism Spectrum Disorders. *Autism Res.* **7**:363–380. [3]

Ekornås, B., A. J. Lundervold, T. Tjus, and M. Heimann. 2010. Anxiety Disorders in 8–11-Year-Old Children: Motor Skill Performance and Self-Perception of Competence. *Scand. J. Psychol.* **51**:271–277. [3]

Emck, C., R. J. Bosscher, P. C. W. Van Wieringen, T. Doreleijers, and P. J. Beek. 2011. Gross Motor Performance and Physical Fitness in Children with Psychiatric Disorders. *Dev. Med. Child Neurol.* **53**:150–155. [3]

Ernst, M. O., and M. S. Banks. 2002. Humans Integrate Visual and Haptic Information in a Statistically Optimal Fashion. *Nature* **415**:429–433. [3]

Fabbri-Destro, M., L. Cattaneo, S. Boria, and G. Rizzolatti. 2009. Planning Actions in Autism. *Exp. Brain Res.* **192**:521–525. [3, 20]

Feldman, A. G., D. J. Ostry, M. F. Levin, P. L. Gribble, and A. B. Mitnitski. 1998. Recent Tests of the Equilibrium-Point Hypothesis (Lambda Model). *Motor Control* **2**:189–205. [3]

Filippetti, M. L., M. H. Johnson, S. Lloyd-Fox, D. Dragovic, and T. Farroni. 2013. Body Perception in Newborns. *Curr. Biol.* **23**:2413–2416. [3]

Forssberg, H., H. Kinoshita, A. C. Eliasson, et al. 1992. Development of Human Precision Grip. *Exp. Brain Res.* **90**:393–398. [3]

Fournier, K. A., C. J. Hass, S. K. Naik, N. Lodha, and J. H. Cauraugh. 2010. Motor Coordination in Autism Spectrum Disorders: A Synthesis and Meta-Analysis. *J. Autism Dev. Disord.* **40**: 1227–1240. [3]

Franklin, David W. W., and D. M. Wolpert. 2011. Computational Mechanisms of Sensorimotor Control. *Neuron* **72**:425–442. [3]

Friston, K. J., J. Mattout, and J. M. Kilner. 2011. Action Understanding and Active Inference. *Biol. Cybern.* **104**:137–160. [3, 6]

Frith, U. 2012. Why We Need Cognitive Explanations of Autism. *Q. J. Exp. Psychol.* **65**:2073–2092. [3, 4]

Frith, U., J. M. Morton, and A. M. Leslie. 1991. The Cognitive Basis of a Biological Disorder: Autism. *Trends Neurosci.* **14**:433–438. [3]

Gallese, V., C. Keysers, and G. Rizzolatti. 2004. A Unifying View of the Basis of Social Cognition. *Trends Cogn. Sci.* **8**:396–403. [3, 15]

Gallese, V., M. J. Rochat, G. Cossu, and C. Sinigaglia. 2009. Motor Cognition and Its Role in the Phylogeny and Ontogeny of Action Understanding. *Dev. Psychol.* **45**:103–113. [3]

Gidley Larson, J. C., A. J. Bastian, O. Donchin, R. Shadmehr, and S. H. Mostofsky. 2008. Acquisition of Internal Models of Motor Tasks in Children with Autism. *Brain* **131**:2894–2903. [3]

Gori, M., M. Del Viva, G. Sandini, and D. C. Burr. 2008. Young Children Do Not Integrate Visual and Haptic Form Information. *Curr. Biol.* **18**:694–698. [3, 7, 15]

Gowen, E., and A. F. Hamilton. 2012. Motor Abilities in Autism: A Review Using a Computational Context. *J. Autism Dev. Disord.* **43**:323–344. [3]

Green, D., T. Charman, A. Pickles, et al. 2009. Impairment in Movement Skills of Children with Autistic Spectrum Disorders. *Dev. Med. Child Neurol.* **51**:311–316. [3]

Hamilton, A. F. 2008. Emulation and Mimicry for Social Interaction: A Theoretical Approach to Imitation in Autism. *Q. J. Exp. Psychol.* **61**:101–115. [3]

————. 2013a. The Mirror Neuron System Contributes to Social Responding. *Cortex* **49**: 2957–2959. [3]

_____. 2013b. Reflecting on the Mirror Neuron System in Autism: A Systematic Review of Current Theories. *Dev. Cogn. Neurosci.* **3**:91–105. [3]

Hamilton, A. F., R. M. Brindley, and U. Frith. 2007. Imitation and Action Understanding in Autistic Spectrum Disorders: How Valid Is the Hypothesis of a Deficit in the Mirror Neuron System? *Neuropsychologia* **45**:1859–1868. [3]

Hernik, M., and V. Southgate. 2012. Nine-Months-Old Infants Do Not Need to Know What the Agent Prefers in Order to Reason About Its Goals: on the Role of Preference and Persistence in Infants' Goal-Attribution. *Dev. Sci.* **15**:714–722. [3]

Heyes, C. 2001. Causes and Consequences of Imitation. *Trends Cogn. Sci.* **5**:253–261. [3]

Hickok, G., and M. Hauser. 2010. (Mis)Understanding Mirror Neurons. *Curr. Biol.* **20**:R593–R594. [3, 9]

Hughes, C. 1996. Control of Action and Thought: Normal Development and Dysfunction in Autism: A Research Note. *J. Child Psychol. Psychiatry* **37**:229–236. [3]

Ito, T., E. Z. Murano, and H. Gomi. 2004. Fast Force-Generation Dynamics of Human Articulatory Muscles. *J. Appl. Physiol.* **96**:2318–2324; discussion 2317. [3]

Iverson, J. M. 2010. Developing Language in a Developing Body: The Relationship between Motor Development and Language Development. *J. Child Lang.* **37**:229–261. [3]

Jenni, O. G., A. Chaouch, J. Caflisch, and V. Rousson. 2013. Correlations between Motor and Intellectual Functions in Normally Developing Children between 7 and 18 Years. *Dev. Neuropsychol.* **38**:98–113. [3]

Johansson, R. S., and K. J. Cole. 1992. Sensory-Motor Coordination During Grasping and Manipulative Actions. *Curr. Opin. Neurobiol.* **2**:815–823. [3]

Johnson, M. H. 2012. Executive Function and Developmental Disorders: The Flip Side of the Coin. *Trends Cogn. Sci.* **16**:454–457. [3]

Johnson-Frey, S., M. E. McCarty, and R. Keen. 2004. Reaching Beyond Spatial Perception: Effects of Intended Future Actions on Visually Guided Prehension. *Vis. Cogn.* **11**:371–399. [3]

Jongbloed-Pereboom, M., M. W. Nijhuis-van der Sanden, N. Saraber-Schiphorst, C. Crajé, and B. Steenbergen. 2013. Anticipatory Action Planning Increases from 3 to 10 Years of Age in Typically Developing Children. *J. Exp. Child Psychol.* **114**:295–305. [3]

Jovanovic, B., and K. Drewing. 2014. The Influence of Intersensory Discrepancy on Visuo-Haptic Integration Is Similar in 6-Year-Old Children and Adults. *Front. Psychol.* **5**:57. [3]

Kanakogi, Y., and S. Itakura. 2011. Developmental Correspondence between Action Prediction and Motor Ability in Early Infancy. *Nat. Commun.* **2**:341–341. [3]

Karasik, L. B., C. S. Tamis-LeMonda, and K. E. Adolph. 2011. Transition from Crawling to Walking and Infants' Actions with Objects and People. *Child Dev.* **82**:1199–1209. [3]

Karl, J. M., and I. Q. Whishaw. 2014. Haptic Grasping Configurations in Early Infancy Reveal Different Developmental Profiles for Visual Guidance of the Reach versus the Grasp. *Exp. Brain Res.* **232**:3301–3316. [3]

Karmiloff-Smith, A. 2012. Challenging the Use of Adult Neuropsychological Models for Explaining Neurodevelopmental Disorders: Developed versus Developing Brains. *Q. J. Exp. Psychol.* **66**:37–41. [3]

Kawato, M., and D. M. Wolpert. 1998. Internal Models for Motor Control. *Novartis Found. Symp.* **218**:291–304; discussion 304–307. [3]

King, B. R., M. Oliveira, J. L. Contreras-Vidal, and J. E. Clark. 2012. Development of State Estimation Explains Improvements in Sensorimotor Performance across Childhood. *J. Neurophysiol.* **107**:3040–3049. [3]

King, B. R., M. M. Pangelinan, K. A. Kagerer, and J. E. Clark. 2010. Improvements in Proprioceptive Functioning Influence Multisensory-Motor Integration in 7- to 13-Year-Old Children. *Neurosci. Lett.* **483**:36–40. [3]

Konczak, J., and J. Dichgans. 1997. The Development toward Stereotypic Arm Kinematics During Reaching in the First 3 Years of Life. *Exp. Brain Res.* **117**:346–354. [3]

Krakauer, M. F. Ghilardi, C. Ghez, and J. W. Krakauer. 1999. Independent Learning of Internal Models for Kinematic and Dynamic Control of Reaching. *Nat. Neurosci.* **2**:1026–1031. [3]

Kuhtz-Buschbeck, J. P., H. Stolze, K. Jöhnk, A. Boczek-Funcke, and M. Illert. 1998. Development of Prehension Movements in Children: A Kinematic Study. *Exp. Brain Res.* **122**:424–432. [3]

Leonard, H. C., R. Bedford, T. Charman, et al. 2013. Motor Development in Children at Risk of Autism: A Follow-up Study of Infant Siblings. *Autism* **18**:281–2891. [3]

Leonard, H. C., and W. L. Hill. 2014. Review: The Impact of Motor Development on Typical and Atypical Social Cognition and Language: A Systematic Review. *Child Adolesc. Ment. Health* **19**:163–170. [3]

Libertus, K., and A. Needham. 2010. Teach to Reach: The Effects of Active vs. Passive Reaching Experiences on Action and Perception. *Vision Res.* **50**:2750–2757. [3]

MacNeil, L. K., and S. H. Mostofsky. 2012. Specificity of Dyspraxia in Children with Autism. *Neuropsychology* **26**:165–171. [3]

Marr, D. 1982. Vision: A Computational Investigation into the Human Representation and Processing of Visual Information. New York: W. H. Freeman. [1, 3, 20]

Matthews, P. B. 1991. The Human Stretch Reflex and the Motor Cortex. *Trends Neurosci.* 14:87–91. [3]

Miall, C., and D. M. Wolpert. 1996. Forward Models for Physiological Motor Control. *Neural Netw.* **9**:1265–1279. [3]

Michel, E., M. Roethlisberger, R. Neuenschwander, and C. M. Roebers. 2011. Development of Cognitive Skills in Children with Motor Coordination Impairments at 12-Month Follow-Up. *Child Neuropsychol.* **17**:151–172. [3]

Moore, D. G., and R. George. 2011. ACORNS: A Tool for the Visualisation and Modelling of Atypical Development. *J. Intell. Disab. Res.* **55**:956–972. [3]

Morton, J. M. 2004. Understanding Developmental Disorders: A Causal Modelling Approach. Oxford: Blackwell. [3]

Nardini, M., R. Bedford, and D. Mareschal. 2010. Fusion of Visual Cues Is Not Mandatory in Children. *PNAS* **107**:17041–17046. [3]

Pascolo, P. B., and A. Cattarinussi. 2012. On the Relationship between Mouth Opening and "Broken Mirror Neurons" in Autistic Individuals. *J. Electromyogr. Kinesiol.* **22**:98–102. [3]

Pickering, M. J., and A. Clark. 2014. Getting Ahead: Forward Models and Their Place in Cognitive Architecture. *Trends Cogn. Sci.* **18**:451–456. [3]

Pratt, M. L., H. C. Leonard, H. Adeyinka, and E. L. Hill. 2014. The Effect of Motor Load on Planning and Inhibition in Developmental Coordination Disorder. *Res. Dev. Disabil.* **35**:1579–1587. [3]

Reddy, V. 2008. How Infants Know Minds. Cambridge, MA: Harvard Univ. Press. [3]

Rigato, S., J. Begum Ali, J. L. J. van Velzen, and A. J. Bremner. 2014. The Neural Basis of Somatosensory Remapping Develops in Human Infancy. *Curr. Biol.* **24**:1222–1226. [3]

Rigoli, D., J. P. Piek, R. Kane, and J. Oosterlaan. 2012a. An Examination of the Relationship between Motor Coordination and Executive Functions in Adolescents. *Dev. Med. Child Neurol.* **54**:1025–1031. [3]

_____. 2012b. Motor Coordination, Working Memory, and Academic Achievement in a Normative Adolescent Sample: Testing a Mediation Model. *Arch. Clin. Neuropsychol.* **27**:766–780. [3]

Rizzolatti, G., and C. Sinigaglia. 2010. The Functional Role of the Parieto-Frontal Mirror Circuit: Interpretations and Misinterpretations. *Nat. Rev. Neurosci.* **11**:264–274. [3, 9, 15]

Roebers, C. M., and M. Kauer. 2009. Motor and Cognitive Control in a Normative Sample of 7-Year-Olds. *Dev. Sci.* **12**:175–181. [3]

Rosenbaum, D. A., F. Marchak, H. Barnes, et al. 1990. Constraints for Action Selection: Overhand versus Underhand Grips. In: Attention and Performance, ed. M. Jeannerod, pp. 321–342. Hillsdale, NJ: Lawrence Erlbaum. [3]

Schilbach, L., B. Timmermans, V. Reddy, et al. 2013. Toward a Second-Person Neuroscience. *Behav. Brain Sci.* **36**:393–414. [1, 3, 20]

Schmitz, C., N. Martin, and C. Assaiante. 2002. Building Anticipatory Postural Adjustment During Childhood: A Kinematic and Electromyographic Analysis of Unloading in Children from 4 to 8 Years of Age. *Exp. Brain Res.* **142**:354–364. [3]

Skerry, A. E., S. Carey, and E. S. Spelke. 2013. First-Person Action Experience Reveals Sensitivity to Action Efficiency in Prereaching Infants. *PNAS* **110**:18728–18733. [3]

Sommerville, J. A., A. L. Woodward, and A. Needham. 2005. Action Experience Alters 3-Month-Old Infants' Perception of Others' Actions. *Cognition* **96**:B1–11. [3]

Southgate, V., and K. Begus. 2013. Motor Activation During the Prediction of Nonexecutable Actions in Infants. *Psychol. Sci.* **24**:828–835. [3]

Southgate, V., K. Begus, S. Lloyd-Fox, V. di Gangi, and A. F. Hamilton. 2014. Goal Representation in the Infant Brain. *NeuroImage* **85**:294–301. [3]

Southgate, V., G. Csibra, and M. H. Johnson. 2008. Infants Attribute Goals Even to Biomechanically Impossible Actions. *Cognition* **107**:1059–1069. [3]

Southgate, V., M. H. Johnson, I. El Karoui, and G. Csibra. 2010. Motor System Activation Reveals Infants' on-Line Prediction of Others' Goals. *Psychol. Sci.* **21**:355–359. [3]

Southgate, V., M. H. Johnson, T. Osborne, and G. Csibra. 2009. Predictive Motor Activation During Action Observation in Human Infants. *Biol. Lett.* **5**:769–772. [3]

Spunt, R. P., E. B. Falk, and M. D. Lieberman. 2010. Dissociable Neural Systems Support Retrieval of How and Why Action Knowledge. *Psychol. Sci.* **21**:1593–1598. [3]

Stöckel, T., C. M. L. Hughes, and T. Schack. 2012. Representation of Grasp Postures and Anticipatory Motor Planning in Children. *Psychol. Res.* **76**:768–776. [3]

Thelen, E., and L. B. Smith. 1996. A Dynamic Systems Approach to the Development of Cognition and Action. Cambridge, MA: MIT Press. [3, 4, 17]

Todorov, E., and M. I. Jordan. 2002. Optimal Feedback Control as a Theory of Motor Coordination. *Nat. Neurosci.* **5**:1226–1235. [3]

van der Meer, A. L. 1997. Keeping the Arm in the Limelight: Advanced Visual Control of Arm Movements in Neonates. *Eur. J. Paediatr. Neurol.* **1**:103–108. [3]

van Swieten, L. M., E. van Bergen, J. H. G. Williams, et al. 2010. A Test of Motor (Not Executive) Planning in Developmental Coordination Disorder and Autism. *J. Exp. Psychol. Hum. Percept. Perform.* **36**:493–499. [3]

von Hofsten, C., and L. Ronnqvist. 1988. Preparation for Grasping an Object: A Developmental Study. *J. Exp. Psychol. Hum. Percept. Perform.* **14**:610–621. [3]

Wang, S. S. H., A. D. Kloth, and A. Badura. 2014. The Cerebellum, Sensitive Periods, and Autism. *Neuron* **83**:518–532. [3]

Wang, Y., and A. F. Hamilton. 2012. Social Top-Down Response Modulation (STORM): A Model of the Control of Mimicry in Social Interaction. *Front. Hum. Neurosci.* **6**:153–153. [3]

Warlaumont, A. S., J. A. Richards, J. Gilkerson, and D. K. Oller. 2014. A Social Feedback Loop for Speech Development and Its Reduction in Autism. *Psychol. Sci.* **25**:1314–1324. [3]

Weigelt, M., and T. Schack. 2010. The Development of End-State Comfort Planning in Preschool Children. *Exp. Psychol.* **57**:476–782. [3]

Wolpert, D. M., K. Doya, and M. Kawato. 2003. A Unifying Computational Framework for Motor Control and Social Interaction. *Phil. Trans. R. Soc. B* **358**:593–602. [2, 3]

Zalla, T., N. Labruyère, A. Clément, and N. Georgieff. 2010. Predicting Ensuing Actions in Children and Adolescents with Autism Spectrum Disorders. *Exp. Brain Res.* **201**:809–819. [3]

Zmyj, N., J. Jank, S. Schütz-Bosbach, and M. M. Daum. 2011. Detection of Visual-Tactile Contingency in the First Year after Birth. *Cognition* **120**:82–89. [3]

Parenting Classes, Parenting Behavior, and Child Cognitive Development in Early Head Start

A Longitudinal Model

Mido Chang, Boyoung Park, and Sunha Kim

Introduction

Parental involvement in children's education has been an important issue because it is a critical resource for children's success in school. Research has consistently indicated that parental involvement relates positively to school achievement. Many educational practitioners are making an effort to evoke parents' involvement in parenting workshops, volunteering in class activities, or various other opportunities. These efforts lead to better behavioral and academic outcomes for children (Bailey, Silvern, & Brabham, 2004; Flouri, 2004; Li, 2006; Reutzel, Fawson, & Smith, 2006; Senechal, 2006; St. Clair & Jackson, 2006; Sy & Schulenberg, 2005; Yan & Lin, 2005). Early studies on parental involvement in preschool programs have also indicated its benefits on children's cognitive and social development. When mothers participated in a program to improve verbal interaction, preschool children of low-income families showed significant cognitive development (Madden, Levenstein, & Levenstein, 1976); when mothers participated in parent-child intervention programs, 1- or 2-year-old toddlers displayed substantially improved cognitive development (Bronfenbrenner, 1974). Pfannenstiel and Seltzer (1985) also showed that preschoolers whose parents participated in a parent education program displayed significantly higher intelligence, language ability, and social development.

The findings of early studies substantiated the importance of intervention programs that first encourage parents to participate in parental education programs and later guide them in daily practice of their gained knowledge and skills to promote their

Mido Chang, Boyoung Park, and Sunha Kim, "Parenting Classes, Parenting Behavior, and Child Cognitive Development in Early Head Start: A Longitudinal Model," *School Community Journal*, vol. 19, no. 1, pp. 155-174. Copyright © 2009 by Academic Development Institute. Reprinted with permission. Provided by ProQuest LLC. All rights reserved.

children's cognitive and social development. Despite the proven importance of parent education, recent studies on the effects of parental classes in preschool or childcare programs have been under-represented. Moreover, research on the impact of parenting classes for children who are preschool age or younger have been less studied than those for school-age children.

This study examines the effects of parental involvement for infant and toddler preschoolers from low-income families by using Early Head Start (EHS) data. EHS constitutes a nationally representative dataset which contains variables of various family backgrounds and types of parental involvement. Among the types of parental involvement, we particularly paid attention to the effects of parenting classes on parental language and cognitive stimulation, parent-child interactive activities, and children's cognitive outcomes.

The study was guided by the following research hypotheses:

- The parents who participated in parenting classes from EHS would demonstrate more parental language and cognitive stimulation, as measured by home observation and by video recording, than those who did not.
- The parents who participated in parenting classes from EHS would demonstrate more parent-child interactive activities than those who did not.
- The children of parents who participated in parenting classes from EHS would demonstrate higher scores on the cognitive evaluation.

Theoretical Background

Parental Involvement and Parenting Classes

Early studies on preschool programs emphasized parental involvement on the basis of its benefits for preschool children's cognitive development. Bronfenbrenner (1974), in a review paper based on nine empirical studies examining parent-child intervention programs, asserted that intervention programs encouraging parental involvement led to substantial cognitive development of toddlers and preschool children. Bronfenbrenner also highlighted the importance of a parent intervention program when children are very young by showing that gains in children's IQ from the effects of parent intervention programs were highest when the children were one or two years of age, while the effects were weak if children were as old as five years.

In a similar vein, Madden et al. (1976) showed significant cognitive development of preschool children from low-income families after two years of their mothers' engagement in a verbal interaction modeling program. Specifically, through this intervention, mothers were taught to interact verbally while playing with their children to promote the children's intellectual and socioemotional development. Pfannenstiel and Seltzer (1985) also found that preschoolers whose parents participated in a similar parent education program (Parents as Teachers) showed, at the end of the program, significantly higher intelligence, language ability, and social development in comparison with national norms. Parents in the program learned how to facilitate the cognitive, social, linguistic, and physical development of their children from the time of prenatal development to the age of three.

Similarly, recent studies have evidenced the positive effects of Parents as Teachers (PAT) Programs on a large scale (Pfannenstiel, Seitz, & Zigler, 2003; Zigler, Pfannenstiel, & Seitz, 2008). Pfannenstiel et al. (2003) studied a PAT program for 2,375 public kindergarten school children in the state of Missouri. The program in their study was designed in such a way that PAT-certified educators taught parents to build knowledge according to their children's developmental stages and to highlight the importance of parental involvement to build solid parent-child relationships. The unique feature of their PAT program was a home visit and customized program component to cater to the needs of individual children. For example, the educators partnered with parents to promote better understanding of various children's developmental issues and to provide solutions for them. The PAT program was successful in helping parents, especially from low-income families, and in getting their children ready for school. Parents who attended the PAT program were more actively engaged in promoting their children's cognitive development: they read books to their children more frequently and enrolled their children more in preschool programs than did those who had not been in the PAT program.

Zigler et al. (2008) extended their earlier study of the PAT program by collecting longitudinal data on 5,721 children's school performance from kindergarten to third grade. The authors confirmed the positive effect of the PAT program on children's school readiness and academic performance at third grade. Furthermore, parents who attended the PAT program demonstrated a great deal of improvement in parenting practices, which was important for influencing school readiness and the academic performance of their children. Also, combined with a quality preschool program, the PAT program was effective in narrowing the gap between poor and affluent children in terms of school readiness and academic performance.

Contrary to the results of the studies cited above, some studies have not indicated the same positive effects. Specifically, even the above-mentioned programs did not consistently show the same results. For example, when Madden, O'Hara, and Levenstein (1984) examined the effects of a mother-child verbal interaction program at a three-year, post-program evaluation, they could not find the same significant cognitive child development that their earlier study found. Furthermore, when Scarr and McCartney (1988) implemented in Bermuda the same verbal interaction modeling program previously used by Madden, O'Hara, and Levenstein, they were not able to find a significant effect on preschooler cognitive development, even immediately after the program. Similarly, when Owen and Mulvihill (1994) evaluated the Parents as Teachers program using a statistically robust method—a quasi-experimental longitudinal design—they reported no significant difference in children's outcomes between experimental and control groups. On the same note, based on their analysis of previous early intervention research, White, Taylor, and Moss (1992) concluded that there was no compelling evidence to prove the significant effects of parental involvement. Instead, they called attention to a need for a specific direction in parental involvement and a systematic exploration regarding which kinds of parental involvement are effective for which children.

Recent studies relating to parental involvement have diverged from early studies that focused on the effects of parent classes for children with behavior problems from lower socioeconomic status (SES) backgrounds. Many studies have been conducted to examine the effects of a parenting class based on the Incredible Years Program and have found a positive effect on decreasing behavior problems. The Incredible Years offers 12 weekly parent classes and teaches parents how to discipline and parent children, in addition to promoting children's social skills. By implementing the Incredible Years for parents with low income, Gross et al. (2003) found that toddlers whose parents attended parent classes showed a greater improvement in their behaviors when compared to other toddlers whose parents did not attend. Also, by extending the Incredible Years Program to two more years to promote a better transition from preschool to kindergarten, Webster-Stratton, Reid, and Hammond (2001) showed a greater conduct improvement both at home and in school among children of mothers who attended parent classes. Hartman, Stage, and Webster-Stratton (2003) implemented advanced components, teaching interpersonal communication and problem-solving skills along with the basic components of the Incredible Years Program, to serve parents of children with behavior and/or attention problems. The authors found that children whose parents attended parent classes decreased their conduct and/or attention problems. When the Incredible Years was implemented in England, Jones, Daley, Hutchings, Bywater, and Eames (2007) found that preschoolers with both conduct and attention problems showed greater improvement if their parents attended parent classes, when compared to other preschoolers.

Similar to the Incredible Years Program, another clinical parenting class program has proved to have similar positive effects on improving conduct disorders in children. The Parenting the Strong-Willed Child (PSWC) class offers six weekly sessions and teaches principles and strategies for parenting children with conduct disorders. By providing the PSWC program to parents of children with behavior disorders, Conners, Edwards, and Grant (2007) reported that children showed less intensity and frequency of disorders in comparison with other children whose parents did not attend the classes. By referring to other empirical studies that showed the same positive effects of a PSWC class, Long (2007), who developed the PSWC program, reported the benefits of these clinical parent classes. Beyond discussing current trends in parenting classes, Long also emphasized the need to benefit "average" parents who do not have children with serious problems.

Parental Involvement in Head Start

Since 1965 when Head Start was launched for the first time, parental involvement has been a critical factor in the program's success. The Head Start Program Performance Standards, which are mandatory for these programs, require parent participation in multiple ways, such as policymaking and operations, curriculum development, parenting classes, home visits, and volunteering in the classroom (Head Start Bureau, 1998). Because Head Start believes that parents are the primary and most important resources to support children's development and learning, the regulation requires that

Head Start agencies must provide opportunities for parents to enhance their parenting skills, knowledge, and understanding of the educational and developmental needs and activities of their children and to share concerns about their children with program staff. [Head Start Program Performance Standards 1304.40 (e) (3)]

While the regulation requires Head Start facilities to provide opportunities for parental involvement in the program, it also allows each program autonomy in planning and implementing parental involvement to meet the different needs and goals of the children and families involved in the program [Head Start Program Performance Standards 1304.40 (a)]. Parenting classes are one of the common types of parental involvement in Head Start. These classes cover various topics, such as early childhood education curriculum, behavior guidance, health and nutrition, preventing violence, early literacy skills and activities, and transition to kindergarten (Head Start Bureau, 1993).

The implementation of Early Head Start (EHS) was largely attributed to the studies of brain functioning for infants and toddlers during the 1980s and 1990s and their emphasis on the importance of cognitive development of young children. In particular, a Carnegie Corporation research report, "The Quiet Crisis," strongly influenced the launch of EHS by warning, "American children under the age of three and their families are in trouble, and their plight worsens everyday" (1994). In response to this report, it was recommended that the Advisory Committee on Head Start Quality and Expansion be established to serve families with children under the age of three. Later, Congress expanded EHS to serve pregnant women and low-income families with infants and toddlers (Early Head Start, 2000). Like Head Start, Early Head Start also mandates parental involvement but gives local programs leeway in planning and implementation.

Methods

Analyses

The main statistical tools for this study were a two-level longitudinal hierarchical linear modeling (HLM) and a multivariate analysis. The HLM analyzed the longitudinal effects of parenting classes on parental cognitive stimulation and children's cognitive development (Bayley MDI scores) after controlling for the effects of the other covariates using three waves of data. The multivariate analyses examined the effects of parenting classes on the parental cognitive and language stimulation and the parent-child interactive activities at 36 months of age.

Multilevel analysis, also referred to as hierarchical linear modeling (HLM), is a statistical methodology for examining hierarchical or nested data. For example, children who are nested in a particular school tend to have more aspects in common than do children from different schools. Multilevel analysis takes into account correlations caused by sharing common factors among children in the same school (Hox, 2002; Raudenbush & Bryk, 2002). Analyzing longitudinal data through a multilevel analysis offers researchers great advantages. This approach has been shown to overcome several methodological limitations associated with traditional repeated measures designs: it is free from the strong assumption (compound symmetry) of repeated measures; it allows for unbiased parameter estimation, even when the data show a high degree of correlation within the levels; and it is highly flexible with respect to the number and spacing of observations, in the sense that it does not require equal spacing or an equal number of observations. This flexibility makes longitudinal multilevel analysis a breakthrough when it comes to the handling of missing data, which has been a major problem for longitudinal data analysis (Hox; Kreft & de Leeuw, 1998; Lee, 2000; Raudenbush & Bryk).

The two-level HLM models were analyzed using the two longitudinal models: In the first longitudinal model, the association of the three waves of parenting classes and the composite score of parental cognitive stimulation was examined; in the second longitudinal model, the relation between the three waves of parenting classes and children's MDI scores was explored. We used the three waves of parenting classes by specifying the variable as a time-varying variable. In this way, we were able to examine the direct effect of parenting classes on dependent variables as well as the longitudinal effect.

The HLM model at level-1 measured the initial score and change (growth) rate of a dependent variable, and the longitudinal effect of a parenting class on the dependent variable. Level-2 was designed to show the interaction effects of the individual variables with the change rate of a dependent variable and a parenting class (*ParClass*) only at the initial point (intercept). (See Appendix A for the detailed model specifications of level-1 and level-2; all Appendices available from the authors upon request; contacts are at the end of this article.)

The multivariate analyses were also adopted to examine the effects of parenting classes on the two forms of parental cognitive and language stimulation and the five parent-child interactive activities. The multivariate analyses were a suitable statistical tool due to multiple dependent variables and their correlated aspects (two types of parental cognitive and language stimulation and five parent-child interactive activities) within each set.

The two forms of parental cognitive and language stimulation were parents' language and cognitive stimulation by Home Observation for Measurement of the Environment (HOME) and parents' cognitive stimulation by video recording of parent-child interaction at 36 months of age. The five activities were measured as parent-child play, parent-child outside activities, reading once or more per day, reading bedtime routine, and reading frequency.

Data and Variables

This study used the Early Head Start Research and Evaluation (EHSRE) database, which contains a three-year, large-scale data, allowing for investigation of the longitudinal effects of parenting classes on parenting behaviors and children's cognitive development. In 1996, the Administration on Children, Youth, and Families (ACYF) initially funded 143 Early Head Start programs. Among those programs, only 17 programs were selected for an evaluation and included in the EHSRE to have a balance of rural/urban locations and racial/ethnic composition. The data collection method of the EHSRE was the random assignment of children and their families to the Early Head Start program (EHS) and to the control group at the onset of programs. While the EHS group received planned services, the children of the control group could not receive any services from Head Start until the child reached the age of 3, although they could receive other services in the community. At the design stage of evaluation, 1,513 families were assigned to the EHS, while 1,488 families were assigned to the control group. After an initial adjustment, the EHS data was composed of 1,503 children of the program group and 1,474 children of the control group (Inter-University Consortium for Political and Social Research, 2004).

As stated in the purpose of the study, the chief predictor was the degree of participation of mothers in parenting classes. The variable of parenting classes in the study indicated whether mothers attended parenting classes at 6, 15, and 26 months after enrollment. Although the EHSRE used random assignments for the Early Head Start programs, it did not employ random assignments with the parenting classes. As shown in Table 8.1, the frequencies of mothers who participated in parenting classes from the control and the EHS were quite different, but they showed constant participation rates over the time. We used the three waves of parenting class variables by specifying them as a time-varying variable. In other words, at each wave the effect of parenting classes was differently associated with the dependent variables, and those different associations revealed the longitudinal effect.

TABLE 8.1 Frequency Table for Participants of Parenting Classes Classified by Three Waves and Program Status (EHS vs. Control Groups)

| | | Parenting Class | | |
		No	Yes	Total
6 months after enrollment in EHS	Control	827	182	1009
	EHS	613	461	1074
15 months after enrollment in EHS	Control	875	134	1009
	EHS	633	442	1075
26 months after enrollment in EHS	Control	872	138	1010
	EHS	687	384	1071

To reduce the selection bias for the effect of parenting classes, which was caused by non-randomization, we controlled for the effects of important predictor variables that could significantly influence the cognitive development of children: teenage status of the mother at random assignment (*Teenmom*), mother's education (*Momedu*), mother's primary language (*Momlang*), adult male in the household at baseline (*Madult*), mother's previous experience of Head Start programs (*PreHead*), family poverty level (*Povty*), child's gender (*Gender*), child's age at random assignment (*Age*), and the program status (*Hdst*).

We analyzed three sets of dependent variables: parent's language and cognitive stimulation, parent-child interactive activities, and Bayley MDI scores. The first set of dependent variables, parent's language and cognitive stimulation, were used to explore the relation between parental education and the quality of parent-child interactions, which can be critical factors in promoting a child's cognitive development. The two raw scores (parent's language and cognitive stimulation as determined by home observation and by video recording) were used as dependent variables in the multivariate analyses. We also created a composite variable by combining the two variables for the longitudinal analysis. The composite variable was created by converting the two raw scores into standardized scores and combining them into one. As the second set of dependent variables, we used five parent-child interactive activities: parent-child play, parent-child outside activities, reading once or more per day, reading bedtime routine, and reading frequency at 36 months of age by specifying another set of dependent variables. Finally, we also paid attention to the Bayley MDI scores at the ages of 14, 24, and 36 months as dependent variables for a longitudinal analysis to examine the effects of parenting classes on the degree of children's mental development.

Results

Our data analysis included descriptive statistics and correlations to determine the bivariate relations among all variables in the first step. The total number of children in the EHS database was 2,977; the total number of mothers who participated in the study was 2,960. Among those, 643, 576, and 522 mothers participated in the 6-, 15-, and 26-month parenting classes, respectively (See Table 8.1 for detailed information). When we looked at the total number of participants, 665 mothers from the program and 300 mothers from the control group participated in one or more parenting class.

As a preliminary analysis, we also performed a bivariate correlation whose results revealed that parenting classes had significant connections with a child's cognitive development indices, justifying the importance of further advanced analyses. The correlation of parenting classes with Bayley MDI at 36 months was 0.127 ($p < 0.01$), with home language cognitive stimulation being 0.169 ($p < 0.01$), and with parent cognitive stimulation being 0.121 ($p < 0.01$), as shown in Table 8.2.

The second analysis was on the longitudinal effect of parenting classes on the composite score of parental cognitive and language stimulation. The effect was significant, having the coefficient of 0.246 ($p < 0.01$) as shown in Table 8.3. In other words, when mothers participated in parenting classes, the mothers showed increased cognitive and language stimulation over the years.

We performed additional analyses to examine the effects of parenting classes on the two separate measures of parental cognitive stimulation. The result of multivariate analysis presented in Table 8.4 indicates that the effects of parenting classes were pronounced for both HOME language cognitive stimulation ($F = 14.159$, $p < 0.01$) and video parent cognitive stimulation ($F = 12.483$, $p < 0.01$). Therefore, when mothers went to parenting classes, increased parental cognitive stimulations in parent-child interactions were noticed over time. This finding shares the observations from early literature (Bronfenbrenner, 1974; Madden et al., 1976). Specifically, our results verified the results of Madden et al. (1976), in which the authors showed that parents of low-income families demonstrated improved verbal interaction with children during play time when they attended an intervention program. In addition, our result is a new addition to the literature in terms of the longitudinal effects of parenting classes on the role of parental behavior in helping foster children's cognitive and language development. Figure 8.1 highlights the effect of parenting classes on parent cognitive stimulation by HOME, while Figure 8.2 displays the effect by video observation.

TABLE 8.2 Descriptive Statistics and Correlation Coefficients of Parenting Classes and All Nine Dependent Variables at 36 months

	1.	2.	3.	4.	5.	6.	7.	8.	9.
1. Parenting Class	—	.127**	.169**	.121**	.106**	.057*	.126**	.136**	.133**
2. Bayley MDI Score		—	.364**	.277**	.133**	-.033	.159**	.197**	.222**
3. HOME: Language & Cognitive Stimulation			—	.296**	.383**	.169**	.288**	.357**	.440**
4. Video: Parent Cognitive Stimulation				—	.129**	.056*	.146**	.132**	.172**
5. Parent-Child Play					—	.389**	.231**	.555**	.691**
6. Parent-Child Outside Activities						—	.083**	.203**	.256**
7. Reading Bedtime Routine							—	.410**	.384**
8. Read Daily								—	.817**
9. Reading Frequency									—
N	2081	1658	1861	1658	2076	2061	2099	2072	2072
Mean	.25	90.63	10.49	3.77	4.36	2.86	.31	.54	4.53
SD	.434	12.634	2.018	1.125	.850	.702	.462	.498	1.143

* $p < 0.05$; ** $p < 0.01$

TABLE 8.3   The HLM Analysis Result Using Composite Scores of Parental Cognitive and Language Stimulation at 14, 24, and 36 Months as Dependent Variables

Fixed Effect	Coefficient	SE	T-Ratio	DF	p
Initial Score	–2.442	0.166	–14.737	1096	0.000
Growth Effect	0.290	0.027	10.731	1105	0.000
Parenting Class Effect on Growth	0.246	0.061	3.996	2598	0.000

FIGURES 8.1 & 8.2   Relationships Between Parenting Classes and Language & Cognitive Stimulation by Observation and by Video Recording at 36 Months

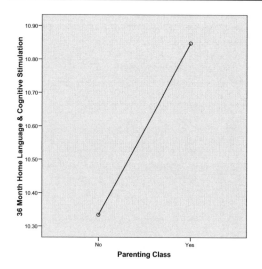

FIGURE 8.1   Home Observation

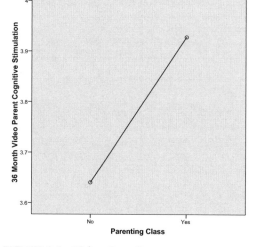

FIGURE 8.2   Video Recoding

TABLE 8.4   The Multivariate Analysis Result Using Language and Cognitive Stimulation by HOME Observation and by Video Recording at 36 Months as Dependent Variables

Source	Dependent Variable	SS	df	MS	F	p	η^2
Parenting Class	H. L. & C. S.[1]	45.971	1	45.971	14.159	.000	.151
	V. L. & C. S.[2]	14.416	1	14.416	12.483	.000	.082
Error	H. L. & C. S.[1]	2636.386	812	3.247			
	V. L. & C. S.[2]	937.718	812	1.155			
Total	H. L. & C. S.[1]	3106.049	822				
	V. L. & C. S.[2]	1021.193	822				

[1] Home Language & Cognitive Stimulation
[2] Video Language & Cognitive Stimulation

In the next analysis, we paid attention to the effects of parenting education on parent-child activities. As Table 8.5 and Figures 8.3–8.7 show, the results of multivariate analysis demonstrate that participation in parenting classes resulted in a statistically significant increase in parent-child activities, with the exception of parent-child outside activity (F = .125, $p > 0.05$). Specifically, parent-child play (F = 10.121, $p < 0.01$; $\eta^2 = 0.031$), reading bedtime routine (F = 17.272, $p < 0.01$; $\eta^2 = 0.069$), reading daily (F = 21.820, $p < 0.01$; $\eta^2 = 0.060$), and reading frequency (F = 20.918, $p < .01$; $\eta^2 = 0.062$) showed significant results with effect sizes ranging from 0.031 to 0.069. Importantly, three reading activities showed significant relationships with parenting education, although the effect sizes were small. Our Figures 8.3–8.7 also confirmed the multivariate results, with increased activities patterns when mothers participated in a parenting class, although careful interpretation is required because of their effect sizes.

Along with results on increased cognitive stimulation, the results of increased parent-child activities by those participating in a parenting class also support previous research findings (Bailey, Silvern, & Brabham, 2004; Bronfenbrenner, 1974; Senechal, 2006; Sy & Schulenberg, 2005; Yan & Lin, 2005).

TABLE 8.5 The Multivariate Analysis Results Using Parent-Child Activities as Dependent Variables at 36 Months

Source	Dependent Variable	SS	df	MS	F	p	η^2
Parenting Class	Parent-Child Play	7.262	1	7.262	10.121	.002	.031
	Parent-Child Outside Activities	.064	1	.064	.125	.724	.001
	Reading Bedtime Routine	3.550	1	3.550	17.272	.000	.069
	Read Daily	5.130	1	5.130	21.820	.000	.060
	Reading Frequency	26.785	1	26.785	20.918	.000	.062
Error	Parent-Child Play	741.907	1034	.718			
	Parent-Child Outside Activities	525.707	1034	.508			
	Reading Bedtime Routine	212.527	1034	.206			
	Read Daily	243.087	1034	.235			
	Reading Frequency	1324.024	1034	1.280			
Total	Parent-Child Play	765.944	1044				
	Parent-Child Outside Activities	531.084	1044				
	Reading Bedtime Routine	228.322	1044				
	Read Daily	258.712	1044				
	Reading Frequency	1411.680	1044				

FIGURES 8.3–8.7   Relationships Between Parenting Classes and Parent-Child Activities at 36 Months

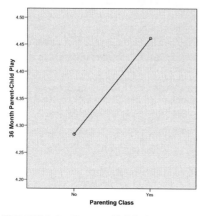

FIGURE 8.3   Parent-Child Play

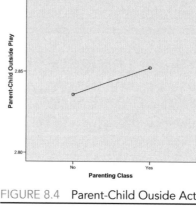

FIGURE 8.4   Parent-Child Ouside Activities

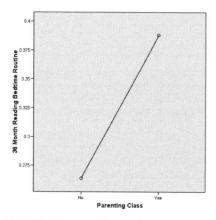

FIGURE 8.5   Reading Bedtime Routine

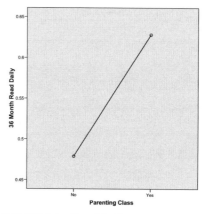

FIGURE 8.6   Read Daily

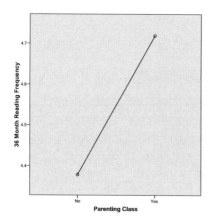

FIGURE 8.7   Reading Frequency

In the last analysis, we analyzed the effect of parenting classes on children's Bayley MDI scores using a longitudinal hierarchical linear modeling. Our analysis revealed that the children whose mothers had a parenting class demonstrated significantly higher MDI scores than those whose mothers had not gone to parenting class (β_{20} = 1.438, $p < 0.05$). To present a clear understanding, we present only the effects of the initial score, the growth rate, and a parenting class on children's Bayley MDI score in Table 8.6. The effects of other independent variables and the other statistical results of the full model are presented in Appendix B (all Appendices

TABLE 8.6   The HLM Analysis Result Using Bayley MDI Scores at 14, 24, and 36 Months as Dependent Variables

Fixed Effect	Coefficient	SE	T-Ratio	DF	p
Initial Score	85.366	1.392	61.312	1109	0.000
Growth Effect	−3.589	0.248	−14.488	2566	0.000
Parenting Class Effect on Growth	1.438	0.567	2.537	2566	0.012

available from authors upon request). Figure 8.8 also illustrates the difference of children's Bayley MDI scores from the two parent groups.

Although this significant result is the final objective of providing parenting classes for the parents of low-income families, it takes extra caution to interpret the results because there may be other factors that determine improved cognitive development of children which we did not consider in the analysis. Despite our caution in asserting a direct association between the effects of parenting classes and children's cognitive development, this result shares similar findings with prior studies which showed parenting classes as being significantly associated with children's intellectual development (Bronfenbrenner, 1974; Madden et al., 1976; Pfannenstiel & Seltzer, 1985).

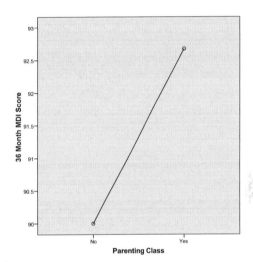

FIGURE 8.8   Relationship Between Parenting Classes and Child's MDI Score at 36 Mos.

Lastly, we paid attention to the effects of the variables we controlled for (covariates) in examining the effects of parenting classes on the three sets of dependent variables. As stated in the methods section, we controlled for the effects of the variables because they could influence the outcome variables and thus confound the effects of parenting classes. At the same time, they could be important variables to consider. Our analyses allowed us to see the results of the covariates along with the interpretation of parenting classes. For longitudinal and multivariate analyses for Bayley MDI scores, the effects of the teenage status of the mother (*Teenmom*), mother's education (*Momedu*), adult male in the household (*Madult*), and child's gender (*Gender*) were significant. High child Bayley MDI scores were observed when the mother was a teenager or had higher education; the child was a girl; or a male adult lived in the household. Both longitudinal and multivariate analyses for parental cognitive stimulation indicated that the effects of the mother's teenage status (*Teenmom*), mother's education (*Momedu*), mother's primary language (*Momlang*), family poverty level (*Povty*), and child's gender (*Gender*) were significant. For the multivariate analysis using parent-child interactive play, the mother's education (*Momedu*) and mother's primary language (*Momlang*) were significant predictors as shown in Appendix C. The detailed information is presented in Appendices B and C (available from the authors upon request).

Discussion

Overall Findings

The long-term goal of this study is to provide sound, empirical research findings on the effects of active parental involvement in children's cognitive development and educational success for low-income families and to support parental outcomes and child well-being. Keeping the long-term goal in mind, the stated short-term objectives of the paper were to investigate the effects of parenting classes on parental cognitive and language stimulation, parent-child interactive activities, and children's cognitive development in Early Head Start participants. As Early Head Start has mandated multi-dimensional parental involvement, such as class volunteering, council meetings, staff-parent conferences, and parenting classes, the study considered parental involvement as an important determinant to change parental behavior and, in turn, to boost the cognitive development of children from low SES families. The study selected the effect of parenting classes as a main predictor variable among available variables of parental involvement. It was guided by prior research in which parenting classes made a direct impact on parental behaviors and children's cognitive development (Bronfenbrenner, 1974; Madden et al., 1976), but this type of investigation has been under-represented in recent research. The findings of our study can be summarized as follows: when compared to the parents who did not participate in parenting classes, those who attended parenting classes: (1) increased their children's cognitive and language stimulation over the years; (2) engaged in more parent-child activities such as parent-child play, reading bedtime routines, reading daily, and reading frequency; and (3) had children with higher scores in the Bayley assessment over the three waves.

As shown in the summary of our findings, we supported all three hypotheses with our analysis results, although they show small effect sizes. Thus, our study mirrored prior studies in which participation in a parental education program had a favorable outcome (Bronfenbrenner, 1974; Madden et al., 1976; Pfannenstiel & Seltzer, 1985), although there exists a difference in the impact of the program effects. In interpreting our findings, however, we were careful not to make a direct cause-effect link, considering that our results are based on survey questionnaires. Although we tried to control for many possible extraneous variables in the study (the teenage status of the mother at random assignment, mother's education, mother's primary language, adult male in the household, mother's previous experience of Head Start programs, family poverty level, child's gender, child's age at random assignment, and the program status), there still exist many factors determining parental behaviors, parent-child interaction, and children's cognitive development. For example, self-selection would remain as a major confounding effect when examining the effects of parenting classes on those dependent variables. The strongly motivated mothers would naturally participate in the parenting classes; thus the motivation rather than the program effects may play a major role in increasing cognitive and language stimulation and parent-child interactions. Therefore, we are cautious about an interpretation that declares the improved outcomes of those dependent variables are due to the effect of parenting classes. Another limitation of this study is the reliance on self-reported data. The participation in parenting classes was a response in the parent interview. With self-reporting methods, a social desirability response bias is of particular concern. Therefore, we suggest that further study is needed to consider the effect of self-selection for parental involvement; we further suggest collecting the data by a means other than self-report.

It is also important to note that there may be many other psychosocial and contextual outcome factors that this study did not consider. Therefore, we recommend that the EHSRE collect child outcome data on pre-academic and behavioral competencies as well as other contextual variables; at the same time we suggest that future studies explore the effects of parenting classes on other psychological and social factors for mothers and children.

We also urge the EHSRE to include program factors from each local Early Head Start program, such as structure, curriculum, child-teacher ratios, parent involvement, teacher qualifications, training, and professional development. As we explained regarding its regulations, Head Start allows each local program autonomy in planning and implementing curricula, including parental involvement programs. Therefore, it is very important to consider the effects of different local programs in examining the effects of parental involvement to gain insights about important determinants for successful programs.

Despite the limitations, this study has important implications regarding potential benefits of parenting classes for both parents and children, especially those from low SES backgrounds. Therefore, this study suggests that an evaluation study of parenting classes for low-income families would be possible using an experimental design with direct causal-effect interpretation. Moreover, the practices and impacts of parenting classes for children who are preschool age or younger have been relatively less studied than those for school-age children, although the importance of parental involvement has been emphasized more often than not. As Early Head Start staff recognizes parents as important resources for the education of children, it is important to encourage parents with young children to learn appropriate parenting skills and to help them maximize interactions with their children at home.

As Edwards, Pleasants, and Franklin (1999) have shown, young children learn not through academic activities such as paper-and-pencil tasks or rote memorization, but from parent-child interactions, including reading books, having open-ended conversations, singing songs, doing creative art projects, and pretend play. Thus, it is very important to have parents recognize the importance of play and learn to stimulate cognitive development in play scenes. Therefore, to conclude, the present study suggests that early childhood education programs should provide parenting classes for children's parents. In these classes, practical ideas about interacting with children, as well as the importance of parental roles in education, should be taught. The contents of parenting classes may include (1) the importance of positive interaction between parents and children, (2) how to play with children at home, (3) good activities for children's literacy and cognitive development, and (4) how to arrange the home environment to promote their children's development and learning. The more children gain exposure to cognitive stimulation in a preschool program and at home during early childhood, the more ready they will be for schooling later.

References

Bailey, L. B., Silvern, S. B., & Brabham, E. (2004). The effects of interactive reading homework and parent involvement on children's inference responses. *Early Childhood Education Journal, 32*(3), 173–178.

Bronfenbrenner, U. (1974). *A report on longitudinal evaluations of preschool programs. Volume II: Is early intervention effective?* (No. [OHD] 76-30025). Washington, DC: U.S. Department of Health, Education and Welfare.

Conners, N. A., Edwards, M. C., & Grant, A. S. (2007). An evaluation of a parenting class curriculum for parents of young children: Parenting the strong-willed child. *Journal of Child and Family Studies, 16*(3), 321–330.

Currie, J., & Thomas, D. (1999). Does Head Start help Hispanic children? *Journal of Public Economics, 74*(2), 235–262.

Edwards, P. A., Pleasants, H. M., & Franklin, S. H. A. (1999). *Path to follow: Learning to listen to parents.* Westport, CT: Heinemann.

Flouri, E. (2004). Correlates of parents' involvement with their adolescent children in restructured and biological two-parent families: The role of child characteristics. *International Journal of Behavioral Development, 28*(2), 148–156.

Gross, D., Fogg, L., Webster-Stratton, C., Garvey, C., Julion, W., & Grady, J. (2003). Parent training of toddlers in day care in low-income urban communities. *Journal of Consulting and Clinical Psychology, 71*(2), 261–278.

Hartman, R. R., Stage, S. A., & Webster-Stratton, C. (2003). A growth curve analysis of parent training outcomes: Examining the influence of child risk factors (inattention, impulsivity, and hyperactivity problems), parental, and family risk factors. *Journal of Child Psychology and Psychiatry, 44*(3), 388–398.

Head Start Bureau. (1993). *Head Start parenting education resource directory.* Washington DC: Author.

Head Start Bureau. (1998). *The Head Start Program Performance Standards Part 1304.* Retrieved July 2, 2007, from http://eclkc.ohs.acf.hhs.gov/hslc/Program%20Design%20and%20Management/Head%20Start%20Requirements/Head%20Start%20Requirements

Hox, J. J. (2002). *Multilevel analysis: Techniques and applications.* Mahwah, NJ: Lawrence Erlbaum.

Inter-University Consortium for Political and Social Research. (2004). *Early Head Start Research and Evaluation (EHSRE) Study, 1996–2001.* Ann Arbor, MI: Author.

Jones, K., Daley, D., Hutchings, J., Bywater, T., & Eames, C. (2007). Efficacy of the Incredible Years basic parent training programme as an early intervention for children with conduct problems and ADHD. *Child: Care, Health and Development, 33*(6), 749–756.

Kreft, I., & de Leeuw, J. (1998). *Introducing multilevel modeling.* Thousand Oaks, CA: Sage.

Lee, V. E. (2000). Using hierarchical linear modeling to study social context: The case of school effects. *Educational Psychologist, 35*(2), 125–141.

Li, G. (2006). What do parents think? Middle-class Chinese immigrant parents' perspectives on literacy learning, homework, and school-home communication. *School Community Journal, 16*(2), 27–46.

Long, N. (2007). Special section: Learning from experience: Shifting from clinical parent training to broader parent education. *Clinical Child Psychology and Psychiatry, 12*(3), 385–392.

Madden, J., Levenstein, P., & Levenstein, S. (1976). Longitudinal IQ outcomes of the mother-child home program. *Child Development, 47*(4), 1015–1025.

Madden, J., O'Hara, J., & Levenstein, P. (1984). Home again: Effects of the Mother-Child Home Program on mother and child. *Child Development, 55*(2), 636–647.

Owen, M. T., & Mulvihill, B. A. (1994). Benefits of a parent education and support program in the first three years. *Family Relations, 43*(2), 206–212.

Pfannenstiel, J. C., Seitz, V., & Zigler, E. (2003). Promoting school readiness: The role of the Parents as Teachers program. *NHSA Dialog, 6*(1), 71–86.

Pfannenstiel, J. C., & Seltzer, D. A. (1985). *New Parents as Teachers project: Evaluation report.* Jefferson City, MO: Missouri State Department of Elementary and Secondary Education.

Raudenbush, S. W., & Bryk, A. S. (2002). *Hierarchical linear models: Applications and data analysis methods* (2nd ed.). Thousand Oakes, CA: Sage.

Reutzal, D. R., Fawson, P. C., & Smith, J. A. (2006). Words to Go!: Evaluating a first-grade parent involvement program for "making" words at home. *Reading Research and Instruction, 45*(2), 119–159.

Scarr, S., & McCartney, K. (1988). Far from home: An experimental evaluation of the Mother-Child Home Program in Bermuda. *Child Development, 59*(3), 531–543.

Senechal, M. (2006). Testing the home literacy model: Parent involvement in kindergarten is differentially related to grade 4 reading comprehension, fluency, spelling, and reading for pleasure. *Scientific Studies of Reading, 10*(1), 59–87.

St. Clair, L., & Jackson, B. (2006). Effect of family involvement training on the language skills of young elementary children from migrant families. *School Community Journal, 16*(1), 31–41.

Sy, S. R., & Schulenberg, J. E. (2005). Parent beliefs and children's achievement trajectories during the transition to school in Asian American and European American families. *International Journal of Behavioral Development, 29*(6), 505–515.

Webster-Stratton, C., Reid, M. J., & Hammond, M. (2001). Preventing conduct problems, promoting social competence: A parent and teacher training partnership in Head Start. *Journal of Clinical Child & Adolescent Psychology, 30*(3), 283–302.

White, K. R., Taylor, M. J., & Moss, V. D. (1992). Does research support claims about the benefits of involving parents in early intervention programs? *Review of Educational Research, 62*(1), 91–125.

Yan, W., & Lin, Q. (2005). Parent involvement and mathematics achievement: Contrast across racial and ethnic groups. *Journal of Educational Research, 99*(2), 116–127.

Zigler, E., Pfannenstiel, J., & Seitz, V. (2008). The Parents as Teachers program and school success: A replication and extension. *The Journal of Primary Prevention, 29*(2), 103–120.

Discussion Questions

1. What is the main focus of Piaget's Cognitive Developmental Theory?
2. Explain and provide examples for Piaget's four stages of cognitive development?
3. Based on your understanding, explain the roles of schema, assimilation, accommodation, and equilibration in human cognitive development?
4. What is reversibility?
5. How can adults apply Piaget's stages of cognitive development to the learning and development of young children?

UNIT III

PHYSICAL DEVELOPMENT

Selection from the Developing Toddler and Early Childhood

Susan Whitbourne and Cynthia R. Davis

Motor Development and Functioning

During the early toddler years, **fine motor skills**, or the control over small movements of the body such as fingers, hands, feet, and parts of the face and mouth, develop at the same time as the child's knowledge of the environment, what he wants to do, and what is necessary to go about doing it, for example, turning a door knob. His motor skills are refined so objects can now be used as tools, such as holding a spoon in an appropriate way to feed himself, or adequately controlling a crayon to draw with it. Fine motor skills also become more precise, effective, and efficient so acts can be carried out with increasing independence (Gerber, Wilks, & Erdie-Lalena, 2010). **Gross motor skills**, on the other hand, involve the activation and coordination of large muscle groups and include movements such as walking, running, and jumping. These, too, are accomplished with increasing coordination and refinement as the child grows older. Table 5-2 shows some ~ne motor skills and gross motor skills that develop across this time period.

The child's newly developing independence comes with some psychological challenges for both the child and parent. It is necessary for parents to set limits on what a child can and cannot do independently, such as going up and down stairs, slicing a tomato, or pushing a playmate. When a child is not allowed to or unable to perform an activity on their own, this can lead to frustration and anger that may result in crying, screaming, or tantrums. This limit- and

MYTHS AND MISCONCEPTIONS

An adult's brain is more active than a child's. Myth

A 3-year-old has a brain twice as active as an adult's. Fact

Susan Whitbourne and Cynthia R. Davis, Selection from "The Developing Toddler and Early Childhood," *Lifespan Development: Biopsychosocial Perspectives*, pp. 111-113, 328-368. Copyright © 2018 by Cognella, Inc. Reprinted with permission. Susan Whitbourne and Cynthia R. Davis, Selection from "The Developing Toddler and Early Childhood," Lifespan Development: Biopsychosocial Perspectives, pp. 111-113, 328-368. Copyright © 2018 by Cognella, Inc. Reprinted with permission.

Emma was the best decision I made, and we have a son, Sawyer, who is now 4 himself. When I was pregnant with Sawyer, I did not want to know the sex of the baby, because I thought of the higher risk of autism in boys. I also didn't want Emma or Sawyer to have vaccinations until their first year of school because of all the talk back then about potential links to autism. Sawyer did well until 15 months, still, he lost eye contact and some verbal skills, and like Abby he showed some repetitive behaviors. He was diagnosed with PDD-NOS, but with all of his therapy, play groups, and his social skills, he is doing great. On the surface you don't see autism.

In many ways, we treat Abby the same way we do Emma and Sawyer. There is no special treatment because she has autism. Everyone is the same. For example, she gets her things taken away and she has her "time outs" when she's disobedient. I certainly do not regret my decision to have more children now. Both Sawyer and Emma know how different Abby is, but they love her a lot.

Think about what you would do in this situation after reading the chapter, and then decide the following:

- If you were the pediatrician who first identified the speech delay, what referrals would you have made?
- If you were the speech pathologist who made the first observation, would you have pushed for follow-up or would you have waited to see how Abby's behaviors progressed?
- If you were Yoly, would you have followed the advice of the first specialist? Would you have questioned some of the behaviors Abby continued to exhibit before she was diagnosed?
- If you were a doctor or specialist delivering an autistic spectrum disorder diagnosis to a parent, how would you be sensitive to their feelings and reactions?
- If you were a stranger seeing a child like Abby having a tantrum, what would your response be?
- If you were Yoly and Mark, would you want to have more children?
- If you were Yoly, what would your outlook be for Abby's future?

boundary-testing that a child acts out is quite normal, and it is recommended that caregivers provide a safe and structured environment with well-defined rules for children to test their physical and emotional limits.

TABLE 9.1 Gross Motor Skills and Fine motor Skills Across Early Childhood (Kaneshiro, 2014)

Age	Gross Motor Development	Fine Motor Development
Generally	• Becoming more skilled at running, jumping, early throwing, kicking, catching a bounced ball	
At about age 3	• Pedaling a tricycle	• Drawing a circle • Drawing a person with three parts • Beginning to use children's blunt-nose scissors • Self-dressing (with supervision)
At about age 4	• Becoming able to steer well • Hopping on one foot, and later balancing on one foot for up to 5 seconds	• Drawing a square • Using scissors, and eventually cutting a straight line • Putting on clothes properly • Managing a spoon and fork neatly while eating
At about age 5	• Doing a heel-to-toe walk	• Spreading with a knife • Drawing a triangle

FIGURE 9.1   Children with Down syndrome don't development motor skills in the same way or at the same rate as other children because of low muscle tone, greater flexibility in their joints, and less overall strength. They can receive physical therapy to promote the eventual development of more optimal posture, movement patterns, and a strong foundation for exercise across the lifespan (Winders, 2012).

Source: Copyright © 2012 Depositphotos/ginosphotos1.

References

Gerber, R. J., Wilks, T., & Erdie-Lalena, C. (2010). Developmental milestones: Motor development. *Pediatrics in Review, 31,* 267–277. doi:10.1542/pir.31-7-267

Kaneshiro, N. K. Z., D. (2010). Sudden Infant Death Syndrome. Retrieved February 15, 2018, from https://www. texashealth.org/allen/health-information/?productId=617&pid=1&gid=001566

Physical Development During the First Two Years

Megan Clegg-Kraynok, Kelvin L. Seifert, and Robert J. Hoffnung

Source: Bolyuk Rostyslav/Shutterstock.com.

CHAPTER OUTLINE

PHYSICAL DEVELOPMENT

The Newborn

Growth during Infancy

Infant States: Sleep and Arousal

Motor Development

Nutrition During the First Two Years

Impairments in Infant Growth

Megan Clegg-Kraynok, Kelvin L. Seifert, and Robert J. Hoffnung, "Physical Development During the First Two Years," *Child and Adolescent Development: A Chronological Approach*, pp. 105-126, R1-R36. Copyright © 2019 by Academic Media Solutions. Reprinted with permission.

Focusing Questions

- What do infants look like when they are first born? How do we know if they are healthy?
- How much do children grow during infancy?
- What changes occur in the brains of infants?
- How do infants' sleep and wakefulness patterns change as infants get older?
- What motor skills evolve during infancy?
- What do infants need nutritionally?
- What factors can impair growth during infancy?

Anne was looking at the journal she had kept about her daughter since Michelle was seven months old.

- April 9: For two weeks, she has been sleeping through the night! Maybe it helped to start nursing her just before bedtime—but it's so hard to tell. She is starting to enjoy bedtime stories, too; babbles at the book and points at the pictures.
- June 10: Michelle has been crawling all over—mostly after the dog. Gets mad, cries when Huggins walks away; struggles to crawl after him; but then forgets all about him.
- August 10: Here's Michelle's latest words: "dada" (daddy), "tigg'n" (Tigger, the cat), "buh" (book). Maybe not polished English, but she's getting there. At this rate, I'm going to lose track of her full vocabulary soon.

As Anne can attest, during the first months of life a baby's behaviors evolve rapidly. In this chapter, we trace some of these changes through the first two years of life. We begin by discussing young infants' physical growth: what they look like, how they sleep, hear, and see, and what behaviors they can already perform at birth. We also look at variations in growth and in infants' nutritional needs in the first months of life. In Chapter 6, we take a second look at infants' development, this time from a cognitive perspective. We explore infants' perceptions and representations of their surroundings and how they learn from their world even before they learn to speak. Finally, we consider one of the most universal yet remarkable of all human accomplishments: the acquisition of language.

As we will see, when compared to other parts of the childhood and adolescence, development during infancy shows more obvious growth and more discontinuity, but less diversity. Growth occurs now as at no other time of life! Babies change daily, putting on pounds and inches and acquiring new skills. "You can almost *see* them grow," said one mother. Growth—both physical and psychological—continues throughout life, but never in quite such an obvious way as in infancy. The very speed of infant growth creates important *dis*continuities: a child who cannot talk at six months, for example, is well on her way to talking at eighteen months.

As we will see, babies also show diversity. Not every infant acquires language, for example, in quite the same sequence or with the same timing. But compared to the important developments of adolescence, infant developments are among the most predictable of the lifespan, both in timing and in nature. It is possible to predict within a few months either way, for example, when most infants will take their first step or speak their first word. Such accurate predictions are rarely possible for adolescents and adults.

Physical Development

The Newborn

As we saw in the last chapter, birth continues rather than initiates physical development. Most organs have already been working for weeks, or even months, prior to this event. The baby's heart has been beating regularly, muscles have been contracting sporadically, and the liver has been making its major product, bile, which is necessary for normal digestion after birth. Even some behaviors, such as sucking and arm stretching, have already developed. Two physical functions, however, do begin at birth: breathing and ingestion (the taking in of foods). These fundamental physical functions constitute the basic physical continuities that must last a lifetime. The baby's heart is the same one that will be beating eighty years and more than two billion heartbeats later; her lungs and stomach will grow larger, but they will be the same lungs and stomach taking in oxygen and food decades later when she has become elderly.

The First Few Hours

When first emerging from the birth canal, the newborn infant (also called a **neonate**) definitely does not resemble most people's

neonate A newborn infant.

stereotypes of a beautiful baby. Regardless of race, skin often looks rather red. If born a bit early, the baby may also have a white, waxy substance called *vernix* on the skin, and the body may be covered with fine, downy hair called *lanugo*. If the baby was born vaginally rather then delivered surgically, its head may be somewhat elongated or have a noticeable point on it; the shape comes from the pressure of the birth canal, which squeezes the skull for several hours during labor. Within a few days or weeks, the head fills out again to a more rounded shape, leaving gaps in the bones. The gaps are sometimes *called fontanelles,* or "soft spots," although they are actually covered by a tough membrane that can withstand normal contact and pressure. The gaps eventually grow over, but not until the infant is about eighteen months old.

Immediately after birth, many hospitals and midwives recommend Kangaroo Mother Care, which includes skin-to-skin contact between the newborn and mother for a period of time as well as breastfeeding (Boundy et al., 2016). Kangaroo Care has been linked to lower rates of infant hypothermia, hypoglycemia, and mortality as well as higher levels of oxygen in the blood (Boundy et al., 2016).

Is the Baby All Right? The Apgar Scale

The **Apgar Scale** (named after its originator, Dr. Virginia Apgar) helps doctors and nurses to decide quickly whether a newborn needs immediate medical attention. The scale consists of ratings that are simple enough for non-specialists to make, even during the distractions surrounding the moment of delivery (Apgar, 1953). To use it, someone present at the delivery calculates the baby's heart rate, breathing effort, muscle tone, skin color, and reflex irritability and assigns a score of zero to two on each of these five characteristics. Babies are rated one minute after they emerge from the womb and again at five minutes. For each rating, they can earn a maximum score of two, for a total possible score of ten, as Table 5.1 shows. Most babies earn eight, nine, or ten points, at least by five minutes after delivery. A baby who scores between five and seven points at one minute is given immediate special medical attention, which usually includes an examination by a pediatrician while oxygen is held under the baby's nose, and is then carefully observed to make sure that the Apgar scores increase to between eight and ten points at the five-minute retest. Monitoring continues during the next few hours and days for any problems that may develop (American Academy of Pediatrics, 2013a; Brazelton & Nugent, 1997).

> **Apgar Scale** A system of rating newborns' health immediately following birth based on heart rate, strength of breathing, muscle tone, color, and reflex irritability.

Size and Bodily Proportions

A newborn baby weighs about 7.5 pounds and measures about twenty inches lying down. Her length matches her adult size more closely than her weight does: her twenty inches represent more than one-quarter of her final height, whereas her 7.5 pounds amount to only a small percentage of her adult weight.

Babies' proportions and general physical appearance may have psychological consequences by fostering *attachments*, or bonds, with the people who care for them. Such bonds promote feelings of security. The cuteness of infants' faces in particular seems to help. No matter what their racial or ethnic background, most babies have unusually large foreheads, features that are concentrated in the lower part of the face, eyes that are large and round, and cheeks that are high and prominent. A pattern of babyish features occurs so widely among animals, in fact, that biologists who study animal behavior suspect it has a universal and genetically based power to elicit parental or nurturing responses among adult animals (Archer, 1992; Lorenz, 1970). Mother in some species of ducks, for example, take care of baby ducks even when the babies are not their own. Among human parents

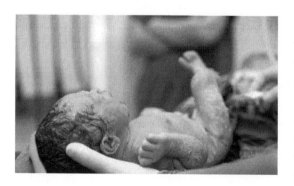

This neonate was delivered moments before the photo was taken. Notice the vernix coating much of the newborn's body.

Source: Naypong/Shutterstock.com.

TABLE 10.1 The Apgar Scale Score

Characteristic	Score		
	0	**1**	**2**
Heart rate	Absent	Less than 100 beats per minute	More than 100 beats per minute
Efforts to breathe	Absent	Slow, irregular	Good; baby is crying
Muscle tone	Flaccid, limp	Weak, inactive	Strong, active motion
Skin color	Body pale or blue	Body pink, extremities blue	Body and extremities pink
Reflex irritability	No response	Frown, grimace	Vigorous crying, coughing, sneezing

Source: Apgar (1953).

Two adorable brown bear cubs.

Sources: (left) Alena Ozerova/Shutterstock.com; *(right)* Voldymyr Burdiak/Shutterstock.com.

and children, attachments may start with this sort of inherent attraction of parents to infants, though, of course, it deepens as additional personal experiences accumulate across the lifespan.

Growth in Infancy

Infants experience a remarkably high rate of growth—they gain height and weight more rapidly during their first two years than at any other point during their post-birth lifetimes. And while increases in height and weight will be clearly evident and frequently measured by pediatricians (because gains in height and weight are indicative of the infant's overall health), less visible growth in the brain will also produce dramatic changes in the infant.

Physical Growth

While actual gains in height and weight can vary from infant to infant, on average, infants double their weight from 7.5 pounds at birth to about 15 pounds by the age of five months, and triple their weight to about 22 pounds by their first birthday (see Figure 10.1). Weight is gained less rapidly during the second year of life, with the average twenty-four-month-old weighing about 28 pounds, approximately four times the weight of a newborn. Young infants tend to have a plump, soft look that results from the accumulation of fat. Body fat helps the infant maintain a constant body temperature. By their first birthday, infants will have lost much of their "baby fat," a trend that continues until puberty (Fomon & Nelson, 2002).

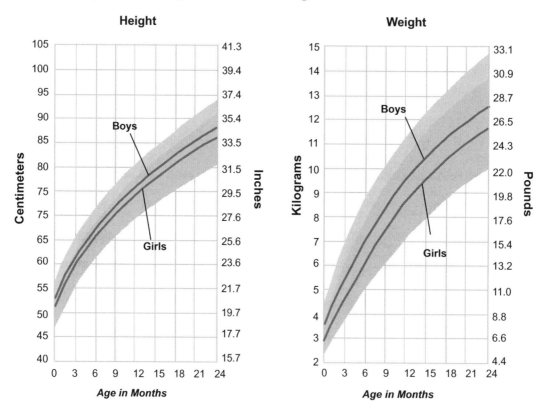

Height and Weight Growth during the First Two Years

FIGURE 10.1   Growth Curves for the First Two Years

During infancy, rapid gains in height (left chart) and weight (right chart) are evident. On average, boys are slightly taller and heavier than girls are, but differences are minimal and are often overshadowed by increasing variability in height and weight within groups of boys and girls.

Infants also gain height, adding approximately ten inches (twenty-five centimeters) to their newborn length of twenty inches (fifty centimeters) by their first birthday, and will continue to get taller during their second year, achieving an average height of about thirty-four inches (eighty-six centimeters) by their second birthday, which is roughly half of their adult height (see Figure 5.1). Body proportions are also changing during the first two years, revealing differences in growth for various parts of the body. At birth, the baby's head accounts for one-quarter of the newborn's total height. In other words, the head is more developed than the torso and limbs. By age two, the head accounts for one-fifth of the total height, as growth of the torso and limbs proceeds at a greater rate than the growth of the head. By adulthood, the head will account for approximately one-eighth of the total height of the average adult. As we will see in Chapter 14, adolescents also experience asymmetrical growth that makes them look gangly rather than like adorable baby ducklings.

WHAT DO YOU THINK?

What do you think attracts parents to their newborn children? Explore this question with the parents of a physically handicapped infant. How did they feel about their child (and about themselves) when the child was born?

Brain Growth

While the head may not be growing as rapidly as the rest of the body, significant development is occurring in the brain and central nervous system during the first two years of life. The **central nervous system** consists of the brain and nerve cells of the spinal cord, which together coordinate and control the perception of stimuli, as well as motor responses of all kinds. The more complex aspects of this work are accomplished by the brain, which develops rapidly from just before birth until well beyond a child's second birthday. In fact, it will be at least two decades until the brain is fully mature (Stiles & Jernigan, 2010). At seven months past conception, the baby's brain weighs about 10 percent of its final adult weight, but by birth, it has more

central nervous system The brain and nerve cells of the spinal cord.

neurons Nerve cell bodies and their extensions or fibers.

synaptogenesis The forming of connections, or *synapses*, between neurons.

than doubled to about 25 percent of final adult weight. By the child's second birthday, the brain has tripled to about 75 percent of its final adult weight (Freund et al., 1997).

Most of this increase results not from increasing numbers of nerve cells, or **neurons**, but from the development of a denser, or more fully packed, brain. This happens in two ways. First, the neurons generate many new dendritic fibers that connect them with one another in a process called **synaptogenesis** (see Figure 5.2). At birth, very few neuronal connections or *synapses* exist, but by age two, each neuron may be connected to hundreds or even thousands of other neurons. Growth of the dendrites is the primary reason why brain weight triples from birth to age two (Johnson, 2010). New synapses are formed in response to every experience the child has; in fact,

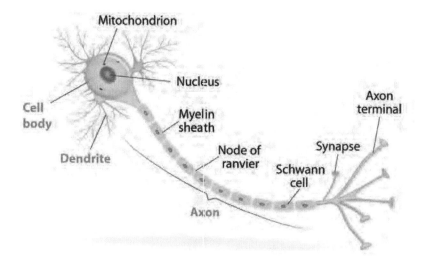

FIGURE 10.2   Anatomy of a Typical Human Neuron
This illustration shows the typical structures of a human nerve cell, including dendrites through which information typically enters the cell, the cell body, the axon covered by a myelin sheath, and the axon terminals through which nerve impulses are passed to adjacent neurons.

Source: Designua/Shutterstock .com.

transient exuberance The rapid but temporary increase in the rate of synaptogenesis and, hence, the number of synapses formed between neurons during infancy.

synaptic pruning The process through which unused synapses and neurons are eliminated.

plasticity The degree to which a developing structure or organ (like the brain) can be influenced by the environment.

during infancy, more synapses are formed than are necessary, a phenomenon described rather colorfully as **transient exuberance**, due to the temporarily rapid and overproductive nature of synaptogenesis at this time. Because more synapses form in response to every experience during infancy and childhood than are needed, many of these synapses are never used again. Consistent with the adage "use it or lose it," unused synapses are eliminated in a process called **synaptic pruning**. When redundant and unused synapses and neurons are eliminated, the nervous system functions more efficiently.

An important consequence of the transient exuberance that occurs during infancy is that it heightens the **plasticity** of the brain, which is the degree to which the brain reacts to experiences with the environment. Plasticity plays a central and often protective role in infant development. If an infant is raised in an enriched environment that provides lots of stimulation and nurturance, the production of synapses is amplified. However, if the infant is raised in an environment with little stimulation, the brain responds by forming and retaining fewer synapses. We can illustrate this with an explanation that is often offered for the superior verbal abilities of firstborn children when compared to their laterborn siblings. Firstborn children, at least until the second child is born, are the recipients of all of their caregivers' attention. This verbally enriched and supportive environment leads to the proliferation of synapses in the regions of the brain responsible for language—areas of the cerebral cortex in the left hemisphere of the brain. Parental attention must be divided among siblings when laterborns arrive, creating an environment for laterborns that is not as verbally-enriched as that experienced by the firstborn child (Frank, Turenshine, & Sullivan, 2010; Glass, Neulinger, & Brim, 1974), leading to lower scores on measures of verbal ability for laterborn children.

Environmental deficiencies can have long-term effects if they are severe and exposure is prolonged during infancy and early childhood. One longitudinal study in Great Britain found that "early adversity"—measured by ratings of the childhood home environment, including cleanliness, age, state of repair, and crowdedness, along with ratings of hygiene and cleanliness of the children themselves (prior to age four)—was associated with lower scores on a variety of cognitive measures through childhood and adolescence that persisted into adulthood (Richards & Wadsworth, 2004). However, plasticity serves in a protective capacity as well, as indicated in infants who suffered left-hemisphere strokes. The areas of the brain responsible for understanding and producing language are localized in the left hemisphere of the brain. However, after an intervention that included intense verbal stimulation, the right hemisphere assumed control of verbal comprehension and production, and language was able to develop normally (Rowe et al., 2009). The plasticity of the brain is greatest during infancy and early childhood, when the rates of synaptogenesis and synaptic pruning are highest.

An additional, important change in the brain during infancy that has a great impact on development is **myelination**, a process in which certain brain cells called *glia* produce fatty sheathing, or *myelin,* that gradually encases

> **myelination** The process through which myelin, a fatty sheathing, covers the axon of some neurons.

the neurons and their fibers. The myelin serves to protect and insulate the axons of neurons, allowing them to conduct neural impulses much more quickly. Myelination occurs rapidly during infancy and childhood, and then continues at a slower rate until about age thirty (Taylor, 2006).

> **DO YOU THINK?**
>
> Do you think that everyone grows at the rates described? Did you? What factors might lead to more or less growth during infancy? If possible, find out how tall you were on your second birthday and multiply that figure by two. How close is that number to your current height? Why might the numbers be different?

An important function of the brain is to control infants' states of sleep and wakefulness. The brain regulates the amount of stimulation infants experience, both externally and internally. Thus, periodic sleep helps infants to shut out external stimulation and thereby allows them to obtain general physical rest while strengthening and consolidating memories of what they have learned while awake. And, somewhat paradoxically, sleep may provide the opportunity for the brain to stimulate itself.

Infant States: Sleep and Arousal

Perhaps one of the biggest surprises for first-time parents is how little time they actually have to interact with their newborn babies while the babies are alert and responsive. Also, the sometimes irregular sleep patterns of newborns can prove to be both physically and emotionally challenging for parents. These challenges are compounded when new parents receive conflicting information about how to help their babies sleep better or longer when they seek advice on the subject.

Sleep

In the days immediately after birth, newborns sleep an average of sixteen hours per day, although some sleep as little as eleven hours a day and others as much as twenty-one (Michelsson et al., 1990). By age six months, babies average just thirteen or fourteen hours of sleep per day, and by twenty-four months, only eleven or twelve. But these hours still represent considerably more sleeping time than the six to eight hours typical for adults. So if infants sleep so much, why are their parents so tired?

REM sleep A stage of sleep in which one's body is paralyzed, but one's eyes and brain are very active. REM sleep is believed to be important for memory consolidation.

non-REM sleep The stages of sleep that vary from light sleep to very deep, restorative sleep. The deeper stages of non-REM sleep play a pivotal role in helping us feel rested, growing, repairing cells, and bolstering immune function.

As Figure 5.3 shows, newborns divide their sleeping time about equally between relatively active and quiet periods of sleep. The more active kind is named **REM sleep**, after the "*r*apid *e*ye *m*ovements," or twitchings, that usually accompany it. In the quieter kind of sleep, **non-REM sleep**, infants breathe regularly and more slowly, and their muscles become much limper. It takes approximately

Developmental Changes in Sleep Requirements

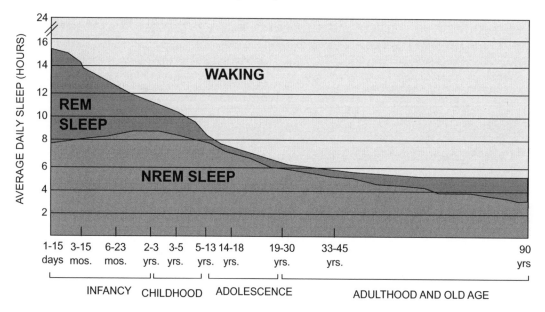

FIGURE 10.3   Developmental Changes in Sleep Requirements
Sleep changes in nature as children grow from infancy to adulthood. Overall, they sleep less, and the proportion of REM (rapid-eye-movement) sleep decreases sharply during infancy and childhood.

sixty minutes for an infant to cycle through REM and non-REM sleep, as compared to a ninety-minute cycle for adults. This discrepancy in the duration of infant cycling and adult cycling is thought to be one reason for new parents' exhaustion: Their sleep cycles are being continually interrupted by their infant's waking, fragmenting their sleep much like someone with a sleep disorder (Montgomery-Downs, Insana, Clegg-Kraynok, & Mancini, 2010).

Unfortunately for parents, a baby's extra sleep time does not usually include long, uninterrupted rest periods, even at night. In the first few months, it is more common for the baby to waken frequently—often every two or three hours—but somewhat unpredictably. Studies of brain development suggest that much of the unpredictability may result from the physical immaturity of the baby's nervous system: his brain may have frequent, accidental "storms" of impulses because it is not yet fully formed (Fransson et al., 2009; Sheldon et al., 1992). In most cases, the irregularities pose no problem to an infant, though as the "Focusing On" feature describes, in some children irregularities of neural activity may be related to "crib death," or sudden infant death syndrome, in a very small percentage of infants. Once a baby's sleep begins to consolidate into longer periods of wake and sleep, these periods have a tendency to "drift" so that a baby who is mostly sleeping through the night one week may be awake most of the night a few weeks later, another reason new parents are so sleepy (Kaltman & Engelmann, 1953; Parmelee et al., 1964).

> **sudden infant death (SIDS)** Sudden infant death syndrome (or "crib death"), an unaccountable death of an infant in its sleep.

FOCUSING ON ...

Sudden Infant Death Syndrome

Each year, about one out of every two thousand young infants dies during sleep for no apparent reason. Doctors call this phenomenon **sudden infant death syndrome (SIDS)**, or "crib death." The problem is most frequent among infants between ages two months and four months, although SIDS can affect babies as young as one month and as old as one year. Even though the rate of SIDS has been reduced by 50 percent since 1994, it is the leading cause of death among infants who survive the first few weeks after delivery (AAP Task Force on SIDS, 2011).

SIDS is disturbing because it is so mysterious. Typically, parents put a seemingly healthy baby down to sleep as usual, but when they come in to get her up again, they discover she is dead. Sadly, because the baby had exhibited no health problems, the parents often blame themselves for the death, suspecting that somehow they neglected their child or hurt him in some way (Kaplan, 1995). Even more unfortunately, friends and relatives often concur in blaming the parents, simply because they can think of no other way to explain SIDS. Other obvious causes simply do not happen. The baby does not choke, vomit, or suffocate; she just stops breathing.

What causes SIDS? One theory is that SIDS is an exaggerated form of normal *sleep apnea*, temporary cessations of breathing during sleep (Hunt, 1992). Another theory suggests that SIDS occurs primarily at a special transition in development, just when inborn reflexive control of breathing begins to fade in importance but before infants have firmly established voluntary control of breathing. For most infants, this transition occurs at about two to four months of age, just when SIDS strikes most often. A third theory suggests that SIDS infants suffer from heart problems: their nervous systems may fail to prompt regular, strong heartbeats and in essence cause them to suffer a heart attack. Unfortunately, no clear evidence points to any of these

(continued)

alternative explanations. Recent neuroscience research suggests that prenatal exposure to nicotine appears to alter receptors in the brain stem that play a role in the governance of certain autonomic functions (like heart rate and respiration). In preterm infants, prenatal exposure to nicotine impairs their recovery from *hypoxia*—low levels of oxygen in the blood—that might result from an obstruction, like a soft blanket, pillow, or stuffed animal, interfering with their supply of oxygen (AAP Task Force on SIDS, 2011).

If medical researchers could identify a basic cause, they would help future infants at risk for SIDS. Those babies could wear monitors that would indicate interruptions in breathing (if lungs are the problem) or heart rate (if that is the problem) and prompt parents or medical personnel to give the baby immediate, appropriate help. But so far, the use of monitors has not been practical on a widespread scale because they can be cumbersome, cause a lot of unnecessary alarm, and occasionally fail to function properly.

Medical research has identified several factors that make a particular family or infant more likely to experience SIDS (American Academy of Pediatrics, 2013b; Byard & Cohle, 1994). Very young mothers and fathers (younger than twenty years) stand a greater chance of having a SIDS infant, as do mothers who smoke cigarettes or have serious illnesses during pregnancy. Mothers who are poorly nourished during pregnancy also carry more risk than mothers who keep reasonably well nourished. Infants who begin daycare before four months of age also appear to be at higher risk for SIDS. Preliminary data indicate that 20 percent of SIDS deaths occur when the infants are being cared for someone other than a parent, and one-third of those deaths occurred during the first week of day care. But certain babies also are at greater risk for SIDS independent of their parents' qualities or behaviors. Boys die of SIDS more often than girls do, for example, and infants born small (less than seven pounds) die more often than larger infants do. These relationships do not mean, however, that being a boy or being small actually *causes* SIDS; they imply only that for reasons still not understood, SIDS seems to strike boys and small infants more frequently.

Even taken together, these factors do not predict SIDS very accurately. The vast majority of high-risk infants do not die, whereas some infants with few risk factors die from SIDS. This circumstance creates problems in translating the studies of risk factors into concrete recommendations for medical personnel and parents because taking the risk indications too literally can arouse fears in parents unnecessarily. The most useful recommendations tend to be valid for all families, whether or not they are at risk for SIDS (Carroll & Siska, 1998). For example, the American Academy of Pediatrics (2013b) offers the following recommendations as part of their safe sleep policy for all children:

- Infants should sleep on their backs until age one for every sleep; sleep positioners like foam wedges or rolled blankets designed to encourage side-sleeping should not be used.
- Consider the use of pacifiers for naptime and nighttime sleep.
- Infants should sleep on a firm surface that is covered by a fitted sheet.
- Soft objects, loose bedding, bumper pads, top sheets or blankets, and stuffed animals should not be in the baby's sleep area.
- Specifically designed sleep clothing (e.g., sleepers, snug-fitting pajamas) should be used instead of blankets.
- The temperature in the room should be comfortable for a lightly clothed adult.
- Never allow smoking in rooms where babies sleep. These are good pieces of advice for everyone, but unfortunately, they do not guarantee complete protection from SIDS. For parents whose babies do die, many hospitals and communities have created support groups in which couples can share their grief and come to terms with it.

What Do You Think?

If you were counseling a parent who lost a baby to SIDS, what would be your most important concern? What might you say to the parent? What might you also say to a relative of the parent who suspects that neglect may have caused the death?

Parents' Response to Infant Sleep and Arousal

The unpredictability of infants' sleep can create chronic sleep deprivation in many parents; as a group, in fact, parents of infants and toddlers—along with older teenagers—are among the most sleep-deprived people in society (Coren, 1996). Research has demonstrated that new mothers obtain about seven hours of sleep each day, which is not significantly less than the average adult gets (Mongtomery-Downs et al., 2010). So why are new parents so much more tired than the rest of us? As noted above, when babies wake up to be fed or changed, parents' sleep cycles are interrupted, causing sleep fragmentation similar to various sleep disorders (Insana & Montgomery-Downs, 2013; Montgomery-Downs et al., 2010). In fact, there is evidence that new fathers may be sleepier than new mothers are; most men do not get paternity leave and, therefore, cannot "make up" for disrupted sleep with daytime napping (Insana & Montgomery-Downs, 2013). Parents' fatigue is aggravated by living arrangements common in modem Western society. Unlike in many non-Western societies, where babies often sleep in the same bed the mother does (something that the American Academy of Pediatrics warns against), infants in our society are often "stationed" in an adjoining room, or at least in a separate bed across the room—an arrangement that makes assisting the baby more disruptive. Furthermore, many non-Western households may have a number of adults or older relatives regarded as capable of calming a baby at night. In our society, in contrast, a household commonly has only two adults, or even just one. The scarcity of "qualified" helpers places a disproportionate burden of nighttime child care on parents, and eventually contributes to fatigue.

Infants spend more time sleeping than doing anything else. Unfortunately, their sleep may not occur at night, so chronic sleep deprivation and sleep fragmentation is a real problem for most parents, particularly primary caregivers. If possible, it is helpful for the caregiver to nap at the same time as the baby. However, because of discrepancies in the time it takes infants (sixty minutes) and parents (ninety minutes) to complete a sleep cycle, even this is not optimal.

Source: Alliance/Shutterstock.com.

The "cure" for nighttime fussiness eventually depends on physical maturation, but parents can also influence their infant's sleep patterns by developing regular (though not rigid) times for and methods of waking, feeding, and sleeping that involve the infant. One study found that infants change toward more adult-like levels of wakefulness and sleep within six weeks after arriving home, provided routines are (relatively) regular (Bamford et al., 1990; Rivkees, 2003). Another found that regularity offers dividends later in childhood: comparisons of Dutch and American families found fewer sleep problems among the young children of Dutch families, whose culture encourages regularity of daily routines more strongly than North American society does (Harkness & Keefer, 1995).

The advice to strive for (relatively) regular routines is widely supported among parent advice experts, but note that it makes assumptions about families that are not always true. In some families, routines cannot be made regular because of competing pressures from other children, because of exhaustion from work or from earlier ill-timed wakings or feedings, or because the family has only one parent. Under these conditions, parents need additional support from friends, extended family, or social service workers. They cannot do it all themselves.

States of Arousal

As Table 5.2 shows, infants exhibit various states of arousal, from sleep to full wakefulness. As they get older, their patterns of arousal begin to resemble those of older children (Ferber & Kryger, 1995). The largest share of time, even among older infants, goes to the most completely relaxed and deepest form of sleep.

Obviously, a fully alert state is a time when babies can learn from their surroundings, but it may not be the only time. During REM sleep, infants' heart rates speed up in reaction to sounds, suggesting that infants may process stimulation even while asleep. But the meaning of a faster heart rate is ambiguous: changes in it may also show neural *dis*organization or an inability to shut out the world. Babies who are born prematurely confirm this possibility because they show more variability in heart rate than full-term babies when they hear sounds in their sleep (Spassov et al., 1994).

In addition to responding to external stimulation during REM sleep, the brains of infants also appear to be engaging in self-stimulation (Roffwarg, Muzio, & Dement, 1966) in this sleep phase. For quite some time, researchers have been wondering what is occurring in the minds of infants during REM sleep—are they dreaming? While this question has not been answered definitively, the brain-wave patterns of young infants in REM sleep differ from those of adults who are

TABLE 10.2 States of Arousal in Infants

State	Behavior of Infants
Non-REM sleep	Complete rest; muscles relaxed; eyes closed and still; breathing regular and relatively slow
REM sleep	Occasional twitches, jerks, facial grimaces; irregular and intermittent eye movements; breathing irregular and relatively rapid
Drowsiness	Occasional movements. but fewer than in REM sleep; eyes open and close; glazed look; breathing regular, but faster than in non- REM sleep
Alert inactivity	Eyes open and scanning; body relatively still; rate of breathing similar to drowsiness, but more irregular
Alert activity	Eyes open, but not attending or scanning; frequent, diffuse bodily movements; vocalizations; irregular breathing; skin flushed
Distress	Whimpering or crying; vigorous or agitated movements; facial grimaces pronounced; skin very flushed

Source: Ferber and Kryger (1995).

dreaming, suggesting that infants are not dreaming, or at least they are not dreaming in the same way that adults dream. However, at about three or four months of age, the brain-wave patterns of infants in REM sleep become similar to those of adults who are dreaming (Zampi, Fagioli, & Salzarulo, 2002).

WHAT DO YOU THINK?

How do parents deal with differences in children's sleep patterns? Ask a classmate or friend who is a parent of more than one child, or ask your own parent(s) how he or she responded to sleep differences in the children as infants. Combine your information with that of several other classmates. Do you see any trends?

Sensory Acuity

If you have not spent much time around infants, you may share William James' (1890) conclusion that "the baby, assailed by eyes, ears, nose, skin, and entrails at once, feels it all as one great blooming, buzzing confusion" (p. 462). William James was trained as a physician and was a professor of philosophy at Harvard University during the late nineteenth and early twentieth centuries. His writings on the intersection of physiology and philosophy helped to establish and shape the new discipline of psychology. James was pondering what parents have questioned for ages: how can infants, new to this world and with no knowledge or point of reference with which to interpret their experiences, interpret the information flooding their senses? What do they sense, and what is their understanding of it? Are they truly confused amidst the blooming buzz of sensory signals? Since James' 1890 description of infants, more than a century of research that utilized new methodologies and technologies revealed some surprising capabilities regarding the sensory acuity of infants.

Visual Acuity

Infants can see at birth, but they lack the clarity of focus or *acuity* (keenness) characteristic of adults with good vision. When looking at stationary contours and objects, newborns see more clearly at short distances, especially at about eight to ten inches—about the distance, incidentally, between a mother's breast and her face. Their vision is better when tracking moving objects, but even so their overall vision is rather poor until about one month of age (Seidel et al., 1997).

Visual acuity improves a lot during infancy, but it does not reach adult levels until the end of the preschool years. An older infant (age one to two) often has 20/30 or 20/40 vision, meaning he can see fine details at twenty feet that adults can see at thirty or forty feet. This quality of vision is quite satisfactory for everyday, familiar activities; in fact, many adults can see no better than this, without even realizing it. But this level of visual acuity does interfere with seeing distant objects.

Color vision also improves dramatically during the few months after birth. Specialized neurons called cones that are located in the retina at the back of the eye enable humans to see color, but these cones are immature at birth (Kellman & Arterberry, 2006). One-month-old infants can distinguish between black, red, and white, and their attention is drawn to bold, high-contrast color patterns. By approximately four months of age, their ability to see colors, including soft pastels and subtle differences between hues, is similar to that of adults (Franklin, Pilling, & Davies, 2005).

Auditory Acuity

Auditory acuity refers to sensitivity to sounds. Infants can hear at birth, but not as well as adults. Any sudden loud noise near an infant, such as that caused by dropping a large book on the floor, demonstrates she can hear. Such a sound produces a dramatic startle reaction, called a *Moro reflex:* The neonate extends her limbs suddenly, sometimes shakes all over, and may also cry. Not all noises produce this reaction; pure tones, such as the sound of a flute, cause relatively little response. Complex noises containing many different sounds usually produce a stronger reaction; a bag of nails spilling on the floor, for example, tends to startle infants reliably.

Regardless of the type of sound, infants tend to exhibit a preference for higher-pitched sounds than lower tones. This fact has sometimes led some experts to suggest that infants have a "natural" preference for female—that is, high-pitched—human voices. Studies of voice preferences, however, have not confirmed this possibility consistently, probably because newborns' range of special sensitivity lies well above the pitch of even female voices and because male and female voices usually are more similar in overall quality than gender stereotypes suggest. Instead, it is more accurate to say that infants prefer sounds in the middle range of pitches, which is the range most similar to human voices, male or female. Recent research on infant auditory preferences has indicated that infants exhibit a distinct preference for human speech sounds over other human and nonhuman vocalizations (Shultz & Vouloumanos, 2010), especially those that are expressed in higher pitches (Fernald & Kuhl, 1987) such as the babbling of other infants (Masapollo, Polka, & Ménard, 2016).

Tactile, Taste, and Olfactory Acuity

Newborns and infants are sensitive to touch (i.e., *tactile acuity*), as all caregivers who have comforted a crying baby by swaddling the child in a blanket or by cradling the child in their arms can attest. Also, as will be addressed in the next section, infants respond reflexively to physical contact—turning toward a touch on the cheek or closing their hands around objects that touch their palms—abilities that are present at birth (Futagi, Toribe, & Suzuki, 2009).

Can infants feel pain? This question has been the focus of much debate during the past few decades, but an increasing body of behavioral and neurological evidence seems to indicate that they can (Warnock & Sandrin, 2004; Williams et al., 2009). The degree to which infants experience pain is still being researched and is complicated by the subjective nature of the perception of pain. For example, in one study involving a control group of newborns whose heels were pricked, the newborns cried loudly in response to the pain- inducing prick. However, an experimental group of newborns who were first given a drop of sucrose before receiving the heel prick exhibited little response to the prick (Harrison et al., 2010).

As for taste and smell (technically called "olfaction"), infants reveal well-developed acuity, even prior to birth. Preferences for sweet tastes have been demonstrated by fetuses who swallow more frequently after an artificial sweetener has been added to their amniotic fluid (Booth et al., 2010). Infants smile and lick their lips when presented with sweet substances (Steiner et al., 2001), and they pucker and grimace when presented with sour or bitter substances (Kaijura, Cowart, & Beauchamp, 1992). Researchers have argued that infant preferences for sweet tastes may have evolutionary survival advantages, as breast milk tends to

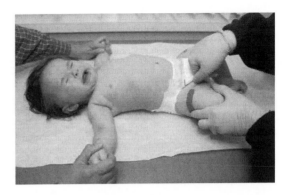

Can infants feel pain? Any parent who has taken a baby to the doctor for a vaccination can attest that their baby feels pain.

Source: Darren Brode/ Shutterstock.com.

be sweet (Liem & Mennella, 2002). Infants also respond with facial expressions that suggest pleasure or disgust when presented with pleasant and unpleasant smells, and by four days after birth, they can discriminate between their own mother's breast smell and that of another lactating mother, keeping their heads turned toward pads with their own mother's scent (Porter & Reiser, 2005).

WHAT DO YOU THINK?

Do parenting books agree with our comments that young infants have the use of vision and hearing? That babies can feel pain and have very well-developed senses of taste and smell? Check the comments made in two or three books about the capabilities of newborn babies. Do they seem consistent, or at least not *inconsistent*?

Given the remarkable sensory acuity of infants, parents may be partly right when they claim their newborn child recognizes them even from birth. What parents may be noticing is their newborn's immediate responsiveness to sights, sounds, smells, taste, and touch. They are right to exclaim over it: by taking an interest in the environment, infants create conditions where they can begin organizing (or *perceiving)* stimuli and attaching meanings to them. As we will see in the next section of this chapter, certain kinds of lines, shapes, and contours are especially interesting to a young infant. So are certain kinds of sounds. Fortunately for the development of family ties, parents are able to provide many of the most interesting sights and sounds with their own faces and voices; and partly in this way, attachments between parents and children are born.

Motor Development

Infants begin life with more than two dozen inborn **reflexes**, or automatic responses to specific stimuli. Table 10.3 summarizes the

reflex An involuntary, automatic response to a stimulus. The very first movements or motions of an infant are reflexes.

TABLE 10.3 Major Reflexes in Newborn Infants

Reflex	Description	Development	Significance
Survival Reflexes			
Breathing reflex	Repetitive inhalation and expiration	Permanent, although becomes partly voluntary	Provides oxygen and expels carbon dioxide
Breathing reflex	Repetitive inhalation and expiration	Permanent, although becomes partly voluntary	Provides oxygen and expels carbon dioxide
Rooting reflex	Turning of cheek in direction of touch	Weakens and disappears by six months	Orients child to breast or bottle
Sucking reflex	Strong sucking motions with throat, mouth, and tongue	Gradually comes under voluntary control	Allows child to drink
Swallowing reflex	Swallowing motions in throat	Permanent, although becomes partly voluntary	Allows child to take in food and to avoid choking
Eyeblink reflex	Closing eyes for an instant ("blinking")	Permanent, although gradually becomes voluntary	Protects eyes from objects and bright light
Pupillary reflex	Changing size of pupils smaller in bright light and bigger in dim light	Permanent	Protects against bright light and allows better vision in dim light
Primitive Reflexes			
Moro reflex	In response to a loud noise, child throws arms outward arches back, then brings arms together as if to hold something	Arm movements and arching disappear by six months, but startle reaction persists for life	Indicates normal development of nervous system
Grasping reflex	Curling fingers around any small object put in the child's palm	Disappears by three months; voluntary grasping appears by about six months	Indicates normal development of nervous system
Tonic neck reflex	When laid on back, head turns to side, arm and leg extend to same side, limbs on opposite side flex	Disappears by two or three months	Indicates normal development of nervous system
Babinski reflex	When bottom of foot stroked, toes fan and then curl	Disappears by eight to twelve months	Indicates normal development of nervous system
Stepping reflex	If held upright, infant lifts leg as if to step	Disappears by eight weeks, but later if practiced	Indicates normal development of nervous system
Swimming	If put in water, infant moves arms and legs and holds breath	Disappears by four to six months	Indicates normal development of nervous system

most important ones. A few reflexes, such as sucking, clearly help the baby to adapt to the new life outside the womb. Others look more like evolutionary vestiges of behaviors that may have helped earlier versions of *Homo sapiens* to cope, for example, by clinging to their mothers at the sound of danger. A few reflexes, such as blinking, breathing, and swallowing, persist throughout a person's life, but most reflexes disappear from the infant's repertoire during the first few months. Their disappearance, in fact, helps doctors to judge whether a baby is developing normally. Newborn reflexes that persist over many months may suggest damage to the nervous system or generally impaired development (El-Dib et al., 2012; Menkes, 1994).

The First Motor Skills

Motor skills are voluntary movements of the body or parts of the body. They can be grouped conveniently according to the size of the muscles and body parts involved. *Gross motor skills* involve the large muscles of the arms, legs, and torso. *Fine motor skills* involve the small muscles located throughout the body. Walking and jumping are examples of gross motor skills, and reaching and grasping are examples of fine motor skills.

Viewed broadly, the sequence in which skills develop follows two general trends. The **cephalocaudal principle** ("head to tail") refers to the fact that upper parts of the body become usable and skillful before lower parts do. Babies learn to turn their heads before learning to move their feet intentionally, and they learn to move their arms before they learn to move their legs. The **proximodistal principle** ("near to far") refers to the fact that central parts of the body become skillful before peripheral, or outlying, parts do. Babies learn to wave their entire arms before learning to wiggle their wrists and fingers. The former movement occurs at the shoulder joint, near the center of the body, and the latter occurs at the periphery.

> **motor skills** Physical skills using the body or limbs, such as walking and drawing.
>
> **cephalocaudal principle** The tendency for organs, reflexes, and skills to develop sooner at the top (or head) of the body and later in areas farther down the body.
>
> **Proximodistal principle** Growth that exhibits a near-to-far pattern of development, from the center of the body outward.

Gross Motor Development in the First Year Almost from birth, and before reflex behaviors disappear, babies begin doing some things on purpose. By age four weeks or so, most babies can lift their heads up when lying on their stomachs. At six or seven months, many babies have become quite adept at using their limbs; they can stick their feet up in the air and "bicycle" with them while a parent struggles valiantly to fit a diaper on the moving target. At ten months, the average baby can stand erect, but only if an adult helps. By their first birthday, one-half of all babies can dispense with this assistance and stand by themselves without toppling over immediately (Savelsbergh, 1993). By age seven months, on the average, babies become able to locomote, or move around, on their own. At first, their methods are crude and slow; a baby might simply pivot on her stomach, for example, to get a better view of something interesting. Consistent movement in one direction develops soon after this time, although the movement does not always occur in the direction the baby intends!

The toddler on the left is watching his older, preschool-aged sister use a pincer grasp to perform a more precise operation using the toy tools on the workbench.

Source: Glenda/Shutterstock.com.

Reaching and Grasping Even newborn infants will reach for and grasp objects they can see immediately in front of them. They often fail to grasp objects successfully; they may make contact with an object but fail to enclose it in their fingers. This early, crude reaching disappears fairly soon after birth, only to reappear at about four or five months of age as two separate skills, reaching and grasping (Pownall & Kingerlee, 1993). During their second year, infants gain increased control over the movements of their fingers, producing a *pincer grasp* in which the thumb and forefinger are brought together to pick up small objects. These skills soon serve infants in many ways. For example, by their second birthday most babies can turn the pages in large picture books one at a time, at least if the paper is relatively indestructible. But they can also point at the pages without grasping for them. The pincer grasp also allows for improved self-feeding with their hands, fingers, and ultimately, utensils (Ho, 2010).

Walking A reasonably predictable series of events leads to true walking in most children; Figure 10.4 describes some of these milestones. While the development of walking, overall,

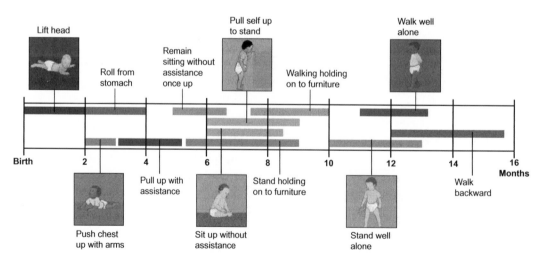

FIGURE 10.4 Milestones of Motor Development
Walking alone is one of the major physical achievements of the first year of life. Quite a few other physical skills usually develop prior to walking, as the figure shows. Note, though, that skills appear at different times for different individuals. Some skills may even appear "out of sequence" in some children.

tends to follow a progression of "stages," on any given day, infants will exhibit creativity and resourcefulness when it comes to their mobility, so caregivers should not be alarmed if their own infant moves around a room in a manner that is unconventional (Adolph, 2008).

> **WHAT DO YOU THINK?**
>
> If motor skills develop partly through learning, why not just deliberately teach infants to walk? What do you think would be the result of doing so? Do similar considerations apply for certain other important developments in infancy?

By about twelve to thirteen months, most children take their first independent steps. Well before two years, they often can walk not only forward but backward or even sideways. Some two-year-olds can even walk upstairs on two feet instead of on all fours. Usually, they use the wall or a railing to do so. Usually, too, coming downstairs proves more difficult than going up; one solution is to creep down backward, using all four limbs.

Cultural and Sex Differences in Motor Development

Differences in motor development exist among cultures and between the sexes, though they are not always large or dramatic. Certain African cultures, for example, give their infants unusually frequent chances to sit upright and to practice their "walking" reflex when held at a standing position by adults and older children (LeVine, 1994; Munroe et al., 1981). These opportunities seem to stimulate toddlers in these societies to learn to walk earlier and better than North American toddlers do. Early walking, in turn, may prove especially valuable in these societies, which do not rely heavily on cars, bicycles, or other vehicles that make walking less important. Yet, early walking may also be a genetic trait (at least partially) for these groups; without comparable training in reflex walking for North American infants, there is no way to be sure.

Yet differences in motor skills do not always appear where we might expect. Take the Navaho and Hopi tribes, whose infants spend nearly all of their first year bound and swaddled tightly to a flat board, with their arms and legs extending straight down along their bodies (J. Whiting, 1981; van Sleuwen, 2007). Apparently as a result, Navaho and Hopi toddlers do tend to acquire walking a little later than Anglo-American children do. But they do not show delays in other skills inhibited by swaddling—notably, reaching and grasping—and the deficit in walking disappears by the end of the preschool years in most cases (Connelly & Forssberg, 1997).

Culture aside, do boys and girls differ, on average, in motor development? The answer depends on distinguishing what infants *can* do from what they typically *actually* do. What they can do—their competence—has relatively little relationship to their sex. Girl and boy babies sit upright at about the same age, for example, and stand and walk at about the same time. Similar equality exists for all of the motor milestones of infancy.

How infants use their time is another matter. Almost as soon as they can move, boys show more activity than do girls. The trend begins even before birth, when male fetuses move about in their mothers' wombs more than do female fetuses (Moore & Persaud, 1998). After birth,

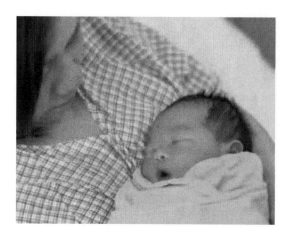

Swaddling infants, as has been done with this Asian baby girl, is practiced in many cultures. Swaddling tends to slow motor development at first, but not permanently. It may also allow caregivers to carry infants with them during daily activities—a circumstance that could make the skills of vocalizing less urgent to develop.

Source: szefei/Shutterstock.com.

the trend continues: girls spend more time using their emerging fine motor skills. Of course, the differences in use of time may stem partly from parents' encouragement (praise) for "gender-appropriate" behaviors. Given the young age of the children, though, and the fact that activity actually precedes birth, part of the difference must come from genetic endowment: an inborn tendency to be more (or less) active.

It is important to note that whatever their source, sex differences in infants' motor development are only averages and, in any case, rather slight. As groups, boys and girls are more alike than different, and numerous individual boys are less active than numerous individual girls, despite "average" behavior. As a practical matter, it is therefore more important for parents and teachers to respond to the qualities of the individual children for whom they are responsible than to stereotypical "gender" averages.

Nutrition during the First Two Years

As obvious as it sounds, the physical developments in infancy depend on good nutrition throughout the first two years. Like adults, babies need diets with appropriate amounts of protein, calories, and specific vitamins and minerals. For various reasons, however, infants do not always get all the nutrients they need. Often poverty accounts for malnutrition: parents with good intentions may be unable to afford the right foods. In other cases, conventional eating practices interfere: despite relatively expensive eating habits, such as going to fast-food restaurants, some families may fail to provide their children with a balanced diet.

Compared with older children, infants eat less in overall or absolute amounts. A well-nourished young baby in North America might drink somewhat less than one liter (about .95 quarts) of liquid nourishment per day. This amount definitely would not keep an older child or a young adult well nourished, although it might prevent starving. In proportion to their body weight, however, infants need to consume much more than older children or adults do. For example, every day a three-month-old baby ideally should take in more than two ounces of liquid per pound of body weight, whereas an eighteen-year-old needs only about one-third of this amount (Queen & Lang, 1993). If adolescents or young adults drank in the same proportion to their body)' weights, they would have to consume six quarts of liquid per day. That is equivalent to twenty-five cups per day, or about one cup every forty-five minutes during waking hours!

Breast Milk versus Formula

Someone (usually parents) must provide for an infant's comparatively large appetite. Whenever breastfeeding is possible, health experts generally recommend human milk, usually in conjunction with a Vitamin D supplement, as the sole source of nutrition for at least the first six months or so of most infants' lives and as a major source for at least the next six months. In some cases, of course, this recommendation proves difficult or impractical to follow. Babies who need intensive medical care immediately after birth cannot be breast-fed without special arrangements. Some women have difficulty producing milk. Also, for one reason or another, some women may choose not to breast-feed, for example, if they are taking medications that might be passed on to the baby, Also, for one reason or another some women choose not to breast-feed. For example, if a woman is taking medications that might be passed on to the baby or if job situations make breastfeeding difficult she may choose to not breast-feed. For these infants, formulas can be either safer or more convenient.

Why do pediatricians recommend breastfeeding? First, human milk seems to give young infants more protection from diseases and other ailments. Second, human milk matches the nutritional needs of human infants more closely than formula preparations do, and the makeup of human milk changes over time to meet infant nutritional needs; in particular, it contains more iron, an important nutrient for infants. Third, breastfeeding better develops the infant's jaw and mouth muscles because it requires stronger sucking motions than bottle feeding does and because it tends to satisfy infants' intrinsic needs for sucking better than a bottle does. Fourth, breastfeeding may encourage a healthy emotional relationship between mother and infant, simply because it involves a lot of close physical snuggling (La Leche League International, 1991). Breastfeeding also provides benefits to mothers: it is less expensive than formula, and it aids in postpartum weight loss, helps reduce risk for postpartum hemorrhaging, and has been linked to a reduced risk for breast, ovarian, and uterine cancer later in life (Dermer, 2001). After about six months, infants can be introduced gradually to solid foods such as strained cereals mixed with breastmilk and strained fruits. As babies become tolerant of these new foods, parents can introduce others that sometimes require a more mature digestive system, such as strained meats and cooked eggs. Overall, the shift to solid foods often takes many months to complete (see Table 10.4 for guidelines about how to do this). As it occurs, parents must

In recent decades, increasing numbers of mothers have chosen to breast-feed their babies, as recommended by most pediatricians. For a significant number of parents and infants, however, partial or complete bottle-feeding remains a valuable option—for example, if fathers wish to be involved in feeding or if the mother's work schedule makes breastfeeding difficult.

Source: Ery Azmeer/Shutterstock .com.

TABLE 10.4 Changing Nutritional Needs during Infancy

Age	Parents May Begin
Birth–4 months	Complete diet of breast milk or baby formula, Vitamin D supplement as directed
4–6 months	Puréed single-grain cereal, preferably iron-fortified; begin with one to two teaspoons and work up to one-half cup, twice per day
6–8 months	Puréed vegetables or fruit, one at a time; begin with one to two teaspoons and work up to one-fourth to one-half cup per serving, twice per day
	"Finger" foods (e.g., chopped banana, bits of dry cereal)
10–12 months	Puréed meats or poultry, beginning with one to two teaspoons and working up to one-fourth to one-half cup per serving, three to four times per day.
	Soft but chopped foods (e.g., lumpy potatoes)
	Whole milk, one-half cup per serving, four to five times per day.
24 months	Milk, one-half cup per serving, four to five times per day.

Source: Adapted from the International Food Information Council, 1993, and the USNLM, 2011.

begin paying more attention to their baby's overall nutritional needs because many solid foods lack the broad range of nutrients that breastmilk and formula provide.

Poor Nutrition

Often, North American diets fail to provide enough of three specific nutrients: vitamin A, vitamin C, and iron. Prolonged deficiencies of vitamins A and C seem to create deficits in motor ability and deficiency of iron appears to lead to deficits in cognitive performance (Black et al., 2011; Pollitt, 1995). For about 4 to 5 percent of infants, these nutritional deficiencies are serious and require immediate remedy. For another group of about the same size, the nutritional deficiencies are less severe but are still a cause for concern. In developing countries worldwide, approximately one in three children suffers

> **stunting** Being excessively short in stature—falling under the fifth percentile for height for one's age—caused by chronic undernourishment.

from severe malnutrition (UNICEF, 2009). If undernourishment is prolonged, it may produce a condition called **stunting**, which, as the term implies, results in stunted growth—specifically, falling below the fifth percentile in height for one's age when compared to typical growth norms (Abukabar et al., 2010).

Even when undernourished infants appear healthy and "bright," they may be at risk for later developmental problems because poorly nourished families often experience other serious deprivations, such as poor sanitation, inadequate health care, and lack of educational opportunities. Under these conditions, it may not take much to turn mild under nourishment into severe malnutrition and thus reduce cognitive and motor performance to below satisfactory levels.

Overnutrition

In affluent, calorie-loving societies such as our own, the problem often is not lack of food but getting too much of calorie-rich, nutrient-poor foods. Social circumstances make it difficult for parents to keep convenience food and "junk" food from their children (or to avoid it themselves!). Food manufacturers and fast-food restaurants have discovered that foods sell better if they contain high amounts of fat, sugar, and salt, and low amounts of fiber—all of which are violations of well-established nutritional guidelines (Wootan & Liebman, 1998). The short-term result during infancy can be **overnutrition**: too many calories, too much of the wrong nutrients, and not enough of other nutrients. The longer-term result can be to establish food preferences that may create health risks when the infant becomes a child and later an adult. A toddler who eats too much ice cream and chips may be "cute"; an adult who does so experiences greater risk for heart problems, diabetes, and certain forms of cancer (Bronner, 1997).

> **overnutrition** Diet that contains too many calories and is therefore unbalanced.

Note that although overnutrition can increase an infant's weight, weight itself is not a cause for *medical* concern in infancy as long as the baby is only moderately above (or below) the average. Infants born bigger or heavier than usual tend to have diets relatively higher in calories. They also tend to drink more milk (via either breast or bottle) and other liquids than usual, and to shift earlier to solid foods. Some parents fear that heavier infants are prone to becoming overweight or obese as children or adolescents, but the evidence for this is inconclusive; some researchers have found that weight in infancy correlated little with weight in childhood and even less with weight in adulthood (Williams & Kimm, 1993). However, other researchers have found significant correlations between weight statuses during infancy (e.g., "overweight" or "obese") with weight statuses during childhood or adolescence (Gunnarsdottir & Thorsdottir, 2003; Harrington et al., 2010; Zhang et al., 2013). Parents sometimes feel concerned about a heavy infant for essentially social and psychological reasons: the paradox of a society that makes overnutrition too easy is that it also values thinness in physical appearance too much. As an infant grows into a child and then an adolescent, he or she will inevitably be affected by the social value placed on thinness. We discuss the results of this development in Chapter 11, in conjunction with discussing extremely overweight (or *obese)* children. In the meantime, though, it will be the child's parents who worry about weight on the child's behalf.

> **WHAT DO YOU THINK?**
>
> If you (or a partner) were expecting a child, would you prefer that the baby be breast-fed or bottle-fed? Discuss this question with a classmate of the *same* sex; then compare your responses with those of a classmate of the *opposite* sex. Do your responses differ?

Impairments in Infant Growth

Within broad limits, healthy infants grow at various rates and become various sizes, and most of the time the differences are no cause for concern. But a small percentage do not grow as large as they should, beginning either at birth or a bit later during infancy. When a baby's size or growth is well below normal, it *is* a major cause for concern, both for the infant and for the infant's parents. At the extreme, it can contribute to infant mortality.

Low-Birth-Weight Infants

A small percentage of newborns are considered **low-birth-weight** infants if they are born weighing less than 2,500 grams, or about 5.5 pounds. The condition can result from several factors. One of the most common causes is malnourishment of the mother during pregnancy. But other harmful practices, such as smoking cigarettes, drinking alcohol, or taking drugs, also

> **low birth weight** A birth weight of less than 2,500 grams (about 5.5 pounds).

can depress birth weight. Mothers from certain segments of the population, such as teenagers and those from very low-SES backgrounds, are especially likely to give birth to low-birth-weight babies, most likely because of their own poor nourishment or their lack of access to good prenatal care. But even mothers who are well nourished and well cared for sometimes have infants who are smaller than is medically desirable. Multiple births (e.g., wins, triplets) usually result in small babies; so do some illnesses or mishaps, such as a serious traffic accident that causes damage to the placenta.

Consequences for the Infant   When birth weight is very low (less than 2,500 grams), infants' reflexes tend to be a bit sluggish, weak, and poorly organized (Brooten, 1992). Such infants do not startle as reliably or grasp as automatically and strongly at objects. Their muscles often seem flabby or overly relaxed. After delivery, the infants must cope with many tasks for which they are inadequately prepared physically, including breathing and digesting food. They also have trouble regulating their own sleep to keep it peaceful, sustained, and smooth.

Neurological limitations often can persist for the first two or three years of life, causing the baby to develop specific motor skills a bit later than other infants. A four-month-old baby who is small due to being born two months preterm, for example, in many ways resembles a two-month-old born at full term; both infants have lived eleven months from conception. Some of the delay may reflect stresses associated with early birth (such as parents' overprotectiveness) rather than the physical effects of early birth as such. Unless they are extremely small, though, most low-birth-weight infants eventually develop into relatively normal preschoolers (Goldson, 1992). This conclusion was supported by a sophisticated study of monozygotic and dizygotic twins in addition to single births that allowed the researchers to control for maternal, environmental, and genetic factors (Datar & Jacknowitz, 2009). The results revealed very small consequences of low birth weight on cognitive and motor development at age two for most of the children in the study, but negative effects on growth were still evident at age two.

Consequences for the Parents   Although low birth weight can worry parents, the condition does not impair relationships with a child in the long term unless the parents are also under additional stresses elsewhere in their lives (Gross et al., 1997). In the short-term, though, low-birth-weight infants lack responsiveness, and initially need intensive care. These circumstances can create distance between parents and child at a time when parents want very much to reach out (literally and figuratively) and connect with their newborn. As the more mature members of the relationship, most parents are capable of understanding the reasons for the distance and of delaying their expectations for response from their child. The reflexive "social smile" normally shown at around two months, for example, may not come until age three or four months. If other stresses of life get in the way, though, waiting for the infant to finally "act normally" may be difficult or even impossible. Poverty, preexisting family conflicts, medical problems of parents, and the like put parents of low-birth-weight infants somewhat more at risk and in need of additional support from professionals, family members, and friends.

Failure to Thrive

An infant or a preschool child who fails to grow at normal rates for no apparent medical reason suffers from a condition called **failure to thrive**. About 6 percent of North American children exhibit this condition at one time or another, although not necessarily continuously (Cole & Lanham, 2011; Woolston, 1993). In some ways, the condition resembles malnutrition, especially when it occurs in developing nations.

> **failure to thrive** A condition in which an infant seems seriously delayed in physical growth and is noticeably apathetic in behavior.

Failure-to-thrive and malnourished children both develop motor and cognitive skills more slowly than usual; both experience higher rates of school failure and learning disabilities; and both are more likely to live in disadvantaged circumstances and to have parents who are enduring physical or emotional stress.

At one time, professionals tended to attribute failure to thrive to lack of nurturing and love between parent and child. A more complex picture may be closer to the truth: failure to thrive may have many sources, both physical and psychological, and depend on both the child and the environment. Consider this pattern: An infant has a genetically quiet, slow-to-respond temperament, making it more difficult for her mother to establish emotional contact. If the mother also is experiencing a number of other stresses (low income, illness, or disapproval of the new baby from others), the relationship between mother and infant is put at risk. A vicious cycle may develop of poorly timed feedings and ineffective efforts to nurture the infant, who persistently resists the mother's love and even her food. Parents in this situation often can benefit from professional help and support in learning new patterns of interacting with their babies.

Infant Mortality

In the past several decades, health care systems in North America and around the world have substantially improved their ability to keep infants alive. The **infant mortality rate**, the proportion of babies who die during the first year of life, has declined steadily during this century. In 1950 in the United States, about twenty-nine out of every one thousand infants died; six decades

> **infant mortality rate** The frequency with which infants die compared to the frequency with which they live.

TABLE 10.5 Infant Mortality in Selected Nations

Nation	Infant Mortality (per 1,000 live births) Nation	Nation	Infant Mortality (per 1,000 live births)
Japan	2.0	United Kingdom	4.3
Singapore	2.4	New Zealand	4.3
Finland	2.5	Poland	4.4
Norway	2.5	Canada	4.5
Sweden	2.6	Greece	4.6
Hong Kong	2.7	Hungary	4.9
South Korea	3.0	United States, whites	5.1
France	3.2	Latvia	5.2
Italy	3.3	United States, average	5.8
Spain	3.3	Chile	6.6
Belgium	3.4	Russia	6.8
Germany	3.4	United States, nonwhites	11.1
Israel	3.4	Mexico	11.6
Austria	3.4	China	12.0
Ireland	3.6	Saudi Arabia	13.2
Netherlands	3.6	Rwanda	29.7
Switzerland	3.6	South Africa	31.0
Denmark	4.0	India	39.1
Australia	4.3	Afghanistan	110.6

Sources: CDC (2012a); Central Intelligence Agency (2017).

later, this number was fewer than six out of every one thousand infants (CDC, 2012a). The averages conceal wide differences within society, some of which are listed in Table 10.5. In fact, there is also variability within the United States: infant mortality rates are higher in poorer states, like Mississippi, with a rate of nine out of every one thousand births, than in Massachusetts, with a rate of four out of every one thousand (United Health Foundation, 2016). Families with very low incomes are about twice as likely to lose an infant as families with middle-level incomes. Likewise, African-American families are twice as likely as white families to lose an infant, perhaps because of the historical correlation of race with income level and access to health care in American society. The strongest correlate with mortality is not race, however, but level of family income. As a rule of thumb, infants born to families with lower incomes are much more likely to die than infants born to families with higher incomes. Though this trend may be easy to believe when comparing poor with middle-income families, it actually holds for the full range of income in society (Finch, 2003; Pritchett, 1993). That is, infants born to middle-income families are *also* more likely to die than infants born to extremely wealthy families. The pattern holds no matter what the race or ethnic background of the child.

On average, infant mortality rates in the United States and Canada are two or three times lower than those in many less developed countries. Even so, infant mortality in the United States actually is *higher* than in numerous other developed nations, including Canada, Japan, Sweden, France, and Great Britain (Central Intelligence Agency, 2017). Cross- cultural investigations of infant mortality rates in European countries have given further clues about the reasons for the relatively high U.S. rate and have suggested ways to improve it. The research overwhelmingly indicates that parents need social supports as much as they need access to basic medical services and knowledge. Most European countries provide pregnant mothers with free prenatal care, for example, and also protect women's right to work during and after pregnancy. Pregnant women get special, generous sick leave, get at least four months of maternity leave *with pay*, and are protected from doing dangerous or exhausting work (such as night shifts). Policies such as these communicate support for pregnant mothers and their spouses in ways not currently available in the United States.

Chapter Summary

- **What do infants look like when they are first born? How do we know if they are healthy?** The average newborn has rather red-looking skin, is often covered with a waxy substance, and has a skull somewhat compressed on the top. The health of newborns born in hospitals is assessed quickly after delivery with the Apgar Scale. The average newborn at full term weighs about 7½ pounds. Regardless of cultural background, the newborn's bodily proportions make the infant look appealing to adults and may foster the formation of attachments with adults.
- **How much do children grow during infancy?** Infants grow very rapidly during the first two years of life, tripling their weight by their first birthday and adding approximately 50 percent to their length by this same time. The torso and limbs of infants grow more rapidly than their heads, enabling their bodies slowly "catch up" to the advanced development of their heads.
- **What changes occur in the brains of infants?** The brains of infants gain mass rapidly during infancy due to important changes in the neurons and to infants' experiences with their environments. Neurons become myelinated, which improves their efficiency, and they form many new synapses as infants have new experiences and acquire new skills. The efficiency of the nervous system is enhanced by the synaptic pruning process that eliminates redundant or unused synapses.
- **How do infants' sleep and wakefulness patterns change as infants get older?** Infants sleep almost twice as much as adults do, but the amount of sleep gradually decreases as they get older. The interruptions in their sleep contribute to fatigue in their parents.

- **What motor skills evolve during infancy?** Infants are born with a number of innate reflexes, but quickly develop certain motor skills during the first year, including reaching, grasping, and walking. Motor skills develop differently depending on cultural background, biological sex, and social gender roles.
- **What do infants need nutritionally?** Infants need more protein and calories per pound of body weight than older children do. Compared to formula and bottle feeding, breastfeeding has a number of practical and psychological advantages. After weaning from breast or bottle, infants need a diet rich in protein and calories. Most North American families can provide these requirements, but many cannot. A common problem in North American diets is overnutrition, which can create health risks in the long term.
- **What factors can impair growth during infancy?** One of the most important impairments to early growth is low birth weight, because the condition leads to difficulties with breathing, digestion, and sleep, and impairs normal reflexes. The problems low-birth-weight infants experience can sometimes put stress on their relationships with parents, but not necessarily. For a variety of reasons, infants sometimes fail to thrive normally. Infant mortality has decreased in the recent past, but in the United States, it is still higher than it should be.
- **How do infants' senses operate at birth?** At birth, infants already can see and hear, but with less accuracy or acuity than adults do. They have well-developed senses of taste, smell, and touch, and infants demonstrate the ability to combine information from multiple senses to better allow them to function in their environments.

Key Terms

Apgar Scale (p. xx)
central nervous system (p. xx)
cephalocaudal principle (p. xx)
failure to thrive (p. xx)
infant mortality rate (p. xx)
low birth weight (p. xx)
motor skills (p. xx)
myelination (p. xx)
neonate (p. xx)
neurons (p. xx)
non-REM sleep (p. xx)
overnutrition (p. xx)
proximodistal principle (p. xx)
plasticity (p. xx)
reflex (p. xx)
REM sleep (p. xx)

stunting (p. xx)

sudden infant death syndrome (SIDS) (p. xx)

synaptic pruning (p. xx)

synaptogenesis (p. xx)

transient exuberance (p. xx)

References

Abukabar, A., Holding, P., Vijver, F. J. R., Newton, C., & Baar, A. V. (2010). Children at risk for developmental delay can be recognized by stunting, being underweight, ill health, little maternal schooling or high gravity. *Journal of Child Psychology and Psychiatry, 51*, 652–659.

Adolph, K. E. (2008). Learning to move. *Current Directions in Psychological Science, 17,* 213–218.

American Academy of Pediatrics. (2013a). *Apgar scores.* Retrieved from http://www.healthychildren. org/ English/ages-stages/prenatal/delivery-beyond/pages/ Apgar-Scores

American Academy of Pediatrics. (2013b). *A child care provider's guide to safe sleep.* Retrieved from http://www.healthychildren.org/English/familylife/ work-play/ Pages/A-Child-Care-Provider%27s-Guide-to-Safe-Sleep

American Academy of Pediatrics Task Force on Sudden Infant Death Syndrome (AAP Task Force on SIDS). (2011). SIDS and other sleeprelated deaths: Expansion of recommendations for a safe infant sleeping environment. *Pediatrics, 128,* 1341–1367.

Apgar, V. (1953). A proposal for a new method of evaluation in the newborn infant. *Current Research in Anesthesia and Analgesia, 32,* 260.

Bamford, F., Bannister, R., Benjamin, C., Hillier, V., Ward, B., & Moore, W. (1990). Sleep in the first year of life. *Developmental Medicine and Child Neurology, 32,* 718–724.

Black, M. M., Quigg, A. M., Hurley, K. M., & Pepper, M. R. (2011). Iron deficiency and iron-deficiency anemia in the first two years of life: Strategies to prevent loss of developmental potential. *Nutrition Reviews, 69,* S64–S70.

Booth, D. A., Higgs, S., Schneider, J., & Klinkenberg, I. (2010). Learned liking versus inborn delight: Can sweetness give sensual pleasure or is it just motivating? *Psychological Science, 21,* 1656–1663.

Brazelton, T. B., and Nugent, J. (1997). *Neonatal behavioral assessment scale* (4th ed.), New York, NY: Cambridge University Press.

Bronner, F. (Ed.) (1997). *Nutrition policy in public health.* New York, NY: Springer.

Brooten, D. (Ed.) (1992). *Low-birth-weight neonates.* Philadelphia: Lippincott.

Byard, R., & Cohle, S. (1994). *Sudden death in infants, children, and adolescents.* New York, NY: Cambridge University Press.

Carroll, J., & Siska, E. (1998). SIDS: Counseling parents to reduce the risk. *American Family Physician, 57*(9) [On-line]. Available: www.sids.org.

Centers for Disease Control and Prevention (CDC). (2012a). *National vital statistics reports, 61* (No. 6). Hyattsville, MD: National Center for Health Statistics. Retrieved from http://www.cdc.gov/nchs/ data/nvsr/nvsr61/nvsr61_06.pdf

Central Intelligence Agency. (2017). *The world factbook.* Washington, DC: Author. Retrieved from https:// www.cia.gov/library/publications/the-worldfactbook/rankorder/2091rank.html

Cole, S. Z., & Lanham, J. S. (2011). Failure to thrive: An update. *American Family Physician, 83,* 829–834.

Connelly, K., & Forssberg, H. (Eds.) (1997). *Neurophysiology and neuropsychology of motor development.* London: MacKeith Press.

Coren, S. (1996). *Sleep thieves.* New York, NY: Free Press.

Datar, A., & Jacknowitz, A. (2009). Birth weight effects on children's mental, motor and physical development: Evidence from twins data. *Maternal and Child Health Journal, 13,* 780–794.

Dermer, A. (2001). A well-kept secret: Breastfeeding's benefits to mothers. *New Beginnings, 18*(4), 124–127.

El-Dib, M., Massaro, A. N., Glass, P., & Aly, H. (2012). Neurobehavioral assessment as a predictor of neurodevelopmental outcome in preterm infants. *Journal of Perinatology, 32,* 299–303.

Ferber, R., & Kryger, M. (Eds.). (1995). *Principles and practice of sleep medicine in the child.* Philadelphia: Saunders.

Fernald, A., & Kuhl, P. (1987). Acoustic determinants of infant preference for motherese speech. *Infant Behavior and Development, 10,* 279–293.

Finch, B. K. (2003). Early origins of the gradient: The relationship between socioeconomic status and infant mortality in the United States, *Demography, 40,* 675–699.

Fomon, S. J., & Nelson, S. E. (2002). Body composition of the male and female reference infants. *Annual Review of Nutrition, 22,* 1–17.

Frank, T., Turenshine, H., & Sullivan, S. J. (2010). *The effect of birth order on personality, intelligence and achievement.* Paper presented at the 118th Annual Convention of the American Psychological Convention, San Diego, CA.

Franklin, A., Pilling, M., & Davies, I. (2005). The nature of infant color categorization: Evidence from eye movements on a target detection task. *Journal of Experimental Child Psychology, 91,* 227–248.

Fransson, P., Skiold, B., Engstrom, M., Hallberg, B., Mosskin, M., Aden, U., ... & Blennow, M. (2009). Spontaneous brain activity in the newborn brain during natural sleep—an fMRI study in infants born at full term. *Pediatric Research, 66,* 301–305.

Futagi, Y., Toribe, YH., & Suzuki, Y. (2009). Neurological assessment of early infants. *Current Pediatric Reviews, 5,* 65–70.

Glass, D. C., Neulinger, J., & Brim, O. C. (1974). Birth order, verbal intelligence, and educational aspiration. *Child Development, 45,* 807–811.

Goldson, E. (1992). The longitudinal study of very low birth-weight infants and its implications for interdisciplinary research and public policy. In C. Greenbaum, & J. Auerbach (Eds.), *Longitudinal studies of children at psychological risk: Cross-national perspectives* (pp. 43–64). Norwood, NJ: Ablex.

Gross, R., Spiker, D., & Haynes, C. (1997). *Helping low-birth-weight, premature babies*. Stanford, CA: Stanford University Press.

Gunnarsdottir, I., & Thorsdottir, I. (2003). Relationship between growth and feeding in infancy and body mass index at the age of 6 years. *International Journal of Obesity and Metabolic Disorders, 27,* 1523–1527.

Harkness, S., & Keefer, C. (1995, February). *Cultural influences on sleep patterns in infancy and early childhood.* Paper presented at the annual meeting of the American Association for the Advancement of Science, Atlanta.

Harrington, J. W., Nguyen, V. Q., Paulson, J. F., Garland, R., Pasquinelli, L., & Lewis, D. (2010). Identifying the "tipping point" age for overweight pediatric patients. *Clinical Pediatrics, 49,* 638–643.

Harrison, D., Bueno, M., Yamada, J., Adams-Webber, T., & Stevens, B. (2010). Analgesic effects of sweet-tasting solutions for infants: Current state of equipoise. *Pediatrics, 126,* 894–902.

Ho, E. S. (2010). Measuring hand function in the young child. *Journal of Hand Therapy, 23,* 323–328.

Hunt, C. (Ed.). (1992). *Apnea and SIDS*. Philadelphia: Saunders.

Insana, S. P., & Montgomery-Downs, H. E. (2013). Sleep and sleepiness among first-time postpartum parents: A field-and laboratory-based multimethod assessment. *Developmental Psychobiology, 55*(4), 361–372.

James, W. (1890). *The principles of psychology*. Boston: Henry Holt.

Johnson, W. (2010). Understanding the genetics of intelligence: Can height help? Can corn oil? *Current Directions in Psychological Science, 19,* 177–182.

Kaijura, H., Cowart, B. J., & Beauchamp, G. K. (1992). Early developmental change in bitter taste responses in human infants. *Developmental Psychobiology, 25,* 375–386.

Kaplan, L. (1995). *No voice is ever wholly lost*. New York, NY: Simon & Schuster.

Kellman, P. J., & Arterberry, M. E. (2006). Infant visual perception. In W. Damon, & R. M. Lerner (Eds.), *Handbook of child psychology: Vol. 2. Cognition, perception, and language* (6th ed.). Hoboken, NJ: Wiley.

La Leche League International. (1991). *The womanly art of breastfeeding* (5th ed.), New York, NY: Plume Books.

LeVine, R. (1994). *Child care and culture: Lessons from Africa,* New York, NY: Cambridge University Press.

Liem, D. G., & Mennella, J. A. (2002). Sweet and sour preferences during childhood: Role of early experiences. *Developmental Psychology, 41,* 388–395.

Masapollo, M., Polka, L., & Ménard, L. (2016). When infants talk, infants listen: Pre-babbling infants prefer listening to speech with infant vocal properties. *Developmental Science, 19*(2), 318–328.

Menkes, J. (1994). *Textbook of child neurology* (5th ed.). Philadelphia: Williams and Wilkins.

Michelsson, K., Rinne, A., & Paajanen, S. (1990). Crying, feeding and sleeping patterns in 1 to 12-month-old infants. *Child: Care, health and. development, 116,* 99–111.

Montgomery-Downs, H. E., Insana, S. P., Clegg-Kraynok, M. M., & Mancini, L. M. (2010). Normative longitudinal maternal sleep: The first 4 postpartum months. *American Journal of Obstetrics and Gynecology, 203*(5), 465-e1.

Moore, K., & Persaud, T. (1998). *The developing human: Clinically oriented embryology* (6th ed.). Philadelphia: Saunders.

Munroe, R., Munroe, R., & Whiting, J. (1981). Male sex-role resolutions. In *Handbook of cross-cultural human development,* New York, NY: Garland.

Parmelee, A. H., Wenner, W. H., & Schulz, H. R. (1964). Infant sleep patterns: From birth to 16 weeks of age. *Journal of Pediatrics, 65*(4), 576–582.

Pollitt, E. (Ed.). (1995). *The relationships between undernutrition and behavioral development in children.* Washington, DC: American Institute of Nutrition.

Porter, R. H., & Reiser, J. J. (2005). Retention of olfactory memories by newborn infants. In R. T. Mason, P. M. LeMaster, & D. Müller-Schwarze (Eds.), *Chemical Signals in Vertebrates.* New York, NY: Springer.

Pownall, T., & Kingerlee, S. (1993). *Seeing, reaching, and touching: Relationships between vision and touching in infants.* New York, NY: Harvester and Wheatsheaf.

Pritchett, L. (1993). *Wealthier is healthier.* Washington, DC: The World Bank.

Queen, P., & Lang, C. (1993). *Handbook of pediatric nutrition.* Gaithersburg, MD: Aspen Publishers.

Richards, M., & Wadsworth, M. E. J. (2004). Long term effects of early adversity on cognitive function. *Archives of Disease in Childhood, 89,* 922–927.

Rivkees, S. A. (2003). Developing circadian rhythmicity in infants. *Pediatrics, 112,* 373–381.

Rowe, M. L., Levine, S. C., Fisher, J. A., & Goldin-Meadow, S. (2009). Does linguistic input play the same role in language learning for children with and without early brain injury? *Developmental Psychology, 45,* 90–102.

Savelsbergh, G. (1993). *Development of coordination in infancy.* New York, NY: North-Holland.

Seidel, H., Rosenstein, B., & Pathak, A. (Eds.). (1997). *Primary care of the newborn* (2nd ed.). St. Louis: Mosby.

Sheldon, S., Spire, J., & Levy, H. (1992). *Pediatric sleep medicine.* Philadelphia: Saunders.

Shultz, S., & Vouloumanos, A. (2010). Three-month olds prefer speech to other naturally occurring signals. *Language Learning and Development, 6,* 241–257.

Spassov, L., Curzi-Dscalovi, L., Clairambualt, J., Kauffman, F., Eiselt, M., Medigue, C., & Peirano, P. (1994). Heart rate and heart-rate variability during sleep in small-for-gestational-age newborns. *Pediatric Research, 35,* 500–505.

Steiner, J. E., Glasser, D., Hawilo, M. E., & Berridge, I. C. (2001). Comparative expression of hedonic impact: Affective reactions to taste by human infants and other primates. *Neuroscience & Biobehavioral Reviews, 25,* 53–74.

Stiles, J., & Jernigan, T. L. (2010). The basics of brain development. *Neuropsychology Review, 20,* 327–348.

Taylor, M. J. (2006). Neural bases of cognitive development. In E. Bialystok & F. I. M. Craik (Eds.), *Lifespan cognition: Mechanisms of change.* New York, NY: Oxford University Press.

United Health Foundation. (2016). *America's health rankings: Infant mortality rates.* Retrieved from http://www.americashealthrankings.org/MS/IMR

United Nations International Children's Emergency Fund (UNICEF). (2009). *The state of the world's children: Maternal and newborn health, 2009.* Retrieved from http://www.unicef.org/sowc09/index.php

U.S. National Library of Medicine (USNLM). (2011). *Age-appropriate diet for children.* Retrieved from http://www.nlm.nih.gov/medlineplus/ency/ article/002455.htm

van Sleuwen, B. E., Engelberts, A. C., Boore-Boonekamp, M. M., Wietse, K., Schulpen, T. W. J., & L'Hoir, M. P. (2007). Swaddling: A systematic review. *Pediatrics, 120,* 1097–1106.

Warnock, F., & Sandrin, D. (2004). Comprehensive description of newborn distress behavior in response to acute pain (newborn male circumcision). *Pain, 107,* 242–255.

Whiting, J. W. M. (1981). Environmental constraints on infant care practices. In R. Munroe, R. H. Monroe, & B. B. Whiting (Eds.), *Handbook of cross-cultural development.* New York, NY: Garland Press.

Williams, A., Khattak, A. Z., Garza, C. N., & Lasky, R. E. (2009). The behavioral pain response to heelstick in preterm neonates studied longitudinally: Description, development, determinants, and components. *Early Human Development, 85,* 369–374.

Williams, C., & Kimm, S. (1993). *Prevention and treatment of childhood obesity.* New York, NY: New York Academy of Sciences.

Woolston, J. (1993). *Eating and growth disorders.* Philadelphia: Saunders.

Wootan, M., & Liebman, B. (1998). Ten steps to a healthy 1998. *Nutrition Action Health Letter, 25*(1), 1, 6–10.

Zampi, C., Fagioli, I., & Salzarulo, P. (2002). Time course of EEG background activity level before spontaneous awakening in infants. *Journal of Sleep Research, 11,* 283–287.

Zhang, J., Himes, J. H., Guo, Y., Jiang, J., Yang, L., Lu, Q., Ruan, H., & Shi, S. (2013). Birth weight, growth and feeding pattern in early infancy predict overweight/obesity status at two years of age: A birth cohort study of Chinese infants. *PLoS ONE, 8,* 1–8.

Physical and Cognitive Development During Early Childhood

Megan Clegg-Kraynok, Kelvin L. Seifert, and Robert J. Hoffnung

Source: Gserban/Shutterstock.com.

FOCUSING QUESTIONS

- What pathway does physical growth normally take during early childhood?
- How is poverty related to children's health?
- When do children achieve bladder control?
- What motor skills do children acquire during the preschool years?
- How does children's growth affect parents and other adults?
- What are the special features and strengths of preschoolers' thinking?
- How does the language of preschool children differ from that of older children?
- What social and cultural factors account for variations in preschoolers' language and speech?
- What constitutes good early childhood education?

Megan Clegg-Kraynok, Kelvin L. Seifert, and Robert J. Hoffnung, Selection from "Physical Development During Early Childhood," *Child and Adolescent Development: A Chronological Approach*, pp. 183-197, R1-R36. Copyright © 2019 by Academic Media Solutions. Reprinted with permission.

"Kitty run!" says Zöe, age three. She is pointing to the neighborhood cat.

"Yes," replies her father. "She's chasing a bird."

Zöe nods and says, "Bird gone now. Bad kitty?" and looks to her father for confirmation.

"It's OK this time," says her father. "The bird flew away soon enough."

At this, Zöe walks off to find the cat, curious to learn what else it might do.

Two features of this incident are especially noteworthy: Zöe's language and her mobility. Little more than a year ago, neither could have occurred. As a preschooler, however, she is developing the ability to deal with her world in symbols, in this case through oral language. She is also developing new physical skills that serve her interests and abilities; for example, she can walk up to the cat simply to learn more about it.

In the next two chapters, we look in detail at physical and cognitive development during early childhood. Many of the examples will suggest relationships between the two domains, as well as their impact on the third domain of psychosocial development. The fact that preschoolers sleep less than they did as infants, for example, is the beginning of a lifelong trend that will affect both child and parents, creating new options for each. For the child, staying awake longer facilitates attending school; for parents, the child's attending school makes adult-focused activities, such as a job or a hobby, easier to arrange than before their children began school. Parents who are ready for the growth and changes in their preschoolers but do not feel pressured to hurry those changes will likely influence their children's development in many positive ways. The changes will also set the stage for even more indirect forms of parenting typical of later phases of childhood and adolescence, discussed in Chapters 13 and 16.

PHYSICAL DEVELOPMENT

Influences on Normal Physical Development

Physical growth during the preschool years is relatively easy to measure and gives a clear idea of how children normally develop during this period. Table 11.1 and Figure 11.1 show the two most familiar measurements of growth, standing height and weight. At age two, an average child in North America measures about thirty-three or thirty-four inches tall, or about two feet, ten inches. Three years later, at age five, he or she measures approximately forty-three inches, or about one-third more than before. The typical child weighs twenty-seven to twenty-eight pounds by age two but about forty-one pounds by age five. Meanwhile, other measurements change in less obvious ways. The child's head grows about one inch in circumference during these years, and body fat decreases as a proportion of total bodily tissue.

For a preschool child who is reasonably healthy and happy, physical growth is remarkably smooth and predictable, especially compared to many cognitive and social developments. Overall, physical growth contains no discrete stages, plateaus, or qualitative changes such as those Piaget proposed for cognitive development. At the same time, however, important differences develop among individual children and among groups of children. Often the differences simply

TABLE 11.1   Average Height and Weight during Early Childhood

Age (Years)	Girls		Boys	
	Height (inches)	**Weight (pounds)**	**Height (inches)**	**Weight (pounds)**
2	33.5	26.5	34.1	28.6
3	37.0	30.9	37.4	31.7
4	39.8	35.0	40.2	35.3
5	42.3	39.7	42.9	40.8

Source: Centers for Disease Control and Prevention (2000).

create interesting physical variety among children, but sometimes they do more than affect appearance. Being larger (or smaller) than usual, for example, can make a child stronger (or less strong) than others of the same age, and therefore more (or less) able to master certain sports or other physical activities. Size can also affect how parents and other adults respond to the child; larger children may seem older and be treated as such, whether or not they are psychologically ready. For both reasons, a child might gain (or lose) self-confidence, and even gain (or lose) popularity among peers.

The overall smoothness of growth means that childhood height and weight can predict adult height and weight to a significant extent, although not perfectly. A four-year-old who is above average in height tends to end up above average as an adult. Nevertheless, correlation between childhood height and adult height is imperfect because of individual differences in nutrition and

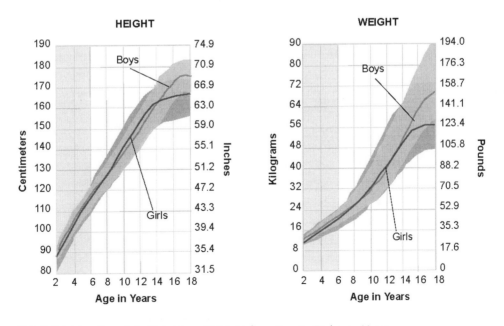

FIGURE 11.1   Growth in Height and Weight from Two to Eighteen Years

health and, most of all, in the timing of puberty. In particular, children who experience puberty later than average tend to grow taller than children who experience it early (Sanfilippo et al., 1994; Yousefi et al., 2013)—a source of diversity that we will say more about in Chapter 13 in connection with adolescence and its impact.

Genetic Background

Most dimensions of growth are influenced substantially by heredity. Tall parents tend to have tall children, and short parents usually have short children. Weight shows similar patterns, although it can be influenced strongly by habits of exercise and diet.

Races and ethnic groups around the world also differ slightly in average growth patterns (Eveleth & Tanner, 1990), and general trends demonstrate that children born in countries with low to middle income are more likely to be low birth weight (5.5 pounds or less) and to exhibit slower growth throughout childhood (Adair et al., 2013). Children from Asian groups, such as Chinese and Japanese, tend to be shorter than European and North American children are. The latter, in turn, tend to be shorter than children from African societies are. Shape differs among these groups as well, although the differences do not always become obvious until adolescence. Asian children tend to develop short legs and arms relative to their torsos, and relatively broad hips. African children do just the opposite: they tend to develop relatively long limbs and narrow hips. Keep in mind, though, that these differences are only average tendencies. Racial and ethnic groups tend to overlap in size and shape more than they differ (that is what makes us all human!). From the point of view of parents, teachers, and other professionals, the most important physical differences among children are individual ones: there are large and small children in every racial and ethnic group, among both boys and girls, and in every community (Doherty, 1996). If you are responsible for children as individuals, recognizing their individual differences is likely to be your priority.

As a result of improvements in nutrition and health care, children in industrialized nations are often taller than in earlier times. But there are important variations among societies—even among industrialized ones—that apparently are influenced genetically.

Source: wckiw/Shutterstock.com.

Nutritional Needs during the Preschool Years

For a time, a young preschooler (such as a three-year-old) may eat less than he or she did as a toddler and become much more selective about foods as well. Michael, the son of one of the authors, ate every meal voraciously as a two-year-old; a year later, he rarely finished a meal, even though he was significantly taller and heavier by then. Elizabeth, his sister, followed a similar but more pronounced pattern. As a toddler, she ate most foods except ice cream ("Too sweet," she said!), but as a young preschooler, she sometimes hardly ate—though she did decide then that she liked ice cream. Later, their appetites returned. As a nineteen-year-old, Michael routinely ate about twice as much as other members of the family did. Elizabeth, at sixteen, was no longer a picky eater—and became especially enthusiastic about ice cream.

Parents may worry about such changes, but in fact, they are normal and result from the slowing down of growth after infancy. Preschool children simply do not need as many calories per unit of their body weight as they did immediately after birth. They do need variety in their foods, however, just as adults do, to ensure adequate overall nutrition. Given preschoolers' newfound selectiveness about eating, providing the variety needed for good nutrition sometimes can be a challenge to parents and other caregivers.

How can one ensure healthy variety in a preschool child's diet? Experts generally discourage coercion ("Eat your vegetables because I say so!") because it teaches children to associate undesired foods with unpleasant social experiences (Endres & Rockwell, 1993; Ventura & Worobey, 2013). They also discourage using sweet foods and drinks as a reward for eating undesired foods ("If you eat your vegetables, then you can have your ice cream") because it implicitly overvalues the sweets and undervalues the undesired food still further. For children who are particularly picky and who do not like to try new foods, sticker rewards for trying new foods have been successful (Corsini et al., 2013). In addition, providing many opportunities for children to try foods, even vegetables the children "don't like," in conjunction with nonfood reinforcement like a sticker increases liking for those vegetables (Fildes, van Jaarsveld, Wardle, & Cooke, 2014). The best strategy seems to be casual, repeated exposure to the food without insisting that the child eat it (Andrien, 1994). Getting children involved in age-appropriate food preparation, such as tearing and washing lettuce, cleaning and breaking apart cauliflower or broccoli, and weighing pasta, was linked to children eating more overall, including vegetables (van der Horst, Ferrage, & Rytz, 2014). Observations of children's eating habits confirm what parents often suspect as well: children's food preferences are influenced by the adult models around them. In the long term, preschoolers tend to like the same foods as their parents and other important adults. More generally, they practice many of their parents' other health behaviors (such as exercise) as well.

The Connection between Health and Poverty

In settings of middle and high socioeconomic status, preschool children as a group are among the healthiest human beings alive, though not as healthy as they will become in childhood, adolescence, and young adulthood. They experience comparatively few major illnesses as long as they get enough of the right things to eat and as long as their parents have reasonable access to modern medical care. As parents often note, preschoolers do experience frequent minor illnesses: various respiratory infections, ear infections, and stomach flus. These typically strike a young child several times per year, which is three or four times as often as for adults and about twice as often as for school-age children (Engels, 1993). For well-fed children whose families have access to medical care, however, these illnesses rarely prove serious or life threatening. Colds and flu do cause worry, as well as create challenges for working parents in arranging childcare.

But this optimistic picture of preschoolers' health may be misleading. Since 1997, when the Children's Health Insurance Program (CHIP), which provides low- or no-cost insurance to children whose families make too much to qualify for Medicaid but cannot afford insurance, passed, rates

WHAT DO YOU THINK?

How do you suppose parents evaluate their child's height and weight? Explore this problem by asking two or three parents how satisfied they are with their child's height and weight. Do you think parents' feelings have any relationship to the actual size of their child?

of uninsured children have decreased significantly. This trend has stabilized with the passage of the Affordable Care Act (ACA), so that currently, only 5 percent of children lack health insurance coverage (Artiga & Ubri, 2017). However, most states that did not accept the Medicaid expansion of the ACA have uninsured child rates of 10 percent or higher (Kenney et al., 2014). Moreover, temporary funding of CHIP and possible repeals of ACA make many children vulnerable to losing access to medical care. Young children from these families are substantially less healthy than are those from middle- and high-SES families. Low-SES preschoolers contract 25 to 50 percent more minor illnesses than do preschoolers as a whole, and they are more often malnourished and face food insecurity, meaning that they chronically lack the quantity and quality of food to thrive, as well as essential vitamins, iron, and protein (American Academy of Pediatrics, 1993; McCurdy, Gorman, Kisler, & Metallinos-Katsaras, 2012; Wilkinson, 1996). Children growing up at or near the poverty level are also substantially more likely to be overweight or obese (McCurdy et al., 2012).

Whether in North America or around the world, minor illnesses combined with malnourishment put children's health at risk for additional illnesses, both minor and major. Malnourishment also contributes to delays in social, language, and cognitive development, possibly because it leads to lack of energy and lack of interest in new experiences. In one study based in Kenya (Africa), even a temporary food shortage (due to a few months of local drought) impaired children's health and school performance two years later (McDonald et al., 1994).

How can we counteract these problems? In general, strategies can focus either on individuals and their particular communities or on systematic reorganization of the health care system and food security systems as a whole. Among individually oriented strategies, an important one is to educate children and families about health and nutrition. For example, pamphlets can be distributed in schools or medical clinics, and public health professionals can make presentations in classrooms, community clubs, or churches. However, these efforts work best when they are multifaceted, including education in combination with improving access to high-quality food and health care. The "Focusing On" feature proposes additional alternatives.

Educational activities can be effective if they build on the knowledge of health and nutrition low-SES parents and their children already have and avoid assuming the public is completely ignorant about these matters. Good programs also improve individuals' self-efficacy about engaging in health-promoting behaviors, and as noted earlier, work best when public policy (like changes to the health care system or expanding programs such as the Supplemental Nutrition Assistance Program) makes engaging in health-promoting behaviors easier. In this sort of situation, it is helpful to organize intervention programs aimed at providing parents and children with the knowledge they need. However, such programs must respect the culture and economic situations of the families, which usually influence food preferences in major ways. Put simply, certain foods acquire symbolic

FOCUSING ON ...

Reforming Children's Health Care

In all societies, the health care system provides less help to poor families than to well-off ones. Low-SES mothers receive less medical attention during pregnancy, causing health problems in themselves or their fetuses to be overlooked, and are more likely to give birth to a low birth-weight infant (Krans & Davis, 2014). Infants of low-income mothers are less likely to receive checkups from a doctor and less likely to be seen by a doctor if they get sick (Bury, 1997; Wilkinson, 1996). However, children who have access to Medicaid and CHIP, described next, are much more likely to get checkups and to see health professionals early in an illness (Rudowitz, Artiga, & Arguello, 2014).

Why does access to health care depend so heavily on personal income? In the United States, medical services for the poor are paid through Medicaid, a federally sponsored insurance program created in the 1960s. It pays for some basic health services, such as taking a child with an ear ache to a general practitioner, but it reimburses the doctor only up to a certain point. Doctors who charge more price themselves out of the market for low-SES families, which have significantly fewer doctors and clinics to choose from but children who experience more illnesses than do children from higher-SES families (Fitzgerald et al., 1994). In 1997, the Children's Health Insurance Program (CHIP) was created, which assists states in providing insurance to children whose families cannot afford insurance but make too much money for Medicaid eligibility. As of 2017, nearly nine million children in the United States were enrolled in CHIP (Medicaid, 2018).

Though there have been significant strides in improving access to health care for children and adults alike, many children still lack access to health care. In some states, uninsured rates for children are over 15 percent, due in part to lack of parents' awareness of eligibility (Rudowitz, Artiga, & Arguello, 2014).

How can society and concerned individuals reduce these economically based inequalities in health care? Numerous reforms have been proposed centering on one of three ideas: community involvement, prevention, and reorganization of services. Reforms that focus on community involvement seek to reduce the psychological and geographical distance between medical staff and the people they serve. Some hospitals and cities have established small community health clinics in areas of greatest need (the inner city). They hire medical staff who establish rapport with the parents and children who seek help, recruit local community members to serve on their governing and advisory boards, and charge low fees based on families' ability to pay.

Reforms that focus on primary prevention seek to keep disease from striking in the first place. These actions often deal with relatively healthy children (who have not gotten sick yet) and the conditions that make illness likely rather than illness itself. Lead poisoning is a good example: community health experts often cite lead as one of the most hazardous health threats to preschool children (Tesman & Hills, 1994). Lead accumulates in the body and eventually damages the nervous system and can cause death. People pick it up accidentally from many sources, but the most prominent culprit is the interior wall paint used in about 75 percent of all homes and apartments built before 1980. Because there is no cure for lead poisoning, prevention strategies have dominated the response of the health care profession: educating parents to the dangers, pressing for legislation outlawing lead-based paints (and lead-based gasoline), removing leaded paint in some homes, and checking/ remediating local water systems when tap water tests high for lead content.

Reforms that focus on reorganization generally involve more self-conscious planning of medical services. Immunization and health-screening programs based in schools, for example, allow programs to reach a higher percentage of children than programs in community health clinics (Behrman, 1993; Behr-man & Stacey, 1997; Jacob et al., 2016). "Front-line" professionals often can improve access dramatically without compromising quality of care: most childhood illnesses, for example, can be treated effectively by a nurse as long as the nurse knows when a particular illness deserves referral to the doctor and appropriate specialized services are indeed available.

What Do You Think?

1. Look back on your own elementary school hearing or eye tests from the point of view of the teachers and nurses. Can you see any limitations to "mass screening," as well as advantages to it?

2. Is there a case to be made for *limiting* health care to the poor? What would it be? And what might be the long-term implications of limiting health care?

WHAT DO YOU THINK?

Suppose you are a teacher or caregiver at a childcare center, and one of your children often seems hungry throughout the day. How could you tell whether the child is undernourished or simply has a big appetite? Compare your strategies for answering this question with those of a classmate.

meanings (such as turkey for American Thanksgiving), regardless of their precise nutritional value. Other foods may never be tried, no matter how worthwhile they are nutritionally, because they cost too much or seem too strange or foreign to a particular family or cultural group.

Bladder Control

Sometime during the preschool years, to parents' great relief, most children acquire control of their bladder. The process includes many false starts and accidents. Most commonly, daytime

In the long run, successful bladder control depends on both physical growth and the child's own motivation. Forcing children prematurely to control themselves may produce results, but only in the immediate future.

Source: Maurizio Milanesio/ Shutterstock.com.

control comes before nighttime control, generally beginning between the ages of two and three (Bloom, Seeley, Ritchey, & McGuire, 1993) and becoming reliable for most children by the age of four (Jansson, Hanson, Sillén, & Hellström, 2005), although individual children vary widely and somewhat unpredictably. Typically, too, daytime control of the bladder occurs at very nearly the same time. Some pediatricians believe this fact implies that children decide when they wish to begin exercising control, perhaps to begin feeling more grown up. In the early stages of toilet training, therefore, reminders and parent-led visits to the toilet may make little difference to most toddlers. Nonetheless, they may help in the long term as a form of behavioral conditioning: a child comes to associate seeing and sitting on the toilet with the relief of emptying a full bladder, as well as with the praise parents confer on the child for successes.

Nighttime bladder control often takes much longer to achieve than daytime control. About one-half of all three-year-olds still wet their beds at least some of the time, and as many as one in five six-year-olds do the same (American Psychiatric Association, 1994). The timing of nighttime control depends on several factors, such as how deeply children sleep and how large their bladders are. It also depends on anxiety level; worried children tend to wet their beds more often than relaxed children do. Unfortunately, parents sometimes contribute to young children's anxieties by becoming overly frustrated about changing wet sheets night after night.

Achieving bladder control reflects the large advances children make during the preschool years in controlling their bodies in general. It also reflects parents' accumulated efforts to encourage physical self-control for their children. The combined result is that children of this age can begin focusing on what they actually want to do with their bodies.

Motor Skill Development

As young children grow, they become more skilled at performing basic physical actions. Often a two-year-old can walk only with considerable effort; hence the term *toddler*. But a five-year-old can walk comfortably in a variety of ways: forward and backward, quickly and slowly, skipping and galloping. A five-year-old also can do other vigorous things that were impossible a few years earlier. Running, jumping, and climbing all occur with increasing smoothness and variety. Children can carry out certain actions that require accuracy, such as balancing on one foot, catching a ball reliably, or drawing a picture.

In this section, we examine in more detail how children reach milestones such as these. Because family conditions vary a great deal, we will make certain assumptions. In particular, we will assume children have no significant fears of being active—that they have a reasonably (but not excessively) daring attitude toward trying out new motor skills, they are in good health, and their physical growth has evolved more or less optimally. These assumptions do not hold for all children or families, as we note later in this section, but they make a good starting point for understanding motor development.

Fundamental Motor Skills

Healthy preschool children obviously have moved well beyond the confines of reflex action, which constituted the first motor skills of infancy. From ages two to about five, they experiment with the simple voluntary actions that adults use extensively for their normal activities, such as walking, running, and jumping (Kalverboer et al., 1993). For older children, these actions usually are the means to other ends. For very young children, they lie very much in the foreground and frequently are goals in themselves. Table 11.2 summarizes some of these activities.

Walking and Running

From a child's point of view, walking may seem absurd at first: it requires purposely losing balance, then regaining balance rapidly enough to keep from falling (Rose & Gamble, 1993).

WHAT DO YOU THINK?

Imagine how you would talk to a parent who was concerned about the child's bed-wetting at night. What would you say? If you or your instructor can arrange it, try acting out a meeting to discuss bed-wetting between a concerned parent and a childcare center worker or director.

TABLE 11.2 Milestones in Preschool Motor Development

Approximate Age	Gross Motor Skill	Fine Motor Skill
2.5–3.5 years	Walks well; runs in straight line; jumps in air with both feet	Copies a circle; scribbles; can use eating utensils; stacks a few small blocks
3.5–4.5 years	Has a walking stride 80 percent that of adult; runs at one-third adult speed; throws and catches large ball, but is stiff-armed	Buttons with large buttons; copies simple shapes; makes simple representational drawings
4.5–5.5 years	Balances on one foot; runs far without falling; can "swim" in water for short distance	Uses scissors; draws people; copies simple letters and numbers; builds complex structures with blocks

Note: The ages given above are approximate, and skills vary with the life experiences available to individual children and with the situations in which the skills are displayed.

Source: Kalverboer et al. (1993).

As older infants, children still must pay attention to these facts, even after a full year or so of practice. Each step is an effort in itself. Children watch each foot in turn as it launches (or lurches) forward; they may pause after each step before attempting the next. By their second or third birthday, however, their steps become more regular and their feet get closer together (Adolph et al., 2012). Stride, the distance between feet in a typical step, remains considerably shorter than that of a typical adult. This makes short distances easy to walk but long distances hard to navigate for a few more years.

Jumping

At first, a jump is more like a fast stretch: the child reaches for the sky rapidly, but her feet fail to leave the ground. Sometime around her second birthday, one foot, or even both feet, may finally leave the ground. Such early successes may be delayed, however, because the child may thrust her arms backward to help herself take off, as though trying to push herself off the floor. Later, perhaps around age three, she shifts to a more efficient arm movement—reaching forward and upward as she jumps—which creates a useful upward momentum.

Success in these actions depends partly on the type of jump the child is attempting. Jumping down a step is easier than jumping across a flat distance, and a flat or broad jump is easier than a jump up a step. By age five or so, most children can broad-jump across a few feet, although variations among individuals are substantial.

Throwing and Catching

For infants and toddlers, first throws may consist of simply waving an object, releasing it suddenly, and watching it take off. Once intentional throwing begins, however, children actually adopt more stereotyped methods initially, using a general forward lurch, regardless of the ball's size or weight. As skill develops, children vary their movements according to the size of the ball.

Catching proceeds through analogous phases, from stereotyped, passive extension of arms to flexible movement of hands in a last-minute response to the oncoming ball.

Fine Motor Coordination: The Case of Drawing Skills

Not all motor activities of young children involve the strength, agility, and balance of their whole bodies. Many require the coordination of small movements but not strength. Tying shoelaces calls for such **fine motor coordination**; so do washing hands, buttoning and zipping clothing, eating with a spoon, and turning a doorknob.

> **fine motor coordination** Ability to smoothly carry out small movements that involve precise timing but not strength.

One especially widespread fine motor skill among young children is drawing. In North American culture, at least, virtually every young child tries using pens or pencils at some time and often tries other artistic media as well. The scribbles or drawings that result probably serve a number of purposes. At times, they may be used mainly for sensory exploration; a child may want to get the feel of paintbrushes or felt-tip pens. At other times, drawings may express thoughts or feelings; a child may suggest this possibility by commenting, "It's a horse, and it's angry." Children's drawings also probably reflect their knowledge of the world, even though they may not yet have the fine motor skills they need to convey their knowledge fully. In other words, children's drawings reveal not only fine motor coordination but also their self-concepts, emotional and social attitudes, and cognitive development.

Drawing shows two overlapping phases of development during early childhood. From about two and a half to four years of age, children focus on developing nonrepresentational skills, such as scribbling and purposeful drawing of simple shapes and designs. Sometime around age four, they begin attempting to represent objects (Coles, 1992). Yet, although representational drawings usually follow nonrepresentational ones, the two types stimulate each other simultaneously. Children often describe their early scribbles as though they referred to real things, and their practice at portraying real objects helps them to further develop their nonrepresentational skills (Coates & Coates, 2006).

Prerepresentational Drawing

Around the end of infancy, children begin to scribble. A two-year-old experiments with whatever pen, crayon, or pencil is available, almost regardless of its color or type, behaving like an infant and like a child. As with an infant, efforts focus primarily on the activity itself: on the motions and sensations of handling a pen or pencil. But like an older child, the two-year-old often cares about the outcome of these activities: "That's a Mommy," he says of his drawing, whether it looks much like one or not. Contrary to a popular view of children's art, even very young children are concerned not only with the process of drawing but with the product as well (Broughton et al., 1996).

A child's interest in the results of her drawing shows up in the patterns she imposes on even her earliest scribbles. Sometimes, she fills up particular parts of the page quite intentionally—the whole left side, say, or the complete middle third. And she often emphasizes particular categories of

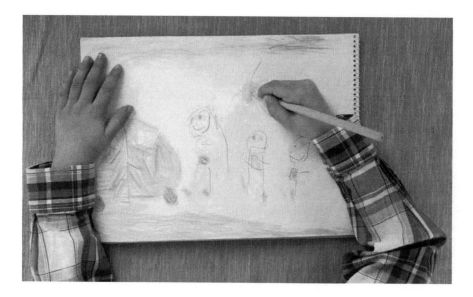

Skills that require fine motor coordination—like creating this drawing—develop through identifiable steps or stages. At first, children tend to make random marks or scribbles; later, they coordinate these into patterns; still later, they coordinate patterns into representations of objects that become increasingly recognizable by parents and teachers.

Source: borisow/Shutterstock.com.

strokes: lots of straight diagonals or many counterclockwise loops. Different children select different types of motions for emphasis, so the motions are less like universal stages than like elements of a personal style.

Representational Drawing

While preschool children improve their scribbling skills, they also develop an interest in representing people, objects, and events in their drawings. This interest often far precedes their ability to do so. A three-year-old may assign meanings to scribbles or blobs in his drawing; one blob may be "Mama," and another may be "our house." Events may happen to these blobs, too: Mama may be "going to the store" or "looking for me." During the early childhood years, and for a long time thereafter, the child's visual representations are limited by comparatively rudimentary fine motor skills. Apparently, children know more, visually speaking, than their hands can portray with pens or brushes. Only as children reach school age do their drawings of people become relatively realistic.

What happens to drawing skills beyond the preschool years depends on a child's experiences and on the encouragement (or lack thereof) received from others. Drawings in later years become even more realistic—more "photographic" or draftsmanlike in style. But not all children stay with art in the long term, due to the combined influence of competing academic interests, the priorities of friends, or even dislike of a teacher. We will discuss these types of influence again in Chapter 13 in connection with social and motivational changes during middle childhood.

Gender Differences in Physical Development

As is true during infancy, preschool boys and girls develop at almost exactly the same average rates. This applies to practically any motor skill of which young children are capable, and it applies to both gross and fine motor skills. Any nursery classroom, therefore, is likely to contain children of both sexes who can run very well and children of both sexes who can paint well or tie their shoelaces without help. This is especially true among younger preschool children (age three or four).

By the time children begin kindergarten (usually at age five), slight gender differences in physical development and motor skills appear, with boys tending to be (slightly) bigger, stronger, and faster (Kalverboer et al., 1993) and with better ball skills, while girls demonstrate better manual dexterity (Junaid & Fellowes, 2006). Yet these differences are noticeable only as averages and only by basing the averages on very large numbers of children. Despite the slight differences, therefore, more than 95 percent of children are more skillful and bigger than some members of *both* sexes, and less skillful and smaller than certain others of both sexes.

By the time children start school, a few children in any community are bigger, stronger, and faster than *any* other children, and most of them are boys. Furthermore, these few individuals may get much more than their share of attention because of their superior physical skills. This contributes to the (mistaken) impression that boys are larger and more skillful than girls *in general*. In this way (among many others) are stereotypes born.

The differences in motor skills might be more accurately called *gender* differences than *sex* differences because they probably derive partly from the social roles boys and girls begin learning early in the preschool years. Part of the role differences includes how preschool children spend their time. Preschool boys do spend more time than girls in active and rough-and-tumble play, and girls spend more time doing quiet activities such as drawing or playing with stuffed animals. Children of both sexes, furthermore, reinforce or support one another more for engaging in gender-typed activities, behavioral shaping that is often less flexible for boys than for girls (Davies, 1991; Kite, Deaux, & Haines, 2008). These differences may create the twin impressions that boys are less capable of fine motor skills and that girls are physically weaker, or at least are less inclined toward gross motor activity.

Variations in Motor Skill Development

Although the preceding sections may have implied that young children acquire motor skills at highly similar rates, in reality they show considerable variability in both fundamental and fine motor skill development. At age three, some children already can walk fast and catch a ball skillfully, but others are still having trouble with both tasks. At age five, some children can use scissors skillfully to cut out shapes for kindergarten art projects, but others still find scissors difficult or even mystifying. Whatever the motor skill, individual children will vary at it.

Like other human differences, these probably result from variations in experience, motivation, and biological endowment. Because of family background or preschool educational experiences, some children may be encouraged more than usual toward active play. Not surprisingly, they develop the skills for active play—like running, jumping, or throwing—sooner

On the average, boys and girls develop motor skills at almost the same rate during the preschool years, but marked differences emerge among individuals within each sex, even at this age.

Source: ESB Professional/Shutterstock.com.

than children who experience less encouragement for active play. Weight also plays a role. Children who are overweight or obese lag behind their normal-weight peers in gross motor skills—a gap that grows over time (D'Hondt et al., 2013). Research has demonstrated that children with parents who engage in more physical activity, particularly if that activity is with their children, are more active, skilled, and healthy (Hinkley et al., 2008; Loprinzi & Trost, 2010; Spurrier et al., 2008).

Experience also plays a large role in drawing or other fine-motor activities. Some children receive more encouragement and opportunity than others. Early successes breed satisfaction with the emerging skills and encourage the development of motivation to refine the initial skills further. Before long, as we saw earlier in the case of gender differences in motor skill development, small initial differences in opportunity and skill become larger differences in skill and motivation.

Biological and genetic background probably also plays a role in motor skill development, although for most children it is hard to sort out how strong these influences are. The most obvious evidence for biological influence—as well as for the questionability of its importance—is the experiences of children with physical disabilities. A child born with cerebral palsy (a disorder of the nervous system that impairs motor coordination) may not learn to walk, jump, throw, or draw at the same times or to the same extent as a child who never experiences this condition. Yet contrary to common stereotypes of children with disorders, the motor development of a child with cerebral palsy is *not* determined solely by the disorder; it is

WHAT DO YOU THINK?

Suppose you are a childcare center worker, and one of your four-year-olds seems to be especially clumsy at throwing and catching a ball. Should you do something about this, and if so, what should you do? Consult with a classmate for a second opinion. Would you feel the same way if the child seemed clumsy or "uninspired" at drawing?

also determined by the child's opportunities and encouragement to learn new motor skills. The final motor achievements of children with this disorder will show diversity just as will the achievements of peers without disorders, and some of the diversity will be the result of education, not biology (Smith, 1998).

The Impact of Children's Growth on Adults

Even though physical growth unfolds largely independently of other forms of development in infancy, growth interacts indirectly in a number of ways with a child's social relationships. A child's physical appearance and particular motor skills can affect how adults and older children respond to the child. A family's attitudes, as well as their economic and social circumstances, can affect opportunities for children to acquire physical skills, and constrain opportunities as well.

Effects of Appearance

From birth—and despite the biases from their own parents—children vary in how attractive their faces seem to adults and other children. As a rule, some individuals look younger than others of the same age. In general, having a young-looking face depends on having large features and a large forehead; that is, facial features should be wide-set and located relatively low on the front of the skull. Even slight changes in these proportions—just a fraction of an inch—can make an adult seem many years older or younger, an infant seem six months older or younger, or a preschooler seem one or two years older or younger.

In general, younger-looking children are also rated as more attractive than older-looking children by both adults and peers, and adults tend to expect more mature behaviors from older-looking children (Parsons, Young, Kumari, Stein, & Kringelbach, 2011). This coincidence of stereotypes—of youthfulness and attractiveness—may contribute to differences in how parents and other adults respond to preschoolers as individuals. Parents and other caregivers need to be made aware of these possibilities, even if differences in response stem partly from innate human reactions to infantile (or babylike) appearance.

Effects of Motor Skills

Consider the changes in size that preschool children experience. A two-year-old often is still small enough to be handled. When necessary, parents can pick up and move a child from one place to another, physically removing the child from danger, and carrying the child (at least partway) if a distance is too far. By age five, a child often has outgrown these physical interactions, not only figuratively but literally. Parents or other adults may still lift and cuddle the child sometimes in play or in an emergency, but they probably are beginning to avoid doing so on a regular basis. To a significant extent, the child may now simply be too bulky and tall. More and more rarely can parents save the child from danger by picking the child up or by speeding the child along a long hallway by carrying the child piggyback. Parents must somehow get children to do these things for themselves.

Usually, of course, parents succeed at this task. By age five, a child can think and talk about her own actions much more than before, and these improvements help guide her own actions. The handling that used to be literal now becomes mostly figurative. Now *handling* means negotiating and discussing with the child rather than lifting her up or carting her around.

Improvements in motor skills also change the agenda for a child's daily activities. A two-year-old may spend a good part of his day experimenting with fundamental skills: walking from one room to another, tearing toilet paper to shreds, or taking pots and pans out of a cupboard. These activities often are embedded in an active social and cognitive life: the child may smile (or frown) at his parents while he works and may "talk" about what he is doing as well. But the motor aspects of his activities absorb a significant part of his attention throughout the day. The child may return repeatedly to a staircase, for instance, as though compelled to get the hang of climbing it; no reward needs to lie at the top step except the satisfaction of a job well done.

A two-year-old's parents therefore must spend a lot of time ensuring that the child comes to no physical harm during motor explorations. They must make sure the child does not fall down the stairs, tumble into the toilet bowl, or discover a sharp knife among the pots. Their role as safety experts can dominate their contacts with the child, particularly if the child is active. Table 11.3 lists common accidents, remedies, and preventions.

By the end of early childhood, minute-to-minute physical surveillance recedes in importance, even though, of course, a concern about safety remains. Rules about dangers make their appearance ("Don't climb on that fence; it's rickety"), along with the hope that a five-year-old can remember and follow the rules at least some of the time. The shift toward rules also results from increasing confidence in the child's motor skills. Now parents are apt to believe their child can go up and down stairs without stumbling very often—and they are usually right.

During the preschool period, many parents discover a special need for patience in their dealings with their children. Simple actions such as tying shoelaces or putting on socks may take longer than before, simply because children now insist on doing many of these things themselves. For similar reasons, walking to the store may now take longer; a three- or four-year-old may prefer to push the stroller rather than ride in it, thus slowing everyone down. And preschoolers may have their own agenda on a walk, such as noticing little rocks on the sidewalk or airplanes in the sky, which differ from parents' goals. On good days, these behaviors offer some of the joys of raising children, but on bad days, they often irritate even the most patient of parents.

TABLE 11.3   Common Accidents, Remedies, and Preventions among Preschoolers

Accidents	What to Do	How to Prevent
Drowning	Unless you are trained in water safety, extend a stick or other device. Use heart massage and mouth-to-mouth breathing when and as long as needed.	Teach children to swim as early in life as possible. Supervise children's swim sessions closely. Have children stay in shallow water.
Choking on small objects	If a child is still breathing, do not attempt to remove object; see a doctor instead. If breathing stops, firmly strike child twice on small of back. If this does not help, grab child from behind, put your fist just under his or her ribs, and pull upward sharply several times.	Do not allow children to put small objects in their mouths. Teach them to eat slowly, taking small bites. Forbid vigorous play with objects or food in mouth.
Cuts with serious bleeding	Raise cut above level of heart; apply pressure with cloth or bandage. If necessary, apply pressure to main arteries of limbs.	Remove sharp objects from play areas. Insist on shoes wherever ground or floor may contain sharp objects. Supervise children's use of knives.
Fractures	Keep injured limb immobile; see a doctor.	Discourage climbing and exploring in dangerous places, such as trees and construction sites. Allow bicycles only in safe areas.
Burns	Pour cold water over burned area; keep it clean; then cover with *sterile* bandage. See a doctor if burn is extensive.	Keep matches out of reach of children. Keep children well away from fires and hot stoves.
Poisons	On skin or eye, flush with plenty of water. If in stomach, phone poison control center doctor for instructions. Induce vomiting only for selected substances.	Keep dangerous substances out of reach of children. Throw away poisons when no longer needed. Keep syrup of ipecac in home to induce vomiting, but use *only* if advised by doctor.
Animal bites	Clean and cover with bandage; see a doctor.	Train children when and how to approach family pets. Teach them caution in approaching unfamiliar animals.
Insect bites	Remove stinger, if possible. Cover with paste of bicarbonate of soda (for bees) or a few drops of vinegar (for wasps and hornets).	Encourage children to recognize and avoid insects that sting, as well as their nests. Encourage children to remain calm in the presence of stinging insects.
Poisonous plants (e.g., poison ivy)	Remove affected clothing. Wash affected skin with strong alkali soap as soon as possible.	Teach children to recognize toxic plants. Avoid areas where poisonous plants grow.

Source: Adapted from O'Keefe (1998).

The new motor skills that preschoolers develop bring new risks and create new safety concerns for parents and other caregivers. What hazards may be waiting for this boy? And how should adults deal with them?

Source: Viacheslav Nikolaenko/Shutterstock.com.

Effects of Differences in Families

A child's growth has a different impact on adults depending on the priorities of parents and on the circumstances of the family and community to which the child belongs. What seems like a risky behavior to one parent (e.g., climbing up on a large boulder) may seem like constructive skill building to another, with consequent differences in encouragement or prohibitions for the child. What seems like a healthy amount of weight for a child to one parent may seem skinny (or plump) to another, with consequent differences in parents' unconscious appraisals of the child's attractiveness.

But settings and circumstances matter as well. In families with many children and few adults, child minding may become the responsibility of older siblings as much as (or more than) of adults. In extended families—those with nonparental relatives living at home or nearby—child minding may become partly the responsibility of other adult relatives. If parents work (or if a single parent works), relatives or other "caregivers for hire" take on much of the responsibility. All of these circumstances alter the settings in which preschoolers grow and the relationships that become prominent during early childhood. Some settings may provide the child with safer places for physical exploration than do other settings, resulting in fewer worries about safety expressed by caregivers. Some families may include so many children that differences in a particular child's physical appearance make little difference simply because caregivers are distributing their attention widely among many children or activities. Individual parents may or

WHAT DO YOU THINK?

How did your own parents' work schedules, the number of children in your family, and family finances influence the joy or irritation they experienced? Did the *number* of parents raising you (one or more than one) make a difference?

may not be aware that alternatives to their particular childcare arrangements exist, and because they often have not participated in the alternatives, they may find them hard to appreciate. But the range of childcare arrangements is very real, as is the range of opportunities they offer to young children (Cannella, 1997).

From Preschooler to Child

The physical changes we have talked about in this chapter create new relationships with parents and other caregivers, who in turn stimulate further changes. Preschoolers' new motor skills may stimulate adults to encourage various talents actively and with more focus than before. Once catching and throwing make their appearance, playing ball becomes a possibility; once scribbling stabilizes, skillful and interesting drawing seems just around the corner. And so parents and other interested adults encourage children toward these new skills, among others. Sometimes, the teaching and learning seem easier now, too, because adults no longer have to monitor a child's every move and can concentrate increasingly on the goals of movements. Just a few years before, "one false step" might have meant a child would literally fall. But now, this term has become only a metaphor for mistakes in general, not for physical mishaps specifically.

The cognitive developments of early childhood are equally influential on relationships, and we will investigate these changes in the next chapter.

Chapter Summary

- **What pathway does physical growth normally take during early childhood?** Between the ages of two and five, growth slows down and children take on more adultlike bodily proportions. Usually growth is rather smooth during the preschool period, though genetic, social, and nutritional differences can affect growth to some extent. Children's appetites often are smaller in the preschool years than in infancy, and children become more selective about what they eat.
- **How is poverty related to children's health?** The general health of a child is associated with the economic resources of the child's family, with higher-SES preschoolers tending to be healthier than lower-SES preschoolers. A number of possible causes for the association exist, including greater access to health care among well-off families.

- **When do children achieve bladder control?** Children tend to achieve daytime bladder control early in the preschool period. Nighttime bladder control tends to come later in the period.
- **What motor skills do children acquire during the preschool years?** Preschoolers acquire and refine many fundamental motor skills, including walking, jumping, throwing, and catching. Fine motor skills such as drawing also emerge during this period, progressing from prerepresentational to representational drawings. Children vary in motor skill development because of both their biological endowment and their experiences.
- **How does children's growth affect parents and other adults?** Preschoolers' changing facial features, size, and motor skills influence parents' responses and methods of childrearing to some extent. Because of differences in circumstances, families respond uniquely to differences in children's growth.

Key Terms

fine motor coordination (p. 227)

References

Adair, L., Fall, C., Osmond, C., Stein, A., Martorell, R., Ramirez-Zea, ... & Victoria, C. (2013). Associations of linear growth and relative weight gain during early life with adult health and human capital in countries of low and middle income: Findings from five birth cohort studies. *Lancet, 382*, 525–534.

Adolph, K. E., Cole, W. G., Komati, M., Garciaguirre, J. S., Badaly, D., Lingeman, J. M., ... & Sotsky, R. B. (2012). How do you learn to walk? Thousands of steps and dozens of falls per day. *Psychological Science, 23*(11), 1387–1394.

American Academy of Pediatrics. (1993). *Pediatric nutrition handbook*. Elk Grove Village, IL: Author.

Andrien, M. (1994). *Social communication in nutrition: A methodology for intervention*. Rome: Food and Agricultural Organization of the United Nations.

Behrman, J., & Stacey, N. (Eds.) (1997). *The social benefits of education*. Ann Arbor, Mich. University of Michigan Press.

Behrman, R. (Ed.) (1993). *The future of children: School-linked services*. Los Altos, CA: Center for the Future of Children. The David and Lucille Packard Foundation.

Bloom, D. A., Seeley, W. W., Ritchey, M. L., & McGuire, E. J. (1993). Toilet habits and continence in children: An opportunity sampling in search of normal parameters. *Journal of Urology, 149*(5), 1087–1090.

Broughton, D., Eisner, E., & Ligtvoet, J. (Eds.) (1996). *Evaluating and assessing the visual arts in education*. New York, NY: Teachers College Press.

Bury, M. (1997). *Health and illness in a changing society.* New York, NY: Routledge.

Cannella, G. (1997). *Deconstructing early childhood education: Social justice and revolution.* New York, NY: Peter Lang Publishers.

Centers for Disease Control and Prevention (CDC). (2000). *2 to 20 years: Boys stature-for-age and weight-for-age percentiles.* Retrieved from http:// www.cdc.gov/growthcharts/data/set1clinical/cj41l021.pdf

Centers for Disease Control and Prevention (CDC). (2000). *2 to 20 years: Girls stature-for-age and weight-for-age percentiles.* Retrieved from http:// www.cdc.gov/growthcharts/data/set1clinical/cj41l022.pdf.

Coates, E., & Coates, A. (2006). Young children talking and drawing. *International Journal of Early Years Education, 14*(3), 221–241.

Coles, R. (1992). *Their eyes meeting the world: Drawings and paintings of children.* Boston: Houghton Mifflin.

Corsini, N., Slater, A., Harrison, A., Cooke, L., & Cox, D. N. (2013). Rewards can be used effectively with repeated exposure to increase liking of vegetables in 4–6-year-old children. *Public Health Nutrition, 16*(05), 942–951.

Davies, B. (1991). Accomplishment of genderedness in preschool children. In L. Weis, P. Altbach, G. Kelly, & H. Petrie (Eds.), *Critical perspectives in early childhood education.* Albany, NY: State University of New York Press.

D'Hondt, E., Deforche, B., Gentier, I., De Bourdeaudhuij, I., Vaeyens, R., Philippaerts, R., & Lenoir, M. (2013). A longitudinal analysis of gross motor coordination in overweight and obese children versus normal-weight peers. *International Journal of Obesity, 37*(1), 61–67

Doherty, D. (Ed.). (1996). *Measurement in pediatric exercise science.* Champaign, IL: Human Kinetics Press.

Endres, J., & Rockwell, R. (1993). *Food, nutrition, and the young child* (4th ed.), Columbus, Ohio: Merrill.

Eveleth, P., & Tanner, J. (1990). *Worldwide variation in human growth* (2nd ed.), New York, NY: Cambridge University Press.

Fildes, A., van Jaarsveld, C. H., Wardle, J., & Cooke, L. (2014). Parent-administered exposure to increase children's vegetable acceptance: A randomized controlled trial. *Journal of the Academy of Nutrition and Dietetics, 114*(6), 881–888.

Fitzgerald, H., Lester, B., & Zuckerman, B. (1994). *Children of poverty: Research, health, and policy issues.* New York, NY: Garland.

Hinkley, T., Crawford, D., Salmon, J., Okely, A. D., & Hesketh, K. (2008). Preschool children and physical activity: A review of correlates. *American Journal of Preventive Medicine, 34*(5), 435–441.

Jacob, V., Chattopadhyay, S. K., Hopkins, D. P., Morgan, J. M., Pitan, A. A., Clymer, J. M., & Community Preventive Services Task Force. (2016). Increasing coverage of appropriate vaccinations: A community guide systematic economic review. *American Journal of Preventive Medicine, 50*(6), 797–808.

Jansson, U. B., Hanson, M., Sillén, U., & Hellström, A. L. (2005). Voiding pattern and acquisition of bladder control from birth to age 6 years—A longitudinal study. *Journal of Urology, 174*(1), 289–293.

Junaid, K. A., & Fellowes, S. (2006). Gender differences in the attainment of motor skills on the movement assessment battery for children. *Physical & Occupational Therapy in Pediatrics, 26*(1–2), 5–11.

Kalverboer, A., Hopkins, B., & Geuze, R. (1993). *Motor development in early infancy and late childhood.* New York, NY: Cambridge University Press.

Kenney, G., Alker, J., Anderson, N., McMorrow, S., Long, S., Wissoker, D., ... & Brooks, T. (2014). *A first look at children's health insurance coverage under the ACA in 2014.* Health Reform Monitoring Survey. Retrieved from http://hrms.urban.org/briefs/ Childrens-Health-Insurance-Coverage-under-the-ACA-in-2014.html

Kite, M. E., Deaux, K., & Haines, E. L. (2008). Gender stereotypes. In F. Denmark, & M. A. Pauldi (Eds.), *Psychology of women: A handbook of issues and theories* (pp. 205–236). Westport, CT: Greenwood Publishing Group.

Krans, E. E., & Davis, M. M. (2014). Strong start for mothers and newborns: Implications for prenatal care delivery. *Current Opinion in Obstetrics & Gynecology, 26*(6), 511–515.

Loprinzi, P. D., & Trost, S. G. (2010). Parental influences on physical activity behavior in preschool children. *Preventive Medicine, 50*(3), 129–133.

McCurdy, K., Gorman, K. S., Kisler, T. S., & Metallinos-Katsaras, E. (2012). Maternal mental health and child health and nutrition. In V. Maholmes & R. B. King (Eds.), *The Oxford handbook of poverty and child development* (pp.124–144). New York, NY: Oxford University Press.

McDonald, M., Sigman, M., Espinosa, M., & Neumann, C. (1994). Impact of a temporary food shortage on children and their mothers. *Child Development, 65,* 404–415.

O'Keefe, M. (Ed.). (1998). *Brady emergency care* (8th ed.). Upper Saddle River, NJ: Prentice-Hall.

Parsons, C. E., Young, K. S., Kumari, N., Stein, A., & Kringelbach, M. L. (2011). The motivational salience of infant faces is similar for men and women. *PloS ONE, 6*(5), e20632.

Rose, J., & Gamble, J. (1993). *Human walking* (2nd ed.). Baltimore: Williams and Williams.

Rudowitz, R., Artiga, S., & Arguello, R. (2014). *Children's health coverage: Medicaid, CHIP, and the ACA.* Retrieved from http://kff.org/healthreform/ issue-brief/ childrens-health-coveragemedicaid-chip-and-the-aca/

Sanfilippo, J., Finkelstein, J., & Styne, D. (Eds.) (1994). *Medical and gynecological endocrinology* Philadelphia: Hanley and Belfus.

Smith, D. (1998). *Inclusion: Schools for all students.* Belmont. CA: Wadsworth.

Spurrier, N. J., Magarey, A. A., Golley, R., Curnow, F., & Sawyer, M. G. (2008). Relationships between the home environment and physical activity and dietary patterns of preschool children: A cross-sectional study. *International Journal of Behavioral Nutrition and Physical Activity, 5*(1), 31.

Tesman, J., & Hills, A. (1994). Developmental effects of lead exposure in children. *Social Policy Report: Society for Research on Child Development, 8*(3).

van der Horst, K., Ferrage, A., & Rytz, A. (2014). Involving children in meal preparation. Effects on food intake. *Appetite, 79,* 18–24.

Ventura, A. K., & Worobey, J. (2013). Early influences on the development of food preferences. *Current Biology, 23*(9), R401–R408.

Wilkinson, R. (1996). *Unhealthy societies: The afflictions of inequality.* New York, NY: Routledge.

Yousefi, M., Karmaus, W., Zhang, H., Roberts, G., Matthews, S., Clayton, B., & Arshad, S. H. (2013). Relationships between age of puberty onset and height at age 18 years in girls and boys. *World Journal of Pediatrics, 9*(3), 230–238.

Promoting Physical Activity in Preschoolers

A Review of the Guidelines, Barriers, and Facilitators for Implementation of Policies and Practices

No
Line Tremblay, Céline Boudreau-Larivière, and Krystel Cimon-Lambert
Laurentian University

Promoting healthy physical activity (PA) behaviours in children between the ages of 0 to 5 years has immediate impacts on the health and well-being of children and serves as a powerful strategy to prevent or minimise the occurrence of chronic diseases in later life. Although children are naturally inclined to partake in active play, their PA levels generally fall below the current Canadian PA recommendations. Given that more than 50% of Canadian children spend 6 hours or more per day in day care settings (home and centres), implementing PA interventions through careful policy development within these settings represents a strategic way to help increase PA levels in young children. Parents and early childhood educators, through their perceptions and beliefs, play an important role in fostering healthy PA behaviours in preschoolers. The purpose of this review article is to summarise the PA guidelines for young children, to discuss the effects of PA and sedentary behaviours on several aspects of children's development and functioning, to describe the barriers and facilitators of PA and sedentary behaviours in preschoolers, and to present recommendations to increase opportunities for PA in the day care setting.

Keywords: preschool children, physical activity, determinants, guidelines, policies

Line Tremblay, Department of Psychology, Laurentian University; Céline Boudreau-Larivière. School of Human Kinetics, Laurentian University; Krystel Cimon-Lambert, Department of Human Development. Laurentian University.

Correspondence concerning this article should be addressed to Line Tremblay, Department of Psychology, Laurentian University. Sudbury, Ontario, Canada, P3E 2C6. E-mail: ltremblay@laurentian.ca

Line Tremblay, Céline Boudreau-Larivière, and Krystel Cimon-Lambert, "Promoting Physical Activity in Preschoolers: A Review of the Guidelines, Barriers, and Facilitators for Implementation of Policies and Practices," *Canadian Psychology*, vol. 53, no. 4, pp. 280-290. Copyright © 2012 by Canadian Psychological Association. Reprinted with permission. Provided by ProQuest LLC. All rights reserved.

There is an assumption among parents, early childhood educators, and even by some researchers that young children are sufficiently active and that the amount and intensity of their natural physical activities are adequate (Alpert, Field, Goldstein, & Perry, 1990; Timmons, Naylor & Pfeiffer, 2007). However, this assumption contradicts the trends in the increasing rates of overweight and obese children. For example, recent epidemiological data show that the percentage of Canadian children and adolescents classified as overweight or obese darted from 14% to 31% among boys, and from 14% to 25% among girls, during the past two decades, and results indicate this upward trend is likely to continue (M. S. Tremblay. Shields, Laviolette. Craig. & Janssen, 2010). Improving physical activity (PA) and nutrition behaviours of children and youth in the school setting in particular is regarded as a critical intervention strategy for enhancing population health in the long term. Although a number of studies have investigated proexercise and antiobesity initiatives implemented in primary and secondary school-based programs (see, for instance, the *Canadian Journal of Public Health,* 2010, Supplement 2. on school health and the references therein), there is a paucity of research aimed at determining the prevalence and effectiveness of PA programs targeting *preschool children in day care settings*. Given that over half of Canadian children are in some form of child care and that one quarter of these children attend day care centres (Statistics Canada, 2003), there is great potential to implement PA interventions aimed at developing healthy PA behaviours in early childhood, thereby enhancing children's health in the short term and fostering lifelong healthy PA behaviours to curtail the prevalence of chronic diseases in later life.

Accordingly, the objective of this article is to review research evidence for promoting and increasing PA in preschoolers and the need for policies, preschool PA programs, as well as training and education for parents and for early childhood educators.

Definitions and Guidelines

PA is defined as any physical movement resulting from skeletal muscle contraction and energy expenditure (Caspersen. Powell, & Christenson. 1985; Goran, 1998). The Canadian Society for Exercise Physiology recommends that infants aged less than 1 year be physically active several times daily through interactive floor-based play, and that children aged 1 to 4 years accumulate at least 180 min of PA at any intensity throughout the day to progress toward at least 60 min of energetic play by the age of 5 years (M. S. Tremblay et al., 2012a). In comparison, the National Association for Sport and Physical Education (2009) in the United States recommends that preschoolers accumulate at least 60 min of structured (organized) PA and 60 min of unstructured (informal) PA per day.

Sedentary behaviour is defined as any waking behaviour characterised by an energy expenditure equal or less than 1.5 metabolic equivalent (MET) while in a sitting or reclining posture (M. S. Tremblay et al., 2012b; M. S. Tremblay, Colley. Saunders, Healy, & Owen, 2010). Sedentary activities in young children include watching TV and videos; playing on the computer; playing video games; sitting; or reclining in a stroller, high chair, or car seat. TV- and video-viewing behaviours have been found to dominate, compared with other sedentary activities, during early to middle childhood. In fact, TV viewing is the most frequently studied sedentary activity among children and is commonly used as a proxy for sedentary behaviour (Must & Tybor, 2005). Of particular concern is that early exposure to TV viewing is associated with sedentary behaviours later in primary school (Pagani, Fitzpatrick, Barnett, & Dubow, 2010), as well as into adolescence and adulthood (Janz. Burns, & Levy. 2005; Kemper, Post, Twisk, & van Mechelen, 1999; Pale, Baranowski, Dowda, & Trost, 1996; Pate et al., 1999; Raitakari et al., 1994). Accordingly, the Canadian Society for Exercise Physiology recommends that parents of children less than 4 years of age minimise the time spent being sedentary to no more than l hr at a time, avoid screen time in children below the age of 2 years, and limit screen time of 2- to 4-year-old children to under 1 hr per day (M. S. Tremblay et al., 2012b) and to a maximum of 2 hr for 5- to 6-year-old children (Canadian Society for Exercise Physiology. 2012c).

Effects of PA and Sedentary Behaviours

The benefits of PA are numerous and include several aspects of development, such as motor skill acquisition, psychosocial functioning, cognition, and physical health (M. S. Tremblay et al., 2012a).

Motor Skill Development

PA is part of any child's normal development. It manifests itself as play that can be described as enjoyable behaviour, seemingly purposeless, beginning in infancy, peaking during childhood, declining during adolescence, and taking three forms—rhythmic stereotypies, defined as purposeless, repetitive gross motor movements such as body rocking and foot kicking (infancy); exercise play (preschool years); and rough-and-tumble play in primary school (Pelligrini & Smith, 1998). If deprived of these natural physical activities, children tend to compensate when they have the opportunity to play (Pelligrini & Smith, 1998), which supports the contention that PA play is necessary for a child's development. A first aspect of development considered as primarily affected by PA is motor skills.

There is strong evidence that PA benefits gross motor skill development (Emck, Bosscher, Beek, & Doreleijers. 2009; Fisher et al., 2005; Sääkslahti et al., 2004; M. S. Tremblay et al., 2012a; Williams et al., 2008). which is critical for the development of higher level fine motor skills such as writing (Woodward & Swinth, 2002). Improvements in motor skills also show positive impacts on other aspects of the child's functioning. For example, a systematic review (Emck et al., 2009) of controlled studies and population studies of school-age children (6 to 12 years old) with emotional, behavioural, and developmental and psychomotor delays shows strong evidence of a relationship between motor skills and self-perceived competence (academic as well as athletic, Goodway & Rudisill, 1996).

Socioemotional Functioning

Improvement of motor and athletic skills, as well as practicing PA itself, also shows important positive outcomes on the social-emotional functioning and well-being of children (C. Branta. Haubenstricker, & Seefeldt, 1984; Emck et al., 2009; M. S. Tremblay et al., 2012a), which is likely to persist throughout development. For instance, a systematic review of the literature, including studies using both controlled and correlational methodologies for all ages, show that physically active adolescents show less emotional distress, irrespective of gender, class, or health status (Paluska, & Schwenk, 2000). Being physically active in groups and in games provides children the opportunity to learn new skills (Bailey, 2005), such as solving conflicts and cooperating. and to develop friendships (Hansen, Larson, & Dworkin, 2003), which, in turn, increase socioemotional adjustment and self-esteem (Emck et al., 2009; Wang & Veugelers, 2008; Wang, Wild, Kipp, Kuhle, & Veugelers, 2009). Some positive socioemotional outcomes of PA were also found in clinical populations such as children with attention-deficit hyperactivity disorder. In particular, PA led to improvements in athletic skills, which, in turn, increased social acceptance and more positive social interactions with peers (Lopez-Williams et al., 2005). This example illustrates the benefit of enhancing athletic skills in children with behavioural and emotional problems and encouraging their participation in team sports. In contrast, a prospective and longitudinal study of 1,314 children, using parents' and teachers' reports of TV exposure and academic and psychosocial functioning, shows that higher levels of early childhood TV exposure predicts greater chances of peer rejection experiences later in primary school, which is explained by the authors as being linked to more time spent alone and inactive during TV viewing, leaving less time for important social interactions (Pagani et al., 2010). In addition, childhood obesity, which is a by-product of inactivity, has negative consequences on psychosocial functioning, including negative stereotypes, peer rejection, and negative self-image (Dietz, 1998; Lobstein, Baur, & Uauy, 2004).

PA and physical education reportedly reduce antisocial and aggressive behaviours in children. For example, using direct observations, validated tests of motor development, interviews, and questionnaires administered to teachers, C. F. Branta and Goodway (1996) reported a significant reduction of aggressive behaviours in 192 at-risk prekindergarten and 101 fourth-grade children living in poor urban communities. The intervention took place in a 3-year period and was aimed to teach the children the notions of personal space and force control, which, in turn, increased their conflict resolution skills as well as physical skills (C. F. Branta & Goodway, 1996). Similarly. Bundy and colleagues (2009) found that their PA intervention targeting 150 5- to 7-year-old children, which consisted of adding purposeless material (such as tires, hay bales, or cardboard boxes) on the playground, resulted in a reduction of aggressive behaviours; an increase in children's cooperation, group play, and creativity; and resilience when experiencing minor injury, as measured by teachers' reports. Thus, keeping children active, teaching them the benefit of PA early, and thus permitting them to develop good habits may lead to a secondary benefit, which is to keep them away from socially undesirable behaviours such as bullying.

Cognitive Functioning

Improved cognitive functioning and academic performance is another interesting benefit of PA, although the underlying mechanisms are not yet well understood. It is suggested that natural occurrence of exercise play can improve cognitive performance (Pelligrini & Smith, 1998). Furthermore, children who are more physically active achieve better grades (C. Branta et al., 1984). A more recent large-scale study in a representative sample of U.S. children revealed that kindergarten and first-grade girls who were the least physically active (0 to 35 min of PA per week) performed significantly lower on standard math and reading tests compared with girls in the moderate and highly active categories (70 to 300 min per week; Carlson et al., 2008). These authors did not find any significant difference among boys. Evidence from longitudinal studies also suggests that TV viewing during the early years has a negative impact on cognitive development of children (Pagani et al., 2010; Schmidt, Rich, Rifas-Shiman. Oken, & Taveras, 2009). Schmidt and colleagues (2009) reported that TV exposure from birth to the age of 2 years negatively impacted cognitive functioning at the age of 3 years, but this effect disappeared when taking into account the mother's level of education and cognitive skills. Pagani and colleagues (2010) reported that early exposure to TV (29 and 53 months) predicted a more passive learning behaviour in the classroom and lower mathematical achievement later in the fourth grade. Increasing PA levels and limiting sedentary behaviour, TV viewing in particular, are therefore correlated with better cognition and academic performance. Although the studies we reviewed were conducted using large sample sizes with a good methodology, more research is certainly needed to better understand how sedentary behaviours and PA influence cognitive processes.

Physical Health

The most obvious beneficial effects of PA are those linked with physical health, and these health effects are observed in people of all ages, including young children. The first effect of PA that is well recognised and strongly supported by research is adiposity. Although there is no single cause of obesity, it is well accepted that healthy weight maintenance results from the balance between energy expenditure via PA and energy intake through healthy eating habits (Cameron, Norgan, & Ellison, 2006: Harris. Kuramoto, Schulzer. & Retallack. 2009; Hill & Peters, 1998; Wardle, Guthrie, Sanderson, & Rapoport, 2001). However, the relationship between PA and obesity in children is complex and not straightforward. This relationship is moderate and depends on the level or intensity of PA. It seems that high-intensity PA in preschool and primary schoolchildren who are overweight is necessary to achieve a reduction in body mass index (BMI; Moore et al., 2003; Moore, Nguyen, Rothman, Cupples, & Ellison, 1995). Considering that PA in young children is associated with lower body fat later in adolescence (Kemper et al., 1999; Moore et al., 1995, 2003), and that excess weight and obesity in young children is linked to increased risks of weight problems throughout childhood and into adulthood (Clarke & Lauer. 1993; Evers, Arnold, Hamilton, & Midgett, 2007; Freedman, Khan, Dietz, Srinivasan, & Berenson, 2001; Magarey, Daniels, Boulton, & Cockington, 2003), focused efforts to increase PA levels in young children to regulate body composition are warranted.

The association between sedentary behaviours such as TV viewing and adiposity in preschoolers is less clear. Some researchers (DuRant, Baranowski, Johnson. & Thompson, 1994) found no association between TV viewing and BMI, whereas others identified that TV viewing became positively associated with BMI when children reached about 6 years of age (Jago, Baranowski, Baranowski, Thompson, & Greaves. 2005) and continued to increase in primary school (Pagani et al., 2010; Proctor et al., 2003). Inconsistencies in results may be explained by the evidence linking sedentary behaviours with unhealthy eating behaviours (J. E. Brown, Broom, Nicholson, & Bittman, 2010; Pagani et al., 2010; L. Tremblay & Rinaldi, 2010), that is, the negative impact of inactivity can be counterbalanced by providing children with a healthy diet. Research also suggests an additive effect of both PA and sedentary behaviours. For example, children who are highly active and who watch less TV have been found to have lower weight than children who combined low activity level with high TV viewing (Janz et al., 2005; Proctor et al., 2003).

In children and adolescents. PA improves other health parameters, such as blood pressure reduction and increased lean muscle mass and bone mineral density (Harris et al., 2009). Controlled studies assessing PA intervention programs (gross and fine motor skills training) in preschool children showed that a gross motor skills program, coupled with calcium supplements, increase bone mass and bone strength; however, this effect was not found to persist 2 years after the program completion (Binkley & Specker, 2004). More recently, Wosje and colleagues (2009) used accelerometer measures, as well as parents' reports, and found that limiting TV viewing to less than 2 hr per day, not PA, predicted greater gains in bone mass and bone mineral density of 3- to 7-year-old children, which was independent of children's adiposity levels, suggesting a direct effect of inactivity on bone development.

In preschoolers, research has shown that naturally occurring exercise play can improve cardiorespiratory functioning and thermoregulation (Pelligrini & Smith, 1998). M. S. Tremblay and colleagues (2012a) reviewed evidence that higher levels of PA were associated with better cardiometabolic health during the early years. For example, an aerobic exercise training program led to improvements in children's cardiovascular fitness compared with a control group of children who engaged in playground free play (Alpert et al., 1990). Outdoor play in particular has been found to represent higher intensity PA and has been shown to correlate with better heart health, such as reduced risk of coronary heart disease as well as lower blood pressure and blood cholesterol levels (Sääkslahti et al., 2004). Sedentary behaviour in children, on the other hand, is associated with cardiovascular and metabolic risk factors, such as high blood pressure, dyslipidaemia, hyperinsulin-emia, and/or insulin resistance (Reilly et al., 2003). Finally, we reviewed only one study positively linking PA and sleep in young children, supporting the belief that spending energy in active play helps children to fall asleep at night (Sääkslahti et al., 2004).

Finally, and similarly to M. S. Tremblay and colleagues (2012a), we did not find any study assessing the risks associated with increased PA in young children. However, in older children and adolescents, there are risks associated with exercise for those who partake in competitive sports. There is some evidence, mainly based on a small number of clinical studies, of higher risks of disordered eating, affect regulation problems, exercise addiction behaviours, and substance use/

doping in children and adolescent athletes compared with nonathletes (Purper-Ouakil, Michel, Baup. & Mouren-Simeoni, 2002). Furthermore, excessive PA is sometimes linked to overtraining and has been documented to induce symptoms of depression (Paluska & Schwenk, 2000). There is certainly a great need for more research to clearly assess this risk. The unanswered question is whether PA promotion in preschool children can lead to such unhealthy exercise-related behaviour later in development. To our knowledge, no study thus far has investigated this issue.

Facilitators and Barriers of PA and Sedentary Behaviours

There are two main sources of influence on young children's PA and sedentary behaviours. The first source is the parents and family environment and the second is the early childhood educators and school environment. Parents influence their children's involvement in PA through their own PA habits and by encouraging and supporting, or by discouraging, sport practices (L. Tremblay, Rinaldi, Cimon-Lambert, & Lariviére, 2012; Zecevic, Tremblay, Lovsin, & Lariviére, 2010). As many children spend a large proportion of their time in out-of-home care, such as preschool child care centres or home day cares, these settings offer an ideal opportunity for the early development of healthy behaviours, including PA (Bower et al., 2008; Eveline, Valery, Jessica, Use, & Greet, 2012). Several factors have been identified to influence PA and sedentary behaviours in day care settings. They include parents' and teachers' perceptions and attitudes, home and school environments, and policies.

Parents' Perception

Research findings suggest that parents hold several beliefs about their young children's PA levels, risks for obesity, gender differences, and their role and influence on their children's PA activity behaviours. Canadian data show that between 55% and 75% of parents believe that their preschoolers are sufficiently active, as they report that their child is engaged in at least 60 min of PA per day (Irwin, He, Bouck, Tucker, & Pollett, 2005; Tucker & Irwin, 2008; Zecevic et al., 2010). Zecevic and colleagues (2010) reported that parents' perceptions of their child's PA level were not different from their day care teachers, suggesting that this perception that children are sufficiently active is shared by some early childhood educators. Parents also report an average of 9 to 14 hr of weekly media consumption (TV, video games, and computer) in preschool-age children (Funk, Brouwer, Curtiss, & McBroom, 2009), with greater sedentary time spent in low-activity playing during the weekend (Pagani et al., 2010; Siiakslahti et al., 2004).

Data collected using objective measures of PA, such as direct observation and using accelerometers, tell a different story. It is estimated that preschool children spend most (from about 50% to 90%) of their free play time engaged in sedentary activity (Dowda, Pate, Trost, Almeida, & Sirard, 2004; Sallis. Patterson, McKenzie, & Nader, 1988) and are engaged in vigorous physical exercise for only a few minutes each hour (Benham-Deal, 2005; Carlson et al., 2008; Danner, Noland, McFadden, DeWalt, & Kotchen. 1991; Pate, Pfeiffer, Trost, Ziegler, & Dowda, 2004).

Research conducted in Canada and elsewhere using objective measures of PA (Alhassan, Sirard, & Robinson, 2007; Colley et al., 2011; Eveline et al., 2012), or direct behavioural systematic observations (Bower et al., 2008; W. H. Brown et al., 2009), consistently shows that children spend, in general, more than two-thirds of their waking time in sedentary activities, that only 4% to 17% engage in moderate to vigorous PA (MVPA), and that only a small proportion (4% to 13%) of children will accumulate the recommended 60 min of MVPA per day. In addition, according to a Statistics Canada report (2003), Canadian children between the ages of 2 and 11 years watched an average of 14.6 hr of TV per week, or approximately 2 hr every day, which is a full 1 hour more than the recommended daily allotment for this age group, as set by the Canadian Paediatric Society (2002) and the Canadian Society for Exercise Physiology (2012c, 2012d). There is strong evidence that activity levels of most children are therefore inadequate, and, accordingly, parents must not assume and trust that their children are accumulating enough PA to meet the daily recommendations.

Another well-documented parental perception regarding PA and health behaviours pertains to body size perception. Research consistently shows that a large proportion (75% to 85%) of parents of overweight children believe that their child is of normal weight (for a review, see L. Tremblay et al., 2012; L. Tremblay, Lovsin. Zecevic. & Lariviére, 2011) and therefore are not likely to consider the need for changing lifestyle habits, such as increasing PA for their child and their family (Maynard. Galuska, Blanck, & Serdula, 2003; L. Tremblay et al., 2012; West et al., 2008). The reason for these misperceptions is not yet fully understood, but it is suggested that adults tend to perceive chubbiness in young children as normative and healthy (L. Tremblay et al., 2011, 2012). However, this perceived "baby fat" (which is. in reality, a surplus of weight) that parents and adults believe goes away on its own only appears to decrease with growth. In fact, although the child's weight to height ratio (BMI) slightly decreases until about 6 years of age, it begins to increase again and continues to climb throughout the remainder of childhood. This phenomenon is known as the adiposity rebound (Heelan & Eisenmann, 2006). Findings from a large-scale study showed that children who had an early versus late adiposity rebound were 6 times more likely to be obese in adulthood (Whitaker, Wright, Pepe, Seidel, & Dietz, 1997), which demonstrates that excess weight gain during the early years may put children at a greater risk of becoming obese as adults. Thus, it is important to acknowledge parents' and adults' misperceptions related to recognising their child's unhealthy weight and, furthermore, to convince parents of the importance of PA as a means to regulate their child's body composition.

A third well-documented perception associated with PA behaviours takes its origins in gender stereotypes. Parents tend to perceive that, compared with boys, girls are less physically active (Zecevic et al., 2010) and that they need less PA (Hinkley, Salmon, Okely. Crawford, & Hesketh, 2011). Parents also tend to be more concerned about good motor skill development in boys than in girls (Toftegaard-stoeckel, Groenfeldt, & Andersen, 2010), suggesting a double standard regarding athletic skills development. One consequence of these findings is that boys tend to perceive themselves as more physically competent than girls, which may be a contributing factor as to why girls are indeed less physically active than boys (Colley et al., 2011; Hinkley,

Crawford, Salmon, Okely, & Hesketh, 2008; Sallis et al., 1993). It has been suggested that the underlying biological differences between boys and girls (i.e., male hormones such as testosterone determine activity level and aggressiveness) explains this gender difference in PA levels (Pelligrini & Smith, 1998). However, several findings call into question the biological hypothesis. First, there is no difference between boys and girls in the amount of early gross motor rhythmic stereotypies, and differences appear only later, when comparing levels of exercise play and rough-and-tumble play, which are higher in boys than in girls (Pelligrini & Smith, 1998) but independent of motor skill development as assessed by teachers (Toftegaard-stoeckel et al., 2010). Second, gender differences in PA levels are most prominent at high levels of activity. For instance, gender differences are only evident in moderate- and vigorous-intensity PA (Finn. Johannsen, & Specker. 2002; Pate et al., 2004) and not in low-intensity PA and sedentary activities (Pate et al., 2004; Taylor et al., 2009). Higher levels of moderate- to vigorous-intensity PA in boys compared with girls (Finn et al., 2002; Pate et al., 2004), however, appear to have little impact on curtailing the increased rates of obesity in boys (31% for boys compared with 25% for girls; M.S. Tremblay et al., 2010), suggesting that other factors, including genetics, eating habits, and environments promoting obesity and sedentary behaviours (Cameron et al., 2006; Hill & Peters, 1998; L. Tremblay et al., 2012), for which there is no gender differences, may be contributing factors. Third, gender differences disappear when measures of PA are made in a context of structured play compared with unstructured play such as recess (Eveline et al., 2012). Fourth, lack of parental support for PA and role modelling is a stronger predictor of low PA for girls than for boys (Dowda, Dishman, Pfeiffer, & Pate. 2007; Thompson. Humbert. & Mirwald. 2003). As a whole, there is no consistent evidence or theoretical basis to imply that PA and motor skills would be more important for the physical development of boys than for girls.

Altogether, these findings support the alternative social hypothesis in explaining gender differences in PA. As low-activity playing is related to higher BMI in girls and not in boys (Sääkslahti et al., 2004), and because structured activity appears to be a more important determinant of PA levels in girls (Eveline et al., 2012), there is a need to address parents' perceptions and education about gender stereotypes as related PA. considering that parental and adult feedback is a main determinant of a young child's perception about him/herself (L. Tremblay et al., 2012).

The last parental perception on PA relates to their role as a model for their child's PA behaviours. Although parents recognise their role in providing opportunities for PA through structured activities, such as taking children to swimming class (Hinkley et al., 2011), some parents believe that support is enough to facilitate PA in their preschoolers and that being physically active themselves is not required (Irwin et al., 2005). However, research shows that parents' PA levels, objectively measured using accelerometers, is positively and significantly associated with children's PA levels (Oliver, Schofield. & Schluter. 2010). Children are 4 times more likely to be highly active if their parents support their child's PA and 2 times more likely to be more active if parents are physically active themselves (Zecevic et al., 2010). Effective intervention strategies aimed at increasing PA should therefore not only target children but also their parents' PA habits and attitudes toward sport and PA.

Early Childhood Educators' Perceptions and Attitudes

Parental perceptions of PA, as it relates to themselves and to preschool children, can be partly explained by the confidence expressed by some parents that their child's day care provides higher quality and more structured PA experience than what is provided at home (Irwin et al., 2005). As already discussed, over 50% of preschoolers spend most of their awake time being sedentary, in both home day cares and day care centres, and are therefore not meeting the Canadian Society for Exercise Physiology PA recommendations. The issue is whether the role of day care settings in providing opportunities for MVPA is acknowledged and, if so, why this goal is not met.

Some research findings highlight the effect of teachers' perceptions, attitudes, and personal preferences to explain the failure to meet PA guidelines. Copeland, Kendeigh, Saelens, Kalkwarf, and Sherman (2012) found that children's outdoor playground time depends solely on the teacher's decision, which is based on the individual teacher's own preference, such as not liking cold weather, an intolerance to noise and chaos outdoors, or on the amount of work involved in preparing children to go outside. In addition, it was found that teachers rarely assume their role as a facilitator for children's PA and even often disengage themselves on the playground by sitting, standing by the fence, or socializing with other teachers (W. H. Brown et al., 2009; Copeland et al., 2012). One possible explanation for such behaviours is teachers' concerns for safety issues and a duty to protect the children. A study conducted by Bundy and colleagues (2009), which consisted of scattering loose parts or material within the school ground, such as car tires and boxes, demonstrated that teachers' anxiety and concerns for safety increased, despite the fact that the frequency or severity of physical injury was unaltered during the intervention compared with pretest measures. Finally, teachers' training and competency in physical education was pointed out as a possible limitation to increasing PA in children; however, the number of studies testing this hypothesis is limited and contradictory. For example. Bower and colleagues (2008) found that PA training and education were associated with better PA promotion and encouragement by teachers. On the other hand, the type of lesson or intensity of PA was not different whether the activity was taught by a regular classroom teacher or a teacher specialized in physical education (Eveline et al., 2012). Interestingly, to reduce the time that children are sedentary, it was recommended that teachers should both reduce the time spent on teaching rules and techniques and permit pupils to free play or help the teachers set up the equipment. Regardless of a teacher's training, higher proportions of MVPA seem to occur when the teacher offers opportunities for structured PA (W. H. Brown et al., 2009).

Home and School Environments

For parents, the most significant barriers to increasing PA in their children are associated with time (having to cope with work, home schedule, and demands), family composition (having several children of different ages), weather and seasons, financial resources (fees to use facilities), access (having to drive to bring the family to the community facilities), and safety issues (strangers in parks; Hinkley et al., 2011; Irwin et al., 2005). Both parents and teachers recognise that gathering and group activities increase PA in children compared with when children are alone (Hinkley et al., 2011). However, such activities require more space, such as big backyards and large school playgrounds, which were also identified as increasing PA (Hinkley et al., 2011), whereas smaller indoor rooms were associated with less MVPA (Eveline et al., 2012). Larger outdoor spaces that foster group play may explain why outdoor activities are found to be associated with higher levels of MVPA compared with indoor play (W. H. Brown et al., 2009; Eveline et al., 2012; Hinkley et al., 2011). However, simply increasing outdoor play is not sufficient to increase PA levels in preschool children (Alhassan et al., 2007). Adding structured activity seems to specifically increase MVPA, at least in girls (Eveline et al., 2012). In addition, the types of equipment and toys available can help to increase PA levels (Bower et al., 2008; W. H. Brown et al., 2009; Hinkley et al., 2011). For example, obstruction equipment, such as tunnels or soft blocks, increases locomotion behaviour, as they allow for more activity, whereas throwing equipment, such as balls, are related to lower levels of MVPA (W. H. Brown et al., 2009). In addition, Bundy and colleagues (2009) showed that loose equipment with no specific function, such as boxes, increases PA by facilitating creativity and pretend play in preschoolers.

Effect of Policies

A PA policy is defined as a formal statement or decision related to PA within organisations that define the priorities and the set of actions to be carried out to fulfill those priorities. The school setting is recognised as a key strategic milieu for implementing policies aimed at improving the health of children through improved nutrition and increased PA. In 2008, the World Health Organization published the School Policy Framework to implement the Global Strategy on Diet, PA, and Health. Within this document, policy options that support healthy eating and PA in schools are described (World Health Organization. 2008). The majority of Canadian provinces and territories have nutrition policies and guidelines for schools and many have structured daily PA or physical education for kindergarten through Grade 12 (Veugelers & Schwartz, 2010). The development and evaluation of PA programs targeting preschoolers in day care settings has been identified by the World Health Organization (2008) as a priority area requiring focused attention as well as further research to determine the long-term effectiveness of PA programming in this target age group. A similar objective was developed by the Ontario Ministry of Health and Long-Term Care (2005) through their Active 2010 program.

PA policies of day care and preschool facilities refer to child care written statements and guidelines related to active/inactive time, such as TV use, a statement supporting PA, play environment use, and education (Bower et al., 2008).

The Day Nurseries Act (1990) indicates that children over 30 months of age that are in attendance for 6 hours or more in a day should play outdoors for at least 2 hours each day, weather permitting, and that day care facilities should offer activities designed to promote the development of gross and fine motor skills. This Act also stipulates that activities should foster language, cognitive, social and emotional development, and should also provide opportunities for active and quiet play. The policies and protocols for the implementation of these day care guidelines are generic, rather than specific, and therefore do not take into account variations from one day care setting to another in areas such as physical resources, community support, and socioeconomic factors. Although new guidelines for increasing activity levels in young children are now available (Canadian Society for Exercise Physiology, 2012a, 2012b), there is a need to provide clear guidance to day care settings on specific methods for implementing these recommendations. Providing inexpensive as well as easy-to- implement and effective strategies for increasing activity levels for this age group, as well as tools for measuring the effectiveness of these strategies on health fitness and movement skills, is necessary. The horizontal integration of PA health initiatives and services (Pan Canadian Joint Consortium for School Health, 2010) is likely the best course of action for assisting day care providers in maximizing opportunities for PA in preschool-age children. In particular, focused efforts in increasing stakeholder engagement (parents, early childhood educators, nongovernmental organisations) are important elements in the development and/or refinement and implementation of PA policies in day care settings in offering support and advocacy for the benefits of PA (Pan Canadian Joint Consortium for School Health, 2010). Clearer policies are required for programming, the physical environment, and the training of early childhood educators, day care staff, and parents that collectively foster PA in young children.

There is some evidence that PA policies positively influence PA and reduce sedentary opportunities in preschoolers (Bower et al., 2008). The decision to implement PA policies in preschools, as well as defining the objective of these policies, depend on the way society sees its role as well as the roles of adults involved with children. Early childhood educators and day care providers are concerned with child safety, nutrition, as well as cognitive and socioemotional development of children. Accordingly, providing the best possible PA opportunities may not be high on their list of priorities, despite their best intentions. Furthermore, according to Bundy and colleagues (2009), society's contemporary discourse is to protect children from all risks of physical injury to the extent that we do not tolerate even minor injuries, such as bruises, that are a natural and universal part of growing up, thus creating what is called "surplus safety." The consequence of this well-intended position is indeed to increase the risk of childhood obesity by reducing children's active and independent play, as well as depriving them of opportunities for emotional, intellectual, and social development (Bundy et al., 2009).

Recommendations and Conclusions

Parents and early childhood educators play a pivotal role in fostering healthy PA behaviours in children. Effective intervention strategies aimed at increasing PA in day care settings should therefore not only target children but also their parents' and day care providers' PA habits and attitudes toward sport and PA. Policies around parental and teacher education and training should therefore be at the forefront. PA policies related to day care programming should also provide more specific- guidelines related to structured outdoor play to help reach target PA levels for preschoolers. This process can be facilitated through the horizontal integration of community-based PA services and resources.

Based on the information reviewed herein, we recommend the steps outlined in the following sections to day care managers, parents, early childhood educators, and preschool program developers.

Policies on Increasing PA Activity Levels in Preschool Children

Based on strong evidence provided by studies using objective, direct measures, as well as correlational research designs showing that preschool children are not sufficiently active, and based on the recognition by the World Health Organization, the Canadian Society for Exercise Physiology, and the Ontario Ministry of Health and Long-Term Care of the importance of PA programs targeting this age group, the following recommendations are made:

1. PA recommendations should be clearly stated and made a priority within the day care program curriculum, that is, to implement a minimum of 1 hr of structured and 1 hr of unstructured PA per day in the regular curriculum (for example, two 30-min blocks of structured play and two 30-min blocks of unstructured play).
2. Both structured and unstructured activity periods should each include at least a total of 30 min of MVPA. Examples of MVPA to increase strength and endurance include dancing or exercising with music, mini-Olympic games where children must go through a series of obstacles such as tunnels, throwing balls to a target, running, or fast walking (i.e., continuous movement to increase, then maintain, a higher heart rate).

Benefits of PA in Preschool Children

Literature reviews, controlled studies, and population studies provide strong evidence of the positive effect of PA on motor skills development and socioemotional development. Therefore, the following recommendations are made:

1. Structured and unstructured PA should be planned and prepared according to the following objectives: (a) increase gross motor skills and athletic skills, (b) develop psychomotor coordination, (c) develop endurance and strength, (d) provide opportunity for social interaction and problem solving, and (e) familiarize children with competition and games role-playing.
2. The types of PA should be diverse, playful, and engaging for young children.

Examples of activities to develop motor skills, athletic skills, and psychomotor coordination include throwing, catching, and bouncing a ball varying in size; jumping and kicking using obstacles varying in difficulty level; and galloping, hopping, and jumping. Using a mat, children can learn different rolling movements. Walking on a line traced on the floor helps to increase balance. Activities that increase social interaction include group or team games such as ball games. Children can also participate in small teams. Indoor or outdoor play time with loose materials permits unstructured and group activity.

Adults as Facilitators and as Role Models

Parents and educators are regarded as having a significant influence on shaping young children's PA habits, though further studies are required to better understand the intricacies of this impact. Based on our current knowledge, we recommend the following:

1. Teachers' should actively participate to maximize children's engagement in PA.
2. Whenever possible, organise activities that include parents and other family members.
3. Parents should view themselves as PA role models. Being active will encourage their children to imitate their healthy behaviours.

Home and Day Care Environments

Based on a small number of studies, there is some evidence that the day care and family home environment has an impact on the frequency and the intensity of children's PA, which leads us to recommend the following:

1. The day care environment should include larger spaces, both indoor and outdoor. When outdoor play is not possible because of weather conditions, using a large indoor space such as a gymnasium is recommended. Day cares housed within schools should be given access to such spaces. Communities should support day cares located near recreation centres or schools by creating a framework to provide access to gymnasiums at no cost or reduced cost.
2. Materials that increase locomotion and MVPA for structured and unstructured activities, such as tunnels, soft blocks, slides with stairs, and any safe type of obstruction equipment, should be available. Furthermore, loose equipment with no specific purpose such as cardboard boxes, which facilitate spontaneous group play and creativity, should also be made available.
3. Day care curricula should include workshops delivered by PA specialists outlining the benefits of PA and healthy lifestyle and strategies to increase PA levels, supplemented with books, videos, or stories portraying physically active children and their parents.

Addressing Parents' Attitudes and Perceptions

There is strong evidence of parental misperceptions about their young children's PA activity levels, as well as their child's weight status and needs for change in lifestyle, as demonstrated by a large number of both controlled and correlational studies converging with similar results. This suggests that day care program developers need to take into account parents as important facilitators of their child's health and PA habits. Therefore, information should be provided to parents about the following:

1. The importance of an objective assessment of their child's health and weight status by a paediatrician or family doctor, as well as an objective assessment of their child's PA levels compared with the Canadian Society for Exercise Physiology's recommendations for PA and sedentary behaviours.

2. The importance and benefits of PA for their children, as well as strategies to help increase PA of the family, such as making safe space at home for the children to be active (such as mats in the basement), family play time at the park or in the backyard, walking after meals, parking at a distance from shopping mall doors, and so forth. For families living in Canada, wintertime can be perceived as problematic for achieving the recommended levels of PA; parents may consider bringing their children to the local shopping malls, playgroups, indoor recreation facilities, or community centres where they can run and walk. Preschoolers can be initiated to outdoor winter activities such as skating and skiing.

3. Community resources for PA. Some parents are unaware of programs or falsely believe that the costs for access to such facilities or programs are too high, which is often not the case.

In brief, the lifelong practice of PA and active behaviours takes root during early childhood, underscoring the importance of fostering healthy PA behaviours early in development (Oliver et al., 2010). The most active children tend to stay active, whereas the least active children tend to remain the least active (Pate et al., 1996, 1999). Taken together with the evidence that sedentary behaviours are more stable than PA behaviours over time (Janz et al., 2005; Pate et al., 1999; Raitakari et al., 1994; Sääkslahti et al., 2(K)4; Taylor et al., 2009). it is clearly apparent that early PA intervention programs targeting young children within day care settings and in general have great potential to help develop healthy PA behaviours in young children, leading to sustained health and wellness benefits throughout life.

References

Alhassan, S., Sirard, J. R., & Robinson. T. N. (2007). The effects of increasing outdoor play time on physical activity in Latino preschool children. *International Journal of Pediatric Obesity, 2.* 153–158. doi: 10.1080/17477160701520108

Alpert, B., Field, T., Goldstein. S., & Perry, S. (1990). Aerobics enhances cardiovascular fitness and agility in preschoolers. *Health Psychology,* 9. 48–56. doi: 10.1037/0278-6133.9.1.48

Bailey, R. (2005). Evaluating the relationship between physical education, sport and social inclusion. *Educational Review. 57,* 71–90. doi: 10.1080/ (X)l 3191042000274196

Benham-Deal, T. (2005). Preschool children's accumulated and sustained physical activity. *Perceptual and Motor Skills, 100.* 443–450. doi: 10.2466/pms. 100.2.443-450

Binkley, T., & Specker, B. (2004). Increased periosteal circumference remains present 12 months after an exercise intervention in preschool children. *Bone.* 35. 1383–1388. doi: 10.IOI6/j.bone. 2004.08.0l2

Bower, J. K., Hales, D. P., Tate, D. F., Rubin, D. A., Benjamin. S. E., & Ward. D. S. (2008). The child-care environment and children's physical activity. *American Journal of Preventive Medicine. 14. 23–29.* doi: 10.1016/j.amepre.2007.09.022

Branta, C., Haubenstricker. V., & Seefeldt. V. (1984). Age changes in motor skills during childhood and adolescence. *Exercise. Sport and Science Review. 12.* 467–520. doi: 10.1249/(XXX)3677-198401 (MX)-(XX)15

Branta, C. F., & Goodway. J. D. (1996). Facilitating social skills in urban school children through physical education. *Peace and Conflict: Journal of Peace Psychology. 2*. 305–319. doi: 10.1207/s 15327949pac0204_3

Brown, J. E., Broom. D. H., Nicholson, J. M., & Bittman. M. (2010). Do working mothers raise couch potato kids? Maternal employment and children's lifestyle behaviours and weight in early childhood. *Social Science A Medicine, 70*. 1816–1824. doi: 10.1016/j.socscimed.20l().()l .040

Brown, W. H., Pfeiffer. K. A., McIver. K. L., Dowda, M., Addy. C. L., & Pate. R. R. (2009). Social and environmental factors associated with preschoolers' nonsedentary physical activity. *Child Development, 80*. 45–58. doi: 10.111 l/j. 1467-8624.2008.01245.x

Bundy, A. C., Luckett. T,. Tranter, P. J., Naughton, G. A., Wyver. S. R., Ragen. J., & Spies. G. (2009). The risk is that there is "no risk": A simple, innovative intervention to increase children's activity levels. *International Journal of Early Years Education. 17*. 33–45. doi: It). 1080/09669760802699878

Cameron. N., Norgan, N. G., & Ellison. G. T. H. (2006). *Childhood obesity: Contemporary issues.* Society for the Study of Human Biology Series. Boca Raton, FL: Taylor & Francis Group.

Canadian Paediatric Society, (2002). *News Releases A Advisories*. Retrieved from http://www.cps.ca/english/media/NewsReleases/2002/ TVTurnoffWeek.htm

Canadian Society for Exercise Physiology, (2012a). *Canadian physical activity guidelines for children (aged 5–11 years)*. Retrieved from http:// www.csep.ca/guidelines

Canadian Society for Exercise Physiology, (2012b). *Canadian physical activity guidelines for the early years (aged 0–4)*. Retrieved from http://www.csep.ca/guidelines

Canadian Society for Exercise Physiology, (2012c). *Canadian sedentary behaviors guidelines for children (aged 5–11 years)*. Retrieved from http://www.csep.ca/guidelines

Canadian Society for Exercise Physiology, (2012d). *Canadian sedentary behaviors guidelines for the early years (aged 0–4)*. Retrieved from http://www.csep.ca/guidelines

Carlson, S. A., Fulton. J. W., Lee, S. M., Myanard. M., Brown. D. R., Kohl. H. W., & Dietz. W. H. (2008). Physical education and academic achievement in elementary school: Data from the early childhood longitudinal study. *American Journal of Public Health. 98*. 721–727. doi: 10.2105/AJPH.2007.117176

Caspersen, C. J., Powell. K. E., & Christenson. G. M. (1985). Physical activity, exercise, and physical fitness: Definitions and distinctions for health-related research. *Public Health Reports. 100(2)*. 126–131.

Clarke, W. R., & Lauer, R. M. (1993). Does childhood obesity track into adulthood? *Critical Reviews in Pood Science and Nutrition. 33,* 42.3-430. doi: 10.1080/10408.399309527641

Colley, R. C., Garriguet, D., Jansen. L., Craig. C., Clarke, J., & Tremblay. M. S. (2011). Physical activity of Canadian children and youth: Accelerometer results from the 2007–2009 Canadian Health Measures Survey. *Health Report. 22,* 15–23.

Copeland, K. A., Kendeigh, C. A., Saelens. B. E., Kalkwarf. H. J., & Sherman. S. N. (2012). Physical activity in child-care centers: Do teachers hold the key to the playground? *Health Education Research. 27*. 81–100 (K). doi: 10.1093/her/cyr038

Danner, F., Noland, M., McFadden, M., DeWalt, K., & Kotchen. J. M. (1991). Description of the physical activity of young children using movement sensor and observation methods. *Pediatric Exercise Science. 3.* 11–20.

Day Nurseries Act. (1990). Government of Ontario. Service Ontario Web site, http://www.e-laws. gov.on.ca/html/regs/english/elaws_regs_ 900262_e.htm

Dietz, W. H. (1998). Health consequences of obesity in youth: Childhood predictors of adult disease. *Pediatrics. 101,* 518–525.

Dowda, M., Dishman, R. K., Pfeiffer, K. A., & Pate, R. R. (2007). Family support for physical activity in girls from 8th to 12th grade in South Carolina. *Preventive Medicine: An International Journal Devoted to Practice and Theory. 44.* 153–159. doi: 10.1016/j.ypmed.2006.10.001

Dowda, M., Pate, R. R., Trost. S. G., Almeida, M. J. C. A., & Sirard, J. R. (2004). Influences of preschool policies and practices on children's physical activity. *Journal of Community Health: The Publication for Health Promotion and Disease Prevention. 29.* 183–196. doi: 10.102.3/ B:JOHE.0000022025.77294.af

DuRant, R. H., Baranowski, T., Johnson, M., & Thompson. W. O. (1994). The relationship among television watching, physical activity, and body composition of young children. *Pediatrics. 94.* 449−455.

Emck, C., Bosscher, R., Beek, P., & Doreleijers, T. (2009). Gross motor performance and self-perceived motor competence in children with emotional, behavioural, and pervasive developmental disorders: A review. *Developmental Medicine & Child Neurology, 5/,* 501–517. doi: 10.1 11 l/j.1469–8749.2009.03337.x

Eveline, V. C., Valery. L., Jessica, G., Use. D. B., & Greet. C. (2012). Preschoolers physical activity levels and associations with lesson context. teachers behavior, and environment during preschool physical education. *Early Childhood Research Quarterly, 27.* 221–230. doi: 10. lOl6/j. ecresq.2Ol 1.09.007

Evers, S., Arnold, R., Hamilton. T., & Midgett, C. (2007). Persistence of overweight among young children living in low' income communities in Ontario. *Journal of the American College of Nutrition, 26,* 219–224.

Finn, K., Johannsen, N., & Specker, B. (2002). Factors associated with physical activity in preschool children. *The Journal of Pediatrics, 140.* 81–85. doi: 10.1067/mpd.2OO2.12069.3

Fisher, A., Reilly, J. J., Kelly. L. A., Montgomery. C., Williamson, A., Paton. J. Y., & Grant. S. (2005). Fundamental movement skills and habitual physical activity in young children. *Medicine & Science in Sports & Exercise, 37.* 684–688. doi: 10.1249/01 .MSS.0000159138 .48107.7D

Freedman, D. S., Khan. K. K., Dietz. W. H., Srinivasan. S. R., & Berenson. G. S. (2001). Relationship of childhood obesity lo coronary heart disease risk factors in adulthood: The Bogalusa Heart Study. *Pediatrics, 108.* 712–718. doi: 10.1542/peds.108.3.712

Funk, J. B., Brouwer. J., Curtiss. K., & McBroom. E. (2009). Parents of preschoolers: Expert media recommendations and ratings knowledge, media-effects beliefs, and monitoring practices. *Pediatrics, 123.* 981-988. doi: 10.1542/peds.2008–1543

Goodway, J. D., & Rudisill. M. E. (1996). Influence of a motor skill intervention program on perceived competence of at-risk African American preschoolers. *Adapted Physical Activity Quarterly. 13.* 288–301.

Goran, M. I. (1998). Measurement issues related to studies of childhood obesity: Assessment of body composition, body fat distribution, physical activity, and food intake. *Pediatrics, 101.* 505–518.

Hansen, D. M., Larson. R. W., & Dworkin. J. B. (2003). What adolescents learn in organized youth activities: A survey of self-reported developmental experiences. *Journal of Research on Adolescence. 13.* 25–55, doi: 10.1111/1532-7795.1301006

Harris, K. C., Kuramoto. L. K., Schulzer. M., & Retallack. J. E. (2009). Effect of school-based physical activity interventions on body mass index in children: A meta-analysis. *Canadian Medical Association Journal. 180.*719–726. doi: 10.1503/cmaj.080966

Heelan, K. A., & Eisenmann. J. C. (2006). Physical activity, media time, and body composition in young children. *Journal of Physical Activity & Health, 3.* 200–209.

Hill.. J. O., & Peters. J. C. (1998). Environmental contribution to the obesity epidemic. *Science. 280.* 1.371–1.374. doi: 10.1 126/science.280.5368.1371

Hinkley, T., Crawford. D., Salmon. J., Okely, A. D., & Hesketh, K. (2008). Preschool children and physical activity. A review of correlates. *American Journal of Preventive Medicine, 34,* 435–441.

Hinkley, T., Salmon. J., Okely, A. D., Crawford, D , & Hesketh, K. (2011). Influences on preschool children's physical activity: Exploration through focus groups. *Family & Community Health: The Journal of Health Promotion 8 Maintenance. 34.* .39–50.

Irwin, J. D., He. M., Bouck, L. M. S., Tucker, P., & Pollett, G. L. (2005). Preschoolers' physical activity behaviours: Parents' perspectives. *Canadian Journal of Public Health. Revue canadienne de sante publique, 96,* 299–303.

Jago, R., Baranowski, T., Baranowski, J. C., Thompson. D., & Greaves, K. A. (2005). BMI from 3–6y of age is predicted by TV viewing and physical activity, not diet. *International Journal of Obesity, 29.* 557- 564. doi: 10.1038/sj.ijo.0802969

Janz, K. F., Burns, T. L., & Levy. S. M. (2005). Tracking of activity and sedentary behaviors in childhood: The Iowa Bone Development Study. *American Journal of Preventive Medicine. 29,* 171–178. doi: 10.1016/j .amepre. 2005.06.001

Kemper, H. C. G., Post. G. B., Twisk, J. W. R., & van Mechelen, W. (1999). Lifestyle and obesity in adolescence and young adulthood: Results from the Amsterdam Growth And Health Longitudinal Study (AGAHLS). *International Journal of Obesity, 23.* s34-s40. doi: 10.1038/ sj.ijo.080088l

Lobstein, T., Baur, L.,. & Uauy. R. (2004). Obesity in children and young people: A crisis in public health. *Obesity Reviews. 5.* 4–104. doi: 10.111 l/j. I467–789X.2004.00133.x

Lopez-Williams. A., Chacko, A., Wymbs, B. T., Fabiano, G. A., Seymour. K. E., Gnagy. E. M., Morris, T. L. (2005). Athletic performance and social behavior as predictors of peer acceptance in children diagnosed with attention-deficit/hyperactivity disorder. *Journal of Emotional and Behavioral Disorders. 13.* 173–180. doi: 10.1177/106342660501.30030501

Magarey, A. M., Daniels. L. A., Boulton. T. J., & Lockington, R. A. (200.3). Predicting obesity in early adulthood from childhood and parental obesity. *International Journal of Obesity, 27,* 505–513. doi: 10.1038/ sj.ijo.0802251

Maynard, I. M., Galuska, D. A., Blanck. H. M., & Serdula, M. K. (2003). Maternal perceptions of weight status of children. *Pediatrics, III,* 1226–1231.

Ministry of Health and Long-Term Care. (2005). *Active 2010; Ontario's Sport and Physical Activity Strategy.* Retrieved from Ontario Government Web site, http://www.mhp.gov.on.ea/en/aetive-living/about/ about2010.asp

Moore, L. L., Gao, D., Bradlee, M. L., Cupples. L. A., Sundarajan- Ramamuni. A., Proctor, M. H., ... Ellison. R. C. (2003). Does early physical activity predict body fat change throughout childhood? *Preventive Medicine: An International Journal Devoted to Practice and Theory. 37.* 10–17.

Moore, L. L., Nguyen. U.-S. D. T., Rothman. K. J., Cupples, L. A., & Ellison. R. C. (1995). Preschool physical activity level and change in body fatness in young children: The Framingham Children's Study. *American Journal of Epidemiology. 142,* 982–988.

Must, A,. & Tybor. D. J. (2005). Physical activity and sedentary behavior: A review of longitudinal studies of weight and adiposity in youth. *International Journal of Obesity, 29,* S84-S96. doi: 10.1038/sj.ijo .0803064

National Association for Sport and Physical Education. (2009). *Active Start: A statement of physical activity guidelines for children front birth to age* 5 (2nd ed.). Retrieved from http://www.aahperd. org/naspe/ standards/nalionalGuidelines/ActiveStart.cfm

Oliver, M., Schofield. G. M., & Schluter. P. J. (2010). Parent influences on preschoolers' objectively assessed physical activity. *Journal of Science and Medicine in Sport, 12,* 403–409. doi: 10.1016/j. jsams.2009.05.008

Pagani, I. S., Fitzpatrick, C., Barnett, T. A., & Dubow, E. (2010). Prospective associations between early childhood television exposure and academic, psychosocial, and physical well-being by middle childhood. *Archive of Pediatrics A Adolescent Medicine, 164,* 425–431. doi: IO.I(X)l/ archpediatrics.2010.50

Paluska, S. A., & Schwenk, T. L. (2000). Physical activity and mental health: Current concepts. *Sports Medicine, 29,* 167–180. doi: 10.2165/ (0000)7256–2000290.30-0003

Pan Canadian Joint Consortium for School Health. (2010). Facilitating health and education sector collaboration in support of comprehensive school health. *Canadian Journal of Public Health, 101,* S18–SI9.

Pate, R. R., Baranowski. T., Dowda, M., & Trost. S. G. (1996). Tracking of physical activity in young children. *Medicine A Science in Sports A Exercise, 28,* 92–96. doi: 10.1097/00005768–199601(XX)-(XX)19

Pate, R. R., Pfeiffer. K A., Trost, S. G., Ziegler. P., & Dowda. M. (2004). Physical activity among children attending preschools. *Pediatrics. 114.* 1258–1263. dot : 10.1542/peds.2003-1088-L

Pate, R. R., Trost, S. G., Dowda, M., Ott, A. E., Ward. D. S., & Saunders, R. (1999). Tracking of physical activity, physical inactivity, and health- related physical fitness in rural youth. *Pediatric Exercise Science. 11,* 364–376.

Pelligrini, A. D., & Smith P. K. (1998). Physical activity play: The nature and function of a neglected aspect of play. *Child Development, 69,* 577–598.

Proctor, M, H., Moore. L. L., Gao. D., Cupples, L. A., Bradlee. M. L., Hood. M. Y., & El I ison, R. C. (2003). Television viewing and change in body fat from preschool to early adolescence: The Framingham Children's Study. *International Journal of Obesity, 27,* 827–833. doi: I0.I0.38/sj.ijo.0802294

Purper-Ouakil. D., Michel, G., Baup. N., & Mouren-Simeoni, M.-C. (2002). Psychopathology in children and adolescents with intensive physical activity: Case study and overview. *Annales Médico- Psychologiques, 160.* 543–549. doi:10.1016/S0003-4487(02)0023.3-0

Raitakari, O. T., Porkka, K V. K., Taimela. S., Telanta. R., Räsänen. L., & Viikari, J. S. A. (1994). Effects of persistent physical activity and inactivity on coronary risk factors in children and young adults. The Cardiovascular Risk in Young Finns Study. *American Journal of Epidemiology, 140.* 195–205.

Reilly, J. J., Methven. E., McDowell. Z. C. Hacking. B., Alexander. D., Stewart. L., & Kelnar. C. J. H. (2003). Health consequences of obesity. *Archives of Disease in Childhood, 88.* 748–752. doi:10.11.36/adc.88.9 .748

Sääkslahti, A., Numminen. P., Vaind. V., Helenius. H., Tammi, A., Viikari, J., & Valimaki, I. (2004). Physical activity as a preventive measure for coronary heart disease risk factors in early childhood. *Scandinavian Journal of Medicine and Sciences in Sport, 14.* 143–149. doi: 10.111 l/j . 1600-0838.2004.00.347.x

Sallis, J. F., Nader. P. R., Broyles. S. L., Berry. C. C., Elder. J. P., McKenzie. T. L., & Nelson, J. A. (1993). Correlates of physical activity at home in Mexican-American and Anglo-American preschool children. *Health Psychology, 12.* 390-398. drvi: 10.1037/0278-6133.12.5.390

Sallis, J. F., Patterson. T. L., McKenzie. T. L., & Nader. P. R. (1988). Family variables and physical activity in preschool children. *Journal of Developmental Behavioral Pediatrics, 9,* 57–61.

Schmidt, M. E., Rich, M., Rifas-Shiman. S., Oken, E., & Taveras. E. M. (2009). Television viewing in infancy and child cognition at .3 years of age in a US cohort. *Pediatrics, 123,* e.370-e.375. doi: 10. l542/peds.2008- 3221

Statistics Canada. (2003). *Television Viewing 2002. The Daily. November 21, 2003.* Retrieved from http://www.statean.ca/Daily/English/O3ll2l/ dO3H21a.htm

Taylor, R. W., Murdoch, L., Carter, P., Gerrard. D. F., Williams. S. M., & Taylor. B. J. (2009). Longitudinal study of physical activity and inactivity in preschoolers: The FLAME study. *Medicine A Science in Sports A Exercise. 41.* 96–102. doi: 10.1249/MSS.()bOI3e.3181849d81

Thompson, A. M., Humbert. M. L., & Mirwald. R. L. (2003). A longitudinal study of the impact of childhood and adolescent physical activity experiences on adult physical activity perceptions and behaviors. *Qualitative Health Research. 13.* 358–377. doi: 10.1177/1049732302250332

Timmons, B. W., Naylor. P.-J. & Pfeiffer. K. A. (2007). Physical activity for preschool children—how much and how? *Applied Physiology, Nutrition, and Metabolism, 32.* SI22–SI34. doi: 10.1139/HO7-112

Toftegaard-stoeckel. J., Groenfeldl. V., & Andersen. L. B. (2010). Children's self-perceived bodily competencies and associations with motor skills, body mass index, teachers' evaluation, and parents' concerns. *Journal of Sports Sciences, 28.* 1369–1375. doi: 10.1080/02640414.2010.510845

Tremblay, L., Lovsin, T., Zecevic. C., & Lariviére. M. (2011). Perceptions of self in 3–5 year old children: A preliminary investigation into the early emergence of body dissatisfaction. *Body Image, 8,* 287–292. doi: 10. IOI6/j.bodyim.2011.04.004

Tremblay, L., & Rinaldi. C. (2010). The prediction of preschool children's weight from family environment factors: Gender-linked differences. *Eating Behaviors. II,* 266–275. doi: 10.IOI6/j. eatbeh.2010.07.005

Tremblay, L., Rinaldi. C., Cimon-Lambert. K . & Lariviére, M. (2012). Toward an effective prevention of pediatric obesity; the role of parental feeding strategies and body weight perceptions on the development of young children" healthy eating habits. In L. V. Berhardt (Ed.). *Advances in medicine and biology* (Vol. 28. pp. 125–150). Hauppauge. NY: Nova Science.

Tremblay, M. S., Colley, R., Saunders. T. J., Healy. G. N., & Gwen. N. (2010). Physiological and health implications of a sedentary lifestyle. *Applied Physiology, Nutrition, and Metabolism, 35,* 725–740. doi: 10.1139/HI0-079

Tremblay, M. S., LeBlanc. A. G., Carson. V., Choquette. L., Conner-Gorber, S., Dillman. C., Spence. J. (2012b). Canadian sedentary behavior guidelines tor the early years (aged 0–4 years). *Applied Physiology, Nutrition, and Metabolism. 37. .370-380.* doi:IO.1139/h2012-019

Tremblay, M. S., LeBlanc, A. G., Carson, V., Choquette, L., Conner-Gorber, S., Dillman, C., Timmons. B. W. (2012a). Canadian physical activity guidelines for the early years (aged 0–4 years). *Applied Physiology, Nutrition, and Metabolism, J7,* 345–356. doi: 10.1139/h2012-018

Tremblay, M. S., Shields, M., Laviolette. M., Craig, C. L., & Janssen. 1. (2010). Fitness of Canadian children and youth: Results from the 2007–2009 Canadian Health Measures Survey. *Health Report, 21,* 7–20.

Tucker, P., & Irwin. J. D. (2008). Physical activity behaviors during the preschool years. *Child and Health Education, I,* 134–145.

Veugelers, P. J., & Schwartz, M. E. (2010). Comprehensive school health in Canada. *Canadian Journal of Public Health. Rerue canadienne de sante publique, 101,* S5–S8.

Wang, F., & Veugelers. P. J. (2008). Self-esteem and cognitive development in the era of the childhood obesity epidemic. *Obesity Reviews. 9,* 615–623. doi: 10.111 l/j. 1467-789X.2008.00507.X

Wang, F., Wild, T. C., Kipp, W., Kuhle, S., & Veugelers. P. J. (2009). The influence of childhood obesity on the development of self-esteem. *Health Reports. 20.* 21–27.

Wardle, J., Guthrie, C. A., Sanderson. A., & Rapoport. L. (2001). Development of the children's eating behaviour questionnaire. *Journal of Child Psychology and Psychiatry, 42,* 963–970. doi: 10.1111/1469-7610.00792

West, D. S., Raczynski, J. M., Philips, M., Bursae, Z., Gauss. C. H., & Montgomery, B. E. E. (2008). Parental recognition of overweight in school-age children. *Obesity, 16,* 630–636. doi: 10.1038/ oby.2007.108

Whitaker, R. C., Wright, J. A., Pepe. M. S., Seidel. K. D., & Dietz. W. H. (1997). Predicting obesity in young adulthood from childhood and parental obesity. *The New England Journal of Medicine, 337,* 869-873. doi: 10.1056/NEJM199709253371301

Williams, H. G., Pfeiffer, K. A., O'Neill, J. R., Dowda, M., McIver. K. L., Brown, W. H., & Pate, R. R. (2008). Motor skill performance and physical activity in preschool children. *Obesity, 16,* 1421–1426. doi:10.1038/oby.2008.214

Woodward, S., & Swinth, Y. (2002). Multisensory approach to handwriting remediation: Perceptions of school-based occupational therapists. *American Journal of Occupational Therapy, 56,* 305–312. doi: 10.5014/ajot.56.3.305

World Health Organization. (2008). *School policy framework: Implementation of the WHO Global Strategy on diet, physical activity and health, Geneva, Switzerland.* Retrieved from http://www.who.int/dietphysicalactivity/SPF-en-2008.pdf

Wosje, K. J., Khoury. P. R., Claytor. R. P., Copeland. K. A., Kalkwarf, H. J., & Daniels. S. R. (2009). Adiposity and TV viewing are related to less bone accrual in young children. *The Journal of Pediatrics, 154,* 79–85.

Zecevic, C. A., Tremblay. L., Lovsin, T., & Lariviére, M. (2010). Parental influence on young children's physical activity. *International Journal of Pediatrics, 2010,* 1-9. doi:10.1155/2010/468526

Studying Environmental Influence on Motor Development in Children

Carl Gabbard and Ruy Krebs

Abstract

There is a good argument that in order to truly understand the influences that shape child motor development, one must consider environmental influences that reflect the multilevel ecological contexts that interact with the changing biological characteristics of the child. Although there are theories typically associated with motor development that mention environmental influence (e.g., constraints, affordances), none provide the comprehensive framework comparable to the works of Bronfenbrenner (1979, 2005). With this paper, we address the need for environmental considerations, highlight Bronfenbrenner's work and application to the field of motor development, and provide examples for research using two contemporary themes.

Over the last 25 years, there has been a substantial increase in the presence of motor development research in top-tier journals of human development, psychology and neuroscience. This trend is due in large part to acknowledgement that level of motor development is a critical factor in child behavior. Additional evidence for this emergence is the observation that aspects of motor development are mentioned with increasing frequency in broad-based theoretical treatises within the fields of cognitive psychology, developmental neuropsychology, developmental psychobiology, and neuroscience (e.g., Andres, Olivier, & Badets, 2008; Fernandino & Iacoboni, 2010; Johnson, Spencer, & Schöner, 2008; Piek, Dawson, Leigh, & Smith, 2008). Contemporary

Carl Gabbard and Ruy Krebs, "Studying Environmental Influence on Motor Development in Children," *Physical Educator*, vol. 69, no. 2, pp. 136-149. Copyright © 2012 by Phi Epsilon Kappa Fraternity. Reprinted with permission. Provided by ProQuest LLC. All rights reserved.

research has answered numerous questions concerning how the body learns and controls movement, and what effects movement has on human development (e g., physical growth, muscle, bone, cardiorespiratory system, and cognitive ability).

Although some mention in prominent theories of motor development is given to environmental factors, to a much greater extent, focus has been on the biological determinants of behavior, with the goal of gaining an understanding of the processes that underscore the dynamic and self-organizing properties associated with perception and action. However, few researchers would disagree with the notion that in order to truly understand the complex nature of human motor development, environmental determinants should be considered. This aspect of study represents the primary intent of this paper. Here, we will briefly address the need for environmental considerations, suggest a framework for study, and provide examples for research using two contemporary themes.

According to Lerner (2002), human development is the product of changing relations between the developing person and his or her changing multilevel environmental contexts. Understanding how biological levels dynamically interact with levels of contexts (aka, contextualism) stresses the interrelation of all levels. Complementing this general view of development, Gabbard (2008) defines motor development as the study of change in motor behavior [and underlying processes] as influenced by biological and environmental factors; that is, the interaction of changing biological systems and environmental contexts.

The importance of considering the environment in the study of motor development was emphasized in several works of Thelen; for example, "The first assumption of the dynamic approach is that developing organisms are complex systems composed of very many individual elements embedded within, and open to, a complex environment" (Smith & Thelen, 2003, p. 343), and "... the coherence [of perception and action] is generated solely in the relationships between the organic components and the constraints and opportunities of the environment" (p. 344). In 2000, the National Academies addressed the issue of environmental effect by noting "Research indicates that early relationships are especially critical and that cultural values and practices provide the context for these bonds" (Shonkoff & Phillips, 2000). More recently, in 2009 the International Journal of Sport Psychology devoted an issue to ecological approaches to studying cognition and action in sport and exercise. One of the theoretical views discussed was the works of Bronfenbrenner (Krebs, 2009); the focus of the present article.

Bronfenbrenner's Bioecological Theory

Bronfenbrenner's bioecological theory (1979, 1988, 1992, 2005, Bronfenbrenner & Morris, 2006), describes the hypothesized (varied) systems of the environment and the interrelationships among the systems that have the potential to shape the individual. In 1979 he proposed that the ecology of human development was "the scientific study of progressive, mutual accommodation between an active, growing human being and the changing properties of the immediate settings in which the developing person lives'" (p. 21). From this perspective, he designed a systemic model to illustrate the four levels of the environment. An illustration of the four systems is shown in Figure 13.1.

Although early versions of the model did not focus on the biological aspects of the individual at the core of the model, most writings inferred that the environment and biology influenced individual development. The model emphasizes the broad range of situations and contexts individuals may encounter as described by four distinct systems: the microsystem, mesosystem, exosystem, and macrosystem. In brief, these systems represent the environmental settings and relationship ranging from the home, to the community, and to the culture in which one lives. Aside from the more obvious influence of the home, a relevant example is city government (parks), which is responsible for the quality of play and

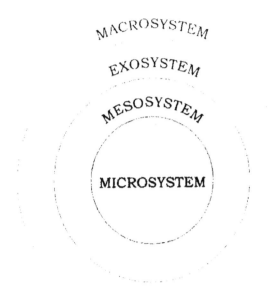

FIGURE 13.1   An Illustration of Bronfenbrenner's *Bioecological Theory*

recreational opportunities, such as youth sports, playgrounds, and swimming facilities. Also included in this framework are sociohistorical contexts. For example, females of today are much more likely to participate in athletic endeavors than they were 20 years ago. As will be discussed in a subsequent section, settings and events within systems represent 'affordances;' opportunities for developing and maintaining motor skill.

Bronfenbrenner viewed a child's development within the context of the system of relationships that form his or her environment. The model describes complex "layers" of the environment, each having a potential effect on a child's development. A more recent update of the model highlights the child's own biology as a primary agent (i.e., the PPCT model to be described in a subsequent section). The interaction between factors in the child's maturing biology, his immediate family/community environment, and the societal landscape fuels and guides development. Change or conflict in any one layer may cause a ripple effect on other layers. To study a child's development, we must look not only at the child and his or her immediate environment, but also at the interaction of the larger environmental context, which provides affordances for growth and development. A summary of the systems follows. We do wish to note that with earlier versions of the model (before 1995). Bronfenbrenner included the 'Chronosystem' (not shown here), which at the time was designed to reflect past influences of the other systems on the person. For example, the longitudinal effects of parenting, school physical education, or social trends on adult physical activity. Bronfenbrenner included this system after analyzing paradigms used in research in human development and noted that the concept of "time" was predominately treated as being synonymous with chronological age. With the goal of using time not only for describing individuals according to age, but also for ordering and explaining events in their historical sequence and context, he proposed the chronosystem; a construct that was later dropped and fused with the now popular Process-Person-Context-Time (PPCT) model introduced in 1995.

Microsystem

Here people can readily engage in face-to-face interaction; the most immediate and earliest influences are the family, along with local neighborhood or community institutions such as the school, religious institutions and peer groups, as well as the specific culture with which the family identifies. For example, parents provide toys and opportunities to move and learn in physical environments. Other influential opportunities (affordances) are provided by schools (e g., physical education, fitness and sport activities) and the local neighborhood (playgrounds, parks pools, walk and bike trails).

Mesosystem

This comprises the interrelations among two or more contexts within the microsystem. For example, the connection between the child's family, school, church, and neighborhood. Each of the contents in the microsystem affects each other. Perhaps this can best be explained in the context of living communities. Places where the child's welfare is a consideration at multiple levels. For example, single-mothers maybe assisted with keeping their child active by an after-school program, community youth sports, and church activities.

Exosystem

This refers to one or more settings that do not involve the developing person directly as an active participant. The exosystem includes things like television and acquaintances. These are things they do not have an active role in, but might affect them indirectly. For example, television viewing can have a strong impact on a child's attitude toward physical activity and a healthy lifestyle. Fortunately, more programs and advertisements are incorporating the 'active body' and 'healthy eating' ideals. And as inferred with the next system (macrosystem), much of this promotion comes via political action.

Macrosystem

This is the societal, cultural, and global influence. The macrosystem consists of the overarching pattern of micro-, meso-, and exosystem characteristics of a given culture, subculture or other broader social context, including laws and governmental policies. For example, political influence may provide needed mandates for physical education and resources for active environments; this applies to the local, state and national levels. National and state programs for education and health can have a huge impact on child development.

The PPCT Model

Whereas the systems model (Figure 13.1) theoretically represents broad-based influences on and options for studying human development, the likelihood of undertaking such a venture in its entirety is arguably not feasible for most researchers (we view the model as a general framework for variable selection). With the idea of providing a more applicable model with focus on the individual, Bronfenbrenner (1995) introduced the Process-Person-Context-Time (PPCT) model; a model that in recent years has garnered the attention of the research community interested in the environment influence on human (biological) development. More specific, this construct encompasses particular forms of interaction between organism and environment, called prox-imal processes, which operate over time, and are posited as the primary mechanism producing human development. The power of such processes to influence development is a function of the characteristics of the developing person, and the immediate and more remote environmental context and the time periods, in which the proximal processes take place The model allows for examination of:

Process: fused and dynamic relation of the person and context

Person: biological, cognitive, and emotional characteristics

Context: nested levels or systems of the ecology

Time: multiple dimensions of temporality. Bronfenbrenner referred to time as the historical period through which the person lives, and the timing of biological and social transitions as they relate to the culturally defined age, role expectations, and opportunities occurring throughout the life course.

Research Using the Model

A literature review indicates that several dissertations/theses, books, and a few journal pub-lications have reported variations of Bronfenbrenner's model(s) with attention to: health (e g., diabetes, alcohol/substance abuse, mental health, pediatric injury, etc) (Liles & Juhnke, 2008; Schwebel & Brezausek, 2007; Swick & Williams, 2006; Yu & Stiffman, 2007; Garcia & Saewyc, 2007), social development (Barrow, Armstrong, Vargo, & Boothroyd, 2007; Logsdon, Hertweck, Ziegler, & Pinto-Foltz, 2008), and cognitive aptitude (Harden, Turkheimer, & Loehlin, 2007).

In regard to the general field of motor behavior, a few studies have been reported on the timely issue of physical activity (Gilmer, Harrell, Miles, & Hepworth, 2003; Salmon & Tim-peno, 2007) and children's sport (Bengoechea & Johnson, 2000; Côté & Hay, 2002; Stefanello, 1999). For example, Tudge, Odero, Hogan, and Etz (2003) used the PPCT to focus on the relations between school-relevant activities (including play) of preschool-aged children and teachers' subsequent perception of the children's competence once they had entered school. They observed 3-year-olds' engagement in everyday activities (Process) and their initiation of those activities (Person) over a period covering the equivalent of an entire waking day. Children were drawn from two social classes (Context). The preschool observations were followed by two consecutive years of teacher reports of academic competence following entry into elementary school (Time). Of more direct relevance to the movement domain and the suggestion of models like Bronfenbrenner's, Salmon and Timperio (2007) conducted a review of the literature regarding the environmental effects on children's physical activity. Their findings were that several contextual factors have been reported. For example, safety concerns (e.g., road safety, crime and concerns about strangers), social interaction (e.g., child peers, neighborhood relationships, other children live in neighborhood close by), and urban design (e.g., connectivity of streets, access and availability of public open spaces and sports facilities). The authors went on to state that unfortunately, no single report has been published using a broad-based ecological model (such as Bronfenbrenner's model). Furthermore, they recommended that "there is a need for conceptual models that take such complexities into account, and need for multilevel study designs that incorporate individual-level influences, proximal social influences and influences within the broader environment in order to better understand physical activity behavior" (p. 196).

However, in reference to more basic child physical growth and motor development issues, surprisingly, reports are in short supply. This void seems especially perplexing given the developmental (time related) nature of the field.

Using the Model with Studies of Motor Development

In addition to the theme issue in the *International Journal of Sport Psychology,* other researchers have pointed-out the promise of Bronfenbrenner's model in understanding the environmental effect on motor behavior. For example, Bengoechea (2002) noted in *Quest* that "Bronfenbrenner's model provides a comprehensive and dynamic conceptual framework for understanding human development" (p. 1). In the author's review of Bronfenbenner's work with application to the study of sport talent development, Krebs (2009) noted that the PPCT design with the emphasis on the discovery process, had not yet been tested in the field of the sport sciences.

It is not uncommon for contemporary developmentalists to consider two other environmental theories with the study of children's motor development; both of which, complement Bronfenbrenner's systems perspective and PPCT model.

Gibson's Ecological Perspective (1988, 2002), which typically focuses in the infant's perception of environmental stimuli and opportunities, derives the concept of affordances. The environment provides affordances that invite and challenge the child to perceive and act on information. In addition to the more obvious set of affordances such as toys, materials, apparatus, and availability of space, stimulation and nurturing by parents (and others) provide the additional component of events. The notion of affordances emphasizes that there is an ecological fit between the individual and the situation. The study of affordances in perception and as agents for change has been given considerable attention in the motor development and ecological psychology literature. Arguably, affordances in the environment via the various systems are one of the basic constructs in Bronfenbrenner's model. For example, the family and community and what it affords the child.

Newell's Constraints Model (Newell, 1986) combines both the biological and ecological systems perspective. This is applied by describing the constraints to behavior in reference to the individual, the task to be performed, and the environment in which it is to be executed. With this model, the term constraint refers to factors that either facilitate or restrict development. Underscoring this view is the perspective that new motor behaviors emerge as a result of changing individual (organismic), environmental, and task constraints. Environmental constraints can be related to the physical environment or sociocultural factors. This may include gravity (terrain), surface, space, temperature, and characteristics of the home. For example, the space and terrain that an infant has available to move in is a constraint on the development of locomotion. A major difference between this model and Bronfenbrenner's work is the multi-systems framework that arguably provides a better delineation of environmental contexts. More specific, the Constraints model was designed to focus on the person and his or her 'immediate' interactions with equipment or the environment, not factors creating or influencing the environment For example, specific effects of the microsystem (family, community) and macrosystem (cultural, political action) that could be change agents. However, the Constraints model combined with considerations of the multilevel and complex nature of ecological systems (described by Bronfenbrenner), hints at considerable promise for quality broad-based research.

Although each of the three models—Gibson's, Constraints, and Bronfenbenner's—has unique features and intentions for use, there is a key similarity worthy of note. Each stresses the importance of studying human development in context of the environmental setting and specific task. From another perspective, perhaps it is not too far out of reason to view Bronfenbenner's PPC and perhaps even T (Time), as constraints to development. However, Bronfenbenner's model, with its broad scope, arguably affords additional detail for studying the developmental course via 'process' interacting with the individual, and the construct of 'time.' Furthermore, when making a general comparison of Bronfenbrenner's model with the application of Gibson's work, the element of 'time' also seems to favor the former.

The following are two application examples for the PPCT model using what may be described as 'frontier' motor development issues (obviously, these are examples, not a definitive list).

Environmental Influence on Fundamental Motor Skill Ability and Later Physical Activity Level in Children

With the national interest in obesity levels in children and adults, researchers have sought to examine factors that may play a role in the attainment and continuance of physical activity across the lifespan—fundamental motor skill ability has been mentioned as one of those factors (e.g., Barnett, van Beurden, Morgan, Brooks, & Beard, 2009; Hardy, King, Farrell, Mcniven, & Howlett, 2009; Wrotniak, Epstein, & Dorn, 2006). Considerations for research include:

- *Person*—assessment of fundamental motor skills (e.g., running, throwing, catching, jumping) and physical fitness variables (e.g., cardiorespiratory endurance, muscular endurance, flexibility, body composition).
- *Process*—type, duration and frequency of play, sport, physical education, and recess; including physical education and youth sport instruction.
- *Context*—family characteristics (socioeconomic status, number of parents in the home, number of siblings, parent education, parents physical activity levels, parent attitudes

toward and knowledge of physical fitness and motor skills, daycare activity, community resources (facilities [play affordances], access, safety, crime, urban design).

- *Time*—systematic assessment (e.g., every three or six months) of the above variables over a designated timeframe (e.g., preschool to grade school to adolescence).

The Relation Between Early Motor Development and Cognitive Ability

The literature indicates that there is a resurgence of interest in the role of early motor development in cognitive ability and academic performance (e g., Bumin & Kavak, 2008; Piek et al., 2008; Wuang, Wang, Huang & Su, 2008). With that in mind, the following research considerations seem relevant:

- *Person*—assessment of birth status (e g., gestational age, birthweight), fine- and gross-motor ability, and cognitive and academic aptitude and ability.
- *Process*—type, duration and frequency of play (in- and outdoor), sport instruction, school instruction (both academic and physical education), and recess.
- Context—family characteristics (e.g., socioeconomic status, number of parents in the home, number of siblings, parent education), and affordances in and around the home (e.g., toys, equipment, playgrounds, parks, and daycare).
- *Time*—systematic assessment (e.g., every three or six months) of the above variables over a designated timeframe (e g., infancy to preschool, to grade school to adolescence).

Final Remarks

The primary intent of this paper was twofold: one, to bring attention to the need for studying and gaining a better understanding of environmental effects on child motor development; and second, to highlight a promising theoretical framework for that endeavor. For those that are students of research and active researchers looking for a theoretical framework and strategy for studying and understanding motor development from the perspective of the changing (biological) individual and multilevel environmental influence, Bronfenbrenner's views provide an array of options. Underscoring the importance of such endeavors is the reasonable notion that to change developmental status and foster positive future behaviors, one must identify and understand direct and indirect influences on human development. For those not interested in conducting research, this information also has applications. For example, teachers, administrators, and program directors interested in enhancing child development, and in this case, motor development, can use this information to affect change from a multi-level approach. What does the child need from the family, school, community, and government? Each context (local community) and person is likely to be unique. To approach the question from a diverse perspective, a diverse and multi-level framework is needed; such as that described here.

Perhaps Bronfenbrenner said it best when stating, "No society can long sustain itself unless its members have learned the sensitivities, motivations, and skills involved assisting and caring for other human beings" (2005, p. 14).

References

Andres, M., Olivier, E., & Badets, A. (2008). Action, words, and numbers: A motor contribution to semantic processing? *Current Directions in Psychological Science, 17*(5), 313–317.

Barnett, L. M., van Beurden, E., Morgan, P. J., Brooks, L. O., & Beard, J. R. (2009). Childhood motor skill proficiency as a predictor of adolescent physical activity. *Journal of Adolescent Health, 44*(3), 252–259.

Barrow, F. H., Armstrong, M. I., Vargo, A., & Boothroyd, R. A. (2007). Understanding the findings of resilience-related research for fostering the development of african american adolescents. *Child and Adolescent Psychiatric Clinics of North America, 16*(2), 393–413.

Bengoechea, E. G. (2002). Integrating knowledge and expanding horizons in developmental sport psychology: A bioecological perspective. *Quest, 54*(1), 1–20.

Bengoechea, E. G., & Johnson, G. (2001), Ecological systems theory and children's development in sport: Toward a process-person-context-time research paradigm. *Avante, 7,* 20–31.

Bronfenbrenner, U. (1979). *The ecology of human development: Experiments by nature and design.* Cambridge, MA: Harvard University Press.

Bronfenbrenner, U. (1995). Developmental ecology through space and time: a future perspective. In P. Moen, G. H. Elder & K. Lüscher (Eds.), *Examining lives in context: Perspectives on the ecology of human development* (pp. 599–618). Washington, D. C.: American Psychological Association.

Bronfenbrenner, U. (1988). Interacting systems in human development. Research paradigms: Present and future. In N. Bolger, A. Caspi, G. Downey & M. Moorehouse (Eds.), *Person in context: Developmental processes* (pp. 25–49). New York. NY: Cambridge University Press.

Bronfenbrenner, U., & Morris, P. (2006). The bioecological model of human development. In W. Damon & R. M. Lerner (Series Eds.) & R. M. Lerner (Vol. Ed.), *Handbook of child psychology: Vol. 1. Theoretical models of human development* (6th ed. pp. 793–828). New York: John Wiley.

Bronfenbrenner, U., & Morris, P. (1998). The ecology of developmental processes. In W. Damon, & R. M. Lerner, Richard M. (Eds.), *Handbook of child psychology: Volume 1: Theoretical models of human development* (5th ed.) (pp. 993–1028). Hoboken, NJ: John Wiley & Sons.

Bronfenbrenner, U. (2005). Bioecological theory of human development. In U. Bronfenbrenner (Ed.), *Making human being human: Bioecological perspectives on human development* (pp. 3–15). Thousand Oaks, CA: Sage.

Bumin, G., & Kavak, S. T. (2008). An investigation of the factors affecting handwriting performance in children with hemiplegic cerebral palsy. *Disability Rehabilitation, 30,* 1374–85.

Côté, J., & Hay, J. (2002). Family influences on youth sport performance and participation. In J. M. Silva & D. Stevens (Eds.), *Psychological foundations of sport* (pp. 503–519). Boston, MA: Allyn & Bacon.

Fernandino, L., & Iacoboni, M. (2010). Are cortical motor maps based on body parts or coordinated actions? *Brain and Language, 112*(1), 44–53.

Gabbard, C. (2008). *Lifelong motor development* (5th ed.). San Francisco, CA: Benjamin Cummings.

Garcia, C. M., & Saewyc, E. M. (2007). Perceptions of mental health among recently immigrated Mexican adolescents. *Issues in Mental Health Nursing. 28*(1), 37–54.

Gibson, E. J. (1988). Exploratory behavior in the development of perceiving, acting, and the acquiring of knowledge. *Annual Review of Psychology, 39,* 1–41.

Gibson, E. J. (2002). *Perceiving the affordances: A portrait of two psychologists.* Erlbaum: Mahwah, N. J.

Gilmer, M. J., Harrell, J. S., Miles, M. S., & Hepworth, J. T. (2003). Youth characteristics and contextual variables influencing physical activity in young adolescents of parents with premature coronary heart disease. *Journal of Pediatric Nursing, 18*(3), 159–168.

Harden, K. P., Turkheimer, E., & Loehlin, J. C. (2007). Genotype by environment interaction in adolescents' cognitive aptitude. *Behavior Genetics, 37*(2), 273–283.

Hardy, L. L., King, L., Farrell, L., Mcniven, R., & Howlett, S. (2009). Fundamental movement skills among Australian preschool children. *Journal of Science and Medicine in Sport,* in press, available online.

Johnson, J. S., Spencer, J. P., & Schöner, G. (2008). Moving to higher ground: The dynamic field theory and the dynamics of visual cognition. New *Ideas in Psychology, 26*(2), 227–251.

Krebs, R. (2009). Bronfenbrenner's bioecological theory of human development and the process of development of sports talent. *International Journal of Sport Psychology, 41*(1), 108–135.

Lerner, R. M. (2002). *Concepts and theories of human development* (3rd ed.). Hillsdale, NJ: Lawrence Erlbaum.

Liles, R. G., & Juhnke, G. A. (2008). Adolescent Diabetic Control: Using the Process-Person-Context-Time Model. *Journal of Counseling & Development, 86*(1), 75–84.

Logsdon, M. C., Hertweck, P., Ziegler, C., & Pinto-Foltz, M. (2008). Testing a Bioecological Model to Examine Social Support in Postpartum Adolescents. *Journal of Nursing Scholarship. 40*(2), 116–123.

Newell, K. M. (1986). Constraints on the development of coordination. In M. G., Wade, & H. T., Whiting (Eds.), *Motor development in children: Aspects of coordination and control* (pp. 341–361). Martinus Nijhoff Publishers: Amsterdam.

Piek, J. P., Dawson, L., Leigh, M., & Smith, N. G. (2008). The role of early fine and gross motor development on later motor and cognitive ability. *Human Movement Science, 27,* 668–681.

Salmon, J., & Timperio, A. (2007). Prevalence, trends and environmental influences on child and youth physical activity. *Medicine in Sport Sciences, 50,* 183–199.

Schwebel, D. C., & Brezausek, C. M. (2007). Nocturnal awakenings and pediatric injury risk. *Journal of Pediatric Psychology, 33*(3), 323–332.

Shonkoff, J. P., & Phillips, D. A. (Eds.), (2000). *From neurons to neighborhood: The science of early childhood development.* The National Academies Press.

Smith, L. B., & Thelen, E. (2003). Development as a dynamic system. *Trends in Cognitive Sciences, 7*(8), 343–348.

Stefanello, J. M. F. (1999). A participação da criança no desporto competitivo: uma tentativa de operacionalização e verificação empirica da proposta teórica de Bronfenbrenner [Child's participation in competitive sport: a temptative of operationalization and empirical verification of Bronfenbrenner's theoretical proposal]. Doctoral Dissertation, Universidade de Coimbra, Portugal.

Swick, K. J., & Williams, R. D. (2006). An analysis of Bronfenbrenner's bio-ecological perspective for early childhood educators: Implications for working with families experiencing stress. *Early Childhood Education Journal, 33*(5), 371–378.

Tudge, J. R. H., Odero, D. A., Hogan, D. M., & Etz, K. E. (2003). Relations between the everyday activities of preschoolers and their teachers' perceptions of their competence in the first years of school, *Early Childhood Research Quarterly, 18*(1), 42–64.

Wrotniak, B. H., Epstein, L. H., & Dorn, J. M. (2006). The relationship between motor proficiency and physical activity in children. *Pediatrics, 118,* 1758–65.

Wuang, Y. P., Wang, C. C., Huang, M. H., & Su, C. Y. (2008). Profiles and cognitive predictors of motor functions among early school-age children with mild intellectual disabilities. *Journal of Intellectual Disability Research, 52,* 1048–1060.

Yu, M., & Stiffman, A. R. (2007). Culture and environment as predictors of alcohol abuse/dependence symptoms in American Indian youths. *Addictive Behavior, 32*(10), 2253–2259.

Major Initiatives Related to Childhood Obesity and Physical Inactivity in Canada

The Year in Review

Mark S. Tremblay

Abstract

This manuscript briefly reviews 15 significant initiatives related to childhood obesity and physical inactivity in Canada between September 2010 and September 2011. These include the: announcement of a Federal-Provincial-Territorial framework for action to promote healthy weights; implementation of the nutrition labeling initiative; launch of the CBC "Live Right Now" campaign; announcement of the Public Health Agency of Canada's innovation strategy funding related to obesity; publication of the Canadian Health Measures Survey physical activity findings; release of new Canadian physical activity and sedentary behaviour guidelines; launch of ParticipACTION's "Think Again" campaign; workshop on building trust to address the epidemic of obesity; start of the Canadian Pediatric Weight Management Registry; initiation of "Our Health Our Future: A National Dialogue on Healthy Weights"; release of the Active Healthy Kids Canada Report Card on Physical Activity for Children and Youth; National Obesity Summit; Nature Play Day and Sports Day in Canada; development of the Canadian Assessment of Physical Literacy; and the creation of Active Canada 20/20—A National Physical Activity Plan. The diversity and intensity of activity addressing the childhood obesity and physical inactivity "epidemic" in Canada is encouraging and must be maintained and enhanced.

Key words: Obesity; overweight; motor activity; exercise; sedentary behaviour; policy

Mark S. Tremblay, "Major Initiatives Related to Childhood Obesity and Physical Inactivity in Canada: The Year in Review," *Canadian Journal of Public Health*, vol. 103, no. 3, pp. 164-169. Copyright © 2012 by Canadian Public Health Association.
Reprinted with permission. Provided by ProQuest LLC. All rights reserved.

Substantial increases in childhood obesity in Canada were observed several years ago[1] and have been confirmed on several occasions.[2,3] This is cause for concern because accumulating evidence shows that childhood obesity is related to morbidity and mortality in adulthood.[4] New, robust measures of the physical activity level of Canadian children indicate that only 4% of girls and 9% of boys[5] are meeting the new Canadian Physical Activity Guidelines[6] and Canada consistently receives failing grades on the Active Healthy Kids Canada Report Card which assesses the physical activity of Canadian children and youth.[7,8] Clearly, this is an important public health crisis and requires attention, resources and adaptations from all sectors.[9] The purpose of this review is to highlight 15 major initiatives that demonstrate the breadth and depth of efforts directed towards this issue in Canada between September 2010 and September 2011. The initiatives are presented in the order in which they occurred in the year in review. An attempt was made to include examples from several sectors but no systematic inclusion or exclusion criteria were applied and clearly many other important initiatives also occurred in this time period. Briefly summarizing these initiatives not only catalogues and consolidates these activities, but also provides information to other jurisdictions that are searching for possible solutions to the global challenge of childhood obesity and inactivity. A similar "year in review" was published in 2007.[10]

Major Initiatives in Canada—September 2010 to September 2011

F-P-T Framework for Action to Promote Healthy Weights

In September 2010, the Federal, Provincial and Territorial (F-P-T) Ministers of Health and/or Health Promotion/Healthy Living adopted a framework for action to promote healthy body weights, with a particular emphasis on curbing childhood obesity.[11] The framework for action is meant to build on the principles identified in the Pan-Canadian Healthy Living Strategy[12] and Declaration on Prevention and Promotion[13] through three integrated strategies:

- making childhood overweight and obesity a collective priority for action among multiple government departments and sectors of Canadian society;
- coordinating efforts on three key policy priorities—supportive environments, early action, nutritious foods; and
- measuring and reporting on collective progress.

The framework has a vision where "Canada is a country that creates and maintains the conditions for healthy weights so that children can have the healthiest possible lives."[11] The Declaration on Prevention and Promotion[13] commits to pursuing this vision through five guiding principles articulating that: prevention is a priority; prevention is the hallmark of a quality health system; prevention is the first step in management; health promotion has many approaches that should be used; health promotion is everyone's business. Further details on the framework can be found at: http://www.phac-aspc.gc.ca/hp-ps/hl-mvs/framework-cadre/indexeng.php.

Health Canada and FCPC Nutrition Labeling Initiative

In October 2010, Health Canada and the Food and Consumer Products of Canada (FCPC) announced the launch of a major nutrition labeling initiative. FCPC (http://www.fcpmc.com/home.asp) is the national industry association in Canada representing the food and consumer products industry. This government–industry collaboration includes a multi-faceted approach to explain the percent daily value to consumers, through messaging to appear on food packages, in-store, and in national media (print, television, online), directing Canadians to Health Canada's educational website. The website (www.healthcanada.gc.ca/dailyvalue) provides information and tips on how to use the percent daily value to make informed, healthy choices when purchasing food products by providing support to understand the nutrition labeling that clearly states the calories per serving and the percent of daily value of various macro- and micro-nutrients provided by one serving of the product. FCPC reports that 34 companies have joined the effort to provide Canadians with information they need to make informed food choices (http://www.fcpc.ca/adult-education/index.html).

Launch of CBC "Live Right Now" Campaign

In early January 2011, CBC (Canada's National Public Broadcaster) with support and guidance from Advisory Board Partners representing stakeholder groups, healthy living program delivery partners and content expert groups, launched a comprehensive, integrated, corporate-wide media-based campaign to promote healthy active living and healthy body weights. The "Live Right Now" campaign is a national initiative designed to inspire Canadians to join together and change the health of the country. The idea is built around the small steps everyone can take in their life to improve their health. Omnipresent messaging and branding was achieved through the exceptional communication reach of CBC through television, radio and on-line media, in both official languages. A variety of semi-sensational efforts fueled the campaign, including:

- "Village on a Diet"—a weekly reality television program that followed the people of Taylor, British Columbia in their quest to lose one ton of body weight in 10 weeks.
- "Million Pound Challenge"—an on-line challenge to Canadians to collectively pledge and lose one million pounds.
- Daily Challenges—healthy active living challenges for individuals and groups to provide constant variety and motivation.
- Media personality involvement—well-known media personalities from CBC provide regular reminders during their programs and participate in awareness-raising events across the country (e.g., mall appearances, fitness challenges).

Details on the CBC "Live Right Now" campaign are available at http://www.cbc.ca/liverightnow.

PHAC Innovation Funding Announcement Related to Obesity

The Public Health Agency of Canada (PHAC), through its Innovation Strategy (http://www.phac-aspc.gc.ca/ph-sp/fund-fonds/indexeng.php), released two strategic calls in 2010 for applications for government funding for Phase 1 projects (pilot or feasibility) aimed at preventing or managing obesity. In January 2011, the funding announcements were made for both strategic funding streams. The "Achieving Healthier Weights in Canadian Communities" call for proposals had a prevention focus and 37 projects were funded up to $250,000 each, with a 12–15 month project timeframe. The "Managing Obesity Across the Lifecycle: An Interventions Approach" call for proposals had an obesity treatment and management focus and 5 projects were funded up to $250,000 each, also with a 12–15 month project timeframe. Pending the feasibility and success of these Phase 1 projects, some will be eligible to apply for Phase 2 support (greater financial support over a longer period to extend the reach and/or scope of the project). More details on the solicitation process are available at http://www.phacaspc.gc.ca/ph-sp/fund-fonds/ahwcc-apscc-eng.php.

Publication of CHMS Physical Activity Findings

The Canadian Health Measures Survey (CHMS) conducted by Statistics Canada is the most comprehensive direct health measures survey ever completed in Canada.[14] This nationally representative survey is now an ongoing cross-sectional survey. Cycle 1 was completed in 2007–2009 and included, for the first time, a direct measurement of the physical activity and sedentary behaviours of Canadians. Physical activity was measured for 7 consecutive days using Actical accelerometers.[15] In January 2011, the physical activity results were released through a media advisory and two peer-reviewed manuscripts: one focused on children[5] and one on adults.[16] The results indicated that 7% of children[5] were meeting the new Canadian Physical Activity Guidelines,[6] assessed as accumulating 60 minutes of moderate- to vigorous-intensity physical activity (MVPA) on at least 6 days per week. The findings also showed that boys are more active than girls (9% versus 4% meet the guidelines); physical activity declines with increasing age; physical activity declines with increasing adiposity in boys; and Canadian children and youth are sedentary for approximately 8.6 hours per day (62% of waking hours).[5] These findings help to substantiate the health-related fitness findings from the CHMS released in 2010 that demonstrated that Canadian children today are taller, heavier, fatter, rounder, weaker and less flexible than in 1981.[17]

Release of New Canadian Physical Activity and Sedentary Behaviour Guidelines

In January 2011, the Canadian Society for Exercise Physiology (http://www.csep.ca), in partnership with ParticipACTION (http://www.participACTION.com), released the new Canadian Physical Activity Guidelines for Children, Youth, Adults, and Older Adults.[6] These new guidelines were based on a rigorous, systematic and transparent review and consultation process[6] and provided an update to the previous guidelines released between 1998 and 2002. The guidelines were developed in consultation with domestic and international experts with an intention to harmonize the physical activity recommendations with other countries and jurisdictions. The new guidelines state:

"For health benefits, children (aged 5–11 years) and youth (aged 12–17 years) should accumulate at least 60 min of moderate- to vigorous-intensity physical activity daily. This should include:

- vigorous-intensity activities at least 3 days per week.
- activities that strengthen muscle and bone at least 3 days per week.

More daily physical activity provides greater health benefits."[6]

In February 2011, approximately 3 weeks after the release of the new Canadian Physical Activity Guidelines, the Canadian Society for Exercise Physiology released the first-ever Canadian Sedentary Behaviour Guidelines for School-aged Children and Youth.[18] These guidelines were prompted by the very high levels of sedentary behaviour among children and youth[5,7,8] and emerging evidence of the health risks associated with sedentary behaviour independent of physical activity.[19] The guidelines state that:

"For health benefits, children (aged 5–11 years) and youth (aged 12–17 years) should minimize the time they spend being sedentary each day. This may be achieved by:

- limiting recreational screen time to no more than 2 hours per day; lower levels are associated with additional health benefits.
- limiting sedentary (motorized) transport, extended sitting and time spent indoors throughout the day."[18]

The release of these new guidelines generated significant national media attention with nearly 100 million media impressions for the two releases combined. Dissemination strategies are in place with various stakeholder groups in an effort to maximize the public health impact of the release of the new guidelines. The new guidelines and related materials are available at http://www.csep.ca/english/view.asp?x=804.

Launch of ParticipACTION's "Think Again" Campaign

In January 2011, Canada's internationally renowned physical activity social marketing and communications organization "ParticipACTION"[20,21] launched its latest mass media campaign called "Think Again". ParticipACTION has an adult brand awareness of approximately 85% in Canada[20] and has been very successful in raising awareness of the importance of, and opportunities for, physical activity. The Think Again campaign is targeted to mothers of children aged 6–12 years and was created because most Canadian mothers are concerned about the level of inactivity in Canadian children, but think that it does not apply to their own children. Therefore, the campaign goals are to make mothers aware that it is likely that their own children are not active enough and to motivate them to take action to get their children more active. The campaign includes short television commercials, posters and online materials. More details on ParticipACTION and the Think Again campaign can be found at http://www.participaction.com/enus/Home.aspx.

Building Trust to Address the Epidemic of Obesity

In February 2011, a workshop was held in Toronto on "Building Trust to Address the Epidemic of Obesity and Chronic Diseases". The workshop included thought leaders from industry, government, academia and the not-for-profit sectors. This workshop was the latest in a series of discussions on the importance of authentic trust to improve the prospects for intersectoral and intrasectoral collaborations on obesity. The need for multisectoral approaches and partnerships is recognized and promoted,[9] yet the trust and motivation surrounding many partnerships and initiatives are questioned.[22] The discussions to date have expressed the need to move beyond the "cordial hypocrisy" that currently infects many public–private partnerships. A recently published commentary stated that "When they partner, health organizations become inadvertent pitchmen for the food industry. They would do well to remember that corporate dollars always introduce perceived or real biases that may taint or distort evidence-based lifestyle recommendations and health messages."[22] The "building trust" discussions aim to reduce the rate and incidence of obesity through more and better intersectoral and intrasectoral partnerships anchored on trust. More details on the building trust initiative can be found at http://www.youtube.com/watch?v=sZh8jAqeLAU.

A spinoff of the building trust initiative was the development of *The Partnership Protocol*,[23] a roadmap created by a multisectoral steering committee that documented the principles and approach for successful private/not-for-profit partnership in physical activity and sport. *The Partnership Protocol*, released in November 2010, explains seven guiding principles for effective partnerships (share each other's equity; stay true to who you are; acknowledge and manage risk; create compelling communications; inspire, motivate and activate your stakeholders; be clear; measure and evaluate) and outlines a three-phased approach to effective partnerships, including assessing potential partners, building partnerships and managing partnerships. *The Partnership Protocol* is designed to help organizations establish, build and sustain effective partnerships using the advice and best practices of a wide variety of experts from the world of academia, business and not-for-profit organizations.[23]

Canadian Pediatric Weight Management Registry Begins

Pediatric obesity researchers in Canada obtained research funding to develop a pan-Canadian pediatric weight management registry (CANPWR) to examine the health of obese youth, the effectiveness of pediatric weight management in Canada, and to create a research platform to enable future interventions to be examined. This prospective cohort study began enrolling patients in February–March 2011 who were newly referred to pediatric weight management programs across Canada. Children and adolescents presenting to Canadian pediatric weight management programs are approached for interest by the clinical teams and consent is obtained for those interested in being a part of the registry. This pilot and feasibility phase of CANPWR involves five sites (Vancouver, Edmonton, Hamilton, Ottawa, Montreal). Harmonized core measures are in place and include socio-demographic, medical history, anthropometric, clinical chemistry, lifestyle behaviour and psychosocial measures. The study objectives are to:

1. assemble a common database of health outcomes and their determinants in obese youth;
2. characterize health status, changes in health over time and key determinants of metabolic and psychosocial health status before and after intervention of obese children receiving weight management care; and
3. establish and pilot a multi-centre, web-based data platform of standardized measures and data management processes to support the national pediatric weight management registry.

More details on CANPWR are available at http://www.obesitynetwork.ca/page. aspx?menu=51&app=225&cat1=577&tp=2&lk=no.

Our Health Our Future: A National Dialogue on Healthy Weights

Emanating from the first initiative described in this paper, the framework endorsed by multisectoral ministers[11] was followed by a launch, in March 2011, of *Our Health Our Future: A National Dialogue on Healthy Weights*, to engage Canadians in a discussion on physical activity, healthy eating and healthy weights, leading to a national summit in the fall of 2011. *Our Health Our Future* recognizes that a complex system of factors contribute to overweight and obesity, and that to address the causes of obesity we need to change the social and physical environments that influence children's and families' eating habits and physical activity levels. This initiative recognizes that all Canadians can play a role in identifying ways to create the conditions that support healthy eating, physical activity and healthy weights. The goal of *Our Health Our Future* is to kick-start a longer-term societal shift to support healthy weights by making the environments where children live, learn and play more supportive of physical activity and healthy eating.

Our Health Our Future works through an online idea forum and submissions centre (www. ourhealthourfuture.gc.ca) where youth, parents, caregivers and all Canadians can share their perspectives on the factors that contribute to childhood obesity and options that can influence and support healthy choices. Key stakeholders—including youth, non-governmental organizations, national Aboriginal organizations, media and industry—were invited to face-toface dialogues across the country to explore areas for joint and/or complementary action. The outcomes led to the development of a report and recommendations for action for the F-P-T Health/ Healthy Living Ministers.

In February 2011, the F-P-T Ministers of Sport, Physical Activity and Recreation (SPAR) announced a commitment to take action to support sport, physical activity and healthy weights. Ministers recognized that the after-school time period constitutes a prime opportunity for increased physical activity among children and youth. In an effort to achieve the 2015 physical activity targets for children and youth set in 2008, Ministers agreed to explore opportunities to work with other departments and stakeholders to identify shared approaches aimed at increasing physical activity in the after-school period. The Ministers also endorsed the Declaration on Prevention and Promotion and the document "Curbing Childhood Obesity: A FPT Framework for Action to Promote Healthy Weights,"[13] and agreed to work with Ministers of Health and Health Promotion/Healthy Living who released these initiatives in September 2010.[11,13]

Release of Active Healthy Kids Canada Report Card

On April 26, 2011, Active Healthy Kids Canada released their seventh Annual Report Card on Physical Activity for Children and Youth.[8] The Active Healthy Kids Canada Report Card provides comprehensive, evidence-informed assessments of the "state of the nation" with respect to physical activity for Canadian children and youth. The preparation and distribution of the report card is meant to serve as an accountability index for all Canadians, a surveillance mechanism, an advocacy tool for physical activity leaders and organizations, a policy driver and a process for identifying research and surveillance needs. The 2011 Report Card indicated substantial room for improvement, assigning a failing grade overall, substantiated by evidence from the CHMS[5] and the CANPLAY survey from the Canadian Fitness and Lifestyle Research Institute.[24] Active Healthy Kids Canada has a mandate to "power the movement to get kids moving" and the report card provides recommendations for action to "improve the grade", challenging all stakeholders to increase the physical activity of children and youth. The media attention the report card release receives each year has had an incredible impact, with between 100–160 million media impressions each of the past three years. Details of the report card process and evaluations are being published[25] and copies of all reports cards from the past seven years are available at https://www.activehealthykids.ca.

Canadian Obesity Network "National Obesity Summit"

In late April 2011, the Canadian Obesity Network hosted its *2nd National Obesity Summit* (http://www.con-obesitysummit.ca). The four-day Summit attracted almost 800 delegates from across Canada and as far away as China, South Africa and Australia. Workshops, symposia, free communication sessions, poster presentations, social events and award ceremonies created ample opportunity for learning, discussion and networking. National, provincial and local media interest were strong, as was social media with almost 500 Tweets from the event reaching upwards of 80,000 people.

Nature Play Day and Sports Day in Canada

In his best-selling book *Last Child in the Woods,* Richard Louv coined the phrase "nature-deficit disorder" to describe the progressive withdrawal of contemporary-living children from nature and the outdoors.[26] The book served as a call to action and the Child and Nature Alliance of Canada (http://www.childnature.ca) responded with a number of initiatives, including an invitation to all Canadians and communities to celebrate outdoor play and join the Child and Nature Alliance for Nature Play Day. This Canadawide day of playing in nature was about finding a simple way to connect with nearby nature in backyards, local parks, schoolyards, rooftop gardens, or wherever. Communities, schools, businesses and households across Canada were invited to participate and register Nature Play Day events on the Child and Nature Alliance map. The first annual Nature Play Day Canada was held on June 15, 2011. More details are available at http://www.child-nature.ca/nature-play-day-canada.

On September 17, 2011, the second annual *Sports Day in Canada* celebrated sport, from grass-roots to high-performance levels, in communities across Canada. *Sports Day in Canada* capped off a week of thousands of local sporting events and activities, open houses and try-it days showcasing sport at all levels, and included a special television broadcast on CBC Sports. *Sports Day in Canada* is presented by CBC Sports (http://www.cbc.ca/sports), ParticipACTION (http://www.Participaction.com) and True Sport (http://www.truesportpur.ca/en/home) and is guided by a committee of national sporting organizations and their networks of coaches, athletes and enthusiasts across the country. It is an opportunity for all Canadians to celebrate the power of sport to build community, fortify our national spirit and facilitate healthy, active living. For more details, see http://sportsday.cbc.ca.

Canadian Assessment of Physical Literacy Developed

The aim of physical education, community sport and active living initiatives is to systematically develop physical competence so that children are able to move efficiently, effectively and safely and gain an understanding of what they are doing. The outcome—"Physical Literacy"—is as fundamentally important to children's education and development as numeracy and literacy. Physical literacy is a construct that captures the essence of what a quality physical education or a quality community sport/activity program aims to achieve. It is the foundation of characteristics, attributes, behaviours, awareness, knowledge and understanding related to healthy active living and the promotion of physical recreation opportunities.[27,28] Physical literacy is deemed to have four core domains: a) physical fitness (cardio-respiratory, muscular strength and flexibility), b) motor behaviour (fundamental motor skill proficiency), c) physical activity behaviours (objectively-measured daily activity), and d) psychosocial/cognitive factors (awareness, knowledge and understanding).[27,28]

No aggregate assessment of physical literacy exists. For the past two years, the Healthy Active Living and Obesity Research Group (HALO) at the Children's Hospital of Eastern Ontario Research Institute (http://www.haloresearch.ca) has been working on developing the Canadian Assessment of Physical Literacy (CAPL) to address this assessment gap. This effort has required reviewing the existing literature, evaluating existing assessment protocols, developing new assessment protocols, pilot testing various iterations of the CAPL, and developing scoring and reporting systems. Funding has been received from many stakeholder groups and funding agencies, and this broad base of support is indicative of the need for such an instrument. To date, nearly 2,000 children have been tested using various iterations of the CAPL. A final version for children aged 9–12 years will be available in 2012.

Creation of "Active Canada 20/20"

Though Canada has the Pan-Canadian Healthy Living Strategy,[12] at present it has no national physical activity strategy. Led by ParticipACTION, and with broad sector involvement, *Active Canada 20/20—A Physical Activity Strategy for Canada* is the response to an urgent national need to increase physical activity and reduce sedentary living. *Active Canada 20/20*, which is nearing completion, will provide a clear vision and a change agenda describing what Canada must do to increase physical activity and reduce sedentary behaviour, thereby reducing future disease risk and achieving the many benefits of a society that is active and healthy. It is designed to engage decision makers and rally the collaborative, coordinated and consistent efforts of all stakeholders at every level to make a difference for the well-being and sustainability of our communities, our country, our social programs and, most importantly, our people. For more information on *Active Canada 20/20,* see http://www.activecanada2020.ca/home.

Conclusion

With concern over the increasing prevalence of non-communicable diseases (NCDs) worldwide, the United Nations convened a high-level meeting in New York on September 19, 2011

TABLE 14.1   Summary of Initiatives Highlighted in the Year in Review

Policy

- F-P-T Framework for Action to Promote Healthy Weights
- Public Healthy Agency of Canada's innovation strategy funding related to obesity
- Active Canada 20/20—A National Physical Activity Plan
- Nutrition labeling initiative

Campaigns/Advocacy

- CBC "Live Right Now" campaign
- ParticipACTION's "Think Again" campaign
- Nature Play Day and Sports Day in Canada

Research/Research Dissemination/Guidelines

- Canadian Health Measures Survey physical activity findings
- Canadian Physical Activity and Sedentary Behaviour Guidelines
- Active Healthy Kids Canada Report Card on Physical Activity and Youth
- Canadian Pediatric Weight Management Registry
- Development of the Canadian Assessment of Physical Literacy

Conferences/Workshops/Consultations

- Workshop on building trust to address the epidemic of obesity
- National Obesity Summit
- Our Health Our Future: A national dialogue on healthy weights

to endorse a declaration on the prevention and control of NCDs.[29] Canada, among many other countries, immediately endorsed the United Nations declaration. NCDs—chiefly cardiovascular diseases, cancers, chronic respiratory diseases and diabetes—now represent nearly two thirds of global deaths, with a disproportionate number of deaths occurring in developing countries. The declaration states that "prevention must be the cornerstone of the global response to NCDs". Resolving the global childhood obesity and inactivity crisis must in turn be the cornerstone of any global prevention initiative.

The diversity and intensity of activity surrounding the childhood obesity and inactivity "epidemic" in Canada is encouraging (see Table 14.1 for summary). To achieve success and to have a positive influence on the health of Canadian children and the environments where they live, learn and play, interventions and policy changes will need to be developed, implemented, monitored and evaluated; recommendations will need to be acted upon; ongoing research and surveillance will be required; and clinical practice will require adaptations. All sectors (governments, industry, health care, media, communities, schools, and families) must participate in an aggressive, informed and sustained movement to recalibrate the behaviours of Canadian children to achieve sustained and pervasive healthy living outcomes. Going forward, it will be important to assess the impact and implementation of the programs listed in this brief review while also holding various sectors and agencies accountable for the implementation of existing and future recommendations for action.

References

1   Tremblay MS, Willms JD. Secular trends in body mass index of Canadian children. *CMAJ* 2000;163(11):1429–33; erratum 2001;164(7):970.

2   Shields M. Overweight and obesity among children and youth. *Health Rep* 2006;17(3):27–42.

3   Janssen I, Shields M, Craig CL, Tremblay MS. Prevalence and secular changes in abdominal obesity in Canadian adolescents and adults, 1981 to 2007–2009. *Obes Rev* 2011;12(6):397–405.

4   Reilly JJ, Kelly J. Long-term impact of overweight and obesity in childhood and adolescence on morbidity and premature mortality in adulthood: Systematic review. *Int J Obes* 2011;35:891–98.

5   Colley RC, Garriguet D, Janssen I, Craig CL, Clarke J, Tremblay MS. Physical activity levels of Canadian Children and Youth: Results from the 2007–2009 Canadian Health Measures Survey. *Health Rep* 2011;22(1):15–24.

6   Tremblay MS, Warburton DER, Janssen I, Paterson DH, Latimer AE, Rhodes RE, et al. New Canadian Physical Activity Guidelines. *Appl Physiol Nutr Metab* 2011;36(1):36–46.

7   Active Healthy Kids Canada. Healthy Habits Start Earlier Than You Think—The Active Healthy Kids Canada Report Card on Physical Activity for Children and Youth. Toronto, ON: Active Healthy Kids Canada, 2010.

8   Active Healthy Kids Canada. Don't Let This Be The Most Physical Activity Our Kids Get After School. The Active Healthy Kids Canada Report Card on Physical Activity for Children and Youth. Toronto: Active Healthy Kids Canada, 2011.

9   Committee on Prevention of Obesity in Children and Youth, Institute of Medicine. Preventing Childhood Obesity: Health in the Balance. Washington, DC: National Academies Press, 2005.

10 Tremblay MS. Major initiatives related to childhood obesity and physical inactivity in Canada: The year in review. *Can J Public Health* 2007;98:457–59.

11 Curbing Childhood Obesity: A Federal, Provincial, and Territorial Framework for Action to Promote Healthy Weights. 2010. Available at: http://www.phac-aspc.gc.ca/hp-ps/hl-mvs/framework-cadre/index-eng.php (Accessed December 2, 2011).

12 Secretariat for the Intersectoral Healthy Living Network, F/P/T Healthy Living Task Group, and the F/P/T Advisory Committee on Population Health and Health Security (ACPHHS). The Integrated Pan-Canadian Healthy Living Strategy. Ottawa, ON: Minister of Health, 2005. Available at: http://www.phacaspc.gc.ca/hl-vs-strat/pdf/hls_e.pdf (Accessed December 2, 2011).

13 Creating a Healthier Canada: Making Prevention a Priority. A Declaration on Prevention and Promotion from Canada's Ministers of Health and Health Promotion/Healthy Living. 2010. Available at: http://www.phac-aspc.gc.ca/hp-ps/hl-mvs/declaration/intro-eng.php (Accessed December 2, 2011).

14 Tremblay MS, Wolfson M, Connor Gorber S. Canadian Health Measures Survey: Background, rationale and overview. *Health Rep* 2007;18(Suppl.):7–20.

15 Colley RC, Connor Gorber S, Tremblay MS. Quality control and data reduction procedures for accelerometry-derived measures of physical activity. *Health Rep* 2010;21(1):63–70.

16 Colley RC, Garriguet D, Janssen I, Craig CL, Clarke J, Tremblay MS. Physical activity levels of Canadian adults: Results from the 2007–2009 Canadian Health Measures Survey. *Health Rep* 2011;22(1):7–14.

17 Tremblay MS, Shields M, Laviolette M, Craig CL, Janssen I, Connor Gorber S. Fitness of Canadian children and youth: Results from the 2007–2009 Canadian Health Measures Survey. *Health Rep* 2010;21(1):7–20.

18 Tremblay MS, LeBlanc AG, Janssen I, Kho ME, Hicks A, Murumets K, et al. Canadian Sedentary Behaviour Guidelines for School-aged Children and Youth. *Appl Physiol Nutr Metab* 2011;36(1):59–64.

19 Tremblay MS, Colley RC, Saunders TJ, Healy GN, Owen N. Physiological and health implications of a sedentary lifestyle. *Appl Physiol Nutr Metab* 2010;35:725–40.

20 ParticipACTION. The Mouse that Roared: A marketing and health communications success story. *Can J Public Health* 2004;95(suppl. 2):S1–S44.

21 Tremblay MS, Craig CL. ParticipACTION: Overview and introduction of baseline research on the 'New' ParticipACTION. *Int J Behav Nutr Physical Act* 2009;6:84.

22 Freedhoff Y, Hebert PC. Partnerships between health organizations and the food industry risk derailing public health nutrition. *CMAJ* 2011;183(3):291–92.

23 The Partnership Protocol—principles and approach for successful private/not-for-profit partnership in physical activity and sport. ParticipACTION, October, 2010. Available at: http://www.participaction.com/en-us/For-Partners-And-Stakeholders/Research-Library. aspx (Accessed December 2, 2011).

24 Tudor-Locke C, Craig CL, Cameron C, Griffiths JM. Canadian children's and youth's pedometer-determined steps/day, parent-reported TV watching time, and overweight/obesity: The CANPLAY Surveillance Study. *Int J Behav Nutr Physical Act* 2011;8:66.

25 Colley RC, Brownrigg M, Tremblay MS. The Active Healthy Kids Canada Report Card on Physical Activity for Children and Youth. *Health Promot Pract* 2012; doi:10.1177/1524839911432929.

26 Louv R. *Last Child in the Woods—Saving Our Children from Nature-Deficit Disorder.* Chapel Hill, NC: Algonquin Books of Chapel Hill, 2005.

27 Tremblay MS, Lloyd M. Physical literacy measurement—the missing piece. *Phys Health Educ J* 2010;76(1):26–30.

28 Lloyd M, Colley R, Tremblay MS. Advancing the debate on 'fitness testing' for children: Perhaps we're riding the wrong animal. *Pediatr Exerc Sci* 2010;22:176–82.

29 United Nations General Assembly. Political declaration of the High-level Meeting of the General Assembly on the Prevention and Control of Noncommunicable Diseases. Sixty-sixth Session, September, 2011.

Discussion Questions

1. Describe the importance of physical activity in early childhood life.
2. In your own opinion, how might limitations in physical and motor development impact other areas of development for children? Provide examples.
3. What are some milestones of the physical development of infants and toddlers? Explain your answer.
4. How does physical development affect the cognitive development of infants? Why?
5. How can adults help infants and toddlers develop their physical and motor skills?

UNIT IV

SOCIAL AND EMOTIONAL DEVELOPMENT

The Developing Toddler and Early Childhood

Susan Whitbourne and Cynthia R. Davis

Emotion Regulation

Emotion regulation is the ability to self-regulate and adjust emotions and emotional expression in a way that is appropriate for a given social situation. It operates alongside executive functioning and many of the cognitive functions under its control. Emotion regulation is a cognitive task, primarily maintained by the caregiver at first who serves as an external regulator letting the child know what is acceptable behavior and what is not. Then gradually, over time, the child is able to self-regulate without the help of a caregiver.

Emotions are fundamental to organizing cognitive processes, learning, and behaviors. These cognitive processes help us interpret and regulate our emotions in a given social context, so that emotions and cognition work together. In many cases emotions need to be calmed, but in other cases it is appropriate and sometimes necessary for a child to become excited or upset—for example, if they are hurt or in danger and need the help of a caregiver. Like many of our human characteristics and behaviors, think of emotion regulation on a continuum as presented in Table 15.1. As you can imagine, the display of appropriate emotions is closely tied to cultural norms.

Emotion Displays

There is a long-held theory that six basic emotions are universal across the human species: happy, surprise, fear, disgust, anger, and sadness. This theory, also known as a "universality hypothesis," argues that based on our evolutionary past and our biological makeup the expression of these emotions is universal because we all use the same facial movements to convey these states (Susskind et al., 2008). However,

Susan Whitbourne and Cynthia R. Davis, *Selection from "The Developing Toddler and Early Childhood,"* Lifespan Development: Biopsychosocial Perspectives, pp. 116-119, 328-368. Copyright © 2018 by Cognella, Inc. Reprinted with permission.

TABLE 15.1 Characterizations of Emotion Regulation in Children (Carlson & Wang, 2007)

Under-controlled	• Low in emotion regulation, impulsive, and high in emotional intensity • Easily frustrated and prone to reactive aggression
Optimally regulated	• Controlled but flexible and use adaptive means of coping with emotions • Described as relatively popular and socially competent
Highly inhibited	• Exhibit self-control but lack flexibility • Tend to be socially withdrawn and sad or anxious

more recent research suggests that there are discrete variations in the ways different cultures convey these emotions. For example, in Westerners, these six emotions each have distinct facial movements. But among Easterners, there is some overlap in facial movements across emotions such as fear, disgust, and anger. Westerners use facial muscles to convey these different emotions, whereas Easterners tend to use eye movements of varying intensity to differentiate among certain basic emotions.

We need to consider what certain cultures deem appropriate for emotional expression in a particular social context. These learned behaviors are known as **emotional display rules** (Ekman & Friesen, 1969). Display rules often go hand in hand with the value a culture places on a particular emotion. If a culture values sadness over disgust, then the emotional expression of disgust is more likely to be repressed. Differences in emotional display rules according to cultural norms has been widely studied in a number of countries including the United States, Japan, Hong Kong, South Korea, Italy, England, Russia, Costa Rica, and Canada; and studies have shown differences among certain ethnic groups within the United States.

One could point to research showing that Japan does not permit expressions of anger, contempt, and, disgust as much as certain North American cultures (Safdar et al., 2009). However, culture and its display rules are not the only things that govern an emotional expression. There are also individual factors that lead to the display of emotions. Maybe you saw U.S. gymnast McKayla Maroney on the medal podium at the 2012 Summer Olympics. She thought her performance was better than the gold medalist's and made a face that perhaps conveyed her disagreement with the judges' decision. During the same year, silver medalist Kōhei Uchimura did not expect to do well going into the competition but his emotional expression conveys happiness and content.

Research also shows even across different cultures, men tend to express anger, contempt, and disgust more than women and women tend to express sadness and fear more than men do (Safdar et al., 2009). In a comparison of Dutch and Iranian children, researchers found that Iranian children used more display rules in their expression of emotions. They were more likely to do so with family members than friends. Dutch children were more likely to exhibit display rules with their friends rather than their families. Iranian children stated they used display rules with family members for the good of others and for self-protective reasons (Novin, Banerjee, Dadkhah, & Rieffe, 2009). The same researchers also examined the strategies children of different cultures use for dealing with emotionally charged situations. Chinese children were more likely to be tolerant of an aggressor, whereas Dutch children were more likely to confront the aggressor to achieve their personal goals (Novin, Rieffe, Banerjee, Miers, & Cheung, 2011).

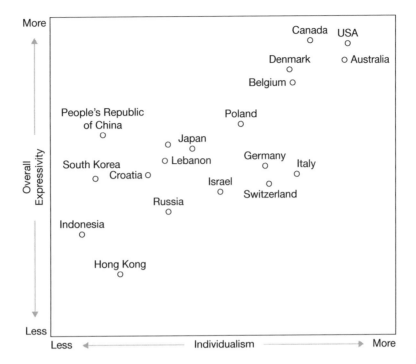

FIGURE 15.1 Note that countries with lower scores on individualism also tend to have lower scores on emotional expressivity, whereas countries with higher scores on individualism tend to have higher scores on emotional expressivity (adapted from Matsumoto, Yoo, & Fontaine, 2008).

Note: Much of this relationship is carried by the relationship between individualism with happiness and surprise.

Source: "Mapping Expressive Differences Around the World: The Relationship Between Emotional Display Rules and Individualism Versus Collectivism." *Journal of Cross Cultural Psychology*, vol. 39, no. 1.

As with executive functioning, emotion regulation can be seen in infancy when in an effort to self-soothe an infant may suck a pacifier or her thumb, avert her gaze, turn her head, or seek proximity to a caregiver when distressed. Toddlers will engage in some of these and other behaviors in an attempt to regulate. For example, a toddler might be told they cannot play with a particular object, so they will distract themselves by playing with another toy. Typically developing children become increasingly better at emotion regulation as social demands become greater.

As one might expect, successful emotion regulation in preschoolers is associated with social competence and positive engagement with peers (Carlson & Wang, 2007). Emotion regulation has even been associated with pediatric obesity. Researchers believe this connection lies within the vagus nerve, a large **cranial nerve** that connects the brain directly to the abdomen to relay information between the brain and the body's organs. The vagus nerve is responsible for telling the brain when the stomach is full and is linked to physiological responses to coping, and thus, emotion regulation. Therefore, it may be children who have a difficult time with emotion regulation also have challenges knowing when they are full. Another possible explanation is the notion of "emotional eating," or eating as a way of coping with stress or negative emotions. Emotional eating has been demonstrated in adulthood, but it is unclear whether children respond to stress in these same ways and whether they, too, are prone to emotional eating (Graziano, Calkins, & Keane, 2010). Another possibility for the link between emotion regulation and childhood obesity is that childhood stressors increase allostatic load and activate hormones from the hypothalamic-pituitary-adrenal axis. The body tries to prepare for a "fight or flight" response and seeks out high fat, and high energy food that can lead to fat storage and obesity (Davis, under review).

References

Carlson, S. M., & Wang, T. S. (2007). Inhibitory control and emotion regulation in preschool children. *Cognitive Development, 22*, 489–510. doi:10.1016/j.cogdev.2007.08.002

Ekman, P., Sorenson, E. R., & Friesen, W. V. (1969). Pan-cultural elements in facial displays of emotion. *Science, 164*(3875), 86–88.

Graziano, P. A., Calkins, S. D., & Keane, S. P. (2010). Toddler self-regulation skills predict risk for pediatric obesity. *International Journal of Obesity, 34*, 633–641.

Novin, S., Banerjee, R., Dadkhah, A., & Rieffe, C. (2009). Self-reported use of emotional display rules in the Netherlands and Iran: Evidence for sociocultural influence. *Social Development, 18*, 397–411. doi:10.1111/j.1467-9507.2008.00485x

Novin, S., Rieffe, C., Banerjee, R., Miers, A. C., & Cheung, J. (2011). Anger response styles in Chinese and Dutch children: A socio-cultural perspective on anger regulation. *British Journal of Developmental Psychology, 29*, 806–822. doi:10.1348/2044-835x.002010

Safdar, S., Friedlmeier, W., Matsumoto, D., Yoo, S. H., Kwantes, C. T., Kakai, H., & Shigemasu, E. (2009). Variations of emotional display rules within and across cultures: A comparison between Canada, USA, and Japan. *Canadian Journal of Behavioural Science, 41*, 1.

Susskind, J. M., Lee, D. H., Cusi, A., Feiman, R., Grabski, W., & Anderson, A. K. (2008). Expressing fear enhances sensory acquisition. *Nature Neuroscience, 11*, 843–850.

The Role of Play in Social and Emotional Development

Peter Gray

Playing with other children, away from adults, is how children learn to make their own decisions, control their emotions and impulses, see from others' perspectives, negotiate differences with others, and make friends. In short, play is how children learn to take control of their lives.

Lessons from Informal Sports

Imagine an old-fashioned sandlot game of baseball. A bunch of kids of various ages show up at a vacant lot, hoping they'll find others to play with. Some come on foot, others by bicycle; some alone, some with friends. Someone brings a bat, another brings a ball (which may not be an actual baseball), and several have fielders' gloves. There are enough people for a game, so they decide to play. The two reputably best players serve as captains, and they choose sides. They lay out the bases—hats, Frisbees, or any objects of suitable size. There aren't enough players to fill all the positions, so they improvise. No adult is present to tell the kids what to do or to settle disputes; they have to work everything out for themselves. This way of playing baseball is actually *play*. It is an activity chosen and directed by the players themselves and done for its own sake, not for some external reward.

Now imagine a Little League game. It's played on a manicured field, which looks like a smaller version of the fields where professional games are played. Most kids are driven there, partly because it's far from home and partly because their parents are behind this activity. Many parents stay for the game, to show their support for their young players. The teams are predetermined, part of an ongoing league. Each team has an adult coach, and an adult umpire calls balls, strikes, and outs. An official

Peter Gray, "The Role of Play in Social and Emotional Development," *Free to Learn: Why Unleashing the Instinct to Play Will Make Our Children Happier, More Self-Reliant, and Better Students for Life*, pp. 157-180, 245-246, 249-264. Copyright © 2013 by Perseus Books Group. Reprinted with permission.

score is kept, and over the course of the season wins and losses are tracked to determine the championship team. Some of the players really want to be there; others are there because their parents coaxed or pushed them into it.

The informal, self-directed way of playing baseball or any other game contains valuable lessons that formal, adult-directed games do not. Here are five such lessons, among the most valuable that anyone can learn in life.

Lesson 1: To keep the game going, you have to keep everyone happy.   The most fundamental freedom in all true play is the freedom to quit. In an informal game, nobody is forced to stay, and there are no coaches, parents, or other adults to disappoint if you quit. The game can continue only as long as a sufficient number of players choose to continue. Therefore, everyone must do his or her share to keep the other players happy, including the players on the other team.

This means that you show certain restraints in the informal game beyond those dictated by the stated rules, which derive instead from your understanding of each player's needs. You don't run full force into second base if the second baseman is smaller than you and might get hurt, even though it might be considered good strategy in Little League (where, in fact, a coach might scold you for *not* running as hard as possible). This attitude is why children are injured less frequently in informal games than in formal sports, despite parents' beliefs that adult-directed sports are safer.[1] If you are pitching, you pitch softly to little Johnny, because you know he can't hit your fastball. You also know that even your teammates would accuse you of being mean if you threw your fastest pitches to someone so young. But when big, experienced Jerome is up, you throw your best stuff, not just because you want to get him out but also because anything less would be insulting to him. The golden rule of social play is not, *Do unto others as you would have them do unto you.* Rather, it is, *Do unto others as they would have you do unto them.* The equality of play is not the equality of sameness, but the equality that comes from granting equal validity to the unique needs and wishes of every player.

To be a good player of informal sports you can't blindly follow rules. Rather, you have to see from others' perspectives, to understand what others want and provide at least some of that for them. If you fail, you will be left alone. In the informal game, keeping your playmates happy is far more important than winning, and that's true in life as well. For some children this is a hard lesson to learn, but the drive to play with others is so strong that most eventually do learn it if allowed plenty of opportunity to play—plenty of opportunity to fail, suffer the consequences, and then try again.

Lesson 2: Rules are modifiable and player-generated.   Because nothing is standardized in an informal game, the players have to make up and modify rules to adapt to varying conditions. If the vacant lot is small and the only ball available is a rubber one that carries too well, the players may decide that any ball hit beyond the lot's boundary is an automatic out. This causes the players to concentrate on placing their hits, rather than smashing them. Alternatively, the strongest players may be required to bat one-handed, with their nondominant hand, or to bat with a broomstick rather than an actual bat. As the game continues and conditions change, the rules may evolve further. None of this happens in Little League, where the official rules are inviolable and interpreted by an adult authority. In the formal game, the conditions must fit the rules rather than the other way around.

The famous developmental psychologist Jean Piaget noted long ago, in a classic study of children playing marbles, that children acquire a higher understanding of rules when they play under their own direction than when they are directed by adults.[2] Adult direction leads to the assumption that rules are determined by an outside authority and thus not to be questioned. When children play just among themselves, however, they come to realize that rules are merely conventions, established to make the game more fun and more fair, and can be changed to meet changing conditions. For life in a democracy, few lessons are more valuable.

Lesson 3: Conflicts are settled by argument, negotiation, and compromise. In the informal game, the players not only make and modify the rules, but also act as umpires. They decide whether a hit is fair or foul, whether a runner is safe or out, whether the pitcher is or isn't being too mean to little Johnny, and whether Julio should have to share his brand-new glove with someone on the other team who doesn't have a glove. Some of the more popular players may have more pull in these arguments than others, but everyone has a say. Everyone who has an opinion defends it, with as much logic as he or she can muster, and ultimately consensus is reached.

Consensus doesn't necessarily mean complete agreement. It just means that everyone *consents;* they're willing to go along with it for the sake of keeping the game going. Consensus is crucial if you want the game to continue. The need for consensus in informal play doesn't come from some highfalutin moral philosophy; it comes from practical reality. If a decision makes some people unhappy, some of them may quit, and if too many quit, the game is over (as noted under Lesson 1). You learn in informal games that you must compromise if you want to keep playing. If you don't have a king who decides things for you, you have to learn how to govern yourselves.

Once I was watching some kids play an informal game of basketball. They were spending more time deciding on the rules and arguing about whether particular plays were fair than they were playing the game. I overheard a nearby adult say, "Too bad they don't have a referee to decide these things, so they wouldn't have to spend so much time debating." Well, is it too bad? In the course of their lives, which will be the more important skill—shooting baskets or debating effectively and learning how to compromise? Kids playing sports informally are practicing many things at once, the least important of which may be the sport itself.

Lesson 4: There is no real difference between your team and the opposing team. In an informal game, the players know from the beginning that their division into two teams is arbitrary and serves only the purpose of the game. New teams are chosen each time. Billy may have been on the "enemy" team yesterday, but today he is on your team. In fact, teams may even change composition as the game goes along. Billy may start off on the opposing team, but may move over to yours, for balance, when two of your teammates go home for supper. Or if both teams are short of players, Billy may catch for both. The concept of "enemy" or "opponent" in informal sports lies very clearly in the realm of play, not reality. It is temporary and limited to the game itself. In that sense the informal game resembles a pure fantasy game in which Billy pretends to be an evil giant trying to catch and eat you.

In contrast, in formal league sports, teams remain relatively fixed over a series of games, and the scores, to some degree, have real-world consequences—such as trophies or praise from adults. The result is development of a long-lasting sense of team identity and, with it, a sense that "my team is better than other teams"—better even in ways that have nothing to do with the game and may extend to situations outside of the game. A major theme of research in social psychology and political science concerns ingroup-outgroup conflict. Cliques, gangs, ethnic chauvinism, nationalism, wars—these can all be discussed in terms of our tendency to value people we see as part of our group and devalue those we see as part of another group. Formal team sports feed into our impulse to make such group distinctions, in ways that informal sports do not.[3] Of course, enlightened coaches of formal sports may lecture about good sportsmanship and valuing the other team, but we all know how much good lecturing does for children—or for adults, for that matter.

Lesson 5: Playing well and having fun really are *more important than winning.* "Playing well and having fun are more important than winning" is a line often used by Little League coaches after a loss, rarely after a win. But with spectators watching, with a trophy on the line, and with so much attention paid to the score, one has to wonder how many of the players believe that line, and how many secretly think that Vince Lombardi had it right. The view that "winning is the only thing" becomes even more prominent as one moves up to high school and then to college sports, especially in football and basketball, which are the sports American schools care most about. As they move up the ladder from children's leagues to high school to college to professional, an ever smaller number make the teams. The rest become spectators for the rest of their lives, growing fat in the stands and on the couch—*unless* they learn to play informally.

In informal sports, playing well and having fun really are more important than winning. Everyone knows that; you don't have to try to convince anyone with a lecture. And you can play regardless of your level of skill. The whole point of an informal game is to have fun and stretch your own skills, sometimes in new and creative ways that would be disallowed or jeered at in a formal game. You might, for example, try batting with a narrow stick, to improve your eye. You might turn easy catches in the outfield into difficult over-the-shoulder catches. If you are a better player than the others, these are ways to self-handicap, which make the game more interesting for everyone. In a formal game, where winning matters, you could never do such things; you would be accused of betraying your team. Of course you have to be careful about when and where to make these creative changes in your play, even in the informal game. You have to know how to do it without offending others or coming across as a show-off. Always, in informal play, you have to consult your inner social guide.

In my experience, both as a player and observer, players in informal sports are much more intent on playing beautifully than on winning. The beauty may lie in new, creative ways of moving that allow you to express yourself and stretch your physical abilities while still coordinating your actions to mesh with those of others. The informal game, at its best, is an innovative group dance, in which the players create their own moves, within the boundaries of the agreed-upon rules, while taking care not to step on each other's toes. I've played formal games, too, where varsity championships were at stake, and those were not creative dances. If stepping on toes helped you win those games, you stepped on them.

Which is better training for real life, the informal game or the formal one? The answer seems clear to me. Real life is an informal game. The rules are endlessly modifiable and you must do your part to create them. In the end, there are no winners or losers; we all wind up in the same place. Getting along with others is far more important than beating them. What matters in life is how you play the game, how much fun you have along the way, and how much joy you give to others. These are the lessons of informal social play, and they are far, far more important than learning the coach's method for throwing a curveball or sliding into second base. I'm not against formal sports for kids who really want them, but such sports are no substitute for informal play when it comes to learning the lessons we all must learn to live a satisfying life.

In an essay about informal sports as they are played at the Sudbury Valley School, Michael Greenberg, a former student at the school, presented some of these same thoughts more poetically than I. He wrote, in part:

> In all the years of playing very physical games like football, soccer, and basketball [at Sudbury Valley], there has never been an injury beyond a minor cut or bruise. People play all these sports in their regular clothes without any of the standard protective equipment that is normally required. How can this be explained when people wearing protective pads injure each other with alarming frequency? Because in a regimented, performance-oriented way of looking at sports (or life), making sure you don't hurt someone becomes less important than winning. So it doesn't matter how much you talk about "sportsmanship" or how many safety pads you wear, people are going to get hurt. When you approach sports (or life) as a fun, exciting process, as something that is done for the sheer joy and beauty of doing it, then not hurting someone, not impairing their ability to enjoy the same process, becomes a top priority. ... To participate in an activity where the clash of unequal bodies is transformed through teamwork, pursuit of personal excellence, responsibility, and restraint into a common union of equal souls in pursuit of meaningful experience has been one of the most profound experiences of my life. I am sure it has had a similar effect on others.[4]

Lessons from Sociodramatic Play

Children learn valuable social lessons in all sorts of free social play, not just in informal sports. As illustration, here's a real example of the kind of imaginative play that researchers refer to as *sociodramatic* play, where children adopt roles and act out story lines together. All over the world, such play predominates among children in the age range of three to six.

Annie (age five years, eleven months) and Beth (five years, two months) were video-recorded by researchers Hans Furth and S. R. Kane as they played an imaginary game in the dress-up area of their after-school day-care center.[5] Annie started the game by saying, "Let's pretend that we had a ball tomorrow night and we had to get our stuff ready." Beth responded by picking up a dress and saying, "This was my dress," thereby demonstrating her implicit acceptance of the play idea and her eagerness to get the prop she wanted most. For the next twenty minutes, the two picked their clothing and accessories and discussed what would happen at the ball. Much of this time was spent haggling over who would play which role and who would get to use which props. They haggled over fancy items of clothing, a telephone, a table, a pair of binoculars, and where each would sleep the night before the ball. In each little argument, each girl gave reasons why she "needed" or "should have" that prop or role, but did so tactfully so as not to offend the other player.

Then, when Annie and Beth had come to a fairly satisfactory agreement on these issues, another little girl, Celia (age four years, nine months) came into the dress-up area from outdoors and asked to join them. They let her in, and then all three began a new round of negotiations about props and roles to include Celia. Each girl felt strongly about such matters as which clothes she would wear, what exactly would happen at the ball, and who was older and had higher status in the play. For the play to go on, they had to reach consensus on every major issue.

For example, Annie and Beth both thought that Celia, the youngest and smallest of the three, should be the "little sister," but Celia emphatically refused that role. To mollify her, Annie and Beth agreed that Celia could be the "big sister." Then, to preserve their relative status, Annie and Beth elevated themselves to the rank of mothers. There was some discussion of whether Celia could have two mothers, since "really, a person can have only one mother," which they resolved by deciding that one would be the stepmother. All three girls wanted to be named Gloria, which they decided was okay. All three girls wanted to marry the prince and become a queen. Beth and Annie acknowledged that in real life the prince could marry only one of them, but decided that "just for pretend" it would be okay for him to marry both of them. However, the idea of his also marrying Celia was too much for them to accept, even in their play, so they refused Celia's request that he marry her, too. To placate her, however, they elevated Celia still further to the role of "big sister princess."

These three girls were already skilled social players, and they were clearly becoming more skilled through the kind of practice that this play episode illustrates. Among the biggest lessons of such play are those of self-assertion, negotiation, and compromise. Each girl had to present her case skillfully to come as close as possible to getting what she wanted without upsetting the other players. In their manner of speech, the girls demonstrated that they understood the necessity of gaining consensus. For example, their proposals on how to play usually took the form of suggestions rather than demands. Most proposals ended with tag questions, such as "okay?" or "all right?" or "right?"

In their negotiations the girls frequently referred to certain rules that had become, by tradition, regular rules of play among the children in this day-care center. One was the finder's rule. Whoever first found or claimed a prop was generally the one who got to use it. However, an even higher rule, which could trump the finder's rule, was the fairness rule. It would not be right for one child to have all or most of the desired props; they had to be divided in a way that seemed at least reasonably fair to all. Players in all sorts of games are emphatic in their insistence on fairness, though they may disagree about the nature of that ideal state and how to reach it.

Another rule often invoked (not by this name) was the consistency rule. The play had to be internally consistent. For example, when Annie, who was eager for the ball to get under way, impulsively announced that the ball was about to begin, Beth reminded her that they had already decided that it wouldn't begin until the next day. They had to have a pretend night of sleep before the ball could begin. Annie understood and immediately conceded the point. The play also, to some degree at least, had to be consistent with the girls' understanding of how things are in the real world. Sometimes they could bend that rule, as when they decided that both Annie and Beth would marry the prince, but such bending required discussion, agreement, and, generally, acknowledgment that this was not how things worked in reality. As they played, the girls also affirmed and consolidated their understandings of certain conventions and rules in the real world. According to Furth and Kane's analysis, sociodramatic play is a means by which young children develop and exercise mental models of the society in which they live. In the researchers' words, children "construct society" through their play.

The three little girls were playing, doing what they wanted to do. But because what they wanted to do was to play an elaborate make-believe game with the other girls, they couldn't do *exactly* what they wanted to. They had to work out compromises and agreements with the others, and they had to control their impulses to cohere with the roles and story lines they had agreed upon. This is the magic of children's social play. By doing what they want to do, which is to play with other children, children learn to compromise and *not* do exactly what they want to do. Celia wanted to become a queen, but she was okay being "big sister princess." All of the girls wanted the most beautiful dress-up clothes, but they had to divide them up in a way that seemed fair enough to each of them. Annie at some point wanted the ball to start immediately—she was so eager for the prince to propose to her—but she had to control this impulse to maintain consistency with the narrative that the girls had already decided upon. All of this self-control and compromise occurred with no adult intervention. In fact, adult intervention would have ruined it. The children clearly enjoyed exercising their own power, intelligence, and capacity for self-restraint as they negotiated with one another, with no adult input at all.

I used this example of play because it was recorded and available, but there is nothing unique about it. Watch any group of little children playing together, who have had extensive experience at such play, and you will see amazing social minds at work. But watch from a distance, inconspicuously. If you watch boys you may find that they are not as tactful as Annie, Beth, and Celia in their negotiations, but they, too, generally figure out ways to meet one another's needs for the sake of the game.

It's not possible to conduct long-term experiments to see if children who are allowed more opportunity for play of this sort develop greater social skills than those who aren't, but correlational studies and short-term experiments, as well as common sense, strongly support this hypothesis. Children who engage in more sociodramatic play have, by various measures, been shown to demonstrate more empathy, and more ability to understand what another person thinks, knows, or desires, than do children who engage in less.[6] Moreover, several short-term experiments conducted in preschools have shown that when some children are provided with extra opportunity to engage in sociodramatic play and others are not, those in the extra-play groups later exhibit higher performance on various measures of social perspective-taking and ability to get along with others than do those in the control groups.[7]

Children's Play in the Holocaust

We turn now from the sweet scene of three little girls in the dress-up area of a playroom to terrible scenes—children in Nazi concentration camps. If play were a luxury, children here would not have played. But play is not a luxury. Play is children's means of making sense of their environment and adapting to it, as best they can, regardless of the type of environment. In the remarkable book *Children and Play in the Holocaust,* historian George Eisen, using diaries and interviews of survivors as evidence, described play among Jewish children in Nazi ghettos and concentration camps.[8]

In the ghettos, the first stage in concentration before prisoners were sent off to labor and extermination camps, parents tried desperately to divert their children's attention from the horrors around them and to preserve some semblance of the innocent play the children had known before. They created makeshift playgrounds and tried to lead the children in traditional games. The adults themselves played in ways aimed at psychological escape from their grim situation, if they played at all. For example, one man traded a crust of bread for a chessboard, because by playing chess he could forget his hunger. But the children would have none of that. They played games designed to confront, not avoid, the horrors. They played games of war, of "blowing up bunkers," of "slaughtering," of "seizing the clothes of the dead," and games of resistance. At Vilna, Jewish children played "Jews and Gestapomen," in which the Jews would overpower their tormenters and beat them with their own rifles (sticks).

Even in the extermination camps, the children who were still healthy enough to move around played. In one camp they played a game called "tickling the corpse." At Auschwitz-Birkenau they dared one another to touch the electric fence. They played "gas chamber," a game in which they threw rocks into a pit and screamed the sounds of people dying. One game of their own devising was modeled after the camp's daily roll call and was called *klepsi-klepsi,* a common term for stealing. One playmate was blindfolded; then one of the others would step forward and hit him hard on the face; and then, with blindfold removed, the one who had been hit had to guess, from facial expressions or other evidence, who had hit him. To survive at Auschwitz, one had to be an expert at bluffing—for example, about stealing bread or about knowing of someone's escape or resistance plans. Klepsi-klepsi may have been practice for that skill.

In play, whether it is the idyllic play we most like to envision or the play described by Eisen, children bring the realities of their world into a fictional context, where it is safe to confront them, to experience them, and to practice ways of dealing with them. Some people fear that violent play creates violent adults, but in reality the opposite is true. Violence in the adult world leads children, quite properly, to play at violence. How else can they prepare themselves emotionally, intellectually, and physically for reality? It is wrong to think that somehow we can reform the world for the future by controlling children's play and controlling what they learn. If we want to reform the world, we have to reform the world; children will follow suit. The children must, and will, prepare themselves for the real world to which they must adapt to survive.

Children's use of play to adapt to trauma has also been observed in other situations closer to home. For instance, a group of children who, unfortunately, had seen a man fall twenty feet to the ground and suffer serious injury outside their nursery school window were much distressed by this experience. For months afterward they played, on their own initiative, at such themes as falling, injury, hospitals, and death.[9] Children who have experienced terrorist attacks against them or their parents have likewise been observed to play at themes that involve re-enactment coupled with some sort of soothing.[10] The soothing in their play may involve repair and mending of damages, protection and nurturance for those left behind, or the eventual triumph of good over evil.

Even children who have never experienced any particular trauma, beyond the little ones everyone experiences, often play at emotion-arousing, traumatic scenes. In doing so, they may be steeling themselves to deal with all sorts of unpredictable but inevitable unhappy and painful events. Researcher Gisela Wegener-Spöhring has described instances of such play among normal, well-adjusted kindergarteners in Germany.

For example, she described a scene of "whipping play," in which a popular boy sat bound in a chair while being whipped, with relatively hard blows with a leather strap, by his playmates.[11] To comfort him as he was being whipped, two girls gave him blocks as bananas to eat. The boys doing the whipping stopped occasionally to give him pretend drinks of water. This appeared to be highly enjoyable play for all of the participants, on the important life theme of pain and soothing for pain. According to Wegener-Spöhring, the only real violence related to this play occurred when the kindergarten teacher came over and stopped it, because she felt it was aggressive. Wegener-Spöhring contends that disruption of good play, when there is no good reason to do so, is always an act of violence and tends to produce a violent reaction. When the whipping game was forcibly stopped, the children's tempers turned bad. They began knocking over chairs and misbehaving in other ways, in apparent acts of rebellion.

The Value of "Dangerous" Play

Researchers who study play in animals have suggested that a major evolutionary purpose of play is to help the young learn how to cope with emergencies.[12] Juvenile mammals of all species deliberately and repeatedly put themselves into awkward, moderately dangerous, moderately frightening situations in their play. As they playfully gallop, leap, and chase one another around they continuously alternate between losing and regaining control of their bodily movements. When goat kids jump, for example, they twist and turn in ways that make it difficult to land.

Young monkeys and apes playfully swinging in trees choose branches that are sufficiently far apart and high enough off the ground to create a degree of fear, but not so high that a fall would cause serious injury. Young chimpanzees seem especially to enjoy games of dropping freely from high branches and then catching onto lower ones at the last moment before hitting the ground.

Young mammals of nearly all species play chase games. They race after one another and take turns at being the pursued and the pursuer. For most species, the apparently preferred position in such chases is that of being pursued.[13] A typical game—for a pair of young monkeys, lambs, or squirrels, for example—starts with one youngster playfully attacking the other and then running off while looking back to be sure that the provoked playmate is pursuing. Observers of monkey play have noted that the chased animal generally shows more evidence of delight in the game—such as a broad playface (the monkey equivalent of a smile)—than does the pursuer.[14] Apparently, the reward for chasing is the opportunity to take a turn at being chased. When the pursuer catches and "tags" the other (typically with a playful nip), the erstwhile pursuer turns and joyfully becomes the pursued. Notice that the preferred position is the position of greatest vulnerability. The one who is running away has less control over what is happening, has less opportunity to stop and take a break, and is more vulnerable to falling and injury than is the one who is running after. The vulnerability itself seems part and parcel of the sense of thrill.

In addition to chasing games, young mammals, especially young males, engage in a great deal of playful fighting. Depending on the species, they butt heads, attempt to throw each other to the ground, attempt to pin each other, and try to give each other playful nips at specific target locations. Unlike in a real fight, in a play fight the larger and more skilled animal deliberately self-handicaps to avoid dominating the playmate. Detailed studies of juvenile rats play fighting suggest that for this species at least, each animal prefers to be in the subordinate position, which, again, offers the greatest physical and emotional challenge.[15] One rat will self-handicap to allow the playmate to get into the attack, on-top position and then will struggle to recover. Over time, the playmates alternate, so each can practice recovering from the vulnerable position.

Even casual observation shows that human children, like other young mammals, deliberately put themselves into fear-inducing, vulnerable positions in their play. They do this as they climb high in trees, dive off high towers or cliffs, leap over crevices from rock to rock, perform tricks on playground equipment, or skateboard down banisters. In their playful fighting, young children, like other young mammals, alternate between getting into and out of vulnerable positions.[16] The stronger partner self-handicaps, to allow the weaker partner to break free from being pinned and to allow that partner to get into the attack position, so both can experience the thrill of being in the vulnerable position and escaping from it. In all of this, young humans are much like the young of other mammals, and they are apparently learning the same crucial lessons.

Think about the universal pleasure of chasing games. The three-year-old girl squeals with almost unbearable joy as she flees from the terrible monster, in the form of her father or big brother, who threatens to catch her and eat her for breakfast. In every human chasing game I can think of, the preferred position is that of being chased. In nightmares and in real life, nothing is more terrifying than being chased by a predator or monster. But in play, nothing is more delightful.

The most universal and basic of all human chasing games is tag. Children everywhere play it, and the goal, always, is to spend as much time being chased, and as little time chasing, as possible. The punishment for being caught is that you become "it," and then you must serve time as chaser until you catch someone and can once again enjoy being chased. As children grow older they play increasingly sophisticated versions of tag, with rules that give additional structure to the game. A typical example is "fox and geese," which my childhood friends and I played on ice skates, on paths carved through the snow on frozen ponds in Minnesota. The preferred position always was to be a goose, not the fox. If you were caught, you had to be the fox until you caught someone and could again be a goose. Hide-and-seek and dodgeball are not exactly chasing games, but they, too, follow the rule: the preferred position is to be pursued. Punishment for being found, or for being hit by the ball, is that you have to be a pursuer.

Even formal team sports, such as soccer, American football, basketball, and hockey, can be understood as complex versions of tag. The joy lies in running across a field or court—kicking or carrying or dribbling a ball, or pushing a puck, toward some goal—while a horde of "enemies" chase after you. Baseball, too, is a form of tag. The batter, after hitting the ball, tries to run around a specified loop, from one safe point to another, while the other team tries to tag him out. In all such games, the teams alternate between offense and defense, and the preferred position is offense, in which you are chased as you run through "enemy" ground.

In many such vigorous activities, children are testing their own fear as well as their physical prowess. The combination of fear and joy is the feeling we call thrill. In such play children must be in charge of their own activities, because only they know how to dose themselves with the right amount of fear. Children swinging on swing sets or climbing trees or ropes know how high to go to generate the level of fear that for them creates excitement but not terror. No parent, coach, or gym teacher can ever make that judgment for them. In the "whipping game" described by Wegener-Spöhring, the boy being whipped would have signaled the whipping to stop if it became too painful. In all forms of playful fighting and chasing, each child has the right to call time-out or to quit if the emotional or physical challenge becomes too great. Without that right, the activity is no longer play.

In our culture today, parents and other adults overprotect children from possible dangers in play. We seriously underestimate children's ability to take care of themselves and make good judgments. In this respect, we differ not just from hunter-gatherer cultures (as described in Chapter 2), but from all traditional cultures in which children played freely. Our underestimation becomes a self-fulfilling prophecy—by depriving children of freedom, we deprive them of the opportunities they need to learn how to take control of their own behavior and emotions.

The Decline of Empathy and the Rise of Narcissism

As I discussed in Chapter 1, the decline of children's free play since about 1955 has been accompanied by a continuous rise in anxiety, depression, and feelings of helplessness in young people. Related to these findings, there has also been an increase in narcissism and decline in empathy.

Narcissism refers to an inflated view of the self, which tends to separate the self from others and prevent the formation of meaningful two-way relationships. Since the late 1970s, it has been assessed in normative groups of college students using the Narcissistic Personality Inventory (NPI), a questionnaire designed to tap the degree to which people are primarily concerned about themselves versus the degree to which they are concerned about others. *Empathy* is more or less the opposite of narcissism. It refers to a tendency to connect emotionally with others, to see things from others' point of view, and to feel sympathy for others' misfortunes. It has been assessed in normative groups of college students since the late 1970s with a questionnaire called the Interpersonal Reactivity Index. Scores on these questionnaires reveal a significant rise in narcissism over the years and a significant decline in empathy.[17] The questionnaire scores are apparently valid measures; they correlate with real-world behaviors. For example, people who score high on narcissism have been found to overrate their own abilities compared to those of others, to lash out angrily in response to criticism, and to commit white-collar crimes at higher rates than the general population.[18] Those who score low on empathy are more likely than the average person to engage in bullying and less likely to volunteer to help people in need.[19]

From all I have said in this chapter, it should be no mystery why a decline in play would be accompanied by a rise in emotional and social disorders. Play is nature's way of teaching children how to solve their own problems, control their impulses, modulate their emotions, see from others' perspectives, negotiate differences, and get along with others as equals. There is no substitute for play as a means of learning these skills. They can't be taught in school. For life in the real world, these lessons of personal responsibility, self-control, and sociability are far more important than any lessons that can be taught in school.

In addition to the correlational evidence and logical arguments linking a decline in play to a stunting of emotional and social development, there is also experimental evidence. We obviously can't conduct long-term experiments in which human children are deliberately deprived of play. However, such experiments can and have been conducted with animals. In some experiments, for example, rhesus monkeys have been raised with just their mothers and then compared to other rhesus monkeys who were raised more normally, with access to peers as well as mothers.[20] Monkey mothers interact in many ways with their young, but they do not play with them, so those in the former group were deprived of play throughout their development. Not surprisingly, when tested as young adults, they were found to be abnormal in many ways. They showed excessive fear and excessive aggression. When placed in a novel environment, which would elicit a small degree of fear in a normal monkey, these monkeys reacted with terror and did not adapt to the environment over time as a normal monkey would. When placed with peers, they failed to respond appropriately to the other animals' social signals and invitations. When a peer attempted to groom them, for example, they would lash out aggressively rather than accept the friendly overture. They also failed to show appropriate aggression-reducing signals in the presence of other monkeys and were therefore attacked more often than normal monkeys.

Similar experiments have been conducted with rats, with similar results. Rats raised without peer playmates exhibit abnormally high levels of both fear and aggression in various behavioral tests.[21] In one set of experiments, some otherwise peer-deprived young rats were allowed to interact for an hour per day with a playful peer while others were allowed to interact for an hour per day with a peer that had been rendered nonplayful by injection of the drug amphetamine.[22] Amphetamine knocks out the play drive in young rats without knocking out other social behaviors. The result was that rats with experience playing with a peer behaved much more normally in adulthood than did those with the same amount of exposure to a nonplayful peer. Apparently the essential interactions between young rats for normal emotional and social development occur in play. In other experiments, play-deprived young rats showed abnormal patterns of brain development. Without play, neural pathways running from frontal areas of the brain—areas known to be crucial for controlling impulses and emotions—failed to develop normally.[23]

It may seem cruel to raise young monkeys, and even young rats, in conditions where they cannot play freely with peers, for the sake of science. But if that is cruel, then what can we say about our current "normal" practice of depriving human children of free play with other children for the sake of protecting and educating them? It's cruel indeed, and dangerous.

What About Video Games?

The one form of play that hasn't declined in recent decades is video games. Some people blame such games, along with television, for the decline in outdoor play. They argue that television programming and video play are so seductive that they hold children at the screen and keep them from other activities. I understand the argument and see why it is compelling to some, but it doesn't fit well with my own observations or with researchers' findings from systematic surveys.

At Sudbury Valley, students can play and explore in whatever ways they like for as long as they like. All of them have unlimited access to computers and television, and almost all of them play and enjoy video games. But most of them also spend lots of time playing and exploring in the fields and woods outdoors. Surveys of game players in the general population, likewise, indicate that kids who are free to play outdoors as well as with video games usually, over time, choose a balance between the two.[24] Those who seem to become addicted to the games are generally those for whom other satisfying forms of play are not available.[25] Video-game play appears to compete much more with television watching than with outdoor play for children's free time. Overall, according to surveys, gamers do not play outdoors any less than do non-gamers, but they do watch less television.[26] In fact, one recent large-scale study of factors promoting outdoor play among children in Holland revealed—to the surprise of some—that children who had a computer or a television in their own room played outdoors significantly *more,* not less, than did otherwise comparable children who had neither in their room.[27]

It seems to me that the decline in children's outdoor play has been caused primarily by the rise of parental fears and by other societal changes (described in Chapter 10) that have reduced children's opportunities to play freely outdoors. The increased video play seems to have come about for two reasons. First, the games really are fun and are becoming more so all the time as the technology and thought that goes into producing them has advanced. Second, as kids are more and more monitored and controlled by adults in the real world, the virtual world has emerged as a place where many of them can still be free. The nine-year-old may not be allowed to walk to the corner store by himself, but he is allowed to enter into and explore freely an exciting virtual world filled with all sorts of dangers and delights.

When kids are asked, in focus groups and surveys, what they like about video games, they generally talk about freedom, self-direction, and competence.[28] In the game, they make their own decisions and strive to meet challenges that they themselves have chosen. At school and in other adult-dominated contexts they may be treated as idiots who need constant direction, but in the game they are in charge and can solve difficult problems and exhibit extraordinary skills. In the game, age does not matter—skill does. In these ways, video games are like all other forms of true play. Far from contributing to the generational rise in anxiety, depression, and helplessness, video games appear to be a force that is helping to relieve those afflictions. This seems to be especially true in recent times, with the emergence of so-called massively multiplayer online role-playing games, such as *World of Warcraft,* which are far more social than previous video games and offer endless opportunities for creativity and problem solving.[29]

In these online games, players create a character (an avatar) that has unique physical and psychological traits and assets, and as that character, enter an extraordinarily complex and exciting virtual world simultaneously occupied by countless other players, who in their real-life forms may be anywhere on the planet. Players go on quests within this virtual world, and along the way they meet other players, who might become friends or foes. Players may start off playing solo, avoiding others, but to advance to the higher levels they have to make friends and join with others in mutual quests. Making friends within the game requires essentially the same skills as making friends in the real world. You can't be rude. You have to understand and abide by the etiquette of the culture you are in. You have to learn about the goals of a potential friend and help that individual to achieve those goals. Depending on how you behave, players may put you on their *friends* list or their *ignore* list, and they may communicate positive or negative information about you to other players. The games offer players endless opportunities to experiment with different personalities and ways of behaving, in a fantasy world where there are no real-life consequences for failing.

Players in these games can also form special-interest groups called *guilds.* To join, players must fill out an application, much like a job application, explaining why they would be valuable members. Guilds typically have structures similar to companies in the real world, with leaders, executive boards, and even recruitment personnel. Such games are in many ways like the imaginative sociodramatic games of preschool children, but played in a virtual world, with communication by online text, and raised up many notches in sophistication to fit the interests and abilities of the older children, teenagers, and adults who play them. Like all sociodramatic games, they are anchored in an understanding of the real world, and they exercise concepts and social skills that are relevant to that world. A study commissioned by the IBM Corporation concluded that the leadership skills exercised within these games are essentially the same as those required to run a modern company in the real corporate world.[30]

Much of the early research on video games was motivated by fears that the violent content in some of the games would increase young people's violent behavior in the real world. For those who have taken the trouble to examine it seriously, that research has quelled the initial fears.[31] There is no evidence that killing animated characters on a screen increases a person's likelihood of harming people in real life. In fact, some studies suggest that the pretend violence of video games helps young people learn to control and regulate their emotions, perhaps in much the same way that "dangerous" outdoor play does. One study, for example, revealed that college students who regularly played violent video games felt *less* hostility, and also less depression, after a frustrating mental task than did college students who rarely or never played such games.[32] I have to admit that I personally cannot play video games, or watch movies, that include graphic depictions of violence, because I find them revolting. But nothing in the research literature leads me to argue that there is any moral virtue in my avoiding such games and movies. I never forbade my children from such pretend violence, and they have grown up to be completely nonviolent, morally virtuous citizens.

More recently, researchers have begun to pay attention to the *positive* effects of video games. Several experiments have shown that playing fast-paced action video games can quite markedly increase players' scores on tests of visuospatial ability, including components of standard IQ tests.[33] Other studies suggest that depending on the type, video games can also increase scores on measures of working memory (the ability to hold several items of information in mind at once), critical thinking, and problem solving.[34] In addition, there is growing evidence that kids who previously showed little interest in reading and writing are now acquiring advanced literacy skills through the text-based communication in online video games.[35] And as I already mentioned, there is at least some evidence that playing high-action, emotion-arousing games helps young people learn to regulate their emotions in stressful situations. To date there has been little formal study of the social benefits of video games, but many anecdotal reports attest to such benefits, and what research has been done suggests that frequent video game players are, on average, better adjusted socially than their nonplaying peers.[36]

The route to getting our kids outdoors is not to throw away the computer or the television set, no more than it is to throw away the books we have in our homes. These are all great sources of learning and enjoyment. Rather, the route is to make sure kids have real opportunities to play freely outdoors, with other kids, without interference from adults. Kids in today's world need to become highly skilled with computers, just as hunter-gatherer kids needed to become highly skilled with bows and arrows or digging sticks. To develop such skills, they need freedom and opportunity to play with computers, the primary tools of today. But for healthy development, they also need freedom and opportunity to play outdoors, away from the house, with other kids. The key words here are *freedom* and *opportunity*—not coercion.

Notes

1   For a discussion of the high frequency of serious injuries in formal youth sports, see Hyman (2009).
2   Piaget (1932/1965).

3   For a classic study showing how formal team sports can create and exacerbate conflicts between groups of boys, see Sherif et al. (1961).

4   M. Greenberg (1992).

5   Furth (1996); Furth and Kane (1992).

6   Connolly and Doyle (1984); Elias and Berk (2002); Jenkins and Astington (1996); Newton and Jenvey (2011).

7   Burns and Brainerd (1979); Dockett (1998, described by Smith, 2005); Saltz, Dixon, and Johnson (1977).

8   Eisen (1988).

9   Brown et al. (1971).

10 Chazan and Cohen (2010).

11 Wegener-Spöhring (1994).

12 Spinka et al. (2001).

13 Suggested originally by Groos (1898) and more recently confirmed by others (see Fairbanks, 2000; Power, 2000). Exceptions, however, occur in the case of predatory animals, including wolves and dogs, where the preferred position in chase games is that of pursuer.

14 Power (2000), p. 194.

15 Pellis et al. (2010).

16 Aldis (1975), p. 187.

17 Konrath et al. (2011); Twenge and Foster (2010).

18 Blickle et al. (2006); Judge et al. (2006); Thomaes et al. (2009).

19 Konrath et al. (2011).

20 Herman et al. (2011).

21 Pellis and Pellis (2011); Bell et al. (2010).

22 Hall (1998); Einon et al. (1978).

23 Pellis and Pellis (2011).

24 For reviews, see Goldstein (2011) and Przybylski et al. (2010).

25 Przybylski et al. (2009).

26 Goldstein (2011).

27 Aarts et al. (2010).

28 McLeod and Lin (2010); Olson (2010); Przybylski et al. (2010); Yee (2006).

29 Barnett and Coulson (2010).

30 Reaves and Malone (2007).

31 Ferguson (2010).

32 Ferguson and Rueda (2010).

33 Green and Bavelier (2003); Spence and Feng (2010).

34 Akilli (2007).

35 Black and Steinkuehler (2009).

36 Durkin and Barber (2002); Ferguson (2010); Olson (2010).

Bibliography

Aarts, M., Wendel-Vos, W., van Oers, H. A. M., van de Goor, I. A. M., & Schuit, A. J. (2010). Environmental determinants of outdoor play in children: A large-scale cross-sectional study. *American Journal of Preventive Medicine, 39,* 212–219.

Akilli, G. K. (2007). Games and simulations: A new approach in education? In D. Gibson, C. Aldrich, & M. Prensky (Eds.), *Games and simulations in online learning: Research and development frameworks* (pp. 1–20). Hershey, PA: Information Science.

Aldis, O. (1975). *Play-fighting.* New York: Academic Press.

Barnett, J., & Coulson, M. (2010). Virtually real: A psychological perspective on massively multiplayer online games. *Review of General Psychology, 14,* 167–179.

Black, R. W., & Steinkuehler, C. (2009). Literacy in virtual worlds. In L. Christenbury, R. Bomer, & P. Smargorinsky (Eds.), *Handbook of adolescent literacy research,* 271–286. New York: Guilford.

Blickle, G., Schlegel, A., Fassbender, P., & Klein, U. (2006). Some personality correlates of white-collar crime. *Applied Psychology 55,* 220–233.

Brown, N. S., Curry, N. E., & Tittnich, E. (1971). How groups of children deal with common stress through play. In N. E. Curry & S. Arnaud (Eds.), *Play: The child strives toward self-realization.* Washington, DC: National Association for the Education of Young Children.

Burns, S. M., & Brainerd, C. J. (1979). Effects of constructive and dramatic play on perspective taking in very young children. *Developmental Psychology, 15,* 512–521.

Chazan, S., & Cohen, E. (2010). Adaptive and defensive strategies in post-traumatic play of young children exposed to violent attacks. *Journal of Child Psychotherapy, 36,* 133–151.

Connolly, J. A., & Doyle, A. (1984). Relation of social fantasy play to social competence in preschoolers. *Developmental Psychology, 20,* 797–806.

Durkin, K., & Barber, B. (2002). Not so doomed: Computer game play and positive adolescent development. *Applied Developmental Psychology, 23,* 373–392.

Eisen, G. (1988). *Children and play in the Holocaust: Games among the shadows.* Amherst: University of Massachusetts Press.

Elias, C. L., & Berk, L. E. (2002). Self-regulation in young children: Is there a role for sociodramatic play? *Early Childhood Research Quarterly, 17,* 216–238.

Fairbanks, L. A. (2000). The developmental timing of primate play: A neural selection model. In Parker, S. T., Langer, J., & McKinney, M. L. (Eds.), *Biology, brains, and behavior: The evolution of human development,* 131–18). Santa Fe, NM: School of American Research Press.

Ferguson, C. (2010). Blazing angels or resident evil? Can violent video games be a force for good? *Review of General Psychology, 14,* 68–81.

Ferguson, C., & Rueda, S. M. (2010). The Hitman study: Violent video game exposure effects on aggressive behavior, hostile feelings, and depression. *European Psychologist, 15,* 99–108.

Furth, H. G. (1996). *Desire for society: Children's knowledge as social imagination,* 149–173. New York: Plenum.

Furth, H. G., & Kane, S. R. (1992). Children constructing society: A new perspective on children at play. In H. McGurk (Ed.), *Childhood social development: Contemporary perspectives*. Hillsdale, NJ: Erlbaum.

Goldstein, J. (2011). Technology in play. In Anthony D. Pellgrini (Ed.), *The Oxford handbook of the development of play,* 322–337. Oxford: Oxford University Press.

Green, C. S., & Bavelier, D. (2003). Action video game modifies visual selective attention. *Nature, 423,* 534–537.

Greenberg, D. (1992). Sudbury Valley's secret weapon: Allowing people of different ages to mix freely at school. In D. Greenberg (Ed.), *The Sudbury Valley School experience,* 3rd ed., 121–136. Framingham, MA: Sudbury Valley School Press.

Groos, K. (1898). *The play of animals*. New York: Appleton.

Herman, K. N., Paukner, A., & Suomi, S. J. (2011). Gene X environment interactions in social play: Contributions from rhesus macaques. In A. D. Pellgrini (Ed.), *The Oxford handbook of the development of play,* 58–69. Oxford: Oxford University Press.

Hyman, M. (2009). *Until it hurts: America's obsession with youth sports and how it harms our kids*. Boston: Beacon Press.

Jenkins, J. M., & Astington, J. W. (1996). Cognitive factors and family structure associated with theory of mind development in young children. *Developmental Psychology, 32,* 70–78.

Judge, T. A., LePine, J. A., & Rich, B. L. (2006). Loving yourself abundantly: Relationship of the narcissistic personality to self—and other perceptions of workplace deviance, leadership, and task and contextual performance. *Journal of Applied Psychology, 91,* 762–776.

Konrath, S. H., O'Brien, E. H., & Hsing, C. (2011). Changes in dispositional empathy in American college students over time: A meta-analysis. *Personality and Social Psychology Review, 15,* 180–198.

McLeod, L., & Lin, L. (2010). A child's power in game-play. *Computers & Education, 54,* 517–527.

Newton, E., & Jenvey, V. (2011). Play and theory of mind: Associations with social competence in young children. *Early Child Development and Care, 181,* 761–773.

Olson, C. K. (2010). Children's motivation for video game play in the context of normal development. *Review of General Psychology, 14,* 180–187.

Pellis, S. M., & Pellis, V. C. (2011). Rough and tumble play: Training and using the social brain. In A. D. Pellgrini (Ed.), *The Oxford handbook of the development of play,* 245–259. Oxford: Oxford University Press.

Pellis, S. M., Pellis, V. C., & Bell, H. C. (2010). The function of play in the development of the social brain. *American Journal of Play, 2,* 278–296.

Piaget, J. (1932; 1965). *The moral judgment of the child*. New York: Free Press.

Power, T. G. (2000). *Play and exploration in animals and children*. Mahwah, NJ: Lawrence Erlbaum Associates.

Przybylski, A. K., Rigby, C. S., & Ryan, R. M. (2010). A motivational model of video game engagement. *Review of General Psychology, 14,* 154–166.

Przybylski, A. K., Weinstein, N., Ryan, R. M., & Rigby, C. S. (2009). Having versus wanting to play: Background and consequences of harmonious versus obsessive engagement in video games. *CyberPsychology & Behavior, 12,* 485–492.

Reaves, B., & Malone, T. W. (2007). *Leadership in games and work: Implications for the enterprise of massively multiplayer online role-playing games.* Seriosity Inc. Published online at www.seriosity.com/downloads/Leadership_In_Games_Seriosity_and_IBM.pdf.

Saltz, E., Dixon, D., & Johnson, J. (1977). Training disadvantaged preschoolers on various fantasy activities: Effects on cognitive functioning and impulse control. *Child Development, 48,* 367–380.

Sherif, M., Harvey, O. J., White, B. J., Hood, W. E., & Sherif, C. S. (1961). *Intergroup conflict and cooperation: The Robbers Cave experiment.* Norman: University of Oklahoma Book Exchange.

Smith, P. K. (2005a). Play: Types and functions in human development. In B. J. Ellis & D. F. Bjorklund (Eds.), *Origins of the social mind.* New York: Guilford.

———. (2005b). Social and pretend play in children. In A. D. Pellegrini & P. K. Smith (Eds.), *The nature of play: Great apes and humans,* 137–212. New York: Guilford.

Spence, I., & Feng, J. (2010). Video games and spatial cognition. *Review of General Psychology, 14,* 92–104.

Spinka, M., Newberry, R. C., & Bekoff, M. (2001). Mammalian play: Training for the unexpected. *Quarterly Review of Biology, 76,* 141–168.

Thomaes, S., Bushman, B. J., DeCastro, B. O., & Stegge, H. (2009). What makes narcissists bloom? A framework for research on the etiology and development of narcissism. *Development and Psychopathology, 21,* 1233–1247.

Twenge, J. M., & Foster, J. D. (2010). Birth cohort increases in narcissistic personality traits among American college students, 1982–2009. *Social Psychological and Personality Science, 1,* 99–106.

Wegener-Spöhring, G. (1994). War toys and aggressive play scenes. In J. H. Goldstein (Ed.), *Toys, play, and child development,* 84–109. Cambridge: Cambridge University Press.

Yee, N. (2006). Motivations for play in online games. *Cyberpsychology & Behavior, 9,* 772–775.

Social-Emotional Learning

Poonam Desai, Vicky Karahalios, and Schevita Persuad

Social justice is not only included in the practice standards of the National Association of School Psychologists (NASP, 2010), it is also an emerging topic within the education, psychology, and school psychology literatures. Social justice is defined as the need for all people to be treated equally, with fairness and respect, where all receive the goods and services to which they are entitled (North, 2006). Shriberg et al. (2008), in examining definitions and perspectives of social justice in school psychology practice, define social justice as "ensuring the protection of rights and opportunities for all," with a particular focus on advocacy, elements of cultural diversity, and recognizing and addressing institutional power" (p. 459). As school psychologists are among the main providers of mental health services in schools, they have the potential to translate the above social justice definitions into practice by advocating for equitable social and emotional supports for all students.

In addition to recent research and professional standards of practice focusing on social–emotional supports, attention has been brought to mental health competence in schools at the international, federal, and state levels. Research suggests that many other nations are implementing social–emotional learning (SEL) in educational institutions to foster social development (Bird & Sultmann, 2010; Hallam, 2009). New bipartisan legislation brought forth The Academic, Social, and Emotional Learning Act of 2013 (H.R. 1875), which will expand the availability of evidence-based programs to more settings through advanced teacher and administrative training in SEL initiatives. Policy makers, state legislators, educators, and communities at all levels are moving toward embracing a vision of schooling in which SEL competencies are a priority in the classroom.

Poonam Desai, et al., "Social-Emotional Learning," *Communique*, vol. 43, no. 1, pp. 14-16. Copyright © 2014 by National Association of School Psychologists. Reprinted with permission. Provided by ProQuest LLC. All rights reserved.

What is SEL?

Social–emotional learning (SEL) is the umbrella term for the many different kinds of prevention programs that draw from public health, mental health, and juvenile justice perspectives to address the social development of children in schools (Hoffman, 2009). The Collaborative for Social Emotional Learning (CASEL) describes five core competencies in SEL programming including: self-awareness (knowing your strengths and limitations), self-management (being able to stay in control and persevere through challenges), social awareness (understanding and empathizing with others), relationship skills (being able to work in teams and resolve conflicts), and responsible decision-making (making ethical and safe choices). The literature has suggested that SEL is an essential part of education, encouraging the establishment of environments that increase students' abilities to coordinate emotion, cognition, and behavior, so they can achieve positive academic, health, and citizenship outcomes (Graczyk et al., 2000).

SEL programs focus on a wide range of behaviors in school including externalizing behaviors, internalizing behaviors, empathy, social problem solving, caring for others, positive coping skills, and perspective taking, to name a few (Bird & Sultmann, 2010; Caldarella, Christensen, Kramer, & Kronmiller, 2009; Durlak, Weissberg, Dymnicki, Taylor, & Schellinger, 2011). The most compelling evidence for the effectiveness of SEL is Durlak and colleagues' (2011) meta-analysis of 213 school-based, universal SEL programs involving 270,034 kindergarten through high school students. Positive outcome gains were identified in attitude toward self and others, positive social behavior, conduct problems, emotional distress, and academic performance (Durlak et al., 2011). Results further showed that programs can be conducted as effectively by regular school staff as by outside providers and can be successful across a range of ages and geographic areas. Research also suggests that SEL programs promote greater emotional well-being for staff, reduced bullying incidents, and system-wide school policy change (Hallam, 2009).

While much research supports the positive effects of SEL programming for students, recent surveys of NASP members currently practicing in Pre-K through 12th grade settings found that school psychologists were not well informed about evidence-based SEL programs (McKevitt, 2012). Thus, documentation of the positive effects of SEL programming is not translating into practitioner knowledge of types and uses of SEL programs, nor into implementation.

Components of an SEL Curriculum Reflective of Social Justice

Selecting and implementing SEL programs reflective of social justice requires consideration of both the accessibility and the content of the curriculum. Briggs (2012) offers guiding questions for school psychologists examining their own and their school's social justice practices, modified here to represent SEL considerations:

- Whose voices are being heard and whose are not being heard in this situation?
- How can I call stakeholders (e.g., school staff, students, families, community members) to action in a manner that will be heard?

- What are the perspectives of school stakeholders regarding how the school as a whole is supporting the healthy development of children? What do they identify as needs and priorities?
- Do school SEL curricula align with the diverse needs and lives of students?
- Do SEL and behavioral data highlight discrepancies in access and success?
- Is there a group of students who experience bullying or discrimination or students who need specific types of support?
- What research-based interventions can I draw from in developing an SEL intervention?
- Are the interventions respectful of the context of each child, and do the interventions support each child in making decisions for himself or advocating for himself?

Keeping these guiding questions in mind, it is then the role of the social-justice-oriented school psychologist to critically reflect on his or her practices and those of the school, and to critically consider potential SEL curricula using a lens of cultural sensitivity, availability of resources, and multicultural awareness.

Accessibility

Though numerous curricula are available to schools, accessibility of these programs remains a critical consideration in choosing SEL curricula. Many evidence-based SEL programs require significant financial investment. For example, the social–emotional programs with *Positive* or *Potentially Positive* effectiveness ratings (as reported by What Works Clearinghouse) range from no-cost to approximately $3,000 per student (U.S. Department of Education, Institute of Education Sciences [IES], 2011; IES, 2013). Indeed, low- or no-cost SEL programs exist and are available to schools; however, research on these programs is limited. As previously noted, social justice involves ensuring the protection of rights and opportunities for all (Shriberg et al., 2008). The high cost of evidence-based SEL programs limits access to effective curricula and brings into question whether the current selection of SEL programs truly focuses on expanding opportunities for social–emotional development for all students or only for the students whose schools can afford SEL programs. That being said, the authors recognize that school psychologists must work within the confines of financial limitations, and encourage practitioners to seek cost-effective, evidence-based curricula where possible.

Content

Schools with access to SEL programs must also consider the content of the available SEL curricula and the audience for which the curricula is intended. Many of the SEL programs have aimed to provide more focus on culture and diversity; however, the focus has been broad and ambiguous (Caldarella et al., 2009; Durlak et al., 2011). Most studies suggest they do this by using their programs in diverse racial and economic settings. This is a start, but the programming often remains the same regardless of the student population.

According to Shriberg and Moy (2014), highly effective social justice practices are rooted in multiculturalism and actively utilize two core social justice actions: collaboration and advocacy. Hoffman (2009) translates this idea to SEL through the examination of SEL programming, yielding a new tenet of increased focus on culture in SEL curricula to address the differences in students and in their understanding of mental health and emotional competence. Hoffman suggests that the language of SEL programs' outcome measures and goals are based on White American perspectives of emotional control that do not take into account the different types of SEL that could foster greater emotional well-being. For example, previously mentioned studies aimed to decrease externalizing behaviors, increase prosocial behaviors, and increase coping strategies. All of these ideas, which are explicitly taught, do not take the perspectives of other cultures or other means of obtaining positive social development.

Though norming data are difficult to find for many programs and curricula, practitioners can consult program websites or request research that establishes the efficacy of a particular program with a population similar to the one the school psychologist works with. The meta-analysis of SEL studies conducted by Durlak et al. (2011) reveals the demographics and implementation-duration data for SEL studies, including: "More than half the programs (56%) were delivered to elementary school students ... [and] nearly one third of the reports contained no information on student ethnicity (31%) or socioeconomic status (32%)" (p. 412).

School teams charged with the task of selecting an SEL program may, led only by effectiveness ratings, choose and implement an SEL program intended for a group of students different from those students enrolled in their school. Considerations by the SEL team should include research studies' age groups, ethnicity, socioeconomic status, school type, curriculum delivery setting and personnel, as well as duration of implementation. However, limitations in norming groups or research data do not preclude schools from successfully implementing culturally sensitive SEL curricula. School psychologists are familiar with the adaptations necessary for academic and behavioral interventions, and this ability to modify interventions extends to SEL programs. SEL programs ensure the protection of rights and opportunities for all by lending themselves to modification. Modifications viewed through a social justice lens are enhanced by contributions of school staff members, students, families, and community members. Ideally, the social–emotional learning program provides structure to these contributions and ideas for altering lessons to meet the needs of a wide range of students and families. Ultimately, local outcome data will show whether such modifications have been successful in delivering improved results for students.

When modifying SEL curriculum to meet the needs of individual students or communities, consider the message of the SEL program, as well as the specific skills and traits the program promotes. In her analysis of the current approach to social–emotional learning, Hoffman (2009, p. 438) asks, "Does a curriculum in emotional skills, for example, adequately engage with or reflect cultural diversity, or does it presume a single model of emotional competency valid across all cultural contexts?" For instance, many social–emotional learning programs foster the development of emotion management and self-control. Consider the implications and characteristics of these skills for various cultures and for those from differing socioeconomic statuses. All families, groups, or communities may not view emotional expression in the same way. Subsequently, an SEL program placing emphasis on emotion control runs counter to the skills these families, groups, and communities intend to teach their children. Similarly, while a skill such as maintaining eye contact when in conversation is a valued interpersonal skill in the

United States, other cultures may see this as a sign of disrespect. These specific considerations, as well as others, are explored more fully in the following section.

What School Psychologists Can Do

The components of a SEL curriculum reflecting social justice should be among the foremost considerations school psychologists should take when advocating for SEL implementation and choosing specific SEL curricula. The application of social justice is complementary to multitiered systems of support; however, a social justice framework more strongly considers the cultural and ecological context in which the SEL instruction takes place (Shriberg & Moy, 2014).

For practitioners attempting to advocate for implementing SEL curriculum at a more integrated level, the following talking points related to social justice may be helpful when speaking with administration:

- SEL programs may be costly at the outset, but they can save money in the long term. Good SEL curricula can positively impact behavior, interpersonal relations between staff and students, attendance, and academics. SEL curricula are not only meant to be intervention agents, but also prevention agents (Durlak, 2011; Greenberg et al., 2003; Weissberg, Payton, O'Brien, & Munro, 2007).
- Higher levels of interventions can be supported through staff initiatives and cost-effective evidence-based practices.
- SEL programs can be part of a larger school climate initiative, which gives the school a common language, encourages conversations between different members of the school community, and can increase student and staff satisfaction (Collie, Shapka, & Perry, 2012).

Other practitioners may want to integrate socially just SEL practices into their school culture and into MTSS initiatives, and may be in the process of choosing an SEL curriculum or have SEL curricula already chosen. Regardless, we recommend the following steps for practitioners seeking a more integrated and socially just approach to bringing and expanding SEL programs in their schools.

- Determine your school's needs using a school-wide assessment or screener. Along with administration and staff, create specific and measurable goals for students based on SEL standards (see your state's or another's for reference; McKevitt, 2012).
- Choose an evidence-based SEL curriculum that promotes positive school culture, utilizes a common language for the school to adopt, and teaches specific social, emotional, and behavioral skills. It should also meet the goals you developed for the school and be cost-effective to implement (McKevitt, 2012).
- Do your research. Find out which populations the curriculum has been tested on. If the population is comparable to your own school's population, then move forward with it. If the populations are drastically different, think about how the curriculum would fit in with

the school community, how it could be adapted, and whether or not another curriculum might best fit the needs of your school (Kress & Elias, 2006; McKevitt, 2012).

- Get input from the school community, including parents, as to what skills they would like to see their students learn and how the community can support these goals. Parents should be seen as equal partners in SEL implementation, not simply as home enforcers. Schools should ensure that SEL curricula reflects parents' values and are culturally responsive, thus encouraging a socially just practice and increasing the likelihood of home support.
- Create an implementation plan. You will not only be working with teachers to implement the universal SEL curriculum, but also putting in place higher tiers of intervention for students who continue to struggle (McKevitt, 2012).
- If your school or district struggles to find the funds to get good SEL programs, look into grants. CASEL's website offers a PDF listing SEL resources and funding options for schools and district (see https://static.squarespace.com/static/513f79f9e4b05ce7b70e9673/t/52fbdd36e4b0a0ce2c93a95c/1392237878883/funding-and-resources-national-5-3-11.pdf).

Multitiered Systems of Support

Speaking on a broad basis, school initiatives are often fragmented and focus on addressing specific problems "without an adequate understanding of the mission, priorities, and culture of schools" (Sarason, 1996). According to Greenberg and colleagues (2003, p. 467), "Programs that are insufficiently coordinated, monitored, evaluated, and improved over time will have reduced impact on student behavior and are unlikely to be sustained." Taking these ideas into account, the authors have compiled the following recommendations for tiered SEL interventions.

Tier 1
Suggestions for the implementation of Tier 1 universal interventions include the following.

- Ensure teachers elicit feedback from students and parents regarding the applicability of the curriculum. Empower students and parents to participate in conversations regarding SEL initiatives from the outset (Kress & Elias, 2006; McKevitt, 2012).
- Find specific ways to involve families and community members in SEL efforts. For instance, hold family nights where some of the SEL skills are explored among families through a facilitated discussion (include food, if possible!). Bring in community members to discuss how they use different SEL skills in their work (this not only gets students thinking about future careers, but how SEL skills are applicable to all careers).
- Work with teachers to ensure that they adapt the curriculum to be more culturally sensitive, as needed (e.g., matching names in the curriculum to common names from the student body; reworking examples and situations to reflect more commonly experienced issues; Kress & Elias, 2006; McKevitt, 2012).
- Make sure a variety of extracurricular activities are available for students to participate in. Students should have a way to explore their interests and engage in positive peer social interactions (Brown & Evans, 2005).

Tier 2

Suggestions for the implementation of Tier 2 targeted interventions include the following.

- Ensure that higher levels of intervention are adapted to the specific needs of students. For instance, counseling groups can be great Tier 2 interventions, but pay attention to who makes up the group (Is it homogeneous or heterogeneous?) and what content is covered (Does it apply to everyone? Is it culturally sensitive?).

- To the extent appropriate, make sure you get to know the background of students involved in higher levels of intervention. Are events from their past or from the school's current practices possibly contributing to their current difficulties? What does their home support look like? Do they have access to adequate housing and food? These are simple questions, but often crucial to understanding and responding to a student's particular needs (Humphrey, Lendrum, Wigelsworth, & Kalambouka, 2009).

- Pay attention to the messages you send at higher levels of intervention. Are you simply trying to teach impulse control, or are you challenging students to become the best versions of themselves they possibly can? Are you teaching that bullying is bad, or are you teaching children how to be leaders and what behaviors that entails? (Elias, DeFini & Bergmann, 2010).

- Check in with family members about the acceptability of the intervention and involve them. You can ask parents to come in for a brief meeting to help brainstorm how they can develop a parallel plan at home to support interventions in culturally acceptable way. Make parents your partners (Durlak et al., 2011).

- Involve community members by asking them to speak in classes or to small groups as extensions of evidence-based programs. Choose leaders in the community who serve important roles, whom students likely respect, and who are representative of the student and community demographics.

- Create a student leadership team comprised of current and potential student leaders that is focused on empowering students to take ownership of their own social and emotional literacy. As a faculty sponsor, the school psychologist could encourage this team to plan school SEL events, become models for practicing SEL skills, and critically reflect on school and student practices (Kress & Elias, 2006).

Tier 3

Suggestions for the implementation of Tier 3 intensive interventions include the following.

- Help children requiring more intensive interventions participate in school activities that are acceptable to them. This helps them to pursue interests and engage in positive peer and adult relationships (Brown & Evans, 2005).

- Ensure parents are valued as equal partners. You may consider bringing parents in for a special meeting to discuss collaboration with the school regarding behavioral expectations, at-home support, encouragement of positive behaviors and interests, and other issues. Home visits (a highly underutilized tool) also help to get parents on board with school initiatives.

- To the extent possible, individualize the higher tiers of intervention to the student's specific needs, interests, and motivations. If you struggle to connect with the student, spend more time getting to know the student in an environment where he or she feels more comfortable. If the student resists working with you due to background or demographics, find a staff member to whom the student might be more responsive (Humphrey et al., 2009).

Conclusion

Research has made it clear that SEL programming in schools can be essential to developing key skills in social, academic, interpersonal, and self-regulatory domains. School psychologists not only need to become more knowledgeable about the wide range of SEL programs and curricula available, but they should also advocate for these programs through a social justice lens to create more equitable access to quality SEL programming.

By looking at schools' needs through a social justice framework, new and important considerations may arise. We have presented some of these considerations here, particularly in the area of advocacy for socially just SEL curricula and integrating SEL curricula in a socially just manner. Although the evidence base is still expanding, curricula are always changing, and costs of these curricula may be prohibitive for some, resources are still available to provide support in decision-making and funding. Current research (available through the websites of CASEL, What Works Clearinghouse, NASP, and other education-focused research organizations), educational legislation, NASP standards of practice, professional organizations, grants, and awards are all common and useful available resources. Ultimately, it is up to the school community, led by the school-based practitioner, to take the next big step of advocating for and adapting evidence-based practices in a socially just manner.

References

Bird, K. A., & Sultmann, W. F. (2010). Social and emotional learning: Reporting a system approach to developing relationships, nurturing well-being and invigorating learning. *Educational and Child Psychology, 27*(1), 143–155.

Briggs, A. (2012). The school psychologist as social justice advocate. In D. Shriberg, S. Y. Song, A. H. Miranda, & K. M. Radliff (Eds.), *School psychology and social justice: Conceptual foundations and tools for practice.* (pp. 294–310). New York, NY: Routledge.

Brown, R., & Evans, W. P. (2005). Developing school connectedness among diverse youth through extracurricular programming. *Prevention Researcher, 12*(2), 14–17.

Caldarella, P., Christensen, L., Kramer, T. J., & Kronmiller, K. (2009). Promoting social and emotional learning in second grade students: A study of the Strong Start curriculum. *Early Childhood Education Journal, 37*(1), 51–56. doi:10.1007/s10643-009-0321-4

Collie, R. J., Shapka, J. D., & Perry, N. E. (2012). School climate and social–emotional learning: Predicting teacher stress, job satisfaction, and teaching efficacy. *Journal of Educational Psychology, 104*(4), 1189–1204. doi:10.1037/a0029356

Durlak, J. A., Weissberg, R. P., Dymnicki, A. B., Taylor, R. D., & Schellinger, K. B. (2011). The impact of enhancing students' social and emotional learning: A meta-analysis of school-based universal interventions. *Child Development, 82*(1), 405–432. doi:10.1111/j.1467-8624.2010.01564.x

Elias, M. J., DeFini, J., & Bergmann, J. (2010). Coordinating social-emotional and character development (SECD) initiatives improves school climate and student learning. *Middle School Journal (j3), 42*(1), 30–37.

Graczyk, P. A., Matjasko, J. L., Weissberg, R. P., Greenberg, M. T., Elias, M. J., & Zins, J. E. (2000). The role of the Collaborative to Advance Social and Emotional Learning (CASEL) in supporting the implementation of quality school-based prevention programs. *Journal of Educational and Psychological Consultation, 11*(1), 3–6.

Greenberg, M. T., Weissberg, R. P., O'Brien, M. U., Zins, J. E., Fredericks, L., Resnik, H., & Elias, M. J. (2003). Enhancing school-based prevention and youth development through coordinated social, emotional, and academic learning. *American Psychologist, 58*(6–7), 466–474. doi:10.1037/0003-066X.58.6-7.466

Hallam, S. (2009). An evaluation of the Social and Emotional Aspects of Learning (SEAL) programme: Promoting positive behaviour, effective learning, and well-being in primary school children. *Oxford Review of Education, 35*(3), 313–330. doi:10.1080/03054980902934597

Hoffman, D. M. (2009). Reflecting on social emotional learning: A critical perspective on trends in the United States. *Review of Educational Research, 79*(2), 533–556. doi:10.3102/0034654308325184

Humphrey, N., Lendrum, A., Wigelsworth, M., & Kalambouka, A. (2009). Implementation of primary social and emotional aspects of learning small group work: A qualitative study. *Pastoral Care in Education, 27*(3), 219–239. doi:10.1080/02643940903136808

Kress, J. S., & Elias, M. J. (2006). Building learning communities through social and emotional learning: Navigating the rough seas of implementation. *Professional School Counseling, 10*(1), 102–107.

McKevitt, B. (2012). School psychologists' knowledge and use of evidence-based, social–emotional learning interventions. *Contemporary School Psychology, 16*, 33–45.

National Association of School Psychologists. (2010). *Model for comprehensive and integrated school psychological services.* Retrieved from http://www.nasponline.org/standards/2010standards/2_PracticeModel.pdf

North, C. E. (2006). More than words? Delving into the substantive meaning(s) of "social justice" in education. *Review of Educational Research, 76*(4), 507–535. doi:10.3102/00346543076004507

Sarason, S. B. (1996). *Revisiting "The culture of the school and the problem of change".* New York, NY: Teachers College Press.

Shriberg, D., Bonner, M., Sarr, B. J., Walker, A., Hyland, M., & Chester, C. (2008). Social justice through a school psychology lens: Definition and applications. *School Psychology Review, 37*(4), 453–468.

Shriberg, D., & Moy, G. (2014). Best practices in social justice advocacy for school psychologists. In P. L. Harrison & A. Thomas (Eds.), *Best practices in school psychology: Foundations*. Bethesda, MD: National Association of School Psychologists.

U.S. Department of Education, Institute of Education Sciences, National Center for Education Evaluation and Regional Assistance, What Works Clearinghouse. (2011). *Children classified as having an emotional disturbance: The Incredible Years*. Retrieved from http://ies.ed.gov/ncee/wwc/pdf/intervention_reports/wwc_incredibleyears_111511.pdf

U.S. Department of Education, Institute of Education Sciences, National Center for Education Evaluation and Regional Assistance, What Works Clearinghouse. (2013) *Early childhood education interventions for children with disabilities: Social skills training*. Retrieved from http://ies.ed.gov/ncee/wwc/pdf/intervention_reports/wwc_socialskills_020513.pdf

Weissberg, R. P., Payton, J. W., O'Brien, M. U., & Munro, S. (2007). Social and emotional learning. *Moral education: A handbook, 2*, 417–418.

Related Communiqué Resources

School Psychology, Juvenile Justice, and the School to Prison Pipeline (Dec 2010)

Advancing Social Justice Through Primary Prevention (Jun 2009)

Social Justice in School Psychology: Moving Forward (Jun 2009)

Applying Social Justice Principles Through School-Based Restorative Justice (Nov 2009)

Social Justice Action Strategies for School Psychologists: Three Perspectives (Dec 2008)

Perceptions of Head Start Teachers about Culturally Relevant Practice

Margaret Gichuru, Jeanetta G. Riley, and Jo Robertson

Introduction

Children bring a variety of cultural, linguistic, and social backgrounds into the preschool classroom. When teachers consider these backgrounds, they are better able to create environments that reflect children's cultures and to design learning experiences that build on children's prior experiences. Through these environments and experiences, bridges are created between home and school to more fully meet children's needs (Hyland, 2010) and allow them to "participate fully and meaningfully in the construction of knowledge" (Ladson-Billings, 2009, p. 104).

Teachers' abilities to implement culturally relevant practices in their classrooms can enhance children's school success, help to develop and maintain children's self-identities, and foster cultural awareness among the children (Compton-Lilly, 2006; Ladson-Billings, 2009).

The definitions of culturally relevant practice are varied. Gay (2000) uses the term culturally responsive teaching and explains it as the teacher's use of students' cultural backgrounds and understandings to create more effective instructional experiences that were more likely to engage students in the learning and increase academic achievement.

Ladson-Billings (1995, 2009) defines culturally relevant teaching as empowering students by helping them to succeed academically, to develop deeper understandings of the significance of the values and traditions of their own cultures, and to critically analyze societal beliefs and perspectives about cultural issues. According to Ladson-Billings (2009), when teachers help students make connections between

Margaret Gichuru, et al., "Perceptions of Head Start Teachers about Culturally Relevant Practice," *Multicultural Education*, vol. 22, no. 2, pp. 46-50. Copyright © 2015 by Caddo Gap Press. Reprinted with permission. Provided by ProQuest LLC. All rights reserved.

what they learn in school and their everyday lives, students are more likely see the worth in the learning and in themselves.

Each of these definitions has in common the need to create a bridge between the school and the students' everyday lived experiences within their home and community. This requires that teachers learn about the general cultural values, expectations, and language of their students' cultural groups (Gay, 2002; Hyland, 2010).

However, to effectively implement culturally relevant practices involves more than the teacher's awareness of diversity within the classroom (Gay, 2000). Teachers must fully understand the "cultural particularities of specific ethic groups" (Brown, 2007, p. 59) and, according to Gay (2000), have "the courage to dismantle the status quo" (p. 13) regarding educational policies and procedures that perpetuate differences in educational opportunities for diverse students.

According to Copple and Bredekamp (2009), early childhood teachers must learn about the family and community specific to the individual child to be effective. However, to enact culturally relevant practice involves moving beyond learning about family and community and toward a more complete understanding of each child's ethnic and cultural identity (Gay 2000).

Thus, early childhood teachers need general knowledge about the various cultures of children in their classrooms and specific knowledge about individual children's specific cultural identities to create relevant learning experiences that reflect children's cultures and to tap into the "funds of knowledge" (Moll, Amanti, Neff, & Gonzalez, 1992) children bring with them into the classroom. Culturally relevant practices help children celebrate and respect their linguistic and cultural backgrounds thus increasing opportunities for positive learning experiences.

When teachers incorporate knowledge of children's family and community cultures into the classroom, they can create a bridge between the children's home and school (Gilliard, Moore, & Lemieux, 2007). Recently, Head Start programs have enrolled higher numbers of children from diverse cultural backgrounds with 42% of the programs indicating that diversity of their communities had increased in the past five years (Cheri, et, al., 2011). Kentucky has developed Migrant Head Start programs to meet the needs of that growing population (Kentucky Head Start Association, n.d.). This trend requires teachers to understand culturally relevant practices and how to implement them in their classrooms.

While studies about how teachers create and implement culturally relevant practices have increased over the past decade, few include teachers of preschool age children. Morrison, Robbins, and Rose (2008) searched six databases for research studies since 1995 that investigated culturally relevant practice and found 45 studies. Of these 45, only two specifically addressed preschool teachers. With this paucity of studies involving preschool teachers, more research into culturally relevant practice in preschool environments is needed.

A previous investigation by three of the current authors about culturally diverse families of Head Start children and their perspectives of their children's school experiences (Riley, Gichuru, & Robertson, 2012) led to the current study. The results of the first study indicated that the families were very satisfied with their children's experiences in Head Start; however, the families voiced few particulars about experiences of their children that were specific to their cultural backgrounds. Therefore, the current study was designed with the purpose of investigating how children's cultural backgrounds are reflected in Head Start classrooms based on the perceptions of seven Head Start teachers.

Methodology

This qualitative study examined how children's cultural backgrounds are reflected in Head Start classrooms from teachers' perspectives. The study was an extension of the researchers' previous investigation examining how families of diverse cultural backgrounds viewed their children's experiences in Head Start.

Investigators for this study were from diverse backgrounds. One of the investigators is a native of South Korea, one is originally from Kenya, and two are of Caucasian background from the United States. The diverse backgrounds of the investigators and their interest in qualitative research have been the catalyst for the research.

A purposeful sample of seven participants was recruited (Creswell, 2007; Maxwell, 1996). Directors of the three Head Start grantees in which the families from the previous study had children enrolled were contacted and asked to identify preschool teachers who had children in their classrooms from culturally diverse backgrounds. The participants were chosen and asked to provide in-depth descriptions of their experiences from their own perspectives (Bogdan & Biklen, 2003).

Data Collection

The investigators contacted the teachers to explain the observation and interview process; each teacher agreed to participate in the study. All teachers were female. One teacher was Hispanic, two were African American, and four were Caucasian. The teachers' educational backgrounds ranged from associate degree to master's degree in education. The demographics of the class-rooms included African-American, Latino, and Caucasian children.

Investigators developed an observation and an interview protocol for the systematic gathering of data. Each teacher was observed in her classroom or center setting for two to three hours using the observation protocol (see Appendix A). Additionally, a semi-structured interview using an interview protocol (see Appendix B) was conducted for approximately one hour after each observation. Interviews were audio taped.

Before interviewing each participant, the investigators explained the purpose of the interview to the participant. During each interview, the investigators used open-ended questions to generate qualitative data and provide in-depth information. Additionally, the investigators used prompts for clarification and elaboration of information collected from the participants' perspective. Follow up questions were also asked to clarify the teacher's answers and what was observed in the teacher's classroom. After each observation and interview, observation notes were typed, and the audio tapes were transcribed verbatim.

APPENDIX A

Observation Protocol for Observing in Teachers' Classrooms

Classroom Environment:

1. Environment and classroom materials represent cultural and ethnic background of children and families. (e.g., books, dolls, puppets, photos, posters, words in various languages, puzzles, dress up clothes, musical instruments, etc.).
2. Participation of all children is encouraged and facilitated by teacher.

Communication:

1. Children's primary language used by adults in the classroom (use of child's home language if different than English).
2. Newsletters and other communications sent home to families are translated for families, if needed.
3. Teachers talk with children about their personal interests and family.

Curriculum:

1. Children are being taught about their own culture.
2. Children are introduced to other cultures through positive experiences (exploring similarities/differences in the cultures of people).

APPENDIX B

Interview Protocol Questions for Teachers in Study

1. Demographic information:
   a. educational background.
   b. experience in teaching/working with children & families.
   c. professional development training about culture and/or cultural experience for young children.
2. In your initial contact when you meet with families, what do you talk about?
   Throughout the year, how do you communicate what the children are learning to their families?
3. Please tell me any challenges that you have in communicating with families.
4. How do you let the families know why you emphasize what the children are learning?
   If reading is part of the answer: What about families who do not read? What about the families who do not read English?
5. What are some examples of activities that you provide that reflect the child's/family's interests and priorities?
6. What are some things you consider as you plan and implement your curriculum?
   Are there other things that you consider?
7. How are the families involved in the children's education?
8. What have you done to help all children feel accepted in your classroom?

Data Analysis

Data analysis occurred after all observations and interviews were conducted. Data were analyzed through coding and recoding observation notes and interview transcriptions (Creswell, 2007). Using the questions from the protocol, categories of meaningful words and phrases were established. Words and phrases were identified as meaningful when the ideas the words conveyed were used by several participants at different Head Start sites.

Meaningful words and phrases for each of the protocol questions were examined to determine initial patterns, categories, and themes for each question. Upon rereading of the notes and transcripts, data were recategorized when investigators determined new categories were needed or data needed to be rearranged.

Findings and Discussion

The purpose of this study was to explore how Head Start Program teachers reflect children's cultural backgrounds in the classrooms. Three themes emerged from the data analysis: influence of children's interest and development on curriculum, reflection of diversity within the physical environment, and communication between teacher and families.

Children's Interest and Development Influence Curriculum

There is increased global recognition of the importance of including children's ethnic and cultural knowledge in their curriculum (Fuller, 2007; Nsamenang, 2008). In this study, teachers perceived that children's interests, needs, and development influenced their curriculum choices. Teachers were observed in their classrooms talking with children about their home life and various family activities in the home or community.

The interviews indicated that the teachers used home visits to gather information and understand the children's interests and needs. One participant elaborated on what they discussed during the visits:

> We [the teachers] ask the parents what are their goals in all those developmental areas. Like language. What do we want them to learn about language? What do we want them to learn about society? What do we want them to learn about physical development? We look at their goal sheet, and if there are areas that their parents may have had concerns about or questions about, we work with the child, and then we address it. We have the parent visits with the family advocate. If they have any questions or concerns they can address those with her. We ask them ... whenever they're in we try to ask them, hey, you know what's going on with you? What's going on at home? How do you feel about things that are going on in the classroom?

When asked about professional development on the topic of cultural diversity, the teachers did talk about trainings. In spite of the teachers' indications of experiencing training about cultural diversity, most of the training involved surface level issues, generally about the use of the child's home language. Embedding the children's cultures into the daily curriculum to enhance children's understanding of their own cultural identity and that of their peers was not mentioned in any depth by most of the teachers. For example, one participant stated,

> They sent us on trainings, and they talk about how it's important to be culturally diverse, and you know, make sure that we use the language of the children mostly when they're young.

Another participant indicated,

> Every year we have an ELL (English Language Learners) training. And in some of those trainings we've talked about different cultures.

In contrast to most of the participants, one participant had trained others about diversity. She believed that diversity went beyond race,

> Diversity can lend itself to somebody's parents being in jail and somebody's not ... A single parent home vs. a mom and dad in the home ... All of those things add to diversity.

However, when asked how she had gained knowledge about diversity to be able to train others, she chuckled as she talked about finding information on the internet,

> I sought it out for myself. And then the more that I did with it, my supervisor was like, hey we need to have more stuff with it. So then we wound up having like a training for us.

Her trainings focused on books with characters of various ethnicities and on helping her audiences develop a different understanding of diversity as they thought about their curriculum:

> I did several trainings on diversity. I did language and literacy training about just bringing in multicultural books and just things about diversity to try to get them to think out of the boxes more than just a black face and a white face and an Asian face in the room. If you're going to meet your children's needs you've got to understand that they have much more in common than they do different. And because of that, you can meet the diverse needs. ... And with me, with the diversity training with the books, that really impacted my participants heavily. Because they didn't know there were a lot of books about black children or by black authors.

The Reflection of Diversity within the Physical Environment

The classroom environment created by the teachers reflected the diversity of the children. Observations indicated that the teachers displayed posters with pictures of culturally diverse children and families, labeled shelves in English and Spanish, and included items such as books, dolls, music CDs, and figures of people representing various cultures in their classrooms.

The materials were sensitive to the children's cultural backgrounds. In her interview, one teacher mentioned the families' reactions when they saw labels in both English and Spanish, "Parents are pleased with labeling classroom materials in English and Spanish." Another teacher mentioned that at the beginning of the semester families of the children in her class were requested to bring family pictures that she framed and placed around the room. She said, "They want to come in because they want to see their pictures and feel connected to it."

Although some of the teachers who had children from a Hispanic background in their classes spoke primarily English, they made an effort to use simple Spanish words and phrases while speaking to children who spoke English as a second language. In one observation, a teacher who was English speaking attempted to use words and phrases in Spanish language when interacting with children during center time and outdoor play.

Additionally, the teachers used both English and Spanish in classroom activities and displays. In one observation, the calendar activities, counting, and a song about the days of the week were conducted in both English and Spanish. Teaching immigrant children and English language learners works best if children are not forced to abandon their native language (California Department of Education, 2007). In addition, classroom learning for preschoolers is enriched when teachers encourage the use of home language while children acquire English (California Department of Education).

Communication between Teacher and Families

It is important for early childhood professionals to have effective communication skills and the ability to establish relationship with families of young children from diverse cultural and linguistic backgrounds. Through interactions, the families are able to share about their culture, ethnicity, and language with the professionals and receive culturally and linguistically appropriate services (Hains, Lynch, & Winton, 2000).

In this study, communication methods reflected the teachers' efforts to include family priorities and interests. In addition to the home visits, the teachers held parent-teacher conferences, sent newsletters and parent-child activity ideas to families, and had translators available, if needed, to communicate with the families. An example of how teachers collected information during the initial home visit was explained by one participant:

> We talk about the traditional things, allergies in food, and we actually have a family conference form that talks about what they want as a parent for their child to learn about the world, about themselves, about communication.

Participants offered various ways in which they stayed in communication with families to acknowledge and include families in the children's learning experiences. One participant noted that she maintained an open door policy and invited families to visit and share their cultures. The teachers also discussed parent-teacher conferences and what the conversations were about during the conferences:

> ... during parent conference, let them (parents) know, you know, how the children are progressing. I have some of their work in their folders, you know, for them to look at. You know, then if they have any questions or comments, they let me know.

Furthermore, one of the teachers explained that the family advocate who spoke Spanish, held parents meetings during the year. During the first meeting, the advocate asked the parents what activities they wanted to do during the year with their children at the school. The parents decided that they wanted to repeat the Mexican independence celebration they had carried out in the school the previous year:

> ... they again wanted to do the celebration that we had last September, but they wanted to add some more things into it. So, it was really the parents that came together from both classrooms and said that that was something they wanted to do.

One participate explained how the families were directly involved in sharing items about their culture and how she used them in the classroom,

> They send ... sometimes I get books, sometimes I get fingerplays ... They want us to know about their cultures.

Another participant said that many families' priority is to have their children acquire academic skills and learn to speak English,

> I think the big thing to the family is that they can write their name and then I guess the family really wants them to speak English.

Another participant mentioned what parents were concerned about during their parents' conferences,

> They just want to know how is my child doing? You know can my child count?

In contrast, another teacher noted how the families rarely asked questions of her other than whether their child would be fed while at school. Additionally, she noted how she tried to encourage family member to feel welcome in her classroom:

> ... your Latino culture, they really think highly of teachers. They think I guess more like a priest, you know. So it's hard to get them to come into the classroom. So like last year, we had a sign out sheet in here [a room just outside the classroom door], sign in and out sheet, but they would never step into the classroom. So I've moved it inside cause I want them to feel a part of it.

Conclusion and Implications

This study provides initial insight into the scope of how culturally relevant practices are implemented in seven Head Start classrooms. Moreover, it raises awareness about Head Start teachers' understandings of culturally relevant practice and examines the importance of teachers developing knowledge and skills that will facilitate effective implementation of culturally relevant practices in the classrooms.

Although the teachers in this study made efforts to communicate with all families, most of the communication tended to be one-way, from the teacher to the family. According to Graham-Clay (2005), one-way communication between families and the school setting is typical. Limited communication with families who are learning English or do not speak English is exacerbated when written notes and newsletters are incorrectly interpreted or when children take the primary responsibility of interpreting messages to their parents (Gou, 2006).

Matthews and Jang (2007) reported on an extensive study conducted by the Center for Law and Social Policy concerning immigrant families and their experiences in relation to child care. Families in the study consistently brought up language as a barrier in building connection with their children's teachers. In an effort to reduce language as a barrier, a language access plan was developed to expand communication beyond typical translation of documents and use of interpreters to reaching out to leaders within community organizations, such as the church.

More open two-way communication between teachers and families allows families to share their desires for their children, in turn providing teachers with better understandings of the children's cultures and how to design and implement culturally relevant teaching. To assist Head Start teachers' efforts to develop more effective two-way communication, administrators can encourage teachers to make continuing efforts to develop on-going relationships with families, thus encouraging families to engage in open, two-way communication.

Furthermore, an understanding by administrators and others who make policy that teachers need support in developing respectful and responsive methods for two-way communication may be an initial step in providing necessary personnel to assist in reducing language as a barrier for family involvement.

The teachers in the current study indicated they had participated in training about cultural diversity. The training focused on including materials in the classroom depicting people of diverse cultures and the importance of children continuing to use their home language when it is different from English. There was limited training about how to embed the children's cultures into the daily curriculum and of how to help children understand their own cultural identity and that of their peers.

Additionally, although the classroom environments that the teachers created included materials of various cultures; they were not necessarily individualized to the children in the classroom nor did the teachers make explicit connections between materials and children's understandings about various cultures.

Training that provides exposure to issues of cultural diversity is a starting point; however, on-going professional development that allows participants opportunities to build understandings of diversity are needed. McDermott and Varenne (1995) emphasized the importance for educators understanding the value of making the connections between children's cultural practices to their academic growth and not to consider their cultural backgrounds as a distraction to their school learning.

Additionally, Vesely and Ginsburg (2011) discussed a study in which administrators provided early childhood professionals with professional development opportunities to enhance their practices for working with diverse immigrant families. In the study, sustained professional learning was essential for professionals to deepen their understanding of different cultures through home visits and supporting the diverse families' access to available social services. Continued professional development is essential for teachers to develop the knowledge, skills, and dispositions needed to effectively work with culturally diverse children and their families.

This study examined seven Head Start teachers' perceptions of how they implemented culturally relevant practice in their Head Start classrooms. Even though teachers expressed limited training about integrating the children's cultures into their everyday curriculum and supporting children's comprehension about their cultural identity, they made an effort to create a culturally relevant environment. The teachers used materials that reflected diversity, created a curriculum that focused on children's interests and developmental needs, and ensured communication was maintained between themselves and the children's families.

While the findings of this qualitative study are not meant to be generalized to the larger population, they do suggest a need for increased opportunities for more in-depth learning about culturally relevant practices for early childhood educators. Furthermore, examination of how these learning opportunities help teachers to incorporate children's culture into the daily curriculum at a deeper, more meaningful level and to bridge communication barriers between home and school are needed.

References

Bogdan, R. C., & Biklen, S. K. (2003). *Qualitative research for education: An introduction to theories and methods* (4th ed.). Boston: Allyn & Bacon.

Brown, M. (2007). Educating all students: Creating culturally responsive teachers, classrooms, and schools. *Intervention in School and Clinic, 43*(1), 57–62.

California Department of Education Child Development Division. (2007). *Preschool English learners: Principles and practices to promote language, literacy, and learning—A resource guide.* Sacramento: California Department of Education Press.

Cheri, V. A., Boller, K., Xue, Y., Blair, R., Aikens, N., Burwick, A., Shrago, Y., Carlton, B. L., Kalb, L., Mendenko, L., Cannon, J., Harrington, S., & Stein, J. (2011). *Learning as we go: a first snapshot of early head start programs, staff, families, and children.* OPRE Report #2011-7, Washington, DC., U.S. Department of Health and Human Services.

Compton-Lilly, C. (2006). Identity, childhood culture, and literacy learning: A case study. *Journal of Early Childhood Literacy, 6*(1), 57–76.

Copple, C., & Bredekamp, S. (2009). *Developmentally appropriate practice in early childhood programs serving children birth though age 8* (3rd ed.). Washington, DC: National Association for Education of Young Children.

Creswell, J. W. (2007). *Research design: Quantitative and qualitative approaches* (2nd ed.). Thousand Oaks, CA: Sage.

Fuller, B. (2007). *Standardized childhood: The political and cultural struggle over early education.* Palo Alto, CA: Stanford University Press.

Gay, G. (2000). *Culturally responsive teaching: Theory, research, and practice.* New York: Teachers College Press.

Gay, G. (2002). Preparing for culturally responsive teaching. *Journal of Teacher Education, 53*(2), 106–116.

Gilliard, J. L., Moore, R. A., & Lemieux, J. J. (2007). In Hispanic culture, the children are the jewels of the family: An investigation of home and community culture in a bilingual early care and education center serving migrant and seasonal farm worker families. *Early Childhood Research and Practice, 9*(2). Retrieved from http://ecrp.uiuc.edu/v9n2/gilliard.html

Gou, Y. (2006). Why didn't they show up? Rethinking ESP parent involvement in K-12 education. TSEL *Canada Journal, 24*(1), 80–95. Retrieved from http://www.teslcanadajournal.ca/index.php/%20tesl/article/viewFile/29/29

Gregg, K., Rugg, M. E., & Souto-Manning, M. (2011). Fostering family-centered practices through a family-created portfolio. *The School Community Journal, 21*(1), 53–70. Retrieved from http://www.adi.org/journal/2011ss/GreggRuggSouto-Manning-Spring2011.pdf

Hains, A. H., Lynch, E. W., & Winton, P. J. (2000). *Moving towards cross-cultural competence in lifelong personnel development: A review of the literature* (CLAS Technical Report No. 3). Champaign: University of Illinois at Urbana-Champaign, Early Childhood Research Institute on Culturally and Linguistically Appropriate Services.

Hyland, N. E. (2010). Social justice in early childhood classrooms: What the research tells us. *Young Children 65*(1), 82–87.

Kentucky Head Start Association. (n.d.). *Scope of services provided*. Retrieved September, 4, 2013, from http://www.khsa.org/wp/?page_id=115

Ladson-Billings, G. (1995). But that's just good teaching: The case for culturally relevant pedagogy. *Theory into Practice, 34*(3), 159–165.

Ladson-Billings, G. (2009). *The dream-keepers: Successful teachers of African-American children*. San Franscico: Jossey-Bass.

Matthews, H., & Jang, D. (2007). *The challenges of change: Learning from the child care and early education experiences of immigrant families*. Washington, DC: Center for Law and Social Policy. Retrieved from http://www.clasp.org/admin/site/publications/files/0356.pdf

Maxwell, J. A. (1996). *Qualitative research design: An interactive approach*. Thousand Oaks, CA: Sage.

McDermont, R., & Varenne, H. (1995). Culture as disability. *Anthropology and Education Quarterly, 26*(3), 324–348.

Moll, L. C., Amanti, C., Neff, D., & Gonzalez, N. (1992). Funds of knowledge for teaching: using a qualitative approach to connect homes and classrooms. *Theory into Practice, 31*(2), 132–141.

Morrison, K. A., Robbins, H. H., & Rose, D. G. (2008). Operationalizing culturally relevant pedagogy: A synthesis of classroom-based research. *Equity & Excellence in Education, 41*(4), 433–452.

Nsamenang, A. B. (2008). (Mis)understanding ECD in Africa: The force of local and imposed motives. In M. Garcia, A. Pence, & J. Evans (Eds.), *Africa's future, Africa's challenge: Early childhood care and development in Sub-Saharan Africa* (pp. 135–149). Washington, DC: World Bank.

Riley, J. G., Gichuru, M. & Robertson, J. (2012). Perceptions of culturally diverse head start families: A focus group study. *Multicultural Education, 20*(1), 33–37.

Vesely, C. K., & Ginsberg, M. R. (2011). Strategies and practices for working with immigrant families in early education programs. *Young Children, 60*(1), 84–89.

Discussion Questions

1. Indicate what factors can influence social and emotional development in childhood.
2. How can adults support and encourage a child's social and emotional development?
3. Why do adults (parents/caregivers) play an essential role in the social and emotional development of an infant or toddler?
4. What is the role of attachment style with child social–emotional development?
5. Considering attachment theory, what types of attachment styles do you have? Explain.

UNIT V

LANGUAGE AND SPEECH

Cognitive Development During Early Childhood

Megan Clegg-Kraynok, Kelvin L. Seifert, and Robert J. Hoffnung

Language Acquisition during the Preschool Years

For most children, language expands rapidly after infancy. They learn words, form ever-longer sentences, and engage in more-complex dialogue. Fairly early in the preschool years, most children have mastered the basic sounds, or *phonology,* that make their first language meaningful and distinctive. They have also made a good beginning at acquiring a vocabulary of single words. We described both of these achievements in Chapter 6 in connection with infants' cognitive development. Now, during early childhood, children's most striking achievements involve *syntax,* or the way the child organizes utterances, and *pragmatics,* or knowledge about how to adjust utterances to the needs and expectations of different situations and speakers. As it turns out, these twin achievements show both diversity and uniformity across children, and therefore, they raise important questions about language acquisition and how parents and other caregivers can influence it. In this section, we look at these questions, beginning with preschoolers' achievements in the area of syntax.

The Nature of Syntax

The **syntax** of a language is a group of rules for ordering and relating its elements. Linguists call the

> **syntax** Rules for ordering and relating the elements of a language.

elements of language *morphemes. Morphemes* are the smallest meaningful units of language; they include words as well as a number of prefixes and suffixes that carry meaning (the /s/ in *houses* or the /re/ in *redo)* and verb-tense modifiers (the /ing/ in *going).*

Megan Clegg-Kraynok, Kelvin L. Seifert, and Robert J. Hoffnung, Selection from "Cognitive Development during Early Childhood"," *Child and Adolescent Development: A Chronological Approach,* pp. 206-215, R1-R36. Copyright © 2019 by Academic Media Solutions. Reprinted with permission.

Syntactic rules operate on morphemes in several ways. Sometimes, they mark important relationships between large classes or groups of words. Consider these two pairs of sentences:

1a. Roberto helped Barbara.   1b. Barbara helped Roberto.

2a. Frank helps Ruije.   2b. Frank helped Ruije.

These sentences differ in meaning because of syntactic rules. In the first pair, a rule about the order, or sequence, of words tells us who is giving the help and who is receiving it: the name preceding the verb is the agent (the helper), and the name following the verb is the recipient (the "helpee"). In the second pair, the morphemes /es/ and /ed/ tell something about when the event occurred; adding /es/ to the end of the word signifies that it is happening now, but adding /ed/ means it happened in the past. These rules, and many similar ones, are understood and used by all competent speakers of the language. Unlike textbook authors, however, the speakers may never state them and may be only barely aware of them.

Unfortunately, for a child learning to talk, some syntactic rules have only a small range of application, and still others have irregular exceptions. Most words, for example, signal pluralization (the existence of more than one) by having an /s/ or /es/ added at the end; *book* means one volume, and *books* means more than one. But a few words use other methods to signal the plural. *Foot* means one, and *feet,* not *foots,* means more than one; *child* means one and *children* more than one; and *deer* can mean either one animal or several.

Thus, in acquiring syntax, a young child confronts a mixed system of rules. Some apply widely and regularly, and others apply narrowly and exceptionally. Added to these complexities is the fact that the child often hears utterances that are grammatically incomplete or even incorrect. Somehow, he or she must sort these out from the grammatically acceptable utterances while at the same time trying to sort out the various syntactic rules and the contexts for using them.

Beyond First Words: Semantic and Syntactic Relations

Before age two, children begin linking words when they speak. Initially the words seem to be connected by their *semantic relations,* or the meanings intended for them, rather than by *syntactic relations,* the relations among grammatical classes of words such as nouns, verbs, and adjectives. This is particularly true when the child is still speaking primarily in two-word utterances (sometimes called *duos).* As the mean length of a child's utterances increases to three words and more, syntactic relations become much more noticeable.

Duos and Telegraphic Speech

These ideas were documented in a classic set of three case studies of early language acquisition by Roger Brown (1973). When the children Brown observed were still speaking primarily in two-word utterances, their utterances were organized around eight possible semantic relationships; these are listed in Table 19.1, along with examples. The meanings of the utterances were determined by the intended relationships among the words, and the intentions of the preschool speakers often were discernible only by observing the context in which the utterances were made.

TABLE 19.1   Semantic Relations in Two-Word Utterances

A child's earliest utterances are organized not according to adultlike grammar but according to particular semantic or meaning-oriented relationships such as those listed in this table. Often the intended, underlying relationships are ambiguous and can be discerned only by an attentive, observant adult at the time of the utterance.

Relationship	Example
Agent + action	Baby cry
Action + object	Eat cookie
Agent + object	Bobby cookie
Action + locative (location)	Jump stair
Object + locative	Teddy bed
Possessor + possessed	Mommy sandwich
Attribute + object	Big dog
Demonstrative + object	There Daddy

"Mommy sandwich" could mean "the type of sandwich Mommy usually eats," or "Mommy is eating the sandwich," or "Mommy, give me a sandwich," all depending on the conversational context.

The reason for the ambiguity is that two-word utterances leave out indicators of syntactic relationships. One syntactic indicator is word order: due to word order, "the boy chased the girl" means something different than "the girl chased the boy." Children who still speak in duos do not use word order randomly, but they do tend to be less predictable about it than more linguistically mature children, whose utterances can be several words long. Another indicator of syntactic relationships is inflections, prepositions, and conjunctions. An older child will add *'s* to indicate possession (as in "Mommy's sandwich") and use words such as *in* and *on* to indicate location (as in "jump on the stair"). Leaving these indicators out makes the speech sound stilted and ambiguous; therefore, it is also called **holographic speech** or *telegraphic speech*— presumably because it sounds like a telegram. Telegraphic speech is characteristic of children's first efforts to combine words (around eighteen months to two years), but it can persist well after children begin using longer, more syntactic utterances some of the time.

> **holographic speech** When a single word is used to communicate a thought, such as when a child says "up" instead of "pick me up."

Regularities and Overgeneralizations

After highly individual beginnings, certain aspects of syntax develop in universal and predictable patterns. English-speaking children have a tendency to know more nouns than verbs, a bias that is not as marked among children learning languages such as Korean or Mandarin. In many Asian languages, verbs end sentences, likely making them "stick out" to the children (Hoff, 2008). The present progressive form *-ing* occurs quite early in most children's language, the regular plural morphemes *-s* and *-es* somewhat later, and articles such as *the* and *a* still later (Hoff, 2008; Marcus et al., 1992).

At a slightly older age, most English-speaking children begin using auxiliary verbs to form questions, but they do so without inverting word order, as adults normally do. At first, a child will say, "Why you are cooking?" and only later "Why are you cooking?" This suggests that language acquisition involves more than just copying adult language; after all, adults rarely model incorrect forms. To a certain extent, children's language seems to compromise between the new forms children hear and the old forms they already can produce easily.

Sometimes, in fact, early syntax becomes *too* regular, and children make **overgeneralizations**. Around age three, preschool children often make errors, such as always adding *–ed* to indicate past tense, even when it is not appropriate as in the sentence: "I runned faster than Maddie." The child uses the wrong but more regular form as opposed to the correct but irregular forms of an earlier age. Usually by early school age, they shift back again, although not necessarily because anyone teaches or forces them to do so. Apparently, their overgeneralizations represent efforts to try out new rules of syntax that they have finally noticed.

> **overgeneralizations** When children use common rules of speaking in all situations, even when inappropriate, such as adding *–s* to indicate a plural form such as, "Do you see all the deers?"

The Predisposition to Infer Grammar

As these examples suggest, and as research confirms (Marcus et al., 1992), young children seem to infer grammatical relationships, rather than simply copy others' speech. The tendency was first documented about sixty years ago in a research study by Hilda Berko (1958), but it is still used in many current tests of children's language development (Brindle, 2015; McDaniel et al., 1996). Instead of asking children about real words, the experimenter in Berko's classic study showed them pictures of imaginary creatures and actions that had nonsense words as names. With one picture, a child was told, "Here is a wug." Then he was shown two pictures and told, "Here are two of them. Here are two _____." Most children, even those as young as two and a half, completed the sentences with the grammatically correct word, *wugs*. Because they could not possibly have heard the term before, they must have applied a general rule for forming plurals, one that did not depend on copying any language experiences specifically but came from inferring the underlying structure of many experiences taken together. The rule most likely operated unconsciously because these children were very young indeed.

The Limits of Learning Rules

Preschoolers' skill at acquiring syntactic rules, however, obscures a seemingly contradictory fact about the acquisition of syntax: much syntax must be learned by rote. As we have pointed out, most children use irregular forms (such as *foot/feet*) correctly before they shift to incorrect but more regular forms. The most reasonable explanation for the change is that they pick up the very first sentence forms simply by copying, word for word, the sentences they hear spoken. Presumably, they copy many regular forms by rote, too, but the very regularity of these forms hides the haphazard, unthinking way in which children acquire them.

Although children eventually rely on rule-governed syntax, they probably still learn a lot of language by rote. Many expressions in a language are *idiomatic,* meaning they bear no logical relation to normal meanings or syntax. The sentence "How do you do?", for example, usually is not a literal inquiry as to how a person performs a certain action; and the sentence "How goes it?", meaning "How is it going?", does not even follow the usual rules of grammar. Because words and phrases such as these violate the rules of syntax and meaning, children must learn them one at a time.

Mechanisms of Language Acquisition

Exactly how do children learn to speak? For most children, several factors may operate at once. In general, current evidence can best be summarized as follows: language seems to grow through the interaction of an active, thinking child with certain key people and linguistic experiences. The preceding sections describe in part this active, thinking child; the upcoming sections describe some possible key interaction experiences.

Reinforcement

A commonsense view, one based essentially on behaviorist principles, is that children learn to speak through reinforcement. According to this idea, a child's caregivers reinforce vocal noises whenever they approximate a genuine word or utterance, and this reinforcement causes the child to vocalize in increasingly correct (or at least adultlike) ways (Skinner, 1957). In the course of babbling, an infant may happen to say "Ma-ma-ma-ma," to which his proud parent smiles and replies cheerfully, "How nice! You said 'Mama'!" The praise reinforces the behavior, so the infant says "Ma-ma-ma-ma" more often after that. After many such experiences, parents begin to reinforce only closer approximations to *mama,* leading finally to a true version of this word. The process would be an example of *shaping.*

Among preschool children, the same process could occur if parents reinforced correct grammatical forms and ignored or criticized errors or relatively immature utterances. Parents might respond more positively to the sentence "I have three feet" than to the sentence "I have two foots." According to the principles of reinforcement the child would tend not only to use the correct version more often but also to generalize the correct elements of this sentence to other, similar utterances.

Analysis of conversations between parents and children confirms this possibility, at least in indirect form and for the early stages of language acquisition. One study compared parents' responses to simple but grammatical sentences made by their two- and three-year-old children to their responses to ungrammatical utterances (Penner, 1987). Parents did not correct their children's grammar directly, but they were more likely to elaborate on the child's topic if the utterance was a grammatical one.

Imitation and Practice

In some sense, children obviously must imitate their native language to acquire it. This is an idea borrowed from the social learning variety of behaviorism. In daily life, though, the process of imitation is

Much learning happens through imitation and practice. These boys see both reading and social skills demonstrated by their grandmother and then practice the same skills themselves.

Source: rSnapshotPhotos/ Shutterstock.com.

subtle and often indirect. Children do not imitate everything they hear, but most copy certain selected utterances, often immediately after hearing them. Sometimes the utterances chosen for imitation involve familiar sentence forms that contain new, untried terms, and sometimes they contain familiar terms cast into new, untried forms. The imitated terms and forms return later in the child's spontaneous speech. At first, these utterances resemble the rote learning mentioned earlier, and they seem to help the child by emphasizing or calling attention to new morphemes and syntax.

Imitation may also help children acquire language by initiating playful practice with new expressions. The child in essence plays around with the new forms she learns and in doing so consolidates her recently acquired knowledge, just as she does in other forms of play. Because quite a bit of language play remains unobserved by adults, its extent is hard to judge, but a lot obviously does go on even in children as young as two years (Messer, 1994). Children ages eighteen to thirty months who had older siblings diagnosed with autism demonstrated delays in communication, language, gesturing, and social skills, suggesting that such imitation may be maladaptive as well (Toth, Dawson, Meltzoff, Greenson, & Fein, 2007).

Innate Predisposition to Acquire Language: LAD

The ease and speed children show in acquiring language have caused some linguists and psychologists to conclude that children have an innate predisposition, or built-in tendency, to learn language (Chomsky, 1994). For convenience, the innate tendency is sometimes called the *language acquisition device,* or *LAD.* According to this viewpoint, LAD functions as a kind of inborn road map to language. It guides the child to choose appropriate syntactic categories as he tries to figure out the comparatively confusing examples of real speech that he ordinarily hears. It helps him find his way through the mazelike structure of language with relatively few major errors instead of having to explore and construct his own language map, as the Piagetian viewpoint implies.

The most persuasive reason for postulating the LAD is the *poverty of content* in the speech to which most infants and preschoolers are exposed. According to this argument, the language children encounter is too incomplete and full of everyday grammatical errors (too "impoverished") to serve as a satisfactory guide in learning the grammatical structure of the language (Baker, 1995). Parents sometimes speak in incomplete sentences, sometimes make grammatical errors, and sometimes do not speak at all when speaking might prove helpful to a child learning the language.

However, children who hear a wider variety of words have larger vocabularies that grow more quickly than children who hear fewer, more simple vocabularies (Hoff, 2008). But even in spite of any poverty of content children seem remarkably resilient in acquiring language. Children isolated from language through parental neglect, for example, have learned some language later in life, but their language usually is limited in amount and complexity. In a less tragic example, identical twins often create a private language that they speak only with each other. In many cases, their private language seems to delay normal language development, though the delay rarely causes serious lasting damage to their development (Mogford, 1993).

A final piece of evidence that a LAD exists is that preschool children do not simply copy their parents' language directly, yet they seem to figure out and use many of its basic syntactic relationships remarkably well. Berko's "wug" experiment discussed earlier illustrates this ability dramatically. In forming plurals they have never heard spoken before, children seem to demonstrate a grammatical skill that is more innate than learned.

The Limits of LAD

Although this evidence suggests that children have a built-in ability to acquire language, it does not show that experience plays no role at all. The evidence from twins and neglected children emphasizes just the opposite: that certain experiences with language may be crucial, especially early in life. Ordinarily, almost every preschooler encounters these experiences. They may consist of hearing others talk and of being invited to respond to others verbally. But the fact that they happen to everyone does not mean that children do not learn from them; it means only that what children learn is universal.

Furthermore, experiences affect the version of language children acquire, even when they supposedly grow up in the same language community. As pointed out earlier, children vary in the vocabulary they learn and in the grammar they use; even by age three or four, children often do not define grammatical categories as abstractly as adults do or necessarily in the same way other children do. Most preschoolers eventually revise their grammatical categories to coincide with conventional adult grammar, thus obscuring their individuality. But as we will see in Chapter 8, large differences persist in older children's styles of communicating, even after they have mastered the basic structure of language.

All things considered, the fairest conclusion we can draw is a moderate one: that children are both predisposed to acquire language and in need of particular experiences with it. Skill with language is neither given at birth nor divorced entirely from other cognitive development. A special talent for language may be given to all normal children, however, and many crucial experiences for developing that talent may happen to occur rather frequently among infants as they grow up.

Parent-Child Interactions

Certain kinds of verbal interactions apparently help children acquire language sooner and better. Parents can help by speaking in relatively short sentences to their preschoolers and using more concrete nouns than pronouns, though this also depends on whether the task or topic at hand calls for concrete or abstract ideas (Hoff-Ginsberg, 1997). For children under the age of eighteen months, parents can make sure that they respond to children's speech with information that relates to what the child is doing or experiencing (Hoff, 2008). In the following pair of comments, the first helps a child learn language more than the second does:

> *Parent 1:* Take your shoes off. Then put your shoes in the closet. Then come kiss Mama goodnight.

> *Parent 2:* After you take off your shoes and put them in the closet, come kiss me goodnight.

As we noted in Chapter 6, the simplified style of the first set of comments is one aspect of a version of language called **infant-directed speech**, or sometimes "motherese." Another aspect of this version is the use of a high-pitched voice. Infant-directed speech is used intuitively by adults with young children and even by older children with younger children (Messer, 1994).

infant-directed speech The style or register of speech used by adults and older children when talking with a one- or two-year-old infant.

One of the most helpful kinds of verbal interactions is *recasting* a child's utterances: repeating or reflecting back what the child says, but in slightly altered form. For instance:

> *Child:* More milk.

> *Parent:* You want more milk, do you?

Recasting helps because it highlights slight differences among ways of expressing an idea. In doing so, it may make the child more aware of how she expresses her idea—its form or organization—as well as call attention to the idea itself.

Most of the techniques for stimulating language development provide young preschoolers with a framework of language that simultaneously invites them to try new, unfamiliar language forms and simplifies and clarifies other aspects of language. Some psychologists call this framework *scaffolding* (Bruner, 1996; Reeder, 1996): like real scaffolds used in building construction, parents' language scaffolds provide a temporary structure within which young children can build their own language structures. As such, it functions much like Vygotsky's zone of proximal

WHAT DO YOU THINK?

Suppose that you were asked to speak to a parent group, and a parent complained about her four-year-old's use of poor grammar. What advice could you give to this parent? Rehearse your comments with a classmate to determine how appropriate they are.

development mentioned earlier: helpful scaffolding changes and grows in response to the child's continuing development, always building a bit beyond the child's current independent abilities but never very far beyond.

These and similar findings have been translated into curricula for education of young children, particularly for those learning English as a second or third language (Proctor, Dalton, & Grisham, 2007) and even of infants (Spodek & Saracho, 1993). Fortunately, the most useful methods of interaction often are those that parents and teachers use intuitively anyway; training for them therefore really consists of emphasizing and refining their use.

Language Variations

Not surprisingly, parents vary in how they talk to their children, and these differences may influence the version of language children acquire as they grow up. It is unclear, however, how language variations affect other aspects of children's development, such as thinking ability. Let's consider three other sources of language variation: gender, socioeconomic status (SES), and hearing ability.

Gender Differences in Language

Within any one community, girls learn nearly the same syntax boys do, but they acquire very different pragmatics, or discourse patterns. Overall, the differences reflect society's gender stereotypes. For example, girls phrase requests indirectly more often than boys do; girls more often say, "Could you give that to me?" instead of "Give me that." Also, they more frequently expand on comments made by others, rather than initiating their own. These differences appear especially in mixed-gender groups and are noticeable not only among adults but also among children as soon as they are old enough to engage in conversation (Coates, 1993; Coates, 2015).

The sexes reinforce their language differences with certain nonverbal gestures and mannerisms. Girls and women tend to maintain more eye contact than boys and men do; they blink their eyelids at more irregular intervals and tend to nod their heads as they listen (Arliss, 1991). Boys and men use eye contact less in ordinary conversation, blink at regular intervals, and rarely nod their heads when listening.

Gender differences in discourse patterns may contribute to gender segregation: members of each gender may feel that members of the other gender do not really understand them, that they do not "speak the same language." Boys and girls therefore begin drifting apart during the preschool years, almost as soon as they begin using language (Ramsey, 1995), possibly due in part to acquiring language. The emerging segregation, in turn, reinforces gender differences in language patterns (Fagot, 1994). Boys reinforce one another for their assertive discourse style, and girls and their (mostly female) teachers reinforce one another for their "considerate" style. In the end, then, cognitive development supports social development, and social development supports cognitive development.

Socioeconomic Differences in Language

Most research has found low-SES children to be less skilled in using formal, school-like language than middle- or high-SES children (Heath et al., 1991). Research also shows that low-SES children are up to a year behind their higher-SES peers by the age of four, due in part to the infrequency with which they hear adults with large vocabularies speak (Hoff, 2008). In practice, this means low-SES children perform less well in verbal test situations, but outside of those situations, their language differences are less clear-cut. These facts have created controversy about the importance of socioeconomic differences in language development.

What is the significance of socioeconomic differences in tests of language development? Some psychologists point out that most tests of language skills favor middle-SES versions of English in both vocabulary and style of *discourse,* or conversational patterns (Gopaul-McNicol & Thomas-Presswood, 1998; Miramontes et al., 1997), and that several popular verbal intelligence scales confound actual verbal ability with socioeconomic status (Chapman, Fiscella, Duberstein, Kawachi, & Muennig, 2014). This bias is due to the content selected for individual test questions and to the ways tests are normally conducted. A question on one of these tests might ask children to describe a dishwasher, but few low-SES families own this appliance. Other questions might draw on experiences that only middle-SES children usually enjoy, such as trips on airplanes or visits to museums.

Perhaps most important, middle-SES families use styles of discourse that include many "test" questions or questions to which parents already know the answers. At the dinner table, parents may ask their preschooler, "What letter does your name begin with?" even though they already know the answer and their child knows that they know. Exchanges such as these probably prepare young children for similar exchanges on genuine tests by making testing situations seem more natural and homelike.

In contrast, low-SES children more often lack prior experience with "test" question exchanges. They can give relatively elaborate answers to true questions such as "What did you do yesterday morning?" when the adult really does not know the answer. But they tend to fall silent when they suspect the adult already can answer the question (for example, "What are the names of the days of the week?"). Their silence is unfortunate because rhetorical, or "test," questions become especially common when preschoolers enter school and because active participation in questioning and answering helps preschoolers' learning substantially.

Language of Deaf and Hearing-Impaired Children

Children with hearing impairments often do not develop oral language skills as fully as other children do, but they are quite capable of acquiring a language of gestures called

American Sign Language (ASL). In fact, language development in ASL children provides much of the reason for considering ASL a true language, one as useful for communication as any verbal language, such as English.

> **American Sign Language (ASL)** System of non-verbal gesturing that is used by many people who are deaf or hearing impaired and that functions as a language.

How can this be so? Signing consists of subtle gestures of the fingers and hands made near the face. In general, each gesture functions like a morpheme. For example, holding the fingers together gently (which signers call a "tapered O") can mean either *home* or *flower,* depending on whether it is placed near the cheek or under the nose. Other sign-morphemes affect the syntax of expressions: gestural equivalents of -*ing* and -*ed*. Individual signs are linked according to syntactic rules, just as in English. After some practice, signers can "speak" (or gesture) as quickly and effortlessly as people who use English can.

What happens to infants and young children with hearing impairments who grow up learning ASL from their parents as their first language? Studies show they experience the same steps in signing development that speaking children do in language development. At about the age when infants babble, signing children begin "babbling" with their hands, making gestures that strongly resemble genuine ASL signs but that signers recognize as gestural "nonsense" (Marschark, 1993). As with verbal babbling, signing infants apparently engage in gestural babbles playfully when waking up in the morning or going to sleep at night.

Sign language has the qualities of oral language, including grammar, subtlety, and expressiveness. This mother and child are communicating about the child's day at school. Unfortunately, in hearing communities (such as classrooms), it can be hard to appreciate the capacities of sign language.

Source: adriaticfoto/Shutterstock. com.

WORKING WITH CAROLYN EATON, PRESCHOOL TEACHER

Introducing Sign Language to Young Children

Carolyn Eaton teaches in a nursery school that serves only children who are deaf or who have moderate or severe hearing impairment. Everyone in the school communicates in American Sign Language (ASL): teachers, the children themselves, and (as much as possible) the parents. When they start the program, the children and parents often know very little ASL.

Kelvin: *How do they acquire this new language? Carolyn talked about some of the ways.*

Carolyn: In a lot of ways, the program really looks like any other nursery program, though maybe one with a lot of language emphasis. We always have a theme for the week. That's how we organize the vocabulary, the signs.

Kelvin: *Can you give an example of a theme?*

Carolyn: Last week's theme was "The Three Little Pigs." I told the story in ASL and read a picture book—one of the children had to hold it because I needed two hands to sign with. I emphasized key signs, like the ones for pig and three and the signs for brick, and straw, and house. I invited the children to make those signs with me when I came to them in the story.

Kelvin: *Do you do other things related to the week's theme?*

Carolyn: We'd have other conversations—in ASL, of course—about pigs and animals. And about trusting strangers, for that matter—that's in that story too! We might act out the story at some point, with signs instead of words. It depends partly on the vocabulary and fluency of the children.

Kelvin: *Is it harder to understand preschoolers' signing than adults'?*

Carolyn: It varies with the child, just like oral language. Most three- and four-year-olds tend to use less complex sign vocabulary and simpler expressions than adults. I found it hard at first to simplify my signing appropriately, the way you simplify oral language for young hearing children. There's a signing equivalent of "motherese" that you have to learn, or you won't be understood.

Kelvin: *I noticed a parent today in the class signing to the kids. Does that happen a lot?*

Carolyn: We have a parent volunteer just about every day. Because not all parents can volunteer, we have the kids take home a page each day that describes what's going on in the class and shows drawings of the signs we're currently emphasizing. We encourage the parents to learn them and use them at home. We also run two signing classes for the families of the preschoolers to help them communicate with their signing child.

Kelvin: *Is it hard for them to learn?*

Carolyn: Like everything else, people vary a lot. Some start learning immediately as soon as they learn that their child will always be deaf, and they're fluent by the time the child is a toddler. Others still haven't learned by the time the child is in grade school.

Personally, I think it has a lot to do with how accepting the parents are of the child's hearing impairment. If they're still grieving over the child's loss, they make less progress at ASL.

Kelvin: *Your program does seem language oriented—ASL oriented, that is.*

Carolyn: It really is, though we also deal with all the other stuff that happens to children—friendships among peers, for example. Did you see that argument between two kids that was going on just as you were arriving today?

Kelvin: *It looked fierce, judging by the children's faces. What was it about?*

Carolyn: Well, Billy wrecked a roadway that two other kids had made in the sand table. They were upset, signed Billy to get lost, and that got Billy upset. That's when I stepped in.

Kelvin: *I noticed how intently you were looking at Billy when you gave him a "talking to."*

Carolyn: I sure was—but in all ASL conversations, not just scoldings, you have to look to see the signs. You get good at reading people's moods that way too, especially if you learn signing as early as these children did.

What Do You Think?

1. Judging by Carolyn's comments, how does the acquisition of ASL resemble the acquisition of oral language? How does it differ?

2. Among speech-language pathologists and deaf people generally, there has been heated debate about whether to emphasize ASL experiences, even if they sometimes segregate children from the hearing community, or to emphasize oral language experiences, even if hearing-impaired children have trouble acquiring them. How might you decide between these alternatives? Compare your thoughts on this issue with one or two classmates' thoughts.

When signing infants reach ages two and three, they experience a phase of one-word signing similar to the holophrases often observed among speaking children. They also experience two-word, telegraphic signing. As with speech, their signs at this point often omit important syntactic gestures and do not follow the usual conventions of word order (or, in this case, signing order) (Bellugi et al., 1993; Goldin-Meadow, 2008). Signing vocabulary increases rapidly during the early preschool period, in amounts comparable to the increases speaking children experience. Even the kinds of words acquired parallel those speaking children acquire; signing preschoolers tend to learn signs for dynamic, moving objects first, as is true for speaking children. The "Working With" interview with preschool teacher Carolyn Eaton describes some of these developments.

Still another reason to consider ASL a true language comes from observations of hearing preschoolers whose parents purposely used both English and ASL during the period when the children normally acquired language (Prinz & Prinz, 1979). During their preschool years, these children became thoroughly bilingual, using ASL and English interchangeably. Especially significant, however, were their patterns of language development, which essentially paralleled those shown by conventionally bilingual children. A clear example concerned vocabulary. Like verbal bilinguals, these children first acquired a single vocabulary that intermingled elements from both ASL and English but included few direct translations. If children understood and used the sign for "tree," they would be unlikely to understand and use the spoken word *tree*. The children eventually acquired translations and thus finally possessed duplicate vocabularies. But acquiring duplicate terms took several years, just as it does with verbally bilingual children.

Language Deficits or Language Differences?

Although we have presented gender differences, socioeconomic differences, and American Sign Language as variations on language development that are equally worthy, society as a whole does not always agree with this assessment. In certain situations, each variation tends to be considered unsatisfactory, and the speaker (or, for ASL, the signer) may be considered deficient in linguistic or cognitive ability. The discourse patterns associated with females are often considered less satisfactory for learning and discussing mathematics, for example, than the discourse patterns associated with males (Walkerdine, 1997). In school, therefore, some girls are more likely to be judged less competent in math than they really are. Students with a language background other than English, whether it is Spanish, ASL, or something else, are at risk for being considered "unintelligent" simply because they cannot communicate fluently in the particular land of language—middle-class oral and written English—that historically has dominated schooling at all levels. Language biases pose a challenge for anyone who works with children professionally (Gopaul-McNicol & Thomas-Presswood, 1998). However, as we will see in Chapter 8, where we look further at bilingualism and its effects, there are ways to overcome language biases and to honor the diversity and talents of all children.

References

Arliss, L. (1991). *Gender communication.* Englewood Cliffs, NJ: Prentice-Hall.

Baker, C. (1995). *English syntax* (2nd ed.). Cambridge, MA: MIT press.

Bellugi, U., Van Hoek, K., Lillo-Martin, D., & O'Grady, L. (1993). The acquisition of syntax and space in young deaf signers. In D. Bishop, & K. Mogford (Eds.), *Language development in exceptional circumstances* (pp. 132–149). Hillsdale, NJ: Erlbaum.

Berko, J. (1958). The child's learning of English morphology, *Word, 14,* 150–177.

Brindle, J. A. (2015). Waali plural formation: A preliminary study on variation in noun class realization. *Journal of African Languages and Linguistics, 36*(2), 163–192.

Brown, R. (1973). *A first language: The early stages.* Cambridge, MA: Harvard University Press.

Bruner, J. (1996). *The culture of education.* Cambridge, MA: Harvard University Press.

Chomsky, N. (1994). *Language and thought.* Wakefield, RI: Moyer Bell Publishers.

Coates, J. (1993). *Women, men, and communication* (2nd ed.), New York, NY: Longman.

Coates, J. (2015). *Women, men and language: A sociolinguistic account of gender differences in language.* Routledge.

Fagot, B. I. (1994). Peer relations and the development of competence in boys and girls. In C. Leaper (Ed.), *Childhood gender segregation: Causes and consequences: New directions for child development* (pp. 53–66). San Fiancisco: Jossey-Bass.

Goldin-Meadow, S. (2008). How children learn language: A focus on resilience. In K. McCartney, & D. Phillips (Eds.), *Blackwell handbook of early childhood development* (pp. 252–273). Malden, MA: Blackwell Publishing.

Gopaul-McNicol, S., & Thomas-Presswood, T. (1998). *Working with linguistically and culturally different children.* Boston: Allyn and Bacon.

Heath, S., Mangolia, L., Schlecter, S., & Hull, G. (Eds.). (1991). *Children of promise: Literate activity in linguistically and culturally diverse classrooms.* Washington, DC: National Education Association.

Hoff, E. (2008). Language experience and language milestones during early childhood. In K. McCartney, & D. Phillips (Eds.), *Blackwell handbook of early childhood development* (pp. 233–251). Malden, MA: Blackwell Publishing.

Hoff-Ginsberg, E. (1997). *Language development.* Pacific Grove, CA: Brooks/Cole.

Marcus, G., Pinker, S., Ullman, M., Hollander, M., Rosen, T., & Xu, F. (1992). Overregularization in language acquisition. *Monographs of the Society for Research on Child Development, 57*(4, Serial No. 228).

Marschark, M. (1993). *Psychological development of deaf children.* New York, NY: Oxford.

McDaniel, D., McKee, C., & Smith, H. (1996). *Methods of assessing children's syntax* Cambridge, MA: MIT Press.

Messer, D. (1994). *The development of communication: From social interaction to language.* New York, NY: Wiley.

Miramontes, O., Nadeau, A., & Commins, N. (1997). *Restructuring schools for linguistic diversity.* New York, NY: Teachers College Press.

Mogford, K. (1993). Language development in twins. In D. Bishop & K. Mogford (Eds.), *Language development in exceptional circumstances* (pp. 80–95). Hillsdale, NJ: Erlbaum.

Penner, S. (1987). Parental responses to grammatical and un-grammatical child utterances. *Child Development, 58,* 376–384.

Prinz, P., & Prinz, E. (1979). Simultaneous acquisition of ASL and spoken English. *Sign Language Studies, 25,* 283–296.

Proctor, C. P., Dalton, B., & Grisham, D. L. (2007). Scaffolding English language learners and struggling readers in a universal literacy environment with embedded strategy instruction and vocabulary support. *Journal of Literacy Research, 39*(1), 71–93.

Ramsey, P. (1995). Changing social dynamics in early childhood classrooms. *Child Development, 66,* 764–773.

Reeder, K. (Ed.). (1996). *Literate apprenticeships: The emergence of language and literacy in the preschool years.* Norwood, NJ: Ablex.

Skinner, B. F. (1957). *Verbal behavior.* New York, NY: Appleton-Century-Crofts.

Spodek, B., & Saracho, O. (Eds.). (1993). *Language and literacy in early childhood education.* New York, NY: Teachers' College Press.

Toth, K., Dawson, G., Meltzoff, A. N., Greenson, J., & Fein, D. (2007). Early social, imitation, play, and language abilities of young non-autistic siblings of children with autism. *Journal of Autism and Developmental Disorders, 37*(1), 145–157.

Walkerdine, V. (1997). Redefining the subject in situated cognition theory. In D. Kirschner & J. Whitson (Eds.), *Situated cognition: Social, semiotic, and psychological perspectives* (pp. 57–70). Mahwah, NJ: Erlbaum.

The Developing Toddler and Early Childhood

Susan Whitbourne and Cynthia R. Davis

Language Development

The capacity for speech and language development is innate in human, but it is also profoundly affected by the social environment. Groundbreaking case studies in the field of psychology demonstrate that speech and language suffer without input from an enriching social environment. One of the most famous case studies in the field of psychology involved a young girl names Genie who was almost entirely isolated from a social environment at a young age. It helped psychologists understand why speech and language cannot develop without input and interaction with others.

We know young children can readily communicate without using of words. Crying, smiling, and gazing, among other things, signal what's happening in an infant's mind. These forms of communication and the ability to put thoughts into words, are known as **expressive language**. As children grow, thoughts develop, or are conceptualized, in their minds. Children choose the words available to them to express a thought and sounds and speech are produced to vocalize that thought. Many caregivers experienced toddlers who are very adept at expressing the word "no," either verbally with words, vocally with sounds, or nonverbally with actions. Another means of language communication in toddlers, **receptive language**, is children's ability to understand what is being communicated to them. A child's response, whether verbal or behavioral, most often indicates a capacity for receptive language. Table 20.1 shows a young child's capacity for language as it develops. At the same time, children and adults with certain motor impairments may be unable to respond to communication to indicate they understand what's being said.

Susan Whitbourne and Cynthia R. Davis, Selection from "The Developing Toddler and Early Childhood," *Lifespan Development: Biopsychosocial Perspectives*, pp. 120-125, 328-368. Copyright © 2018 by Cognella, Inc. Reprinted with permission.

TABLE 20.1 Language milestones during the toddler years and early childhood (Wilks, Gerber, & Erdie-Lalena, 2010)

Age	Language Milestone
12 to 15 months	• Can point to body parts • Can point to familiar objects when named • Shakes head to communicate "no" • Repeats words • Mimics sounds (cat's meow)
18 to 24 months	• Has approximately a 50-word vocabulary • Understands pronouns • Refers to self as "me" • Can produce two-word sentences (noun + verb) • Communicates wants (want dada) • Communicates socially (hi mama) • 50% of speech is understandable by a stranger
2 years to 3 years	• Vocabulary increases • Can produce three- to four-word phrases • Can answer questions • Communicates to learn (asks "what" questions) • Understands concept of "one" • Follows two-step commands
3 to 4 years	• Communicates to learn ("why" questions) • Becomes reliable reporter of events that occurred in the past • Understands what's being communicated to her well • 75% is understandable by a stranger
4 to 5 years	• Can follow more complex instructions • Speech is completely understandable to strangers

Adapted from R. Jason Gerber, Timothy Wilks, and Christine Erdie-Lalena, Developmental Milestones: Motor Development, Pediatrics in Review, vol. 31, no. 7. American Academy of Pediatrics, 2010.

The social environment impacts many factors that contribute to a child's ability to communicate and possess language skills. Studies have shown that early cognitive stimulation is fundamental to language development. Caregiving behaviors such as reading, teaching, verbal interactions, and the availability of learning materials including games and toys all contribute to language development (Cates et al., 2012).

A child's gender is associated with early language development. Research shows that "females produce sounds at an earlier age, use words sooner, develop larger vocabularies, display greater grammatical complexity, spell better, and read sooner than males" (Lovas, 2011). Nevertheless, female children show relatively small advances during early childhood over their male counterparts, and these differences typically disappear by the age of 5. It's believed that differences at the biological and social level contribute to these early abilities. Biologically speaking, during the prenatal stage females are exposed to different types and amounts of hormones that result in

THEORY THEN AND NOW

Theory then: Noam Chomsky first proposed that humans have an instinctive capacity, called the Language Acquisition Device, based in the brain that allows us to understand rules of grammar and to use language to communicate.

Theory now: He later put forth the notion of Universal Grammar, which states language development requires three components: (1) the innate ability to develop language based on humans' unique genetic makeup; (2) stimulation from the environment; and (3) factors independent of innate abilities and the environment.

Many contend that there are "critical periods" for the development of language. In other words, if we don't develop this ability during early childhood, our ability to develop it at all is in jeopardy. The longer a person goes without the tools for language development (based on the three requirements of Universal Grammar) the less likely they are to develop language. Those who don't develop this ability by the time puberty ends are unlikely to develop it at all (Pinker, 1994). Universal Grammar, which proposes the principles of grammar are the same across all languages, has come into question in recent years, given what we know about the complexity of languages as well as developments in our understanding of cognition that have put forth new explanations for humans' capacity for language.

accelerated brain development, which leads to differences in perception and attention between the sexes. Socially speaking, on average, female infants tend to make more eye contact, and participate in joint attention more often than males do. Because of these differences, females engage differently with the verbal and nonverbal behaviors of caregivers, leading to increases in language development during early childhood. Research also shows that parents tend to speak more and in more meaningful ways to their young daughters than to their sons (Lovas, 2011).

Hearing impairment. Two to three of every 1,000 children are born with some degree of hearing impairment, and most states in the United States perform mandatory newborn hearing tests to determine if some kind of hearing impairment exists (Natonal Institute of Health, 2013). Hearing impairments in young children may be a result of genetically inherited traits, or environmental factors, including fetal alcohol syndrome and prenatal infections in the mother, such as chlamydia. Other environmental factors that could lead to hearing loss are mumps or meningitis, exposure to certain toxins, some types of brain tumors, or injuries that result in ruptured ear drums. Hearing impairment can range from mild, to profound, to total deafness, and is referred to as prelingual deafness if the impairment exists at birth or occurs prior to the child's acquisition of language.

Children with severe to profound hearing impairments spend less time communicating with their caregivers. In turn, children with hearing impairments tend to show greater language acquisition difficulties that may lead to attention difficulties and behavioral problems (Barker et al., 2009; Tasker, Nowakowski, & Schmidt, 2010).

Until recently children with hearing impairments relied on hearing aids, which amplify sound for ears that have been damaged in some way. Now it is somewhat more common for a person with a hearing impairment to receive cochlear implants. Rather than simply amplifying sound, cochlear implants artificially stimulate the cochlear (auditory) nerve and send auditory information directly to the brain, bypassing the damaged parts of the ear all together. The "sounds" experienced are somewhat different, but for children under 2 years of age, cochlear implants can improve joint attention abilities, language skills, and speech, sometimes putting them on par with their peers without hearing impairments.

Second language learners. Young children are especially adept at acquiring language. Language acquisition is believed to have a critical period of development during early childhood as the brain undergoes the rapid production and pruning of neurons and synapses. It is a critical skill for the individual to obtain during this developmental period. Therefore, acquiring a second language during toddlerhood and early childhood can be easier than when it is learned later in life. In fact, second language learning is one area in which children are far superior to adults. Figure 20.1 shows that a person's ability to learn and speak a second language declines as they age.

The "critical" period for language development, however, depends on which aspect of language we're talking about. Phonetic language learning, how to say and make movements with the mouth to produce certain sounds, occurs during infancy and the first year of life. Syntactic learning, or learning various language rules to produce statements that make sense and sound correct for any given language, peaks from 18 months to 3 years of age. Many parents and caregivers describe (and research supports the notion of) an "explosion" of vocabulary starting at 18 months. Learning new vocabulary continues across the lifespan as we are always able to learn new words and terms in the languages we speak (Kuhl, 2010).

Speech and language delays. Roughly 7% of children exhibit speech and language delays when they begin elementary school. These delays can include vocabulary, understanding grammar

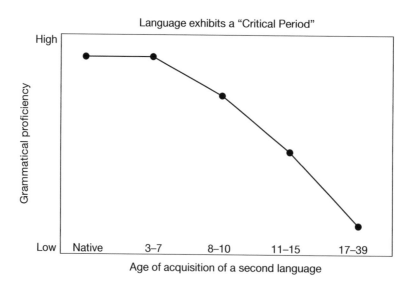

FIGURE 20.1   The relation between age of acquisition of a second language and language skill (adapted from Johnson & Newport, 1989, as cited in Kuhl, 2010).

Source: "Critical Period Effects in Second Language Learning: The Influence of Maturational State on the Acquisition of English as a Second Language." *Cognitive Psychology,* vol. 21.

THEORY THEN AND NOW

Theory then: Language learning was due to the development of the corpus callosum, the area of the brain responsible for communication between the left and right hemispheres (Lenneberg, 1967).

Theory now: The way neurons develop early in infancy maximizes a child's ability to detect, process, and understand the basic language she is exposed to. Think about the simplistic ways in which many parents and caregivers speak to their children. Once the basics are established (in English, for example, the adjective "good" should come before the noun "boy"), they set the stage for learning the primary language completely, be it English or Arabic, and they delay the ability to learn language patterns that do not conform to those "basics" (Kuhl, 2010).

To put it another way, the brain, as it learns a language, is creating a pattern of neurons for English that is like a round hole, and the more complex rules for English that are learned across childhood are like a round peg. The rules (the round peg) fit the neuron patterns (round hole). However, the pattern for Arabic may be like a square hole. Trying to learn the language sounds and rules for Arabic (a square peg) if you are an English speaker would be like to trying to fit a square peg into a round hole! However, if you're learning both English and Arabic in early childhood, the brain will have created patterns to accommodate the learning of both languages.

rules, interpreting meaning, sound production, and knowing how language is used in varying social contexts. There are some established risk factors for language delays. For example, did you know that by kindergarten children from higher socioeconomic status backgrounds have been exposed to roughly 32 million more words than children from lower socioeconomic status backgrounds (Wilks, Gerber, & Erdie-Lalena, 2010)? Learning English as a second language may contribute to delays in one or both of the languages a young child is exposed to. And as we've discussed, providing a rich cognitive environment is critical in supporting language development (Boyle, 2011).

If a language delay is not addressed, it can affect a child's ability to read, their social development and behaviors, as well as their mental health and well-being in adulthood. At the same time, it can sometimes be hard to tell whether a language delay is the sole or primary problem, or whether the language delay is the result of an additional or larger problem. Young children with language delays may also be within the range of a "normative" developmental timeline, therefore the problem may be overlooked (Boyle, 2011).

MYTHS AND MISCONCEPTIONS

Educational videos promote children's language development (Wilks et al., 2010). **Misconception**

Educational videos often do not take into account and cannot provide the subtle interactive components necessary for speech promotion and language development. **Fact**

Reading to young children and interventions designed to increase the frequency and complexity of language exposure, promote speech and language development. **Fact**

References

Barker, D. H., Quittner, A. L., Fink, N. E., Eisenberg, L. S., Tobey, E. A., & Niparko, J. K. (2009). Predicting behavior problems in deaf and hearing children: The infuences of language, attention, and parent–child communication. *Development and Psychopathology, 21*, 373–392. doi:10.1017/S0954579409000212

Boyle, J. (2011). Speech and language delays in preschool children. *BMJ, 343*. doi:10.1136/bmj.d5181

Cates, C. B., Dreyer, B. P., Berkule, S. B., White, L. J., Arevalo, J. A., & Mendelsohn, A. L. (2012). Infant communication and subsequent language development in children from low-income families: The role of early cognitive stimulation. *Journal of Developmental & Behavioral Pediatrics, 33*, 577–585. doi:510.1097/DBP.1090b1013e318264c318210f.

Kuhl, P. K. (2010). Brain mechanisms in early language acquisition. *Neuron, 67*, 713–727. doi:10.1016/j.neuron.2010.08.038

Lovas, G. S. (2011). Gender and patterns of language development in mother-toddler and father-toddler dyads. *First Language, 31*, 83–108. doi:10.1177/0142723709359241

National Institute of Health. (2013). *Newborn hearing screening. Research Portfolio Online Reporting Tools*. Retrieved from http://report.nih.gov/nihfactsheets/ViewFactSheet.aspx?csid=104

Pinker, S. (1994). *The language instinct: The new science of language and mind* (Vol. 7529). London: Penguin.

Tasker, S. L., Nowakowski, M. E., & Schmidt, L. A. (2010). Joint attention and social competence in deaf children with cochlear implants. *Journal of Developmental and Physical Disabilities, 22*, 509–532. doi:10.1007/s10882-010-9189-x

Wilks, T., Gerber, R. J., & Erdie-Lalena, C. (2010). Developmental milestones: Cognitive development. *Pediatrics in Review, 31*, 364–367. doi:10.1542/pir.31-9-364

Why Early Language Matters

Betty Bardige

I f you're a parent or a grandparent, you've probably seen a poster that quotes Robert Fulghum's classic essay, "All I Really Ever Needed to Know I Learned in Kindergarten."

Here, according to Fulghum, are the essential guidelines for a meaningful life, phrased in the simple language in which they are communicated to young children during their first experiences with schooling:

> Share everything.
>
> Play fair.
>
> Don't hit people.
>
> Put things back where you found them.
>
> Clean up your own mess.
>
> Say you're sorry when you hurt somebody.
>
> Wash your hands before you eat.
>
> Flush.
>
> Warm cookies and cold milk are good for you.
>
> Live a balanced life—learn some and think some and draw and paint and sing and dance and play and work every day some.
>
> Take a nap every afternoon.
>
> When you go out into the world, watch out for traffic, hold hands, and stick together.
>
> Be aware of wonder ...[1]

Fulghum's wisdom is shared by elementary school teachers, who recognize that the critical capacities that enable children to succeed in school and in life are social and emotional. Children who are "ready for school" are able to get along with others, to keep their impulses under control, to empathize, help out, and do their part, to take

Betty Bardige, "Why Early Language Matters," *At A Loss For Words: How America Is Failing Our Children*, pp. 32-48, 218-220. Copyright © 2005 by Temple University Press. Reprinted with permission.

on challenging tasks, persist in the face of frustration, and accept setbacks with good humor, and to approach learning with a sense of wonder. Preschool teachers might also add their signature instruction to Fulghum's list: "Use your words."

Research supports these common sense ideas. In his classic book, *Emotional Intelligence*,[2] Daniel Goleman summarizes a vast body of research on the development of social and emotional competence and its critical contribution to success in all areas of life. He explains how emotional factors can "hijack" judgment and interfere with learning. These truths are encoded in our language, in terms like "paralyzing fear," "blind rage," "overwhelming stress," and "irresistible desire."

Goleman goes on to explain how children can be taught Fulghum's basics: emotional control, empathic understanding, more accurate reading of social cues, strategies for positive conflict resolution and helpful intervention on behalf of others, belief that effort makes a difference, and effective social problem-solving techniques. His examples extend well beyond early childhood as he traces the ongoing growth of these critical capacities.

Early educators and parents who urge children to "use your words" are laying a strong foundation for emotional intelligence. They teach young children to ask for what they want instead of whining, to convince a playmate to share instead of grabbing a toy, to negotiate instead of hitting, to assert their rights in the face of bullying, to talk themselves through challenges and puzzles, and to request help when they need it.

This foundation builds a "sturdy stage" for later development. Children who, as young preschoolers, become skilled at making and keeping friends generally have an easy time with the transition to formal schooling.[3] Those who cannot keep up with the verbal repartee of their peers may be stigmatized or rejected; those who have difficulty controlling their aggression or containing their frustration are likely to experience continuing problems. The words children hear and the words they can say play a surprisingly important role in their emotional and social development, which in turn play often underestimated roles in their ability to learn.

In his book, *The Vulnerable Child*,[4] psychologist Richard Weissbourd tells the stories of children who fail, who get caught in downward spirals of low school achievement, friendlessness, victimization or aggression, and poor emotional health. Some of these children have experienced classic "risk factors"—poverty, divorce, parental depression or substance abuse, or biological vulnerabilities such as chronic illnesses or mild disabilities. Others seem to be in the wrong place at the wrong time. For them, small problems, unaddressed, escalate into difficulties that become stubborn and pervasive. Dr. Weissbourd repeatedly points out that healthy development at one point is not a guarantee of smooth sailing later on. Likewise, many problems can be addressed and transcended; others may be made moot by a change of scene or a new beginning. Yet Weissbourd's stories—drawn from around the country and including children from all walks of life—show us why shaky foundations make children vulnerable. When adversity strikes in any of its myriad forms, children whose foundations for mental health, academic achievement, social participation, or peer acceptance are fragile are likely to get into deeper and deeper trouble.

Psychologists use the concept of "resilience" to describe much, though not all, of what Goleman means by "emotional intelligence" and to denote the opposite of vulnerability. Resilience is the ability to cope with difficulty, rather than being defeated or overwhelmed by it or responding in a way that is destructive or self-destructive. Resilient children "bounce back"; they thrive despite adversity. Many of them are "survivors" who "beat the odds." Resilient children are not necessarily "tough" or "invulnerable." They can be hurt—and may even be hurt very badly—but their scars do not lead to permanent incapacitation or lifelong handicap, unless the trauma is so severe as to overwhelm their resilience.

Resiliency is in part inborn. It helps to have a flexible or easy-going temperament, a sunny disposition, and a strong physical constitution. It also helps to be physically attractive; as children who look appealing are more likely to get help.[5] However, the real keys to resilience are capacities that can be learned and developed, and most of these involve facility with language. Indeed, these capacities rest upon strong early language foundations. It turns out that early communication patterns—including responsiveness, affirmation, encouragement to use words, sharing of information, and engagement in extended conversations—are important for resiliency and emotional intelligence, just as they are for vocabulary development.[6]

So what does the research on resiliency tell us? In a retrospective study of adults who had managed to thrive despite childhoods spent in troubled families,[7] Drs. Steven and Sybil Wolin identified seven "resiliencies," or protective factors. These are:

- *Relationships*: mentors, friends, support networks; the ability to pull others in and keep them connected, to ask for help when needed, and to make others want to help
- *Insight*: the habit of asking tough questions that pierce the denial and confusion in troubled families; the ability to describe what is happening and to analyze why, to recognize patterns and make predictions, and to use language to represent difficulties and challenges as problems that can be solved
- *Independence*: emotional and physical distancing from a troubled family; the use of school as a sanctuary and as an arena for success; the tendency to "master" pain by focusing on one's own accomplishments and positive relationships
- *Initiative*: a push for mastery that combats feelings of helplessness
- *Creativity*: the ability to express feelings and represent experience through the arts, including writing, drama, visual arts, and music
- *Humor*: the ability to laugh at oneself, to appreciate irony, to look on the bright side, and to use levity to make difficult situations easier to bear
- *Morality*: concern for others and a desire to do good
- Dr. Linda Gilkerson and her colleagues have studied interactions between children and their parents or other caregivers in minute detail to see just how adults help children to develop resilience. Their findings underscore the key role of early relationships and especially of language.

Dr. Gilkerson presented these findings at a national conference on early childhood mental health by sharing a dramatic case study.[8] "Angie" was a child with multiple risk factors. She was born into poverty in a rough urban neighborhood, the only child of young parents who split up soon after her birth. Her father continued to stalk her mother, and would beat her severely when he could find her. Angie and her mother moved often, but they could never escape for long.

Eventually, Angie's mother became despondent and began using drugs. When Angie was ten, her mother killed her father in self-defense. Angie saw the argument and ran inside just in time to avoid seeing the shot.

Knowing only this much of her story, most people would expect Angie to be in serious academic and emotional trouble as an adolescent and young adult. Research backs up these dire predictions. Poverty (especially during the early childhood years, when the brain is most vulnerable to nutritional deficiencies, toxic substances, over- or understimulation, and psychological trauma), being raised by a single parent, maternal depression, parental substance abuse, having a parent who is the victim of violence, witnessing violence, frequent unplanned and disruptive moves, and living in poor neighborhoods with correspondingly poor schools are all proven risk factors. Because risk factors tend to compound each other, having three or more tends to lead to "rotten outcomes," such as emotional and behavior problems, school failure and drop out, substance abuse, delinquency, teen pregnancy, difficulty in obtaining and holding employment, and perpetuation of cycles of victimization and abuse. In one study, children with two risk factors were four times as likely to develop social and academic problems as those with one or none; four risk factors increased the risk tenfold.[9]

Angie defied these odds, and, at age eighteen, entered a four-year college with a full scholarship. She had all of the classic hallmarks of resilience—adult mentors outside of her family (most recently, her French teacher, who drove her to college and helped her register), obvious intelligence and verbal ability, demonstrated independence and initiative in caring for herself and her mother and taking challenging high school courses, concern for others expressed through active volunteer involvement in school-based community service activities, insight into her own strengths and the challenges she faced, and a healthy sense of humor.

But where did these strengths come from? Dr. Gilkerson traced them to Angie's early relationship with her mother. In videotapes from Angie's first year, we see Angie's mother holding her, talking to her, responding to her bids for attention and for brief time-outs from interaction and stimulation, engaging in the "dance" of communication that facilitates "secure attachment" and a sense of "basic trust." In Angie's second and third years, we see her mother encouraging her emerging verbal abilities by listening intently to what she is trying to say, responding to her attempts to communicate by repeating and expanding her language, encouraging her to use words, complying with her requests, soothing her with comforting words and songs, telling and reading her simple stories, encouraging and answering her questions, and sharing information. Later, we see Angie's mother helping her learn to read, teaching her, and helping her with schoolwork.

Dr. Gilkerson points out some of the specifics. Like other parents or caregivers of resilient children, Angie's mother uses language to help make Angie's world more predictable and encourages Angie to do the same. She gives Angie time words, like "soon," "tomorrow," "Friday," and "after lunch," so that Angie can anticipate events. She prepares Angie for transitions and new experiences by telling her what to expect and coaching her on how to behave. She provides explanations that make things that appear scary (like masked trick-or-treaters) less so. She takes advantage of "teachable moments" to encourage her daughter's learning, and also deliberately introduces books, questions, and information to expand Angie's knowledge.

Again, we see the power of language to reduce or prevent fear or stress and to keep potentially destructive behavior in check. Children who master such language at a young age have several advantages:

- They learn constructive ways to calm themselves and reduce their own stress and impulsivity.
- They are seen by teachers and other adults as more mature and competent.
- They are liked by peers, who can trust them not to be overly impulsive or aggressive and who enjoy playing with them because they can use language to keep the play going.
- They approach challenges as problems to be solved, and get lots of practice in effective problem-solving techniques—including the technique of asking for help.
- Their learning and emotional wellness are enhanced, and enhance each other.

Claudia Cooper[10] analyzed the written work and behavior of elementary school students whose language and home and school learning had been followed since they were toddlers. All of the children came from low-income families. Many were thriving, though others were not. Cooper found, not surprisingly, that children whose homes and schools had been more stimulating and supportive were more emotionally resilient. These children were also more expressive in their writing.

Young children's language development—and the security of the relationships that facilitate it—has a strong influence on their emotional development, which in turn influences their adjustment to school, their interest in learning, and therefore their learning and academic achievement. Yet children whose families do an excellent job of supporting their emotional and social development may still be at a loss for words if they enter schools where their language and style of communicating is not fully understood and appreciated, if they haven't learned sufficient vocabulary, or if they are unaccustomed to the type of literary language that they will encounter as early readers.[11] Because in our culture schooling relies on verbal and written communication, language facility has a direct as well as indirect influence on academic outcomes.

Verbal facility and "emotional intelligence" are intertwined, but they are not the same. We all know people who are verbally "smart" and emotionally "out of touch" or socially "clueless," as well as people who struggled with formal education but whose emotional wisdom and ability to bring people together make them leaders in their communities. At the same time, we can see how "using words" contributes to both emotional adjustment and academic achievement in schools with high verbal demands. Early language learning prepares children for the social challenges of school, making it easier for them to concentrate on learning. It also paves the way for learning to read.

Children who read independently on grade level by the end of grade three are likely to complete high school and go on to college. According to a panel of experts convened by the National Academy of Sciences, "A person who is not at least a modestly skilled reader by the end of third grade is quite unlikely to graduate from high school."[12] Children who come in with stronger prereading skills are, not surprisingly, more likely to become proficient readers in the primary grades.[13]

But this is not the whole story. Third grade is used as a marker because this is the first time that a group-administered paper-and-pencil test can be used effectively with nearly all of the children.[14] With younger children, such tests often produce inconsistent results because children who know the answers may not demonstrate their knowledge in the test-taking situation. They may not fully understand the directions, may not realize that they are supposed to do the problems quickly, may have difficulty sitting still or holding the pencil, or may simply decide that the instructions make no sense and it would be better to follow their own logic, as illustrated by the following story:

> A first grader, taking a paper and pencil vocabulary test, was asked to "put an x on the girl's knee." She started to follow the instruction, then changed her mind and carefully drew an x above the girl's ear. "What are you doing?" her teacher asked. "I said to put the x on the girl's knee." "I know," replied the child nonchalantly, "but that would look ugly. I put it in her hair so that it would look like a pretty ribbon."

Third grade is also a watershed. In kindergarten, first, and second grade, most children are learning to decode—to translate printed words into spoken ones. The texts that they can read themselves are often way below their comprehension level. They are filled with short and regularly spelled or common words, as well as pictures, repeated words and phrases, and context clues that make the decoding easier. By the end of third grade, children are expected to read at their comprehension level. At that point, if not sooner, learning to read gives way to reading to learn. Now children with larger vocabularies have an obvious advantage. Knowing more words enables them to read more difficult texts more easily. Not only can they read the words whose meanings they know, these words provide a context for other, unfamiliar words that helps to make their meaning clear. Thus good readers extend their vocabularies and enhance their reading prowess, often without even realizing that they are learning new words.

E.D. Hirsch, Jr., president of the Core Knowledge Foundation, argues that the "reading gap" between children from more and less advantaged backgrounds is better described as a "language gap" or "verbal gap." "Such a shift in terminology might reduce public confusion between 'reading' in the sense of knowing how to decode fluently, and 'reading' in the sense of being able to comprehend a challenging diversity of texts. It is the second, comprehension, deficit, based chiefly on a vocabulary deficit, that constitutes the true verbal gap indicated in the NAEP [National Assessment of Educational Progress] scores."[15]

It is not difficult to teach most children specific prereading skills, such as identifying letters, writing their names, and matching words that begin or end with the same sound. Programs for four-year-olds that explicitly teach these skills often produce dramatic gains in kindergarten and first grade, with graduates scoring above their peers on reading tests given in their classrooms. Yet these gains can be short-lived and may "fade out" by the end of second or third grade.[16]

Although more recent research shows that children's gains as a result of high quality Head Start and other early education and family support programs have long-term persistence,[17] some early studies had found only short-term effects.[18] At least part of the explanation seems to be that some early programs, which reached only four- and five-year-olds in part-day classes, offered too little too late. They imparted specific skills, but they didn't do enough to enhance children's vocabularies and their expressive language use.

The Abecedarian Project, led by Craig Ramey, showed the power of a high quality, comprehensive program that started in the first year of life.[19] Dr. Ramey and his colleagues worked with children of very low-income mothers who had not completed high school, beginning when the children were less than a year old. They provided a high quality early education program for the children, full day, five days a week, year round. In addition, they provided support to the mothers through home visiting. Children in their program and in the control group (children from the same pool who were not lucky enough to be randomly assigned to the program, or "intervention") received nutrition and health care support.

Using state-of-the-art individually administered developmental tests, the researchers tracked children's intellectual performance at regular intervals. Significant differences in average scores between the children receiving the intensive intervention (treatment group) and those who weren't (controls) were apparent by eighteen months and continued throughout the project (see Figure 21.1).

Considering that the children in the study had not been expected to be "ready for school" by age five, the Abecedarian Project's results were remarkable. In this group of children living in poverty, whose mothers lacked a high school education, the average IQ was the same as that for the general population. In addition, although 40 percent of the children in the control

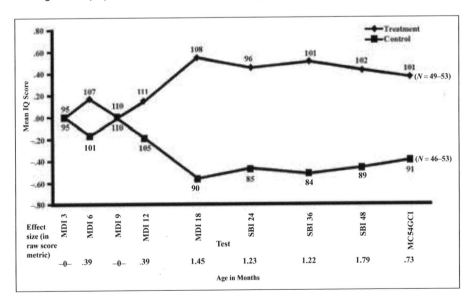

FIGURE 21.1   Abecedarian Project Results: Average Intellectual Performance Scores of Treatment Group and Controls Across the Preschool Years.

Source: Ramey, C. T., Campbell, F. A., Burchinal, M., Skinner, M. L., Gardner, D. M., and Ramey, S. L. (2000) Persistent effects of early childhood education on high-risk children and their mothers, *Applied Developmental Science*, 4(1): 2–14.

group received IQ scores in the "developmentally delayed" or "retarded" range at age four, only 5 percent of the children in the treatment group scored this low.

A follow-up study of the Abecedarian Project participants and controls produced even more remarkable findings.[20] The researchers provided enhanced support in grades K-2 to half of each group. This support included continuing consultation for their classroom teachers to help strengthen and individualize the curriculum, support for their parents in helping with schoolwork and educational activities at home, summer programs designed to maintain academic progress, and individually tailored learning activities.

Not surprisingly, students benefited from this support whether or not they had received the early learning program. However, when reading, math, and IQ scores were compared at the end of third grade, the importance of early learning became clear. Children who had received both enriched early education services *and* special support in their first years of elementary school scored the highest, followed by those who had received *only* the enriched early learning program! The children who had received support only in kindergarten, first, and second grade did not do as well as those who had been involved only in the preschool program (see Figure 21.2).

The effect of the early learning program was strongest on reading, because that was where children who had not had the enriched preschool experience were most likely to earn low scores. Over time, the impact of the K-2 support washed out; at age fifteen it had a small effect on reading, none on mathematics, and none on the likelihood of repeating a grade. However, the impact of the enriched preschool program continued to be striking—a ten-point difference in IQ scores, significantly higher reading and mathematics achievement, and significant reduction in the likelihood of being retained in a grade or placed in special education!

For children who are living in poverty and whose parents lack education, there is considerable evidence that high quality early education programs make a difference, especially when they begin before age three and provide intensive services. Hart and Risley's work[21] may explain why.

In 1965, Hart and Risley were working with a half-day preschool program designed to boost the cognitive functioning and school readiness of low-income children. They zeroed in on language, and developed methods of measuring the growth in children's vocabularies, as evidenced in their daily conversations in the classroom and on the playground. This method involved tape-recording the children, transcribing their words, and keeping track of words that were new or were used in new ways.

Using vocabulary growth as an outcome measure, Hart and Risley tracked the impact of various educational strategies. They also compared the children in the preschool, all of whom came from poor families, with counterparts in a university-based preschool, all of whom came from professional families. Their most successful intervention involved a theme-based curriculum centered around field trips. Teachers would use books, puzzles, and other educational materials and lots of formal and informal discussion to prepare children for a trip to the bank or fire station, introducing specialized vocabulary that would be reinforced during the trip and then practiced in pretend play.

The children eagerly lapped up the new words, concepts, and experiences, and used their new vocabulary as they played "bank," "store," "fire station," and "farm" in the house corner and block

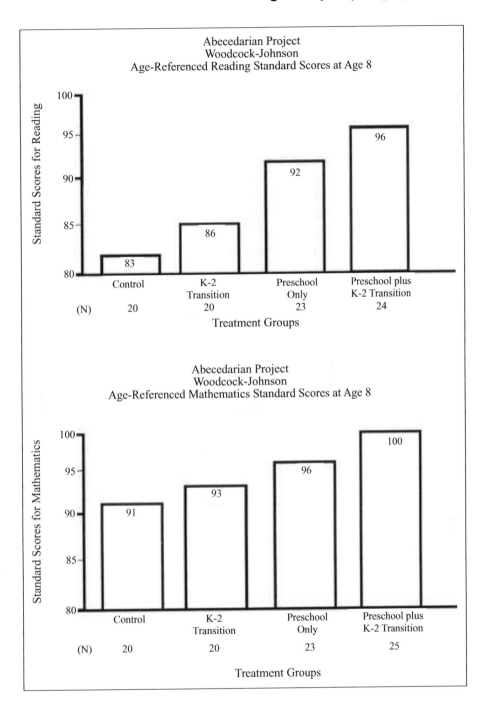

FIGURE 21.2   Abecedarian Project Results Through Grade 2.

Source: Ramey, C. T., Campbell, F. A., Burchinal, M., Skinner, M. L., Gardner, D. M., and Ramey, S. L. (2000) Persistent effects of early childhood education on high-risk children and their mothers, *Applied Developmental Science*, 4(1): 2–14.

area and on the playground. Yet, when the researchers looked at the rates at which the children's overall vocabularies were growing, they still fell short of those of the wealthier children in the university-based preschool. The ever-widening gap did not bode well for their educational futures.

Concluding that they were providing too little too late, Hart and Risley decided to look at what children in different income strata were learning in their everyday home interactions in their first three years.

Hart and Risley observed forty-two children and their families for one hour a month for two and a half years, beginning when the children were ten months old. They carefully tracked the children's emerging "in use" vocabularies, as they had in their preschool observations. In addition, they recorded and analyzed everything that was said to the child during their observations.

After years of intensive analysis, Hart and Risley were able to substantiate some remarkable conclusions:

- There were wide differences among the families in the amount of language used, and especially in the amount of language addressed to the child. These differences, which were strongly associated with social class, are reflected in the size and rate of growth of children's vocabularies.
- Children who heard more words developed larger vocabularies by age three.
- The children whose parents were on welfare heard an average of about nine million words spoken to them in ordinary conversation by the time they were three, those from working class families heard about eighteen million, and those from professional families heard nearly thirty-three million! (These estimates were arrived at by multiplying the average number of words the researchers recorded per hour by the number of hours that the typical child would be awake. The hidden assumption, of course, is that children are spending most of their waking hours with their parents, or with people who talk to them about as much as their parents do. That assumption was more likely to be valid in 1982, when Hart and Risley began their work, than it would be today.)
- Not only the number of words addressed to the child, but also key features of parents' communication styles (described in the next two points) contributed to children's vocabularies and IQ scores at age three and to their vocabulary and general language scores in third grade.
- Not surprisingly, children who heard more "yeses" and encouragement—including repetition or expansion of their language, answers to their questions, praise, and approval—and proportionally fewer "no's"—did significantly better.
- Other communication style features that made a difference included *language diversity* (measured by the number of different nouns and descriptive words parents used per hour), *symbolic emphasis* (a measure of information richness and decontextualization derived by counting nouns, modifiers, and past tense verbs and dividing by the number of utterances), *guidance style* (giving children choices, measured by looking at the proportion of questions vs. commands), and *responsiveness* (listening; letting the child take the lead).

The features of parents' communication styles that Hart and Risley identified as making a difference in their children's language development are similar to what experts identify as "good" quality in child care and early education programs (I've italicized key words to highlight the similarities):

For infants and toddlers:

- Staff members *do a lot of talking* to babies and toddlers, engage in verbal play, *name and talk about objects, pictures, and actions*, read books to children and say nursery rhymes, *respond* to children's crying, gestures, sounds, words, and maintain eye contact while talking to the child
- Caregivers are patient with a crying baby or upset toddler.
- Staff are *warm and affectionate*, initiate verbal and physical play, and *show delight in children's activity.*

For preschoolers:

- *Frequent adult–child conversations*
- *Language is used primarily to exchange information* with children and for social interactions.
- Staff *add information* to *expand on children's ideas.*
- Staff *encourage communication* between children.
- Staff use *nonpunitive discipline methods*, model social skills, and help children develop appropriate social behavior. [22]

When centers and family child-care homes fall down on quality, it is most likely to be in those areas of quality that matter most for vocabulary and expressive language development.[23] When too many children are present, it is difficult to find time and quiet space for intimate, responsive adult–child conversations. When teachers are inadequately trained, they are less likely to be responsive to children's early attempts to communicate, to offer children choices and use positive guidance, or to use decontextualized language, expand on children's ideas, and ask open-ended questions that encourage reasoning and explanation. When the classroom or family child-care home lacks an intentional curriculum, whether preplanned or emerging from the children's interests, language used by adults and children alike is likely to be less diverse and less rich in information.

For children growing up in poverty, and for those whose homes do not provide good quality language experience, good quality early care and education programs can make an enormous difference. So can home-visiting programs that teach parents to engage in language-promoting interactions—if they are well designed, sufficiently intensive, and offered during the critical language acquisition years.[24] Several of these programs are described in more detail in Chapter 9. Here, we discuss just one of these programs, the Parent–Child Home Program, because its graduates have been followed for many years in several studies. One of these studies,[25] done in Pittsfield, MA, followed program children and matched controls through high school graduation. Program children were half as likely as their counterparts to drop out of high school. In several shorter duration studies, program children scored at average or above average levels on elementary school reading and math tests, despite their initial disadvantages of poverty and often also of language differences.[26]

The Parent–Child Home Program provides twice weekly home visits, beginning when the child is between eighteen and twenty-four months and continuing for two years. The home visitor, who speaks the family's language and often comes from their neighborhood, brings a book or a toy and shows the parent how to use it to support the child's language learning. The sessions are intended to be fun for all participants. The intervention is simple and relatively inexpensive. It is also extremely well targeted. It provides very frequent services during the critical two years when children are learning language, it engages the parent as a partner, and it develops habits of reading, playing together, and encouraging a child's questions that will continue long after the program ends. No wonder it has such a powerful impact!

What about children who are not growing up in poverty? Do high quality programs make a difference for them?

The Infant Health and Development Program[27] was designed as a replication of the Abecedarian Project, but with babies who were considered at risk because of low birth weight or prematurity or both rather than because of severe social disadvantages. Some of the children in this study were born to undereducated single mothers living in poverty; others had parents who were college graduates. By age three, children in eight sites who had received health, home visiting, and family support services along with very high quality early education, full day/full year, from six weeks through age three, scored on average thirteen points higher on an IQ test than did counterparts with similar backgrounds who only received the health, home visiting, and family support services (see Figure 21.3).

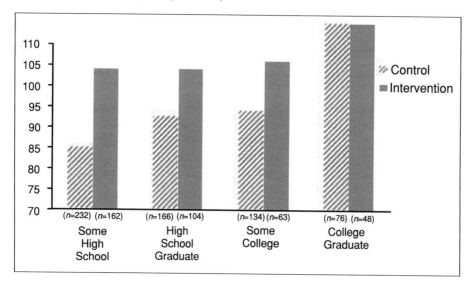

FIGURE 21.3   Infant Health and Development Program (IHDP) Results. Children's IQ at 36 months: Maternal Education × Treatment Group.

Source: Ramey, C. T., Campbell, F. A., and Ramey, S. L. (1999) Early intervention: Successful pathways to improving intellectual development, *Developmental Neuropsychology*, 16(3): 385–392.

Furthermore, only children of college graduates scored higher than children who had received the enriched early education and whose parents had not completed college. In fact, the children in the early intervention programs whose parents had not completed high school did almost as well as those whose parents had taken some college courses. The scores of the intervention group children whose mothers had not completed high school, like those of the intervention children whose mothers were better educated, were higher on average than those of children in the general population, in spite of the initial biological risk factors that had made them eligible for participation in the study!

The Infant Health and Development Program services ended when the children were three. At that point, the children who had received the enriched early education programs showed higher receptive vocabularies, on average, than their counterparts who had not had this opportunity. When the services ended, however, these two groups of children were likely to have the same chance of getting, or not getting, the opportunities to use their words and gain new ones in frequent, stimulating conversations with the adults charged with their care. In contrast to the Abecedarian Project, which continued to at least age five, the Infant Health and Development Project did not show significant IQ advantages for former participants at age eight. Neither were there clear advantages in reading scores.[28]

Putting all of this research together, we can see that it is essential for children to learn Fulghum's basics and know how to use their words before they get to school. But that is not enough. Children also need to learn a lot of words. And they need a lot of ongoing encouragement to use them in a variety of ways.

When children are given the opportunity, learning and using lots of words is easy, natural, and fun. It is what two- and three- and four-year-olds do. We need to find ways to ensure that all of our children get those opportunities.

The learning opportunities and encouragement of communication must begin early to build a strong foundation; they must also continue. As summarized by Ed Zigler, Matia Finn-Stevenson, and Nancy Hall, authors of *The First Three Years and Beyond*, "Evidence tells us that support and intervention in the early years are critical but that this period is not the only time that helps to define how we will evolve as individuals, nor is it the only period during which course corrections can be made and help given to improve children's lives and optimize their potential."[29] But the course corrections can be costly, both in the resources spent on remedial efforts and in the pain experienced by the child who is academically or socially out of step with his peers and with the expectations of his society.

The 2001 Elementary and Secondary Education Act,[30] championed by both President George W. Bush and Senator Edward Kennedy, set forth a key challenge for the United States: "Close the achievement gap." As our leaders have recognized, we cannot afford to be a society that leaves nearly a third of our children behind because they cannot meet the educational standards we set.

Many experts believe that we can close the gap if—and most likely only if—we start early. How early is early enough is less a matter of scholarly debate than of political will. The scholars are in agreement: for health care and parenting support, birth is too late to start.[31] In the critical realm of language development, we must ensure warm, responsive caregiving in the first year.

And we must begin *at least by age two* to assure the rich, engaging conversations that promote the development of robust vocabulary and expressive language.

There may be nothing more important to children's school and work success than early language development, and there is nothing more important to children's early language development than adults who regularly talk with them in enticing, encouraging ways. Yet while we provide many different, often expensive, interventions to help older children who are not doing well, we are doing frighteningly little to influence the everyday interactions between adults and young children that shape development and set the stage for success.[32] Indeed, providing high quality programs for two- and three-year-olds and the adults who interact with them may be the best educational investment we can make.

These high quality programs can take place wherever children are: at school, at home, in community settings such as playgrounds, churches, and libraries, or in a combination of places. They don't have to be formal or esoteric. But they can't be scattershot. Young children are relentless learners by nature. They need lots and lots of learning opportunities, each and every day. They need the critical mass of meaningful conversation that Hart and Risley, Snow, and other researchers have identified: conversation addressed to the child, sufficiently decontextualized, rich in vocabulary, filled with information and positive affect; encouraging of interaction; responsive to their questions and other communications; and affirming of their efforts, curiosity, and growing selves.

In the next two chapters, we will visit a number of settings where children are routinely engaged in rich and interesting conversation, and see how teachers, caregivers, and well-supported parents help very young children build a "sturdy stage" for later learning.

References

1   R. Fulghum (1993) *All I Ever Really Wanted to Know I Learned in Kindergarten*, Mass Market Paperback, pp. 6–7.

2   D. Goleman (1995) *Emotional Intelligence*, New York: Bantam Books.

3   M. Segal and D. Adcock (1983) *Making Friends*, New York: Prentice Hall.

4   R. Weissbourd (1997)*The Vulnerable Child: What Really Hurts America's Children and What We Can Do About It*, New York: Perseus Publishing.

5   E. E. Werner (1987) Vulnerability and resiliency in children at risk of delinquency: A longitudinal study from birth to adulthood, In J. D. Burchard and S. N. Burchard (eds.), *Primary Prevention of Psychopathology, Vol. 10: Prevention of Delinquent Behavior*, Newbury Park, CA: Sage, pp. 16–43.

6   See zero to three's 1992 report, *Heart Start: The Emotional Foundations of School Readiness* (Washington, DC: zero to three Press, www.zerotothree.org) for a discussion of how parenting and caregiving practices help children to develop "Confidence, Curiosity, Self-Control, Ability to Relate to Others, Capacity to Have an Impact and be Persistent, Capacity to

Communicate (including Learning to Talk), and Cooperation," seven social–emotional "keys" to school readiness.

7   S. Wolin and S. Wolin (1993) *The Resilient Self: How Survivors of Troubled Families Rise Above Adversity*, New York: Villard Books.

8   L. Gilkerson (2001) Factors that place young children at risk, Plenary session presented at *Building Our Future Conference on the Emotional Roots of School Readiness*, Miami Beach, FL, October 17–19. The case described here comes from Dr. Dorothy Norton's research in Chicago. See D. G. Norton, (1996) Early linguistic interaction and school achievement: An ethnographical, ecological perspective, *ZERO TO THREE*, 16: 8–14; D. G. Norton (1994) My mommy didn't kill my daddy, In J. D. Osofsky and E. Fenichel (eds.), *Caring for Infants and Toddlers in Violent Environments: Hurt, Healing, and Hope*, Washington, DC: zero to three Press; and D. G. Norton (1993) Diversity, early socialization and temporal development: The dual perspective revisited, *Social Work*, 38: 82–90.

9   Werner, *Primary Prevention of Psychopathology*, Vol. 10, pp. 16–43.

10 C. R. Cooper (2001) *Who Are these Writers?: An Exploration of the Connections Between Expressiveness in Children's Writing and Their Psychosocial Profiles*, Ed.D. Thesis, Harvard Graduate School of Education.

11 For a compelling case study, see V. Purcell-Gates (1995) *Other People's Words: The Cycle of Low Literacy*, Cambridge, MA: Harvard University Press.

12 National Research Council (1998) *Preventing Reading Difficulties in Young Children*. Committee on the Prevention of Reading Difficulties in Young Children. Catherine E. Snow, M. Susan Burns, and Peg Griffin (eds.). Washington, DC: National Academy Press, p. 21.

13 F. J. Morrison, E. M. Griffith, G. Williamson, and C. L. Hardaway (1995) The nature and sources of early literacy, Paper presented at the biennial meeting of the Society for Research in Child Development, Indiannapolis, IN; H. W. Stevenson, T. Parker, A. Williamson, A. Hegion, and E. Fish (1976) Longitudinal study of individual differences in cognitive development and scholastic achievement, *Journal of Educational Psychology*, 68: 377–400, cited in *From Neurons to Neighborhoods*.

14 S. L. Kagan, E. Moore, and S. Bredekamp (eds.) (1995) *Reconsidering Children's Early Development and Learning: Toward Shared Beliefs and Vocabulary*, Washington, DC: National Goals Panel.

15 E. D. Hirsh, Jr. (2001) Overcoming the language gap, *Education Week*, May 2, 2001.

16 See U.S. Department of Health and Human Services (December 2003) *State Funded Pre-Kindergarten Programs: What the Evidence Shows* (http://aspe.hhs.gov/hsp/ state-funded-pre-k/index.htm) for a summary of short and longer term effects of prekindergarten programs and a discussion of the fade-out phenomenon.

17 E. Zigler and S. Styfco (1993) *Head Start and Beyond: A National Plan for Extended Childhood Intervention*, New Haven, CT: Yale University Press. High quality programs that contain both early education and family support components are likely to have a stronger long-term impact than programs that provide only one or the other. H. Yoshikawa (1995) Long-term effects of early childhood programs on social outcomes and delinquency, *Future of Children*, 5: 51–75.

18 After Head Start's first summer, researchers reported dramatic gains in IQ scores. The designers were skeptical: How could a six-week intervention make such a difference? Had children become smarter or more knowledgeable, or had they just become more comfortable and motivated in the testing situation? The media frenzy led to inflated expectations, which turned to disappointment that nearly killed the program when the gains were not sustained. E. Zigler, M. Finn-Stevenson, and M. Hall (2002) *The First Three Years and Beyond: Brain Development and Social Policy*, New Haven, CT: Yale University Press.

19 C. T. Ramey and F. A. Campbell (1984) Preventive education for high-risk children: Cognitive consequences of the Carolina Abecedarian Project (Special Issue), *American Journal of Mental Deficiency*, 88: 515–523, Available at www.circ.uab.edu/craigramey/abceffect.htm.

20 C. T. Ramey and F. A. Campbell (1991) Poverty, early childhood education, and academic competence: The Abecedarian experiment, In A. C. Huston (ed.), *Children in Poverty*, New York: Cambridge University Press, pp. 190–221.

21 B. Hart and T. Risley (1995) *Meaningful Differences in the Everyday Experience of Young American Children*, Baltimore, MD: Paul H. Brookes Publishing Company.

22 S. Helburn and B. Bergmann (2002) *America's Childcare Problem: The Way Out*, New York: Palgrave, pp. 70–71 and 66–67.

23 S. W. Helburn (ed.) (1995) *Cost, Quality, and Child Outcomes in Child Care Centers*, Technical Report, Denver, CO: Department of Economics, Center for Research in Economic and Social Policy, University of Colorado at Denver.

24 S. Powers and E. Fenichel (1999) *Home Visiting: Reaching Babies and Families "Where They Live,"* Washington, DC: zero to three Press.

25 P. Levenstein, S. Levenstein, J. A. Shiminski, and J. E. Stolzberg (1998) Long-term impact of a verbal interaction program for at-risk toddlers: An exploratory study of high school outcomes in a replication of the Mother–Child Home Program, *Journal of Applied Developmental Psychology*, 19: 267–285.

26 P. Levenstein, J. M. O'Hara, and J. Madden (1983) The Mother–Child Home Program of the Verbal Interaction Project, In Consortium for Longitudinal Studies (ed.), *As the Twig is Bent*, Hillsdale, NJ: Lawrence Erlbaum Associates.

27 C. T. Ramey, D. M. Bryant, B. H. Wasik, J. J. Sparling, K. H. Fendt, and L. M. LaVange (1992) Infant Health and Development Program for low birth weight, premature infants: Program components, family participation, and child intelligence, *Pediatrics*, 89(3): 454–465.

28 J. Brooks-Gunn, C. M. McCarron, P. H. Casey, M. C. McCormick, C. R. Bauer, J. C. Bernbaum, J. Tyson, M. Swanson, F. C. Bennett, D. T. Scott, J. Tonascia, and C. Meinert (1994) Early intervention in low-birth-weight premature infants: Results through age 5 years from the Infant Health and Development Program, *Journal of the American Medical Association*, 272(16): 1257–1262.

29 E. Zigler, M. Finn-Stevenson, and N. Hall (2002) *The First Three Years and Beyond*, New Haven, CT: Yale University Press, p. 211.

30 PL 107–110 The *No Child Left Behind Act* of 2001, signed January 2002 by President George W. Bush.

31   National Research Council and Institute of Medicine (2000) *From Neurons to Neighbor-hoods: The Science of Early Childhood Development.* Committee on Integrating the Science of Early Childhood Development. Jack P. Shonkoff and Deborah A. Phillips (eds.). Board on Children, Youth, and Families, Commission on Behavioral and Social Sciences and Education. Washington, DC: National Academy Press.

32   Rick Weissbourd used this argument to shape the Literacy Action Plan for the City of Cambridge's Agenda for Children. I am indebted to him for this strong position and perspective.

Developing Children's Oral Language Skills Through Dialogic Reading

Guidelines for Implementation

Kylie S. Flynn

Mrs. Thomas was a lead teacher in a public prekindergarten classroom where slightly more than half of her students were eligible for special education services due to a developmental delay (DD), language impairment (LI), or some other diagnosed disability. The remaining students qualified for public prekindergarten via the Title I School Readiness program based on their families' poverty status. Thus, Mrs. Thomas was aware of the at-risk nature of her students and their varying levels of ability. Despite having students with DD and/or LI in her classroom, the district did not provide additional speech and language therapy for these children, even if they had language goals on their individualized education programs (IEPs). Although Mrs. Thomas had over 20 years of experience with prekindergarten and kindergarten children and certifications for both early childhood education and K-12. she did not have special education certification. However, she was very familiar with the IEP process and had worked with a number of students with varying disabilities. Concerned about her students' language development and how to handle their varying levels of language ability, she turned to the What Works Clearinghouse, the online web site of the Institute of Education Sciences (IES) for evidence-based practices. She learned that **dialogic reading** has had very positive effects for language development in young children in a variety of settings (U.S. Department of Education. 2007), so she decided to implement the strategy in her classroom.

Rationale for Implementing Dialogic Reading

With the passage of the No Child Left Behind Act of 2001 and the reauthorization of the Individuals With Disabilities Education Act in 2004, special educators are facing

Kylie S. Flynn, "Developing Children's Oral Language Skills Through Dialogic Reading: Guidelines for Implementation," *Teaching Exceptional Children*, vol. 44, no. 2, pp. 8-16. Copyright © 2011 by Council for Exceptional Children. Reprinted with permission. Provided by ProQuest LLC. All rights reserved.

growing demands to develop children's language and literacy skills through evidence-based practices. Given the developing body of research supporting the premise that literacy begins at infancy (Weikle &Hadadian, 2004), intervention should begin as early as possible with young children who may be at risk for future illiteracy due to poverty, developmental delays, and/or disabilities. To that end, educators need to seek intervention strategies that are grounded in a well-developed body of research. One promising research-based strategy is dialogic reading (DR), which is an interactive picture-book reading technique developed in the late 1980s by Whitehurst and colleagues (Whitehurst et at, 1988).

Whitehurst and Lonigan (1998) defined *emergent literacy* as "the skills, knowledge, and *attitudes* that are developmental precursors to reading and writing" (p. 848). They also suggested that language is one of those important skills in children's literacy acquisition. The connection between literacy development and language is supported by several longitudinal studies (e.g., Bishop & Adams, 1990; Scarborough, 1989; Weikle & Hadadian, 2004) that have indicated a relationship between early oral language abilities and later reading proficiency in children who are typically developing, reading-delayed, and/or language delayed. Because DR focuses on developing children's expressive language skills, it can be an important strategy for addressing the emergent literacy development in young children who may be at risk due to their developmental and/or socioeconomic status. An extensive body of research exists using DR with children ages 2 to 6 years old in a variety of settings, including at home with parents, in subsidized child-care settings (e.g., Head Start), and in early childhood special education programs. DR also meets the What Works Clearinghouse evidence standards for best practices (1ES, 2007).

Dialogic Reading in the Classroom

Although DR was initially studied with parent-child dyads (Arnold, Lonigan, Whitehurst & Epstein, 1994; Briesch, Chafouleas, Lebel, & Blom-Hoffman, 2008; Chow & McBride-Change, 2003; Crain-Thoreson & Dale, 1999; Dale, Crain-Thoreson, Notari-Syverson, & Cole, 1996; Huebner, 2000; Huebner & Meltzoff, 2005; Valdez-Menchaca & Whitehurst, 1992; Whitehurst, et al., 1988; Zevenbergen, Whitehurst, & Zevenbergen 2003), it also can be used with groups of children in a classroom setting. Typically, *shared reading* means the teacher reads the text to the entire class and occasionally points out pictured vocabulary; students take the more passive role of listening. DR differs from typical shared reading in that the teacher works with small groups of children and facilitates their language through a series of prompts. Ultimately, the teacher and students have a conversation (i.e., *dialogue)* about the book; the adult gradually talks less and the children gradually increase their expressive language by talking more. The process focuses primarily on the book's illustrations and is broken down into three levels, each with its own strategy for engaging students (Lonigan, 2006; see Figure 22.1).

In the practice of DR, the teacher shares the book with the children a minimum of three times and often as many as five or six times. Before implementing DR, the teacher gives students a preview of the book and of approximately 10 to 20 illustrations representing age-appropriate vocabulary. The teacher then introduces the book via a more typical shared reading, highlighting print concepts such as the author, illustrator, cover, title, and so on. Then the teacher reads the book out loud, occasionally asking a question about one of the selected illustrations.

Level 1: Introduce New Vocabulary

After introducing the book to the whole class, the teacher meets with small groups of students. The purpose of Level 1 is to introduce specific selected vocabulary words and to facilitate the students' language acquisition through scaffolding. The teacher no longer reads the text, but instead focuses on the illustrations. After posing basic labeling questions (e.g., "What's this?"), the teacher follows up with an attribute and/or function question. An *attribute question* asks about specific features of the picture (e.g., "What color is it?"). A *function question* asks about the utility of the object (e.g., "What do you do with it?"). When introducing new vocabulary, the teacher asks the children to repeat the new word or phrase using a balanced mix of individual and choral responses to ensure participation. Because they do not facilitate the use of expressive language and practice with new vocabulary, pointing questions (e.g., "Point to the monkey.") and yes/no questions are not used, unless working with children who are nonverbal. When most of the students can label at least *75%* of the target vocabulary in a book, the teacher proceeds to Level 2.

**Dialogic Reading
Level 1**

1. Ask "wh" type questions. "What is this?" "What do you call that?"

2. Follow answers with questions. "What color is it? What is it used for?"

3. Have students repeat new words.

4. Help students as needed.

5. Talk about what interests your students.

6. Praise and encourage students.

7. Have fun!!

**Dialogic Reading
Level 2**

1. Ask open-ended questions. "What do you see on this page?" "Tell me more."

2. Follow answers with expansions. Add 1 or 2 words to student's answer.

3. Have students repeat expansions.

4. Help students as needed.

5. Let students choose topics to talk about.

6. Praise and encourage students.

7. Have fun!!

**Dialogic Reading
Level 3**

1. Ask questions related to the story plot. "What did he do next?" "Why was he sad?" "Where are they?"

2. Start asking distancing questions that relate to the student's personal experiences and remote events. "Did you ever see one?" "Have you ever been to a _____?"

3. Help students as needed.

4. Praise and encourage students.

5. Have fun!!

FIGURE 22.1   Dialogic Reading Bookmarks.

Level 2: Practice and Expansions

The purpose of Level 2 is to create opportunities for students to practice the new vocabulary they have learned and to encourage longer responses. Thus, using the same book, the teacher begins to ask open-ended questions (e.g., "What do you see here?" "What's happening on this page?") and to evaluate responses. Initially, students are likely to need encouragement to expand their responses. Thus, the teacher should follow tip one-word responses with an open-ended prompt, such as "Tell me more" or "What else do you see?" Also, in Level 2, the teacher starts using *expansions* (see Figure 22.2) as both a model and a teaching tool.

Expansions elaborate on what the student says by adding a few more words to the student's answer. For expansions to be successful

- Add only one or two words to the student's original response.
- Keep it short and simple.
- Stress the new word(s) and speak slowly.
- Repeat at least part of what the student said; pause after an expansion to see if the child will repeat without a prompt.
- Occasionally ask students to repeat the expansions.

In Level 2, the teacher should manage turn taking by soliciting individual responses. There is no use of higher level questions (e.g., "How do you think the boy is feeling?" "Why do you think the boy is crying?") or prediction questions until Level 3, because children need to be familiar with new vocabulary before using it at a higher level. When most of the students can use most of the vocabulary in expanded phrases or sentences, the teacher proceeds to Level 3.

Student: A cat.
Teacher: A cat is at the veterinarian's.

Student: She on that.
Teacher: Right, she is on the swing

Student: It eating.
Teacher: Good, the giraffe is eating.

Student: Boat.
Teacher: It is a big boat.

Student: I sawed it.
Teacher: You saw the car.

Student: Bird up there.
Teacher: The bird is flying.

FIGURE 22.2   Examples of Expansions.

Level 3: Relate Knowledge to Experience

After students have been exposed to a book in Levels 1 and 2 and can label and discuss most of the pictured vocabulary, the teacher moves on to Level 3 with the same book. At this level, students are encouraged to relate the story to their own experiences; the teacher facilitates conversations about those experiences. For example, introducing a story about a camping trip, Mrs. Thomas asked her students what experiences with camping they had had and allowed them to share those experiences. In this way, the teacher-student dialogue begins to depart from the story but also allows for verbal expression and practice with new vocabulary words; it also builds children's background knowledge.

Level 3 also offers the opportunity to expand student comprehension of a story by using higher level questions about the illustrations, the plot, or the sequence of events. Thus, even though many of the students in Mrs. Thomas's class hadn't had experience camping, this process gave them the opportunity to develop their background knowledge while practicing their comprehension and expression. At Level 3, the goal is generalization of newly acquired vocabulary and knowledge through the use of extending and enriching activities.

> The teacher-student dialogue begins to depart from the story but also allows for verbal expression and practice with new vocabulary words.

Extension and Enrichment Activities

After the book has been read and children are familiar with the book and can accurately answer Level 3-type questions, teachers can turn to extension and enrichment activities. One form of an extension activity is *story retelling:* Students retell the story in their own words without looking at the book or using the pictures as a guide. Another extension activity is *reenactment,* where students act out the story. They might describe what they are doing; speak lines; and describe their character, including the character's clothing and role in the story. Finally, *cooking and art* are creative extension activities that are generally feasible for all children, regardless of age or disability. Cooking activities allow for sensory experiences, including smell, taste, touch, hearing, and sight. Both cooking and art provide for more generalization opportunities and are an excellent way to reinforce targeted vocabulary. Many picture books are appropriate for cooking and/or art extension activities.

Recommendations for Implementation

Book and Vocabulary Selection

In selecting DR books, teachers should choose books with clear and varied illustrations but minimal text; The illustrations are used to introduce new vocabulary and *to* facilitate children's

TABLE 22.1 Suggested Picture Books for Dialogic Reading

Theme	Books
All about me/family	*ABC I Like Me!* (Carlson, 1999) *Leo the Late Bloomer* (Kraus, 1994) *Today I Feel Silly: And Other Moods That Make My Day* (Curtis, 1998) *Alexander & the Terrible. Horrible, No Good, Very Bad* Day (Viorst, 2009)
Fairy tales	*Goldilocks and the Three Bears* (Ransom, 2002) *Juan Bobo Goes to Work: A Puerto Rican Folk Tale* (Montes, 2000) *Three Little Javelinas* (Lowell, 1992) *Where the Wild Things Are* (Sendak, 1988)
Zoo/animals	*Goodnight, Gorilla* (Rathmann, 2002) *Duck on a Bike* (Shannon, 2002) *I Love my Daddy Because . . .* (Porter-Gaylord, 1991) *Little Penguin's Tale* (Wood, 1993) *The Escape of Marvin the Ape* (Buehner, 1999)
Nutrition/food	*If You Give a Moose a Muffin* (Numeroff, 1994) *The Little Red Hen.* (Ottolenghi, 2002) *If You Give a Pig a Pancake* (Numeroff, 2000) *The Monster Who Ate My Peas* (Schnitzlein, 2010) *Good Enough to Eat: A Kid's Guide to Food and Nutrition* (Rockwell, 2009) *The Seven Silly Eaters* (Hoberman, 2000)
Growing things	*Muncha! Muncha! Muncha!* (Fleming, 2002) *Messy Bessey's Garden* (McKissack & McKissack, 2002) *Apple Farmer Annie* (Wellington, 2004) *Tops &Bottoms* (Stevens, 1995) *Flower Garden* (Bunting, 2000)
Under the sea/ocean	*Hello Ocean* (Munoz Ryan, 2001) *Dear Mr. Blueberry* (James, 1996) *The Whale's Song* (Sheldon, 1997) *Don't Eat the Teacher* (Ward, 2002) *My Visit to the Aquarium* (Aliki, 1996)

Note. Many of these publications are available in Spanish as well as English; teachers using the Literacy Express curriculum (Lonigan, 2006) may have access to these publications and additional materials through the Literacy Express Classroom Library.

expressive language (see Table 22.1). Before conducting a DR session, preview the book carefully and select the *vocabulary to introduce* in the lesson. Vocabulary should be

- Developmentally appropriate
- Well depicted in the illustrations
- Novel to the students.

Sticky notes to flag when to introduce a particular word and when to refer to it again later in the book can be helpful when using an unfamiliar book. Other teachers have taped an index card of all the target vocabulary words on the back of the book to use as a reference during the DR session. As teachers become familiar with the books, they simply rely on memory and intuition for introducing the selected vocabulary.

Group Composition and Management

Research is varied about the number *of* children who should participate in a dialogic reading session at one time. Although much of the DR research has been conducted with parent-child dyads (Arnold et al., 1994; Briesch et al., 2008; Chow & McBride-Change, 2003; Crain-Thoreson & Dale, 1999; Dale et al., 1996; Huebner, 2000; Huebner & Meltzoff, 2005; Valdez-Menchaca & Whitehurst, 1992; Whitehurst et al., 1988; Zevenbergen et al., 2003), several studies have also used small groups with six or fewer children (Lonigan & Whitehurst, 1998; Lonigan, Anthony, Bloomfield, Dyer, & Samwel, 1999; Whitehurst, Arnold et al., 1994; Whitehurst, Epstein, et al., 1994) and one study used the whole class (Wasik & Bond, 2001). Keeping in mind that the purpose of DR is to get children talking as much as possible, teachers should base decisions about group size on their classroom organization, management style, student–teacher ratio, and the age of their students. For younger children (e.g., 2 to 3 years old), teachers may want to consider smaller groups with no more than four children. For prekindergarten classrooms with 4- to 5-year-olds, teachers may experiment with groups of five to eight children. Kindergarten and first-grade teachers may be able to manage larger group sizes or whole–class readings that facilitate everyone's participation.

In terms of the frequency and duration of a DR session, although most studies recommended conducting DR daily, few studies mention specifically how long a dialogic reading session should last. Three studies (Huebner & Meltzoff, 2005; Lonigan & Whitehurst, 1998; Valdez-Menchaca & Whitehurst, 1992) suggest conducting dialogic reading in 10-minute sessions. However, it is likely that older children (e.g., 4- to 6-year-olds) could stay engaged for longer sessions lasting up to 20 minutes, Thus, teachers will want to use their professional judgment about the length of their sessions based on the age of their students and their classroom schedules and routines. Bearing in mind the goal of child participation and engagement, teachers can gauge the duration of a session based on the group's level of attentiveness and expression.

In determining group composition, teachers have flexibility and will have to make decisions based on the needs of their students and classroom routines. The advantage of using homogenous grouping is that teachers can work with groups at their appropriate level. In this way, students can proceed through the levels at a pace that is commensurate with their progress and abilities. However, homogenous grouping also has to be balanced with assembling groups of children who get along well and are willing to interact with each other. When heterogeneous groups are used, an advantage is that children with higher levels of linguistic abilities can serve as role models for children who are less verbal. The challenge to this type of grouping is that the teacher must be more mindful of scaffolding at the individual level. For example, if the group is participating in a Level 2 session but one or two children are still at Level 1, the teacher will have to remember to scaffold between the two levels as appropriate. Additionally, depending on the group composition, teachers may want to vary the length of the session or increase the amount of time spent previewing or reviewing. Finally, teachers are encouraged to change the grouping as needed, based on informal assessments of children's vocabulary and expressive language.

Management of the group is vital to successfully conducting DR, because the goal is to be interactive. Thus, it is important to make sure that all students are participating and have opportunities to respond verbally. Students should sit close to the teacher in a way that allows everyone to see the book at the same time, as this will help maintain interest. Teachers should ask questions in such a way that all the students stay involved and engaged in the answer. This interaction can be achieved by having the whole group repeat new information and by providing clear guidelines for turn taking, active listening, and participating. For extremely shy or quiet children, the teacher can begin by asking them only questions to which they know the answer and/or having them repeat or extend answers provided by other students. For more verbal children who may get impatient waiting their turn or who dominate the session, teachers can use a variety of techniques based on overall classroom management or on individual student needs:

- Using a talking "microphone" to delineate the turn-taking process,
- Having the "impatient" child sit in closer proximity to the teacher
- Giving the child an additional role in the group, such as page turner.

> It is important to make sure that all students are participating and have opportunities to respond verbally.

Children with specific delays or disabilities may require more specific accommodations and/or modifications.

Accommodations and Modifications

Teachers can enrich the DR experience for diverse learners by using objects and/or props. Supplementing the Level 1 lesson with physical objects or props may provide a more concrete opportunity for students to learn new vocabulary; As they explore objects with all of their senses, they can discuss and learn new vocabulary, interactive books with Velcro images that can be removed and replaced provide another way to concretely engage children with the book (see Figure 22.3). These books may be particularly beneficial for younger children or those who are nonverbal. Making related props available during center time also provides students with the opportunity to generalize their new vocabulary through developmental play.

Whenever possible, teachers should capitalize on opportunities to integrate paraprofessionals, parent volunteers, and/or specialists (e.g., speech and language pathologists, SLPs, and occupational therapists, OTs) into the classroom, particularly during small-group instruction. Depending on the site and classroom conditions, specialists can participate on a continuum of levels from teaching small group lessons to consulting with the teacher. SLPs can help with

FIGURE 22.3   Sample Interactive Book

Note. TO MARKET, TO MARKET by Anne Miranda. Text copyright ® 1997 by Anne Miranda. Illustrations copyright ® 1997 by Janet Stevens. Reprinted by permission of Houghton Mifflin Harcourt Publishing Company. All Rights reserved.

vocabulary selection and communication systems, and OTs can help with adaptive devices such as specialized seats and pointers. Even without the benefit of specialists, teachers can easily make accommodations and modifications for students with a variety of special needs.

For children with speech and language delays, the DR method offers a valuable opportunity for language practice. Teachers should use short, simple language; provide actual objects as needed in addition to the pictures in the book; allow more time for response; and model correct pronunciation and ask students to repeat. For children with visual impairments, teachers can use big books and/or objects that represent the vocabulary being taught. Similarly, children with hearing impairments will benefit from the use of simple sign language paired with pictures in the book or with the actual objects. The biggest concern for children with motor and physical impairments is their positioning; they need to be positioned in such a way that they can easily see the book and interact with the other group members. Children with cognitive delays will benefit from more time to respond; short, simple teacher prompts; and focusing strategies such as turning the pages of the book.

Final Thoughts

In general, teachers should use the same DR methodology of questioning in Levels 1, 2, and 3, with the addition of more concrete props as necessary. Keep in mind that only for students who are nonverbal is it acceptable to begin with receptive language skills and build to the expressive. Regardless of any disabilities that the children may have, teachers need to group children thoughtfully and scaffold between the different levels when grouping students heterogeneously.

References

Aliki. (1996). *My visit to the aquarium,* New York, NY: HarperCollins.

Arnold, D. H., Lonigan, C. J., Whitehurst. G. J., & Epstein, J. N. (1994). Accelerating language development through picture book reading: Replication and extension to a videotape training format. *Journal of Educational Psychology, 86,* 235–243. doi: 10,1037/0022-0663.86.2.235

Bishop, D. V. M.,& Adams, C. (1990). A prospective study of the relationship between specific language impairment, phonological disorders and reading retardation. *Journal of Child Psychology and Psychiatry and Allied Disciplines, 31,* 1027–1050. doi:10.1111/i.1469-7610.1990 ,tb00844.x

Briesch, A. M., Chafouleas, S. M., Lebel, T. *J., &* Blom-Hoffman, J. A. (2008). Impact of videotaped instruction in dialogic reading strategies: An investigation of caregiver implementation integrity. *Psychology in the Schools,* 45(10), 1–16. doi:10.1002/pits.20346

Buehner, C. (1999). *The escape of Marvin the ape.* New York, NY: Puffin.

Bunting, E. (2000). *Flower garden.* Orlando, FL: Sandpiper.

Carlson, N. L. (1999). ABC *I like me!* New York, NY: Puffin.

Chow, B. W., & McBride-Change, C. (2003). Promoting language and literacy development through parent-child reading in Hong Kong preschoolers. *Early Education and Development, 14,* 233–248. doi: 10.1207/s 15566935eed1402_6

Crain-Thoreson, C., & Dale, P. S. (1999). Enhancing linguistic performance: Parents and teachers as book reading partners for children with language delays. *Topics in Early Childhood Special Education, 19,* 28–39. doi:10.1177 /Q2711214990I90C103

Curtis, J. L. (1998). *Today I feel silly: And other moods that make my day.* New York, NY: HarperCoilins.

Dale, P. S., Crain-Thoreson, C., Notari-Svyerson, A., & Cole, K. (1996). Parent-child book reading as an intervention technique for young children with language delays. *Topics in Early Childhood Special Education, 12,* 213–235. doi: 10.1177/027112149601600206

Fleming, C. (2002). *Muncha! Muncha! Muncha!* New York, NY: Simon &Schuster.

Hoberman, M. A, (2000). *The seven, silly eaters.* Orlando, FL: Sandpiper.

Huebner, C. E. (2000). Promoting toddlers' language through community-based intervention. *Journal of Applied Developmental Psychology, 21,* 513–535. doi:10.1016/S0193-3973(00)00052-6

Huebner, C. E., & Meltzoff, A. N. (2005). Intervention to change parent-child reading style: A comparison of instructional methods. *Journal of Applied Developmental Psychology, 29,* 296–313. doi: 10.1016/j.appdev.2005.02.006

Institute of Education Sciences. (2007, February). *Intervention: Dialogic reading.* Retrieved from http://ies.ed.gov/ncee/wwc/reports/early_ed/dial_read/

James, S. (1996). *Dear Mr Blueberry.* New York. NY: Aladdin.

Kraus, R. (1994). *Leo the late bloomer.* New York, NY: HarperCollins.

Lonigan, C. J., Anthony, J. L., Bloomfield, B,, Dyer, S. M., & Samwel, C. (1999). Effects of two preschool shared reading interventions on the emergent literacy skills of children from low-income families. *Journal of Early Intervention, 22,* 306-322. doi:10.1177 /105381519902200406

Lonigan, C. J. (2006). Literacy express comprehensive preschool curriculum [Educational materials]. Available from http://www.lakeshoreleaming.com

Lanigan, C. J., & Whitehurst, G. J. (1998). Relative efficacy of parent and teacher involvement in a shared-reading intervention for preschool children from low- income backgrounds. *Early Childhood Research Quarterly,*13(2), 263-290. doi:10.1016/50885-2006(99)80038-6

Lowell, S. *The three little javelinas.* Flagstaff, AZ: Rising Moon.

McKissack. P. C., & McKissack, P. (2002). *Messy Bessey's garden* (Rev.). New York, NY: Scholastic.

Miranda, A., & Stevens, J. (1997). *To market, to market.* San Diego, CA: Houghton Mifflin Harcourt.

Montes, M. (2000). *Juan Bobo goes to work: A Puerto Rican folk tale.* New York, NY: G. P. Putnam's Sons.

Munoz Ryan, P. (2001). *Hello ocean.* Watertown, MA: Talewinds.

Numeroff, L. J. (1994). *If you give a moose a muffin.* New York, NY: HarperCollins.

Numeroff, L. J. (2000). *If you give a pig a pancake.* New York, NY: HarperCollins.

Ottolenghi, C. (2002). *The little red lien.* Bel Air, CA: Brighter Child.

Porter-Gaylord, L. (1991). *I love my daddy because ... New* York, NY: Dutton.

Ransom, C. (2002). *Goldilocks and the three bears.* Columbus, OH: School Specialty Publishing.

Rathmann, P. (2002). *Goodnight, gorilla.* New York, NY: G. P. Putnam's Sons.

Rockwell, L. (2009). *Good enough to eat:* A *kid's guide to food and nutrition.* New York, NY: HarperCoilins.

Scarborough, H. S. (1989). Prediction of reading dysfunction from familial and individual differences. *Journal of Educational Psychology, 81,* 101–108. doi: 10.1037/0022-0663.81-1.101

Schnitzlein, D. (2010). *The monster who ate my peas.* Atlanta, GA: Peachtree.

Sendak, M. (1988). *Where the wild, things are.* New York, NY: HarperCollins.

Shannon, D. (2002). *Duck on a bike. New* York, NY: Blue Sky Press.

Sheldon, D. (1997). *The whale's song.* New York, NY: Puffin.

Stevens, J. (199S). *Tops & bottoms.* New York, NY: Harcourt.

U.S. Department of Education. (2007). *What works clearinghouse: Dialogic reading* (WWC Intervention Report). Retrieved from http://ies.ed.gov/ncee/wwc/pdf /WWC_Dialogic_Reading_020807.pdf

Valdez-Menchaca, M. C., & Whitehurst, G. J. (1992). Accelerating language development through picture book reading: A systematic extension to Mexican day care. *Developmental Psychology,* 28(6), 1106–1114. doi: 10.1037/0012-1649.28.6.1106

Viorst, J. (2009). *Alexander and the terrible, horrible, no good, very bad day.* New York, NY: Simon & Schuster.

Ward, N. (2002). *Don't eat the teacher.* New York, NY: Scholastic.

Wasik, B. A., & Bond, M. A. (2001). Beyond the pages of a book: Interactive book reading and language development in preschool classrooms. *Journal of Educational Psychology, 93,* 243–250, doi: 10.1037/0022-0663.93.2.243

Weikle, B., & Hadadian, A. (2004). Literacy, development and disabilities: Are we moving in the right direction? *Early Child Development and Care.* 7, 651–666.

Wellington, M. (2004). *Apple farmer Annie.* New York, NY: Puffin.

Whitehurst, G. J., Arnold, D. S., Epstein, J. N., Angell, A. L., Smith, M., & Fischel. J. E. (1994), A picture reading intervention in day care and home for children from low-income families. *Developmental Psychology,* 30(5), 679-689. doi:10.1037 /00I2-1649.30.5.679

Whitehurst, G. J., Epstein, J. N., Angell, A. L., Payne. A. C., Crone, D. A., & Fischel. J. E. (1994). Outcomes of an emergent literacy intervention in Head Start. *Journal of Educational Psychology.* 86(4), 542–555. doi:10.1037/0022-0663.86.4.542

Whitehurst, G. J., Falco, F. L., Lonigan, C. J., Fischel, J. E., DeBaryshe,B. D., Valdez-Menchaca, M. C., & Caulfield, M. (1988). Accelerating language development through picture book reading. *Development Psychology, 24,* 552–559. doi: 10.1037/0012-1649.24.4.552

Whitehurst, G. J., & Lonigan, C. J. (1998). Child development and emergent literacy. *Child Development,* 69(3), 848-872.

Wood, A. (1993). *Little penguin's tale.* Orlando, FL: Sandpiper.

Zevenbergen, A. A., Whitehurst, G. J., & Zevenbergen, J. A. (2003), Effects of a shared-reading intervention on the inclusion of evaluative devices in narratives of children from low-income families. *Applied Developmental Psychology, 24,* 1–15. doi:10.1016/50193-3973(03)00021-2

You Don't Speak My Language

Betty Bardige

Young children need a "critical mass" of engaging and informative language input, along with lots of opportunities to "use their words" with adults and other children. What happens if the input and communication practice come in more than one language, as is increasingly the case for young children in the United States? What happens when the language a child learns in early childhood is not the language that he will use in school? The answers to these questions are complex—and fascinating. What we as a society do with these answers is affecting more and more of our children—including many of those whose families speak English.

One Child's Ordeal

Six-year-old Jeudry Sanchez spent much of his first day of school in tears. His family had recently moved to Massachusetts from Puerto Rico, and Jeudry spoke only Spanish. His teacher was speaking in English, as were the other children, and Jeudry was overwhelmed by the cacophony of unfamiliar words.

Jeudry's teacher could have mediated the transition for him in his own language—she was a former bilingual education teacher who had been born in Puerto Rico and spoke Spanish fluently. But this was Massachusetts in 2003, where a new state law forbade primary grade teachers from using languages other than English in their classrooms. Its aim, of course, is to get children from immigrant families to become fluent in English as rapidly as possible, but that didn't help Jeudry to cope with coming to a new school in a new country—a transition that can be challenging even without a language barrier.

Betty Bardige, "You Don't Speak My Language," *At A Loss For Words: How America Is Failing Our Children*, pp. 74-86, 221-223. Copyright © 2005 by Temple University Press. Reprinted with permission.

Under the law, Jeudry's teacher was allowed only to offer a few words of comfort in Spanish. She could not use it for teaching or for explaining procedures. This put her at a severe disadvantage in teaching children like Jeudry, for she could not build upon—nor even adequately assess—the knowledge and interests that they brought to school. Fortunately, she was able to pair Jeudry with a Spanish-speaking child whose English was strong enough to follow her lessons and who could help Jeudry understand what he was supposed to do.[1]

Families' Dilemmas

Throughout the United States, children even younger than Jeudry experience similar challenges every day, as they enter classrooms or family child-care settings where their language is not spoken. In many cases, their parents have no choice: they need to work and there are no appropriate child care or early education programs in their community where their child can learn in her home language.

When they have a choice, some families opt for places where teachers and children speak their home language, either because they want their child to learn or maintain the language, or because they believe that he will be happier and more successful in a place where he can "use his words," where they can communicate easily with his teachers, and where adults and children will understand and value his culture. Other parents reason that the sooner their children learn English the better off they will be. They place their young ones in English-speaking settings, and may even use English at home in addition to or instead of their home language. Some of these parents limit their conversations with their babies and young children, under the misconception that hearing their home language will interfere with their child's ability to learn English. Still others search far and wide for settings where their children can learn two languages simultaneously.

Conscientious parents and policy makers who study the research will not find a simple answer as to whether to place their young non-English-speaking children in settings where English is the dominant language or to seek out settings where most of the communication and learning occurs in their home language. The child's age and temperament, his vocabulary and communicative skills in his home language, the "match" of what the setting offers with the child's interests and developmental capabilities, and the quality of the relationships and of the language-related teaching that the child experiences all play critical roles in the speed and depth of children's bilingual learning.[2]

In addition, parents must consider their options for the next step—will their child be able to continue learning in his home language as he adds a second one, or will he be forced to make an abrupt transition? What level of English fluency will be required in order to fully participate in his next school? Will supports be available to help him make the transition? Will his literacy and ongoing learning in his home language be supported, either in school or in an after-school program? In their community, will their child receive better content instruction in bilingual education programs or in English-speaking classrooms?

Here is what we know:

- *Young children who hear and converse in two languages from birth learn both, and rarely confuse them, although they may "borrow" words or phrases from their other language in order to better express their meaning.* Children who hear, babble, and ultimately converse in more than one language as infants are not learning a second language—they are learning two (or more) first languages. Unlike second language learners, they store both in the same areas of their brains.[3]

- *Children who have a firm foundation in one language can build on that knowledge as they learn a second.* Children who have a rich vocabulary in their home language will also have learned a great deal of content that is not language-specific and will have developed a range of strategies for gaining new information. Children who are already good at connecting with others, sharing thoughts and feelings, and using inner language to control their behavior and talk themselves through problems do not need to relearn these skills as they add a new language to their repertoire. They bring these resources to their early childhood classrooms, and to the task of learning a second language.[4]

- *Children learn language from their peers as well as from adults; this is especially true for children three and older.* In Hart and Risley's study,[5] parents provided children with their key language inputs during the first two years, and both the quality and quantity of these inputs made a lasting difference. As the children began to talk, parents were key conversation partners. However, as the children neared their third birthdays, they more frequently sought out other conversation partners and also played more independently, using language to talk to their toys or accompany their play. Preschool play depends upon verbal interaction; children are highly motivated to use the language of their peers as they act out pretend play scenarios together.

- *Children need a basic vocabulary of about 5,000 words in order to learn to read easily.*[6] With appropriately rich early language input and conversational practice, children typically learn at least 5,000 words in their first language by the time they are five, and this oral language foundation prepares them for reading. Children who learn to read in another language can apply their knowledge to English words and use reading as a tool to support their English learning.[7] Children who are learning to read for the first time in a language in which they are not fluent face several obstacles: they may not know the meaning of all of the words they are reading, they may not have sufficient experience with the sounds of the language to recognize common patterns of symbol/sound correspondence, they may not have sufficient fluency with grammar and common usage to recognize which of several guesses make sense in a particular context, and they will likely lack an intuitive understanding of word parts and word formation patterns that can help them to deduce the alphabetic principle and to rapidly analyze and decode new words.

- *Bilingual education programs have a mixed track record, but strong programs that support children in their home languages* can *help them make an effective transition to schooling in a second language.* In the United States, we have tried a variety of approaches to educating children who are not fluent in English when they enter an English-dominant school, including immersing English learners in English-only classes with little or no support, pulling children out for ESL instruction or tutoring until they achieve basic fluency, teaching children content in their home language as they learn English, grouping children with peers who speak their home language, separating children from same-language peers in order to encourage English, and discouraging children from speaking anything but English. The results have been mixed.[8] However, a study commissioned by the U.S. Department of Education found that children in programs that provide native-language content instruction for at least 40 percent of the school day through the fifth grade do better in math and English-language skills than children in English immersion or shorter-duration bilingual programs.[9] This research review has convinced some previously skeptical educators of the value of teaching children content—including reading—in their home language and in English until they have become proficient in both languages.[10]

In countries where most village children speak a native language at home and the official language at school, letting children adapt to the school situation before introducing the new language has proven to be a more effective approach than an abrupt transition. Similarly, a transitional summer program for entering kindergarteners who have spent their early years in the care of non-English-speaking grandparents is proving to be an effective support for English learners in several Massachusetts communities.[11]

Dual immersions, or bilingual/bicultural programs, have been among the most effective[12] and are gaining in popularity in the United States and around the world. In these programs, half of the students and teachers are native speakers of one language and half are native speakers of a second. Generally, half of the day is spent learning in one language and half in the other, and all of the children benefit.

- *Children who learn a language before the age of six or seven are likely to learn both its sound system and grammar as native speakers; those who learn later sometimes have continuing difficulties with pronunciation and with some grammatical forms. However, children who begin instruction or immersion in their second language earlier in their school careers do not necessarily master the language more fully or quickly than children who are exposed to it later, with the exception of its sound system.* Younger children have an advantage in that they have less of the language to learn in order to catch up with peers who learned it as a first language and a longer time in which to practice and learn in the new language; older children, however, are able to build upon general knowledge and communication skills gained in their first language, analyze grammatical forms and patterns, and, in many cases, read the new language before they are verbally fluent and learn new vocabulary through reading.[13]

Parents who do not speak fluent English at home and who want their children to do well in U.S. schools are therefore faced with a dilemma: do they maximize their child's chances for acquiring rich vocabulary, expressive confidence, and breadth and depth of knowledge in their home language, or do they prepare them to enter English-speaking classrooms by challenging them to learn English during their preschool years?

As the United States becomes more linguistically diverse, more and more families face this dilemma. In Los Angeles today, people from 100 different ethnic groups speak 70 different languages.[14] Nineteen percent of U.S. children under eighteen lived with at least one foreign-born parent in 2001, and, although this statistic is not broken down by age, the percentage was higher among the youngest children. Approximately 20 percent of all U.S. births in 2000 were to women who identified themselves as Hispanic, although they were not necessarily Spanish speakers. (Studies indicate that approximately a third of Latinos speak only or mainly Spanish, a third speak only English, and a third are bilingual.[15])

If demographers' predictions are born out, by 2010 one third of our nation's children will live in four states—California, Florida, New York, and Texas—where the majority of children will belong to groups that are today considered ethnic minorities.[16] By 2050, almost half of the residents of the United States will be non-white, and one third will be of Latino or Asian descent.[17] As more and more Americans are born into families whose preferred language is not English, we will need to develop early education programs that can meet their needs for a firm language foundation.

Educating Young Children in Mixed-Language Classrooms

Clearly, children who are not comfortably fluent in the language of play and instruction present a challenge for their preschool and elementary school teachers. Such children may be misdiagnosed as language impaired or developmentally delayed. On the other hand, problems that could benefit from early intervention may be overlooked because they are mistakenly attributed to their difficulties with a second language.[18] More important, when their teachers are not skilled at facilitating their participation, the children can miss out on important opportunities for play and learning that rely on linguistic input and communication.

Young children entering a preschool program where their language isn't widely used generally go through several stages as they learn the language of the classroom.[19] At first, they may simply speak their own language, not realizing that they are not being understood. They then may enter a period of silence, where they gather information about the new language but do not yet use it. Toddlers may babble the new sounds to themselves, just as they babbled the sounds of their home language, but preschoolers are usually too aware of social norms to use the new language in a noncommunicative way. During the "silent" phase, they are likely to rely on nonverbal communication, sometimes using words in their own language for emphasis or approximating words, phrases, and inflections of the new language as they try to make their meaning clear.

Before long, most young children will begin to pick up and repeat key words and stock phrases in the new language. They may use them as one-word labels and requests, or string two or three together in a kind of telegraphic speech, similar to a toddler's early sentences in his first language. At times, they may incorporate words and phrases from their home languages, or substitute rough approximations when they can't find the right words. At this stage they almost always get the word order right, but prepositions, conjunctions, pronouns, and grammatical markers such as plural and past tense endings are more elusive. As teachers and peers respond to and expand their utterances, children begin to pick up the grammar of the new language and to use it with increasing confidence.

Each child, of course, brings a unique temperament, learning style, and set of prior skills and interests to the task of learning a new language. Successful teachers connect with each child, bring out and build upon her strengths, and find ways to encourage and answer her questions—whatever language or nonverbal communication system she uses to ask them.

Well-prepared preschool teachers know how to support second language learners in all aspects of their development. They set up opportunities for children to demonstrate their prior knowledge and acquire new knowledge nonverbally—through drawing, block building, puzzles and games, movement activities, and pretend play. They are also adept at using techniques that facilitate rich vocabulary, expressive fluency, and emergent literacy in a child's first language, and adapting these techniques to benefit second language learners in a mixed-language setting.

- They recognize the cognitive and social–emotional strengths that children have developed through their experiences with their home language, and see their knowledge of two languages as an asset for the individual child and for the class as a whole.
- They help children learn language by talking with them a lot—providing running commentary on what they and the children are doing, encouraging children to repeat new words and to "use their words" (in both their home language and English), showing interest in what children have to say, and responding with words and appropriate clarifying gestures to children's verbal and nonverbal questions.
- They expand and elaborate the children's comments, providing good models without actually correcting grammar, just as they would for toddlers learning their first language and for preschoolers who still typically struggle with the pronunciation of certain words and with exceptions to the grammatical regularities that they have just recently mastered.
- They emphasize key words through repetition and highlight features of language, such as word endings and distinctions among similar sounds, that English learners may not hear if they are not salient in their home language. (Parentese, the way in which adults around the world tend to speak to their babies, uses repetition and emphasis in similar ways.)
- They focus on high-interest vocabulary for all children, and help them appreciate the component parts of words.
- They read frequently to children in small groups and one-on-one, choosing books carefully and using shared reading techniques that highlight new vocabulary and sentence patterns, encourage the children to chime in with repeated or predictable text, and engage the children in conversation about the story and the pictures.
- They help children make connections between written and spoken words—in both of their languages.
- They use carefully worded questions to scaffold children's learning, pushing them to draw upon prior knowledge and then go just a bit beyond what they already know and can do.

- They actively include second language learners in teacher-led discussions, facilitate their inclusion in child-centered play and exploration, and help children who do not share their linguistic background to appreciate and enjoy their contributions.
- They encourage interactions among children, especially pretend play, providing ample opportunities for children to learn and practice new words.
- They take steps to ensure that all children are comfortable in their classroom and that their development is nurtured in all domains. When possible, they use bilingual classroom aides and other children to translate, build bridges, and provide reassurance.
- They consult with each child's parents, as well as with professionals who speak her language and can explain nuances of behavior and culture-specific communication patterns.
- They make extensive use of songs, nursery rhymes, finger plays, and movement games for teaching children each other's languages.
- They bring in books and other materials in each child's home language, and, with the help of parents and other community members, incorporate her home language and culture into the curriculum for the group as a whole.
- They make a point of learning the child's language themselves, and of including words in that language in classroom conversations, displays, and play materials.

Unfortunately, too few of our preschool teachers, and even fewer of the teachers of the one- and two-year-olds who may be learning two languages simultaneously, have the level of preparation needed to employ such techniques consistently and effectively.

Losing Language

One consequence of the lack of preparation of people who work with young children is that some children may not get the input and conversational practice they need to develop a firm foundation—in any language. Another is that without the support of the teachers and peers with whom they are spending a significant amount of their time, children's first language skills may stagnate or diminish as they try to learn a second language. Scholars refer to this as "subtractive bilingualism"—the loss of the first language.

Our language is so intertwined with the way we name and know the world, the way we think and think of ourselves, as well as the ways in which we communicate with others, that it is hard for most of us to imagine "losing" our native languages. Learning a second language should mean just that—adding a new language to one's repertoire. However, language, like the neural connections in our brains, is strengthened with use and can atrophy with disuse.

For many children in the United States today, learning a new language can mean the gradual and sometimes total replacement of their first one, often within a few years.[20] As their schoolmates, neighborhood friends, and perhaps even their parents are increasingly reliant upon English, they find fewer and fewer occasions to use their native language. Unless they are spending a fair amount of time with grandparents or others who prefer their native tongue, or are enrolled in native-language classes to advance their literacy and cultural knowledge, they are likely to retain only the rudiments of the language—the basic grammar and conversational vocabulary they acquired as young children, or, quite often, only a few key words and phrases and well-rehearsed songs or sayings. Even in communities where many children speak their native language, children may pick up subtle and not-so-subtle messages that their language is not the language of learning and that their way of speaking is not the path to success. They may choose to speak English, even though this means cutting ties with family and culture.[21]

Because language is so intimately connected with culture and identity, the consequences of devaluing a child's home language can be devastating. In his autobiography, *Always Running*, Luis Rodriguez describes the linguistic challenges he faced as a Chicano growing up in Los Angeles in the 1950s and 1960s. A gifted child, he reached adolescence having repeatedly failed in school but also showing impressive talent in both visual art and poetry, along with striking resilience and leadership ability.

As he worked with teachers to prepare his writings for a national contest, Luis reflected on his linguistic abilities and disabilities:

> I had fallen through the chasm between two languages. The Spanish had been beaten out of me in the early years of school—and I didn't learn English very well either.
>
> This was the predicament of many Chicanos.
>
> We could almost be called incommunicable, except we remained lucid; we got over what we felt, sensed and understood. Sometimes we rearranged words, created new meanings and structures—even a new vocabulary. Often our everyday talk blazed with poetry.
>
> Our expressive powers were strong and vibrant. If this could be nurtured, if the language skills could be developed on top of this, we could break through any communication barrier. We needed to obtain victories in language, built on an infrastructure of self-worth.
>
> But we were often defeated from the start.[22]

Today, most adults working with young children know better than to "beat out" their native languages. We have seen the disastrous consequences of Bureau of Indian Affairs assimilation efforts earlier in this century. In order to promote "assimilation," children were removed from their homes and sent to boarding schools where their tribal languages were forbidden. Many returned as adolescents to find that they belonged neither on or off their reservations. Their elders called them "the lost generation." The gap that they left in the fabric of their communities contributed to the loss of tribal languages and traditions.

The practice of literally beating children in order to correct their speech is no longer accepted. Early childhood teachers are mandated child abuse reporters, and most receive some training in recognizing signs of physical abuse. Their profession considers even mild spanking to be taboo (as well as ineffective) in an early childhood classroom, even for children whose families use physical discipline. And of course, early childhood teachers are taught to value each child and each family—not to punish children for who they are.

Today, too, we realize that we live in a global economy, where the ability to speak more than one language fluently is an important economic asset. Depriving children of opportunities to practice a language and improve their proficiency and then trying to reteach it to them as a high school course seems like a waste of time. And hearing new languages from peers—perhaps even learning some basic vocabulary—benefits all children, even if they won't have an opportunity to study those languages until they are older.

Still, too often, children pick up messages that their way of speaking is not valued in school or in the larger society. Whether it is their language or their dialect, their first-language-influenced pronunciation or their regional accent, their carryover of phrases and grammatical markers from their first language or the grammatical but nonstandard usage of their English dialect, children's ways of speaking are too often misinterpreted and stereotyped as signs of lesser knowledge or lesser intelligence.[23] These pressures lead some children to hide or reject their linguistic backgrounds, while others may be inappropriately held back in their academic progress because they don't "talk right." Some children become adept at code-switching, speaking one way at home and in their linguistic community and another way at school and in the community at large.

Diversity in the Workforce

The increasing diversity of the young child population is accompanied by increasing diversity among their teachers, child-care workers, and nannies. This is in many ways a good thing: it means that families who want their children to be cared for and taught by adults who can nurture their home language learning and cultural traditions can find such adults in their communities. It means that teachers of increasingly diverse classes can find colleagues who can support their students in their home languages, translate with children and parents, explain cultural differences, and help them to avoid misunderstandings and correct miscommunications. It means that children of many backgrounds can have the opportunity to learn from adults of many backgrounds.

In the best early education and family support programs, children reap the benefits of a diverse early childhood workforce and realize the vision set forth by the Early Childhood Equity Alliance.

We envision a world where all children and families

- feel that they belong,
- have all aspects of their identity affirmed,
- have the resources they need to thrive,
- eagerly learn from each other across cultural and other differences,
- actively address biased behavior through open communication and willingness to grow, and
- work together to challenge and change institutionalized forms of bias.[24]

But the prevalence of close-to-poverty wages in the child-care field and the dearth of opportunities for educational advancement for those not fluent in English means that diversity tends to be greatest in the poorest paid and least trained sectors of the field. English language learners are most likely to work as nannies or caregivers for babies, as aides in center-based classrooms, as unlicensed family child-care providers, and as teachers or licensed providers where licensing requirements are lax. Some, of course, have been well trained to work with young children in their home countries—where publicly supported early childhood programs may be more prevalent and may demand higher credentials than those in the United States. Many, however, have low levels of education and literacy in their home languages and little, if any, early childhood professional training.

Child-care centers on tight budgets, unable to afford or retain staff with strong credentials, hire the best of the available applicants. This often means overlooking language. A common compromise in English-only settings is to place teachers who are English learners with preverbal children, reasoning that their limited vocabulary or difficulties reading English aloud will be less of a handicap than it would be with older children. This means, of course, that babies and toddlers are likely to hear less language, with less varied vocabulary, than if their caregivers spoke to them in a language in which they were comfortable.

This problem can be equally acute for parents seeking to hire nannies. Like Zoë Baird, President Clinton's first choice for attorney general, they may be unable to find an appropriate person to take the job who is not a recent immigrant, either legal or undocumented. Communication between the parents and the nanny may be awkward at first if they are not completely fluent in each other's language, but they will usually share enough words to make themselves understood. The child, however, needs more from his caregiver, especially if they are together for long periods of time. He needs a critical mass of rich language input and engaged conversation—and this may not be forthcoming in either language. Isolated from her own linguistic community, the nanny may use less and less of her home language as she speaks to the child in her emergent English. She may use her home language when she encounters a fellow immigrant, but the child in her charge is likely to be left out of those conversations.

On the other hand, some children are lucky enough to learn two languages—one from their caregiver and one from their parents and other family and community members. This is most likely to occur, of course, when the caregiver is a relative or family friend, or when the parents can at least speak the caregiver's language and reinforce her lessons.

Benefits of Bilingualism

For young children lucky enough to learn two languages well, bilingualism confers unique cognitive and social advantages. Children who learn two languages early in life become aware early on that the same thing can be said in different ways. They gain extensive practice in adapting their communication to the context and to the listener; often they are challenged to shift rapidly from one language to another when a new person enters the conversation or when they and their conversation partners move into a setting where a different language dominates.

Researchers have discovered an interesting phenomenon: apparently coping with the challenge of speaking two languages makes children more flexible in their thinking[25] and improves their scores on verbal and nonverbal IQ tests! In one study, researchers tested 123 kindergarteners and first graders in Puerto Rico. They found a positive relationship between the extent of children's bilingualism and their scores on a nonverbal intelligence test.[26] Studies of English-speaking Canadian children found that those who learned more French in their French-immersion elementary school classrooms made greater gains in IQ than classmates whose French language skills were less advanced.[27] Other studies found that bilingual teens used more sophisticated learning strategies than their monolingual peers.[28]

Perhaps as we both become and participate in a more global community, the United States will commit to catching up with our trading partners and competitors by educating our children in more than one language. We will provide a strong language and literacy foundation in early childhood and sustain it with later schooling. The graduates of our school systems will be able to express and appreciate complex concepts, subtle shades of meaning, technical information, and poetic possibilities in at least two languages.

Today, too many of our children are not acquiring this level of fluency and literacy in even one language, let alone in two or three. Whether they have missed the opportunity to build a strong foundation in their native language, shifted so abruptly from one language to another that they can't follow daily lessons, or "lost" their home language without fully replacing it, they start school behind and have difficulty catching up. Part II—The Quiet Crisis—examines the factors that are placing them at such an acute disadvantage.

Notes

1 Jeudry's story was reported in *The Boston Globe* on the first day the English immersion law, or Unz Initiative, went into effect. A. Vaishnav (2003) School begins, immersed in English, *The Boston Globe*, August 27.

2 P. O. Tabors (1997) *One Child, Two Languages*, Baltimore, MD: Paul H. Brookes Publishing Company. See J. Cruzado-Guerrero (2003) Understanding literacy development in young bilingual children, in *Florida's Child*, Summer 2003 (Tallahassee, FL: Florida Children's Forum) for a discussion of pros and cons of different options for infants, toddlers, and preschoolers.

3 F. Genosee, W. E. Lambert, L. Mononen, M. Seitz, and D. Starch (1979) *Language Processing in Bilinguals*. Also see *From Neurons to Neighborhoods*, pp. 135–136, for a discussion of more recent research on the connections between the timing of second language acquisition and the areas of the brain involved in processing different aspects of the language. Function words and other grammatical information tend to be stored differently by those who learn a language later in life.

4 See C. Genishi (2002) Young English language learners: Resourceful in the classroom, In *Young Children*, July 2002, pp. 66–72.

5 B. Hart and T. Risley (1999) *The Social World of Children Leaning to Talk*, Baltimore, MD: Paul H. Brookes Publishing Company.

6 C. Snow (2002) Ensuring reading success for African American children, In B. Bowman (ed.), *Love to Read*, Washington, DC: National Black Child Development Institute.

7 Reading ability transfers across languages, even when different alphabets are used or when one language is written alphabetically and the other isn't. J. Cummins, M. Swain, K. Nakajima, J. Handscombe, D. Green, and C. Tran (1984) Linguistic interdependence among

Japanese and Vietnamese immigrant students, In C. Rivera (ed.), *Communicative Competence Approaches to Language Proficiency Assessment: Research and Application*, Clevedon, England: Multilingual Matters, pp. 60–81.

8   D. August and K. Hakuta (eds.) (1997) *Improving Schooling for Language-Minority Children: A Research Agenda*, Washington, DC: National Academy Press.

9   J. D. Ramírez, S. D. Yuen, and D. R. Ramey (1991) *Longitudinal Study of Structured English Immersion Strategy, Early-Exit and Late-Exit Transitional Bilingual Education Programs for Language-Minority Children*, San Mateo, CA: Aguirre, International. Prepared for the United States Department of Education under Contract No. 300-87-0156. For a discussion of the implications of these findings for educators of young children, see C. Eggers-Piérola (in press) *Connections and Commitments: Reflecting Latino Values in Early Childhood Programs*, Portsmouth, NH: Heinemann.

10 M. A. Zehr (2004) Study gives advantage to bilingual education over focus on English, *Education Week*, February 4.

11 Elizabeth Schaefer, Administrator, Early Learning Services, Massachusetts Department of Education, personal communication, January 14, 2004.

12 J. Cummins (2001) The academic and political discourse of minority language education: Claims and counter-claims about reading, academic language, pedagogy, and assessment as they relate to bilingual children's educational development. Paper presented at the *International Conference on Bilingualism*, Bristol, April 20, 2001. See http://www.iteachilearn.com/cummins/claims.html for a summary.

13 See *From Neurons to Neighborhoods: The Science of Early Childhood Development* (National Research Council and Institute of Medicine (2000) Committee on Integrating the Science of Early Childhood Development. Jack P. Shonkoff and Deborah A. Phillips (eds.). Board on Children, Youth, and Families, Commission on Behavioral and Social Sciences and Education. Washington, DC: National Academy Press), pp. 134– 136, and B. Mclaughlin (1992) *Educational Practice Report #5: Myths and Misconceptions about Second Language Learning: What Every Teacher Needs to Unlearn* (Washington, DC: National Center For Research on Cultural Diversity and Second Language Learning).

14 V. Washington and J. D. Andrews (eds.) (1999) *Children of 2010*, Washington, DC: Children of 2010 and National Association for the Education of Young Children.

15 Washington and Andrews (eds.), *Children of 2010*.

16 Washington and Andrews (eds.), *Children of 2010*.

17 United States Census Bureau (2001*) Statistical Abstract of the United States: 2001*, Springfield, VA: National Technical Information Service.

18 See Tabors's *One Child, Two Languages* for a discussion of assessment challenges and techniques.

19 P. O. Tabors (2003) What early childhood educators need to know: Developing effective programs for linguistically and culturally diverse children and families, In D. Koralek (ed.), *Spotlight on Young Children and Language*, Washington, DC: National Association for the Education of Young Children.

20   L. W. Filmore (2000) Loss of family languages: Should educators be concerned? *Theory Into Practice*, 39(4): 203–210.

21   L. Tse (2001) *"Why Don't They Learn English?: Separating Fact from Fallacy in the U.S. Language Debate*, New York: Teachers College Press.

22   L. Rodriguez (1993) *Always Running*, New York: Simon and Schuster, p. 219.

23   See S. B. Heath (1983) *Ways with Words: Language, Life and Work in Communities and Classrooms*, Cambridge, UK: Cambridge University Press, for a classic study of the ways in which children in two different working-class communities, one African American and one white, learn to use language and how differences between their ways of speaking and the language of schooling and power lead to unequal opportunity for academic advancement. Unfortunately, a large body of research shows that children who speak English differently continue to be misunderstood, disadvantaged, and discriminated against in schools that do not validate their home language. See L. Delpitt and J. K. Dowdy (eds.) (2003) *The Skin That We Speak: Thoughts on Language and Culture in the Classroom*, New York: New Press.

24   The above vision is part of the mission statement of the Early Childhood Equity Alliance. See www.rootsforchange.net.

25   J. Cummins and M. Swain (1986) Bilingualism in Education: Aspects of Theory, Research and Practice, London: Longman.

26   K. Hakuta and R. M. Diaz (1984) The relationship between degree of bilingualism and cognitive ability: A critical discussion and some new longitudinal data, In K. Nelson (ed.), *Children's Language*, Vol. 5, Hillsdale, NJ: Lawrence Erlbaum Associates.

27   H. C. Barik and M. Swain (1976) A longitudinal study of bilingual and cognitive development, *International Journal of Psychology*, 11: 251–263; B. Harley and S. Lapkin (1984) The effects of early bilingual schooling on first language development, OISE. Mimeo.

28   S. Bochner (1996) The learning strategies of bilingual vs. monolingual students, *British Journal of Educational Psychology*, 66: 83–93.

Prime Time for Language Learning

Betty Bardige

Humans are social animals, and their children come into the world primed to communicate. Language and symbolic thought, the hallmarks of humanity, develop very early. The first five years of life, and especially the years between one and four, are prime time for language learning. The brain is growing and developing rapidly, forming new connections as it learns. These connections, in turn, enable rapid information processing and new learning.[1]

Virtually every child who can physically speak and hear (and many who can't) masters at least one language by age five.[2] Their learning is so rapid that some scientists have postulated a "language instinct" that is hardwired into the brain and activated by hearing, practice, and conversation.[3]

But being able to speak a language fluently is not the whole story. As we saw with Jack and Jill, it is the qualitative differences in the way language is used that matter, and these, like language learning in general, are rooted in early experience.

This chapter zeroes in on the period of dramatic language development that occurs for most children between the ages of one and four. In this short period, children go from grunts and gestures to complex storytelling. This is the time when language learning is easy, when children "burst into language" and parents are constantly surprised by how much their children know. If we want to ensure that all children learn their language well, it makes sense to direct our efforts to the period when they are most eager and able to learn it.

By looking at the developmental milestones that all children traverse and at the experiences that help them attain and build on these milestones, we can gain a deeper understanding of the conditions necessary for healthy development and for optimal language learning. We can see what it is about young children that makes their language learning so rapid and understand what it is that children should be

Betty Bardige, "Prime Time for Language Learning," *At A Loss For Words: How America Is Failing Our Children*, pp. 21-31, 216-218. Copyright © 2005 by Temple University Press. Reprinted with permission.

getting during this time of rapid learning. As we examine parenting, caregiving, and teaching practices that enable children to develop robust vocabularies and effective language use, we can begin to see what it would take to give a child like Jill the essential early language and learning foundation that Jack can take for granted.

Children's language development begins very early. During their first month, babies recognize and turn toward the voices of their most frequent caregivers. They make eye contact, watch eyes and mouths, imitate facial expressions, and begin to learn the turn-taking "dance" of communication exchange.

Although babies' first communications may not be intentional, attentive parents and other caregivers are able to interpret their meanings. For example, they can differentiate between the rhythmic, intense cry that means "I'm hungry," the sharp cry that means "I'm in pain," and the whiney cry that means "I'm uncomfortable." Often without realizing what signals they are noticing, they recognize that when a baby hiccups, tenses her body, tightens her lips, screws up her face, stiffens her body, or curls her toes, the baby is saying "I am overstimulated or overwhelmed and I need to be soothed." Most important, they tune in to the baby's rhythm of interaction. They follow the baby's lead as she makes eye contact, engages in back-and-forth play, signals that she needs a break by briefly turning away, and then resumes the play when she is ready.[4]

Before long, babies are tuning in to the rhythms and inflections of language. Adults the world over speak to babies in a language that psychologists refer to as "Parentese."[5] They use low, smooth murmurs for soothing, rising intonation to elicit or direct attention, a rising and falling pattern to indicate approval, and sharp, quick sounds to mean "Stop!" or "Don't!"[6] Indeed, parents of young babies often discover that it doesn't matter what they say, as long as they say it in Parentese. Often, a baby who fusses when his mother talks on the phone or carries on a conversation with another adult will be perfectly content if his mother continues the conversation while looking at him and adopting the high pitch and singsong inflections of Parentese.

Along with its recognizable melodies, Parentese has features that grab the baby's attention and facilitate language learning. Its high pitch and accompanying eye contact mark it as language, and specifically as language directed to the baby. Words are enunciated more clearly than in typical speech, usually with elongated vowels, making it easier to hear where one word ends and a new one begins. Key words, especially nouns and verbs, are often given exaggerated emphasis, making it easier to associate a word with a thing or action. The speaker often repeats the same sentences over and over with slight variations, giving the baby more opportunities to focus on the key words.[7]

By the time they are six months old, most babies have begun to babble, or to play with speech sounds. At first, babies throughout the world babble the same sounds, but gradually, those not used in languages the baby hears drop out. At the same time, the baby begins to imitate the inflections she hears, and her babbling, though still only gibberish, comes to sound more and more like meaningful sentences. She may also learn to follow simple verbal directions, such as "Wave bye-bye," or "Touch Daddy's nose."

During the first year, the baby will learn to communicate through purposeful nonverbal signs. He will lift his arms to signal "pick me up," push away your hands to signal "I don't want that," point with one finger to tell you to look at something, turn or shake his head to tell you he doesn't want what you are offering. As caregivers interpret and respond to a baby's signs, the baby learns the value of conversational exchanges.

The importance of talking with babies before they can talk themselves cannot be overestimated. The more that researchers study infants, the more astounded they are at the extent of their capabilities and at the rapidity of their learning.[8] Babies can remember and reenact complex events before they can speak.[9] When the adults in their lives give them words—for example, by talking about a recent event, babies' eyes light up as they make connections between the words and the experiences. After a few repetitions of a nursery game like "Pop Goes the Weasel," babies learn to anticipate the "pop" and are excited by their own mastery.

Sometime between the beginning of the second year and the middle of the third, language development really heats up. The toddler begins to put words together into short sentences like "More juice," "Baby crying," and "Daddy bye-bye car." This new ability to combine words allows her to say things she has never heard. As she discovers the power of words to communicate, she uses language for many different purposes: to make requests, call out greetings, direct attention to something she finds interesting, ask questions, describe what she sees or hears or what she is doing, entertain herself and others, protest, and invite interaction. To her parents, it seems as if a minor miracle is occurring.

Some children move from single words to conversation in a rapid burst; others gradually increase the length and complexity of their communications.[10] As the child relies increasingly on language to communicate, his vocabulary development skyrockets. According to Stephen Pinkner, author of *The Language Instinct*, "Vocabulary growth jumps to the new-word-every-two-hours minimum rate that the child will maintain through adolescence."[11] (This "jump," of course, is neither as predictable nor as instinctive as Pinkner portrays it. It is dependent upon opportunities to hear new words repeatedly in meaningful contexts and to practice those words in conversation.)

The typical two-year-old says between 50 and 100 words, but the range of "normal" is quite wide. Three-year-olds who are developmentally on target understand about 2,000 words, and use nearly 1,000 different words in their everyday speech![12]

At about the same time she begins putting words together, the toddler starts to pretend. At first, her pretending looks like deferred imitation: she will put a hat on her head or "drink" from an empty cup. In effect, she is labeling the objects with her actions, showing that she knows what they are for. Soon, however, she will use one object to stand for another. She may "drink" from a block and then hold it out to an adult for a refill, perhaps using words like "cup" or "more milk" to make her intention clear. By their third birthdays, most preschoolers are adept pretenders—acting out a variety of scenarios alone, with friends, with adults, and in their play with toys and small objects. Familiar themes like eating, sleeping, cooking, and going places, or favorite stories from books and videos, are reenacted in skeletal form and gradually elaborated into complicated stories that are played out over and over again with endless variations.

In one of his weekly columns, comic writer Dave Barry gave this description of his two-and-a-half-year-old daughter's favorite pretending game:

> Snow White ... is a game she plays 814,000 times per day, using little figurines to act out the parts. Snow White is played by Snow White. The seven dwarfs are played by six dwarfs (Sleepy is currently missing). The wicked witch is played by a Fisher-Price Little People construction worker, who wears a hard hat, as if to say: "I may be evil incarnate, but, dang it, I am not exempt from OSHA regulations!" The poison apple is played by a plastic apple from Sophie's play kitchen. It's roughly 10 times the size of Snow White's head; even if she didn't eat it, this thing could scare her into a coma. The handsome prince is usually played by a handsome prince, although recently he was misplaced, so Snow White was awakened from her coma by a romantic kiss from: a sheep. It's from the Fisher-Price farm set, and as sheep go, it's reasonably handsome.
>
> Over and over, in Sophie's little hands, these figurines act out the story: Snow White is put to sleep by the giant mutant apple; she is awakened by the handsome prince/sheep; everybody dances around happily, including the hard-hat witch.[13]

When child development experts speak of the preschool period as "the magic years"[14] or say that "play is the work of children,"[15] they are talking about this endlessly compelling pretending.

This explosion of language, symbolization, and sharing of meaning doesn't happen all by itself. Children can hear torrents of words from radio, television, or overheard conversation and pick up none of them. For example, many Dutch children avidly watch German TV, but they don't learn to speak German unless it is spoken in their homes or taught in school. Likewise, hearing children whose deaf parents were advised to keep the TV on for them failed to learn spoken language through that medium.[16] On the other hand, young children who can follow the gist of a conversation that they are not supposed to be listening to often surprise or embarrass their parents by repeating adults' words.

Mother (to Father): I want her to eat some vegetables. Don't give her her M-I-L-K yet.
Three-year-old: But I want my M-I-L-K, right now!

For the most part though, language learning proceeds through practice and interaction.

Healthy young children spend a lot of time practicing language. Parents commonly overhear them talking to themselves, for example, saying "hot," "no," or "touch gently" to remind themselves not to grasp a tempting but dangerous object. Young children also talk to their toys, their hands and feet, and to objects that interest or threaten them, as well as to the people in their lives. In addition, they sometimes repeat words, syllables, and sequences just because they like their sounds. For example, I vividly remember my three-year-old daughter, who loved Beatrix Potter's *Tale of the Flopsy Bunnies*,[17] repeating the phrase "handsome muff" over and over to herself because she liked hearing it, though she had only a rudimentary idea of what it meant. Indeed, researchers have found that practicing nursery rhymes, nonsense ditties, rock lyrics, and tongue twisters helps children develop an awareness of sound patterns that serves as a stepping-stone to reading.

But the real progress occurs through communication. It occurs when a baby's big brother hands her a rattle and she smiles and he says (in Parentese) "Oooh. You like the rattle" and she smiles again and gurgles. It occurs when a toddler says "Wha's dat?" and a parent supplies the name of the object that the child is pointing to. It occurs when a caregiver says "umm, delicious peas" and a two-year-old uses the new word in a sentence like "More peas" or "All done peas" to indicate his desire. It occurs when a teacher reads a book and a child uses the new vocabulary to name or ask about the pictures. It occurs when a child utters a two-word sentence like "Daddy car" and her grandmother expands the sentence as she checks to see if she interpreted it correctly. "Yes, Daddy got in the car. He's going to work."

The basic rules of grammar are relatively easy to learn, and most children master them in predictable stages. They start out by combining two words—subject–verb, possessor–possessed, or adjective–noun—into "sentences" that reflect the word order of their language. As they elaborate these simple sentences into three-, four-, and five-word utterances, they also begin to add grammatical markers, such as plural and past tense endings. At first, children overgeneralize the rules, applying these endings to irregular verbs and nouns with irregular plurals, as in "We goed to the store" or "The sheeps eated up all the grass." Gradually, they learn the exceptions; by age five their usage conforms to the conventions of their community.

Children who as babies hear more than one language spoken by the people around them will learn the grammar of each language separately, and rarely confuse the rules.[18] For example, they will not omit a tense marker like -s or -ed to indicate past or present in English, or use an adjective ending such as -a or -o in Spanish that does not match the gender of the noun it describes, although people who learn a second language as adults tend to make such mistakes. Deaf children whose hearing parents and caregivers do not use sign language will invent their own gestures and gesture sequences, which follow regular grammar-like rules.[19] Only children with rare disorders, such as a specific language disability or some forms of autism, fail to learn the basic patterns of a language.[20]

Late talkers are not necessarily slow in their language learning.[21] It is quite common for children to have difficulty with articulation, which they either outgrow or overcome with a short course of speech therapy. Once they are able to speak clearly, their language development is likely to be very rapid because they already know the meaning of so many words and phrases. During their period of silence or "mumbling" they have been actively communicating—stringing together grunts and gestures to express their wishes, questions, and ideas and responding to the increasingly complex language that is spoken or read to them.

The differences that matter are vocabulary—the aspect of language that gets measured in IQ assessments and college admission tests—and "expressiveness," the extent to which language is used. Children whose homes or child-care environments are rich in books, interesting things to explore and talk about, and people interested in talking about them develop rich vocabularies and use their words in a variety of complex sentences for a variety of purposes. Children with less responsive people to talk to and less to talk about are likely to recognize fewer words and use words in more limited ways. In one study, a group of children entering kindergarten showed a range in receptive vocabulary (number of words understood) scores from 1 year, 9 months to 10 years, 8 months![22]

The good news is that children who are slow to develop their vocabularies can catch up. Unlike grammar and pronunciation, which are learned most easily in early childhood, vocabulary does not get harder to learn as one gets older. The bad news is that "catching up" gets harder and harder as time goes on. This is because children who develop richer vocabularies by age three or four tend to increase their vocabularies at a faster pace, so the gap widens every year. This widening gap should be no surprise. The more words of a sentence or paragraph one understands, the easier it is to pick up new words from the context. Similarly, having a richer vocabulary enables a child to ask more nuanced questions, make more precise observations, draw on more sources for making analogies, and give and understand more detailed explanations or inferences. Thus learning is accelerated, and with it the potential for mastering new words and asking new questions.[23]

So, what do parents and caregivers need to do to ensure that children learn enough vocabulary in their early years to be prepared to succeed in school? Is ordinary experience enough, or do we need to add special training and supports? The best answer seems to be "both." The experiences children need are ordinary ones, but, through no fault of their own and often despite the best efforts of their families, an increasing percentage of our children do not have sufficient access to these ordinary experiences.

Children need help from adults if they are to learn their language well, and adults can do a better job of helping if they know what works. Reading and talking about books, telling simple stories, singing together, reciting nursery rhymes, playing word games, sharing pretend play with props or puppets, asking and encouraging questions, elaborating children's ideas and sentences, and other forms of effective language "teaching" are such fun for children and adults alike that they are easy to incorporate into everyday routines. They feed the constant flow of engaged conversation—with opportunities to hear and practice language, to note the impact of one's words, and to try again and again to make one's meaning clear—that fuels the child's learning.

Most children who spend their days conversing with attentive, responsive, informative, and playful adults will get what they need through ordinary experience. Unfortunately, for far too many American children, this is not the case. The people with whom they spend large portions of their days lack the unhurried time, the skill at teaching young children in a group, the knowledge of techniques for facilitating language and literacy, or the fluency in the language that they use with the children to provide them with enough language input, practice, and feedback. A society that expects all of its children to achieve high levels of literacy needs to intervene during prime time for language learning. In other words, we need public policies and public investments that support parents and other caregivers who are responsible for young children's early learning.

It is not difficult to provide the additional training and support that adults who spend their days with young children need in order to be successful facilitators of their language learning. But it does take resources. Fortunately, we have a large body of research and practical knowledge that can guide us in deploying those resources effectively.

Let's look more closely at the "ordinary" daily experiences that adults provide for children who are learning their language well.

Infants with "attuned" caregivers have an easy time communicating; their caregivers are adept at reading their signals and respond in ways that are comforting and engaging. These babies spend lots of time enjoying back-and-forth "conversations" with looks, gestures, grunts and squeals, babbles, and eventually words. They happily explore an interesting environment and constantly learn how to make new things happen. As the babies show off their skills and discoveries, their caregivers share their delight. Over time, these babies learn that they can use words to connect with people and to influence their behavior.

Toddlers and preschoolers who are developmentally "on target" are hungry for words. Learning to talk, and to use language to give meaning and form to their perceptions and imaginings, is their paramount developmental task. They are driven to practice at every opportunity. They are constantly asking "What's that?" "Where?" "How?" and "Why?" When their questions are answered and encouraged, when the people around them show genuine interest in what they are thinking and what they have to say, their learning proceeds apace. As one grandmother observed, "I'd forgotten how much energy it takes to spend a day with a three-year-old. My granddaughter wants to know everything! I don't think she stopped asking questions or insisting I pretend with her for more than five minutes, unless her mouth was full. And of course, she expected me to have all the answers!"

If keeping up with one three-year-old can be exhausting, how can a teacher or caregiver keep a whole group of young children engaged? A good child-care program, whether home- or center-based, provides ample opportunities for children to explore topics that interest them in depth. In a home, children can join in as adults shop, cook, garden, do household repairs, run errands, and pursue hobbies. They can help prepare for holidays and celebrate the special rituals that their families cherish, or learn firsthand about cultures that are different from their own. They can take walks through the neighborhood and encounter pets, wildlife, rocks, pine cones, fallen leaves, flowers, construction sites, police officers and fire fighters, older children, babies, shopkeepers, and different kinds of vehicles. They can listen to stories or watch videos and then play out the scenarios or retell favorite parts. And of course, they can use books (including library books) to learn new information, find answers to their questions, encounter new stories, revisit old favorites, and spend special time with people they love. With adults to encourage their explorations and accompany them on their travels, young children gather a wealth of information. As they walk through the world with wide-eyed wonder, their vocabularies, pretend play, and constant conversations reveal their ever-expanding knowledge.

In schools and school-like programs, teachers often introduce topics of conversation through curriculum units on popular subjects like the farm, seasons, dinosaurs, or pets. Using books, pictures, games and puzzles, pretend play materials, artifacts, art materials, and occasional visitors or field trips, teachers provide opportunities for children to explore and talk about topics that interest them. Some take their cues from the children, implementing a "project approach"[24] or "emergent curriculum." Building on an interest expressed through a child's pretend play, art work, storytelling, or question, they might begin by gathering a group of children and brainstorming with them what they know about a topic and what they would like to learn. There is ample time for conversation as children plan, investigate, and share their discoveries. Hands-on learning experiences, books, visitors, and field trips provide answers to children's questions—and spark new ones. Children are encouraged to represent their discoveries in a variety of media: pretend play, drawing and painting, sculpting, dictating stories, singing songs, making books with captioned pictures, and working together to create murals, displays, class journals, thank you letters to class visitors and field trip guides, block constructions, and elaborate settings for games like "house," "store," "astronauts," or "animal hospital."

Another approach is to use a prepared curriculum[25] that is rich in language and builds upon children's daily experiences in their families and communities. Such curricula can be purchased commercially or can be put together by a teacher (or better yet, by a team that includes parents as partners). Units can be organized around favorite books, appealing topics such as babies, space, transportation, the circus, or dinosaurs; seasonal themes like holidays, growing plants, or weather; places such as the city, the beach, or the farm; or concepts such as colors, light and shadow, families, or growth and change. The theme provides the topic for conversations in the various areas of the classroom, on the playground, and during small and large group "lessons" where teachers facilitate discussions, read stories, teach games and songs, and impart information. Children have many opportunities to practice new vocabulary in a variety of settings as they interact with each other and with their teachers and as they bring home their creations, discoveries, and questions.

There is no "best" curriculum or teaching approach, but there are common factors among the early childhood education programs that have proven effective in providing children with a strong foundation for literacy and school success[26]:

- warm, secure, and playful relationships with caring adults who come to know each child well, affirm his emerging strengths, and adapt to his interests and preferred ways of learning
- a planful approach to daily activities, balancing active and quiet, individual and group, and child-initiated and teacher-initiated activities, and addressing all areas of the child's development
- "developmentally appropriate practice," that is, using age-appropriate techniques like pretend play and puppetry that are particularly engaging for young children, presenting concepts that children can grasp because they build on what they already know, and choosing activities and lessons that are challenging but not overly frustrating
- lots of reading—of posters, magazines, signs, labels, captions, software, items such as cereal boxes and tickets used in pretend play, notes, cards, letters, and especially books, both read with children and given to them to "read" themselves

In an extensive observational study of low-income toddlers and preschoolers, Catherine Snow and her colleagues recorded their conversations at home and at their child-care programs.[27] They continued to collect data until the children were in grade school, and analyzed their learning outcomes. Their clearest and most striking finding was that children who as preschoolers engage with adults in more "decontextualized" talk, or conversation that goes beyond the here and now to include references to past, future, and imagined events and to abstract ideas, fare better on reading comprehension tests through the sixth grade. Snow also found, as have other researchers, that a large vocabulary at school entry is a strong indicator of later success.[28]

What would happen, we wonder, if all children could engage in rich, interesting, and increasingly decontextualized talk throughout each day in the years between one and four, their prime time for language learning? Could providing these ordinary experiences to all children ensure that nearly all would enter school primed for success? As we shall see in the next chapter, the answer is "Very likely, yes."

Early language experiences have unique power. After reviewing an extensive body of research, an expert panel convened by the National Academy of Sciences to review the science of early childhood development concluded, "What happens during the first months and years of life matters a lot, not because this period of development provides an indelible blueprint for adult well-being, but because it sets either a sturdy or fragile stage for what follows."[29] In the next chapter, we will examine some of this research to gain a fuller understanding of why early language matters so much.

Notes

1   R. Shore (1997) *Rethinking the Brain: New Insights into Early Development*, New York: Families and Work Institute.

2   See *From Neurons to Neighborhoods: The Science of Early Childhood Development* (National Research Council and Institute of Medicine (2000) Committee on Integrating the Science of Early Childhood Development. Jack. P. Shonkoff and Deborah A. Phillips (eds.). Board on Children, Youth, and Families, Commission on Behavioral and Social Sciences and Education. Washington, DC: National Academy Press) for a discussion of the resilience of basic language learning, in the face of obstacles such as limited exposure to language models, sensory impairments, and brain injury, as well as for a full discussion of aspects of language learning that are not resilient and that depend upon experience, opportunities for practice, and interaction.

3   See "An Instinct to Acquire an Art," in S. Pinkner (1994) *The Language Instinct: How the Mind Creates Language*, New York: William Morrow and Company.

4   M. Segal, J. Leinfelder, B. Bardige, and M. J. Woika (forthcoming) *All About Child Care and Early Education*, New York: Allyn & Bacon.

5   A. Gopnik, A. Meltzoff, and P. Kuhl (1999) *The Scientist in the Crib*, New York: William Morrow and Company.

6   Pinkner, *The Language Instinct*.

7   Pinkner, *The Language Instinct*; Gopnik, Meltzoff, and Kuhl, *Scientist in the Crib*.

8   See *From Neurons to Neighborhoods* (National Research Council and Institute of Medicine), *The Scientist in the Crib* (Gopnik, Meltzoff, and Kuhl), and *What's Going on in There? How*

the Brain and Mind Develop in the First Five Years of Life (L. Eliot (1999), New York: Bantam Books) for summaries of recent, fascinating research on what babies can learn and the role of language in supporting that learning.

9   Eliot, What's Going on in There?

10 M. Segal (1998) Your Child at Play: One to Two Years: Exploring, Learning, Making Friends, and Pretending, New York: Newmarket Press.

11 Pinkner, The Language Instinct, pp. 267–268.

12 R. E. Owens, Jr. (2000) Language Development: An Introduction, 5th edn., New York: Allyn & Bacon.

13 D. Barry (2002) Daughter, 2, Will be Allowed to Date in 2048, The Miami Herald, January 27, 2002.

14 S. Fraiberg (1977) The Magic Years, New York: MacMillan Publishing Company.

15 This statement is made frequently by early childhood professionals to argue that young children learn best through play. For example, in the cover story for the November 2003 issue of the American School Board Journal, Kathleen Vail quotes Ed Zigler, director of Yale's Center in Child Development and Social Policy: "We have known for 75 years that an important determiner of growth and development is play." "Play is the work of children."

16 Eliot, What's Going on in There?

17 B. Potter (2002) The Tale of the Flopsy Bunnies, London: Frederick Warne and Company.

18 P. Tabors (1997) One Child, Two Languages: A Guide for Preschool Educators of Children Learning English as a Second Language, Baltimore, MD: Paul H. Brookes Publishing.

19 S. Goldin-Meadow and C. Mylander (1998) Spontaneous sign systems created by deaf children in two cultures, Nature, 391: 279–281.

20 National Research Council and Institute of Medicine, From Neurons to Neighborhoods.

21 About half of the children who are late talkers at two (using fewer than fifty words and no word combinations) are likely to exhibit normal language development by age three; another 25% will be within the range of normal by the time they enter school. (Rescorla and Schwartz, 1990; Thal and Tobias, 1992; cited in From Neurons to Neighborhoods (National Research Council and Institute of Medicine), p. 144.)

22 National Research Council and Institute of Medicine, From Neurons to Neighborhoods, p. 139.

23 See C. Snow (2002) Ensuring reading success for African-American children, In B. Bowman (ed.), Love to Read: Essays in Developing and Enhancing Early Literacy Skills of African-American children, Washington, DC: National Black Child Development Institute, for a discussion of the ways in which vocabulary and reading influence each other.

24 See J. Helm and L. Katz (2001) Young Investigators: The Project Approach in the Early Years, New York: Teachers College Press.

25 When selecting prepared curricula, it is essential to take into account the ages, interests, developmental level, and linguistic and cultural backgrounds of the children. Programs that rely heavily on teacher presentations, worksheets, standardized art projects, and vocabulary drill tend to reduce the amount and richness of conversation in a preschool classroom. On the other hand, play-based approaches that include lots of book reading, pretending,

problem-solving, and exploration along with interesting content and deliberate attention to literacy and math concepts tend to enhance young children's learning in all domains. See *Eager to Learn: Educating Our Preschoolers* (National Research Council (2001) Committee on Early Childhood Pedagogy. Barbara T. Bowman, M. Suzane Donovan, and M. Susan Burns (eds.). Commission on Behavioral Sciences and Education. Washington, DC: National Academy Press) for examples of exemplary practice and a discussion of effective approaches.

26 National Research Council, *Eager to Learn*.

27 The findings of this study are reported in detail in D. K. Dickinson and P. O. Tabors (2001) *Beginning Literacy with Language*, Baltimore, MD: Paul H. Brookes Publishing Company.

28 In her (unpublished) research, Catherine Snow has found that vocabulary at school entry predicts high school reading comprehension. Personal communication, May 16, 2004.

29 National Research Council and Institute of Medicine, *From Neurons to Neighborhoods*, p. 5.

Myths about Early Childhood Bilingualism

Fred Genesee

Competence in two, or more, languages has taken on increased value in recent years in many communities and countries around the world. There are local, national, and global reasons for this. Locally, there are communities where knowing more than one language is an advantage because knowing more than one language facilitates interpersonal communication, enhances job prospects, and enriches one's day-to-day life; this is true in cities such as Montreal, Geneva, New Delhi, among others. Similarly, there are advantages to bilingualism in communities where an indigenous language is spoken, and members of the community want to maintain and revitalise competence in the indigenous language while also learning an important majority language. For example, the Mohawk community near Montreal has developed immersion programs that promote the acquisition of Mohawk among young Mohawk children while ensuring that they also know English and/or French (Jacobs & Cross, 2001). Bi- and even multilingualism are often advantageous for national reasons as well. In countries with policies of official bi- or multilingualism, such as Canada, Switzerland, and South Africa, there are personal, educational, and economic benefits to knowing both or all official languages. The European Union's "1 + 2" policy encourages member states to promote acquisition of the national language along with another European language and a third language so that European citizens can travel and work freely anywhere in the European Union and, also, be competitive globally.

There are yet other advantages to learning more than one language. Research has shown that bilingual individuals enjoy certain neurocognitive advantages in comparison with monolinguals. A bilingual advantage has been demonstrated in the performance of tasks that call for selective attention (e.g., Bialystok, 2001), including tasks that require focusing, inhibiting, and switching attention during problem

Fred Genesee, "Myths About Early Childhood Bilingualism," *Canadian Psychology*, vol. 56, no. 1, pp. 6-15. Copyright © 2015 by Canadian Psychological Association. Reprinted with permission. Provided by ProQuest LLC. All rights reserved.

solving, for example. It has been argued that learning and using two languages calls for selective attention to minimise interference between languages and ensure their appropriate use; this, in turn, enhances the development of executive control processes in general, not only in linguistic domains. These advantages have been found in both childhood and adulthood (Bialystok, Craik, Klein, & Viswanathan, 2004) and are most evident in bilinguals with relatively advanced levels of proficiency in two languages and who use their two languages actively on a regular basis (Bialystok, Peets, & Moreno, 2014).

Notwithstanding the evident professional, personal, social, and cognitive advantages of bi- and multilingualism, parents, educators, policymakers, and health care professionals often express serious concerns about raising or educating children bilingually. These fears are often founded on four myths: (1) the myth of the monolingual brain; (2) the myth that younger is better; (3) the myth of time-on-task; and (4) the myth of bilingualism and children with developmental disorders and academic challenges. These myths have serious theoretical significance as well as practical implications for raising and educating children bilingually. Thus, it is important that their validity be examined scientifically.

Each of these myths is explicated, and research findings relevant to each are reviewed in this article. Evidence is drawn from research on three populations of young learners: preschool children who acquire two languages simultaneously (simultaneous bilinguals); majority language students attending second language immersion/ bilingual programs; and children who acquire a minority language at home but are educated in a majority language in school, such as Spanish-speaking children attending English language schools in the United States. Collectively, these diverse learners are referred to as "dual language learners."

The Myth of the Monolingual Brain

There are often concerns that learning two languages simultaneously from birth stretches the limits of infants' ability to acquire language and that they, therefore, will be confused and unable to differentiate between languages if their parents use both in the home; Paradis, Genesee, and Crago (2011) refer to this as the "limited capacity theory" of bilingual acquisition. It is feared that this, in turn, could result in delays in language development, deviant patterns of development, and possibly even incomplete competence. Viewed from a neurocognitive point of view, these fears can be interpreted to reflect a belief that infants' brains are essentially monolingual and that they treat input in two languages as if it were a single language—what Genesee (1989) dubbed the "unitary language system" hypothesis. Parents in many bilingual families adhere to the one-parent/one-language rule on the assumption that their children need explicit markers of each language so that they do not become confused. Bilingual codemixing by children is often taken as evidence that they are unable to separate their two languages (Genesee, 2002). Evidence from three sources refutes this myth: research on milestones and patterns of language development in children raised bilingually, grammatical constraints on child bilingual codemixing, and bilingual children's use of two languages in conversations.

Much of the research reviewed here was conducted in Montreal with children learning French and English. Montreal is a particular appropriate context for studying this issue because both French and English are prevalent in the community, and both have high status; thus, both are very useful and highly valued and, as a result, motivation to learn both is high. In other words, Montreal is an ideal context for examining children's capacity for dual language learning when learning conditions are propitious. Having said that, there is wide variation in the conditions under which children acquire two languages, and their learning environments can change significantly over time. Amount, quality, and consistency of language exposure can influence all aspects of bilingual acquisition (see Grüter & Paradis, 2014, for detailed discussions of the role of input). In question in the present article is children's capacity for dual language learning in supportive learning environments and not on variation among bilingual children and the extent to which children exposed to two languages actually become fully bilingual.

Language Development

If simultaneous acquisition of two languages is beyond the capacity of typically developing children, then one would expect that, in comparison with monolingual children, bilingual children would be delayed in their language development and, as well, demonstrate different patterns of development. In particular, one would expect that their grammatical development would deviate from what is typical for monolingual children acquiring the same languages because they are unable to acquire differentiated grammars. The notion that the neurocognitive systems that underlie language development are essentially monolingual is evident in early theories of bilingual first language acquisition. A particularly influential theory by Volterra and Taeschner (1978) argued that children who learn two languages from birth initially have fused lexical and morphosyntactic systems; followed by separation of the lexicons of each language, but fused morphosyntactic systems; this is subsequently followed by differentiation of morphosyntactic systems. It was only by 3 years of age that children learning two languages were thought to be truly bilingual (also, see early work by Leopold, 1949).

There are a number of sources of evidence that dispute these concerns and theoretical claims. To begin, children who acquire two languages from birth achieve the same fundamental milestones in language development with respect to babbling, first words, and emergence of word combinations as monolingual children within the same time frame despite the fact that they have less exposure, on average, to each language than monolinguals. For example, in a study of a French-English infant, Maneva and Genesee (2002) found that he engaged in variegated babbling with each parent, one of whom spoke English and the other French, between 10 and 12 months of age, the same age as monolingual children. Similarly, in a much larger study of 73 infants learning Spanish and English in Miami, Kimbrough Oller, Eilers, Urbano, and Cobo-Lewis (1997) found that the onset of canonical babbling did not differ significantly for the bilingual and monolingual infants. Bilingual children, including children learning both a signed and a spoken language and children learning two spoken languages, have also been reported to produce their first words at about the same age as monolingual infants (e.g., Genesee, 2003; Patterson & Pearson, 2004; Petitto et al., 2001). Simultaneous bilingual children are often found to have smaller vocabularies than monolingual children when each language is considered separately, but equivalent or even larger vocabularies when both languages are considered together, what is referred to as conceptual vocabulary (Bedore, Peña, García, & Cortez, 2005). In a longitudinal study of children acquiring French and English in Montreal, Paradis and Genesee (1996) found that they began to produce word combinations within the same timeframe as that found for monolinguals—between approximately 1.5 and 2 years of age (see also Conboy & Thal, 2006; and Marchman, Martínez-Sussmann, & Dale, 2004).

Contrary to the unitary language system hypothesis, moreover, children acquiring two languages demonstrate evidence of differentiated systems from the earliest stages of language development. Maneva and Genesee (2002), for example, found that the babbling of the French-English infant in their study differed depending on whether he was interacting with his English-speaking mother or his French-speaking father and, furthermore, his babbling in each case was similar to that of monolingual infants with respect to the mean length of babbled utterances, syllable load, and syllable type. Detailed examination of the developing grammatical systems of French-English bilingual children in Montreal revealed that, for the most part, they were the same as those of monolingual children (Paradis & Genesee, 1996). Zwanziger, Allen, and Genesee (2005) report evidence of differentiated grammatical development in children acquiring English and Inuktitut which, in contrast to French and English, have radically different morphosyntactic properties. Even under conditions of specific language impairment, bilingual children exhibit similar patterns of grammatical development as monolingual children with impairment (Paradis, Crago, Genesee, & Rice, 2003; Paradis et al., 2011). Taken together, these findings offer convincing evidence that learning two languages simultaneously is no more challenging for the human neurocognitive system than learning one.

Grammatical Constraints on Bilingual Codemixing

When individuals use words from two languages in the same sentence, or what is referred to as "intrautterance codemixing," they run the risk of violating the grammatical constraints of one or both languages. For example, the utterance "I *le* like" (I like it) is ungrammatical since the object pronoun "le" (it) should follow the verb in English. Extensive research on adult bilinguals has shown that they rarely produce incorrect mixed sentences (e.g., Myers-Scotton, 1997). If young children who are learning two languages simultaneously go through a stage when they treat both languages as part of one system, then one would expect them to codemix extensively under the hypothesis that they initially have single lexical system. As well, they should produce many ungrammatical mixed utterances because their grammatical systems are undifferentiated. In an early study on this issue, Genesee, Nicoladis, and Paradis (1995) found that French-English bilingual children (1;10 to 2;02 years of age) in Montreal mixed within utterances less than 3% of the time, on average, far less often than one would expect if they were unable to differentiate between French and English. In an independent sample of young French-English children in Montreal, Sauve and Genesee (2000) similarly found that codemixing within utterances occurred less than 4% of the time, and moreover, there were virtually no grammatical errors when codemixing did occur. The same findings have been reported in studies of children learning other language pairs, for example, French and German (Meisel, 1994), English and Estonian (Vihman, 1998), and Inuktitut and English (Allen, Genesee, Fish, & Crago, 2002). Researchers have also reported that the constraints that operate on children's bilingual codemixing are essentially the same as those that have been reported in adults (Paradis, Nicoladis, & Genesee, 2000). Moreover, there does not appear to be a stage in bilingual first language acquisition when grammatical constraints do not operate, albeit the nature of the constraints may change as children's grammars change. These findings are interesting for two reasons. First, they indicate that these bilingual children had acquired the grammatical constraints of each language; otherwise, how could one explain that they complied with the constraints of each most of the time. Thus, these findings reinforce results reviewed earlier indicating that bilingual children acquire differentiated languages early in development. Second, and even more interesting, they indicate that these children were able to activate and access both language systems at the same time in order to ensure that their mixed utterances followed the constraints of both languages.

Differentiated Use of Two Languages

If simultaneous bilingual children go through an initial unitary language stage, then one would expect them to have difficulty using their languages appropriately. In other words, you would expect them to use each language indiscriminately with conversational partners regardless of their partner's language competence or preferences. However, systematic studies on this issue have revealed that even very young bilingual children are communicatively very competent. For example, in an early study on this issue, Genesee et al. (1995) studied 2-year-old children who were acquiring French and English simultaneously from their parents who used the one parent/one language pattern with their children. They found that these children were able to use their two languages appropriately—they used more of the mother's language with the mother than with the father and, conversely, more of the father's language with the father than with the mother. In a follow-up study, Genesee, Boivin, and Nicoladis (1996) similarly found bilingual children can use their languages appropriately with strangers with whom they have had no prior experience. In a related vein, it has also been found that young bilingual children can adjust their rates of codemixing to match those of unfamiliar interlocutors who changed their rates of mixing from one observation session to the next (Comeau, Genesee, & Lapaquette, 2003). Finally, 2- and 3-year-old bilingual children who used the "wrong language" with a monolingual interlocutor whom they had never met before switched languages when their interlocutors indicated that they did not understand what the child had said (Comeau, Genesee, & Mendelson, 2010). The children switched languages even when their interlocutors used a very general prompt, such as "What?," which did not indicate the source of the breakdown, indicating that managing their two languages was not a challenge. Taken together, this evidence is difficult to reconcile with the myth of the monolingual brain that would predict that bilingual children should not be able to use their two languages differentially and appropriately with others.

The Myth That Younger is Better

It is also widely believed that young children are effective and efficient language learners. As a result, it is generally expected that they will acquire a second language quickly and effortlessly and attain native-like proficiency largely through untutored, natural exposure to the target language. This thinking is based, in part, on the critical period hypothesis of language learning according to which the human neurocognitive abilities that underpin language learning are particularly "plastic" during early development, usually thought to be between birth and 12 to 13 years of age (Long, 1990). Accordingly, it is during this period when language learning is relatively effortless and results in complete mastery of language.

However, the link between age and second language outcomes is not linear and is much more complex than generally thought. To begin, learners who begin to acquire a second language earlier generally also have more exposure to that language than those who begin later. Thus, it is often impossible to separate the effects of age from amount of exposure. To facilitate discussion of research on age effects, age is considered in this section setting aside issues related to amount and quality of exposure; the role of exposure is discussed in the next section. With respect to age and second language acquisition in general, there is evidence that, other things being equal, young second language learners are more likely to attain levels of oral proficiency like those of monolinguals or, at least, greater proficiency than learners who begin to learn a second language when older (Birdsong & Vanhove, in press). However, there is no consensus on how early is early enough to achieve native-like competence that is comparable with that of monolinguals and, in fact, whether monolingual native-like competence is possible even if second language learning begins very early. In this regard, research conducted in Sweden by Abrahamsson and Hyltenstam (2009) examined the language abilities of long-term residents of Sweden who had migrated to Sweden at different ages, including the preschool years. In comparison with native Swedish speakers, most preschool-age immigrants in their study did not demonstrate native-like competence in Swedish as a second language even after more than 20 years of exposure when tested using a battery of diverse and demanding language tests.

In a similar vein, our own research on internationally adopted children from China has shown that they score significantly lower than matched nonadopted children on a variety of standardised measures of language ability, including expressive and receptive vocabulary and grammar (Delcenserie & Genesee, 2014). The adoptees had begun learning the adopted language between 12 and 24 months of age; they had exclusive exposure to the adopted language postadoption; and they were raised in families with higher than average socioeconomic status—all factors that should favour language learning. The adoptees studied by Delcenserie and Genesee did not show similar delays in general cognitive, socioemotional, or nonverbal memory development suggesting that their language development was uniquely affected by their delayed exposure. That these effects are probably due to delayed exposure to the second language and not attrition of the birth language comes from neuroimaging research by Pierce, Klein, Chen, Delcenserie, and Genesee (2014) on 9- to 17-year-old adoptees from China who were also acquiring French. The adoptees' neurocognitive responses to pseudowords that varied in tone, a phonemic feature of Chinese but not French, were compared with those of French monolingual children and children who had acquired Chinese as a first language and continued to use it. The responses of the adoptees did not differ significantly from those of the Chinese-speaking children; in other words, the adoptees evidenced traces of the birth language even after many years of disuse. Taken together, the Abrahamsson and Hyltenstam and Delcenserie and Genesee findings suggest that *monolingual* native-like competence may not be achievable even when second language acquisition begins very early, a point discussed further in the conclusions.

Commonly held beliefs about how easily and effectively young learners can acquire a second language usually do not take into account the complexities of language in the context of schooling. In this regard, education researchers argue that there are significant differences in the language skills used for social communication and those used for academic purposes, although obviously there is extensive overlap (see Genesee, in press, for an expanded discussion). Academic language refers to the specialised vocabulary, grammar, discourse/textual, and functional skills associated with academic instruction and mastery of academic material and skills; it includes both oral and written forms of language (see Genesee, in press, for an expanded discussion). A growing body of evidence indicates that achieving competence in a second language for academic purposes is a more complex process that takes considerably longer than previously thought. For example, in a review of research on the oral language development of second language students in the United States (often referred to as English language learners or ELLs), Saunders and O'Brien (2006) concluded that ELLs, including those in all-English programs, are seldom awarded ratings of "generally proficient" (but not native-like) in English even by Grade 3. None of the studies they reviewed reported average ratings of "native-like" in English until Grade 5. In a longitudinal study of ELLs in Edmonton, Canada, Paradis (2006) found that after 21 months of exposure to English, only 40% performed within the normal range for native-speakers on a test of grammatical morpheme production (e.g., the use of "s" to pluralise nouns or "-ed" to express past tense in verbs), 65% on receptive vocabulary, and 90% on story grammar in narratives. Bolstering these results, findings from a number of reviews and individual studies on proficiency levels in English among ELLs indicate that it can take ELLs between 5 to 7 years to achieve proficiency in English for academic purposes that is comparable to that of monolinguals (Lindholm-Leary & Borsato, 2006; Thomas & Collier, 2002). These findings belie the myth that second language learning is easy even for relatively young learners.

Evidence that younger is not necessarily better and, to the contrary, older may be advantageous comes from evaluations of alternative forms of bilingual (or immersion) education for majority and minority language students in Canada and the United States. In a series of comparative evaluations of alternative forms of French immersion programs in Canada, Genesee (1981) found that, on the one hand, majority language English-speaking students in early immersion (beginning in kindergarten) generally achieved significantly higher levels of second language proficiency than students in programs with a delayed (middle elementary grades) or late (secondary school) starting grade, suggesting that an early start is often better. On the other hand, Genesee also found that students in 2-year late immersion comprised of 80% of instruction in French in Grades 7 and 8 sometimes achieved the same or almost the same levels of second language proficiency as students in early immersion. Harley and Hart (1997) similarly found few significant differences between early partial (50% instruction in each language) and late partial immersion students on a battery of French language tests. Genesee's results are particularly striking since the late immersion students in his studies had had considerably less exposure to the second language than students in early immersion at the time of testing. These findings attest to the ability of older learners to acquire a second language relatively quickly and, arguably, more quickly than younger learners in school contexts (see also Muñoz, 2014).

There are a number of possible explanations of why late immersion students can make such rapid progress in acquiring a second language despite reduced exposure compared with younger students. To mention just two—older students have the benefit of well-developed first language skills and, in particular, they may have well-developed literacy skills in the first language. Literacy skills acquired in one language can facilitate literacy development in a second language through transfer or the use of common underlying cognitive abilities linked to reading and writing (Genesee & Geva, 2006; Riches & Genesee, 2006); this is especially true for languages that are typologically similar and/or have similar orthographies (e.g., French, Spanish, and English). Second, older students may also be faster second language learners than younger students because language teaching and learning in the higher grades is generally more abstract and context-reduced than in the earlier grades. As result, second language learners in higher grades may be able to call on acquisitional strategies that are more analytic and less experiential than is required in the lower grades and that are better developed in older learners.

Further evidence that a late start to second language learning in school can be advantageous comes from research that has examined the relative effectiveness of bilingual versus English-only forms of education for minority language students in the United States who come to school with no or limited in English—that is ELLs. Minority language students in the United States, on average, attain significantly lower levels of achievement in school than their majority language peers; more of them drop out of school; and fewer go on to pursue postsecondary education (Genesee & Lindholm-Leary, 2012). There has been ongoing debate about the best ways to educate such students in order to close the achievement gap with majority language students. It has been proposed that bilingual forms of education in which ELLs receive initial academic instruction, including literacy, in the home language might be one way of enhancing their academic success since it would allow them to acquire literacy skills and keep up with academic instruction in a language they already know while they are learning English. A variety of forms of bilingual education exist that differ with respect to how much instruction is provided in the minority language, ranging from 50% to 90% (see Genesee, 1999, for more details); for example, in the 90:10 model, the home language is used for 90% of instruction in kindergarten to Grade 2, and English is used as a primary medium of instruction beginning in Grade 3. Systematic reviews of evaluations of these programs have concluded that ELLs in bilingual programs score as well as or often better than ELLs in English-only programs on tests of oral proficiency, literacy and other school subjects (e.g., mathematics) in English (see Genesee & Lindholm-Leary, 2012, and Goldenberg, 2008, for reviews); at the same time, bilingual program participants acquire significantly higher levels of competence in the home language, Spanish in most cases. Contrary to the myth that younger is better, these findings indicate delayed instruction in English resulted in better outcomes than early instruction for these students.

The Myth of Time-On-Task

A related belief that is commonly held about language learning in general and second language learning in particular is that the more time spent learning the language, the greater one's competence. This belief is common in educational contexts where the amount of time devoted to specific activities, like teaching specific school subjects, is a reflection of how important we think these activities are. Beginning instruction early in certain subjects, like reading and mathematics, is another manifestation of the importance we attach to time-on-task. An examination of research findings with respect to first and second language learning reveals, as was found for the age factor, that there is not a simple correlation between how much exposure children have to a second language in school or in the home and language proficiency. We have already seen some evidence of this in the monolingual brain section from research showing that despite the fact that simultaneous bilinguals have less exposure to each language as monolinguals, they achieve the same milestones in language development at approximately the same ages as monolingual children, and they demonstrate the same patterns of development in general. However, this is not to say that amount of exposure is not important.

Bilingually raised children seldom have equal exposure to both languages. Understandably, below some minimum level of exposure, bilingual children are likely to demonstrate poor competence in a language. However, simultaneous bilingual children do not need as much exposure in each language as monolinguals in order to achieve comparable levels of competence. How much exposure is needed to perform within monolingual norms depends on what is assessed. In a study of children learning French as a second language in Montreal, Thordardottir (2011) found that 40% to 50% exposure is necessary to perform within monolingual norms on tests of receptive vocabulary, but between 40% and 60% exposure on tests of expressive vocabulary. Moreover, beyond a certain threshold level of exposure, the performance of the bilinguals was not enhanced.

Research on English-speaking students in French immersion programs in Canada similarly illustrates that the influence of time-on-task, like the influence of age, is complex and sometimes unexpected. As noted earlier, alternative forms of French immersion exist and vary with respect to the grade when instruction in French and how much instruction through French is provided. Comparative evaluations of these alternatives reveal that the relationship between exposure and language outcomes depends on whether the language under evaluation is the majority language, English, or a minority language, like French. Thus, on the one hand, students who participate in programs that devote more time to French, the second language, outperform students in immersion programs that devote less time to French (Genesee, 2004). On the other hand, and in contrast, these studies fail to demonstrate a relationship between amount of exposure to English and achievement in English in the long run. More specifically, students in early total immersion who did not receive instruction in or through English until Grade 3 demonstrate the same levels of competence on a variety of measures of English as students in delayed and late immersion even though students in the latter programs have had some instruction in English from kindergarten. The immersion and comparison students participating in these evaluations were comparable with respect to overall academic ability and socioeconomic status, and they often attended the same schools, with immersion being a strand within a larger school. Thus, major factors that might have favoured the immersion students were largely eliminated and, thus, cannot account for these findings.

The question arises how can students who get less instruction in their first language in school score as well as students who get all their instruction in the native language? Two possible explanations are considered here. First, the reduced exposure to English that Canadian students experience in French immersion is offset by their total immersion in English outside school. The exposure to English that immersion students get outside school includes exposure to written forms of the language which, in turn, supports students' acquisition of literacy skills in English even though they are being taught formally to read and write in French. A second explanation for why immersion students do not fall behind in first language development is related to transfer. A great deal of research on second language reading has shown that students with relatively well-developed decoding and reading comprehension skills in one language demonstrate relatively advanced reading skills in their other language (e.g., Erdos, Genesee, Savage, & Haigh, 2011; Riches & Genesee, 2006; see August & Shanahan, 2006, for a review). Thus, as immersion students acquire word decoding and reading comprehension skills in French, their second language, they are also acquiring skills that can be applied to reading English. As a result, immersion students require reduced instruction in English to achieve grade-appropriate levels of competence in reading English.

Similar findings with respect to the importance of exposure to a majority language, like English, in school and acquisition of that language have been found by Lindholm-Leary in her research in the United States (Lindholm-Leary & Borsato, 2006). The students who participated in this research included ELLs who were native speakers of Spanish and had no or limited proficiency in English when they started school. Some ELLs were attending bilingual programs, as described earlier, in which as much as 90% of instruction was provided in Spanish, beginning in kindergarten, while others attended conventional all-English schools. Lindholm-Leary and Borsato (2006) found that, despite their reduced exposure to English, ELLs in the bilingual programs scored as well as, or better than, similar ELLs in all-English programs on standardised tests in English. Lindholm-Leary argued, as have Canadian researchers, that the high status of English along with students' extensive exposure to English outside school minimises the potential negative consequences of reduced exposure to English in these bilingual programs. At the same time, there was a significant positive relationship between amount of exposure to Spanish and students' proficiency in Spanish.

The Myth of Bilingualism and Children With Developmental Disorders and Academic Challenges

Dual language learning during the preschool years or in school is thought to be unsuitable for children with a variety of learning challenges because it is thought that learning two languages or through two languages will exacerbate learning difficulties. This thinking is often applied to children with developmental disorders that implicate language learning difficulties (such as specific language impairment (SLI), Down Syndrome, or Autism Spectrum Disorder), and children with academic challenges that may be due to the child's sociocultural background (such as low socioeconomic and minority ethnic group status) or poor academic ability. As a result, education professionals and speech-language specialists often counsel parents of children with these kinds of challenges to use only one language in the home and/or to enrol them in a monolingual school program. Children with SLI provide a particularly rigorous test of this assumption because SLI is a developmental disorder with a genetic origin (Leonard, 1998) that is specific to language acquisition and is often associated with poor academic outcomes. Thus, it is discussed in some detail here.

Children with SLI exhibit significant delays in early language development and their language competence is noticeably below that of same-age peers. However, they are typical in other aspects of development—they have no known central processing, neurological, cognitive, or socioemotional problems that could account for their language learning difficulties. They can exhibit difficulties with lexical, morphosyntactic, and pragmatic aspects of language, with difficulty learning specific morphosyntactic features of language being an especially robust indicator of SLI. In fact, morphosyntactic problems are often taken as a marker of SLI and, thus, have received the lion's share of research attention (see Paradis et al., 2011, Chapter 9, for a detailed discussion of bilingual and second language learners with SLI).

In one of the earliest studies to examine this issue, Paradis et al. (2003) found that simultaneous bilingual children (7 to 7.6-yearold) with SLI exhibited equivalents levels of morphosyntactic competence and the same profiles of morphosyntactic strengths and weakness as monolingual children with SLI. In other words, bilingual children with SLI were not at greater risk than the monolingual children with SLI. At the same time, the bilingual children were becoming bilingual within the limits of their ability. These results have since been confirmed by many studies examining other language pairs under different sociocultural circumstances (e.g., see Gutiérrez-Clellen, Simón-Cereijido, & Wagner, 2008, for the case of Spanish-English minority language students in the United States). Paradis and Sorenson (2009) have similarly shown that children with SLI who were acquiring French as a second language were not extraordinarily delayed in their language development in comparison with monolingual learners of French as a second language who also had SLI, again indicating that dual language learning does not exacerbate the language difficulties of children with SLI. In a related vein, Down Syndrome and ASD are also developmental disorders with genetic bases that put children at risk for poor language outcomes, along with other difficulties. Investigations of these kinds of children indicate that they do not differ significantly from children with the same disorders who are learning only one language (e.g., Bird et al., 2005; Hambly & Fombonne, 2012; Marinova-Todd & Mirenda, in press), although they do demonstrate more language-related difficulties than children without these disorders. It is difficult to reconcile these diverse findings with the belief that dual language learning puts children with developmental disorders at greater risk for language difficulties than learning only one language.

Students who have poorly developed first language skills or SLI are often considered unsuitable for immersion/bilingual programs because it is feared that their language learning difficulties will be increased, and this, in turn, will jeopardise their overall academic success. This is an important ethical issue since excluding such children from bilingual programs can have significant long-term consequences especially for children living in bilingual families or communities where acquisition of two languages is important. It can also reduce the opportunities children have for employment in jobs that require competence in more than one language when they leave school, a possibility that is growing as globalisation increases. Despite the significance of this issue, there is relatively little empirical investigation of such learners, one exception being work by Bruck in Montreal (Bruck, 1978, 1982). Bruck compared the language and academic performance of Grade 3 immersion students with "impaired" first language skills to comparable students in nonimmersion programs using a battery of language, literacy, and academic achievement tests. She found no significant differences between the two groups, except the impaired immersion students had acquired significantly superior French language proficiency in comparison to the impaired students receiving conventional French-as-a-second language instruction in the monolingual program.

Concerns about the suitability of bilingual forms of education for students who might struggle in school extend beyond students with language learning difficulties per se and include students with low academic ability and students from economically disadvantaged families. Students with these kinds of backgrounds often, although not always, underperform in school in comparison with students without these background characteristics. Research by Genesee on immersion students in Montreal who were at-risk for academic difficulty because of below average levels of academic ability indicates that such students are not differentially handicapped in their first language and academic achievement in comparison to similar students in English-only programs (Genesee, 1976). To the contrary, he found that below average students in early immersion sometimes performed as well as average immersion students on tests of listening comprehension and speaking in their second language, although significantly lower on tests of reading. Genesee also found that the students with academic difficulties benefited from immersion in the form of increased levels of functional proficiency in French. Immersion students from relatively low socioeconomic backgrounds have also been shown to keep pace academically and in English with similar students in all-English programs while, at the same time, acquiring more advanced French language skills (e.g., Bruck, Tucker, & Jakimik, 1975; Holobow, Genesee, & Lambert, 1991).

Conclusions

The findings reviewed in the preceding sections have significant theoretical significance as well as practical implications for parents, educators, and other professionals who work with young dual language learners. Before proceeding, however, it is important to repeat a caveat made earlier. The evidence reviewed here attests to children's capacity to develop dual language competence in early childhood and school settings under favourable conditions. Not all children thrive in dual language families or dual language schools to the same extent. Undoubtedly, the quality of the learning environment in which young children grow up and are educated affects whether or not individual children become fully bilingual and succeed fully in school. Understanding the conditions that favour or disfavour full dual language competence during the preschool years and academic success in dual language programs goes beyond the limitations of this article (see Grüter & Paradis, 2014, and Paradis et al., 2011, for extended discussions of these issues).

With these caveats in mind, taken together, the evidence reviewed here indicates that learning two languages simultaneously is as natural as learning one and that children can acquire full competence in two languages that is comparable with that of monolingual children, given the right learning environment. Evidence indicates that even children with genetic predispositions for language learning difficulties, including SLI, can acquire competence in two languages at the same time during the preschool years (or successively in bilingual school programs) within the limits of their impairment. In other words, their learning difficulties do not impair their language abilities beyond that seen in monolingual children with the same learning challenges. Detailed studies of simultaneous bilinguals indicate that they acquire differentiated language systems from the earliest stages of development that are, moreover, the same as those of monolingual children in most important respects. That the neurocognitive mechanisms that underlie language acquisition have the capacity for dual language learning comes from a number of different sources of evidence, including evidence that they are able to access both languages online during code-mixing and, as a result, avoid violating the grammatical constraints of both languages most of the time. Thus, contrary to early conceptualisations of child bilingual codemixing as indicating confusion and incompetence, it is a sign of linguistic and communicative competence. Studies of the communicative competence of simultaneous bilinguals indicates that they are able to use their two language differentially and appropriate with others and are able to adapt use of their two languages in accordance with their interlocutors' language abilities and preferences—even with unfamiliar interlocutors. There are, of course, differences among bilingual children and between bilingual and monolingual children; but to date most differences appear to be related primarily to characteristics of the learning environment, including the quantity, nature, and consistency of the input that bilingual children receive rather than to the fact of learning two languages per se (Grüter & Paradis, 2014).

Practically speaking, there is no empirical evidence at present to justify restricting children with developmental disorders from learning two languages. At the same time, parents and others who care for children who are being raised bilingually should take active responsibility to ensure that they get adequate exposure to both languages so that they acquire both languages fully. It also seems likely, although evidence on this is anecdotal, that bilingual children need continuous and regular exposure to both languages to ensure full acquisition. Abrupt changes in exposure and/or irregular exposure should probably be avoided, as much as possible.

While the competence of bilingual children is often evaluated by comparing them to mono-lingual children, this is not the only basis of evaluation, nor even the right one. The language proficiency profiles of bilingual children will always be somewhat different from those of mono-linguals, even as they grow into adulthood. This is necessarily so because their acquisition of each language as well as their use of each is distributed across different contexts—simply put, they learn and use each language with different people, in different social and professional contexts, and for different purposes. As a result, whether one examines their vocabulary, grammar, or functional language skills, they are likely to differ from monolinguals who use the same language with everyone, in all contexts, and for all purposes. Thus, differences between bilinguals and monolinguals are to be expected, and they should be analysed and understood with reference to the different environments in which they learn and use each language. The same is true for children who are educated in dual language school programs.

When it comes to educating children bilingually, the evidence consistently indicates that children who speak a majority first language and who participate in second language immersion-type bilingual programs attain the same, or higher, levels of native language proficiency and academic achievement in the long run as children in monolingual programs. In fact, there is some evidence that students in enriched immersion programs outperform students in monolingual programs when tested in the first language even when the two groups are equated for intellectual and socioeconomic factors (Holobow, Genesee, Lambert, Gastright, & Met, 1987). At the same time, students in immersion programs acquire advanced levels of functional competence in a second language. Research on immersion programs in Canada (Genesee, 2007) and the United States (Genesee & Lindholm-Leary, 2013) indicates further that immersion is suitable and effective for a wide variety of learners, including English-speaking students who often struggle in school. Thus, at present, there is no evidence to preclude most students from participating in immersion/bilingual programs, including students who might otherwise be at-risk for academic difficulties. At the same time, second language learning in school settings and the benefits of learning two languages take time. Thus, parents must make a long-term commitment to immersion educa-tion and avoid switching students out of these programs unless there is strong evidence that individual children will perform better in a monolingual program.

Finally, research on children who speak a minority language at home and are schooled in a majority language, such as English in Canada or the United States, indicates that they are not at a disadvantage if they maintain and continue to learn the minority language—in the home or in school, despite the myth that younger is better. To the contrary, there is growing evidence that high levels of competence in the home language, especially in domains related to literacy and schooling, can give minority language children an advantage in school in comparison to other minority language students who have not developed their home languages in these ways (Genesee & Geva, 2006). Minority parents who do not speak the majority language should be encouraged to continue to use the home language with their children, if this is their dominant language (Paradis, in press).

There is still much to learn about early childhood bilingualism. However, there is sufficient research evidence to dispel many common myths held by parents, educators, and profession-als about raising and educating children bilingually. Moreover, findings from dual language acquisition by young children are providing a rich data source for extending current theories of language learning and teaching and extending our understanding of individual differences and contextual factors that influence dual language learning in home and school environments.

References

Abrahamsson, N., & Hyltenstam, K. (2009). Age of onset and nativelikeness in a second language: Listener perception versus linguistic scrutiny. *Language Learning, 59,* 249–306. http://dx.doi .org/10.1111/j.1467-9922.2009.00507.x

Allen, S. E. M., Genesee, F. H., Fish, S. A., & Crago, M. B. (2002). Patterns of code mixing in English-Inuktitut bilinguals. In M. Andronis, C. Ball, H. Elston, & S. Neuvel (Eds.), *Proceedings of the 37th annual meeting of the Chicago Linguistic Society* (Vol. 2, pp. 171–188). Chicago, USA: Chicago Linguistic Society.

August, D., & Shanahan, T. (Eds.). (2006). *Developing literacy in second language learners. Report of the National Literacy Panel on Minority-Language Children and Youth.* Mahwah, USA: Erlbaum.

Bedore, L., Peña, E., García, M., & Cortez, C. (2005). Conceptual versus monolingual scoring: When does it make a difference? *Language, Speech and Hearing Services in Schools, 36,* 188–200.

Bialystok, E. (2001). *Bilingualism in development: Language, literacy, and cognition.* New York, USA: Cambridge University Press. http://dx.doi .org/10.1017/CBO9780511605963

Bialystok, E., Craik, F. I., Klein, R., & Viswanathan, M. (2004). Bilingualism, aging, and cognitive control: Evidence from the Simon task. *Psychology and Aging, 19,* 290–303. http://dx.doi .org/10.1037/0882-7974.19.2.290

Bialystok, E., Peets, K. F., & Moreno, S. (2014). Producing bilinguals through immersion education: Development of metalinguistic awareness. *Applied Psycholinguistics, 35,* 177–191. http:// dx.doi.org/10.1017/ S0142716412000288

Bird, E. K., Cleave, P., Trudeau, N., Thordardottir, E., Sutton, A., & Thorpe, A. (2005). The language abilities of bilingual children with Down syndrome. *American Journal of Speech-Language Pathology, 14,* 187–199. http://dx.doi.org/10.1044/1058-0360(2005/019)

Birdsong, D., & Vanhove, J. (in press). Age of second language acquisition: Critical periods and social concerns. In E. Nicoladis & S. Montanari (Eds.), *Lifespan perspectives on bilingualism.* APA and de Gruyter.

Bruck, M. (1978). The suitability of early French immersion programs for the language disabled child. *Canadian Journal of Education, 3,* 51–72. http://dx.doi.org/10.2307/1494685

Bruck, M. (1982). Language impaired children's performance in an additive bilingual education program. *Applied Psycholinguistics, 3,* 45–60. http://dx.doi.org/10.1017/S014271640000415X

Bruck, M., Tucker, G. R., & Jakimik, J. (1975). Are French immersion programs suitable for working class children? *Word, 27,* 311–341.

Comeau, L., Genesee, F., & Lapaquette, L. (2003). The modeling hypothesis and child bilingual code-mixing. *The International Journal of Bilingualism, 7,* 113–126. http://dx.doi.org/10.1177/ 13670069030070020101

Comeau, L., Genesee, F., & Mendelson, M. (2010). A comparison of bilingual and monolingual children's conversational repairs. *First Language, 30,* 354–374. http://dx.doi.org/10.1177/0142723710370530

Conboy, B. T., & Thal, D. J. (2006). Ties between the lexicon and grammar: Cross-sectional and longitudinal studies of bilingual toddlers. *Child Development, 77,* 712–735. http://dx.doi.org/10.1111/j.1467-8624 .2006.00899.x

Delcenserie, A., & Genesee, F. (2014). Language and memory abilities of internationally adopted children from China: Evidence for early age effects. *Journal of Child Language, 41,* 1195–1223.

Erdos, C., Genesee, F., Savage, R., & Haigh, C. (2011). Individual differences in second language reading outcomes. *The International Journal of Bilingualism, 15,* 3–25. http://dx.doi.org/10.1177/1367006910371022

Genesee, F. (1976). The role of intelligence in second language learning. *Language Learning, 26,* 267–280. http://dx.doi.org/10.1111/j.1467-1770 .1976.tb00277.x

Genesee, F. (1981). A comparison of early and late second language learning. *Canadian Journal of Behavioural Science/Revue canadienne des sciences du comportement, 13,* 115–128. http://dx.doi.org/10.1037/ h0081168

Genesee, F. (1989). Early bilingual development: One language or two? *Journal of Child Language, 16,* 161–179. http://dx.doi.org/10.1017/ S0305000900013490

Genesee, F. (1999). *Program alternatives for linguistically diverse students. Educational Practice Report #1.* Santa Cruz, USA: Center for Research on Education, Diversity and Excellence.

Genesee, F. (2002). Portrait of the bilingual child. In V. Cook (Ed.), *Portraits of the second language user* (pp. 170–196). Clevedon, UK: Multilingual Matters.

Genesee, F. (2003). Rethinking bilingual acquisition. In J. M. deWaele (Ed.), *Bilingualism: Challenges and directions for future research* (pp. 158–182). Clevedon, UK: Multilingual Matters.

Genesee, F. (2004). What do we know about bilingual education for majority language students? In T. K. Bhatia & W. Ritchie (Eds.), *Handbook of bilingualism and multiculturalism* (pp. 547–576). Malden, USA: Blackwell.

Genesee, F. (2007). French immersion and at-risk students: A review of research findings. *Canadian Modern Language Review, 63,* 655–688.

Genesee, F. (in press). Reconceptualizing early childhood education for minority language children. In V. Murphy & M. Evangelou (Eds.), *Early childhood education in English for speakers of other languages.* London, UK: British Council.

Genesee, F., Boivin, I., & Nicoladis, E. (1996). Talking with strangers: A study of bilingual children's communicative competence. *Applied Psycholinguistics, 17,* 427– 442. http://dx.doi.org/10.1017/ S0142716400008183

Genesee, F., & Geva, E. (2006). Cross-linguistic relationships in working memory, phonological processes, and oral language. In D. August & T. Shanahan (Eds.), *Developing literacy in second language learners. Report of the National Literacy Panel on Minority-Language Children and Youth* (pp. 175–184). Mahwah, USA: Erlbaum.

Genesee, F., & Lindholm-Leary, K. (2012). The education of English language learners. In K. Harris, S. Graham, & T. Urdan (Eds.), *APA handbook of educational psychology* (pp. 499–526). Washington, DC, USA: APA Books.

Genesee, F., & Lindholm-Leary, K. (2013). Two case studies of content-based language education. *Journal of Immersion and Content-Based Education, 1,* 3–33. http://dx.doi.org/10.1075/jicb.1.1.02gen

Genesee, F., Nicoladis, E., & Paradis, J. (1995). Language differentiation in early bilingual development. *Journal of Child Language, 22,* 611– 631. http://dx.doi.org/10.1017/S0305000900009971

Goldenberg, C. (2008). Teaching English language learners: What the research does—And does not say. *American Educator, 32,* 8–23.

Grüter, T., & Paradis, J. (Eds.). (2014). *Input and experience in bilingual development.* Amsterdam, The Netherlands: John Benjamins. http://dx .doi.org/10.1075/tilar.13

Gutiérrez-Clellen, V. F., Simon-Cereijido, G., & Wagner, C. (2008). Bilingual children with language impairment: A comparison with monolinguals and second language learners. *Applied Psycholinguistics, 29,* 3–19. http://dx.doi.org/10.1017/S0142716408080016

Hambly, C., & Fombonne, E. (2012). The impact of bilingual environments on language development in children with autism spectrum disorders. *Journal of Autism and Developmental Disorders, 42,* 1342–1352. http://dx.doi.org/10.1007/s10803-011-1365-z

Harley, B., & Hart, D. (1997). Language aptitude and second language proficiency in classroom learners of different starting ages. *Studies in Second Language Acquisition, 19,* 379–400. http://dx.doi.org/10.1017/ S0272263197003045

Holobow, N. E., Genesee, F., & Lambert, W. E. (1991). The effectiveness of a foreign language immersion program for children from different ethnic and social class backgrounds: Report 2. *Applied Psycholinguistics, 12,* 179–198. http://dx.doi.org/10.1017/S0142716400009139

Holobow, N., Genesee, F., Lambert, W. E., Gastright, J., & Met, M. (1987). Effectiveness of partial French immersion for children from different social class and ethnic backgrounds. *Applied Psycholinguistics, 8,* 137–152. http://dx.doi.org/10.1017/S0142716400000175

Jacobs, K., & Cross, A. (2001). The seventh generation of Kahnawà:ke: Phoenix or Dinosaur. In D. Christian & F. Genesee (Eds.), *Bilingual education* (pp. 109–121). Alexandria, USA: TESOL.

Kimbrough Oller, D., Eilers, R. E., Urbano, R., & Cobo-Lewis, A. B. (1997). Development of precursors to speech in infants exposed to two languages. *Journal of Child Language, 24,* 407–425. http://dx.doi.org/ 10.1017/S0305000997003097

Leonard, L. (1998). *Children with specific language impairment.* Cambridge, USA: MIT Press.

Leopold, W. (1949). *Speech development of a bilingual child* (Vol. 4). Evanston, USA: Northwestern University Press.

Lindholm-Leary, L., & Borsato, G. (2006). Academic achievement. In F. Genesee, K. Lindholm-Leary, W. Saunders, & D. Christian (Eds.), *Educating English language learners: A synthesis of empirical evidence* (pp. 176–222). New York, USA: Cambridge University Press.

Long, M. (1990). Maturational constraints on language development. *Studies in Second Language Acquisition, 12,* 251–285. http://dx.doi.org/ 10.1017/S0272263100009165

Maneva, B., & Genesee, F. (2002). Bilingual babbling: Evidence for language differentiation in dual language acquisition. In B. Skarbela, S. Fish, & A. H.-J. Do (Eds.), *Boston University Conference on language development 26 Proceedings* (pp. 383–392). Somerville, USA: Cascadilla Press.

Marchman, V. A., Martínez-Sussmann, C., & Dale, P. S. (2004). The language-specific nature of grammatical development: Evidence from bilingual language learners. *Developmental Science, 7,* 212–224. http:// dx.doi.org/10.1111/j.1467-7687.2004.00340.x

Marinova-Todd, S. H., & Mirenda, P. (in press). Language and communication abilities of bilingual children with ASD. In J. Patterson & Barbara L. Rodriguez (Eds.), *Multilingual perspectives on child language disorders.* Bristol, UK: Multilingual Matters.

Meisel, J. M. (1994). Code-switching in young bilingual children: The acquisition of grammatical constraints. *Studies in Second Language Acquisition, 16,* 413–441. http://dx.doi.org/10.1017/S0272263100013449

Muñoz, C. (2014). Contrasting effects of starting age and type of input on the oral performance of foreign language learners. *Applied Linguistics, 35,* 463–482. http://dx.doi.org/10.1093/applin/amu024

Myers-Scotton, C. (1997). *Duelling languages: Grammatical structure in codeswitching.* New York, USA: Oxford University Press.

Paradis, J. (2006). Second language acquisition in childhood. In E. Hoff & M. Shatz (Eds.), *Handbook of language development* (pp. 387–405). Oxford, UK: Blackwell.

Paradis, J. (in press). Supporting the home language of EAL children with developmental disorders. In V. Murphy & M. Evangelou (Eds.), *Early childhood education in English for speakers of other languages.* London, UK: British Council.

Paradis, J., Crago, M., Genesee, F., & Rice, M. (2003). French-English bilingual children with SLI: How do they compare with their monolingual peers? *Journal of Speech, Language, and Hearing Research, 46,* 113–127. http://dx.doi.org/10.1044/1092-4388(2003/009)

Paradis, J., & Genesee, F. (1996). Syntactic acquisition in bilingual children: Autonomous or interdependent? *Studies in Second Language Acquisition, 18,* 1–25. http://dx.doi.org/10.1017/S0272263100014662

Paradis, J., Genesee, F., & Crago, M. (2011). *Dual language development and disorders: A handbook on bilingualism and second language learning* (2nd ed.). Baltimore, USA: Brookes.

Paradis, J., Nicoladis, E., & Genesee, F. (2000). Early emergence of structural constraints on code-mixing: Evidence from French-English bilingual children. *Bilingualism: Language and Cognition, 3,* 245–261. http://dx.doi.org/10.1017/S1366728900000365

Paradis, J., & Sorenson, D. T. (2009). *Differentiating between English L2 children with typical and impaired language development.* Paper presented at the Boston University Conference on Language Development, Boston University.

Patterson, J. L., & Pearson, B. Z. (2004). Bilingual lexical development: Influences, contexts, and processes. In B. A. Goldstein (Ed.), *Bilingual language development and disorders in Spanish-English speakers* (pp. 77–104). Baltimore, USA: Brookes.

Petitto, L. A., Katerelos, M., Levy, B. G., Gauna, K., Tétreault, K., & Ferraro, V. (2001). Bilingual signed and spoken language acquisition from birth: Implications for the mechanisms underlying early bilingual language acquisition. *Journal of Child Language, 28,* 453–496. http:// dx.doi .org/10.1017/S0305000901004718

Pierce, L., Klein, D., Chen, J. K., Delcenserie, A., & Genesee, F. (2014). Mapping the unconscious maintenance of a lost first language. *Proceedings of the National Academy of Sciences of the United States of America, 111,* 17314–17319.

Riches, C., & Genesee, F. (2006). Cross-linguistic and cross-modal aspects of literacy development. In F. Genesee, K. Lindholm-Leary, W. M. Saunders, & D. Christian (Eds.), *Educating English language learners: A synthesis of research evidence* (pp. 64–108). New York, USA: Cambridge University Press. http://dx.doi.org/10.1017/CBO9780511499913 .004

Saunders, W., & O'Brien, G. (2006). Oral language. In F. Genesee, K. Lindholm-Leary, W. Saunders, & D. Christian (Eds.), *Educating English language learners: A synthesis of research evidence* (pp. 14–63). New York, USA: Cambridge University Press.

Sauve, D., & Genesee, F. (2000, March). *Grammatical constraints on child bilingual code-mixing.* Paper presented at the annual conference of the American Association for Applied Linguistics, Vancouver, Canada.

Thomas, W., & Collier, B. (2002). *A national study of school effectiveness for language minority students' long-term academic achievement.* Santa Cruz, USA: Center for Research on Education, Diversity and Excellence.

Thordardottir, E. (2011). The relationship between bilingual exposure and vocabulary development. *The International Journal of Bilingualism, 15,* 426–445. http://dx.doi .org/10.1177/1367006911403202

Vihman, M. (1998). A developmental perspective on codeswitching: Conversations between a pair of bilingual siblings. *The International Journal of Bilingualism, 2,* 45–84.

Volterra, V., & Taeschner, T. (1978). The acquisition and development of language by bilingual children. *Journal of Child Language, 5,* 311–326. http://dx.doi.org/10.1017/S0305000900007492

Zwanziger, E. E., Allen, S. E. M., & Genesee, F. (2005). Crosslinguistic influence in bilingual acquisition: Subject omission in learners of Inuktitut and English. *Journal of Child Language, 32,* 893–909. http://dx.doi .org/10.1017/S0305000905007129

UNIT V

Discussion Questions

1. What are the five stages of language development? Explain, and provide an example for each stage.
2. What are some factors that influence children's language development, and why is language important in child development?
3. Are infants able to talk or understand adult language? How much do infants know about language? How do children learn a language?
4. What are the language stages for children from 0 to 24 months?
5. What can adults do to help children learn a language? Provide examples.